Series on International Corporate Responsibility
Volume 2

Sponsored by the
Carnegie Bosch Institute for Applied Studies
in International Management
Carnegie Mellon University

Perspectives on International Corporate Responsibility

John Hooker
Ans Kolk
Peter Madsen
Editors

This volume contains a selection of the papers presented at the Second Conference on International Corporate Responsibility, which was held at the University of Amsterdam in 2004. The conference was conducted by the Center for International Corporate Responsibility at Carnegie Mellon University, which believes that advances in business ethics require a truly international approach that accounts for cultural differences. The conference was sponsored by the Carnegie Bosch Institute for Applied Studies in International Management as part of its mission to foster dialogue between managers and researchers on fundamental issues related to the global orientation of business. These conference volumes on international corporate responsibility are now published on behalf of Carnegie Mellon University by the Philosophy Documentation Center.

Related Publications:

International Corporate Responsibility: Exploring the Issues.
ISBN 0-88748-439-5

For more information on these volumes please contact:

Philosophy Documentation Center
P.O. Box 7147, Charlottesville, Virginia 22906-7147
Phone: 800-444-2419 (US & Canada), 434-220-3300; Fax: 434-220-3301
E-mail: order@pdcnet.org; Web: www.pdcnet.org

ISBN 1-889680-45-1

Published by the Philosophy Documentation Center

Perspectives on International Corporate Responsibility

Table of Contents

ICR and Environmental Issues

Regional Studies

Responsible Marketing and ICR Information Strategies

PREFACE

The Center for International Corporate Responsibility at Carnegie Mellon University's Tepper School of Business conducted its second Conference on International Corporate Responsibility in Amsterdam on June 18–20, 2004. The conference was sponsored by the Carnegie Bosch Institute for Applied Studies in International Management (also at Carnegie Mellon University) and managed locally by the Amsterdam graduate Business School, University of Amsterdam. Prominent scholars from eleven countries on six continents, together with a few managers of select multinational corporations, met to analyze, discuss, and debate various issues having to do with the general theme of international corporate responsibility (ICR).

It could be argued that the field of ICR has emerged as a bona fide sub-discipline within the general area of business ethics. The impressive growth of ICR can be measured in a variety of ways. One can point to the heightened awareness of the role that corporate responsibility plays in international affairs on the part of governmental organizations, particularly in Europe. The European Union and its Commission, for example, has done much to entice the European-based multinational enterprises (MNEs) to practice responsibly as they seek profits globally. (As early as 1991, it offered a "green paper" entitled "Promoting a European Framework for Corporate Social Responsibility.") Or, and perhaps even more telling of the new significance of ICR, one could describe the different kinds of "stakeholder groups"—primarily non-governmental organizations (NGOs)—that have set as their mission the promotion and spotlighting of issues having to do with ICR. A brief survey can show that these organizations and their activities are accurate barometers of the increasing importance of ICR.

In general, there are two kinds of these stakeholder groups and NGOs that have a practical interest in the conduct of MNEs. In the first category are NGOs that place various kinds of political pressure on MNEs to raise their level of corporate responsibility or to offer assistance to them in doing so. The various organizations that assist MNEs to perform research for and/or to create audits, transparent accounting, and public statements about their social and/or environmental practices can be labeled "ICR-reporting groups," while NGOs that provide professional services to global corporations on how to be socially responsible can be called "ICR-provider groups." Then, as a final example of these groups, there are stakeholders who are also shareholders and who engage in the ICR-promoting tactic of "socially responsible investing."

Among the examples of the ICR-reporting groups we would include academic organizations that are housed in universities and function like "think tanks." A representative example and one of the first such ICR-reporting groups in academia is the Centre for Social and Environmental Accounting Research (CSEAR) in the Department of Accounting and Finance at the University of Glasgow. Established in 1991, it now has 300 members from over thirty different countries. CSEAR collects and publishes data and information about "the practice and theory of social and environmental accounting and reporting." Under the general rubric that accounting and accountability are interdependent, some of the topics covered in research reports, discussion papers, and scholarly treatises at CSEAR deal with such issues as the economics of sustainability; environmental management; the actual process of social, ethical, and environmental reporting by MNEs; social and environmental cost internalization by markets and organizations; the relationship between social and environmental disclosures and corporate share price performance; and articulation of the standards for social and environmental reports.[1]

There are also a host of commercial organizations that make a business out of ICR-reporting and ICR-providing activities. These entrepreneurial ventures have sprung up all over the world and take international business ethics onto a higher plane, in that they see potential commercial value in this topic. Although they often maintain the legal status of a nonprofit organization, they nonetheless employ the strategies of contemporary businesses by mounting aggressive marketing campaigns, conducting active public relations, and performing quantitative measurement of their activities. An exhaustive list of such enterprises would be much too long to include here, but leading representatives of ICR-reporting and ICR-providing organizations, respectively, are Social Accountability International and CSR Europe.

Social Accountability International is a watchdog agency in that it is "dedicated to the development, implementation, and oversight of voluntary verifiable social accountability standards."[2] Concerned primarily with the issues of improving the quality of workplaces, ethical sourcing practices, and the elimination of sweatshops worldwide, SAI has worked to implement SA8000 as an international corporate standard. Used to prompt auditing and public reporting of unacceptable MNE labor practices, SA8000 models itself after the International Standards Organization and its work in certification and accreditation of quality management (ISO9000 family of standards) and environmental (ISO14000) practices among MNEs. SAI also conducts ongoing research on how to improve the SA8000 standard, maintains a certification program, conducts training for auditors, convenes workshops for consultative organizations from around the world, and hosts international conferences specifically for businesses as well as meetings designed for the edification and education of the public.

CSR Europe is comprised of over sixty-five company members and eighteen national "partner" NGOs from various countries. CSR Europe, as its name suggests, is an NGO dealing with corporate social responsibility issues for European-based MNEs, and it sees its mission as helping companies "achieve profitability, sustainable growth, and human progress by placing corporate social responsibility in the mainstream of business practice."[3] It attempts to achieve these goals by:

- providing over 500,000 business people and partners annually with print and online publications, news of best practices, and tools;
- offering business managers learning, benchmarking, and various capacity-building programs;
- promoting CSR issues in dialogues focusing particularly on European institutions.

Among the "tailored capacity-building programs," which are defined as training courses focusing on particular aspects of corporate social responsibility provided by CSR Europe to their member companies, are corporate social responsibility reporting, finance and social responsibility, business and diversity, and protecting human rights in global business. CSR Europe also maintains a digital databank of information on corporate social responsibility for its member companies. This database contains research publications, articles dealing with corporate social responsibility from the mainstream press, a selection of materials on business best practices and cases, and Internet links to other sources of business ethics information. Finally, in cooperation with the Corporate Register in the United Kingdom, CSR Europe makes various corporate social and environmental reports available to their member companies.

The final stakeholder group in this survey is composed of those who seek to apply financial pressures that will promote ICR in the form of "socially responsible investing" (SRI). SRI is a worldwide movement that employs free market investment principles to promote responsible MNE conduct. The organizations that make up this group are among the most interesting of these stakeholders for two reasons. For one, these groups attempt to influence the activities of MNEs directly through the buying and selling of corporate stock, thereby becoming voting owners of MNEs. Second, many SRI organizations attempt to influence MNE practices by establishing large mutual funds that screen corporations before they can be included in the fund. Often this screening takes the form of a report card on how well MNEs have succeeded in such domains as the environment, social accountability, and financial performance—the so-called "triple bottom line."

There are over 200 SRI mutual funds in the United States today that use screening principles to invest the public's money in an array of equity, balanced, international, bond, index, and money market funds. It may come as no surprise that the principles used to screen such investing are controversial with respect to both the kind of matters screened and the way that these screens are implemented. In any event, according to a 1999 study, 2.16 trillion USD was invested in the U.S. alone in a "socially responsible manner, up a strong 82 percent from 1997 levels."[4] According to the *GreeenMoney Journal*, "more than one out of every nine dollars under professional management in the United States today is involved in socially responsible investing. The $2.16 trillion managed by major investing institutions—including pension funds, mutual fund families, foundations, religious organizations, and community development financial institutions—has remained stable, accounting for 11.3 percent of the total $19.2 trillion in investment assets under professional management in the United States."[5]

In Europe, there were 313 SRI-type funds in 2003, which represented a 12 percent increase in the number of such investment outlets since 2001. SRI in the United Kingdom, Sweden, France, and Belgium accounts for approximately 63 percent of all such investing in Europe. However, European SRI funds are emerging most rapidly in Italy, where they have doubled over the course of an eighteen-month period.[6] The amount of SRI-managed assets in 2003 in Europe was approximately 12.2 billion EUR, with an additional 336 billion EUR in SRI assets held by European institutional investors.

The SRI movement is not restricted to the U.S. and Europe. Australia's Ethical Investment Association recently reported that SRI assets invested there doubled in three years. In Japan, there are now 11 SRI funds with holdings of almost 1 billion USD. There are six global SRI fund options in Hong Kong, one in Korea, and in Malaysia there are thirteen Islamic funds based on Syariah finance principles. There are investment outlets available in the U.S., Canada, and the U.K. that focus solely on Asian markets and screen for social responsibility issues.[7]

What can be taken away from this survey of diverse stakeholder groups is that there is a good deal of concern about ICR and a good number of people who are trying to address it. Based on these examples, it would not be an exaggeration to say that ICR has become an important and central agenda item for global managers and the stakeholders with whom they must work and to whom they have corporate obligations. The above survey shows that ICR has reached a new level of maturity, and the Second International Conference on Corporate Responsibility explored some of the same issues that governments, stakeholders, and others are concerned with and want to push onto center stage.

At the conference, established scholars as well as more junior scholars shared their recent work in the form of academic papers that addressed: international codes of business conduct (part 1 of this volume); socially responsible investments, finance, corporate governance, and reputation (part 2); ICR and globalization (part 3); and environmental issues in different societal contexts (part 4). There were a number of papers that focused on more specialized matters in different parts of the world, such as employment and foreign investments, respectively, in the Philippines and Middle East; corporate decision-making and MNE relations with local communities in Latin America; and the role of German companies in Poland (part 5). Part 6 deals with issues related to responsible marketing, with particular attention to HIV/AIDS, and to the information strategies related to ICR.

In addition to the papers in this volume, the conference also included some hands-on reports from corporations, which offered the participants a practitioner's view of the ICR picture. A keynote presentation by Alan Christie, then vice president of corporate affairs at Levi Strauss Europe, Middle East, and Africa, and chair of the CSR board of directors, began the conference and set the tone for the meeting with a very straightforward and candid account of the successes and failures of the ICR movement on the part of MNEs. A panel of executives that dealt with the issues faced by global coffee companies (Sara Lee/Douwe Egberts and the Ahold Coffee Company) was also well received by participants, as it too gave them a chance to hear first hand about yet another set of ICR challenges from those required to manage them.

The conference was held in the beautiful *Bondsraadzaal*, or council room, in Amsterdam's National Trade Unions Museum (*Vakbondsmuseum De Burcht*), which provided an ambiance conducive to the discussion of ICR. Indeed, it was quite appropriate for the conference to be convened in Amsterdam, the home of the Dutch East India Company—*Verenigde Oostindische Compagnie* or VOC—which is arguably the world's first publicly held corporation that also functioned as a global business. Japan, China, India, the Persian Gulf, Africa, and all of Europe were joined to Amsterdam, thanks to the work of the VOC. Chartered in 1602, it had a long but not so illustrious history, as it leveled competitors and set up a monopoly in the world spice market until 1799, when it was liquidated thanks to mismanagement. The Dutch called VOC's experiment in international business *V(ergaan) O(nder) C(orruptie)*, which roughly translates as "sunk under corruption." Thus the conference scholars were literally surrounded by the lessons of ICR both in and outside of their meeting room.

Notes

1. Centre for Social and Environmental Accounting Research (CSEAR), http://www.gla.ac.uk/departments/accounting/csear/, accessed on November 11, 2004.

2. Social Accountability International, http://www.cepaa.org/AboutSAI/AboutSAI.htm, accessed on November 11, 2004.

3. CSR Europe http://www.csreurope.org/aboutus/default.aspx, accessed on November 11, 2004.

4. Social Investment Forum, http://www.socialinvest.org/areas/news/1999-trends.htm, accessed on November 11, 2004.

5. The GreenMoney Journal, http://www.greenmoneyjournal.com/article.mpl?newsletterid=28&articleid=302, accessed on November 11, 2004.

6. SRI Compass, http://www.sricompass.org/trends/Factsandfigures_page102.aspx#size, accessed on November 11, 2004.

7. The Association for Sustainable & Responsible Investment in Asia (ASRIA), http://www.asria.org/sri/asia/sriasia?expand_all=1, and the Syariah Index, http://www.klse.com.my/website/education/smb_syariahindex.htm, accessed on November 11, 2004.

The Editors

John Hooker is T. Jerome Holleran Professor of Business Ethics and Social Responsibility and Professor of Operations Research at the Tepper School of Business, Carnegie Mellon University, Pittsburgh, Pennsylvania, USA. E-mail: john@hooker.tepper.cmu.edu.

Ans Kolk is Professor of Sustainable Management, Amsterdam graduate Business School, University of Amsterdam, Roetersstraat 11, 1018 WB Amsterdam, The Netherlands. E-mail: akolk@uva.nl.

Peter Madsen is Associate Teaching Professor of Philosophy and Executive Director of the Center for the Advancement of Applied Ethics, Carnegie Mellon University, Pittsburgh, Pennsylvania, USA. E-mail: pm2n@andrew.cmu.edu.

CORPORATE CODES OF CONDUCT AS A GLOBAL BUSINESS STRATEGY

James K. Rowe and Ronnie D. Lipschutz
University of California, Santa Cruz, California, USA

Abstract

We argue that Corporate Social Responsibility (CSR), particularly corporate codes of conduct, has been one of global business's preferred strategies for quelling popular discontent with corporate power. By "business strategy" we mean organized responses, through organizations like the International Chamber of Commerce (ICC), to the threat that public regulation poses to business's collective self-interest. Attention to CSR's historical development reveals it has flourished as discourse and practice at times when corporations became subject to intense public scrutiny. In this essay we outline two periods of corporate crisis, and account for the role codes have played in quieting public concern over increasing corporate power: 1) When developing countries along with Western unions and social activists were calling for a "New International Economic Order" that would more tightly regulate the activity of Transnational Corporations (1960–1976); and 2) When mass anti-globalization demonstrations and high profile corporate scandals are increasing the demand for regulation (1998–Present).

Introduction

> Four hundred years earlier, social responsibility shifted from the church to the state, as government replaced religious institutions as society's predominant force. At the dawning of the twenty-first century, business appears the next likely candidate to carry this mantle. (Makower 1994: 33).

Recent global protest activity, from the streets of Seattle in 1999 to the fences of Cancun in 2003, has been largely impelled by the social, economic, and environmental "externalities" associated with economic globalization (that is, inadequate wages, poor working conditions, deforestation, general environmental degradation). A solution to these externalities being increasingly forwarded by business organizations is private sector self-regulation. Self-regulation—more popularly known as Corporate Social Responsibility (CSR)—is presented as a way to balance the interests of business and society *without* expanding government intervention in the global market place.

What exactly is CSR? CSR is defined by Business for Social Responsibility, a global non-profit organization funded by corporations, as "achieving commercial

pp. 1–45

success in ways that honor ethical values and respect people, communities, and the natural environment" (Business for Social Responsibility 2003). According to Jeremy Moon, Professor of Corporate Social Responsibility at Nottingham University,

> Business social responsibility . . . refers to the voluntary contribution of finance, goods or services to community or governmental causes. It excludes activities directly related to firms' production and commerce. It also excludes activity required under legislation or government direction. (Moon 2002: 385–86)

The common thread that weaves through the various definitions of "Corporate Social Responsibility" is the voluntary nature of the good practices referenced. What makes CSR initiatives "socially responsible" is that they are not mandated by governmental or intergovernmental institutions—they are voluntarily pursued.

The most celebrated mechanism in the CSR toolkit, and our focus in this study, is the corporate code of conduct. The Organization for Economic Cooperation and Development (OECD) defines corporate codes as "commitments voluntarily made by companies, associations, or other entities, which put forth standards and principles for the conduct of business activities in the marketplace" (OECD 1998: 5). But how effective can voluntary and largely unverified corporate efforts to minimize market externalities be?

More and more studies measuring the (in)effectiveness of voluntary corporate codes are being published every day. The results are mixed. Some find promise (Schrage 2004; Kolk, van Tulder, and Welters 1999) whereas others are much more critical (Christian Aid 2004; Zarsky 2002; OECD 2003). The consensus underlying these divergent findings is that, even if voluntary codes have potential, they are not currently addressing globalization's externalities in a sustained way. But if voluntary codes have not proven effective, or if there is at least no consensus on their effectiveness, why then are corporations, intergovernmental organizations like the UN, and even civil society so interested in them? That is the central question guiding this chapter. We begin with the less obvious: unpacking civil society's investment in voluntary codes of conduct.

For labor and social activists, corporate codes of conduct, even if voluntary, can strengthen efforts to hold corporations accountable. Simply put, condemning an organization for unethical behavior is easier when said organization has already and openly agreed that ethical behavior is virtuous. Bama Athreya of the International Labor Rights Fund concretizes this point in relation to her organization's campaign against Nike: "Let's face it, hypocrites are far more interesting than mere wrongdoers, and its been much easier to sensitize press and public to Nike's failure to implement its own code of conduct than to its failure to comply with Indonesian labor laws" (quoted in Klein 2000: 432).

Most labor and social activists supportive of corporate codes of conduct are also mindful of their limits. For one, activists lack the resources to monitor the plethora of trans-national corporation (TNC) activity spanning the globe. Thus, a strategic hope for activists is that voluntary corporate codes of conduct developed by individual companies, and international organizations like the UN and OECD, will nurture more regulation friendly environments both nationally and internationally (Smith 2003). There are thus long-term (gateway to binding social regulation) and short-term (immediate improvements in corporate conduct) rationales for supporting voluntary codes of conduct.

Our aim in this chapter, however, is to question whether the short-term gains provided by CSR and corporate codes are worth the costs. Our argument is that the primary cost of supporting voluntary codes is precisely what global civil society hopes to gain through them: the binding regulation of transnational corporations. We argue that the primary reason for business's trenchant interest in corporate codes is that they are an effective means of quelling popular discontent with corporate power and the political change that discontent might impel. Our research has convinced us to approach corporate codes of conduct less as exemplars of business ethics and more as effective business strategy. By "business strategy," we mean organized responses, through organizations like the International Chamber of Commerce (ICC) and World Business Council for Sustainable Development (WBCSD), to the threat that public regulation (both domestic and international) poses to business's collective self-interest. Thus in simple terms, by unpacking why business is so invested in corporate codes of conduct, we aim to convince civil society and concerned members of the business community to become disinterested.

We support this aim with an historical analysis. Attention to the corporate code of conduct's historical development reveals that it has flourished as discourse and practice at times when corporations and the institutional structures that supported them, became subject to intense public scrutiny. In this paper we examine two recent periods of crisis for the business world—times when the threat of public regulation loomed large:

- 1960–1976: when developing countries along with Western unions and social activists were calling for a "New International Economic Order" that would more tightly regulate the activity of Transnational Corporations.

- 1998 and after: when mass anti-globalization demonstrations and high profile corporate scandals (Enron and WorldCom) are increasing demand for regulation.

By accounting for the corporate codes' role in business's bid to avoid regulation at a time when global opposition to corporate power was even stronger than today (1960–1976), we argue that recent CSR flourishings should be approached with more concern than optimism. In other words, the strategic hope that voluntary mechanisms can create regulation friendly environments is problematic when, historically, corporate codes have been self-consciously invoked by business to avoid social regulation.

World Order Contended: 1960–1976

While what we today term Corporate Social Responsibility began with the emergence of the modern corporation itself at the end of the nineteenth century (see Marchaud 1998 and Nace 2003), the business crisis in the late 1960s and 1970s saw modern CSR discourse take shape. To communicate the depth of this global crisis, we begin our historical account in the United States, where even the putative beneficiaries of American Hegemony and US Corporate power—the American people—were becoming increasingly opposed to corporate power at home and abroad.

The United States Scene

The United States emerged as the world's dominant economic actor in the aftermath of World War II. The US government's encouragement of corporate participation in European economic recovery abetted the outflow of US foreign direct investment. In the post-war era, the TNC became a symbol of American economic power (Gilpin 1975: 139). But while the national economic growth impelled by the internationalization of US capital materially benefited Americans in general, the costs of an increasingly global economy (even if dominated by American corporations), was being felt at home by the mid-1960s.

Mounting unemployment through the 1960s and early 1970s was attributed by organized labor to increasing import penetration as European and Japanese economic power increased, but also to "capital flight"—the closure of American plants and factories, and the shifting of jobs to the developing world.

American labor was not alone in its concerns. Other movements for consumer safety, environmental protection, and social justice were becoming increasingly concerned by the power, flexibility, and unaccountability of transnational corporations operating at home and abroad.

Broad-based concerns over TNC misconduct coalesced and were intensified by the death of Chilean President Salvador Allende on September 11, 1973. Eight months prior to his death, Allende had alerted the UN's General Assembly to plans of the International Telephone and Telegraph Company (an American TNC), to overthrow his democratically elected government with the help of the CIA:

> Last July, the world learned with amazement of different aspects of a new plan of action that ITT had presented to the US government in order to overthrow my government in a period of six months. I have with me the document, dated in October of 1971, that contains the 18-point plan that was talked about. They wanted to strangle us economically, carry out diplomatic sabotage, create panic among the population and cause social disorder so that when the Government lost control, the armed forces would be driven to eliminate the democratic regime and impose a dictatorship. (Allende 1975: 239)

ITT's machinations in Chile impressed themselves on the public consciousness and became a rallying point for activists.

TNC image was not helped when more corporate scandal hit the front pages three years later. For business analyst John Kline: "While corporations were protesting that the isolated, atypical ITT incident had unfairly tarred the image of MNCs in general, nearly 500 of America's top corporations were being drawn into disclosures of improper payments abroad" (Kline 1985: 23). The years 1975 and 1976 brought rolling revelations of bribery of foreign officials, laundered money used for illegal political payments, and secret off-the-book accounts. The TNC, continues Kline, "had exploded on the American public consciousness in an extremely negative fashion. Imagery created by the ITT and bribery incidents helped paint MNCs as suspicious enterprises given to serious abuse if not closely watched and regulated" (Kline 1985: 24).

Public mistrust of TNCs within the US contributed to a regulation-friendly environment that was capitalized on by labor and other social movements. For business historian Archie Carroll, "[t]he late 60s and early 70s was a period during which social movements with respect to the environment, worker safety, consumers, and employees were poised to transition from special interest status to government regulation (Carroll 1999: 6). Indeed, as Judith Richter notes, "between 1965 and 1977, the US Congress enacted 20 new regulatory laws governing, for example, occupational health and safety, consumer product safety, clean air, clean water and toxic waste, and created an elaborate regime for assessing environmental impacts and regulating the financial system" (Richter 2001: 19). This era is nicely summed up by historian Edwin Epstein: "A critical difference throughout much of the 1960s was that federal and state governments were no longer reluctant to enact laws that transformed general public expectations about business responsibilities into specific legal requirements. A new era in the interaction between business and other sectors of society was emerging" (Epstein 1998: 6).

The Global Scene

The friendly regulatory climate within the US during the 1960s and early 1970s was consonant with the global scene. This was a time when post-colonial states were actively seeking the economic and political autonomy self-determination promised in name. Salvador Allende's Chile and some twenty other developing nations passed legislation controlling TNC activities in the late 1960s and early 1970s. Nationalization of foreign corporations reached a peak in the first half of the 1970s (Richter 2001: 20). Allende's speech to the UN General Assembly just prior to his death remains one of the more pithy accounts of developing-country concern and captures the mood of the time:

> The nationalization of basic resources constitutes an historic demand. Our economy could no longer tolerate the subordination implied by having more than 80 percent of its exports in the hands of a small group of foreign companies that have always put their interests ahead of the country in which they make their profits. . . . We are potentially wealthy countries and yet we live a life of poverty. We go here and there, begging for credits and aid and yet we are—a paradox typical of the capitalist economic system—great exporters of wealth. (Allende 1975: 234).

Developing countries were not only nationalizing industries and imposing national regulations on foreign capital, but were also busy pursuing international regulation for TNCs. The UN was a key venue and vehicle for their organizing efforts. The Group of 77—a coalition of seventy-seven developing countries—was formed at the 1964 United Nations Conference on Trade and Development (UNCTAD) to promote an international agenda and structure more responsive to their needs.

The Group of 77 found their break in 1973. This year not only brought the assassination of Salvador Allende, and the strengthened solidarity it forged between less developed countries (LDCs), but also the OPEC orchestrated oil crisis. The quadrupling of world oil prices "resulted in a massive transfer of resources from the developed to the less developed countries, both directly to the oil producing countries themselves, and indirectly to oil-importing Third World countries through the recycling of the capital surpluses of some OPEC member countries (so-called 'petrodollars') by the international banking system" (Hoogvelt and Puxty 1987: 169). Most importantly, for our purposes, the 1973 oil crisis emboldened developing countries and strengthened demands for a reformed global economy.

"Developing countries," for John Kline, "had complained before about MNC abuses, even if they were perhaps less dramatic than the ITT incident. The crucial difference now was that the context for complaints changed when developing countries perceived oil resource power as an indication that they finally had some leverage to effect changes in the international economic system" (Kline 1985: 21).[1] The first manifestation of this newfound power was the 1974 adoption by the UN General Assembly of a declaration on the establishment of a New International Economic Order (NIEO). The understanding that the "colonially imposed 'old' international division of labour coupled with the free—that is, unregulated operations of world markets systematically disadvantages the poorer, ex-colonial countries of Africa, Asia and Latin America" now had the beginnings of an international political program (Hoogvelt and Puxty 1987: 162–3).

Binding international codes of conduct for TNCs were a central component of the program. In 1974 the UN Economic and Social Council (ECOSOC) set up the UN Commission on Transnational Corporations, with the UN Centre on Transnational Corporations (UNCTC) as its special research and administrative body.

The centre was entrusted with three basic tasks:

- monitor and provide reports on the activities of TNCs;
- strengthen the capacity of developing countries in dealing with TNCs; and
- draft proposals for normative frameworks for the activities of TNCs. (Richter 2001: 9)

In 1976, the UN Commission on Transnational Corporations made the formulation, adoption and implementation of a draft UN Code of Conduct on Transnational Corporations one of its top priorities.[2] It must be reiterated that the proposed code would have been comprehensive and legally binding.

The prospect of a comprehensive and legally binding international code regulating the activities of TNCs put the global North on serious alert. While the draft code by itself was not a radical threat to Northern economic interests, there was real concern that it might initiate a dangerous dynamic—that "such an international code might gradually evolve into a mechanism which would unduly limit and restrict . . . the activities which constitute the core responsibilities of business" (McQuade, quoted in Van Der Pijl 1993: 49).

It was soon determined that the "best form of defense against the G-77 onslaught on Western economic interests and values was attack" (Robinson 1983: 164). This "attack" took the form of apparent concession, the OECD Guidelines on Multinational Corporations—a voluntary code of conduct. For John Robinson, a business writer at the time, the voluntary guidelines were a "calculated compromise by Western governments between, on the one hand, the need to sensitise firms to their social, economic, and political responsibilities and, on the other, the need to make the rest of the world aware, and in particular the LDCs negotiating a UN code of conduct for transnational corporations, that the West is not prepared to see excessive constraints imposed on their major creators of wealth: MNCs" (Robinson 1983: 7). Robinson continues: "The speed with which the Guidelines moved from conception to decision was dramatic, and was a direct product of the rich world's belief that it had to go into the UN negotiations on multinationals with a coherent and apparently progressive position with which to confront the developing countries clamour . . . for more radical and compulsory control" (Robinson 1983: 117).[3]

To cut a long story short, suffice it to say that Northern efforts to derail negotiations of a binding code for transnational corporations were successful. By the time negotiations on the code began in 1977, it had already been agreed that it would be voluntary. While a draft code was nearly complete by 1981, negotiations were stalled and more or less abandoned a short time later.[4] For our purposes, the simple point is that the OECD Guidelines were a tool used to forestall more compulsory control being sought at the UN. The year 1976 marks the entrance of the voluntary code of conduct into business's strategic repertoire.

We need to clarify two parts of our narrative. Firstly, the voluntary guidelines drafted at the OECD were not the only reason the binding UN code failed. More important in this regard was the global recession of 1980–1982 (the "Reagan Recession"), brought on by record-high interest rates in the United States and Europe, which caused resource prices to collapse and developing country debt to skyrocket. It also eliminated Third-World economic leverage and replaced talk of an NIEO with the discipline of "structural adjustment." This recession removed any Third-World economic leverage and opened way to talk of "structural adjustment" more than new international economic orders. The recession spurned a general move to the right in developing countries whose economic vulnerability and investment thirst reduced the pressure for comprehensive social regulation.

There are numerous analyses accounting for how the Reagan administration administered the 1980–1982 recession that helped pave the way for neoliberal, or economic, globalization.[5] This is a complicated history that we cannot address here. Our simple point is that the first voluntary code of conduct on the global stage—the OECD Guidelines—was invented to forestall the binding international regulation of TNCs.

John Kline nicely accounts for what business learned about the power of CSR during this period:

> Events in the 1970s forced MNCs onto the defensive. An opportunity now exists to change this posture into a positive forward outlook and plan of action. One step in this direction is to build a public affairs program that uses the intergovernmental code movement as public guidance rather than just defending against it as possible law. Individual MNC codes can play a vital role in this effort, counterbalancing the use of intergovernmental codes as political levers while also creating a better understanding of corporate operations that could preclude more restrictive actions in the future. (Kline 1985: 161)

While some of Kline's recommendations were pursued through the 1980s and into the 1990s, business interest in CSR and codes of conduct faded without the agitations of developing countries, the international trade union movement, and social activists.

As will be discussed below, events through the 1990s would again put TNCs on the defensive, and make Kline's "plan of action" more politically pressing.

Before pursuing recent history, we need to make another clarification regarding the 1960s–1976 period, and our claim that CSR is *business* strategy. As noted the official players in the bid for, and defense against, binding international control of TNCs were developing country *governments*, Northern *governments*, and *intergovernmental* bodies like the OECD and the UN. Where was the business?

The international business lobby—working through the Business and Industry Advisory Committee (BIAC) at the OECD—actively participated in the drafting of the voluntary Guidelines, and the International Chamber of Commerce lobbied hard to derail negotiations on a binding code at the UN.[6] Western transnationals, however, did not have to push their home government hard to resist the code being drafted at the UN. TNCs are great creators of wealth—wealth that contributes to state coffers, finances foreign policy objectives, and trickles down to grease class divisions within First World societies. There are structural reasons for First World states to defend their corporations on the global stage (see Gilpin 1975).

But even given this structural advantage, business learned during the 1960s and 1970s that it had to be much better organized at the international level if it was going to secure its interests. Writing about global struggles between business and labor at the end of the 1970s, John Robinson noted that "Business's task has been uphill, not just because of the general trend towards interventionism, but because of the nature of the adversary organizations. . . . Whereas the trade unions are a relatively homogenous group with an organization to match, 'business' is in fact a collective misnomer for diversified interests with often only a low common denominator" (Robinson 1983: 197). Developing country governments, in conjunction with the international trade union movement, had come close to having a binding code established that would have made doing global business a much more complicated and expensive affair, and could well have spiraled into more profound transformations of the global political economy. This period of crisis taught business that it should not take Northern government support, or the support of international organizations, mainly the UN, for granted.

It is thus in the midst and just after this period of crisis that international business began organizing itself in a sustained way. In 1971, Klaus Schwab established the World Economic Forum (WEF), and in 1973, David Rockefeller established the Trilateral Commission (TLC). The ICC also enjoyed a spike in membership and support during and just after this period.

These business policy and lobby groups can be said to function, in Gramscian terms, as "collective intellectuals" or agents of the capitalist class "entrusted with the activity of organizing the general system of relationships external to business itself" (Gramsci 1971: 6; also see Carroll and Carson 2003: 32). Thus, by "business strategy," we mean strategy developed by these collective intellectuals. Again, while business organizations were heavily involved in the fight against the UN code, this period taught transnational corporate capital that it had to become much more organized—that it needed to become a class not only in-itself, but for-itself.

Before clarifying the development of a transnational class consciousness and its concomitant organizations, we would like to briefly account for domestic business organizing in the US in response to the 1960s and 1970s crisis. Not only was this organizing an important US export, and important to the more "global" story we are telling, but it also provides a nicely focused account of business's rise as a self-consciously political force.

"Attack on the American Free Enterprise System"

Our account begins in 1971 when a US Chamber of Commerce memorandum written by Lewis F. Powell, Jr., was circulated to top business executives.[7] The influential memorandum, entitled "Attack on American Free Enterprise System," perfectly articulates business's political program of the past thirty years, and is worth considering in detail.[8]

Powell's basic argument, like John Robinson's, is that business is losing in the battle over American hearts and minds:

> But what now concerns us is quite new in the history of America. We are not dealing with sporadic or isolated attacks from a relatively few extremists or even from the minority socialist cadre. Rather, the assault on the enterprise system is broadly based and consistently pursued. It is gaining momentum and converts. . . . The most disquieting voices joining the chorus of criticism come from perfectly respectable elements of society: from the college campus, the pulpit, the media, the intellectual and literary journals, the arts and sciences, and from politicians. (Powell 1971)

While Powell's memorandum shows appropriate disdain for business's adversaries, it evinces respect for their ideological and organizing prowess. What progressives have that business lacks, is cohesion. And this cohesion stems from a common project—the radical upheaval or at least radical reform of the free enterprise system. By focusing on "the system" instead of just its individual symptoms (chemical pollution, low wages, unsafe products), progressives have forged powerful alliances among different social movements.

If progressives have found strength and cohesion decrying the system, business can find the same defending it: "If our system is to survive, top management must be equally concerned with protecting and preserving the system itself." And for Powell, this has to be a collective project:

> [I]ndependent and uncoordinated activity by individual corporations, as important as this is, will not be sufficient. Strength lies in organization, in careful long-range planning and implementation, in consistency of action over an indefinite period of years, in the scale of financing available only through joint effort, and in the political power available only through united action and national organizations. (Powell 1971)[9]

Powell's advice was heeded. According to journalist Thomas Edsall: "From 1971 to 1979, the number of corporations represented by registered lobbyists grew from 175 to 650. . . . The National Association of Manufacturers moved to Washington in 1973. . . . [C]hief executive officers of Fortune 500 companies formed the Business

Roundtable in 1972. Membership in the Chamber of Commerce more than doubled, from 36,000 in 1967 to 80,000 in 1974" (Edsall 1990: 248).

For Powell, business's newfound organization and power should be directed towards two fronts: US culture and politics.[10] On the cultural front, Powell argues that business needs to make its presence felt more in the Academe, on television, and in other news media—what he sees as bastions of "liberal" and even "left" thought. Again, his advice was heeded. The period after Powell's memo marked: "growing corporate grants to the Public Broadcasting System, from $3.3 million in 1973 to $22.6 million in 1979; the key role of corporate-funded foundations in the financing of Jude Wanniski's *The Way the World Works* and George Gilder's *Wealth and Poverty*; grants to the Heritage Foundation and the American Enterprise institute; the endowment between 1974 and 1978 of forty 'free enterprise' chairs primarily at liberal undergraduate colleges" (Edsall 1990: 248).

Like Gramsci, Powell felt this cultural war should be guided by political ends:

> [O]ne should not postpone more direct political action, while awaiting the gradual change in public opinion to be effected through education and information. Business must learn the lesson, long ago learned by labor and other self-interested groups. This is the lesson that political power is necessary; that such power must be assiduously cultivated; and that when necessary, it must be used aggressively and with determination—without embarrassment and without the reluctance which has been so characteristic of American business. (Powell 1971)

Again, learning from labor, corporations began organizing Political Action Committees (PACs)—what had previously been the preserve of unions. According to Edsall, "[i]n 1974 there were 89 corporate PACs, in 1978 there were 784, and by the end of 1982 there were 1,467. . . . Labor PACs, in turn, grew only from 201 to 380 in the period from 1972 to 1982" (Edsall 1984: 131). "During the 1970s," writes Edsall, "the political wing of the nation's corporate sector staged one of the most remarkable campaigns in the pursuit of power in recent history. By the late 1970s and the early 1980s, business and Washington's corporate lobbying community in particular, had gained a level of influence and leverage approaching that of the boom days of the 1920s" (Edsall 1984: 107).

Powell ends his memo ominously: "It is time for American business—which has demonstrated the greatest capacity in all history to produce and to influence consumer decisions—to apply their great talents vigorously to the preservation of the system itself" (Powell 1971). Needless to say business has succeeded in its charge.

The problems faced by business in the US—vigorous social movement and a regulatory state—were also shared by business globally. We are now better positioned to account for the rise of a global business consciousness and its related organizations—a process that borrowed from and contributed to the more American story we have just told.

Global Business Becomes *Global* Business

Writing about the 1960 and 1970 period, Stephen Krasner notes how "The South has been able to take two legacies of the North—the organization of political units into sovereign states and the structure of existing international organizations—and use them to disrupt, if not replace, market-oriented regimes over a wide range of issues" (Krasner 1985: 124) The business response to this more global crisis was not perfectly coherent. A main line of tension, speaking generally, was between the *money* and *productive* capitalist fractions. To explain this difference, and the forging of a more global perspective for business, a theoretical digression is required.

Capitalist Fractions and Polanyi's Double Movement

For political economists Henk Overbeek and Kees Van Der Pijl, "[f]ractions of total capital are aggregates of capitalist interests which crystallize around a particular function in the process of capital accumulation" (Overbeek and Van Der Pijl 1993: 3). "*Money Capital*," for Overbeek and Van Der Pijl, "represents the total quantity of commodities, . . . which is at the same time the most general and abstract form of capital. *Productive capital*, even as an abstraction, always refers to tangible 'factors': human labour, raw material, means of production" (Overbeek and Van Der Pijl 1993: 3). Functionaries of the money fraction include investment bankers, while industrialists better represent the productive fraction.

For Overbeek and Van Der Pijl, money capital's more general perspective on markets—its more universal class outlook—interests it in definitively capitalist projects, mainly the opening of new markets, de-regulating existing markets, and reducing barriers to trade and investment. Productive capital has tended to be more parochially minded; its boundedness and thus proximity to tangible factors of production, including human labor and raw materials, predisposes it to protect what appears to money capital as "non-market, non-value aspects of the productive process and its immediate social setting" (Overbeek and Van Der Pijl 1993: 4). In other words, productive capital has tended to be friendlier towards the protective social regulations money capital has been historically interested in removing.

Thus in economic historian Karl Polanyi's terms, money and productive capital, represent the two sides of the "double movement" that has historically characterized market societies. For Polanyi: "Social history in the nineteenth century was thus the result of a double movement. . . . While on the one hand markets spread all over the face of the globe and the amount of goods involved grew to unbelievable dimensions, on the other hand a network of measures and policies was integrated into powerful institutions designed to check the action of the market relative to labor, land and money" (Polanyi 2001: 79).

Polanyi helps clarify the distinctly capitalist quality of productive capital's protective impulse. He thus complicates Overbeek and Van Der Pijl's general account of the more truly capitalist money fraction, and more parochially minded productive fraction. Polanyi's central argument in his influential work of economic history, *The Great Transformation*, is that truly unregulated—or what he terms "disembedded"—economies are impossible: "Our thesis is that the idea of a self-adjusting market implied a stark utopia. Such an institution could not exist for any length of time without annihilating the human and natural substance of society; it would have physically destroyed man and transformed his surroundings into a wilderness" (Polanyi 2001: 3).

Polanyi's rationale for why the purely free market is both myth and dream is that the three most central commodities to market economies—labor, land, and money—are *fictitious*, they are inventions, they need to be continually made and remade. It is worth quoting Polanyi at length in this regard:

> Commodities are here empirically defined as objects produced for sale on the market; markets, again, are empirically defined as actual contacts between buyers and sellers. . . . But labor, land, and money are obviously not commodities; the postulate that anything that is bought and sold must have been produced for sale is emphatically untrue in regard to them. In other words, according to the empirical definition of a commodity they are not commodities. (Polanyi 2001: 75)

Labor and land are the most important "commodities" to consider for our purposes here. Labor, for Polanyi, is "only another name for a human activity which goes with life itself, which in its turn is not produced for sale but for entirely different reasons, nor can that activity be detached from the rest of life" (Polanyi 2001: 75). And land is only another name for nature—what is not produced by humans. Polanyi's point is that incredible work is required to commodify bare life and land—work that markets cannot do on their own. Historically, organized political intervention has always been a prerequisite for the establishment of "free markets": "There was nothing natural about laissez-faire; free markets could never have come into being merely by allowing things to take their course . . . laissez-faire itself was enforced by the state" (Polanyi 2001: 145).

Not only is state intervention integral to the constitution of markets, but perhaps even more importantly for Polanyi, public regulation is necessary to ensure markets do not destroy what makes them possible in the first place: commodified land, labor, and money. There is no logic internal to the market that keeps it from exploiting land and labor in profoundly unsustainable ways. Indeed, with profit as the market's primary engine, there is incentive to extract as much as is humanly and environmentally possible. But both labor and land have natural limits. These limits are for Polanyi, what makes the purely free-market impossible—if these limits are transgressed, markets will destroy their very own bases for existence. States must thus intervene to protect labor and land, and ensure that markets do not destroy themselves.

This intervention, or "counter-movement," is impelled by a confluence of social forces. What we now term "social movements" have been important sparks for protective counter-movements, but so too has business. Indeed, Polanyi provides ample historical evidence of laissez-faire proponents inside and outside of government pursuing interventionist policies without any pressure from social movements: "on the contrary, everything tends to support the assumption that objective reasons of stringent nature forced the hands of the legislators" (Polanyi 2001: 154). Historically even devout capitalists—mostly of the productive ilk—have understood the fundamental limits to labor and land's commodification, and have pushed for state intervention.

Regardless of where the agitation for regulation originated, Polanyi's argument is that state intervention on behalf of society and nature, has historically been integral to the "free-market's" existence.

Thus the brokering of the New Deal in the US, and its corollaries in other Western countries, had the support of productive capital, whose view, especially following the Great Depression, was dominant at the time. "The productive capital perspective," According to Overbeek and Van Der Pijl, "was dominant at the national level in the period from the First World War to the 1950s" (Overbeek and Van Der Pijl 1993: 6).

The 1960s/1970s crisis threw productive capital's protective impulse into relief. Instead of serving to strengthen and enable the free market system, the welfare state had apparently enabled demands that, for business, or "total capital," were looking increasingly illiberal both nationally and internationally. Socialism was only a distant fear—the more imminent concern was the use of the state to more tightly regulate capital domestically and internationally. From capital's perspective, the state was suffering a reverse "legitimation crisis."[11] Instead of revealing its "inherently capitalist nature," the state appeared open—domestically and internationally—to social demands of an uncapitalist, or highly moderating nature. And this opening appeared to be emboldening social forces and enabling even more radical demands. The state was proving a useful weapon in the "Attack on the Free Enterprise System." *It was in the face of this common threat that traditional tensions between money and productive capital subsided.*

This new unity of historical fractions was abetted by transformations in the production process. A more global business outlook had traditionally been the preserve of money capital, but productive capital was finding it increasingly profitable to globalize. Technological advances in transport, telecommunications and, automation, enabled the globalization process but what we term "globalization" is also a *project*—the result of conscious political decisions (Went 2000: 53). According to Robinson and Harris, one of the primary reasons for globalizing production was to weaken domestic labor demands—demands that were posing serious problems for capitalist accumulation, and that were partly enabled by productive capital's protective impulse itself (Robinson and Harris 2000: 27). By moving, or outsourcing production to where labor costs were cheaper—countries in the Global South—both domestic labor's bargaining position was weakened, and more surplus value/profit could be accrued.

It is important to note how crucial racism was/is to the globalization project. A return to Polanyi is useful here. For Polanyi, what moderates over-exploitation of labor and land are human and natural limits—limits that if transgressed, will result in the destruction of the market's very bases of existence. But Polanyi's humanism blinds him to the elasticity of the category "human." While there are general limits to how hard the human body can be worked, determining those limits remains a contextual affair. For Northern capital, Third-World labor can be worked more than First-World labor. Speaking abstractly, the cost of sustaining labor power (reproducing workers) is similar for all laborers. But speaking historically, years of colonialism have produced structural conditions under which Third-World labor power is simply worth less. Third-World laborers can thus be more easily compelled both legitimately (capitalist exchange) and illegitimately (slave labor) to work more for less, and thus produce more profit. And returning to Polanyi's terms, the compulsion to intervene on behalf of destitute Third-World laborers is less for Northern capital because these laborers are lesser humans—a racist interpretation objectified, or made historically real in the global labor market. The important point here, is that globalized production allows "total capital" to push the bounds of "the human" and thus stall the protective impulse integral to market societies.

In the 1960s and 1970s post-colonial states were not only defending against this capitalist "utopia," but were moving to restructure the global economy in profound ways. It was in this context of the failed protective impulse in the North (intensive worker organizing, social movement, and an increasingly regulatory state), the resulting push for globalized production, and the increasing power of Third-World states, *that a new capitalist consensus developed around the traditionally money capital position—the opening of new markets and deregulation of existing ones.*

While the economic liberalism of money capital had enjoyed earlier periods of prominence—much of the nineteenth century for instance (see Polanyi 2001: 3–35)—the late 1970s was novel. The primary difference now was that the globalization of production was contributing to the formation of a new transnational capitalist class (TCC)—one unmoored from the protective impulse of nationally bounded production. For Robinson and Harris, "[a]s national productive structures . . . become transnationally integrated, world classes whose organic development took place through the nation-state are experiencing supra-national integration with 'national' classes of other countries" (Robinson and Harris 2000: 17). The still forming TCC contains elements from both money and productive capital: "transnational corporations and financial institutions, the elite that manage the supranational economic planning agencies, major forces in the dominant political parties, media conglomerates, and technocratic elites and state managers in both North and South" (Robinson and Harris 2000: 2).[12]

Our focus in this study is on "supranational economic planning agencies."[13] This phrase references both multilateral economic institutions like the IMF, WTO, World Bank, and OECD, and business planning forums like the WEF, TLC, and the ICC that are, formally speaking, removed from state apparatuses. More particularly, our focus is on the role of these latter "agencies," mainly the International Chamber of Commerce, in articulating global business vision and strategy.

Global business planning forums are both the product of, and preconditions for, a transnational capitalist class. While organizations like the WEF are enabled by transformations in the production process, they are also integral to the articulation of class-consciousness; it is these organizations that have made the TCC a class not only in-itself, but for-itself. For William Carroll and Colin Carson, global business planning forums "provide intellectual leadership that is indispensable in the ongoing effort to transform transnational capital from an economically dominant class to a class whose interests take on a sense of universalism" (Carroll and Carson 2003: 37). We are not claiming that these forums dictated the business fight-back against encroachments on its interests—the regulatory state—in the North and the South. The business fight-back was more an "accumulation of tactical responses" than the product of centralized strategy making (Zinn 2003: 59). But business policy forums *did* play a crucial role—one that has increased over time—in articulating a self-conscious political program for global business.

What was the program? It is worthwhile, in this regard, to recall business writer John Robinson's doldrums at the end of the 1970s. Not only did Robinson worry that "global business" was only a "collective misnomer for diversified interests with often only a low common denominator," but also that "*there is no binding ideological force which is such a cohesive element in the trade unions' organisation*" (Robinson 1983: 197, emphasis added). Robinson's concerns are jarring for the current reader. As we well know, a new ideological specter was haunting the world.

If the trade union and developing country position can be termed "social democratic," the business position was "neoliberal." If the "social democratic" strategy was to use the state to better regulate Western capital in its home countries, moderate its effects in the global South, and work through international organizations to reform the global political economy itself, the neo-liberal position was to use the state to deregulate markets in the North, open and deregulate markets in the South, and work through international organizations to reform the global political economy itself.

But neoliberalism was not merely reactive. As Stuart Hall remarks in regard to the advent of neoliberalism in the UK:

> If the crisis is deep—"organic"—these efforts cannot be merely defensive. They will be *formative*: aiming at a new balance of forces, the emergence of new elements, the attempt to put together a new "historic bloc," new political configurations and "philosophies." . . . These new elements do not "emerge": they have to be constructed. Political and ideological work is required to disarticulate old formations, and to rework their elements into new ones. (quoted in Overbeek and Van Der Pijl 1993: 14)

Part of what makes neoliberalism formative and "neo" is its attempt to stall the previously *capitalist* impulse to protect the very bases of markets (labor and land) from commodification-to-death. As noted, this requires a radical—though uneven—reformulation of the categories "human" and "nature." This reformulation requires sustained cultural, ideological, political, and economic work on a multiplicity of scales. We cannot account for all of this multi-frontal and leveled work. Our focus is more general—on neoliberalism as a global political-economic project that "seeks to achieve the conditions in each country and region of the world for the mobility and free operation of capital" (Robinson and Harris 2000: 41).

What is confusing about this global and apparently anti-statist project is that its primary vehicles are Northern states, and international economic institutions dominated by Northern governments. As Powell's memo helps us understand, a key plank in the business fight-back has been "state reclamation," or at least clarifying whose side the state is on. Globally, neoliberalism has informed calls for all governments (North/South) to reduce trade and investment barriers (like burdensome regulations), and the intense pressure Northern countries have placed on Southern countries—using multilateral economic institutions like the IMF, World Bank, and WTO—to "liberalize" their national economies. In other words, to deregulate industry, privatize state functions and resources, cut social programs and generally make their economies more open to foreign investment from TNCs mostly based in the First World.

While we agree with Overbeek and Van Der Pijl that "neo-liberalism is the fundamental expression of the outlook of transnational circulating capital" (Overbeek and Van Der Pijl 1993: 15) we are not claiming a passive role for the state in this story. There are structural incentives for rich countries—especially hegemons like the US—to actively pursue a "liberal world economic order" (Gilpin 1975: 142; also see Lake 1983). Our simple claim is that events in the 1960s and 1970s—mainly regulationist claims being made on the state in the North, South, and globally—jarred business into sustained self-organization. This self-organization has enabled an impressive counter-offensive against the "social democratic" bloc that emerged during this period. In other words, it has enabled the emergence of a *radical* political program—neoliberalism—that could not have been so vigorous in content and pursuit without business's sustained self-organization.[14]

Voluntary codes of conduct would not become a crucial part of the neoliberal program until the 1990s. We submit, however, that the threat of a binding UN code contributed significantly to neoliberalism's constitution. For Van Der Pijl, "the threat and the transformative potential of the code of conduct challenge were sufficiently well perceived to fuel a vehement counteroffensive along a much broader front" (Van Der Pijl 1993: 54). Before forging into the next period—when CSR enters into the neoliberal tool-kit in a sustained way—we'd like to briefly account for arguments *against* CSR *within* the business community during the 1960s/1970s period. We do this for two reasons. Firstly to show that business has never fully agreed that CSR is strategically valuable. Secondly, because the particular criticism we unpack comes from an interesting source—Milton Friedman, one of neoliberalism's greatest intellectuals—and has an ironically critical edge we would like to unpack.

"The Social Responsibility of Business is to Increase its Profits"

Milton Friedman's New York Times article "The Social Responsibility of Business is to Increase its Profits" (Friedman 1970) is probably the most-cited commentary on CSR—for and against—from the period. Friedman's basic claim is that corporate spending on socially responsible ends—ends not directly related to the company's business operations—is theft. Socially responsible spending, for Friedman, steals from shareholders who did not sanction such spending, from customers who must pay higher prices for goods, and from employees whose wages are compromised. Publicly minded business ends up distorting the market and hurting society; it is the pursuit of self-interested profit that ultimately leads to collective betterment.

Friedman's argument operates on two related but distinct levels. His first claim is more fundamental: profits and the entrepreneurs who pursue them are inherently good—profit seeking *is* socially responsible. His second claim is more strategic: if the business community relents to calls for social responsibility and does not defend the value of profit seeking in itself, the free market will be imperiled.

As noted, Friedman was writing at a time when there was "wide spread aversion to 'capitalism,' 'profits,' the 'soulless corporation' and so on" (Friedman 1970). He saw business bids for CSR as complicity with these aversions, the telos of which was government regulation—a slippery slope to socialism:

> [CSR] helps to strengthen the already too prevalent view that the pursuit of profits is wicked and immoral and must be curbed and controlled by external forces. Once this view is adopted, the external forces that curb the market will not be the social consciences, however highly developed, of the pontificating executives; it will be the iron fist of Government bureaucrats. (Friedman 1970)

Friedman's calls were not heeded, and he ultimately lost the CSR debate, which for John Kline, "has been resolved in favor of an expanded social contract for business" (Kline 1985: 159). Friedman's argument is worth mentioning, however, because while his "profits-are-everything" philosophy has been historically invoked by CSR advocates as exemplary of free-market thinking gone wrong, his argument has a critical edge worth preserving. Friedman's retort to his critics is provocative and worth quoting at length:

> It may well be in the long run interest of a corporation that is a major employer in a small community to devote resources to providing amenities to that community or to improving its government. That may make it easier to attract desirable employees, it may reduce the wage bill or lessen losses from pilferage and sabotage or have other worthwhile effects. . . . In the present climate of opinion, with its wide spread aversion to "capitalism," "profits," the "soulless corporation" and so on, this is one way for a corporation to generate goodwill as a by-product of expenditures that are entirely justified in its own self-interest. It would be inconsistent of me to call on corporate executives to refrain from this hypocritical window-dressing because it harms the foundations of a free society. That would be to call on them to exercise a "social responsibility"! *If our institutions, and the attitudes of the public make it in their self-interest to cloak their actions in this way, I cannot summon much indignation to denounce them.* At the same time, I can express admiration for those individual proprietors or owners of closely held corporations or stockholders of more broadly held corporations who disdain such tactics as approaching fraud. (Friedman 1970; emphasis added)

Friedman's argument very much resembles our own. Where Friedman differs is his desire for institutions that better recognize profit's inherent value, and thus do not compel companies to fake benevolence. Friedman's desires have become profoundly manifest. But the neoliberal project has resulted in deregulated business environments that ironically, given Friedman's argument, makes CSR all the more necessary to quell public concern. What other commentators understood better than Friedman, and what would become clearer as the neoliberal project consolidated its gains—is that CSR is a crucial mechanism for keeping government and society out of the "business of business."

History's Sequel: 1998–Present

The 1980s were a decade of relative calm for transnational corporate capital. The Berlin Wall crumbled; the Soviet Union disintegrated, and so did, for many commentators, any alternative to the capitalist mode of production and social organization. But while the 1990s were supposed to be the end of history's happy beginning, transnational corporations quickly became lightning rods for global protests against the neoliberal consensus and its deleterious effects—plant closures in the North, brutal labor conditions in the South, unrestricted exploitation of environmental resources worldwide, human rights abuses, corporate concentration, shrinking democratic accountability, etc. Richard Howitt, member of the European parliament, provides a nice summary of recent anti-corporate activity:

> [The] early 1990s saw a stream of exposes of sweatshop conditions within the supply chains of major US clothing suppliers, in particular in Central America. Royal Dutch Shell was attacked relentlessly for its role—or lack of it—in relation to the killing of Ken Saro-Wiwa and oppression of the Ogoni people in, then, non-democratic Nigeria. The 1998 Soccer World Cup was skillfully exploited by activists to highlight child labour in South Asia's sportswear industry. (Howitt 2002: xiii)

In North America, popular frustrations over corporate rule and power crystallized on November 30, 1999, when approximately 60,000 people flooded the streets of Seattle and succeeded in shutting down meetings of the WTO's Third Ministerial.[15] The popularity of the anti-corporate sentiments impelling the mass demonstrations was confirmed by a *Business Week* poll conducted in September 2000. Pollsters asked Americans what they thought of the statement "Business has too much power over too many aspects of our lives." Fifty-two percent said they "strongly" agreed and an additional 30 percent said they agreed "somewhat" (Nace 2003: 10). This is powerful sentiment, especially from the putative beneficiaries of US hegemony and the "liberal world economic order."

Popular anti-corporate sentiments in the US were strengthened when Enron's scandalous bankruptcy hit the front pages. Enron, for five years running, had been named "most innovative" company by none other than *Business Week* magazine (Nace 2003: 178). Its primary innovation, however, was creative accounting that enhanced the company's financial appearance thus inflating stock price. When financial reality finally caught up to appearance, thousands of Enron employees lost their jobs *and* retirement savings. Many thousand more working Americans were impacted. Before going bankrupt, Enron was the seventh largest company in the nation and a favorite, and supposedly secure, investment for various employee pension and retirement plans.[16]

Enron might have been written off as an unfortunate exception to the rule of corporate responsibility, but by "by July 2002, the scandal sheet included over a dozen corporations, including Adelphia, AOL Time Warner, Arthur Anderson, Bristol-Meyers Squibb, Global Crossing, Halliburton, Johnson & Johnson, Qwest Communications, Tyco, WorldCom and Xerox" (Nace 2003: 179). Investors, and ordinary Americans whose retirements are dependent on healthy stock prices—people who may not have been "anti-corporate" before—now had immediate reasons for demanding more government control over corporations. The corporate scandals that turned the century lay bare and popularized concerns of a global anti-corporate movement that was vibrant *before* news of the scandals broke. The growing chorus of peoples from around the world actively opposed to neoliberal globalization and corporate rule has put capital in a defensive position—one it has not had to assume since the mid-1960s and 1970s.

In response to this crisis, business has predictably turned to a trusty tool in its repertoire of contention: "In an era when reputation began to exceed all other factors in determining company sales and value," Richard Howitt writes about the past decade, "executives could not afford to wait for a change in the political wind. The more enlightened ones began to admit to the problem, and say only they could do something about it" (Howitt 2002: xiii). Corporate Social Responsibility is born, again.

The corporate code of conduct has been a favored business response to threatened profits. Whether in response to direct criticism or in scrambles to avoid that criticism, corporations worked hard through the nineties to stem growing frustration with corporate abuses. According to Naomi Klein, all of the decade's major corporate codes were drafted by public-relations firms in the wake of threatening media investigations:

> Wal-Mart's code arrived after reports surfaced that its supplier factories in Bangladesh were using child labor; Disney's code was born of the Haitian revelation; Levi's wrote its policy as an answer to prison labor scandals. Their original purpose was not reform but to "muzzle the offshore watchdog" groups, as Alan Rolnick, lawyer for the American Apparel Manufacturers Association, advised his clients. (Klein 2000: 430)

Every major corporation now has a code of conduct or at least makes mention of commitments to social responsibility on its website and in shareholder literature. Indeed, CSR has become a growth industry. Writing about the past decade, Dwight Justice of the International Confederation of Free Trade Unions (ICFTU), notes how "CSR moved from a concept to become an industry as consultants and enterprises emerged, offering CSR services to business. Among these services were social auditing and reporting as well as 'risk assessment' services" (Justice 2002: 99). "The trade union concern with this industry," Justice continues, "is that is assisting business in redefining the expectations of society instead of responding to them" (Justice 2002: 99). Business has been intent on redefinition since labor and social activists have been working to capitalize on popular discontent and lobby for more market regulation nationally and globally.

One of civil society's more challenging regulatory moves through the nineties was global labor's attempt to link "the ILO with the WTO, hoping that the ILO's rights-oriented culture might join with the WTO's enforcement power and sanctioning process" (Monshipouri 2002: 26). Ian Hurd nicely outlines the WTO's appeal to labor activists:

> The WTO is a strong intergovernmental organization with a clear mandate to review domestic regulation in member states and issue legally binding remedies when states violate the set of agreed-upon rules. This appears to satisfy the institutional structure that many labour-standards advocates seek. Adding new rules to this set (perhaps, for instance, on hours of work or the right to unionise) seems a smaller task than creating an entirely new organization and might be able to take advantage of the unusually strong dispute-settlement mechanisms already built into the WTO. (Hurd 2003: 103)

The "new rules" the labor movement wanted enforced were the ILO's core labor standards including freedom of association, the right to collective bargaining, abolition of forced labor, prevention of discrimination in employment, and a minimum age for employment (O'Brien 2000: 83). The key to having these standards as part of the WTO is, for Robert O'Brien, "that for the first time they would become enforceable and not depend on the whims of individual states. Labour wanted the WTO Sheriff to include core labour standards on its beat" (O'Brien 2000: 83). Labor's bid was ultimately defeated, but was reminiscent of the earlier period, and caused grave concern in the business community.[17]

One way of acknowledging concern with labor rights without compromising capital accumulation is, of course, the voluntary code of conduct. According to a 1997 editorial in the *Journal of Commerce*: "The voluntary code helps defuse a contentious issue in international trade negotiations: whether to make labor standards part of trade agreements. If . . . the sweatshop problem is solved outside the trade context, labor standards will no longer be tools in the hands of protectionists" (quoted in Klein 2000: 437).

Two of the most prominent organizations business has partnered with to solve "the sweatshop problem"—a phrase that serves as a synecdoche for all of neoliberal globalization's externalities, and the protests they impel—have been the OECD and the UN. These organizations were where the battle over compulsory vs. voluntary regulation was fought in the 1970s, and where it is being fought today. The primary difference between now and then, however, is that *both* the OECD and UN are on the same side—that of business and the voluntary code of conduct.[18] Stranger yet, while the OECD offered up its relatively vacuous voluntary Guidelines on Multinational Corporations in 1976 *as a counter* to the UN's binding code of conduct, the OECD's current Guidelines are much more stringent than the UN's recent contribution to the regulation debate—the Global Compact.

Linking the OECD Guidelines and UN Global Compact is the significant contribution made to each by the International Chamber of Commerce. The ICC is not the sole author of these documents but, as will be discussed below, its vision is deeply etched in both. Carroll and Carson nicely articulate the relationship between business policy forms like the ICC and more formal political bodies like the OECD and UN:

> [Business policy forums] operate at one remove from the structural adjustment programmes, "poverty reduction strategies" and other enforcement mechanisms, including the capacity for military intervention, that are the province of statist bodies, whether national or international. They foster discussion of global issues among members of the corporate elite, often in combination with other influential political and professional elites. They facilitate the formation of a moving elite consensus that is framed within one or another variant of neo-liberal discourse. They educate publics and states on the virtues of the neo-liberal paradigm. In sort, they are agencies of political and cultural leadership, whose activities are integral to the formation of a transnational capitalist class. (Carroll and Carson 2003: 53)

The ICC—which terms itself the "voice of world business"—has been the business organization most invested in the strategic deployment of codes of conduct.[19] The remainder of this chapter will track the role both the UN and OECD—with significant prodding from the ICC—have played in forestalling a sustained regulatory solution to the "sweatshop problem."

The OECD Guidelines Redux

What the original OECD Guidelines for Multinational Enterprises had in common with the UN's proposed code of conduct was the recognition that unregulated business activity was causing serious social and environmental externalities. Where the Guidelines differed, however, was the lack of mechanisms for ensuring these problems were addressed in a sustained way. Summing up the gist of the OECD's original guidelines, Susan Aaronson and James Reeves note that "firms would not abuse citizens or the environment in these [OECD] countries, and governments would not try to control these firms" (Aaronson and Reeves 2002: 11). Business, as the current flurry of debate on CSR suggests, did not keep its end of the bargain.

But, as noted, the economic stagnations of 1973–1975 and 1980–1982—primarily the latter—helped weaken public pressure on business and government and changed the terms of the international regulation debate. For John Robinson, writing in the early 1980s, the "shifting emphasis of the OECD . . . from control of multinational companies to encouragement of international investment is now a central part of the strategy of those who, like the US administration, believe that there has been undue stress laid to date, and certainly up until the 1979 review of the Guidelines, on the 'negative' or control aspects of the decisions taken by the OECD council" (Robinson 1983: 146). With the specter of regulation exorcised, the discourse and practice of corporate social responsibility subsided—there is little incentive for business to concern itself with ethics when its conduct is not being heavily scrutinized. While the OECD Guidelines went under review in 1979, 1982, 1984, and 1991, no significant changes were made.

This all changed in 1998. "In 1998," write Aaronson and Reeves, "the OECD again began a review to make the Guidelines more useful and effective" (Aaronson and Reeves 2002: 11). This review was higher stakes than the four previous. This same year, the OECD suffered a major political defeat with the collapse of talks it was hosting on the Multilateral Agreement on Investment (MAI).[20]

While there were indications that negotiations for an investment agreement were under way, the public did not become aware of the MAI and its implications until draft copies of the proposed treaty were leaked to citizen groups in March of 1997. By October of 1997, when the text was first officially released, a large and vocal protest movement was underway. By 1998 Toronto's *Globe and Mail* observed that the OECD governments "were no match . . . for a global band of grassroots organizations, which, with little more than computers and access to the Internet, helped derail a deal" (quoted in Chomsky 1998). The *Financial Times* reported that "fear and bewilderment have seized governments of industrialised countries . . . their efforts to impose the MAI in secret have been ambushed by a horde of vigilantes whose motives and methods are only dimly understood in most national capitals" (Chomsky 1998).

The defeat of the MAI by global civil society stunned the OECD ministers. Canadian Trade Minister Sergio Marchi remarked after talks had collapsed that "the lesson he has learned is that 'civil society'—meaning public interest groups—should be engaged much sooner in a negotiating process, instead of governments trying to negotiate around them" (Perlas 2000).

The OECD responded predictably to the MAI's defeat, and the emergence of a new global protest movement; it revamped its Guidelines for Multinational Corporations, and with a revamped "feel-good" process. Overnight, the OECD moved from a strategy of exclusion—the MAI was being negotiated in secret—to one of accommodation. Civil society organizations that had rallied their constituents against the OECD were now invited to the bargaining table for a high-stakes review of the Guidelines for Multinational Corporations. Susan Aaronson and James Reeves nicely describe the redrafting process:

> The OECD adopted an unusual approach to revising the Guidelines. It hoped to build a broad international constituency by involving a wide range of groups and giving them a stake in the development and implementation of its code. . . . Each group organized and presented a common position to the negotiators and OECD staff. . . . Among the civil society groups involved were World Wildlife, Amnesty International, Friends of the Earth, Tradecraft Exchange, and SOMO of the Netherlands. In this way, the OECD embraced a new strategy for the development of international public policy, with a different approach to transparency and public participation. (Aaronson and Reeves 2002: 12)

Even with the OECD's inclusion of civil society, and the specter of regulation on the streets and the Internet—a rallying cry of the anti-MAI protests was that we must "bring the rule of law to global capital" (Clarke and Barlow 1998: 4)—business gave up very little on the redrafting.

On the surface, the revamped Guidelines look promising. Covering nine areas of business conduct including labor, environment, human rights, and information disclosure, the Guidelines are more comprehensive than most other codes of conduct (Ethical Corporation, unpaginated).[21] They are also the only multilaterally endorsed code of conduct for TNCs (Gordon 2001: 2). According to the OECD, "while observance of the recommendations by enterprises is purely voluntary, adhering governments sign a binding decision to participate in Guidelines implementation and to promote their observance by enterprises operating in or from their territory" (Gordon 2001: 9). OECD governments implement the Guidelines through National Contact Points (NCPs) responsible for promoting the Guidelines, handling inquiries, and helping to resolve issues that arise.[22]

The NGOs that participated in the re-drafting were quick to highlight their concerns in a June 6, 2000, document published soon after the new Guidelines: "Whilst we would prefer to see the text strengthened further, the key test of the Guidelines is their implementation. If adhering Governments fail to implement the Guidelines vigorously, transparently and effectively world-wide, then NGOs will be left with no option but to actively and publicly oppose the Guidelines" (NGOs 2000). The NGOs conclude "unless implementation is conducted in good faith there is a real risk that the Guidelines will be used to justify behaviour and practices by multinational enterprises which undermine sustainability" (NGOs 2000).

It is important to consider what "implementation" means in the context of the non-binding Guidelines. At best, "implementation" means the enaction of a well-resourced National Contact Point that will vigorously promote the Guidelines, and provide an impartial venue for citizens and organizations that want to report irresponsible corporate behavior. "Implementation" does *not* entail active enforcement or the punishment of wrongdoers. Since the text is non-binding, "breaking" the Guidelines is legally impossible. Thus NGO support for the agreement hinges on active promotion of the voluntary Guidelines more than their enforcement.

Even with these minimal criteria for support, NGO threats have not been heeded: "As of this January 2002 writing," report Aaronson and Reeves, "many governments, such as the United States and Mexico, are doing virtually nothing or very little to implement the Guidelines. If, as example, the US does nothing, most citizens will not pressure it to do more, because most Americans have no knowledge that the US and other governments have ever agreed to implement such a code" (Aaronson and Reeves 2002: 13).

Civil society is growing increasingly wary of the OECD, but remains hopeful that the Guidelines will be useful for short-term campaigning, and the longer-term bid for an international and binding regulatory framework. The rationales for civil society's exuberant patience were outlined at a recent "NGO Training and Strategy Seminar on the OECD Guidelines for Multinationals." A strategic point made at the seminar was that even with their non-binding quality, the fact that the Guidelines are endorsed and supported by governments, provides some leverage to those wanting to push for more sustained market regulation. For Peter Pennartz of the International Restructuring and Education Network Europe (IRENE), the "Guidelines provide an opportunity to drag governments back into the arena of corporate social responsibility and pinpoint governments again at their responsibilities towards civil society" (quoted in Smith 2003: 2).[23]

Beyond this larger strategic reason for continuing to use (and tacitly supporting) the Guidelines, the general consensus at the seminar was that since the Guidelines exist, they are worth testing: "the vast majority of participants voted in favour of continuing to use and develop the OECD Guidelines as an instrument in the toolbox for campaigning" (Smith 2003: 11). There is thus a long-term (gateway to binding international framework) and short-term (immediate improvements in corporate conduct) rationale for working with the Guidelines. Our concern with the consensus expressed at the NGO seminar, is that civil society support for the Guidelines will likely forestall the longer-term vision of a binding international framework while providing few short-term payoffs. This concern was voiced at the seminar by Matt Phillips, from Friends of the Earth, who

> looked at the wider picture of campaigning which only brings success at the local level and argued for the need to drive a bigger picture of global change

> which needs binding international rules. He expressed concern about pursuing lots of cases through the OECD Guidelines and the danger that we will only get a whole set of ambiguous outcomes that don't give us any big change to the global development model. (Smith 2003: 7)

To unpack the argument that supporting the Guidelines will compromise bids for a binding regulatory framework, we need to analyze the OECD's logic in drafting the Guidelines. The OECD's strategy is clearly one of co-optation through limited accommodation. One gets a sense of this strategy in a statement made at the NGO seminar by Andre Driessen from OECD's BIAC, summarized here by rapporteur Lisa Smith:

> He sees the Guidelines as a two-way process and doesn't relate to them as a problem, he sees them as a solution. . . . Andre concluded by saying that the debate can continue but the Guidelines should be used for what they are—they are a *compromise*. If we only focus on enforcement a whole part of the Guidelines will be lost. (Smith 2003: 8, emphasis added)

But what has business actually compromised in the redrafting process? What has business given up in order to convince civil society this was largely a legitimate and worthwhile process? Business made two compromises that have captured (or distracted?) the interests of civil society. The first is simply admitting the problem—that corporate conduct has often been unethical during the past decade and that a remedy is required. The second is agreeing that government should play some role (even if extremely limited) in that remedy—the regulation of corporate conduct. We will consider each compromise in turn.

Ceding Ethical Ground/Acceptance of Progressive Norms

This compromise is not meaningless; it subjects business to ethical considerations beyond the bottom line and not previously in its purview. As aforementioned, condemning an organization for unethical behavior is easier when said organization has already and openly agreed that ethical behavior is virtuous.[24] The danger with business's admission of a spotty ethical record, and acceptance of progressive norms, however, is that it takes the sting out of civil society accusations. Since most civil society concerns already have a common-sense appeal (livable wages, the sanctity of human rights, environmental sustainability, etc.) it is perhaps even more striking when business is completely eschewing them, rather than paying discursive lip-service. Business's acceptance of progressive norms has destabilized the ethical ground from which civil society garners its authority. Progressive terms ("sustainability," etc.) have been vacated of meaning while retaining their significance. This is to say that "sustainability" or "human rights" continues *signifying* responsibility and ethical progressivism to the constituents and consumers business wants to target, while *referring* to barely responsible and often irresponsible behavior. In plain terms, business "talks the talk" *so as not* to "walk the walk." Indeed, by overtaking the talk, retaining its significance while vacating its content, business changes what it actually means to walk the walk in the first place. Business has assumed civil society's progressive language without assuming the accompanying practices or policies. While civil society organizations have had some success capitalizing on this contradiction, business has been the big winner from their "compromise"—they understand better than most, especially in our increasingly mediated world, that signifiers often matter more than referents.

Governments and Implementation

The OECD understands that without an emphasis on implementation and enforcement, codes of conduct lack legitimacy. The OECD was sensitized to the power of a disgruntled public in the late 1990s, and takes the legitimacy problem seriously. The OECD's primary challenge in drafting the Guidelines was to solve the legitimacy problem—providing for some level of implementation and enforcement—without shifting the policy paradigm away from voluntary mechanisms. To fully grasp the OECD's challenge, we need to consider the series of studies they commissioned on Corporate Codes of Conduct while, and just after, reviewing and redrafting the Guidelines.[25] These are authoritative studies cited by both sides of the regulation debate. While the OECD's research is ideologically inflected—the organization is definitively on the voluntary side of the regulation debate—these studies can be read as an immanent critique of voluntary regulation in general. The studies cannot hide that voluntary codes of conduct are ineffective at regulating corporate behavior.

In "Codes of Conduct: An Inventory," OECD researchers survey and analyze 233 codes of corporate conduct. The OECD reports that it is interested in codes because they "represent a relatively new way of addressing *certain issues* through mainly non-governmental bodies in ways that seek little direct impact on trade or investment flows" (OECD 1999: 4, emphasis added). But the contents of the report suggest that codes of conduct also have little direct impact on the "certain issues" (human rights abuses, environmental destruction, morbidly low wages) codes are meant to address. "A significant number of company and business association codes included in the inventory," report the OECD researchers, "do not touch on the subject of monitoring at all. Where company codes have relevant provisions, almost all state that in-house staff will oversee implementation of and compliance with the code's standards—both by the company that issues the code and by its suppliers and other business partners. In other words, companies tend to prefer internal procedures or remain silent on this issue" (OECD 1999: 17). The researchers continue: "*The effectiveness of codes in influencing the behavior of corporations depends also on a strong enforcement mechanism. . . .* Not all of the codes surveyed describe responses to breaches of code in great detail" (OECD 1999: 18, emphasis added). A strong enforcement mechanism would entail external monitoring by a second or third party with some punitive powers. But according to a more recent OECD report on CSR, "External monitoring is the least used implementation technique examined—only two percent of the company codes mention it" (OECD 2001b: 11).

These weaknesses in most private initiatives in play are a concern for the OECD. Codes of Conduct have the potential to assuage civil society concern with corporate (mis)conduct while minimally impacting trade or investment flows. But for private initiatives to satisfy (or at least distract) NGOs and labor, they must *at least* speak the language of implementation and enforcement. This is the beauty of the OECD Guidelines. They are voluntary and non-binding while simultaneously emphasizing the importance of implementation. Like with assumption of ethics-speak ("sustainability"), business is busy recuperating the meaning of implementation. "Implementation" still signifies monitoring and enforcement even while it refers to the same old non-binding arrangements. And with the assumption of "implementation-speak," the OECD can claim an impressive advancement in the field of CSR. In the OECD's most recent study "The OECD Guidelines and Other Corporate Responsibility Instruments: A Comparison," the researchers smugly report that "by adding the weight of adhering governments' views to the general public debate on many issues in international business ethics, the Guidelines process has already succeeded in raising the legitimacy and profile of corporate attempts to address these issues. The Guidelines implementation procedures have also been enhanced, especially in relation to the functioning of the National Contact Points. They remain unique" (Gordon 2001: 7). The problem, as noted, is that large segments of civil society agree.

In a recent presentation to the National Policy Association, ANPED's Pieter van der Gaag noted that compared to other CSR initiatives, the Guidelines are an impressive regulative mechanism:

> The OECD Guidelines on the other hand, may have a bigger chance of bringing us the needed fast improvements. The OECD guidelines are a more detailed and complete document. . . . What is also needed is the systemised non-threatening dialogue that is offered by the implementation mechanism of the OECD Guidelines. The value of the different perspectives that are brought in while dealing with difficult issues like supply chain responsibility, implementation on the corporate level of the precautionary principle, human rights, whistleblower protection, and some of the other difficult points in the guidelines will start creating the common understanding needed to build good policy on. (van der Gaag 2001: 3)

Van der Gaag has apparently accepted the OECD's implementation "compromise," along with the consensus language preferred by BIAC. He still believes that government regulation is the only way to ensure corporate responsibility, but thinks the OECD Guidelines, and the forums for exchange it establishes between civil society, business, and government, can lead to such regulation. His strategy is made clear here:

> A combination of worldwide standardised information gathering and verification and multistakeholder dialogue will finally put in place the decision-making mechanism to create and protect sustainable societies. A start should be made with further developing the real-world . . . OECD Guidelines to effective, detailed global standard systems that generate the information needed and provide the space for networked information sharing and dialogue. (van der Gaag 2001: 5)

The hope at the root of van der Gaag's strategy, and which the Guidelines stoke, is that corporations and governments can be convinced through friendly dialogue to change their behavior and accept the civil society call for an international and binding regulatory framework. Speaking generally, this hope flies in the face of one of history's most important lessons—that social and political change comes more from agitation, confrontation and challenge, than friendly conversation between adversaries (Richter 2001: 205). Speaking particularly, van der Gaag's hope contradicts the history being told here—voluntary mechanisms have been consistently invoked to prevent, not abet binding regulation.

It is interesting to note, however, that while van der Gaag is supportive of the Guidelines, he is very critical of most other CSR mechanisms. The other high profile mechanism he considers is the UN's Global Compact. For van der Gaag,

> [t]he global compact and its UN Agency spin-offs are, however, part of a deal that seems to elevate companies above the usual consultative status that every other UN partner, such as NGOs, enjoy, onto an almost co-decisional arrangement. Some of my colleagues believe, and I tend to agree with them, that there will be advertising pay-offs for those companies who have joined, we call it the potential for blue wash. . . . Now this "all is well" approach, coupled with the above concerns may even mean that the Compact will cause a slow-down of the so necessary fast continuous improvement . . . the planet needs so much. (van der Gaag 2001: 3)

Van der Gaag's enthusiasm for the Guidelines and suspicion of the Compact is a common position among activists. While the Compact enjoys some provisional civil society support (Amnesty, Human Rights Watch, ICFTU, etc.), it is a less-respected mechanism.

Our argument, however, is that the Guidelines and Global Compact are different sides of the same coin. Both mechanisms have the same goal—forestalling regulation—but different audiences in mind. The OECD Guidelines are a more stringent and lower profile mechanism meant for a very specific audience—the organized elements of civil society: NGOs and Trade Unions. The Guidelines' concessionary language around implementation has piqued the interest, attention, and hopes of civil society organizations. The Global Compact, a largely vacuous but high profile mechanism, is targeted at the larger public—the Compact mobilizes the UN's profile and legitimacy to quell widespread public concern with corporate power. In other words, the OECD Guidelines are a "Thinking Man's" Global Compact.

The ICC has been a pivotal driver behind *both* documents. While the ICC agree with van der Gaag that "the OECD Guidelines [are] the highest set of standards out there, and in the view of the ICC the most important code of conduct for business in the world," they also co-authored the Compact—what is sometimes termed the "UN-ICC Global Compact" (quoted in van der Gaag 2001: 4). Why the ICC would suggest the Guidelines are better than the Compact they directly crafted is unclear. But the different purposes of these tools are. The following section unpacks the Global Compact's strategic value for business.

The UN Global Compact

What is the Global Compact? The Global compact consists of nine principles, distilled from key environmental, labor, and human rights agreements, that the Secretary General asks business to abide by. Corporate participation is voluntary; there is no screening process, nor is there monitoring or enforcement (Bruno and Karliner 2000: 5).[26] "On the surface, then, the Global Compact is a fairly modest initiative," write Kenny Bruno and Joshua Karliner, "yet it was inaugurated in July 2000 with great fanfare, with the CEOs of corporations such as Nike, Shell, Rio Tinto and Novartis sharing the stage with the Secretary General at UN headquarters in New York" (Bruno and Karliner 2002: 50). The Compact's meaning rests in the disconnect between its modest content and extravagant fanfare.

Fully understanding the Compact, however, requires a brief historical digression. We would like to account for the political shifts that enabled the Compact's profound difference from the 1976 UN Code on Transnational Corporations.

The ICC Goes to Manhattan

As noted earlier, the original UN code on Transnational Corporations, and the Center that was drafting it, was virtually terminated by 1992. This termination was at the behest of the US, Japan, and the European Community. The downsized Center on Transnational Corporations (CTC) was re-oriented towards "helping match up corporations and countries for foreign investments. This change had been an objective of the US as well as some of the UN's most vocal critics, such as the Heritage Foundation" (Bruno and Karliner 2000: 11).

The deathblow to the CTC came at a turning point in world history. Nineteen-ninety-two was one year into the "New World Order" heralded by the fall of the Berlin Wall and the Soviet Union (Bush 1991). The "End of History" was just beginning (Fukuyama 1992). Free market triumphalism was tempered however, by the growing threat, and vocal movements around that threat, of the "end of nature" (McKibben 1989).

As history was putatively screeching to a halt, so to was the earth's carrying capacity. It in this light that the 1992 UN conference on Environment and Development—the Earth Summit—was viewed by business as a threat to the forward march of neoliberal globalization. This threat was not unfounded.

In preparation for the negotiations, the then still running UN Center on Transnational Corporations was asked by the UN Economic and Social Council (ECOSOC) to prepare a set of recommendations on transnational corporations and other large enterprises that governments might use when drafting Agenda 21—the summit's central document (Bruno and Karliner 2002: 25). The business lobby and Northern governments were intent on these recommendations getting dropped. According to Peter Hansen, former director of the UNCTC,

> [t]he Recommendations were focused on Environment and Development. . . . The US and Japan both opposed them, as they had opposed the Center on Transnationals. The US and Japan had also made it quite clear that they were not going to tolerate any rules or norms on the behavior of the TNCs, and that any attempts to win such rules would have real political costs in other areas of the negotiations. (quoted in Bruno and Karliner 2002: 26)

By the time of the negotiations, the UNCTC had been all but disbanded. "Try as the UNCTC staff might," write Bruno and Karliner ". . . they couldn't get the Secretariat to accept their report, which might have laid the groundwork for a set of international standards on corporations and sustainable development" (Bruno and Karliner 2002: 26). Instead official recommendations came, at the behest of Maurice Strong, Earth Summit Secretary General, from the Business Council for Sustainable development—now the World Business Council for Sustainable Development (WBCSD). For Karliner: "The BCSD was made up of the CEOs of some of the world's most powerful corporations. Together with the ICC, the BCSD made sure that most every reference to transnational corporations—some of the world's most environmentally destructive entities—in the Earth Summit texts referred to self-regulation rather than any other mechanism to control their activities" (Karliner 1999: 10). Bruno and Karliner elaborate:

> The WBCSD and ICC, who despite some friction for the most part closely coordinated policies, proceeded to demonstrate what self-regulation meant: making Agenda 21's chapter on business and industry compatible with their positions; lobbying, most often successfully, for the elimination of references to transnational corporations wherever possible throughout Agenda 21; and ensuring that the idea of even a minimal system of international regulations never gained public acceptance. (Bruno and Karliner 2002: 30)

As has historically been the case, business had to at least address the concerns being raised by civil society as part of its strategy to effectively forestall the regulatory solutions being sought. It was in this context that the ICC's Business Charter for Sustainable Development was developed at the Second World Industry conference on Environmental Management in Rotterdam in 1991: "More than 1000 companies signed the nonbinding Charter, which urged that environmental management in a free market setting be recognized 'as among the highest corporate priorities'" (Bruno and Karliner 2002: 28). Borrowing a strategy from the past, business recognized that the best defense against the environmental movements' arguments for more government control over corporate activities was attack. Business and Northern governments entered the Rio conference with the Charter, and its promises that business would clean up its act, in hand.[27] Just before Rio, Stephen Schmidheiny, founder of WBCSD pleaded with business that unless "we promote self-regulation . . . we face government regulation under pressure from the public" (quoted in Bruno and Karliner 2002: 29). The promotion of self-regulation is business's version of the precautionary principle.

Thanks to a concerted effort on behalf of business and Northern governments, the resulting document was business-safe.[28] For Jan-Olaf Willums and Ulrich Goluke from the ICC,

> [i]n general, the feeling among business participants was that the substantive output of UNCED was positive. It could have taken a negative stance on market forces and the role of business, and there was at one time the real possibility that the conference might be pushed to lay down detailed guidelines for the operations of transnational corporations. Instead it acknowledged the important role of business. . . . National governments have now begun to formulate their own policies and programs in accordance with commitments given in Brazil. We expect that these national laws and regulations will not be as stringent, bureaucratic and "anti-business" as some feared before UNCED. (Willums and Goluke 1992: 20–21)

Business successfully fended off the threat it perceived in the early 1990s and enjoyed relative calm until the latter half of the decade.

Birth of the Compact

In 1997 the Asian financial crisis shook confidence in the global market. Of equal concern was the collapse of talks on the MAI months later. This collapse signaled the emergence of a movement more international and broad-based than the burgeoning environmental movement that posed a threat in the early 1990s.[29] As aforementioned, Seattle 99 further evinced growing frustrations with corporate power.

After the failure of the Seattle meetings, the ICC announced that its primary strategic objective was "restoring the momentum of trade liberalization" (CEO 2000b). Something had to be done to counter what ICC Secretary-General Maria Livanos Cattaui called "the growing globaphobia and rising criticism of multinational business that poses a special challenge to the ICC" (quoted in CEO 2000b).

A key plank in the business response to this new threat was to continue its work from the early 1990s, and further secure the UN as an ally in the globalization debate. "Fearing an upcoming backlash against globalization that could threaten corporate-driven trade and investment liberalisation," according to Corporate Europe Observer, "the ICC's charm offensive towards the UN is a very proactive move to ensure that any regulation of the global economy will be tailored to the interests of international business" (CEO 2000a).

The ICC is pursuing two goals. The first is to counter-intuitively *center* the UN as an authority and venue for the globalization debates. As aforementioned, the ongoing concern is that civil society and developing countries will seek to inject the multilateral trade and investment regime with binding regulation. For the ICC "The multilateral trading system should not be called upon to deal with such non-trade issues as human rights, labour standards and environmental protection. To call on it to do so would expose the trading system to great strain and the risk of increased protectionism while failing to produce the required results. The right place for addressing these issues is the UN and its appropriate agencies" (ICC 2000). But the right place must also be the right UN. The ICC's second goal is to continue *decentering* the UN as a venue for capitalism's critics. Business's plan is working.

In 1998, The ICC hosted the Geneva business dialogues "where high-level officials from the WTO, the UN, the EU and the World Bank, and other top decision-makers met with 450 global business leaders" (CEO 2000a). In his address, UN Secretary-General Kofi Annan promised to "build on the close ties between the UN and the ICC" (quoted in CEO 2001: 2). Only seven months prior, at meetings with the ICC, Annan had agreed to "forge a close global partnership to secure greater business input into the world's economic decision-making and boost the private sector in the least developed countries" (CEO 2000a).

The UN's complicity with Business's agenda is not due solely to the ICC's lobbying or strategic prowess—the UN has strategic interests in mind as well. First off, in helping secure greater business input in the world's decision-making, the UN is seeking to increase *its* input in "global policy-making, which, during the last years of intense economic globalisation, has been predominantly controlled by the Bretton Woods institutions (World Bank, International Monetary Fund and the WTO)"

(CEO 2000a). Secondly, the UN has a cash flow problem: "While the US continues to withhold US 1.6 billion it owes, the UN appears to be hoping that the ICC may be an effective lobbyist on its behalf" (Karliner 1999: 9). The ICC has already begun fulfilling its end of the bargain by lobbying heads of state at the 1998 and 1999 G-8 meetings for more UN funding (Karliner 1999: 9).

It is important to note, however, that Annan's and the UN's interest in the ICC is ideological as well as instrumental. While the UN is a far from homogenous organization, Kofi Annan is a proponent of neoliberal globalization. His ideological alignment with the ICC is made clear in a remarkable speech he delivered to the 1999 World Economic forum in Davos, where he first introduced the idea of a Global Compact between the UN and business. Annan's speech wonderfully articulates the political terrain the various sides of the regulation debate find themselves on, and is worth considering in detail.

The Global Compact and the Double Movement

After beginning his speech with the typical There-Is-No-Alternative argument in favor of neoliberal globalization—"Globalization is a fact of life" (Annan 1999: 1)—Annan proceeds with a critique: "The problem is this. The spread of markets outpaces the ability of societies and their political systems to adjust to them, let alone guide the course they take. History teaches us that such an imbalance between the economic, social and political realms can never be sustained for very long" (Annan 1999: 1). For Annan, the Western world's response to the Great Depression provides a model for how we might address globalization's externalities: "In order to restore social harmony and political stability, they adopted social safety nets and other measures, designed to limit economic volatility and compensate the victims of market failures" (Annan 1999: 1). Annan continues: "Our challenge today is to devise a similar compact on the global scale, to underpin the new global economy. . . . Specifically, I call on you—individually through your firms, and collectively through your business associations—to embrace, support and enact a set of core values in the areas of human rights, labour standards, and environmental practices" (Annan 1999: 2).

What is astonishing about Annan's narrative is how he seamlessly moves from a discussion of public regulation during the post-war years to a discussion of private regulation and "shared values" presently. This move is even more remarkable given that Karl Polanyi's theorizing is central to the Compact.

Polanyi finds his way into the UN-ICC endeavor via John Ruggie.[30] Recall that for Polanyi, *public* regulation is necessary for markets to survive. Ruggie and Annan rationalize their emphasis on *private* regulation with reference to deepening globalization. For Ruggie, the public regulation Polanyi thought necessary is impossible to replicate on the global scale. "The reason is obvious," writes Ruggie, "there is no government at the global level to act on behalf of the common good, as there is at the national level. And international institutions are far too weak to fully compensate" (Ruggie 2003: 4).

Ruggie's argument is somewhat disingenuous. For Fred Block,

> [a]t the global level Polanyi anticipated an international economic order with high levels of international trade and cooperation. He did not lay out a set of blueprints, but he was clear on the principles. . . . In other words collaboration among governments would produce a set of agreements to facilitate high levels of international trade, but societies would have multiple means to buffer themselves from the pressures of the global economy. . . . This vision also assumes a set of regulatory structures that would place limits on the play of market forces. (Block 2001: xxxvi)

Ruggie is right that our current political climate is not regulation friendly. But this is a historical and political, not a necessary, fact. Moreover, international institutions are *not* too weak to compensate. This is why global labor has shown such interest in the WTO. Finally, it is not at all clear business is willing or able to regulate itself in the ways Ruggie and Annan hope for.[31]

John Ruggie is not a cynical man. He genuinely believes that corporations can be socially responsible without public regulation. And interestingly, his and Annan's belief is rendered intelligible by Polanyi. Recall that for Polanyi, markets require a regulatory response to survive—otherwise their very bases for existence will be overrun. Annan trusts that business will come to see that its larger interests, its "enlightened self-interest," lies in *effective* (self-) regulation. "Finally," says Annan "I choose these three areas [human rights, labor, and the environment] because they are the ones where I fear that, if we do not act, there may be a threat to the open global market, and especially to the multilateral trade regime" (Annan 1999: 2).

An interesting difference arises, however, in terms of how Annan and the ICC understand this threat. For Annan the threat is "protectionism; populism; nationalism; ethnic chauvinism; fanaticism; and terrorism"—"isms" that all "exploit the insecurity and misery of people who feel threatened or victimized by the global market" (Annan 1999: 4). Unnamed, but lurking on the sidelines of the list is the specter of socialism always threatening to become incarnate at the end of the end of history (everything ends). While business undoubtedly shares these fears, perhaps primary on their list is the very "regulation" Annan celebrated in his account of past responses to economic strife. Unlike the ICC, Annan is not absolutely opposed to regulation, a fact made evident in his speech. But even the mention of distant regulations, and the possibility of future legislation,[32] was enough to put business on the defensive about a document largely in line with their interests. On the day of the Compact's unveiling, an editorial by the secretary-general of the ICC, Maria Livanos Cattaui, appeared in the *International Herald Tribune* that, while mostly supportive in its tenor, warned that "business would look askance at any suggestion involving external assessment of corporate performance, whether by special interest groups or by UN agencies. The Global Compact is a joint commitment to shared values, not a qualification to be met. It must not become a vehicle for governments to burden business with prescriptive regulations" (Cattaui 2000).

Not only does the ICC see the threat differently—*any* kind of legally binding regulation is anathema—it simply does not accept Polanyi's argument. Unlike Annan and the Global Compact office, business assumes that "human" and "natural" limits are elastic—both have, so far, proven profitably pliable. But for Polanyi, as the limits to human and natural commodification are reached, reactionary counter-movements will *inevitably* arise to defend against market externalities. The closer we get to those limits, the more powerful and potentially disruptive the counter-movement will be. Indeed, with Polanyi's analysis in mind, Annan ended his speech with a final warning: "unless [the Compact's] values are really seen to be taking hold, I fear we may find it increasingly difficult to make a persuasive case for the open global market" (Annan 1999: 4).

Ten months after Annan's speech, the streets of Seattle were flooded with over 60,000 people protesting the WTO. Annan appeared vindicated, and business took note. In early May 2000, over 1000 industrialists gathered at the 33rd World Congress of the International Chamber of Commerce in Budapest. In his opening speech ICC president Adnan Kassar warned participants that the main challenge for business today, "takes the form of a highly vocal and well-organized array of special interest groups with their own agendas" (CEO 2000c: 3). According to Corporate Europe Observer, "fears about a backlash to the corporate agenda were a constant worry among participants. Almost every session, regardless of the issue on the agenda, turned into a discussion on how to counter the globalisation-critics" (CEO 2000c: 3). There was general agreement among Congress attendees that Annan's proposed Compact provided a golden opportunity for business to win the globalisation debate (CEO 2000c: 4).

But again, the ICC understands the Compact differently from the UN. Their different positions are registered in the different ways of reading Annan's warning "unless those values are really *seen to be taking hold*, I fear we may find it increasingly difficult to make a persuasive case for the open global market." Taking hold, and seen to be taking hold, are not the same thing. Annan has investment in the former, the ICC would settle for the latter.

We are not arguing that all ICC members and leadership are cynical, but we do think that business has a keener appreciation than most that perception can be a reality unto itself. The Compact is a "golden opportunity" less because it can better regulate and mold the behavior of business, and more because it can better regulate and mold the perceptions of those concerned with increasing corporate power. For Adnan Kassar "What the Global Compact does is to assemble a broad picture of company actions that *demonstrate* corporate citizenship in action in every part of the world" (quoted in CEO 2001: 3, emphasis added). "In the past," Kassar elaborates, such initiatives "were often unnoticed, because they were conducted in isolation" (CEO 2001: 3). The ICC has the tendency to speak of the Compact less as a regulatory (even if self-regulatory!) tool, and more as a mechanism that can advertise all the good corporations are doing in the world—good deeds that have previously been disconnected and unknown.[33] At the ICC's 2000 Congress, plans were announced to enlist "the support of international media organizations to make the business response to the Global Compact even more widely known" (CEO 2001: 6).

Two months after the ICC's congress, the Global Compact was officially announced, and, as aforementioned, with great fanfare. Corporations whose brands had been dragged through the mud were now hand in hand—on the covers of major world newspapers, and television screens worldwide—with a widely recognized force for change in the world. As Kenny Bruno and Joshua Karliner note about the press conference, a synechdoche for the UN-ICC relationship, CEOs like Nike's Phil Knight, got to literally align themselves with "with the UN flag, the symbol of international peace, and with the Nobel prize-winning Mr. Annan" (Bruno and Karliner 2002: 54).

According to the UNDP Guidelines and Procedures for Mobilization of Resources from the Private Sector, when a UN agency "is engaged in a public relations activity within the framework of a corporate relationship, a mutual image transfer inevitably takes place" (quoted in Bruno and Karliner 2000: 7). This mass mediated image transfer is exactly what business has gained from the Compact.[34] As noted, acquiring organized civil society's support has not been a priority for business in its partnership with the UN. Business's primary target is the global public opinion that was turning against it while turning the century: "The twenty-first century started in Seattle," ran the headline of French newspaper *Le Monde* the morning following the November 30 protests. The Compact, simply put, is a sophisticated attempt by business to stem threatening anti-corporate criticisms without making significant changes to the business environment—changes required to address the externalities impelling the protests.

Self-Regulation and the Truncheon

The problem of human and natural limits to commodification, however, is not totally avoidable. These limits might always be contextually determined, but they are still lived and felt by humans worldwide—humans with a stake in their (re)constitution and the (re)constitution of their natural environs. Perhaps the increasingly militarized response to global justice demonstrations should thus be read as a harbinger of neoliberalism's coming contribution to the "countermovement"—to the state intervention required to keep markets open and running.

The OECD Guidelines and UN Global Compact are meant to stem deep frustrations with economic globalization without addressing their material roots. They operate at the level of perception, and have few material effects beyond the forestallment of public regulation. But while they might stall resistance (the telos of which business reads as regulation), resistance will still emerge. And if business does not capitulate to a *public* regulatory solution to the "sweatshop problem," it will need to push for regulation of another, more coercive kind. For now, in democratic countries, the disciplinary underside of voluntary mechanisms like the Global Compact are truncheons, rubber bullets, and tear gas.[35] The consent that business cannot win through voluntary mechanisms will need to be secured with "public regulation" of an overtly violent kind.

Recall that for Polanyi the life of market societies depend on two forms of state intervention. First, speaking generally, state intervention is required for turning humans and nature into labor and land (i.e., commodification of labor and enclosure). Secondly, intervention is required to ensure markets do not ravage the very humans and nature they depend upon. What makes the *neo*liberal political project novel, in the history of market societies, is its ambition and ability (in large thanks to CSR) to stall the regulatory impulse integral to previously liberal societies.

Neoliberalism's legacy, in Polanyi's terms, is its capacity to jam the second half of "the double movement." But this capacity comes with a cost. If human and natural limits are not actively minded, people will resist. Business must thus be prepared to support constant and active 'redefinition' of humans and nature; it must enlist the state in the perpetual pursuit of enclosure. In other words, as natural and human limits are surpassed, new humans and environments will need to be constituted, their limits redrawn (Luke 2003; Rowe 2003). Alternative visions will also need to be suppressed. The underside to self-regulation, whether business is prepared for this eventuality or not, is an increasingly regulatory state of the coercive kind. More pithily: The truncheon is the code of conduct's telos.

There are some indications, however, that codes of conduct and CSR more generally, are losing their luster. In conclusion we would like to highlight three developments in the debate over economic globalization that may suggest a shift away from the self-regulation paradigm.

Concluding Remarks

Our basic argument is that codes of conduct have been historically designed to forestall public regulation more than ensure responsible corporate behavior, and should thus be resisted. This argument is particularly targeted at Civil Society Organizations (CSOs) that see voluntary codes as gateways to more binding regulation.

The first development we would like to report, however, is that our argument is quickly losing its critical bite! A civil society consensus is already forming around the perspective supported here—that the self-regulation paradigm has not fulfilled its promise. The clearest marker of this fast-forming consensus is the recent report published by Christian Aid, *Behind the Mask: The Real Face of Corporate Social Responsibility* (2004). Christian Aid's highly critical report has made media waves (See Macalister 2004b and Frean 2004), and elicited harsh denunciations from the business community (Macalister 2004a). We sense the report harkens more widespread civil society resistance to voluntary codes of conduct like the Global Compact and the OECD Guidelines. "We are advocating a move beyond corporate social responsibility" write the report's authors "to corporate social accountability—meaning that companies in the future will have a legal obligation to uphold international standards" (Christian Aid 2004: 3). The authors continue: "NGO pressure can influence multinationals' policy and practice in certain instances, [but] it is clear that it cannot, by itself, ensure that multinationals uphold environmental and human rights standards. In the long run, international NGOs may be more effective by throwing their collective weight behind the drive for international regulation than by tying up their scant resources in bilateral dialogues" (Christian Aid 2004: 14).

What made the "drive for international regulation" so powerful in the 1960s and 1970s was the impressive coalition between the international trade union movement, Western social activists and developing country governments. This social democratic coalition, broken in the 1980s, is reforming (the second development worth highlighting). We cannot claim trade union resurgence, but as aforementioned, the global justice movement is much larger and stronger than its earlier incarnations. Perhaps more important is the emergence of a new developing country oppositional bloc—the G-20+.

The G-20+ was introduced to the world at the WTO's fifth ministerial meeting in Cancun where developing country governments organized themselves in response to longstanding concerns over agricultural subsidies and trade related intellectual property rights (TRIPS).[36] The G-20+ demands were not met, and the talks collapsed. According to Thomas Palley, an economist with the Open Society Institute: "The G-20+'s emergence represents a significant change in the landscape of multilateral trade negotiation. In the past, developing countries have been out-gunned by the superior negotiating capacities of the EU and US Now, they have shown the ability to contest agendas they find unsatisfactory" (Palley 2003: 1).

The G-20+ alliance is shaky, with less power and cohesion than the G-77, but still holds promise for reformers. The hope is that a coalition between global labor, the global justice movement, and the G-20+ can reach a "grand compromise" with business and Northern governments that includes international and enforceable labor and environmental standards coupled with guaranteed commitments of long-term development aid and debt relief for the developing world (see Shoch 2000 and Palley 2003).

The final development we would like to report on is the compelling set of corporate responsibility Norms being compiled by the UN Sub-Commission on the Promotion and Protection of Human Rights. The legal status of the Norms remains murky, but their supporters see them as the first step towards the aforementioned "grand compromise."

Business sees the Norms similarly and has mounted a coordinated opposition. According to Stefano Bertasi from the ICC: "We have a problem with the premise and the principle that the norms are based on. These norms clearly seek to move away from the realm of voluntary initiatives . . . and [we] see them as conflicting with the approach taken by other parts of the UN that seek to promote voluntary guidelines" (CEO 2004).

The Norms overcame an impressive hurdle in April 2004 when the UN Commission on Human Rights, despite intense business pressure, opted to continue developing them. The Commission's decision was undoubtedly impacted by the widespread civil society support for the UN Sub-Commission's work. In March 2004 nearly 200 CSOs endorsed a statement supporting the Norms (Amnesty International 2004).

The UN Norms are attractive to civil society because they provide a positive alternative to the self-regulation paradigm *and* the UN's general complicity with the ICC. The Norms are seen as a way to interrupt both of these trends—trends that have stalled attempts to regulate corporations in a sustained and enforceable manner. According to Christian Aid, "[We are] part of a growing network of NGOs, policy institutes, legal experts and development specialists arguing for an agreed set of legally binding obligations for business. There is an emerging consensus about the possible scope of such obligations, exemplified by the UN Sub-Commission on the Promotion and Protection of Human Rights' development of a set of norms covering corporate responsibility. The time is ripe to move this consensus towards legal obligations" (Christian Aid 2004: 50). We agree.

Notes

1. Craig Murphy and Enrico Augelli go so far as to suggest that the "Soviet Union was never as much of a fundamental threat to the post-war Western system as OPEC was from 1973 through 1983" (1988: 154).

2. The ICFTU initially proposed the idea of a UN code on TNCs in 1969—international trade union support was central to the push for a binding code.

3. It should be noted that Robinson's *Multinationals and Political Control* is meant as a guide for "the business reader" (Robinson 1983: xv), and is not a critical work on global political economy.

4. The code, along with the UN Center on Transnational Corporations, was officially terminated in 1992. More below.

5. For a particularly good account, see Murphy and Augelli 1988. For Murphy and Augelli, "[t]he global recession engineered by the US made the Third World less powerful in the world trading system than it had ever been before in the entire history of American supremacy within the world economy" (Murphy and Augelli 1988: 165).

6. Indeed, the roots of the OECD guidelines can be found in a voluntary code of conduct adopted by the ICC in 1972. In the introduction to the code, as reported by Van Der Pijl, "it was stated that the aim was to 'create a climate of mutual confidence,' and that it was hoped 'these guidelines will be helpful to the United Nations' and other organizations in their efforts to 'promote constructive discussions of the problem'" (1993: 50). While it might make more sense to mark 1972 as the voluntary code of conduct's birth-year, 1976 saw the voluntary code's emergence, in the form of the OECD Guidelines, as a salient political force.

7. In 1971, the same year the memorandum was published, Nixon appointed Powell to the Supreme Court, where he served, in a surprisingly moderate fashion, until 1987 (see Landay 2002).

8. We are not trying to suggest American business followed Powell's suggestions programmatically. His memo does, however, brilliantly articulate a set of concerns and responses that were disparately circulating at the time; it also *did* make a difference in the world. For one, Powell's memo convinced Joseph Coors, President of the Adolph Coors Company, that American business was "ignoring a crisis" (Landay 2002: 13). Coors was compelled to act. According to Jerry Landay, Coors contributed the "first $250,000 to fund the 1971–72 operations of the Analysis and Research Association (ARA) in Washington, D.C."—the original name for the Heritage Foundation (Landay 2002: 13). As Landay continues, "Heritage became the trend-setting model for scores of policy institutes and lobbying operations that compose the radical-right apparat. Heritage has been a major beneficiary of the Coors Castle Rock Foundation ever since" (Landay 2002: 13). See Landay 2002 for a more extensive account of Powell's direct impact on US business.

9. This quote, interestingly enough, falls under the heading "Responsibility of Business Executives" in Powell's memo. For Powell, it is "socially responsible" for business to organize against assaults on the free-enterprise system. Our project is meant to account for how CSR has become part of the toolbox business uses to fulfill its responsibility to the system that benefits it.

10. It is doubtful Powell ever read Antonio Gramsci's *Prison Notebooks*, but his plan of action deeply resonates with Gramsci's thinking on the modern political terrain. Margaret Kohn provides a nice synopsis: "[Gramsci] realized that unlike Russia's absolutist state, the modern bourgeois state was fortified by institutions like the church, school, political parties, and media. . . . In order to build a counter-hegemonic bloc, the socialist vanguard had to also fight on the terrain of civil society and create a new cultural/moral vision capable of unifying workers and peasants. Socialism had to become the new common sense, embodied in institutions, practices, and beliefs" (Kohn 1999: 218–219). This was a period when the American left was succeeding on Gramscian terms, and one when business was worriedly studying—even if not formally—those terms. As will be discussed below, American business has learned a tremendous amount from leftists and social reformers.

11. Wendy Brown provides a nice definition of this term: "whenever the state was required to ostentatiously intervene on behalf of capital (whether through overt bail-outs and subsidies or slightly more covertly through policies that favored it), the state ran the risk of a 'legitimation crisis' as it tipped its hand in this way. That is, at such moments, the state revealed itself as a 'capitalist' state while its legitimacy depended upon perceived independence from social and economic powers" (Brown 2003: 30).

12. For Robinson and Harris, traditional capitalist fractions are being replaced by a new one: national vs. transnational capital (Robinson and Harris 2000: 10). Given the intensity of globalized production, this fraction does not easily graft onto the former productive/money division.

13. For a more sustained account of the TCC in general see Sklair 2002.

14. It is telling that the phrase "The Washington Consensus"—often used interchangeably with neoliberalism—was coined in 1989 by John Williamson, an analyst working for the Institute of International Economics (IIE)—a corporate funded think-tank established in 1981. The phrase was used to summarize a list of policy reforms in Latin America that the IIE suggested the US pursue. See http://www.iie.com/staff/jwguide.htm#topic3 for Williamson's reaction to the popularity of his term.

15. It is important to recall that the "Battle of Seattle" was not fought solely in Seattle. According to George Katsiaficas there were major demonstrations in "14 US cities; twenty thousand people marched in Paris; eight thousand in Manila, three thousand in Seoul and thousands more around the world. In Mexico city a few days later, ninety-eight people were arrested and tortured for demanding the release of arrested Seattle demonstrators" (Katsiaficas 2002: 29).

16. Apparently Enron's code of conduct has been a hot seller on E-bay (see Vargas 2002).

17. One of the crucial controversies at the 1999 WTO ministerial meeting in Seattle was US President Clinton's desire—stoked by the mass protests outside the meetings—to begin negotiating a labor-standards protocol for the WTO (Hurd 2003: 103). It is unclear how satisfied the global labor movement would have been with Clinton's proposal, but it held some promise for enforced standards. According to Hurd, the proposal failed because of developing country objection—LDCs were concerned the standards were cover for either Western protectionism or neo-imperialism (Hurd 2003: 103). For developing countries, high labor standards meant increased production costs, reduced foreign investment, and reduced competitiveness for their export goods. The failure of the US proposed protocol nicely signifies the impressive political economic shifts that have occurred since the mid-1970s. We would like, however, to problematize the tendency for commentators to suggest that developing countries are now proponents of economic globalization (Kell and Ruggie 1999 is exemplary). First of all, there is an ugly history to the support, or at least consent, Southern governments lend to neoliberal policies. Secondly, an increasing number of Southern governments (Brazil, Venezuela, Argentina, etc.) are opposing the neoliberal model. Indeed, the latest meeting of the WTO in Cancun saw the beginnings of a new Southern oppositional bloc—the Group of 20+. More on the G-20+ below.

18. The OECD and UN, particularly the latter, are not homogenous organizations. But for the most part, their institutional direction is now much more in line with business than civil society. Discussed more below.

19. For William Carroll and Colin Carson, "The ICC's distinctive contribution to transnational class formation is to integrate capitalism's centre with its margins; hence the ICC board blends a smattering of the global corporate elite with various representatives of national and local capital" (Carroll and Carson 2003: 45). The ICC is as a good a representative of 'total capital' as there is.

20. The ICC was heavily involved in these negotiations. According to Corporate Europe Observatory (CEO), the ICC wrote the effective blueprint for the first MAI draft (CEO 2000a). For an analysis of the MAI see Picciotto 1999.

21. While broad in scope, the Guidelines are still weak on specifics. For instance, the human rights language in the text does not tackle high profile concerns like indigenous peoples' rights, or the corporate use of security forces to terrorize employees and stake holding populations. Neither

do the Guidelines, unlike most codes of conduct, include language on wages and benefits including a sustainable living wage (Gordon 2001: 14).

22. Infrastructurally, the NCPs "may be a senior government official or a government office headed by a senior official. Alternatively, the National Contact Point may be organised as a co-operative body, including representatives of other government agencies. Representatives of the business community, employee organisations and other interested parties may also be included" (OECD 2000).

23. The Dutch case is the most promising AND disturbing account of government acting on their "responsibilities towards civil society." Aaronson and Reeves report: "In December 2000, the Dutch Parliament requested the government to link the OECD Guidelines to government subsidies for international trade and investment as well as export credits. The government simply asked all applicants for export subsidies to state that they were aware of and working to comply with the Guidelines. The Business Advisory Group to the OECD complained alleging that this action made the Guidelines 'binding.' . . . Thus, the Dutch government's effort to provide an incentive and to promote the Guidelines has led to international business opposition. . . . [T]he Dutch Government continues to persevere" (Aaronson and Reeves 2002: 16).

24. It should be reiterated that there is not complete consensus on the virtues of CSR within the business community. For many commentators, admitting the virtue of business ethics is too significant a compromise (Henderson 2001).

25. Codes of Corporate Conduct: An Inventory (1999); Codes of Corporate Conduct: Expanded Review of their contents (May 2001); Corporate Responsibility: Results of a fact-finding mission on private initiatives (February 2001); OECD Guidelines and Other Corporate Responsibility Instruments: A Comparison (December 2001).

26. According to the UN website: "The Global Compact is not a regulatory instrument—it does not 'police,' enforce or measure the behavior or actions of companies. Rather, the Global Compact relies on public accountability, transparency and the enlightened self-interest of companies, labour and civil society to initiate and share substantive action in pursuing the principles upon which the Global Compact is based."

27. Like with the case of the 1972 voluntary code forged by the ICC, it is likely the 1991 Business Charter was a benchmark used in formulating the revised OECD Guidelines, and especially the Global Compact.

28. In one glaring example of government-corporate collusion, the Canadian government hosted a series of meetings to coordinate corporate lobbying of the Earth Summit negotiations (Bruno and Karliner 2002: 30).

29. Elements of the global justice movement, of course, grew out of the environmental activism of the late 1980s and 1990s—these movements are deeply intermeshed.

30. John Ruggie is professor of International Affairs and director of the Center for Business and Government at Harvard University. From 1997–2001 he was Assistant Secretary-General and chief advisor for strategic planning to United Nations Secretary-General Kofi Annan. His most oft-cited work on Polanyi is "International Regimes, Transactions and Change: Embedded Liberalism in the Postwar Economic Order," *International Organization* 36 (Spring 1982). It is entirely likely that Ruggie wrote Annan's speech.

31. The simple question rarely addressed in the CSR literature is that if business is truly serious about social responsibility, why are they so vehemently opposed to such responsibilities being formalized in law?

32. "Don't wait for every country to introduce laws protecting freedom of association and the right to collective bargaining" (Annan 1999: 3).

33. For Corporate Europe Observer: "The ICC's approach of presenting isolated, non-verifiable initiatives, however insignificant and unrepresentative of the companies' record, as proof of 'corporate citizenship,' is deeply flawed. For instance, the fact that automobile and arms producer Daimler-

Chrysler uses locally produced coconut fibers in a Brazilian factory producing car components says nothing about the company's overall environmental conduct" (CEO 2001: 3).

34. The Internet is the primary mechanism used to publicize the Compact. It is of note that the ICC eagerly launched its own official website three months before the official Global Compact one was released (CEO 2000b).

35. Eddie Yuen nicely captures the currently uneven, but increasingly generalized police response to "anti-globalization" protestors: "As Genoa, Geneva, and Gothenburg in Europe and the Port of Oakland, Sacramento and St. Louis in the US have shown [we would add Miami], Northern white activists are increasingly being treated like their counterparts in Argentina, the Philippines, or Harlem. Capitalist globalization is now characterized by a race to the bottom for basic freedoms and civil liberties as well as for environmental and working conditions" (Yuen 2004: xiii).

36. Members of the G-20+ include Argentina, Bolivia, Brazil, Chile, China, Cuba, Egypt, Guatemala, India, Indonesia, Mexico, Nigeria, Pakistan, Paraguay, Peru, Philippines, South Africa, Thailand, and Venezuela. More than 51 percent of the world's population and 63 percent of farmers live in the G-20+ countries, which produce more than a fifth of global agricultural output and more than a quarter of farm exports (Capdevilla 2003).

References

Aaronson, Susan, and James Reeves. 2002. "The European Response to Public Demands for Global Corporate Responsibility." Paper prepared for the National Policy Association, http://www.bitc.org.uk/docs/NPA_Global_CSR_survey.pdf (accessed 15 January 2003).

Allende, Salvador. 1975. "Speech to the United Nations," in *International Firms and Modern Imperialism*, ed. Hugo Radice. Baltimore: Penguin Books.

Amnesty International. 2004. "UN Human Rights Norms for Businesses," http://web.amnesty.org/pages/ec-unnorms_2-eng (accessed 23 May 2004).

Annan, Kofi. 1999. "Secretary-General Proposes Global Compact on Human Rights, Labour, Environment, in Address to World Economic Forum in Davos." New York: UN. http://www.un.org/News/Press/docs/1999/19990201.sgsm6881.html (accessed 15 January 2004).

Block, Fred. 2001. "Introduction," in Karl Polanyi, *The Great Transformation*. Boston: Beacon Press.

Brown, Wendy. 1995. *States of Injury: Freedom and Power in Late Modernity*. Princeton, N.J.: Princeton University Press.

———. 2003. "Neo-Liberalism and the End of Liberal Democracy," *Theory & Event* 7(1), at http://muse.jhu.edu/journals/theory_and_event/v007/71brown.html (accessed 19 August 2004).

Bruno, Kenny, and Joshua Karliner. 2000. *Tangled Up in Blue: Corporate Partnerships at the United Nations*. Oakland: CorpWatch. http://www.corpwatch.org/upload/document/tangled.pdf (accessed 20 September 2003).

———. 2002. *Earthsummit.biz: The Corporate Takeover of Sustainable Development*. Oakland: Food First Books.

Bush, George H. 1991. "New World Order: President Bush's Speech to Congress." http://www.al-bab.com/arab/docs/pal/pal10.htm (accessed 15 January 2004).

Business for Social Responsibility. 2003. "Overview of Corporate Social Responsibility," http://www.bsr.org/CSRResources/IssueBriefDetail.cfm?DocumentID=48809 (accessed 17 March 2003).

Capdevila, Gustavo. 2003. "G22 Warmup for post-Cancun Talks," *Asia Times* (October 3, 2003), http://www.atimes.com/atimes/Global_Economy/EJ04Dj01.html (accessed 7 March 2004).

Carroll, Archie B. 1999. "Corporate Social Responsibility," *Business and Society* 38(3): 268–295.

Carroll, William K., and Colin Carson. 2003. "The Network of Global Corporations and Elite Policy Groups: A Structure for Transnational Capitalist Class Formation?" *Global Networks* 3(1).

Cattaui, Maria Livanos. 2000. "Business-UN Compact Could Be at Take-Off Point," *International Herald Tribune* (July 26), http://www.iccwbo.org/home/news_archives/2000/business_compact.asp (accessed 6 June 2003).

Chomsky, Noam. 1998. "Hordes of Vigilantes and Popular Elements Defeat the MAI, For Now," Z-Net, http://zena.secureforum.com/Znet/chomsky/articles/z9807-mai.htm (accessed 5 May 2003).

Christian Aid. 2004. *Behind the Mask: The Real Face of Corporate Social Responsibility.* http://www.christian-aid.org.uk/indepth/0401csr/csr_behindthemask.pdf (accessed 10 February 2004).

Clarke, Tony, and Maude Barlow. 1998. *MAI Round 2: New Global and Internal Threats to Canadian Sovereignty.* Toronto: Stoddart.

Corporate Europe Observatory (CEO). 2000a. "The ICC and the Corporate Cooptation of the UN," ICC Fact Sheet #2, http://www.corporateeurope.org/icc/icc_un.html (February 2003).

________. 2000b. "ICC: Powerhouse of Corporate-Led Globalization," ICC Fact Sheet #1, http://www.corporateeurope.org/icc/icc_intro.html (February 2003).

________. 2000c. "ICC Steps Up Counter-Campaign against Critics of Corporate-Led Globalisation," http://www.corporateeurope.org/observer7/icc.html (February 2004).

________. 2001. "High Time for UN to Break 'Partnership' with the ICC," http://www.corporateeurope.org/un/icc.html (accessed 17 March 2003).

________. 2004. "Shell Leads International Business Campaign Against UN Human Rights Norms," http://www.corporateeurope.org/norms.html (accessed 1 April 2004).

Danaher, Kevin, and Jason Mark. 2003. *Insurrection: Citizen Challenges to Corporate Power.* New York: Routledge.

Edsall, Thomas Byrne. 1984. *The New Politics of Inequality.* New York: W. W. Norton & Co.

________. 1990. "Business in American Politics: Its Growing Power, Its Shifting Strategies," *Dissent* (Spring).

Epstein, Edwin M. 1998. "Business Ethics and Corporate Social Policy: Reflections on an Intellectual Journey, 1964–1996, and Beyond," *Business and Society* 37(1).

Ethical Corporation. 2003. "Analysis: International Standards for Corporate Responsibility," http://www.ethicalcorp.com/content.asp?ContentID=354 (accessed 15 March 2003).

Frean, Alexandra. 2004. "Corporate Aid or Plain Hypocrisy?" *The Times* (February 2), http://business.timesonline.co.uk/article/0,,9075-986592,00.html (accessed 20 September 2004).

Friedman, Milton. 1970. "The Social Responsibility of Business is to Increase its Profits," *The New York Times Magazine* (September 13), http://www.colorado.edu/studentgroups/libertarians/issues/friedman-soc-resp-business.html (accessed 12 March 2003).

Fukuyama, Francis. 1992. *The End of History and the Last Man.* New York: Free Press.

Gilpin, Robin. 1975. *U.S. Power and the Multinational Corporation.* New York: Basic.

Gordon, Kathryn. 2001. *The OECD Guidelines and Other Corporate Responsibility Instruments: A Comparison.* Paris: OECD. http://www.oecd.org/dataoecd/46/36/2075173.pdf (accessed 12 February 2003).

Gramsci, Antonio. 1971. "State and Civil Society," in *Selections from the Prison Notebooks*, ed. and trans. Quintin Hoare and Geoffrey N. Smith. New York: International Publishers.

Henderson, David. 2001. *Misguided Virtue: False Notions of Corporate Social Responsibility.* London: Institute of Economic Affairs.

Hoogvelt, A., with G. A. Puxty. 1987. *Multinational Enterprise: An Encyclopedic Dictionary of Concepts and Terms.* London: Macmillan.

Howitt, Richard. 2002. "Preface," in *Corporate Responsibility and Labour Rights: Codes of Conduct in the Global Economy*, ed. Rhys Jenkins, Ruth Pearson, and Gill Seyfang. London: Earthscan, xiii–xvi.

Hurd, Ian. 2003. "Labour Standards Through International Organisations: The Global Compact in Comparative Perspective," *The Journal of Corporate Citizenship*, iss. 11.

ICC. 2000. "World Business Message for the UN Millennium Assembly on the Role of the UN in the 21st Century," http://www.iccwbo.org/home/statements_rules/statements/2000/millennium_assembly.asp (March 2003).

International Forum on Globalization. 2002. *Alternatives to Economic Globalization: A Better World is Possible.* San Francisco: Berrett-Koehler.

Jones, Marc T. 1996. "Missing the Forest for the Trees: A Critique of the Social Responsibility Concept and Discourse," *Business and Society* 35(1).

Justice, Dwight W. 2002. "The International Trade Union Movement and the New Codes of Conduct," in *Corporate Responsibility and Labour Rights: Codes of Conduct in the Global Economy*, ed. Rhys Jenkins, Ruth Pearson, and Gill Seyfang. London: Earthscan.

Karliner, Joshua. 1999. *A Perilous Partnership: The United Nations Development Programme's Flirtation with Corporate Collaboration.* San Francisco: TRAC—The Transnational Resource and Action Center. http://www.earthrights.org/un/perilous.pdf (accessed 28 October 2003).

Katsiaficas, George. 2002. "Seattle Was Not the Beginning," in *The Battle of Seattle: The New Challenge to Capitalist Globalization*, ed. Eddie Yuen, George Katsiaficas, and Daniel Burton Rose. New York: Soft Skull Press.

Kell, Georg, and John Gerard Ruggie. 1999. "Global Markets and Social Legitimacy: The Case of the 'Global Compact.'" Paper presented at an international conference: Governing the Public Domain beyond the Era of the Washington Consensus? Redrawing the Line Between the State and the Market, York University, Toronto, Ontario, Canada, November 4–6, 1999. http://www.csmworld.org/public/csrdoc/global_market.pdf (accessed 16 February 2004).

Klein, Naomi. 2000. *No Logo: Taking Aim at the Brand Bullies*. Toronto: Vintage Canada.

Kline, John. 1985. *International Codes and Multinational Business: Setting Guidelines for International Business Operations*. London: Quorum Books.

Kohn, Margaret. 1999. "Civic Republicanism Versus Social Struggle: A Gramscian Approach to Associationalism in Italy," *Political Power and Social Theory* 13: 202–235.

Kolk, Ans, Rob van Tulder, and Carlijn Welters. 1999. "International Codes of Conduct and Corporate Social Responsibility: Can Transnational Corporations Regulate Themselves?" *Transnational Corporations* 8(1): 143–180.

Krasner, Stephen. 1985. *Structural Conflict: The Third World Against Global Liberalism*. Berkeley: University of California Press.

Lake, David A. 1983. "International Economic Structures and American Foreign Economic Policy," *World Politics* 35(4).

Landay, Jerry. 2002. "The Powell Manifesto: How a Prominent Lawyer's Attack Memo Changed America." Media Transparency. http://www.mediatransparency.org/stories/powell.htm (February 2004).

Lipschutz, Ronnie D. 2001. "Why Is There No International Forestry Law? An Examination of International Forestry Regulation, both Public and Private," *UCLA Journal of Environmental Law & Policy* 19(1): 155–182.

Liubicic, Robert J. 1998. "Corporate Codes of Conduct and Product Labeling Schemes: The Limits and Possibilities of Promoting International Labor Rights through Private Initiatives," *Law and Policy in International Business* 30: il.

Luke, Timothy W. 2003. "International or Interenvironmental Relations: Reassessing Nations and Niches in Global Ecosystems," *Alternatives: Global, Local, Political* 28(3).

Macalister, Terry. 2004a. "Business in the Community Hits Back at Critics," *The Guardian* (January 26), http://www.guardian.co.uk/business/story/0,3604,1131160,00.html (accessed 15 February 2004).

________. 2004b. "Social Responsibility is Just a PR Tool for Businesses, Says Report," *The Guardian* (January 21), http://www.guardian.co.uk/business/story/0,3604,1127373,00.html (accessed 12 February 2004).

Madison, James, Alexander Hamilton, and John Jay. 2003. *The Federalist Papers*. New York: Signet.

Makower, Joel, and Business for Social Responsibility. 1994. *Beyond the Bottom Line: Putting Social Responsibility to Work for Your Business and the World*. New York: Simon & Schuster.

Marchaud, Roland. 1998. *Creating the Corporate Soul: The Rise of Public Relations and Corporate Imagery in American Big Business*. Berkeley: University of California Press.

McKibben, Bill. 1989. *The End of Nature*. New York: Random House.

Monshipouri, Mahmood. 2002. "The Problems and Possibilities of Overseeing Corporate Conduct: MNCs and the Ethics of Global Responsibility" Paper delivered at the 43rd Annual International Studies Association Convention, New Orleans, March 24–27, 2002.

Moon, Jeremy. 2002. "The Social Responsibility of Business and New Governance," *Government and Opposition* 37(3): 385–408.

Murphy, Craig, and Enrico Augelli. 1988. *America's Quest For Supremacy and The Third World: A Gramscian Analysis*. London: Pinter Publishers.

Nace, Ted, 2003. *Gangs of America: The Rise of Corporate Power and the Disabling of Democracy.* San Francisco: Berrett-Koehler.

NGOs. 2000. "Statement to Governments Adhering to the OECD Multinational Enterprise Guidelines from interested NGOs," http://www.corporate-accountability.org/docs/NGO-comments-OECD_Guidelines.pdf (accesssed 7 March 2003).

O'Brien, Robert. 2000. "The World Trade Organization and Labour," in *Contesting Global Governance: Multilateral Economic Institutions and Global Social Movements*, ed. Robert O'Brien, Anne Marie Goetz, Jan Aart Scholte, and Marc Williams. Cambridge: Cambridge University Press.

Organization for Economic Cooperation and Development (OECD). 1998. "Codes of Corporate Conduct: An Inventory." Paris: OECD. http://www.olis.oecd.org/olis/1998doc.nsf/LinkTo/td-tc-wp(98)74-final (accessed 13 February 2003).

———. 1999. *Codes of Corporate Conduct: An Inventory*. Paris: OECD. http://appli1.oecd.org/olis/1998doc.nsf/LinkTo/td-tc-wp(98)74-final (accessed 12 December 2002).

———. 2000. "The OECD Guidelines for Multinational Enterprises: Decision of the Council. Paris: OECD. http://www.oecd.org/document/39/0,2340,en_2649_34889_1933095_1_1_1_37461,00.html (accessed 6 August 2004).

———. 2001. *Codes of Corporate Conduct: Expanded Review of their Contents*. Paris: OECD. http://www.oecd.org/dataoecd/57/24/1922656.pdf (accessed 13 June 2003).

———. 2001b. *Corporate Responsibility: Results of a Fact-Finding Mission on Private Initiatives.* Paris: OECD. http://www.oecd.org/dataoecd/45/28/1922698.pdf (accessed 13 June 2003).

———. 2003. *Voluntary Approaches for Environmental Policy: Effectiveness, Efficiency and Usage in Policy Mixes.* Paris: OECD.

Overbeek, Henk, and Kees Van Der Pijl. 1993. "Restructuring Capital and Restructuring Hegemony: Neoliberalism and the Unmaking of the Post-War Order," in *Restructuring Hegemony in the Global Political Economy*, ed. Henk Overbeek. London: Routledge.

Palley, Thomas I. 2003. "Possibilities for a New North-South Grand Bargain on Trade," *Foreign Policy in Focus*, http://www.fpif.org/papers/cancun2003.html (accessed 29 February 2004).

Perlas, Nicholas. 2000. "Civil Society, The Third Global Power: The Collapse of the WTO Agenda in Seattle," *Southern Cross Review* http://www.southerncrossreview.org/4/wto.html (accessed 10 October 2003).

Picciotto, Sol. 1999. "A Critical Assessment of the MAI," in *Regulating International Business: Beyond Liberalization*, ed. Sol Picciotto and Ruth Mayne. London: Macmillan Press.

Polanyi, Karl. 2001. *The Great Transformation: The Political and Economic Origins of Our Time.* Boston: Beacon Press.

Powell, Lewis F., Jr. 1971. "Attack on the Free Enterprise System," http://www.mediatransparency.org/stories/powellmanifesto.htm (accessed 20 February 2004).

Richter, Judith. 2001. *Holding Corporations Accountable: Corporate Conduct, International Codes, and Citizen Action.* New York: Zed Books.

Robinson, John. 1983. *Multinationals and Political Control.* New York: St. Martin's Press.

Robinson, William I., and Jerry Harris. 2000. "Towards a Global Ruling Class?: Globalization and the Transnational Capitalist Class." *Science and Society* 64(1).

Rowe, James K. 2003. "States of Nature, Environing the Political: A Response to Timothy W. Luke." *Alternatives: Global, Local, Political* 28(5).

Ruggie, John Gerard. 2003. "Taking Embedded Liberalism Global: The Corporate Connection," http://www.law.nyu.edu/kingsburyb/spring03/globalization/ruggiepaper.pdf (accessed 10 March 2004).

Shoch, James. 2000. "Contesting Globalization: Organized Labor, NAFTA, and the 1997 and 1998 Fast-Track Fights," *Politics & Society* 28(1).

Schrage, Elliott. 2004. "Promoting International Worker Rights through Private Voluntary Initiatives: Public Relations or Public Relations or Public Policy?" University of Iowa Center for Human Rights, at http://www.uichr.org/content/act/sponsored/gwri_report.pdf (accessed 12 May 2004).

Sklair, Leslie. 2002. *The Transnational Capitalist Class*. Oxford: Blackwell.

Smith, Julie. 2003. *Public Summary of Report: International NGO Training and Strategy Seminar on the OECD Guidelines for Multinationals*. Friends of the Earth. http://www.foenl.org/publications/oesdtraining_eng.pdf (accessed 10 June 2003).

van der Gaag, Pieter. 2001. "Global Corporate Social and Environmental Responsibility Regimes: Governments, Stakeholders and How to Use Companies in Creating and Protecting Sustainable Societies." Amsterdam: ANPED. http://www.anped.org/PDF/Carpg.pdf (accessed 10 September 2003).

Van Der Pijl, Kees. 1993. "The Sovereignty of Capital Impaired: Social Forces and Codes of Conduct for Multinational Corporations," in *Restructuring Hegemony in the Global Political Economy*, ed. Henk Overbeek. London: Routledge.

Vargas, Daniel. 2002. "Enron Workers Sell, Sell, Sell Company Stuff Online." *Houston Chronicle* (January 17). http://www.chron.com/cs/CDA/story.hts/business/1215116 (accessed 10 October 2003).

Willums, Jan-O!af, and Ulrich Goluke. 1992. *From Ideas to Action: The ICC Report on The Greening of Enterprise 92*. Oslo: ICC Publishing.

Went, Robert. 2000. *Globalization: Neoliberal Challenge, Radical Responses.* London: Pluto Press.

Yuen, Eddie. 2004. "Introduction," in *Confronting Capitalism: Dispatches from a Global Movement*, ed. Eddie Yuen, Daniel Burton-Rose, and George Katsiaficas. Brooklyn: Soft Skull Press.

Zarsky, Lyuba. 2002. "Beyond Good Deeds: For Multinational Corporations to Adopt Socially Responsible Practices, Voluntary Measures are not Enough," *Forum for Applied Research and Public Policy* 16(4): 14–23.

Zinn, Howard. 2003. *A People's History of the United States: 1492–Present.* New York: HarperCollins.

The Authors

James K. Rowe is a Ph.D. candidate in the Department of Politics, University of California at Santa Cruz, Santa Cruz, CA 95064 USA; e-mail: jkrowe@ucsc.edu.

Ronnie D. Lipschutz is a professor in the Department of Politics, University of California, Santa Cruz; e-mail: rlipsch@ucsc.edu.

FORMULATING A MORAL CORE FOR INTERNATIONAL CODES OF CONDUCT

Duane Windsor
Rice University, Houston, Texas, USA

Abstract

A moral core places ethical considerations superior to business interest. This core must include voluntary prescriptions in various forms to "buy higher, sell lower." International business ethics must somehow address the tradeoff between corporate financial and stakeholder interests. Corporation codes of conduct generally do not define a moral core. Corporate citizenship is typically strategic investment in markets and reputation. There are two practical paths for formulating a moral core. One path is civil lawsuits against multinationals that, successful or not, increase corporate moral sensitivity. The other path is evolution of multilateral codes of conduct embedding negotiated norms for guidance of corporate behavior. Four key cases illustrate: (1) World Bank approach for combating corruption in Chad; (2) a lawsuit against Unocal alleging human rights abuses by Myanmar; (3) a lawsuit against ChevronTexaco alleging environmental and community damages in Ecuadorian Amazonia; and (4) demand by developing countries for relaxing intellectual property rights.

Introduction

The word "code" has a specific meaning in jurisprudence: a code is a systematic written compilation of law promulgated by some governmental authority; and such law commands mandatory compliance. Business codes (issued by corporations or industry associations) and multilateral codes (adopted or proposed by governments or nongovernmental organizations—NGOs) extend this meaning to ethical norms and expectations intended to have the practical effect or force of international law as a result of voluntary compliance. A code should reflect precise expression and logical arrangement (see Kinni 2003). Corporation, industry, and multilateral codes of conduct have become widespread devices for two reasons beyond perceived litigation risks. One reason is the increasing number and diversity of ethical dilemmas encountered in international business. Multilateral codes can assume moral if not legal authority (Frederick 1991). The other reason is strategic: Verschoor (1998) reports a positive link between corporate "ethics code" emphasis (not necessarily ethical behavior) and financial performance measures.

 pp. 47–63

This paper focuses on formulation of a "moral core" for corporation or multilateral codes of conduct applicable to international business operations of multinational enterprises (MNEs). One can readily state a general principle conception: international business ethics concerns "the rightness or wrongness of certain business actions across cultures" (Buller and McEvoy 1999: 326). How a code addresses specific actions defines its core. A corporation- or industry-issued code is necessarily a code of business conduct. Such a privately-issued code expresses business strategies and policies. Whether such a code of business conduct amounts to ethics in action depends on whether the code has a definable and appropriate moral or normative core in some form. In a world of highly variable and often quite minimalist multi-domestic regulation permitting a corporate "race to the bottom" (Berenbeim 1999: 697), a moral core must go beyond variable legal compliance across national jurisdictions. Mere legal compliance is, because mandatory, a trivial moral exercise. A general statement of precepts—e.g., honesty, integrity, and fairness—is also a trivial moral exercise. A moral core necessarily involves addressing the concrete details of business decisions and activities (Kaplan and Norton 2003): "the detailed processes and practices which constitute the day-to-day activities of organizational life *and* which relate to strategic outcomes" (Johnson, Melin, and Whittington 2003: 3).

There must be specific criteria for formulating a morally acceptable code of conduct, whether business or multilateral in origin, and thus for assessing whether a given code of business conduct has a definable much less an acceptable moral core. The task of formulating a moral core is not a simple one: there are serious intellectual disagreements both on general principles and in detail among competing moral frameworks of (a) community utilitarianism (translating roughly to global capitalism as moral community and the global economy expand), (b) stakeholder-oriented rights and duties (translating roughly to international legal and moral constraints on global capitalism), and (c) cultural relativism (translating roughly to multi-domestic capitalism). A particular code may rate highly on one dimension and poorly on another dimension (Buller, Kohls, and Anderson 1991: 769). As Kolk and van Tulder (2003: 53) point out, it is one thing to specify compliance with local laws concerning child labor and another thing to set an international standard for the minimum age defining child labor. Most codes leave definition to host country law, although Sara Lee reportedly sets an international standard of fifteen years of age. Kolk and van Tulder report that, for fifty identifiable corporation child labor codes (about 60 percent US firms and 35 percent European), about 75 percent were in the apparel industry, followed mostly by retailers. There are applicable International Labour Organization (ILO) and UN conventions (Kolk and van Tulder 2003: 51). None of the corporation codes mention home country laws, which would typically be stricter than in host countries. About half mention host country laws, and a quarter international standards; while about 20 percent mention no standards. Of thirty-five firms with explicitly identifiable positions, about 70 percent were multi-domestic and 30 percent universal in orientation. The multi-domestic orientation is marked (see also Kolk and van Tulder 2002; van Tulder and Kolk 2001).

The notion of a moral core draws on Donaldson and Preston's (1995) use of a similar concept in stakeholder theory. Those authors argue that stakeholder theory is at its core normative in orientation. Their particular perspective on normative stakeholder theory is however that ethical reasoning compels a redistribution of existing property rights away from investors and managers to other stakeholders in accordance with relative contribution to the joint production success of the enterprise. The present paper neither endorses nor excludes that particular perspective; initially, it simply makes use of Donaldson and Preston's tripartite formulation. Their normative core is wrapped within next instrumental and finally descriptive dimensions of stakeholder theory. Instrumental stakeholder theory addresses cause-and-effect relationships between means and ends. Descriptive stakeholder theory addresses the empirical and behavioral realities of the firm's world. Adaptation of this tripartite dimensionality to business and multilateral codes of conduct is somewhat different. It is vital to distinguish moral core from instrumental calculation or descriptive-empirical conditions of relative power and moral influence. A moral core identifies "moral significance" in a situation, as distinct from degree of influence over the outcome of the situation or level of urgency to resolve the situation although the latter two dimensions affect feasibility and timing of action (Kohls, Buller, and Anderson 1999: 41). A moral or normative core effectively places ethical considerations superior to immediate business interest. Such a moral core must include prescriptions in various forms to "buy higher, sell lower." Examples are improved labor practices that increase costs; and relaxed intellectual property rights that reduce revenues. That win-lose sacrifice of immediate business interest is good (i.e., enlightened) long-term business strategy (Jensen 2000) or prudent altruism (Friedman 1970) is a separate, instrumental matter. Hillman and Keim (2001) conclude that stakeholder management can be profitable, but that social issue engagement is likely to be costly. Whether a firm should comply with activists' demands depends strategically on circumstances (Hudson and Lusk 2004).

International business ethics must address tradeoffs between corporate financial interests and other stakeholder interests including the public interest. An appropriate moral core does not automatically reduce to stakeholder theory, although it may imply particular tradeoffs whose outcomes amount to redistribution of property rights. Nor does the moral core automatically expand at least yet, contrary to Scherer and Smid (2000), to assume a new purpose of taking dominant responsibility for improvement of world-wide social and environmental conditions due to widespread governmental incapacity. The firm operates within a framework of laws, customary ethics, and multiple stakeholder interests (Friedman 1970); but this framework is still fundamentally a set of constraints on investor and manager wealth creation. Investors and managers pursue self-interested goals that have, however imperfectly, a market utilitarian linkage to social welfare creation. Imperfections (e.g., non-priced negative externalities and other stakeholder or societal harms) are sources of ethical dilemmas. The moral core concerns voluntary self-restraint (Banfield 1985: 337) and prudent altruism (Friedman 1970) on the one hand, and multilateral recognition of moral duties toward and rights of stakeholders and societies on the other hand (see subject matter survey in Barker and Cobb 1999).

Legal compliance and reputation protection (Alsop 2004) are instrumental calculations directed at investor and manager wealth creation within given descriptive-empirical conditions of governmental and stakeholder power to injure the firm. Where a firm can transfer increased costs on to customers or suppliers or employees, the firm has not addressed a moral core of conduct. Any maximizing model requires assumptions about goals, time horizon, and voluntary moral constraints adopted as a sense of duty (Banfield 1985: 337). Pure responsiveness to environmental pressures is not a moral core: "If the actor takes account of such prohibitions only as 'costs' that it might be 'unprofitable' to risk incurring, they are not, of course, moral constraints, but simply environmental conditions, like prices, which he [or she] must take as given" (Banfield 1985: 337). Instrumental action is corporate social responsiveness rather than corporate social responsibility. Responsiveness can lead to corporate socially responsible outcomes. Motive (i.e., intent) and outcome are separable in this respect. (In criminal law, intent may be sufficient to indict even an otherwise innocent action; or an action or its outcome can be criminal without regard for intent.)

Win-win outcomes are obviously desirable. The acid test of a moral core is when the business must accept some win-lose burden on a moral principle. A recent example is Levi Strauss's decision to stop operations in China due to "pervasive" human rights abuses there (Katz and Paine 1994). Levi Strauss, a privately-owned apparel firm, had previously halted operations in Burma on these grounds. Levi Strauss had formulated written guidelines for "Business Partner Terms of Engagement" (defining child labor at less than fourteen or compulsory age for schooling) and "Guidelines for Country Selection" (emphasizing protection of Levi Strauss's global brand image). The Levi "Mission Statement and Aspiration Statement" highlighted "Ethical Management Practices" and its "Code of Ethics" stated a set of ethical values or principles. There was also a statement on environmental philosophy and guiding principles. A China Policy Group applied a "principled reasoning approach" to the issue—resulting in divided views concerning staying versus leaving. CEO Robert Haas ultimately found company guidelines compelling for exiting China. Five years later (April 1998), Levi announced return to manufacturing and selling in China on a judgment that the situation was improving. Activist and labor interests criticized the decision to return. In May 1999, Levi Strauss, Mattel, and Reebok announced they were joining with twenty-one NGOs in endorsing a set of principles governing conduct of business in China.

Corporation codes of conduct frequently do not define a moral core, even if they outline some ethical decision-making procedure and legal-compliance reporting procedure. "Sadly, at many companies ethics and values are just for show. They amount to a lot of paperwork and little more than platitudes. . . . Even after all of the scandals of the past two years, it's still the rare company that makes ethics and values a part of its culture and day-to-day decision making" (Alsop 2004: 57). Alsop cites as notorious examples Enron and Tyco (see Watkins 2003). Code content has often reflected unhappy incidents (e.g., Robertson and Fadil 1998). Typically, corporate codes (see Kaptein 2004 for an empirical study): (1) define and defend corporate interests (e.g., intellectual property rights); (2) command employee loyalty (e.g., non-competition and no conflicts of interest); (3) specify legal compliance (i.e., adherence to statutes and regulations of all governments); (4) recognize stakeholder power (e.g., customer satisfaction focus); and (5) specify internal procedures for reporting misconduct (e.g., corrupt payments) or "gray" difficulties (e.g., facilitating payments) for higher management handling. Legal compliance is a trivial exercise in moral reasoning until one comes to the very real problems of variation in legal standards across countries or of globally footloose corporations without a true national identity. Neither company nor individual have any real moral freedom in the matter of legal compliance. Employee loyalty and subordination of interest are likewise mandatory except in legal and moral matters. One vital ethical matter not typically discussed in a company code of conduct is the handling of civil litigation—delegated to attorneys. Company policy or practice concerning litigation is voluntary. If defendant, the firm may settle or litigate; if plaintiff, the firm may decide not to litigate, or in case of litigation again decide to settle or litigate. Litigation policy typically reflects calculation of outcome likelihoods.

The *Boeing Ethical Business Conduct Guidelines* begin with a set of values and then the "Boeing Code of Conduct." The eight values are leadership (including being "a world-class leader . . . in our financial results"), integrity ("the highest ethical standards" and treating "everyone fairly and with trust and respect"), quality, customer satisfaction, employee cooperation ("people working together"), diverse and involved teamwork, good corporate citizenship (safe workplace, environmental protections, health and well-being of employees and their families, community voluntarism, and philanthropy), and enhancing shareholder value. The intervening four values of quality, customer satisfaction, employee productivity, and diversity and involved teamwork may appear to function as the instrumental linkage between leadership and integrity on the one hand and corporate citizenship and enhancing shareholder value on the other hand. The statement implicitly posits win-win outcomes. The Boeing Code of Conduct instructs employees to (in order of the statement): (a) avoid conflicts of interest; (b) avoid inappropriate personal gain; (c) follow all restrictions on use and disclosure of information; (d) observe "fair dealing" (undefined) in all transactions and interactions; (e) protect all company, customer, and supplier assets; (f) comply with "all applicable laws, rules, and regulations"; and (g) report "any illegal or unethical conduct." Whistleblower litigation and protections require that: "Retaliation against employees who come forward to raise genuine concerns [undefined] will not be tolerated." The booklet then outlines various procedures, including initial advice on "Ethical decisionmaking" in what can be characterized here as "gray areas": careful balancing needs, new problems, multiple considerations, and personal cost. The detailed procedures address specific areas of concern, such as marketing practices or offering of business courtesies or specific US compliance issues. Basically a business code seeks partly to insulate the firm legally against its employees' misdeeds.

No program is fully effective, of course. A recent series of scandals has tarnished Boeing's reputation. In June 2003, Lockheed Martin sued Boeing and three former Boeing employees, alleging theft of proprietary documents used to help win the Evolved Expendable Launch Vehicle program (i.e., rockets used to launch military satellites). The US Air Force rescinded the contract award. In November 2003, Boeing fired its CFO and a former Air Force acquisitions official for secretly discussing the latter's subsequent Boeing job while still working for the government. The Boeing CEO resigned a week later. The former Air Force official, then working for Boeing, pleaded guilty to conspiracy. A government inspector general reported that the Air Force improperly awarded Boeing a $1.32 billion contract for NATO surveillance-plan upgrades negotiated by the former acquisitions official. In May 2005, Boeing announced a settlement with female workers who claimed the firm knew male employees received higher pay and better promotions. The multiplicity of these problems suggests that the formally promulgated code lack any real linkage to organizational culture, ethical climate and behavior, or deterrence effectiveness.

The source of the gap between code and behavior is reasonably traceable. A prevailing global capitalism worldview (Werhane 2000) presumes utilitarian outcomes in development and reasonable rights to practice business freely. Berenbeim (1999: 696–697) reported that MNEs increasingly "prefer to view themselves as transnational rather than multinational entities that compete in a global rather than a multinational environment" and possess a "self image . . . of a single company that seeks growth and profit in a single market." This perspective reduces "business practice" to "a few overriding principles and priorities" (Berenbeim 1999: 697). The simple and universal maxim for wealth creation is "buy low, sell high" to maximize (risk-adjusted) return on invested capital. This worldview embeds certain other assumptions concerning transparency, contract, and negotiation. A firm should then never internalize non-priced negative "externalities" (a proxy here for various undesirable social, environmental, and stakeholder impacts) unless reasonable to do so for legal or strategic considerations. Corporate citizenship is often purely strategic investment in markets and corporate reputation. An MNE can search for markets with weaker public policy and stakeholder power; and seek to influence public policy and corporate reputation.

The remainder of the paper proceeds in the following manner. The next (second) section proposes a preliminary conceptual framework for formulating a moral core in codes of conduct. Paths forward for formulating moral cores in business and multilateral codes appear to be on the one hand some combination of multi-domestic legal compliance and market morality (i.e., global capitalism), and on the other hand some combination of civil litigation and evolution of international norms by multilateral action. It is sufficient that multilateral codes of conduct simply embed negotiated norms (Gauthier 1986) for guidance of corporate behavior. The paper uses four key examples, all with marked local corruption, to illustrate international norm evolution and civil litigation. The third section explains two cases illuminating evolution of international norms and standards. One case is the World Bank approach for combating corruption in Chad and Cameroon while promoting economic development of those two countries through oil production and transportation. A second case examines demand in developing countries for relaxation of MNE intellectual property rights presently guaranteed by the World Trade Organization (WTO TRIPS). The fourth section explains two pending lawsuits illuminating the possible role of civil litigation against MNEs. Anonymous residents of Burma have sued Unocal alleging liability for claimed human rights abuses by the Myanmar regime. Indians have filed a lawsuit against ChevronTexaco claiming liability for alleged damages to environment and indigenous communities in Ecuadorian Amazonia. Civil lawsuits against MNEs, successful or not, may increase corporate moral and ecological sensitivity and suggest multilateral code content.

Proposed Conceptual Framework

Most MNEs are headquartered in the advanced economies. The global economy consists at the country level of highly diverse legal frameworks and value cultures. Globalization creates difficult ethical problems for MNEs (Manakkalathil and Rudolf 1995; Velasquez 2000) beyond those facing domestic enterprise or MNE operations in the advanced economies. The vital case concerns MNEs operating in developing and transition societies. These countries often have natural resources, inexpensive labor, and growing markets. These countries also often feature difficult conditions *inter alia* of corruption, desperate poverty, human rights abuses, lax labor and environmental standards, governmental and stakeholder incapacity, and non-democratic regimes; as well as varying attitudes about values and behaviors. The interaction between MNE and host country cannot be restricted to the typical bargaining model of the international business literature. A moral core must address fair negotiation within the context of voluntary corporate restraint based on understanding and respect for local culture, and of voluntary corporate altruism based on recognition of the specifics of local operating conditions. MNEs have both positive and negative impacts on developing and transition societies. Social goods include combating corruption and human rights abuses. Social bads include damages to natural ecology and local cultures.

Four Logical Paths Forward

Figure 1 illustrates four logical paths forward from the current situation of largely multi-domestic regulations and value cultures for defining the content of corporation and industry codes of conduct. The benchmark path is continued multi-domestic legal compliance. This path is the one most commonly sketched in corporation codes. The second path will not be formally stated as such in corporate codes. But the path is found tacitly in injunctions for bottom line maximization. Market morality (Kolk and van Tulder 2003: 49) essentially argues for what is necessary to the survival and

Figure 1. Logically possible paths forward

prosperity of the firm. It posits a global capitalism operating in a minimally regulated world economy. The typical corporate code reflects a combination of these two logics. A third path forward is civil litigation intended ultimately to alter the decision-making incentives of managers and investors. A fourth path forward is the development of international norms through multilateral agreements of various types. The paper suggests that the two paths can interact to influence future corporation codes.

Legal Compliance and Market Morality

One can address business ethics within the resource-based view (RBV) as a source of competitive advantage (Barney 1991; Barney and Wright 1998), such that one can add ethical capability to strategic, technological, financial, and organizational capabilities (Buller and McEvoy 1999: 326). The essence of the resource-based view is the importance of relative efficiency of net benefit creation in explaining inter-firm performance differences (see Hoopes, Madsen, and Walker 2003). Net benefit creation is the resultant (or sum) of creating greater value (i.e., premium pricing) and/or reducing costs (i.e., relative cost efficiency). The VRIO model (see Peteraf and Barney 2003) emphasizes that resources are valuable (V), rare (R), and inimitable (I); and that the organization (O) has capabilities for exploiting those resource attributes. Resources occur in different forms of physical capital, organizational capital, and human capital.

If one believes that business ethics is invariably smart business practice, then the competitive advantage argument cannot be rejected (Williamson 1999). However, the argument has a peculiar difficulty. The more rare and inimitable the resource, the more valuable it is. Hence, ethical capability yields value where it is relatively unique. If one wants ethical capability to be widespread, then imitation is highly desirable. Ethical capability thus yields temporary rather than sustainable advantage, unless new ethics problems keep arising.

Figure 2 outlines key dimensions of strategic management and corporate social performance theories relevant to the paper's topic. Strategy separates into two main and competing schools of thought (Williamson 1991). The internal perspective on strategy emphasizes organizational development of resources, capabilities, and practices for competitive differentiation as the source of rents (i.e., profits higher than the cost of capital). One might think of resources underlying capabilities in turn underlying practices. The external perspective on strategy emphasizes industrial economic structure and hence market power, collusion, and strategic behavior as sources of rent. Differentiation conveys market power within a niche or an industry, but market power has the general sense of a large market share whether arising in differentiation or not. The dotted arrow connecting internal to external perspective suggests only a loose cause-and-effect relationship. The evidence concerning the relationship between external perspective and interfirm performance differences is disputed. The dotted arrow connecting external perspective to performance suggests again only a loose cause-and-effect relationship. The connection between internal perspective and interfirm performance differences is even weaker (see Ray, Barney, and Muhanna 2004).

The stockholder wealth creation theory argues that the primary purpose and thus goal of the firm, organized by investors as principals and operated by contract manag-

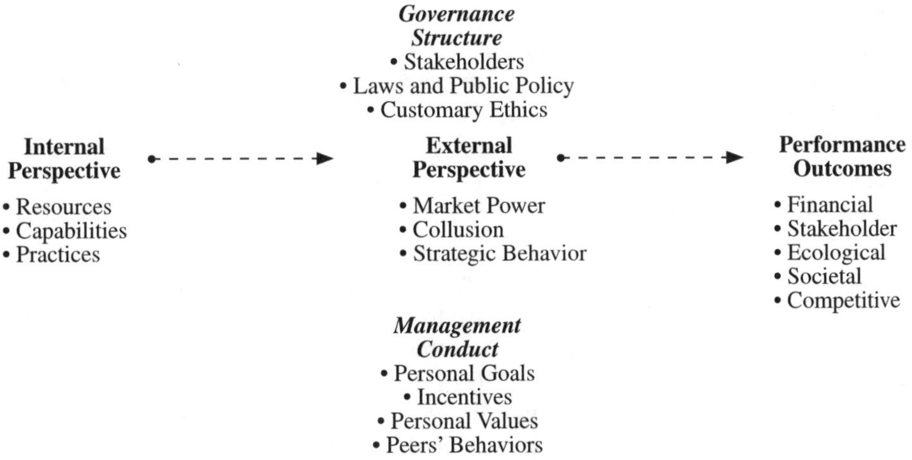

Figure 2. Key dimensions of strategic management and corporate social performance theories

ers as agents, is financial performance (separated unavoidably into current and future dimensions) on behalf of the investors. This theory operates within constraints imposed by laws, public policy, and customary ethics. The theory can extend to apprehend the role and influence of other stakeholders. These constraints and influences are part of the governance structure of the firm. The principal-agent contract is incomplete or imperfect. Management conduct thus reflects some variable combination of personal goals, incentives, personal values, and conduct of peers. Corporate social responsibility theory expands performance outcomes to multiple dimensions in addition to financial performance: e.g., stakeholder, ecological, societal, and competitor impacts.

International Norms and Civil Litigation

Development of international norms moves in the direction of "a new global civil society" (Berenbeim 1999: 698). Multilateral code formulation should involve MNEs, home countries, host countries, NGOs (e.g., TI, ICC), and international institutions (e.g., UN Global Club, WHO Tobacco Free Initiative). The World Trade Organization (WTO) is not a particularly good example, as in various ways (e.g., US tuna and gasoline restrictions) morally or ecologically based trade barriers suffer in favor of economic development. The UN Global Club addresses labor and human rights and ecological practices.

There is useful guidance to other situations in emerging multilateral cooperation against corruption. In December 2003, some 125 nations signed the UN Convention Against Corruption. The OAS in 1996 and the OECD and EU in 1997 adopted multilateral anti-corruption conventions. The EU faces important incentives in anticipated entry of Eastern European transition economies. The UN convention explicitly does not define corruption—to retain flexibility in local circumstances. What the convention signals is consensus against something (corruption) and for something (progress and democracy). If there has to be full definitional agreement, negotiations are apt to fail: the US declined to ratify the Kyoto Protocol. Consent to an agreement, however vague, is a basis for possible future progress, since a consenting party cannot easily withdraw although it may fail to implement its consent.

Lack of multilateral definition of corruption reflects two kinds of problems. One problem is a materiality distinction between bribery and grease. The US Foreign Corrupt Practices Act excuses the latter. In some Latin American countries any payment to a public official is strictly illegal. The other problem is the distinction between bribery and relationship. Corruption is some abuse of a position of monopoly power (market or legal) to obtain private rents. In many countries, relationship is more important than Western-style morality. The vital difficulty is the clash of views. Corruption may be "chaotic" or more systematically "organized." A chief concern is that globalization has intensified corruption into an epidemic of organized corruption subsystems undermining progress and democracy in developing and transition societies. A study of forty-seven countries found that politically connected firms—shareholders and top executives being members of national governments or parliaments—are widespread in highly corrupt countries (Faccio 2003). There are also other linked problems such as money laundering and terrorism financing.

Buller and McEvoy (1999: 332, Table 1) suggest a continuum between polar opposites of local responsiveness and global consistency along which lie three possible configurations for the MNE. Local responsiveness corresponds to a multi-domestic strategy of adaptive business practices (focusing on human resource management) and relativist ethics (i.e., cultural relativism). Local values and norms dominate ethical choices; business practices adapt. Global consistency corresponds to a global strategy of exportive business practices (focusing on human resource management) and universal ethics (i.e., global norms). This global-local distinction corresponds to the horizontal axis of Figure 3. At the center of the continuum in an intermediate position is what one may label, from Buller and McEvoy, transnationalism or cosmopolitanism in contrast to localism and globalism. This configuration corresponds to a transnational strategy of integrative business practices and cosmopolitan ethics. Integrative business practices reflect a combination of local and global; cosmopolitan ethics specifies ethical sensitivity to balances between local and global norms. Corporation codes are likely to follow this approach as a matter of strategic management. Buller and McEvoy (1999: 332) are clear that a particular company need not necessarily follow strictly one of these three configurations. A multi-domestic strategy may combine with some universal ethical standards; a global strategy may honor some local values and norms. These combinations presumably tend toward the transnational configuration.

Figure 3 depicts corporate codes of conduct positioned within four general considerations. These considerations reflect two interdependent dimensions (see Donaldson 1996). One dimension is the tension between global capitalism and domestic localism of value cultures. A second dimension is the tension between multilateral norms and civil litigation on the one hand and multi-domestic regulation of markets and enterprises on the other hand. The design of Figure 3 isolates four outcomes:

- Cultural relativism differentiates the global economy into multi-domestic markets. Values, ethics, and norms differ by culture (i.e., country); and firms conduct themselves by country situation. This outcome leaves domestic corruption to operate by country.

- Multi-domestic legal compliance obeys the laws and regulations of each country. This outcome generates what is typically called the "race to the bottom": MNEs look for the most lax regulatory environments in which to operate and may seek to influence regulations.
- Market morality may be asserted as if a universal ethics grounded in community utilitarian and investors' property rights (see Werhane 2000).
- Regime evolution allows for a kind of rising ethics in which over time international norms emerge despite the conflict of domestic values.

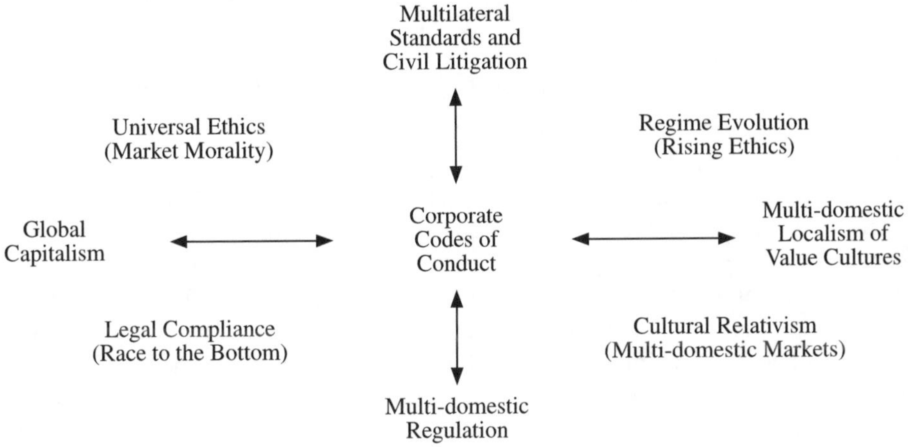

Figure 3. The context for corporate codes of conduct

The intellectual contribution to this situation is some "model of global ethics" (Buller, Kohls, and Anderson 1991: 767; see also Payne, Raiborn, and Ashvik 1997). Buller, Kohls, and Anderson (1997: 172, Table 1) offer a list drawn partly from the literature (see Sethi 2003). A significant part of the list addresses constitutional and political rights of the individual (i.e., "fundamental human rights" taken from Donaldson 1989; see Turcotte 1998). The firm cannot violate these rights, but it is murky as to how the firm can create such rights in developing and transition countries although it may be able to defend them for employees and suppliers. There are also "basic moral norms" (taken from DeGeorge 1993), some of which—such as truthfulness, honoring contracts, and fair dealing—do bear directly on MNEs. Buller, Kohls, and Anderson (1997) stipulate a list of specific ethical norms for MNEs: (1) "no intentional direct harm"; (2) more good than harm in host countries; (3) contribution to host country development; (4) respect human rights of employees (see Liubicic 1998); (5) respect local culture where it does not violate (universal) ethical norms; (6) pay "fair share of taxes"; and (7) cooperation with host governments in "developing and enforcing just background institutions." Presently an MNE can reasonably agree with some but not all of these proposed norms. The authors also commend the Caux Round Table principles for business (Skelly 1995) stipulating: (1) stakeholder responsibilities; (2) concern for economic and social impact; (3) going beyond "the letter of the law toward a spirit of trust"; (4) respect for rules; (5) support for multilateral trade; (6) environmental sensitivity; and (7) avoidance of "illicit operations."

Evolution of International Standards

General precepts for MNEs, given satisfactory profit, are to: (1) understand and appreciate local conditions; (2) apply best feasible practice to those conditions; (3) maximize positive local benefits and compensations; and (4) minimize negative local impacts. The Chad-Cameroon pipeline project and the WTO position on intellectual property rights illustrate the evolution of international standards. Multilateral norms may influence corporation views.

Corruption, Environment, Human Rights, and Local Cultures in Chad

The Chad Cameroon Petroleum Development and Pipeline Project involves ecology and indigenous communities versus development. The routing through Cameroon from Chad endangers black rhino and forest pygmies (Ivanovich 2000). A case study characterizes Chad as one of the riskiest investment locations (Esty and Ferman 2001). Following 1960 independence, there were repeated civil wars. In 1990, an army general seized power through a coup. That regime is reportedly oppressive and a repeated violator of human rights. Neighboring Cameroon is also very poor and under an oppressive regime. The World Bank is very interested in helping development of these two very poor countries. A public-private consortium (ExxonMobil, Petronas of Malaysia, and Chevron with the two governments) will build a pipeline through Cameroon and operate the oilfields in southern Chad. To reduce problems arising from receipts to government, the World Bank developed a Revenue Management Plan for Chad. (Chad will receive some $1.8 billion in cash flow.) Income tax receipts are restricted to general development spending. Royalties and dividends will go into a Special Petroleum Revenue Account, with 10 percent (deposited in foreign financial institutions) going to finance poverty reduction programs; and 85 percent of remaining funds deposited in Chad commercial banks going to finance five civilian sectors of development and 15 percent going to the government. The World Bank and Chad will form an oversight committee for annual review of a detailed expenditure program subject to external audit and World Bank monitoring.

Intellectual Property Rights in Key Products

TRIPS (WTO) requires global protection of intellectual property rights. Rawls's (1971) theory of justice argues that changes in status quo should favor the disadvantaged. Developing countries have different views of patents and software codes—preferring open access (in production) and cheap pricing (in consumption). In Vietnam, some 97 percent of software is pirated, with Microsoft Windows and Office reported available for no more than $10 (*Houston Chronicle* 2003). The essential TRIPS debate over pharmaceuticals is that while developing countries argue that patent protection for MNE drugs raises health costs, drug companies argue that therapeutic substitutes for most patented drugs prevent significant price rises. A key illustration of lower prices involves anti-AIDS drugs. Under pressure, drug firms began negotiating discounted prices country by country in Africa. A serious consideration is likely firms' concern that pricing would subsequently also fall in advanced countries. Even so, most AIDS victims cannot afford the discounted drugs. One study of empirical data suggests that the total annual welfare losses to the Indian economy from withdrawal due to global patent protection of the four domestic product groups in the fluoroquinolone sub-segment of systemic anti-bacterials (i.e., anti-biotics) would be on the order of US $713 million, about 118 percent of the entire segment sales in 2000 (Chaudhuri, Goldberg, and Jia 2003). Foregone profits of domestic producers constitute $50 million (or 7 percent), so the overwhelming portion of the total welfare loss derives from the loss of consumer welfare. Profit gains to foreign producers are estimated to be around $57 million per year (close to foregone profits of domestic producers).

Civil Litigation

An alternative approach is civil litigation against MNEs for alleged damages. The US Alien Tort Claims Act (ATCA), a one-line component of the Judiciary Act of 1789 (the act organizing the federal judiciary) illustrates the possibility. The ATCA was apparently adopted to permit actions by aliens in US federal courts against pirates. In recent years, some 100 lawsuits have attempted to revive and expand reach of the ATCA to US corporations operating abroad. No lawsuit has yet succeeded against an American MNE. Two ongoing lawsuits indicate the potential role for civil litigation in pressuring corporations (in addition to media attention and activist-sponsored boycotts).

Human Rights Abuses in Myanmar

A practical test is at work in US federal court (Coyle 2003; Greene 2003). Unnamed ("John Doe") plaintiffs, citizens of Myanmar (Burma), allege that Unocal (Union Oil of California) bears liability for alleged human rights abuses committed by the Myanmar regime along a joint venture pipeline (*John Doe I, et al., Plaintiffs v. Unocal Corp., et al., Defendants*, US Court of Appeals for the Ninth Circuit, December 3, 2001, argued and submitted, September 18, 2002, filed). Unocal is a passive minority investor in the pipeline built and operated by a Myanmar state enterprise and a French firm, Total, to transport natural gas from the Andaman Sea to Thailand. The state enterprise and the French firm have been dismissed from the case for want of jurisdiction. The Unocal suit was dismissed, then reinstated upon appeal, and is now going to trial. There was also a failed activist effort to revoke the Unocal chapter. The suit occurs under the one-sentence Alien Tort Claims Act of 1789 likely intended to deal with issues arising from piracy. The essential argument alleges that Unocal knew what its Myanmar partner would likely do (if the alleged facts are true) and invested in disregard of that knowledge. International law and federal common law forbid slavery or equivalents, which plaintiffs allege in Myanmar.

Ecological Sustainability in Ecuador

Proposals to establish something like a World Environmental Organization (WEO) along WTO lines have not come to fruition. A 1993 suit filed in US federal district court against ChevronTexaco (merged 2001) alleges liability for damages to environment and indigenous communities in Ecuadorian Amazonia (Kass and McCarroll 2003). About 30,000 residents allege that from 1971 to 1992 Texaco dumped waste into open, unlined pits and spilled oil. Ecuador did not effectively regulate waste disposal. Plaintiffs argue that long-established practice has been reinjecting waste back into wells. A US appeals court ruled in 2002 that a lawsuit should be heard in Ecuador but would be enforceable in the US. ChevronTexaco argues that the suit should be against its subsidiary Texaco Petroleum Co. operating in partnership with Ecuador's state oil company, and that the government of Ecuador, certifying in 1998 Texaco's $40 million cleanup, absolved it of liability. The plaintiffs' basic contention is that those standards were insufficient and Texaco had the capacity for better conduct at the time.

Summary and Conclusions

This paper examines the formulation of a moral core for international codes of conduct, whether adopted by corporations or proposed by industry associations, governmental bodies, or nongovernmental organizations. The typical corporation code does not have a moral core. Rather the typical code stipulates multi-domestic legal compliance and market morality (i.e., survival and prosperity of the firm). The paper explores the potential roles of evolving international norms and increasing civil litigation in developing a moral core for business codes of conduct.

References

Alsop, R. J. 2004. *The 18 Immutable Laws of Corporate Reputation: Creating, Protecting, and Repairing Your Most Valuable Asset*. New York: Wall Street Journal Books through Free Press.

Banfield, E. C. 1985. *Here the People Rule: Selected Essays*. New York: Plenum Press.

Barker, T. S., and S. L. Cobb. 1999. "A Survey of Ethics and Cultural Dimensions of MNCS." *Competitiveness Review* 9(2): 11–18.

Barney, J. B. 1991. "Firm Resources and Sustained Competitive Advantage." *Journal of Management* 17: 99–120.

Barney, J. B., and P. M. Wright. 1998. "On Becoming a Strategic Partner: The Role of Human Resources in Gaining Competitive Advantage." *Human Resource Management* 37: 31–46.

Berenbeim, R. 1999. "The Divergence of a Global Economy: One Company, One Market, One Code, One World." *Vital Speeches of the Day* 65(22) (September 1): 696–698.

Buller, P. F., J. J. Kohls, and K. S. Anderson. 1991. "The Challenge of Global Ethics." *Journal of Business Ethics* 10: 767–775.

———. 1997. "A Model for Addressing Cross-Cultural Ethical Conflicts." *Business & Society* 36: 169–193.

Buller, P. F., and G. M. McEvoy. 1999. "Creating and Sustaining Ethical Capability in the Multi-National Corporation." *Journal of World Business* 34: 326–343.

Chaudhuri, S., P. Goldberg, and P. Jia. 2003. "The Effects of Extending Intellectual Property Rights Protection to Developing Countries: A Case Study of the Indian Pharmaceutical Market." NBER Working Paper No. W10159 (December), available from http://ssrn.com/abstract=478668.

Coyle, M. 2003. "9th Circuit Spurns U.S. Over Alien Tort Claims: A Big Unocal Case Is Still to Be Argued." *National Law Journal* 25(84) (June 9): 1, LexisNexis.

DeGeorge, R. T. 1993. *Competing With Integrity in International Business*. New York: Oxford University Press.

Donaldson, T. 1989. *The Ethics of International Business*. New York: Oxford University Press.

———. 1996. Values in Tension: Ethics Away from Home." *Harvard Business Review* 74(5) (September–October): 48–57.

Donaldson, T., and L. E. Preston. 1995. "The Stakeholder Theory of the Corporation: Concepts, Evidence, and Implications." *Academy of Management Review* 20: 65–91.

Esty, B. C., and C. Ferman, C. 2001. "The Chad-Cameroon Petroleum Development and Pipeline Project." Harvard Business School Cases, Part A, 9-202-010 (revised April 10, 2003), and Part B 9-202-012 (publication date October 29, 2001).

Faccio, M. 2003. "Politically Connected Firms." Working paper, Vanderbilt University, Owen Graduate School of Management, available at http://ssrn.com/abstract=444960.

Frederick, W. C. 1991. "The Moral Authority of Transnational Corporate Codes." *Journal of Business Ethics* 10: 165–177.

Friedman, M. 1970. "The Social Responsibility of Business Is to Increase Its Profits." *New York Times Magazine* (September 13): 32–33, 122, 124, 126.

Gauthier, D. P. 1986. *Morals by Agreement*. New York: Oxford University Press.

Greene, J. 2003. "Gathering Storm: Suits that Claim Overseas Abuse Are Putting U.S. Executives On Alert and Their Lawyers On Call." *Legal Times* (July 21), LexisNexis.

Hillman, A. J., and G. D. Keim. 2001. "Shareholder Value, Stakeholder Management, and Social Issues: What's the Bottom Line?" *Strategic Management Journal* 22: 125–139.

Hoopes, D. G., T. L. Madsen, and G. Walker. 2003. "Why Is There a Resource-Based View? Towards a Theory of Competitive Heterogeneity." *Strategic Management Journal* 24: 889–902.

Houston Chronicle. 2003. "Vietnam Is Leading Move Away from Microsoft to Open Source" (December 4): 3B.

Hudson, D., and J. Lusk. 2004. "Activists and Corporate Behavior in Food Processing and Retailing: A Sequential Bargaining Game." *Journal of Agricultural and Resource Economics* 29: 79–93.

Ivanovich, D. 2000. "OK for African Oil Project Expected, But Its Impact on Two Impoverished Nations Debated." *Houston Chronicle* (June 6): 1C, 5C.

Jensen, M. C. 2000. "Value Maximization and the Corporate Objective Function." In *Breaking the Code of Change*, ed. M. Beer and N. Nohria. Boston, Mass.: HBS Press, 37–57.

Johnson, G., L. Melin, and R. Whittington. 2003. "Micro Strategy and Strategizing: Towards an Activity-Based View." *Journal of Management Studies* 40: 3–22.

Kaplan, R. S., and D. P. Norton. 2003. "Managing Regulatory and Societal Processes." *Balanced Scorecard Report*, Harvard Business School reprint B0307A.

Kaptein, M. 2004. "Business Codes of Multinational Firms: What Do They Say?" *Journal of Business Ethics* 50: 13–31.

Kass, S. L., and J. M. McCarroll. 2003. "Environmental Law: Alien Tort Claims Act." *New York Law Journal* 230 (July 1): 3, col. 1, LexisNexis.

Katz, J. P., and L. S. Paine. 1994. "Levi Strauss and Co.: Global Sourcing" (A). Harvard Business School case 9-395-127 (revised February 27, 1997).

Kinni, T. 2003. "Words to Work By: Crafting Meaningful Corporate Ethics Statements." *Harvard Management Communication Letter* (January): 1–2, C0301E.

Kohls, J. J., P. F. Buller, and K. S. Anderson. 1999. "Resolving Cross-Cultural Ethical Conflict: An Empirical Test of a Decision Tree Model in an Educational Setting." *Teaching Business Ethics* 3: 37–56.

Kolk, A., and R. van Tulder. 2002. "Child Labor and Multinational Conduct: A Comparison of International Business and Stakeholder Codes." *Journal of Business Ethics* 36: 291–301.

———. 2003. "Ethics in International Business: Multinational Approaches to Child Labor." *Journal of World Business* 39: 49–60.

Liubicic, R. J. 1998. "Corporate Codes of Conduct and Product Labeling Schemes: The Limits and Possibilities of Promoting International Labor Rights through Private Initiatives." *Law and Policy in International Business* 30: 111–158.

Manakkalathil, J., and E. Rudolf. 1995. "Corporate Social Responsibility in a Globalizing Market." *S.A.M. Advanced Management Journal* 60: 29–33.

Payne, D., C. Raiborn, and J. Ashvik. 1997. "A Global Code of Business Ethics." *Journal of Business Ethics* 16: 1727–1735.

Peteraf, M. A., and J. B. Barney. 2003. "Unraveling the Resource-Based Tangle." *Managerial and Decision Economics* 24: 309–323.

Rawls, J. 1971. *A Theory of Justice*. Cambridge, Mass.: Belknap Press of Harvard University Press.

Ray, G., J. B. Barney, and W. A. Muhanna. 2004. "Capabilities, Business Processes, and Competitive Advantage: Choosing the Dependent Variable in Empirical Tests of the Resource-Based View." *Strategic Management Journal* 25: 23–37.

Robertson, C., and P. A. Fadil. 1998. "Developing Corporate Codes of Ethics in Multinational Firms: Bhopal Revisited." *Journal of Managerial Issues* 10: 454–468.

Scherer, A. G., and M. Smid. 2000. "The Downward Spiral and the US Model Business Principles: Why MNEs Should Take Responsibility for the Improvement of World-Wide Social and Environmental Conditions." *Management International Review* 40: 351–371.

Sethi, S. P. 2003. *Setting Global Standards: Guidelines for Creating Codes of Conduct in Multinational Corporations*. Hoboken, N.J.: John Wiley.

Skelly, J. 1995. "The Caux Round Table Principles for Business: The Rise of International Ethics." *Business Ethics Magazine*, advertising supplement insert (May/June), cited in Buller, Kohls, and Anderson 1997.

Turcotte, M.-F. 1998. “Commerce with Conscience: Human Rights and Corporate Codes of Conduct.” *Revenue Canadienne des Sciences de l’Administration* 15: 108–109.

van Tulder, R., and A. Kolk. 2001. “Multinationality and Corporate Ethics: Codes of Ethics in the Sporting Goods Industry.” *Journal of International Business Studies* 32: 267–283.

Velasquez, M. 2000. “Globalization and the Failure of Ethics.” *Business Ethics Quarterly* 10: 343–352.

Verschoor, C. C. 1998. “A Study of the Link Between a Corporation’s Financial Performance and Its Commitment to Ethics.” *Journal of Business Ethics* 17: 1509–1516.

Watkins, S. S. 2003. “Ethical Conflicts at Enron: Moral Responsibility in Corporate Capitalism.” *California Management Review* 45(4) (Summer): 6–19.

Werhane, P. H. 2000. “Exporting Mental Models: Global Capitalism in the 21st Century.” *Business Ethics Quarterly* 10: 353–362.

Williamson, O. E. 1991. “Strategizing, Economizing, and Economic Organization.” *Strategic Management Journal* 12: 75–94.

________. 1999. “Strategy Research: Governance and Competence Perspectives.” *Strategic Management Journal* 20: 1087–1108.

The Author

Duane Windsor is Lynette S. Autrey Professor of Management at the Jesse H. Jones Graduate School of Management, Rice University, 6100 Main Street, Houston, Texas 77005, USA; e-mail: odw@rice.edu.

CORPORATE CODES OF CONDUCT: ON THE VIRTUE OF MODESTY

Ian Maitland
University of Minnesota, Twin Cities, USA

Abstract

What are international codes of conduct for? The broad support for such codes masks fundamental differences about their purpose. Corporations see codes of conduct as regimes for regulating their relations with their suppliers in developing countries and—not least—to counter negative publicity. For labor and human rights activists, on the other hand, codes of conduct are levers for forcing positive change in global labor and environmental standards. Here I consider two areas typically covered by codes of conduct—wages and child labor—and identify some of the dangers of using codes to force change. If low wages or child labor are the result of poverty, and can't be fixed by enlightened corporate policies, then codes will at best leave the underlying problems untouched and at worst will aggravate them. I conclude that we should be cautious about using codes to force higher standards.

Introduction

Corporate codes of conduct appear to be all things to all people. That may be the secret of their success. For global companies, codes of conduct serve an external purpose—to protect their brand equity by signaling to the public their commitment to high labor and environmental standards—and an internal purpose—to communicate those standards to management, employees and contractors. For NGOs and activists, codes of conduct are a means of ratcheting up standards of corporate behavior and making global companies more accountable to external stakeholders. For governments, codes of conduct appear to be a flexible and relatively costless alternative to direct regulation of the largely unregulated global economy.

Companies tend initially to adopt codes of corporate conduct to counter negative publicity about their labor or environmental practices. Ironically, companies' sensitivity to threats to their reputation is a byproduct of the same process of globalization of production that has exposed their labor practices to harsh scrutiny. With the outsourcing of production to contract plants in developing countries, American retailers are rapidly becoming "virtual" companies. As a Nike manager plaintively explained when his company first came under fire for its labor practices: "We don't know the first thing about manufacturing. We are marketers and designers" (Barnet

pp. 65–78

and Cavanagh 1994). As a consequence, Nike's brand is its principal asset. Unlike tangible assets like factories or money in the bank, brand equity is vulnerable to shifts in the public's perception of the company. This point has not been lost on critics of the companies who have turned their strength against them. A leading anti-Nike activist, Medea Benjamin, has announced that her strategy is to "make the swoosh uncool" (Egan 1998).

In another irony, activists and the media have globalized their operations as fast as corporate America or Europe. As a consequence, consumers in the developed world have been brought face to face with the conditions under which the goods they buy are made in developing countries. In a sense, consumers are being brought face to face with their own past. The conditions under which workers in the developing world labor are not exceptional or outlandish—rather they hold up a mirror to our own past and have been the norm throughout history. We forget that we are the exception. But, perhaps because none of us has directly experienced these conditions, the result is a case of culture shock, all the more acute because the media rarely explain the context of the images they beam into our homes.

Seen through the lens of, say, CNN, the global economy—along with everything else—is simplified and formatted and scripted to fit the exigencies of the medium and the limited attention span of the audience it is trying to attract. One proven way of gaining ratings and market share is investigative reporting—what used to be called muckraking journalism. Essentially investigative reporting is about exposing conspiracies—preferably in high places, like corporate board rooms, government agencies, and maybe local police departments. If a bridge collapses or school children fall ill because of food poisoning, investigative reporting uncovers who profited from the tragedy. In other words, if there is no human agency—no guilty party to point the finger at—then there is no story. And the media abhor a vacuum—what they call dead air time—because air time is money.

There are obvious exceptions to what I have just said about human agency. Natural disasters involving large-scale loss of life are a case in point. They are a good fit for CNN. They don't require much set-up time, they are highly photogenic, and they tug at our heart strings. But exceptions like this illustrate another iron rule of the mass media: If a story doesn't fit into a two-minute sound-bite or photo-op, then the story does not have legs.

If the message is edited to fit the medium, what does that mean for the reporting of globalization? To win market share, the media exploit the shock value of the conditions under which workers labor in developing countries. It is not that there is anything new about these conditions. What is new is that the media have opened a window in Western homes on to these conditions.

Also the script requires that these conditions be presented not as the result of the workings of impersonal economic forces but as deliberate choices: If workers in Nike's or Reebok's contract plants in Indonesia have to survive on wages of one or two dollars a day, then that is because Nike and Reebok made a conscious decision not to pay them a living wage. If workers are sexually harassed by supervisors, then that is because Nike and Reebok callously turned a blind eye to such practices. If children are discovered stitching soccer balls for Nike, then that is because it is Nike's policy to seek out cheap and docile workers with nimble fingers.

This account of the reporting of globalization is important because it forms the background against which companies adopt codes of conduct. It is no accident that it is companies with household names—and so the most to lose—that are most likely to adopt such codes. If companies, initially at least, adopt codes of conduct in response to some actual or emerging negative publicity, then it is likely that these codes will reflect the media's definition of the problem. If Nike adopts a code of conduct for its contractors in developing countries in order to combat substandard wages, or child labor, or abusive treatment of workers, then that will be seen as an implicit admission on Nike's part that these problems originated in poor management or corporate greed or venality. (No retail company that I know of has tried to mount a serious defense of its contracting practices. Such companies have apparently judged that they cannot win a war of sound bites with their critics. So they have sued for peace with their critics and tried to appease the public by adopting codes of conduct. See Maitland 1997).

On its face, there is plenty of work for codes of conduct: "The popular press is rife with anecdotes about foreign workers who labor for multinational companies for low wages and for excruciating long hours under horrific conditions in low-income countries to produce goods for Western consumers" (Brown, Deardorff, and Stern 2003). However, if low wages or child labor are the result of poverty, and can't simply be fixed by enlightened corporate policies, then codes of conduct at best will leave the underlying problems untouched and at worst will aggravate them. In the rest of this paper, I examine two areas typically covered by corporate codes of conduct—wages and child labor—to identify some of the dangers of addressing these issues by means of codes of conduct.

Two Models of Codes

Before I turn to my two case-studies—of labor practices in the footwear and apparel industries in Southeast Asia and child labor in Pakistan—I need to distinguish between two models or ideal-types of corporate codes of conduct. Although they are analytically distinguishable, in practice most codes of conduct are hybrids.

The first model (what I call a minimalist code) sees codes as a regime for governing the company's relations with its contractors. The purpose of such a code is to rationalize and systematize the norms governing the workplace. It is also intended to disseminate best practice, facilitate communication, and to establish accountability. What distinguishes the minimalist code is that it does not seek to raise the bar but alerts the contractors with which it deals just how high the bar has been set.

The second (or reformist) model sees codes as vehicles for bringing about positive change in the area of global labor standards. It deliberately raises the bar. It attempts to bring corporate behavior into line with (home country) public demands and expectations. It uses multinational corporations as leverage for improving labor conditions and eliminating practices like child labor. It asks companies to lead by example. In Debora Spar's words, "the best way to change a country's laws or practice may well be through the corporations that invest there" (Spar and La Mure 2003). The classic example of a reformist code of conduct is the Sullivan Principles that made corporate law-breaking (of apartheid-era laws) a condition of approval of a company's continuing presence in South Africa.

Nike's corporate code of conduct is a hybrid one. Relevant to our purposes here are two elements in Nike's code. First, Nike has resisted proposals to include a "living wage" provision in its code. Indeed, this was one of the main issues that led to the breakup of President Clinton's Apparel Industry Task Force (predecessor of the Fair Labor Association) (Greenhouse 1998). Nike's code requires contractors to pay the higher of the local minimum wage or prevailing wage. Second, Nike has set minimum age requirements for its apparel factories (age sixteen) and its footwear factories (age eighteen). Nike has also limited overtime, but that will not be considered here.

A minimalist code may be a useful adjunct to management. At worst, it is pretty innocuous. The problems that I will describe are more likely to be associated with attempts to implement the more ambitious "reformist"code of conduct. Do corporate codes of conduct really provide us with leverage for changing the world for the better? If low wages and child labor are the problem, then are corporate codes of conduct the solution?

The Wages of Nike

Sweatshop activists argue that companies have room to raise the wages of workers in contract plants in countries like Indonesia, China, and Vietnam. The theory underlying this claim seems to be that there is a global race to the bottom in which wages are being artificially bid down as developing countries compete for scarce foreign investment. Thus, developing countries have deliberately held down minimum wages or failed to enforce them, with the result that wages are often below workers' minimum physical needs. They have used the military or state power to prevent collective bargaining and to break strikes. They have winked at contract plants' violations of labor rights and wage laws. As a consequence, wages in developing countries are artificially depressed. The AFL-CIO affiliate, the Asian American Free Labor Institute (AAFLI) argued in a 1991 study that "[i]t is most clear that Nike makes great profit from Indonesia, especially from those working in their licensed factories, . . . [but] those people do not enjoy any benefit from Nike's presence" (Loeb 1991).[1] Accordingly, the host country's minimum wage or the local prevailing wage rates are an inappropriate standard for contract plants supplying product to retailers in the US and Europe. Instead, companies should require their contract factories to pay a "living wage."

This story does not square with my own review of the literature about wages paid by Nike in Indonesia, Vietnam, and China, in the apparel, footwear, and textile industries, in the export sectors of developing countries, and more (Maitland 2004).[2] Take Nike's wages first. According to my calculations, in 1997 the lowest paid Nike workers surveyed by a Dartmouth University team were taking home (in cash) more than seven times the national poverty level (counting overtime but excluding in-kind benefits and year-end (13th month) bonus). The local minimum wage was on average more than five times the poverty level.[3]

In Vietnam, the basic entry-level wage for a Nike worker in 1997 was about $45 per month. That was slightly more than the average hourly wage of a wage earner in 1997–1998 (about $40 per month). However, only 20 percent of Vietnamese workers have wage jobs (most of the other 80 percent are self-employed farmers) and those jobs provide, on the average, much better incomes than the jobs that the other 80 percent have. Per capita income in Vietnam in 1998 was about $200 per year (Glewwe 2001).

In 1999, Nike contractors in Indonesia paid hourly wages that were twice or more than the average pay of other production workers in Indonesia (Atma Jaya Catholic University 2001). In 2000, Nike contractors in Vietnam earned annual wages of $670, compared with an average minimum wage of $134. In Indonesia, annual wages were $720, compared with an average annual minimum of $241 (Lim 2000).

These estimates are consistent with more impressionistic evidence going back to 1992. A frequent observation by reporters who visited Nike factories is that Nike workers generally consider themselves lucky and know that their wages are higher than other factories (and much higher than what their parents make in the countryside). The epiphany of *New York Times* columnist Nicholas Kristof is not unusual. Kristof was the newspaper's Far Eastern bureau chief in the 1990s. He has described how he and his wife (and fellow correspondent) tried to find workers who would deplore their lives to the Western media. But he found that "it was almost impossible to find workers to speak to that. They regarded their jobs as so much better than what they had at home" (Karlin 2000).

Activists have charged that Nike workers cannot get by on their wages. But my review found little or no support for that charge (Maitland 2004). On the contrary, news stories consistently reported that Nike workers are able to save up to 75 percent of their incomes (mostly in the range of one-third to one-half of their wages). *The Oregonian*'s Jeff Manning reports that most workers in Asian footwear factories save 30 to 60 percent of their pay (Manning 1997).

Some critics appear to concede that Nike's workers are well-paid by local standards. Thus Nike activist Jeff Ballinger does not deny that "some" of the workers in sweatshops are paid comparably to professors and other professionals in their countries (Oldenburg 1997). And the Interfaith Center on Corporate Responsibility (ICCR) reported that wages paid by suppliers to Nike and Reebok "pay at least the prevailing minimum wage and workers often make more, with their jobs sometimes paying above that of local factories or in some cases professionals, like teachers." (That did not prevent the ICCR from charging that even these wages often don't cover their families' basic food, shelter, and transportation needs) (Ramey 1998).

I also found no support for the charge that the Indonesian government has deliberately kept wages low to attract foreign investment. Over the 1976–1997 period, Islam reports that for the Indonesian economy as a whole, real wages and productivity have grown at 5 percent annually while poverty declined by 29 percentage points (Islam 2002). Wages have not lagged behind productivity growth. Other studies support these findings (e.g., Manning 1998).

Since 1988, on average,[4] the minimum wage in Indonesia has either kept pace with or exceeded wage and productivity growth. From 1988 to 1992, the increase in real minimum wages (national average) was similar to the growth rate in average wages and productivity in manufacturing (around 15 percent per annum). After 1992, minimum wages increased still more rapidly. In the period 1989–1996 they tripled in nominal terms and doubled in real terms (Agrawal 1996: 41) and probably outstripped productivity increases (Manning 1998: 217). In conclusion, contrary to claims that the Indonesian government deliberately held the country's minimum wages low, the Suharto regime used minimum wage increases as a means of buying the support of urban workers. Islam calls the increases a key tool of Bismarckian strategy or policy of "paternalistic authoritarianism" (Islam 2002: 26).

A closely related charge is that the Indonesian government failed to enforce its minimum wage laws. Again, if enforcement was lax, that seems to have changed by the early 1990s. In one of many ironies, the Indonesian military—which activists accused of strike-breaking—by 1993 was being used to enforce the government's higher minimum wages (Manning 1998: 220).

The same is true for Vietnam. I found no evidence that Vietnam artificially repressed its minimum wages in order to attract foreign investment. On the contrary, in Vietnam, workers at foreign-owned enterprises enjoy a *higher* minimum wage than workers employed in state enterprises. There is a separate dollar-denominated minimum wage for such workers. "State-owned factories [in Vietnam] have a minimum wage of $13 per month, but private, foreign companies generally must honor minimum wages in the $35 to $45 per month range, depending on their location. Foreign companies must pay minimum wage that is specified in US dollars, although of course paid in Vietnamese Dong" (Kahle, Boush, and Phelps 2000).

The charge that the Indonesian government deliberately kept the minimum wage low is hard to reconcile with another piece of evidence. Chris Manning points out that even in 1992, Indonesian minimum wages were relatively high. "[T]he gap between the average and minimum wage was already considerably smaller in Indonesia in 1992 than that recorded in several other developing countries, where minimum wages were typically only 20–30 percent of average earnings. . . . By 1994, minimum wages were on a par with wages in lower wage industries and exceeded average wages among younger, less-educated females" (Manning 1998: 218).

Nor is there evidence that the poor have been excluded from the benefits of economic growth in Indonesia. Earlier I cited the 5 percent growth in real wages over the period 1976–1996. In 1966, Western economists like Gunnar Myrdal had written off the Indonesian economy: "As things look at the beginning of 1966, there seems to be little prospect of rapid economic growth in Indonesia" (Myrdal 1969: 489; quoted in Hill 1996: 1). But in the next thirty years, Indonesia's economy grew at a rate of almost 7 percent a year in real terms. By the mid-1990s, Indonesia's per capita income had expanded tenfold (Brauchli 1994) and the fruits of growth were being shared relatively equally among Indonesians. In 1996, Hal Hill, author of *The Indonesian Economy Since 1966*, wrote that "Indonesia's record on poverty alleviation has been a resounding success" (Hill 1996: 1).[5]

If we look beyond the cases of Indonesia and Nike, we find the same story. Rather than trigger a race to the bottom in apparel, textile and footwear manufacturing, globalization has had positive effects on employment and wages. According to the ILO, from 1980 to 1995 wages in clothing manufacture increased in Asia (some 160 percent), Latin American countries, (165 percent), and European countries (some 150 percent) (ILO, 2000). Also, according to the ILO, during the period 1990–1998, hourly labor costs in the Chinese clothing industry increased by more than 60 percent (ILO, 2000).

Also, studies consistently report that plants in export sector pay premium wages or certainly no worse than other sectors (see citations in Maitland 2004). As Kimberly Ann Elliot and Richard B. Freeman (2001) have said,

> [s]weatshop jobs are better than jobs in rural agriculture or the informal sector, particularly for young women who make up the bulk of the sweatshop work force. . . . [F]oreign-owned and export-oriented factories in developing countries offer higher pay and better conditions than those of domestic firms producing for the local market. . . . Wages in footwear and apparel may be at the bottom of manufacturing, but they are generally higher than the minimum wage level in many developing countries and better than conditions in agriculture. . . . While there are situations where workers are misled by employer promises, subjected to forced labor, or paid less than they are promised, workers choose sweatshop jobs because those jobs are the best available alternatives to them.

Child Labor and Codes of Conduct

Should corporate codes of conduct be used proactively to try to reduce child labor in export industries? Some activists have suggested a link between globalization and child labor. The logic of ruthless cost cutting inevitably leads companies to seek out the weakest and most exploitable workers—namely children and young women. Pharis Harvey, executive director of the International Labor Rights Education and Research Fund, has attributed the "growing epidemic of child labor" to a "globalization of production" (Kamm 1993). However, only an estimated 5 percent of child workers are directly employed in export industries.

Nevertheless, in response to a spate of negative publicity (see Crossette 1990; CBS 1995; Silvers 1996; Schanberg 1996) from religious, labor, consumer, and other US groups against child labor, companies like Nike have cracked down on child labor. In 1998 Nike increased the minimum age requirements in its contract factories to sixteen for apparel workers and eighteen for footwear workers. Nike also spearheaded a coalition to eliminate child labor in soccer-ball production in Sialkot, Pakistan. Most child labor occurred in the home. Nike decided that it would source its soccer balls only from centralized stitching centers so that it could monitor the ages of workers. It also launched educational programs for soccer-ball workers (Schrage 2004: 34). Under intense US pressure, including threats of the revocation of trade benefits for specific Pakistani goods, the soccer-ball industry in Sialkot eventually followed Nike's lead in trying to eliminate home-based work. A partnership embracing UNICEF, ILO, Save the Children (UK) and other organizations designed a "social protection program" to complement the monitoring program. The program aimed at providing families of child stitchers with alternative means to replace lost income, through micro-credit loans or by employing adult family members. At least $4.7 million was budgeted for this (Schrage 2004: 36, 40, 42).

The Sialkot project illustrates the perils and pitfalls associated with trying to reduce child labor.[6] The good news is that the Project achieved its first objective which was to assist manufacturers seeking to prevent child labor in the manufacture of soccer balls in Sialkot. (Accusations of child labor in the soccer-ball industry persist, however). Also, as a result of the project, 6000 children were attending schools sponsored by the social protection partners (Schrage 2004: 45–49).

However, the project had unintended (but foreseeable) consequences. Families suffered a 20 percent drop in income. Save the Children estimated that preventing children from earning income by stitching soccer balls could reduce family income by around 23 percent. Most children became involved in other occupations. Reports of displaced children ending up in more hazardous occupations, such as brick kilns and the manufacture of surgical instruments, have been difficult to refute or confirm, but they cannot be discounted (Schrage 2004: 45–49).

Women obtained less or no work stitching soccer balls because cultural and religious barriers prevented them from working outside the home in the company of unrelated men. The cottage industry of soccer-ball stitching had provided women, as well as children, the opportunity to earn income inside the home. Other unintended consequences were that large and medium-sized manufacturers benefited at the expense of their smaller competitors. For manufacturers, the changes to the production process decreased the supply of stitchers and increased labor costs (Schrage 2004: 45–99). Overall, according to Schrage, despite the creation of educational opportunities, the Project has not proved as successful, however, in providing children removed from child labor with educational and other opportunities, changing community and family attitudes toward child labor, or eliminating child labor in other local industries (Schrage 2004: 42).

Studies of the Sialkot soccer industry have failed to back up some of the charges made by US news stories and paint a much more nuanced picture of child labor there. Eighty percent of the children working in the industry were fifteen or older. The total number of children was closer to 15,000 than the 25,000 reported in the US. And only an estimated 2,750 stitchers were under fourteen. Contrary to US reports, no evidence was found that child stitchers were bonded laborers (Schrage 2004: 28, 40, 46).

The children were not working under abusive or hazardous conditions. "In fact, it was generally acknowledged that children who worked stitching soccer balls faced less hazardous conditions and less risk of exploitation than children engaged in many other occupations in Pakistan." Soccer-ball stitching may be one of the least hazardous occupations for children who work in Pakistan (Schrage 2004: 29, 49). Child labor in the soccer-ball industry was widely accepted and legal in Pakistan, and for children fourteen and older it apparently did not violate ILO rules. "Absent any evidence that stitching soccer balls is likely to jeopardize the 'health, safety, or morals' of stitchers, and with no compulsory education in Pakistan, the lowest employment age permissible under the ILO standard would be fourteen" (Schrage 2004: 30, 52). Stitching soccer balls did not necessarily prevent children from attending school. Seventy-two percent of the child stitchers interviewed by Save the Children did not attend school because their parents could not afford to send them.

In other cases, too, US pressure to eliminate child labor has had unintended consequences—or even caused humanitarian disasters. One example is Bangladesh in the early 1990s. One of the world's poorest countries, Bangladesh had managed almost to double its exports of textiles and clothing to America between 1990 and 1993. As a result of American pressure, perhaps 30,000 children were thrown out of their jobs in the country's textile industry. A follow-up study by Oxfam, a British charity, found that far from going to school, many of these children ended up in far more dangerous employment, in welding shops or prostitution (*Economist* 1995: 13).

In the mid-1990s, in response to demands by the National Labor Committee and other activists that American apparel companies stop doing business with Honduran "maquilas" that employed children, the maquilas stopped hiring any workers under sixteen and fired hundreds of employees who were minors. Honduran law permitted children as young as fourteen to work up to thirty-six hours a week with parental permission. All three of the leading Honduran labor federations, including unions that had worked closely with the National Labor Committee in denouncing abuses of workers, disagreed with the NLC's position. The fired teenagers did not return to school. On the contrary, most of the children instead obtained new jobs outside the assembly sector that were lower-paying and more physically demanding, or bought fake documents in an effort to sneak their way back into the apparel plants. The National Labor Committee's Charles Kernaghan conceded that his group's efforts to end child labor had produced unanticipated consequences. "Obviously this is not what we wanted to happen. . . . It's a tragic situation that needs to be resolved," he added. When asked how that should be done, he lamely replied, "I may not be the right person to answer that kind of question since I'm not an economist" (Rohter 1996).

Discussion

What are the implications of these case-studies for corporate codes of conduct? Both illustrate the pitfalls of trying to bring about change by means of corporate codes. This conclusion may not be obvious in the case of wages in contract factories. My findings simply show that contractors already pay premium wages in comparison with other employers in their domestic labor markets and that there is no race to the bottom. But since these wages are so pitifully low (at least by Western standards), why not hike them further, say, by including a living wage clause in corporate codes of conduct?

The objection is that that these higher wages in contract factories will come at the expense of the incomes and the job opportunities of much poorer workers. Higher wages in the formal sector reduce employment there and (by increasing the supply of labor) depress incomes in the informal sector. This fear doesn't just haunt the imaginations of Chicago-school economists. A University of Michigan panel warned that if codes of conduct impose living wages without regard to local labor market conditions, "[a] likely effect . . . in the apparel industry would be a shift of jobs from countries that would require large wage increases to those that would require smaller increases. . . . If this is true, then licensed apparel is unlikely to be produced in the world's poorest countries, where jobs of any kind, but particularly entry-level manufacturing jobs, are so badly needed" (University of Michigan 2000). The ILO has noted that the shift of production from high-wage to low-wage countries has increased employment at the global level in apparel, footwear, and textiles. The alternative would have been for enterprises in developed countries to replace their work forces with capital equipment, as has happened in the industry segments that have been retained in those countries (ILO 2000).

For these reasons, and others, even economists sympathetic to the anti-sweatshop movement are leery about the campaign to raise sweatshop wages. Harvard's Dani Rodrik says, "[t]he worry is that a living wage might cause some workers to lose their jobs" (Bernstein 1999). Kimberly Elliot and Richard Freeman voice the same concern: "[d]emands for living wages in anti-sweatshop campaigns run the greatest risk of backfiring, since such demands could price workers in less developed countries out of some markets" (Elliot and Freeman 2001).[7] Where such economists fear to tread, companies should not rush in. I conclude that Nike and the Fair Labor Association have been prudent in refusing to endorse the living wage concept. Things might be different if the race to the bottom was a reality or if jobs in contract factories were treadmills of drudgery and low wages. But the evidence I have seen (some of which is presented here) suggests that these factories are a step on the ladder of economic development. Wages have not stagnated. The global labor market is working.

With regard to child labor, the evidence shows how even the best-laid plans may have unintended consequences. Elliot Schrage's own verdict is that it is "not clear that the Project [to eliminate child labor in soccer-ball production] has been cost-effective, sustainable, or replicable" (Schrage 2004: 51).

The worst sort of humanitarian intervention is the kind that results in the wholesale firing of child workers. The evidence from Bangladesh and Honduras is that the children simply end up in other jobs—often more hazardous ones that bring in less income. Even where outside agencies help fund schools—as in Sialkot—children continue to work. The alternative would be to deprive their families of significant income that they need to get by. As Schrage notes, "[t]he principal reason children work is poverty. Children in the developing world work mostly to survive" (Schrage 2004: 18).

Critics of globalization appear to argue that globalization may have the effect of stimulating child labor. Economists don't reject this argument out of hand. Theoretically, it is possible that trade liberalization might increase the return to unskilled labor in developing countries (I have argued above that that has been the case) and thus reduce the incentives to invest in skills and education. Another possibility is that the fierce competition among manufacturers to cut production costs may lead them to hire the cheapest labor of all, namely children (Neumayer and de Soysa 2004).[8]

However, these theoretical possibilities appear to be trumped in practice by an income effect. That is, at higher incomes, families have fewer incentives to send their children to work.[9] Here, history seems to be repeating itself. As Robert Heilbroner has written,

> The most important effect of the industrial revolution . . . was its long-term leverage on economic well-being. The ultimate impact of the industrial revolution was to usher in a rise of living standards on a mass scale unlike anything the world

> had ever known before. This did not happen overnight. In 1840, according to the calculations of Arnold Toynbee, Sr., the wage of an ordinary laborer came to eight shillings a week, which were six shillings less than he needed to buy the bare necessities of life. He made up the deficit by sending his children or his wife, or both, to work in the mills." (Heilbroner 1968: 84)

As family incomes rose, children's participation in the labor force declined. Viviana Zelizer has noted the paradox that, as the rapid industrialization in the United States in the 1860s raised the wages of children, child labor went into sharp decline (Zelizer 1985: 5–6, 13).

If these precedents hold, then the most effective attack on child labor will be an indirect one. Only by raising living standards can we uproot the practice. That means more globalization, not less. It also means that we should be cautious about burdening globalization with onerous obligations—such as those spelled out in some codes of conduct—that hinder it from accomplishing its basic mission. Thus I disagree with Ans Kolk and Rob van Tulder when they argue that companies that fire child workers should "take measures that help improve the situation through compensatory programs for the children, such as access to education, food, and health care, and alternative sources of income for the children's families" (Kolk and van Tulder 2002). Companies probably should not fire the children in the first place. But if economic growth is the most effective weapon against child labor, then we should not impose this additional "tax" or disincentive on the very agents of that economic growth. If there are First World responsibilities to child workers in developing countries, then that should be a charge on all of us, not the special responsibility of the companies that operate there.

In the meantime, companies can at least try to do no harm. Ill-considered responses include the massive firing of child workers. But they also include Nike's policy (embodied in its code of conduct) of requiring that workers in their contract footwear factories be at least eighteen years old. If this results in some families being unable to feed themselves, the restriction is probably an immoral one. Given the hue and cry, Nike's policy is understandable, but it is a shame that the company bowed to pressure instead of doing the right thing. With codes of conduct, modesty is a becoming virtue.

Notes

1. Similarly, Robin Broad and John Cavanagh (1995) reject "claims that US [free trade] policies are leading to the growth of huge middle classes—in such countries as China, India and Indonesia—that will drive the world economy in the twenty-first century." Merrill Goozner (1994) claims that, "[a]s the global economy pushes ever deeper into the poorest precincts of the developing world, its benefits aren't trickling down. . . . There is mounting evidence that the rising tide of rapid development is not lifting all boats, especially in China and Indonesia, the first and fourth most populous countries on earth." If the evidence I present in this paper is correct, these charges are flat wrong.

2. See Lim 2001: 39–40 for findings that foreign-owned and contract companies tend to pay higher wages than domestic companies.

3. Based on figures in Calzini et al. 1997.

4. Indonesia has a system of regional minimum wages.

5. The early 1990s were no flash in the pan. See Agrawal 1996.

6. This account is based on Case Study 1, "Addressing child labor in Pakistan's soccer-ball production," in Elliott Schrage's report.

7. Elliot and Freeman don't believe that this danger has materialized yet.

8. Neumayer and de Soysa present strong and robust evidence that more "globalized" developing countries also have a lower incidence of child labor than those that are less open to trade and less penetrated by foreign direct investment.

9. See the literature summarized in Neumayer and de Soysa 2004.

References

Agrawal, Nisha. 1996. "The Benefits of Growth for Indonesian Workers." Policy Research Working Paper 1637, World Bank.

Atma Jaya Catholic University (Centre for Societal Development Studies). 2001. *Workers' Voices: An Interim Report of Workers' Needs and Aspirations in Nine Nike Contract Factories in Indonesia.* Jakarta, Indonesia (prepared for the Global Alliance for Workers and Communities). Available at http://www.theglobalalliance.org/indonsub4.htm.

Barnet, Richard J., and John Cavanagh. 1994. "Just Undo It: Nike's Exploited Workers." *New York Times* (February 13): Section 3, p. 11.

Bernstein, Aaron. 1999. "Sweatshop Reform: How to Solve the Standoff." *Business Week* (May 3):186.

Brauchli, Marcus W. 1994. "Indonesia is Striving to Prosper in Freedom But is Still Repressive." *Wall Street Journal* (October 11): A1.

Broad, Robin, and John Cavanagh. 1995. "Don't Neglect the Impoverished South." *Foreign Affairs* 18 (Winter): 18.

Brown, Drusilla, Alan V. Deardorff, and Robert M. Stern. 2003. "The Effects of Multinational Production on Wages and Working Conditions in Developing Countries." National Bureau of Economic Research Working Paper 9669 (April). Available at http://www.nber.org/papers/w9669.

Calzini, Derek, Jake Odden, Jean Tsai, Shawna Huffman, and Steve Tran. 1997. *Survey of Vietnamese and Indonesian Domestic Expenditure Levels.* Field Study in International Business, The Amos Tuck School, Dartmouth (November 3). Available at http://nike .jp/nikebiz/global/pdf/case/vietnameseandindonesian.pdf.

CBS. 1995. "Eye to Eye with Connie Chung: Children at Work: Pakistani Labor Prominent in Manufacture of Goods for US Sports Companies and UNICEF." Television broadcast (April 6).

Crossette, Barbara. 1990. "Soccer Balls Sustain Pakistan Town." *New York Times* (October 8): D4.

Economist. 1995. "Consciences and Consequences" (June 3): 13.

Egan, Timothy. 1998. "The Swoon of the Swoosh." *New York Times Magazine*, (September 13): 66–70.

Elliot, Kimberly Ann, and Richard B. Freeman. 2001. "White Hats or Don Quixotes? Human Rights Vigilantes in the Global Economy." Working paper w8102, NBER, Cambridge, Mass., January. Available at http://www.nber.org/papers/w8102.

Glewwe, Paul. 2001. Letter to the University of Minnesota Social Concerns Committee (June 6). Available from Ian Maitland, personal communication.

Goozner, Merrill. 1994. "Asian Labor: Wages of Shame: Western Firms Help to Exploit Brutal Conditions." *Chicago Tribune* (November 6): 1.

Greenhouse, Steven. 1998. "Groups Reach Agreement for Curtailing Sweatshops." *New York Times* (November 5): A18.

Heilbroner, Robert L. 1968. *The Making of Economic Society*, 2d ed. Englewood Cliffs, N.J.: Prentice Hall.

Hill, Hal. 1996. *The Indonesian Economy Since 1966*. Cambridge: Cambridge University Press.

ILO. 2000. *Labour Practices in the Footwear, Leather, Textile and Clothing Industries*. Geneva: International Labour Office.

Islam, Iyanatul. 2002. "Poverty, Employment and Wages: An Indonesian Perspective." ILO-JMHLW-Government of Indonesia Seminar on Strengthening Employment and Labour Market Policies for Poverty Alleviation and Economic Recovery in East and Southeast Asia, Jakarta, April 29–May 1, 2002, ILO, p. 37. Available at http://www.ilo.org/public/english/employment/recon/poverty/download/indonesia.pdf.

Kahle, Lynn R., David M. Boush, and Mark Phelps. 2000. "Good Morning, Vietnam; An Ethical Analysis of Nike Activities in Southeast Asia." *Sport Marketing Quarterly* 6: 44.

Kamm, Lynn. 1993. "How Our Greed Keeps Kids Trapped in Foreign Sweatshops." *Washington Post* (March 28): C5.

Karlin, Adam. 2000. "Correspondent Describes Asian Worker Mentality." *The Daily* (University of Washington) (October 20).

Kolk, Ans, and Rob van Tulder. 2002. "Child Labor and Multinational Conduct: A Comparison of International Business and Stakeholder Codes." *Journal of Business Ethics* 36: 291–301.

Lim, Linda Y. C. 2000. "My Factory Visits in Southeast Asia and UM Code and Monitoring (September 6)." Available at http://www.fordschool.umich.edu/rsie/acit/Documents/LimNotes00.pdf.

———. 2001. *The Globalization Debate: Issues and Challenges*. Geneva: International Labour Organisation.

Loeb, Vernon. 1991. "In Indonesia, Nikes are Made on a Shoestring: The Worker who Makes $75 Shoes Gets About 15 Cents an Hour." *Philadelphia Inquirer* (December 22): A1.

Maitland, Ian. 1997. "The Great Non-Debate Over International Sweatshops." *British Academy of Management Annual Conference Proceedings*. London (September): 240–265.

———. 2004. "The Wages of Nike," ms.

Manning, Chris. 1998. *Indonesian Labour in Transition*. Cambridge: Cambridge University Press.

Manning, Jeff. 1997. "Poor Jump at Chance to Work for Nike." (Nike in Asia, second of three parts), *Minneapolis-St. Paul Star Tribune* (November 28).

Myrdal, Gunnar. 1969. *Asian Drama: An Inquiry into the Poverty of Nations*. New York: Pantheon.

Neumayer, Erik, and Indra de Soysa. 2004. "Trade Openness, Foreign Direct Investment and Child Labor." (March). Available at http://ssrn.com/abstract=482649.

Oldenburg, Don. 1997. "Child Labor Debate." *The Washington Post* (September 30): E5.

Ramey, Joanna. 1998. "Religious Investors Ask Nike, Reebok to Hike Offshore Factory Worker Wages." *Women's Wear Daily* (May 21): 4.

Rohter, Larry. 1996. "To US Critics, a Sweatshop; For Hondurans, a Better Life." *New York Times* (July 18): A1.

Schanberg, Sydney. 1996. "Six Cents an Hour." *Life Magazine* (June): 38.

Schrage, Elliot J. 2004. *Promoting International Worker Rights Through Private Voluntary Initiatives: Public Relations or Public Policy?* University of Iowa Center for Human Rights (January). Available at http://www.cfr.org/pdf/Schrage-DOS.pdf.

Silvers, Jonathan. 1996. "Child Labor in Pakistan." *Atlantic Monthly* (February): 79–92.

Spar, Debora, and Lane T. La Mure. 2003. "The Power of Activism: Assessing the Impact of NGOs on Global Business." *California Management Review* 45 (Spring): 81.

University of Michigan. 2000. *The Final Report of The Advisory Committee on Labor Standards and Human Rights*. University of Michigan (May). Available at http://www.umich.edu/~newsinfo/BG/humright.html.

Zelizer, Viviana. 1985. *Pricing the Priceless Child*. New York: Basic.

The Author

Ian Maitland is Professor in the Department of Strategic Management/Organization, Carlson School of Management, University of Minnesota, Twin Cities, MN, USA. E-mail: imaitland@csom.umn.edu.

CORPORATE FINANCE AND ENVIRONMENTALLY RESPONSIBLE BUSINESS

Benjamin J. Richardson
York University, Toronto, Ontario, Canada

Abstract

The financial services sector has the potential to be an important driver for improved corporate social and environmental responsibility through its control over corporate financing. But, so far, only ad hoc policy initiatives have arisen in the European Union and other countries. Because the financial services sector is where wholesale decisions regarding future development, and thus pressures on the environment, arise, the reform of investment and banking services to promote long term investment and better consideration of environmental impacts may be an effective way to promote sustainable development. Reforms such as corporate environmental reporting requirements and lender liability for borrowers' environmental harm, are some of the ways by which an institutional framework for mobilising financial organizations as instruments of environmental regulation could be constructed.

Environmental Governance of Companies through Financial Institutions

Corporate environmental responsibility can be encouraged when those institutions that finance companies incorporate environmental considerations into their lending and investment policies. Unfortunately, the traditional methods of environmental regulation and policy available to governments have not been proven to be effective in this respect (Bosselmann and Richardson 1999: 1–4; Gunningham and Grabosky 1998). One approach to improve this aspect of environmental governance involves the role of the financial services sector (Jeucken 2001). The activities and decisions of ordinary business corporations are affected by financial institutions, such as banks, insurers and investors, which supply the capital and other resources necessary for economic activity. Financial organizations are special types of companies that are in the business of providing loans, financial advice, insurance services and management of investment resources to other firms and individuals. While there already exist some reasons why those that finance corporations might wish to avoid supporting environmentally harmful activities (e.g., where such activities reduce the profitability of an investment), more often than not, barriers exist which cause environmental considerations to be ignored or trivialized in financial institutional decision-making.

 pp. 79–100

This essay introduces how an approach to environmental regulation diffused through the financial services sector could be institutionally constructed, and considers existing reforms in the European Union (EU) and other Western jurisdictions. The approach is to examine the environmental policy relevance of the investment and lending sectors, and how government regulation could be adjusted to facilitate financial organizations' stronger engagement with environmental issues. The broad argument is that corporate environmental responsibility can be advanced when governments work to share environmental regulatory responsibilities with the financial services sector. Because the financial services sector sponsors and profits from much economic development, it arguably should share responsibility for ensuring such development accords with environmental policy goals and standards. There are various factors, however, which can inhibit financial institutions' focus on the environment; principally, where there are insufficient monetary incentives or inadequate environmental information. The aim of government regulation to promote shared environmental governance with this sector must be to ensure that the right directions, incentives and information are available. If this is achieved, then financial institutions should provide a means of transmitting and amplifying primary environmental regulatory standards through the economy.

The EU has advanced the notion of "shared responsibility" for environmental regulation with financial markets. In the European Commission's (EC) *Fifth Environment Action Programme* (1992–2000), the EC envisaged a role for private financial entities in environmental policy, when it declared that "financial institutions which assume the risk of companies and plants can exercise considerable influence—in some cases control—over investment and management decisions which could be brought to play for the benefit of the environment" (European Commission 1997: 27). There are several ways in which financial institutions appear generically relevant to environmental management: as investors, they supply the resources for environmental initiatives; as stakeholders, such as shareholders and lenders, they exercise influence over corporate management; and, as valuers, they price risks and predict the income of companies. Despite this potential, the financial sector has not yet attracted much attention from scholars and policy-makers (Delphi International and Ecological GMBH 1997; Richardson 2002a). Yet, to harness market organizations to facilitate policy goals is not unprecedented in public policy design; the contractual relationship between financial institutions and their customers has long been regulated to ensure public policy objectives and standards are met in relation to consumer protection and fraud control (Cranston 1997: 153).

Getting financial organizations to contribute to systems of environmental governance dovetails with broader trends in changes in systems of public governance in Western nations that are geared toward more delegation and sharing of responsibilities with the private sector. Because of their perceived advantages in terms of management skills, efficiency and client knowledge, in various Western countries private organizations have been enlisted to furnish social services, such as health care and undertake local government services (Donahue 1989). Such shifts can also be understood in terms of the desire of policy-congested states, unable to satisfy competing demands, to find ways to off-load responsibilities to civil society and the market (Habermas 1973; Offe 1987). Various regulatory theorists emphasise that regulators operate increasingly in a pluralistic setting in which effective governance resides in flexible, collaborative mechanisms in which state functions are shared with or devolved to private interests (Rein 1989; Wilson 1980). Unlike "government," which denotes public organizations and rules and implies a demarcation between public and private sectors, "governance" involves complex interdependencies among actors—the interorganizational linkages involving an array of market and nongovernmental bodies. Governance may involve a combination of rules, incentives and informational mechanisms by which the state seeks to steer and co-ordinate the non-government sector (Stoker 1998). Financial organizations such as banks and pension funds are highly relevant to such debates, as they are "gate-keepers" to the economy, supplying development loans for small businesses and equity capital for large public companies. Schemes to more effectively diffuse environmental policy through the market must work with those strategically placed financial institutions that have the capacity to communicate and enforce policy goals and standards.

But the scope for sharing environmental governance with financial organizations must be influenced by the tools chosen for articulating environmental policy through this sector. Banks and other financial service providers are commercial entities interested in profitability, rather than pursuing for their own sake ethically laudable objectives. They are not in the business of subsidising good environmental practices per se. Another consideration is that direct regulatory commands are likely to be politically controversial, and thus vulnerable to implementation failure. There are several reasons why informational, incentive and liability tools should be emphasised in the policy package. Reflexive law theorists such as Teubner (1983) argue that, because of the disaggregation of modern societies into relatively discrete subsystems, such as the market, with their own codes and norms, regulation is more likely to succeed when it deploys less invasive mechanisms that serve to *stimulate* desired behaviour within market actors, producing an enhanced sensitivity to public policy objectives and a readiness to reflect on and adjust organizational policies and procedures accordingly. Corporate environmental reporting is an example of this approach. Economic instruments such as pollution taxes and tradeable emission permits are also considered to have reflexive properties, in that they can explicitly convey in the language of market systems the price of engaging in environmentally exploitative activities (Orts 1995). Sometimes, government conscription of financial organizations in the name of environmental policy will be welcomed for creating new market opportunities, such as requirements for firms to have their environmental performance assessed and certified by private auditors (Grabosky 1995: 530–536). The delegation and assignment of regulatory roles to auditors, accountants and other professions can be useful where they can competently develop appropriate regulatory standards and undertake effective supervision on behalf of the state. Overall, the aim of government regulation should primarily be to make corporate environmental performance relevant to financial institutions' evaluation of corporate *economic* performance. Without such a synergy, environmental standards and rules will likely be resisted by financial organizations as a set of extraneous, irrelevant requirements.

It is also important to understand how differences between countries and business sectors can foster or inhibit governments from bringing financial entities into the environmental policy framework. For example, to mobilise institutional investors as a vehicle for corporate environmental responsibility arguably depends on the existence of extensive equity markets dominated by pension funds and other large investors. In the EU, only the United Kingdom and the Netherlands strongly feature such conditions (Blommestein 1998). Elsewhere, the United States and Australia also have a well-developed institutional investor sector. One of the reasons why Australia and the UK have been among the first countries to introduce ethical investment reforms (as discussed below), appears to be because of the presence in each country of well-developed lobby groups for ethical investment reforms, namely Australia's Ethical Investment Association and the UK Social Investment Forum (UKSIF). In some jurisdictions, notably Germany and Japan, banks play a relatively larger role in corporate financing, and so environmental regulation strategies that seek to mobilise the financial services providers in these nations would need to focus on the banking sector. National traditions and styles of environmental regulation is also an important variable. Countries with a tradition of economic deregulation and use of economic policy instruments may be more receptive to addressing the role of financial organizations. Another important driver toward reform is the existence of supranational institutions and policies with an interest in this subject. Some European developments have occurred against the backdrop of EU policy in the *Fifth Environment Action Programme*. Globally, an emerging catalyst to boost the profile of environmental issues in global financial markets is the United Nations Environment Programme (1992), which has launched a Financial Institutions Initiative wherein banks and other financial entities pledge themselves to specified sustainable development practices.

The shift toward shared governance is not without challenges and potential problems for the state. Dangers range from policy incoherence if the state is unable to strategically direct decision-making, to complete policy failures if private institutions capture and distort regulatory programmes. Rhodes (1997: 54) warns that without effective systems of democratic supervision, governance networks may be less accountable than the state if decisions are largely removed from the traditional governmental apparatus. Because of the risk that shared governance may generate confusion among regulatees and the broader community as to where final authority and policy responsibility lies, it is essential that chains of regulatory control are readily traceable back to the primary government authorities. Careful design of monitoring and oversight mechanisms is needed to ensure the state is able to track and verify implementation of policy goals and ensure governance systems are democratically nourished. Grabosky (1995: 544) sees the challenge as one of 'meta-monitoring,' by which government agencies focus on "strategic surveillance" and "monitoring the overall regulatory system" but engage in "authoritative intervention" where third party resources are lacking.

Apart from the appropriate definition of the institutional relationships between the state and market actors, shared environmental governance raises the question of what environmental policy functions are to be actually *shared*. There is an extensive economics literature which highlights problems markets face in addressing environmental concerns, including undervaluation of ecological properties, discounting of future environmental costs and benefits (Costanza et al. 1997) and an inability to address the problem of scale, or aggregate resource use within biosphere limits (Daly 1992). Decentralised financial markets cannot coordinate society toward specific environmental goals without government direction. The setting of environmental policy goals must derive from an interdisciplinary analysis of ecological, social and economic considerations, undertaken within participatory decision-making systems. Also, financial institutions are unable to offer the same public participation and information rights and procedures that are an integral part of current environmental legislation and administration. Economic analysis can help determine the cost of achieving such ecological standards, but not the substantive merits of environmental objectives, which arises from participatory policy-making. In terms of expertise and management systems, financial service providers also cannot undertake many of the specialist functions of modern environmental agencies in government. Thus, while there should be a place for sharing environmental responsibilities with financial organizations in relation to the financing of green developments and management of pollution risks, it is inconceivable that banks or insurers would operate national parks or be urban planners. The value of the financial services sector lies in its strategic market position that can be manipulated by government rules, information and monetary incentives to enable environmentally sound companies to flourish at the expense of polluters and resource degraders.

The prospects for reform of financial institutions are also likely to be shaped by the increasing transnational character of financial markets. Technological advances and the deregulation of capital markets in Western economies have greatly accelerated the geographical mobility of capital in its search for the most lucrative investments (Walter 1993: 202–204). The globalization of banking and investment services reduces the power of states individually to regulate financial institutions (Braithwaite and Drahos 2000: 7–8). Domestic regulatory moves that threaten economic interests can prompt the migration of financial resources to jurisdictions perceived as offering a more benign regulatory milieu. National regulators may also face capacity and information deficits when attempting to supervise enterprises engaged in complex trans-border commerce. International agreements and institutions are thus necessary to prevent environmentally enlightened financial service providers from suffering competitive disadvantages in their transnational business. While this article does not explore the global regulation of financial bodies, it can be noted that apart from in the EU, the existing international regulatory mechanisms in this sector are largely at an embryonic stage of development. Clearly, a shift to shared environmental governance will unavoidably become more intertwined with internationalised patterns of policy-making involving international organizations and other supranational actors.

Institutional Investors

Opportunities for and Constraints to Environmental Investment

Environmental issues can alter the economic assumptions that underlie an investor's decision to commit capital to an enterprise. Systems of capital investment are where primary decisions regarding future development, and thus pressures on the environment, begin (Schmideiny and Zorraquin 1996). Given that sustainable development stresses maintenance of natural and human capital for posterity, the role of capital markets must be recognised as pivotal to sustainability strategies (England 2000). Financial markets generally provide capital with the objective that it should ideally grow. Whilst there is obviously a difference between financial capital (i.e., economic assets and income) and the broader concept of capital in sustainable development (i.e., natural resources and ecosystem integrity), financial capital is relevant to the environment as it enables major investments to be undertaken, such as technological innovations, which invariably have environmental effects of some form. Sharing environmental governance with this sector of the financial markets relates to encouraging investors to favour environmentally sound companies and to use their financial leverage to make corporate management and policy more mindful of natural resource use and pollution concerns.

Today, capital markets are overwhelmingly dominated by large institutional investors, rather than by individual "amateur" shareholders (Rada and Trisoglio 1992; Brancato 1991). In recent decades, institutional savings have mushroomed as societies make greater private provision for old age in the face of shrinking welfare entitlements. As financial intermediaries, investors assist with risk reduction by pooling and diversifying assets, and by lowering the transaction costs of contracting and information processing (Black 1992). The institutional investment community has a diverse membership, including public and private pension funds, mutual funds, life insurance companies, university foundations and funds managed by banks. A technical distinction can be made between *institutional* investors per se, involving, for example, the investment actions of pension funds using their beneficiaries' monies, and *retail* investments, where individuals directly contribute to a mutual fund that specialises in investing in certain market segments. In both cases, however, a specific investment institution is managing investments. Within the OECD area, insurance companies are the largest investors, followed by pension funds (OECD 1999). Apart from commercial investors such as mutual funds and venture capital funds, there is an assortment of communal financial entities, such credit unions, building societies, industrial and provident associations and public charities, which can make an important contribution to social investment and community regeneration (Hudson 2000: 259–294).

The relationship between financial markets, investors and sustainable development is problematic. There is that evidence that financial markets do not efficiently allocate capital, and that unsustainable, speculative bubbles suck in financial resources whilst inefficient under-investment arises at other times or in other sectors (Baker and Fung 2001). Such capital flows may be associated with adverse social and environmental effects arising from company and project investment choices. These problems have been framed by some commentators as arising from a distinction between the paper investments of the myopic financial markets against real investments in socially useful goods and services (Stanford 1999: 65). Yet, a number of commentators stress the growing benign influence of institutional investors in promoting sustainable development. In their book *The Rise of Fiduciary Capitalism,* Hawley and Williams (2000) identify the institutional investor as a new voice for promoting corporate social and environmental responsibility. This is because institutional investors are 'universal owners' holding a broad portfolio of stocks, and possessing an interest in the health and long-term sustainability of the entire economy rather than the profitability of individual businesses. As fiduciaries, long-term investors and majority owners, Hawley and Williams argue that institutional investors are not concerned with short-term returns on investment, but rather long-term performance to meet the needs of their present and future beneficiaries. Similarly, Monks, in *The New Global Investor* (2001: 105) believes that the universal or "global investor" "is likely to make good decisions for the long-term of society, because it can afford in most cases to take a long-term view, and a diversified view. An ordinary domestic investor may need to reap profits in the short term." Hawley and Williams assert that universal owner status gives institutional investors an interest in public policy governance issues in areas outside traditional macroeconomic issues. They state: "a universal owner that really wants to maximize the shareholder value of its portfolio would need to develop public policy-like positions and monitor regulatory developments and legislation on a number of key issues to the economy as a whole" (Hawley and Williams 2000: 170). Accordingly, businesses in which they invest should be conducted in a financially, socially and environmentally responsible manner that supports a healthy and sustainable economy.

Certainly, the growth of institutional investment funds has pooled mammoth resources capable of exerting significant leverage over corporate environmental activities. And there are many reasons why the environment might be of interest to institutional investors. Pension funds and life insurance companies in particular have long-term financial liabilities, providing a structural incentive to favour lasting, sustainable investment. Further, fund managers have fiduciary responsibilities in trust law and statute to take an active interest in corporate governance (Tasch and Viederman 1995: 125). Ethical screening can appeal to investors because it reinforces notions of socially responsible governance. There is growing evidence of a correlation between corporations that embody socially responsible governance and sustainable development (Sparkes 2002). Good environmental and social performance is often seen as a proxy for a financially well-managed company. Poor environmental performance that threatens firm profitability is a basis for intervention in corporate management or the switching of investments. But there are also countervailing barriers to more environmentally sensitive investment practices, including inadequate information about corporate environmental performance, the absence of appropriate taxes on environmental resource use and pollution, which can thereby make it difficult to measure environmental performance in financially relevant terms, and structural barriers in corporate governance systems that can impede investor shareholder activism.

There is evidence in the EU and internationally of a growing niche market for environmental investment products and funds. In the EU, there were estimated to be some 250 specialist ethical investment funds, taking account of environmental and other concerns, operating in 2001, up from a mere fifty such funds a decade earlier (Sustainable Development Research International Group 2002: 7). In addition to ethical mutual funds, the labour movement has emerged as a force for ethical investment, through union-based pension funds and labour-sponsored venture capital funds (Quarter et al. 2001). The founding of several indices to track ethical investments points to the growing legitimacy of this sector. Leading ethical investment indices include the Dow Jones Sustainability Group Index and the UK's Financial Times Stock Exchange's "ethical index." Yet the total size of ethical investment funds is still small compared to the market capitalization of companies in which they invest; in the UK, ethical investment in September 2001 comprised a mere 3.5 percent share of the investment market, compared to 13 percent in the US (Cerulli Associates 2001). But, encouraging, the growth of ethical investments in recent years has tended to exceed other investments.

When considering such statistics, it is important to recognise that there is no authoritative definition of "ethical investment" that is universally accepted. The discourse of ethical investment has been largely propelled by ethical investment research and lobby organizations and academic commentators, while government policy-makers have issued little guidance or regulation so far. Environmentally responsible investment can be effected in several ways, most commonly through 'ethical screening' involving the inclusion or exclusion of shares in investment portfolios on environmental grounds, and shareholder activism to change corporate policy and practice (Sparkes 1995: 1–18). In North America, there is growing empirical evidence of a correlation between share price movements and corporate environmental performance (Lanoie, Laplante, and Roy 1998; Cormier, Magnan, and Morard 1993). Good environmental achievements are increasingly seen as an indication of business health, whilst negative environmental performance may lead to adverse company publicity or, worse, costly pollution liabilities.

One of the barriers to achieving more widespread acknowledgement of environmental issues among institutional investors is uncertainty concerning the environmental integrity of a product or company performance. Surveys of the financial services sector have revealed a patchy understanding of the relevance of corporate environmental performance (PricewaterhouseCoopers 2001). The lack of corporate reporting on environmental activities and costs is a factor that undoubtedly has contributed to this poor understanding. As discussed later in this article, mandating some level of environmental reporting by businesses is a necessary reform if investors are to be mobilised as instruments of environmental governance.

In common law jurisdictions, such as the US and UK, institutional investor passivity or ignorance may also be explained in terms of the effect of trust law precedents. Trustee investors who are required to invest prudentially on behalf of others (e.g., pension funds) may find the least risky course is to adopt investment strategies similar to their peers. Notions of fiduciary responsibility have been interpreted in the seminal

British cases of *Cowan v Scargill* ((1984) 2 All ER 750) and *Martin v City of Edinburgh District Council* ((1988) SLT 329) as constraining pension fund managers from taking into account ethical factors that may detract from securing the optimal financial return for beneficiaries when choosing investments. However, where an investment fund is established explicitly as an ethical investment vehicle, then the trust law constraints against green investment are largely removed so long as the optimal financial returns within the agreed governing framework of environmental or other investment principles are pursued. In continental Europe, quantitative regulation of investment portfolios is typically applied, such as restrictions on particular classes of investment including foreign securities, real estate and loans.

In many countries, company law rules can also be source of constraints to ethically minded investor activism. Because of legal constraints on concentrated ownership, fiduciary obligations that require extensive diversification to minimise risk and a strong preference for liquidity, institutional investment agents have tended to seek portfolios comprising fragmented holdings across a plethora of companies (Lee 1987: 303). This can reduce the influence of an investor or discourage activism because the stakes may be considered too small given the size of the institution's equity holdings. However, the regulatory trend in Western states has been for securities watchdogs to progressively liberalise rules restricting shareholder proposals from management's proxy statement and other company law obstacles to shareholder activism. Although EU institutions are increasingly setting standards for corporate governance, innovative reforms are still occurring in a number of EU Member States, such as Britain (UK Department of Trade and Industry 2001).

Promoting Ethical Finance

Among the other reforms that can stimulate shared environmental governance with investors are requirements that investment institutions consider the environmental effects of their own activities and publicly report on their policies in this respect. In the UK, for instance, in July 1999, the government promulgated a regulation under the Pensions Act 1995 requiring occupational pension fund trustees to disclose their policies on socially responsible investment and on the exercise of shareholder rights, including voting rights (*Occupational Pension Schemes (Investment, and Assignment, Forfeiture, Bankruptcy etc.), Amendment Regulations 1999*, cl. 2(4)). This UK initiative has inspired similar reforms in the EU and Australia (Richardson 2002b). Legislation requiring pension fund managers to disclose or take account of environmental, social or ethical considerations in their investment policies has arisen in France (Projet de loi sur l'épargne salariale, 7 February 2001. No.2001-152, article 2), Germany (Betriebliche Altersvorsorge: article 10), and Belgium (Projet de loi relative aux pensions complémentaires, article 42). The French example includes obligations to actually take the environment into account, although this requirement pertains only to government sector pension schemes. Another ambitious reform was undertaken in Australia, whereby the Financial Services Reform Act 2001 applied an ethical disclosure obligation on a wider range of investment products including: pensions, managed investment products and investment life insurance products. But, like the UK initiative, none of these examples attempts to statutorily define criteria of ethical investment, and all only weakly address the challenge of monitoring compliance. Recent empirical evidence of the effect of the UK reforms suggests that while there has been a significant increase in adoption of ethical investment policies by pension funds, the quality and implementation of such policies has been weak (Coles and Green 2002).

Beyond environmental disclosure requirements for investors, governments could consider mandating consideration of environmental issues in the regulatory envelope governing financial regulators. During the preparation of the UK's Financial Services and Market Act 2000, which created a single regulator for the financial services industry, the Financial Services Authority, the UKSIF argued before the House of Commons Environmental Audit Committee that there had been no environmental appraisal of the statute's potential consequences. The UKSIF unsuccessfully requested inclusion of a reference to sustainable development in the Authority's mandate; for example, to require best practice in environmental risk management and to encourage the provision of environmental investment and environmental lending products. In the absence of an explicit political mandate, at best financial regulators could be expected to issue guidance notes on environmentally prudent investment practices. Already, the UK Department for Environment and the Corporation of London issued in August 2002 their so-called *London Principles of Sustainable Finance*, which advocate a limited range of measures to improve acknowledgement of the environmental dimensions of financial market activities.

Apart from domestic-sourced rules, the EU Member States are subject increasingly to EU financial law, and, less intrusively, emerging international standards. The EU has issued a plethora of directives and policies to ensure competition in financial services markets (European Commission 2000). But no EU-wide financial services regulator has been established. Environmental concerns have hardly been a feature of EU services financial regulation to date. The EC's proposal in 2000 (COM(2000) 507 final) for a directive on the activities of institutions for occupational retirement provision, omitted any environmental disclosure provisions, although an amendment to the EC's proposal was later unsuccessfully advanced in the European Parliament to provide an obligation to refer to 'ethical and socially responsible investment principles' in the Article 12(1) disclosure of investment policies requirements (European Parliament 2001: 52). Elsewhere, amendments to the EU's Eco-Management and Audit Scheme (2001) and the Eco-Label Regulation (2000) have allowed for their extension to financial services, thereby enabling investment and other financial service products to be more readily assessed and compared in terms of their environmental credentials.

One possibility for future financial services law reform would be to authorise establishment of a specific ethical investment institution that would be free to invest in a range of asset types according to environmental, social and other ethical criteria. Mayo and Mullineux (2000) suggest such an institution could function as a mutual investment fund that is open-ended and working under contract law, and thus able to give priority to environmental and social returns over financial returns. While there appears to be some merit in legislating for a specialist ethical financing vehicle, it poses the risk that mainstream investors (e.g., pension funds) would see the environment as an issue not directly relevant to their own operations. For ethical finance to be integrated into financial markets, it must become embedded in the culture of mainstream financiers. At a minimum, this would seem to require maintenance of obligations on investment institutions to appraise their environmental activities and impacts, and to disclose their ethical investment policies.

Apart from provision of appropriate financial and information incentives to promote environmental investment, there is the nagging issue of the internal governance of investment institutions. In relation to pension funds, for example, there is a growing debate on whether pension fund governance should be democratised to ensure that worker beneficiaries have more say in how their monies are invested (Kodar 2002: 57). Through worker influence over pension fund investments, there could be a shift away from short-term profit focus to long-term real investment. Some labour movement activists are attempting to acquire greater representation on pension fund boards of trustees either through joint or sole trusteeship, or to establish advisory boards to these bodies. In Canada, for example, Quebec pension legislation establishes mechanisms for employee representation on pension management boards (Supplemental Pension Plans Act, 2001). But contrary to the optimism expressed by Drucker (1976) in his book, *Unseen Revolution: How Pension Fund Socialism Came to America*, pension plan beneficiaries generally do not control or direct the corporations in which their pension monies were invested (Rifkin and Barber 1978). The question of how the governance of pension funds and other investment entities should be democratised, and the connections between democratic governance and sustainable development, is beyond the scope of this article, but it is an issue that environmental reformers will need to be mindful of.

Banks

Environmental Issues in Banking

Whereas institutional investors are relevant to environmental financing through their investments in the equity markets, banks are important for their role in providing project finance for specific developments and in funding small, unlisted businesses. Banks are financial intermediaries for the receipt of deposits from members and deployment of such deposits by way of loans and investments for development and consumption purposes. For banks worldwide, environmental issues are becoming a stronger concern for several reasons (Richardson 2002c: 290). First, there is the prospect of direct lender liability where a bank becomes responsible for the environmental liabilities of its clients, such as liability to cleanup contaminated land. Second, environmental problems can generate indirect credit risks for lenders where a borrower experiences financial hardship. Third, there is reputational risk for banks when associated with environmentally controversial developments. In the EU, a number of banks have gone beyond these features of "defensive" banking, involving the avoidance of obvious environmental problems, to the conscious promotion of sustainable development through differential interest rates and other services and incentives provided to encourage environmentally friendly development (Bouma, Jeucken, and Klinkers 2001). Banks in the latter mould include UmweltBank in Germany, the Triodos Bank in the Netherlands, and the UK's Co-operative Bank.

Interest by private banks in environmental matters is also being shaped by reforms to the provision of public development finance. Notably, there have been extensive changes to the operations of the multilateral development banks (MDBs), which have adopted environmental procedures and standards that clients must satisfy for project approvals. The European Bank of Reconstruction and Development (EBRD) has gone the furthest in this respect and is the only MDB to be given a specific environmental mandate in its charter (EBRD 1990, Article 21(vii). Multilateral development bank environmental lending standards can provide benchmarks for private banks interested in environmental issues (Bank of America 2000: 17). Of course, many private banks have not been inspired by the MDB reforms to consider the environment, owing to differences in their loan portfolio, clientele and other aspects of the financial markets they work in, and differences in the regulatory structures by which they are governed.

Nonetheless, the relationship between borrowers and lenders is one of the critical points at which the interests of the environment can be factored into economic decision-making. Lenders often face a long payback period, and their concern for repayment creates, in theory, an interest in the sustainability of the borrower's activities. This interest can be articulated where institutional processes are available that allow banks to share their expertise with and give guidance to their borrowers. In the US, the threat of contaminated site liabilities under the so-called Superfund legislation (Comprehensive Environmental Response, Compensation and Liability Act 1980) has helped catapult environmental concerns to the forefront of banks' analysis of credit arrangements. Most obviously, such liabilities may lower the credit worthiness of the debtor (or guarantor) or reduce the value of any security. Appraising the environmental sequelae of loan proposals helps protect a bank's financial position; projects that incur environmental liabilities may adversely affect a borrower's cash flows and thereby compromise loan repayments. A more ambitious role for banks involves going beyond the mere vetoing of projects posing environmental liabilities, to being a facilitator, steering companies and industries toward best environmental practice. The greatest reach of the banking sector here is in its relationship to small and medium sized enterprises, where banks can be influential through lending practices, by providing information, and offering specialist environmental financial services (Rondinelli and Vastag 1996). But without government intervention to embed environmental standards in banking regulation, banks may be disinclined to voluntarily undertake such a role except where it relates to avoidance of potential environmental liabilities. As with any industry, there are difficulties encouraging banks to take an interest in the environment when it has no obvious correlation with core objectives of profit-making.

Reforming the Banking Sector

Recent EU developments point to some ways in which this problem could be corrected. The EU's Eco-management and Audit Scheme (EMAS) Regulation and Eco-label

Regulation, both voluntary schemes for businesses, have been amended to encompass financial institutions and products. The need to open the EMAS Regulation to the financial sector was acknowledged for several years, as the site-based focus of the original 1993 EMAS Regulation made it not readily adaptable for encompassing the environmental effects of the clients of banks and other financial entities. The EMAS Regulation was revised in March 2001 to extend the scheme to all sectors of economic activity, with a focus on company operations as a whole rather than on specific industrial sites. There is more emphasis in the Regulation on "indirect environmental aspects," defined as including "capital investments, granting loans and insurance services" (Annex, cl. 6.3(b)). In addition, the 1992 Eco-Label Regulation was amended in 2000 to redefine "products" to include "any goods and services," thus implementing earlier European proposals to expand the Eco-Label scheme to the financial services sector. This change means that banking and investment products can be more readily assessed and compared in terms of their environmental credentials, and this should facilitate marketing and reward innovation. These EU innovations point to a style of shared environmental governance that relies on voluntary approaches and market incentives for corporate participation, such as an improved environmental profile among environmentally conscious consumers and productivity gains through reduced waste and resource consumption.

For national banking regulation, no serious consideration has yet been made by governments as to whether environmental policy concerns should be grafted into control systems. Banks are incorporated entities and are hence subject to company law controls. Because of their responsibilities as repositories for people's savings, banks are subject to additional prudential regulation which addresses a range of public policy concerns, principally investor-protection and consumer service standards, through capital adequacy and liquidity requirements (Lastra 1996). Money laundering controls, requiring financial institutions to report suspicious transactions, illustrates the ability of government to harness banks as co-regulators in furtherance of policy objectives. Because of their expertise and access to relevant information financial institutions are at the forefront in efforts to control fraud. Such controls, however, are more easily reconciled with the financial priorities of banks than amorphous environmental concerns. Banks are certainly in a position to demand detailed environmental information concerning the development projects they fund, but the incentives to gather such information are weaker, and it would be inappropriate to expect to banks lacking suitable expertise to take on environmental appraisal responsibilities currently discharged by state authorities. However, banks could at least expect borrowers to comply with environmental legislation and to provide lending on preferential terms to clients that demonstrate a high standard of legislative compliance.

There could be scope within existing regulatory parameters for financial regulators to introduce environmental standards as conditions of banking authorizations. One potentially powerful measure would be to offer financial incentives for banks to introduce differential interest rates (and hence cost of availability of capital) to reflect the environmental risks of different types of development. In the home loan and building financing markets, some lenders are offering "green mortgages" as a way of meeting consumer demand for environmentally friendly, energy-efficient houses. The lending schemes vary in criteria and benefits, but in general the loans offer borrowers higher credit ratios and, sometimes, lower interest rates (Brady 1999). But, as with ethical investment mutual funds, green mortgages is a niche segment of the financial markets currently addressed by only a few institutions, and the incentives for more general practices in the banking sector in this area seem to be lacking. Again, government intervention is required.

Governments could encourage banks to give preferential treatment to projects that meet sustainability criteria by providing tax relief for profits earned on environmental-friendly development loans. The Netherlands has explored the taxation option, and in January 1995 the Dutch government introduced a green investment scheme that allows banks to offer depositors funds whose interest or dividends are exempt from personal taxation. To qualify, the fund must invest at least 70 percent of its assets in environmentally friendly projects. Projects currently certified by the government regulators include renewable energy, organic agriculture and environmental technology (Netherlands Agency for Energy and the Environment 1997). As a result of this initiative, several Dutch banks set up their own green investment funds. The funds have been heavily subscribed to, and because of the large volume of funds consequently generated finance has been available to project proponents on very competitive terms. The attractive interest rates mean investors see gains in funding progressive new projects that were formerly perceived as risky with limited return. Although these unique reforms may be explained by the fact that the Netherlands is a country with a relatively high level of environmental awareness, and a strong tradition of environmental law innovation, other countries may now follow suit given emerging evidence that the Dutch green investment schemes is succeeding to promote sustainable development projects (Bellegem et al. 1997).

Additionally, there could be requirements for banks to commission environmental audits to be undertaken by borrowers, as part of credit appraisal systems used in loan administration procedures. This may require the development of some internal professional competencies in relevant environmental management techniques or the contracting-in or sharing of such competencies for smaller financial institutions. Environmental appraisal by financial institutions should not be a substitute for government environmental impact assessment systems but may operate as a point of initial screening and assist in improving project design before submission to planning permission authorities.

Beyond controls on the operation of banks, governments can promote environmentally responsible lending in the banking sector through appropriately directed liability legislation. Increased lender liability may eventually lead to a reduction in the number of environmentally damaging activities that are financed, and thereby eliminate industries and businesses associated with environmental problems in the market. Environmental lender liability has become a grievance in various industrial economies because of legislative changes or judicial precedents (Lipton 1996). The potential environmental liability of lenders arises from the definitions of "owner," "operator," "permits," or "causes" found in pollution control legislation. A wide interpretation of such words may implicate lenders despite the fact that they had no direct role in causing the contamination. Liability could arise by being the potential owner of a contaminated property through the right to realise the security previously offered by the project borrower; and providing guarantees for firms with potential or actual environmental liability (e.g., firms handling hazardous wastes).

The most persuasive evidence of the effect of government intervention into financial markets is in the US where the behaviour of banks has been profoundly influenced by the implementation of the Comprehensive Environmental Response, Compensation and Liability Act (CERCLA) 1980. This statute may make a lender vicariously liable for contaminated site remediation (Berz 1991; Norton 1995: 358–359). According to a survey by the American Bankers' Association, 62 percent of community commercial banks had rejected loan applications or potential borrowers because of the possibility of environmental liability and 45 percent had withdrawn from lending in known hazardous sectors because of similar concerns (Blackman 1995). Following extensive lobbying by banks, in 1996 the US Congress amended CERCLA to reduce lenders' exposure to environmental liabilities (Asset Conservation, Lender Liability and Deposit Insurance Protection Act of 1996). The US experience has been followed with interest in Europe, where the European Union adopted in April 2004 the Directive on environmental liability with regard to the prevention and remedying of environmental damage. The EU directive avoids specifically attaching liability to financial sponsors, but leaves open the possibility of lender liability where banks exercise operational control over polluting facilities.

More research is needed into the optimal liability regime—one that provides appropriate incentives for banks to eschew funding environmentally contentious developments without stifling potentially socially valuable investments. For instance, whilst the retroactive nature of some environmental liability regimes may further environmental compensation goals, there is little deterrence effect from the penalising of organizations for unforeseeable, non-negligent contamination caused by distant activities (Lyons 1986: 301). This situation can be compounded by joint and several liability rules. The latter is a mechanism for mutual regulation, encouraging each party to only contract with other reputable parties, and thereby creating strong incentives for parties to monitor each other's behaviour (Teubner 1994: 430). Joint and several liability rules seem incongruous with the polluter pays principle in that they encourage the channelling of liability to the deepest pockets, namely financial lenders, rather than the actual contributor of environmental harm (Tietenberg 1989). Joint and several liability can cause "over-deterrence" by deep pocket parties and "under-deterrence" by less solvent parties who may believe that no claims will be brought against them for environmental harm (Gergen 1994: 674). Allowing deep pocket parties to recover contributions from joint tortfeasors generates additional transaction costs and it is of little value if the joint tortfeasors are insolvent. Current economic theory suggests partial lender liability for borrowers' environmental harms is most appropriate (Pitchford 1995).

Further Reforms for Improving Corporate Responsibility through the Financial Services Sector

Some additional reforms to the context in which financial institutions operate are arguably necessary if an effective reorientation of investment and lending patterns toward sustainable development is to be achieved. Investors and lenders would appear to need much stronger financial incentives, clearer environmental information and means of leverage in corporate affairs if they are to effectively promote corporate environmental responsibility.

As a priority, governments should introduce a wider array of economic instruments, notably pollution taxes and tradable emission permits, so that the financial costs or benefits of corporate environmental behaviour are made more transparent and relevant to the calculations of private financiers (Tietenberg 1990; Gunningham and Grabosky 1998: 69–82; Stewart 2000: 171). Investment asset prices should reflect environmental performance if environmental financing is to have an objective basis. Economic instruments should also be applied directly to environmental friendly investments to create tax advantages for such practices. The success of the Dutch tax incentives to promote investment in environmental businesses has already been noted. Eco-taxes directly affect company balance sheets, and financial institutions should support polluter pay charges since as low-energy users they would not be heavily penalised by new charges. With tradable permits, companies that are able to generate cost savings through trade in pollution permits could become more attractive investment opportunities for financial organizations. Creating new markets for environmental goods could significantly augment ethical financing. The UK government's recent Climate Change Levy and Emissions Trading Scheme are in this respect welcome initiatives, but more extensive use of economic instruments as a means of environmental policy is lacking in many countries (Richardson and Chanwai 2003). Until equity and debt prices reflect environmental performance, then ethical investment and lending will remain somewhat arbitrary in determining which businesses are favoured or rejected.

A second area for reform should be imposition of corporate environmental reporting obligations so as to help generate reliable and comprehensive information regarding corporate environmental performance for investors and insurers. Reliable information is crucial to the proper functioning of capital markets, improving accurate pricing of securities and so enabling the market to allocate capital efficiently (Baskin and Miranti 1997: 322). Without material information, investment decisions are likely to be distorted. Disclosure of environmental information can help inform consumers and investors about a firm's level of resource use, emissions and other environmental impacts. Not only does such information feed the ethical concerns of investors, but it also affects the market value of an enterprise by disclosing liabilities and other factors that can affect earnings and profitability. Better environmental information is also crucial for insurers if they are to assess and monitor environmental risks and price premiums accordingly.

Extending requirements for disclosure of environmental costs under securities laws and other company-directed law can facilitate investors' and other stakeholders' scrutiny of the environmental behaviour of firms. Traditional corporate reporting statements have not adequately captured the financial consequences of a company's environmental management. Corporate accounting has been associated with myopic, profit-centred performance measurement (Owen 1992). However, disclosure is a central tenet of emerging voluntary standards such as the CERES Principles and the ISO 14000 series (Tibor and Feldman 1995). Among EU states, mandatory environmental reporting has been instituted in various forms in France, the Netherlands, Sweden, Denmark, and the UK (KPMG 1999: 8). Only in the US are environmental reporting requirements well integrated into mainstream company law through regulations promulgated by the federal Securities and Exchange Commission (SEC) (Geltman 1992: 144). One reason why the SEC (set up in the 1930s) has gone further in corporate disclosure requirements than other jurisdictions is because US policy-makers have long traced the causes of the Great Depression to the failure to establish adequate regulations to ensure investors and other stakeholders have adequate information regarding corporate performance. Environmental reporting requirements are most likely to succeed when regulators provide detailed guidance on reporting criteria and ensure that reports reflect an enterprise's full range of operations, including relationships with subsidiaries and franchisees that may otherwise be exploited by the parent company to disguise its overall environmental impacts.

Thirdly, reforms should be made to systems of corporate governance to enable or direct investee shareholders to be more active in corporate decision-making. Most EU ethical funds use a screening approach, which tends to reduce their influence on corporate environmental practice. As Miller (1991: 7) suggests, "the main arguments against [ethical investment] are that: one cannot hope to change the ways of a major institution simply by buying or selling its shares." Shareholder proposals sponsored by institutional investors are a key means by which institutions can influence company policy (Del Guercio and Hawkins 1999). In some jurisdictions, significant barriers to shareholder activism persist, such as investor portfolio diversification obligations and proxy context rules. The Enron scandal has highlighted the potential huge damage that malfunctioning corporate governance can inflict on pension savings. Various reforms are possible, although the subject raises thorny economic and political concerns to overcome. In theory, financial regulators could require investment institutions to register their share votes, so as to encourage institutions to formulate and express a view on all issues put to a vote at shareholder meetings. Another possibility is the appointment of minority independent directors to corporate boards, nominated by institutional investor groups rather than enterprise management. Beyond measures to stimulate accountability and shareholder involvement, there is the persistent question of whether corporate liability should be broadened, so as to discourage environmentally risky activities (Easterbrook and Fischel 1985). Thus, in principle, imposing liability on institutional shareholding investors for the environmental impacts of their portfolio companies could promote environmentally responsible investment because of the lower liability risks offered by green companies.

Conclusions

This article has argued that because of their gate-keeping role within the economy, financial organizations could become instruments for promoting corporate environmental responsibility. But it is clear that beyond the desire to avoid the traditional kinds of environmental liabilities, the incentives for financial institutions to address the environment systematically currently are often lacking. To date, generally only negative environmental performance has concerned financial markets and there is a paucity of appreciation that a company's environmental management can be a reliable indicator of good business management. Intervention by governments will therefore be necessary to facilitate the integration of environmental concerns into financial markets. Among the regulatory challenges is market uncertainty as to the nexus between environmental performance and business performance, and difficulties in obtaining information that can be understood and efficiently applied by the financial sector. There are also barriers to making the environment sufficiently important to merit the attention of some financial institutions when faced with pressing challenges ranging from market competition to consumer service demands.

In reforming financial markets, government incentive measures (e.g., tax concessions) rather than regulatory commands are likely to be more acceptable and more efficiently implemented. Regulatory measures to facilitate information disclosure on environmental liabilities and ethical investment practices can help allow institutions and customers judge environmental performance. Governments, of course, must also subject their own economic institutions and financial reforms to strategic environmental appraisal and public scrutiny. Environmental policy makers will not achieve sustainable development unless they understand and address the principal economic forces that shape the arenas within which they operate. Of course, it should not be forgotten that environmental reform of the financial services sector alone would not generate sustainable development. Many other well-known features of our environmental law systems—such as national parks, municipal urban planning, and natural resources management regimes—will not become redundant simply because financiers become more environmentally sensitive. But our economies would more likely function within their ecological limits if financiers could be encouraged to use their financial leverage to make corporations more environmentally responsible.

References

Baker, D., and A. Fung. 2001. "Collateral Damage: Do Pension Fund Investments Hurt Workers?" In *Working Capital: The Power of Labor's Pensions*, ed. A. Fung, T. Hebb, and J. Rogers. Ithaca, N.Y.: Cornell University Press.

Bank of America. 2000. 1999 *Environmental Progress Report*. New York: Bank of America.

Baskin, J. B., and P. J. Miranti, Jr. 1997. *A History of Corporate Finance*. Cambridge: Cambridge University Press.

van Bellegem, T., A. Beijerman, and A. Eijs. 1997. *Green Investment Funds: Organic Farming*. Paris: OECD.

Berz, D. R. 1991. "Lender Liability Under CERCLA: In Search of a New Deep Pocket." *Banking Law Journal* 108.

Black, B. S. 1992. "Agents Watching Agents: The Promise of Institutional Investor Voice." *U.C.L.A. Law Review* 39: 813.

Blackman, P. 1995. *Part II of the Environment Act and the Amendments to the Environmental Protection Act 1990*. London: IBC conference on the Environment Act.

Blommestein, H. 1998. "Impact of Institutional Investors on Financial Markets," in *Institutional Investors In The New Financial Landscape*, ed. Organization for Economic Co-operation and Development. Paris: OECD.

Bosselmann, K., and B. J. Richardson. 1999. "Introduction: New Challenges for Environmental Law and Policy." In *Environmental Justice And Market Mechanisms*, ed. K. Bosselmann and B. J. Richardson. London: Kluwer.

Bouma, J. J., M. Jeucken, and L. Klinkers, eds. 2001. *Sustainable Banking: The Greening of Finance*. Sheffield: Greenleaf Publishing.

Brady, S. 1999. "Fannie Mae/NAHB Launch Effort to Develop "Green" Mortgages." *Professional Builder* 6: 1.

Braithwaite, J., and P. Drahos. 2000. *Global Business Regulation*. Cambridge: Cambridge University Press.

Brancato, C. K. 1991. "The Pivotal Role if Institutions in Capital Markets," in *Institutional Investing: Challenges and Responsibilities of the 21st Century*, ed. A. W. Sametz and J. L. Bicksler. Homewood, Ill.: Business One Irwin.

Cerulli Associates. 2001. "The Cerulli Edge—Global Edition." Available at http://www.cerulli.com.

Coles, D., and D. Green. 2002. *Do UK Pension Funds Invest Responsibly?* London: JustPensions.

Cormier, D., M. Magnan, and B. Morard. 1993. "The Impact of Corporate Pollution on Market Valuation: Some Empirical Evidence." *Ecological Economics* 8(2): 135.

Corporation of London and Department of Environment, Food, and Rural Affairs. 2002. *Financing the Future. The London Principles: The Role of UK Financial Services in Sustainable Development*. London: Department of Environment, Food, and Rural Affairs.

Costanza, R., J. Cumberland, H. Daly, R. Goodland, and R. Norgaard. 1997. *An Introduction to Ecological Economics*. Boca Raton, Fla.: St. Lucie Press.

Cranston, R. 1997. *Principles of Banking Law.* London: Clarendon Press.

Daly, H. 1992. "Allocation, Distribution and Scale: Towards an Economics That Is Efficient, Just and Sustainable." *Ecological Economics* 6: 185.

Del Guercio, D., and J. Hawkins. 1999. "The Motivation and Impact of Pension Fund Activism." *Journal of Financial Economics* 52: 293.

Delphi International and Ecological GMBH. 1997. *The Role of Financial Institutions in Achieving Sustainable Development.* London: Delphi International.

Donahue, J. D. 1989. *The Privatization Decision: Public Ends, Private Means.* New York: Basic Books.

Drucker, P. 1976. *Unseen Revolution: How Pension Fund Socialism Came to America.* New York: Harper and Row.

Easterbrook, F. H., and D. R. Fischel. 1985. "Limited Liability and the Corporation." *University of Chicago Law Review* 52: 89.

England, R. W. 2000. "Natural Capital and the Theory Of Economic Growth." *Ecological Economics* 34(3): 425.

European Bank for Reconstruction and Development. 1990. *Agreement Establishing the European Bank for Reconstruction and Development.* OJ L 372, 31/12/1990.

European Commission, Fifth Environment Action Programme. 1992. *Towards Sustainability: A European Community Programme of Policy and Action in Relation to the Environment and Sustainable Development.* Brussels: European Commission.

European Commission. 2000. *Institutional Arrangements for the Regulation and Supervision of the Financial Sector.* Brussels: European Commission.

European Parliament, Committee on Economic and Monetary Affairs. 2001. *Draft Report on the Proposal for a European Parliament and Council Directive on the Activities of Institutions for Occupational Retirement Provision* (8 May). PE 295.986/AM/48-134.

Geltman, E. I. A. G. 1992. "Disclosure of Contingent Environmental Liabilities by Public Companies under the Federal Securities Laws. *Harvard Environmental Law Review* 16: 129.

Gergen, M. J. 1994. "The Failed Promise of the "Polluter Pays" Principle: An Economic Analysis of Landowner Liability for Hazardous Waste. *New York University Law Review* 69: 624.

Grabosky, P. 1995. "Using Non-Governmental Resources to Foster Regulatory Compliance. *Governance* 8(4): 527.

Gunningham, N., and P. Grabosky. 1998. *Smart Regulation. Designing Environmental Policy.* Oxford: Clarendon Press.

Habermas, J. 1973. *Legitimation Crisis.* Boston: Beacon Press.

Hawley, J. P., and A. T. Williams. 2000. *The Rise of Fiduciary Capitalism.* University of Pennsylvania Press.

Hudson, A. 2000. *The Law on Investment Entities.* London: Sweet & Maxwell.

Jeucken, M. 2001. *Sustainable Finance and Banking: The Financial Sector and the Future of the Planet.* London: Earthscan.

Kodar, F. 2002. *Corporate Law, Pension Law and the Transformative Potential of Pension Fund Investment Activism.* LLM Thesis. Toronto: Osgoode Hall Law School, York University.

KPMG. 1999. *International Survey of Environmental Reporting.* London: KPMG.

Lanoie, P., B. Laplante, and M. Roy. 1998. "Can Capital Markets Create Incentives for Pollution Control? *Ecological Economics* 26: 31.

Lastra, R. 1996. *Central Banking and Banking Regulation.* Financial Markets Group.

Lee, W. 1987. "Modern Portfolio Theory and the Investment of Pension Funds." In *Equity and Commercial Relationships*, ed. P. Finn. Sydney: Law Book Company.

Lipton, J. D. 1996. "Project Financing and the Environment: Lender Liability for Environmental Damage in Australia." *Journal of International Banking Law* 11: 7.

Lyons, J. J. 1986. "Deep Pockets and CERCLA: Should Superfund Liability be Abolished? *Stanford Environmental Law Journal* 6: 271.

Mayo, E., and A. Mullineux. 2000. *Regulation of Social Investment.* London: New Economics Foundation.

Miller, A. 1991. *Socially Responsible Investment: The Financial Impact of Screened Investment in the 1990s.* London: Financial Times Business Information.

Monks, R. A. G. 2001. *The New Global Investor.* Albany, Ore.: Capstone Publishing.

Netherlands Agency for Energy and the Environment (Novem). 1997. *Financing Energy and Environmental Technology: The Dutch Way.* The Hague: Novem.

Norton, J. 1995. "Lender Liability in the United States." In *Banks, Liability and Risk*, ed. R. Cranston. London: LLP.

Offe, C. 1987. *Contradictions of the Welfare State.* Boston: MIT Press.

Organization for Economic Co-Operation and Development. 1999. *Institutional Investors: Statistical Yearbook 1998.* Paris: OECD.

Orts, E. W. 1995. "Reflexive Environmental Law." *Northwestern University Law Review* 89(4): 1227.

Owen, D., ed. 1992. *Green Reporting: Accountancy and the Challenge of the Nineties.* London: Chapman & Hall.

Pitchford, R. 1995. "How Liable Should a Lender Be? The Case of Judgement-Proof Firms and Environmental Risk." *American Economic Review* 85: 1171.

PricewaterhouseCoopers. 2001. *Report on Financial Institutions Initiative: Australia.* Sydney: PricewaterhouseCoopers.

Quarter, J., I. Carmichael, J. Sousa, and S. Elgie. 2001. "Special Investment by Union-Based Pension Funds and Labour-Sponsored Investment Funds in Canada." *Industrial Relations* 56(1): 92.

Rada, J., and A. Trisoglio. 1992. "Capital Markets and Sustainable Development." *Columbia Journal of World Business* 27(3/4): 42.

Rein, M. 1989. "The Social Structure of Institutions: Neither Public Nor Private," in *Privatization and the Welfare State*, ed. S. B. Kamerman and A. J. Kahn. Princeton, N.J.: University Press.

Rhodes, R. A. W. 1997. *Understanding Governance: Policy Networks, Governance, Reflexivity and Accountability.* Maidenhead: Open University Press.

Richardson, B. J. 2002a. *Environmental Regulation Through Financial Organizations.* London: Kluwer Law.

———. 2002b. "Pensions Law Reform and Environmental Policy: A New Role for Institutional Investors?" *Journal of International Financial Markets: Law and Regulation* 3(5): 159.

———. 2002c. "Environmental Liability and Banks: Recent European Developments." *Journal of International Banking Law* 17(10): 289.

Richardson, B. J., and K. L. Chanwai. 2003. "Taxing and Trading in Corporate Energy Activities: Pioneering UK Reforms to Address Climate Change." *International Company and Commercial Law Review* 14: 18.

Rifkin, J., and R. Barber. 1978. *The North Will Rise Again: Pensions, Politics and Power in the 1980s.* Beacon Press.

Rondinelli, D. A., and G. Vastag. 1996. "International Environmental Standards and Corporate Policies: An Integrative Framework. *California Management Review* 39: 106.

Schmideiny, S., and F. Zorraquin. 1996. *Financing Change: The Financial Community, Eco-Efficiency and Sustainable Development.* Boston: MIT Press.

Sparkes, R. 1995. *The Ethical Investor.* London: Harper Collins.

———. 2002. *Socially Responsible Investment: A Global Revolution.* New York: John Wiley & Sons.

Stanford, J. 1999. *Paper Boom: Why Real Prosperity Requires a New Approach to Canada's Economy.* Toronto: Canadian Centre for Policy Alternatives.

Stewart, R. B. 2000. "Economic Incentives for Environmental Protection. In *Environmental Law, the Economy and Sustainable Development*, ed. R. L. Revesz, S. Philippe, and R. B. Stewart. Cambridge: Cambridge University Press.

Stoker, G. 1998. "Governance as Theory." *International Social Sciences Journal* 155: 17.

Sustainable Development Research International Group. 2002. *Green, Social and Ethical Funds in Europe in 2001*. Sustainable Development Research International Group.

Tasch, E., and S. Viederman. 1995. "New Concepts Of Fiduciary Responsibility." In *Steering Business Toward Sustainability*, ed. F. Capra and G. Pauli. Tokyo: United Nations University Press.

Teubner, G. 1983. "Substantive and Reflexive Elements in Modern Law." *Law and Society Review* 17: 239.

———. 1994. "The Invisible Cupola: From Causal to Collective Attribution in Ecological Liability." *Cardozo Law. Review* 16(2): 429.

Tibor, T., and I. Feldman. 1995. *ISO 14000: A Guide to the New Environmental Management Systems.* Irwin.

Tietenberg, T. H. 1989. "Indivisible Toxic Torts: The Economics of Joint and Several Liability." *Land Economics* 65(4): 305.

———. 1990. "Economic Instruments for Environmental Regulation. *Oxford Review of Economic Policy* 6(1): 17.

UK Department of Trade and Industry. 2001. *Modern Company Law for a Competitive Economy: Final Report.* London: Department of Trade and Industry.

United Nations Environment Programme (UNEP), 1992. *Statement by Banks on Environment and Sustainable Development.* Nairobi: UNEP. Advisory Committee on Banking and the Environment.

Walter, A. 1993. *World Power and World Money.* New York: Harvester Wheatsheaf.

Wilson, J. Q. 1980. *The Politics of Regulation.* New York: Basic Books.

The Author

Benjamin J. Richardson is Associate Professor at Osgoode Hall Law School, York University, 4700 Keele St., Toronto, Canada, M3J 1P3. E-mail: brichardson@osgoode .yorku.ca.

BEYOND GOOD INTENTIONS: NEW DIRECTIONS FOR INVESTING IN SUSTAINABILITY

Jacob Park
Green Mountain College, Poultney, Vermont, USA

Abstract

This paper examines the rise of socially responsible investment (SRI) as a sustainable finance mechanism and discusses the potential of SRI in steering the banking and financial services industry toward a more socially responsible and environmentally sound model of commerce. I argue in this paper that the potential of SRI to serve as a *sustainable* business mechanism to steer the global financial market toward a new ethical architecture depends on two related factors: (a) continuing institutional and social pressures for greater corporate transparency, and (b) the ability of SRI to become a viable financial instrument outside its traditional markets in emerging and developing economies.

Toward a New Model of Values-Based Investing

To date, the focus of the academic literature and the popular press has been on the possible differences between the financial returns between Socially Responsible Investing (SRI) and traditional investment funds. Leaving aside the technical question of whether there is a tilt toward technology and other growth stocks in the investment portfolio of many SRI funds,[1] there is compelling evidence that SRI fund investors do not have to sacrifice financial performance to uphold their ethical concerns. For instance, the Domini 400 Social Index, one of the earliest and most prominent SRI indices, has beaten its benchmark, the S&P Index, for almost the entire life of the fund. For a ten-year period from April 1994–2004, the Domini 400 Social Index had an averaged annualized return of 12.2 percent compared to the S&P 500's 11.4 percent (Fig. 1).[2]

What this narrow analytical lens leaves out is the role SRI can be expected to play in the broader context of the global banking and financial services (BFS) industry. On the one hand, SRI has already become an important global financial phenomenon. The US Social Investment Forum estimates that one out of eight dollars under professional management in 2003 has been invested according to a socially responsible investment strategy (SIF 2003). On the other hand, SRI is still at best a niche financial instrument that remains outside the global BFS industrial mainstream. There is yet no evidence

 pp. 101–108

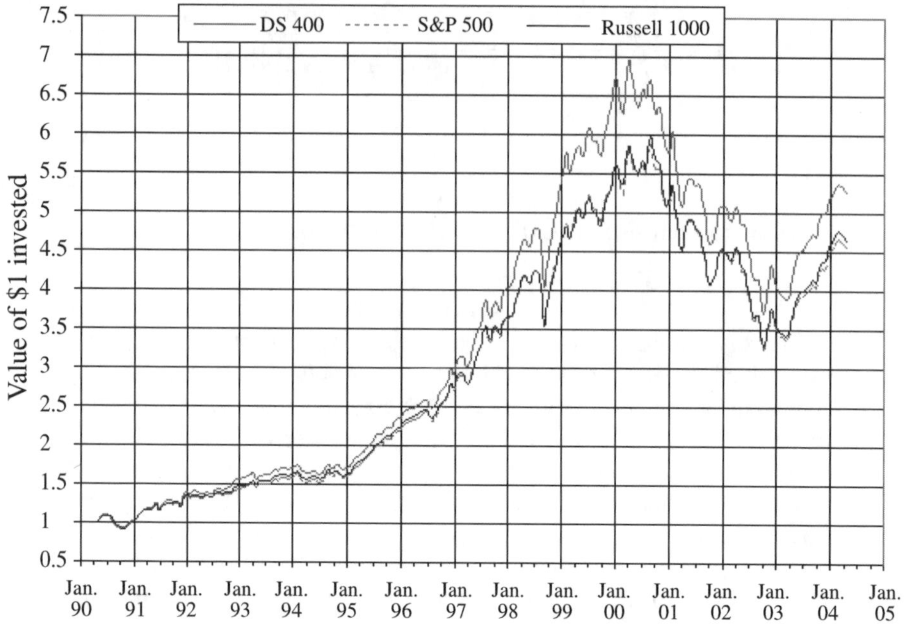

Figure 1. The relative financial performance of the Domini 400 Social Index compared to the S&P 500 and Russell 1000 (May 1990–April 1994). Source: KLD Research & Analytics Inc.

to suggest that the rapid growth in SRI has significantly changed the traditionally laggard role BFS companies have played in terms of disclosing environmentally and socially related information. A 2002 study conducted by the German consulting firm Oekom Research suggests that "more than half of the leading financial institutions around the world proved to be so lacking in transparency that it was impossible to analyze their social and environmental activities in any depth" (Mathias 2002: 8), while a 2001 Benchmark Survey of the State of Global Environmental and Social Reporting concludes that the financial services sector makes up the *largest* percentage of the world's 100 largest firms while representing the *smallest* percentage of the companies that issue sustainability reports (CSR Network 2001).

What is not in dispute is that the SRI and the BFS industry have an important role to play in advancing social, environmental, and ethical business responsibilities in the global economy. The Collevecchio Declaration on Financial Institutions and Sustainability outlines the unique role and responsibility the financial sector has in advancing sustainability: "the financial sector's role of facilitating and managing capital is important; and finance, like communications or technology, is not inherently at odds with sustainability. However, in the current context of globalization, financial institutions play key roles in channeling financial flows, creating financial markets and influencing international policies in ways that are too often unaccountable to citizens, and harmful to the environment, human rights, and social equity."[3]

I argue in this paper that the potential of SRI to serve as a sustainable business mechanism to steer the global financial market toward a new ethical architecture depends on two related factors: (a) continuing institutional and social pressures for greater corporate transparency and (b) the ability of SRI to become a viable financial instrument outside its traditional markets in North America and Europe in emerging and developing economies. To fully examine these factors, the following three issues and questions will be explored in this paper: First, how has SRI developed historically as a financial instrument in North America and Europe? Second, how should we view SRI in the broader sustainability context? Third, what is the future outlook for the SRI as a financial and sustainability mechanism?

SRI Development: From Faith to Global Markets

The origins of the modern SRI movement can be traced to the turbulent period in the 1960s when powerful social undercurrents including environmentalism and anti-war activism fueled a radical change in the way society viewed faith, values, and commerce. SRI funds were once primarily known as ethical funds and, given their strong Judeo-Christian roots, this is not at all surprising. The notion of an "ethical business enterprise" has strong roots in Judeo-Christian traditions, and one can find examples of such a notion in the book of Deuteronomy, dating back more than 3000 years. However, it is arguably the Quaker faith that has made the greatest impact in forging a connection between commercial activities and ethical values in the modern age.

The Quakers were the first group to practice "negative screening" of investments when they avoided investments in the armaments sector for more than 140 years, by faithfully applying their peace traditions to commercial activities. One of the early examples of what we might now call a SRI-like activity was an investment fund established by the Methodist Church in the 1960s that avoided investments in armaments, alcohol, gambling, and tobacco. Since the fund managed by the Methodist Church was closed to outsiders, the first modern example of what we now call a SRI fund was the US Pax World Fund established by two Methodist ministers in 1971. The first investment fund that specifically addressed ecological concerns was the Ecology Fund established by Merlin/Jupiter Company in 1988 (Kreander 2001).

The political unrest in South Africa in the 1960s and 1970s set the stage for another major policy push for SRI and the important connection between ethics and business practices. Reverend Leon Sullivan helped to draft a code of conduct (subsequently known as the "Sullivan Principles") for companies doing business in South Africa. By the early 1980s, the Sullivan Principles had become the rallying cry for anti-apartheid activism. By 1982, the State of Connecticut adopted the Sullivan Principles and other social criteria to guide its investment decision-making, and by 1984, the California Public Employees Retirement System (CalPERS) and the New York Employee Retirement System quickly followed and issued their own guidelines concerning South Africa (IFC 2003).

Today, the global SRI market, at least in the wealthy OECD countries, is well established and, in the case of Europe, is entering a major growth phase. In the US, $2.2 trillion or about 13 percent of the $19.2 trillion under professional management is currently invested in one of the three core social investment strategies—screening, shareholder advocacy, and community investing. There are currently 200 socially screened mutual funds, whose assets total $151 billion. Most impressively, socially responsible mutual funds registered a net inflow of $1.5 billion in 2002, while traditional US equity funds recorded outflows of nearly $10.5 billion (SIF 2003). According to a recent survey by the European Sustainable and Responsible Investment Forum, European institutional SRI (consisting of Austria, Germany, Italy, the Netherlands, Spain, Switzerland, and the United Kingdom) could be as high as 336 billion euros (Eurosif 2003). Even in countries like Japan and the Asia-Pacific region where awareness of social responsibility concerns lag that of North America and Europe, SRI represents one of the few financial instruments that are growing rapidly in size (Table 1).

	Assets ($US Billions)		**Market Capital**
	1999	**2002**	**SRI as % of Total**
US	2160	2300	12%
UK	2	354	19%
Canada	32	30	3.2%
Europe	NA	17.6	1%
Japan	none	2.0	<1%
Australia	6.3	8.3	<5%
Total	2280 (est.)	2710 (est.)	

Table 1. Socially Responsible Investments in OECD Countries and Regions. Source: Adapted from International Finance Corporation (2003), "Towards Sustainable and Responsible Investment in Emerging Markets" Washington DC: IFC.

The growth in the SRI markets of North America and Europe overshadows, however, the almost complete lack of SRI activity in emerging and developing economies, where more than two-thirds of the world population live and work. According to a recent report by the International Finance Corporation, the sum total of SRI assets in emerging markets is approximately $2.7 billion, or 0.1 percent of the $2.7 trillion global SRI market. It is estimated that emerging market assets held by SRI investors in industrialized countries total less than $1.5 billion, while emerging market assets held by SRI investors in the same emerging economies total about $1.2 billion, or nearly 0.04 percent of all SRI worldwide (IFC 2003). This is one of the many institutional hurdles SRI must overcome if it is to become more than just a niche market.

SRI and Sustainability

An impressive number of books, journal articles, and working papers have come out in recent years on a wide range of SRI-related themes, including environmental finance (Labatt and White 2002), greening of the banking sector (Bouma, Jeucken, and Klinkers 2001 and Jeucken 2001), financial community and sustainable development (Schmidheiny 1998), the relationship between environmental regulation and financial organizations (Richardson 2002), links between financial and social/environmental performance (Margolis and Walsh 2001), and a number of popular books on ethical investing that target mainstream investors (Camejo 2002 and Sparkes 2002). Despite these new academic and mainstream works on SRI and related themes, there is still a great deal of confusion about the use and applicability of SRI as a business concept. At the simplest level, SRI can be defined as the integration of personal values and societal concerns with investment decisions while considering both the investor's financial needs and an investment's impact on society. It uses traditional financial analysis but incorporates social and environmental factors into the overall investment decision-making process.

Although three important SRI strategies (screening, shareholder advocacy/engagement,[4] and community investing) have evolved over the years, the most easily understood and common way social and environmental factors have been incorporated into the investment process is through "portfolio screening." Portfolio screening is the process of using social and/or environmental criteria to include (positive screen) or exclude (negative screen) shares of a certain company from an investment portfolio. Though the weighting of the individual screens differ from one SRI fund to another and from one SRI asset management company to another, most SRI funds typically screen, positively and/or negatively, individual firms based on the following criteria: environment (energy intensity, carbon emissions, environmental management system, etc.); workplace practices (equal opportunities, employee welfare and opportunities, anti-discrimination policies, etc.); stakeholder relations (charitable contributions, human rights, engagement with nonprofit/community groups), and in some cases, corporate governance and related board practices.

Smaller SRI fund companies without their own research staff rely on independent research providers, such as KLD Analytics in the US or Ethical Investment Research Service in the UK, for most of their research needs, while larger SRI fund companies rely on their own internal staff to conduct research and shareholder advocacy and/or engage with companies. While the more simplistic process of screening companies out of the portfolio is still used, SRI research as a whole has become much more sophisticated in recent years. New SRI research companies like the UK-based Trucost are starting to use sophisticated economic modeling to assess the environmental externalities that may not be captured in conventional financial accounts. The development of global sustainability indices like the Dow Jones Sustainability as well as the FTSE4Good Index Series have filled a great need for investment indices of the SRI capital markets[5] and have led to greater pressure on companies to disclose relevant environmental and social indicators.

However, is there evidence to suggest companies have actually changed their environmental and social business practices as the result of SRI portfolio screening or shareholder advocacy/engagement? It is yet too early to draw any firm conclusions, but there is some anecdotal evidence to suggest SRI is having a sustainability impact. When CalPERS, the world's largest pension fund with $151 billion in assets, announced that it would start employing SRI principles in its investment management decisions in 2001, the practical result of this decision were initially unclear. A year later, after CalPERS decided that it would divest its investments in Thailand, Indonesia, and Malaysia due to unacceptably low labor, political stability, and financial transparency country rankings, finance and stock market officials in those respective countries began scrambling to adopt policies to improve business practices.

More recently, the FTSE Group, the global index provider and the parent body of the FTSE4Good Index Series, announced that the FTSE4Good Index Series has made a number of positive impacts on the practices of corporate environmental and social responsibility practices among listed companies around the world, including a marked improvement in the number of companies increasing their commitment to international standards such as the UN Global Compact. More than 266 companies have indicated that they've made changes to their environmental management practices (based on the FTSE4Good Index criteria), and sixty-two companies that have been originally on the index have been removed for not adequately meeting human rights and environmental challenges (FTSE 2004).

SRI: Financial and Sustainability Outlook

Will SRI become a sustainable business and policy mechanism to steer the global financial market toward a new ethical architecture? The answer might be a resounding yes if it depended only on the likelihood of greater institutional pressures for corporate transparency and accountability. Not only do social and environmental pressures continue, but they may even accelerate in the case of UK and the EU. They will be spurred on not only by the global SRI movement, but also by international policy initiatives like the Global Reporting Initiative and by national/regional governments (particularly UK and the EU countries) that are placing ever-increasing regulatory pressures to strength disclosure of corporate environmental and social data. It is even possible that other European countries and possibly Japan and other Asian countries may follow the lead of the UK in adopting pension laws that encourage the development of SRI.

The answer to the question becomes more ambiguous if we also take into account the likelihood that SRI will become a viable financial instrument in emerging and developing economies. It is hard to be optimistic when the current total of SRI assets in emerging markets is only $2.7 billion, or 0.1 percent of the $2.7 trillion global SRI market. Yet, we may also be overlooking a small but important trend that is taking place in emerging and developing economies, due to the many and obvious global macro trends favoring SRI (e.g., growing institutional shareholder activism and tightening environmental and social regulatory pressures). Case in point: the Johannesburg Securities Exchange in South Africa required that as of September 1, 2003, all companies listed with the Exchange must comply not only with corporate governance codes, but also must use the Global Reporting Initiative guidelines for disclosing social and environmental performance. In the end, the actual dollar amount may not be as important as the development of the "right" institutional infrastructure and public-private partnerships to steer SRI toward its next phase of development in both the industrialized and emerging/developing economies.

Notes

1. Many SRI funds, particularly those in the US, are partial to companies in the technology sector because Intel, Microsoft, Hewlett-Packard, and other tech companies tend to do well with the funds' screens.

2. The website of KLD Research & Analytics (http://www.kld.com/benchmarks/dsi.html) has a good history and the methodology of the Domini 400 Social Index

3. The Collevecchio Declaration on Financial Institutions and Sustainability (January, 2003) can be found in the Friends of the Earth website (http://www.foe.org/camps/intl/declaration .html).

4. Shareholder advocacy and engagement is the use of shareholder institutional power to influence business behavior (e.g., to be more pro-active on global warming or in addressing waste management issues). It can consist of filing resolutions at a company's annual general meeting or requesting to meet with a company's senior management to engage with the company.

5. Investment indices (most commonly based on a certain geographical region or country) are used extensively by investors (including SRI investors in the case of Dow Jones Sustainability and FTSE4Good index series) worldwide for investment analysis, performance measurement, asset allocation, and for creating a wide range of index tracking funds.

References

Bouma, J. J., M. Jeucken, and L. Klinkers. 2001. *Sustainable Banking: The Greening of Finance*. Sheffield, UK: Greenleaf Publishing

Camejo, Peter. 2002. *The SRI Advantage: Why Socially Responsible Investing Has Outperformed Financially*. Gabriola Island, B.C.: New Society Publishers

CSR Network. 2001. *The 2001 Benchmark Survey: The State of Global, Social and Environmental Reporting*.

European Sustainable and Responsible Investment Forum (Eurosif). 2003. *Socially Responsible Investment among European Institutional Investors*. 2003 Report Available from http://www.eurosif.org.

FTSE. 2004. *Criteria Development and Company Engagement Programme: 2003–2004 Report*. Good Index Series.

International Finance Corporation (IFC). 2003. *Towards Sustainable and Responsible Investment in Emerging Markets*. Washington, D.C.: IFC: 12–13.

Jeucken, Marcel. 2001. *Sustainable Finance and Banking*. London: Earthscan.

Kreander, Niklas. 2001. "An Analysis of European Ethical Funds." Occasional Research Paper No. 33. London: Certified Accountants Educational Trust.

Labatt, S., and R. White. 2002. *Environmental Finance: A Guide to Environmental Risk Assessment and Financial Products*. New York: John Wiley & Sons.

Margolis, Joshua, and James Walsh. 2001. *People and Profits?: The Search for a Link Between a Company's Social and Financial Performance*. Mahwah, N.J.: Lawrence Erlbaum Associates.

Mathias, Alex 2002. "Banks Rate Poorly on CSR." *Environment Finance* 8 (September): 8.

Richardson, Benjamin. 2002. *Environmental Regulation Through Financial Organisations: Comparative Perspectives on the Industrialised Nations*. The Hague: Kluwer Law International.

Schmidheiny, Stephan. 1998. *Financing Change: The Financial Community, Eco-Efficiency, and Sustainable Development*. Cambridge, Mass.: MIT Press.
Social Investment Forum (SIF). 2003. *Report on Socially Responsible Investment Trends in the United States* (updated December 2003). Available at http://www.socialinvest.org.
Sparkes, Russell. 2002. *Socially Responsible Investing: A Global Revolution*. New York: John Wiley & Sons

The Author

Jacob Park is Assistant Professor of Business and Public Policy, Green Mountain College, One College Circle, Poultney, VT 05764-1199, USA. E-mail: parkj@greenmtn.edu.

AN ANALYSIS OF CORPORATE GOVERNANCE ISSUES FOR LARGE JAPANESE MULTINATIONALS SEEN THROUGH THE PRISM OF THREE RECENT CASES

Rae Weston
Macquarie Graduate School of Management, Sydney, Australia

Abstract

This study examines the three major Japanese multinational corporate governance cases of the past decade: Sumitomo Copper, Daiwa Bank, and Mitsubishi Motors. The analysis focuses on three particular matters: Does senior management and the board exhibit a form of "disaster myopia"? Were there clear signs of the impending problems that were ignored? Is there anything distinctive that makes these cases Japanese in character? The first two questions are answered in the affirmative for all three firms, but only the Mitsubishi case exhibits a peculiarly Japanese characteristic.

Introduction

Charkham (1998), Gilson and Roe (1993), Futatsugi (1990), and Sheard (1989) suggest that the Japanese form of corporate governance differs from that in the U.K. and the U.S., while Miles (1998: 63) says that its unusual characteristics "give it the leeway for self dealing whether by individual directors or by member companies."

Ron Bevacqua, Chief Economist at Commerz Securities in Tokyo, was quoted in the *China Daily* (2000) as saying of the Mitsubishi Motors case that the scandal appeared to "highlight Japanese management's ingrained tendency to give short shrift to the interests of outsiders, whether shareholders or consumers."

In this paper we examine the three major Japanese multinational corporate governance cases of the past decade: Sumitomo Copper, Daiwa Bank, and Mitsubishi Motors. Our analysis focuses on three particular matters: first, does senior management and the board exhibit the form of "disaster myopia" that has been a feature of the main bank loss cases of Barings, Allied Irish Banks, and National Australia Bank (Weston 2004); second, were there clear signs of the impending problems that were ignored; and is there anything distinctive that makes these cases Japanese in character? We begin with the Sumitomo case.

 pp. 109–118

Sumitomo

In June 1996 it was reported that an investigation by the U.K. Securities and Investment Board (SIB) had revealed that losses of 1.8 billion USD had been accumulated from unauthorized trading at Sumitomo Corporation, a leading copper dealer. The company attributed blame for the losses to Yasuo Hamanaka, a former head of copper trading, but nevertheless emphasized that it would stand behind its copper market obligations, and recognized that the losses could rise if the copper price fell.

American Metal Market (Burgett and Furukawa 1996) reported that

> [e]xecutives said they learned of the losses June 5 when Hamanaka allegedly admitted to unauthorized trading. The admission followed the discovery in late April and early May of unaccounted-for bank transactions that led to Hamanaka's removal from trading and further investigations led to the confession, executives said. A second unidentified trader who left the company eight years ago was the only other said to have been involved.
>
> Hamanada was known in the copper markets as "Mr. Five Percent" because Sumitomo's copper trading team traded approximately 500,000 metric tons of copper a year, which was 5 percent of the total world demand for copper.
>
> The market Hamanaka had been trading in was the London Metal Exchange forward market for copper. In this market, positions taken are normally for three months, but there is the ability to roll positions forward, thereby deferring the settlement and chrystalisation of profit or loss date. Sumitomo was the largest participant in the physical market for copper, handling twice the volume of its nearest competitor. Hamanaka was quoted in the company's Annual Report in the early 1990s accounting for the company's significance in the market as "attributable to expertise in risk management.

The Economist (1996) speculated that Hamanka may either have managed to convince his company that it owned copper which it did not in fact possess, or had borrowed money to cover his losses.

Sumitomo had had its attention drawn to possible irregularities in its copper market dealings before: first in 1991 by the LME when David Threlkeld, one of its metal brokers, reported being asked by Hamanaka for an invoice for non-existent trades; secondly in 1994 when an inquiry by the U.K. Securities and Futures Authority into the relationship between Winchester and a Chilean trader acting for Codelco led the authority to notify Sumitomo that Winchester had made most of its money acting as a broker for Sumitomo; and, third, in early 1996 when the SIB and the U.S. CFTC began to investigate the copper market, it was clear that the company's activities in the market would be of interest to them. Nevertheless, although the company relieved Hanamaka from trading in early May in order for him to help the two bodies with their inquiries, Sumitomo did not recognize the losses until June 5, and even then its actions were in response to a bank statement it had received that credited the company with funds from a transaction it could not find.

On June 24 the company announced that it was assembling an investigation team, including a New York–based law firm and a U.S. accounting firm as well as four or five of its own executives from other divisions, to look into the copper trade losses.

The president of Sumitomo, Tomichi Akiyama, said that he was "profoundly embarrassed" by the loss.

In July it was established by ring-dealing members of the LME, and announced by Credit Lyonnais Rouse, that "all credit lines and contractual documentation with Sumitomo had been properly processed and authorized by officials designated by Sumitomo to have such powers and such authorities were not exclusively in the hands of Hamanaka." The requirements of the Securities and Futures Act's Adequate Credit Management Policy had been satisfied with respect to these transactions.

By August it had been established that Hanamaka's strategy had been to buy up physical copper, store it in the LME warehouses, and watch demand drive up the price, holding off short sells by purchasing the other sides of those positions. This strategy unwound when Hanamaka was relieved of his trading role in early May and could no longer counter short-selling.

By September the Tokyo prosecutor's office had formed a special unit to investigate the affair, and Sumitomo voluntarily turned over to them data on both its corporate organization and copper trading. In November the prosecutor's office formally indicted Hamanaka on four counts of forgery allegedly in 1993 and 1994, and Sumitomo filed a fraud charge against him. In that claim Sumitomo alleged that Hanamaka had swindled a Hong Kong subsidiary, Sumitomo Corp (Hong Kong) Ltd into buying 770 million USD of copper that existed only on paper and using the proceeds to cover losses from other deals.

At his trial in February 1997 Hamanaka pleaded guilty to charges of fraud and forgery in connection with 2.6 billion USD in losses that Sumitomo had incurred over a ten year period. According to the prosecution case Hanamka and his superior, Saburo Shimizu began forward trading on the LME copper market in late 1985 to speculate without authorization in an attempt to try to recoup a loss they had incurred from physical copper trading in the Philippines. In fact the losses rose to 60 million USD, at which point Shimizu resigned. Both traders felt the losses were too great to report to their superiors. Hanamaka believed it was not impossible to recover the losses through trading.

Hanamaka and a copper merchant firm entered into a contract to supply Sumitomo with a total of 1,194 million metric tons of copper between 1994 and 1997. Almost half of the copper sold in 1995 and 1996 was sold back to the merchant's supplier and never delivered. A term of the contract made it in the traders' interests for prices to rise above a pre-established minimum price, because Sumitomo was obligated under the minimum price provision to buy copper at a price equal to the larger of (a) the market price at the time of shipment and (b) the minimum price set by Sumitomo during a specified time period. Under the price-participation provision, the merchant firm was required to pay Sumitomo 30 percent of the difference between the market price at the time of shipment and the minimum price on futures contracts purchased to hedge the supply contracts. Whenever copper prices rose above the pre-established minimum price, the merchant firm and Sumitomo would share in the price appreciation.

In order to coordinate their trades Hanamaka and the merchant firm established accounts at a number of brokers and authorized access to those accounts by using Sumitomo's name and credit line. To force up prices and liquidate their positions at a profit, Hanamaka and the merchant firm held all of the stocks in LME warehouses at different times during the last quarter of 1995.Between them, Hanamaka and the merchant firm managed to create artificial prices and price relationships.

In a New York lawsuit that alleged manipulation between Sumitomo and a merchant firm, Global Minerals, between June 1994 and June 1996, Sumitomo agreed in August 1998 to pay 99 million USD, and in a California suit agreed to pay 42.5 million USD.

In March 2001 five former directors of Sumitomo agreed to pay a total of 3.55 million USD to the company to settle a shareholder lawsuit over the loss from illegal copper trading. The settlement amounted to approximately half the retirement benefits received by the former directors.

This case bears a striking resemblance to the recent National Australia Bank case where a series of early warning signals were clearly there but were either ignored or their significance not understood. Also as with Sumitomo, where others above Hanamaka clearly permitted the situation to continue, so in the National Australia Bank case management above the currency options dealing team knew that limits were consistently being breached.

Daiwa Bank

Toshihide Iguchi was, from 1991 to 1994, a senior vice president, and, from 1994 to September 1995, an executive vice president of the New York branch of Daiwa Bank. On or before July 21, 1995, Daiwa received a letter addressed to its president, written by Toshihide Iguchi, in which he stated that he had "caused approximately a $U.S. 1.1 billion loss from trading U.S. Treasury bonds at the New York branch," and further, that this trading loss had been compensated for by selling investment securities of the New York branch or selling Treasury bonds that Daiwa held for its clients as their custodian. The letter also revealed that some 377 million USD of U.S. Treasury obligations belonging to Daiwa's customers had been sold without authorization. In his letter Iguchi suggested that Daiwa should minimize the likelihood that these losses would be discovered by the U.S. authorities, specifically by replacing the U.S. Treasury obligations that had been sold without authorization, and that Daiwa should transfer his 1.1 billion USD trading losses to Daiwa's head office.

On July 24, 1995, Daiwa received a second copy of the letter, along with another letter that claimed that there was no possibility that the case would be uncovered in the United States if the Treasury obligations were bought back. On the same day Daiwa's Deputy President, one of its Managing Directors, and the General Manager of its International Treasury Division telephoned Toshihide Iguchi from Japan to discuss the contents of the letters. Four days later, the managing director, the general manager of the New York branch, and the president of Daiwa Trust met with Toshihide Iguchi in New York. At this meeting the managing director said that Daiwa intended to announce the loss "in some form" in late 1995, after the company had announced its financial results for the six-month period ending September 30, 1995, but that in the interim it was imperative that the 1.1 billion USD loss remain a secret.

On September 18, 1995, Daiwa Bank met with a representative of the Federal Reserve Bank and reported that its New York branch had incurred losses of 1.1 billion

USD from trading activities undertaken by Toshihide Iguchi over a period of eleven years. These losses had been reflected neither in the books and records of the bank nor in its financial statements. Their existence had been concealed, as Iguchi had suggested, through liquidations of securities held in the bank's custody accounts and falsification of its custody records. In both 1993 and 1994 the U.S. regulators had warned Daiwa about its poor internal controls. However, it appears that Daiwa misled them by claiming that Iguchi no longer performed both front- and back-office functions.

Daiwa said that the losses had been concealed from U.S. banking regulators for almost two months, and that its officials had directed Iguchi to continue transactions during the two month period so as to avoid disclosure of the losses. Some Japanese Ministry of Finance officials had been informed in early August of Daiwa's losses but neither instructed Daiwa to inform the U.S. authorities nor did so themselves.

In a later interview (Chua-Eoan and Desmond 1995), Iguchi said, "I traded the same bonds for 12 years. It was pretty simple for management to understand. I had several managers over me who should have understood. But the New York branch depended on me so heavily for profits—we were producing more than half their profits—they wanted to keep their eyes closed and they didn't want to know anything."

On October 9, the Bank further announced that its separately federally insured bank subsidiary in New York had incurred losses of some 97 million USD as a result of trading activities, some of them unauthorized, between 1984 and 1987. These losses had not been reflected in the subsidiary's books, records, or financial statements and were concealed from U.S. authorities by transferring the losses to offshore affiliates with the apparent knowledge of senior management. Daiwa alleged that Iguchi was a rogue trader acting alone but had to revise this when it was discovered that at least three other bond traders had been circumventing the bank's reporting requirements for years.

President of the company, Akira Fujita, and his chairman, Sumio Abekama, announced that they would take a pay cut of 30 percent over the next six months as a sign of penance, while other directors would lose between 10 percent and 30 percent of their salaries, and top management would not receive their bonuses.

On October 2, 1995, U.S. federal and state authorities issued cease-and-desist orders requiring Daiwa to cease trading in the United States and to terminate its banking operations by February 1996. Also in October Iguchi pleaded guilty in New York to conspiring with senior bank management to conceal from federal authorities the 1.1 billion USD trading loss. The Japanese Minister of Finance, Masayoshi Takemura, announced "that management must take proper responsibility" for the events, and only a few days later both Fujita and Abekama announced they would resign.

New York federal prosecutors took criminal action against the bank, alleging conspiracy to defraud the Federal Reserve Bank. The bank and its New York manager, Mashahiro Tsuda, were named as defendants. Tsuda was relieved of his duties and subsequently resigned as a director of the bank.

In January 1996, Daiwa Bank sold its U.S. assets to Sumitomo Bank for 65 million USD. In February Daiwa agreed to plead guilty to sixteen criminal charges with respect to the case and to pay a 340 million USD fine. Tsuda agreed to plead guilty to one count of conspiracy to defraud the Federal Reserve Board but still maintained that he had only been following orders from his superiors and from the Japanese Ministry of Finance in concealing the losses.

Daiwa Bank's stockholders undertook a representative action against the directors of Daiwa Bank in the Osaka District Court. The case had two parts: first, an action alleging that the directors had a duty to establish a proper risk management system but had failed to do so, and a second action alleging that the 340 million USD in damages from the plea agreement in the U.S. arose from a breach of the directors' duty. The court concluded that the failure of the risk management process to function at Daiwa Bank was a responsibility of the directors and ordered both current and former top executives of Daiwa to pay the bank 775 million USD in damages for this lack of oversight. Of the eleven executives found to be liable, the former head of the New York branch was judged to be solely responsible for the lack of risk management and was ordered to pay the bank 530 million USD while others, including the President, were found liable for having failed to report the losses to the appropriate authorities.

What pattern can be identified? In the Daiwa case the loss due to fraud was recognized internally but then knowingly concealed from the relevant authorities. It appears from Iguchi's testimony that what he had done was tolerated by his managers because they wanted to perpetuate the profits he was generating for the company. There was an allegation by the company that he was a "rogue trader" operating alone. This proved to be untrue. Eventually the liability reached the president of the bank. There is clear evidence that the authorities had drawn Daiwa's attention previously to possible irregularities.

In the Sumitomo case the company attributed blame for the losses from unauthorized trading in the copper market to its former head of copper trading but nevertheless said that it would stand behind its copper market obligations. There was again clear evidence that the authorities had drawn the company's attention to possible irregularities in its copper market dealings. It was eventually established that managers above the accused trader had properly processed and authorized the trades. Sumitomo had to settle lawsuits arising from the manipulation of the copper market, and in 2001 five former directors of Sumitomo paid some half of their retirement benefits in compensation.

The details of both cases provided in the last two sections suggest that the two companies were not, as suggested by Charkham (1998: 41), pursuing the long-term preservation and prosperity of the family. It seems that the continuation and protection of profits, even though they were improperly earned, was the key factor. This effectively makes them indistinguishable from the Barings and National Australia Bank cases, and they therefore do not have a particularly "Japanese" character. We consider now the third case, Mitsubishi Motors.

Mitsubishi Motors

Mitsubishi Motors Corporation (MMC) was established in 1970 as an automobile manufacturer in Japan and became the country's fourth largest. In 1988 its shares were listed on the Tokyo, Osaka, and Nagoya stock exchanges. Internationally it has a workforce of 65,485, of which 22,666 are in Japan.

In 1998 the company recorded its worst loss in history, with its share price dropping to an all-time low of 208 JPY in October 1998. CEO Katsuhiko Kawasoe introduced a three-year reform program (Renewal Mitsubishi 2001) in an attempt to approve the company's performance.

In order to secure the company's future growth, Kawasoe realised he would have to sell a large stake to a foreign owner. On July 28, 2000, DaimlerChrysler, a German/U.S. auto manufacturer, agreed to acquire a 34 percent stake in Mitsubishi at a cost of 2.1 billion USD.

Just prior to this new shareholding, Japanese Ministry of Transport officials, responding to a tip, searched MMC's headquarters and found documents detailing unreported customer complaints. The company's officials denied accusations that the company had hidden customer complaints. Twelve days later, on July 18, the company admitted it had failed to report customer complaints and announced it would recall 514,000 cars and trucks as well as offering to check others. It said it expected costs of the recall to total 5 billion JPY (47.6 million USD).

An even greater impact on the company resulted when Daimler/Chrysler renegotiated the price of its shareholding down to 1.9 billion USD.

In August MMC admitted that it had systematically hidden complaints from authorities for more than twenty years and in several cases repaired vehicles secretly. The company announced more recalls, bringing the number of vehicles it recalled or offered to check close to one million. This included 200,000 vehicles overseas. The cost of the recall was now estimated at 7.5 billion JPY. The Chief Executive Kawasoe admitted to having no knowledge of the cover-up until internal investigations submitted their findings to the government.

The Economist reported on August 26 that MMC's management had been insisting that there was no cover-up, but that Kawasoe subsequently admitted that the company had deliberately failed for more than twenty years to pass on to the transport ministry reports of faults in cars, buses, and trucks. Internal investigation revealed that the cover-up was part of a deliberate management policy, since recalls were considered humiliating by MMC, due to the fact that Japan's auto manufacturers are recognized for producing vehicles of superior quality and durability. At this point Kawasoe said, "Unfortunately I have no option but to admit that the report reflects a truly regrettable state of affairs at our company," and he went to the transport minister's office to present the company's report and bowed "for nearly a minute at the most humble angle, the 45-degree bottom-of-the-barrel bow." This followed the tradition of exorcising wrongs with a public apology.

Kawasoe insisted he would not resign over the scandal and blamed a lack of respect for rules and regulations on the part of company officers and employees as the cause of the state of affairs. Despite the fact that MMC managers ordered a change in procedures in 1997, the departments in charge of complaints reverted to its illegal ways soon thereafter. Three directors were aware of the practice of hiding customer complaints. By the end of August, representatives from MMC's major shareholders (CEOs of Mitsubishi Heavy Industries, Bank of Tokyo-Mitsubishi, and Mitsubishi Corporation) met with Kawasoe and insisted on Kawasoe's resignation so as to take responsibility for the scandal. Investigators revealed that MMC had kept dual sets of records on customer complaints on its computing systems, one for the authorities and one to be hidden.

In October, MMC established an internal Quality Issues Action Committee, which formulated an action plan to raise quality levels in development, production, sales, after-sales service, and all other processes in order to prevent a reoccurrence of the situation.

In early February 2001 criminal charges were laid against nine of MMC's current and former managers, including Vice Presidents Saturo Toyama and Hikoichi Motoyama. No charges were laid against former CEO Katsuhiko Kawasoe.

In the same month, MMC announced a further recall affecting 1.35 million cars—401,106 in Japan and 950,000 in the U.S.—at an estimated cost of 17 billion JPY and reported its biggest anticipated net loss of 200 billion JPY for the year ending March 31, 2001. Sales figures continued to decline for the fifth consecutive month. In an attempt to reduce its debt of 1.2 trillion JPY by 2002, MMC also announced a reduction in its workforce by 9,500 over three years, a reduction in the number of models produced from twenty-four to twelve, and the closure of a car manufacturing plant.

MMC's organisation was based on the keiretsu model, with 48.51 percent of the shareholding retained by companies aligned with MMC (Table 1). A separate audit committee usually undertakes the evaluation of the CEO's performance within Japanese companies, but Yasui (1998) argues that the committee usually consists of ex-employees or business partners. According to MMC's 1999 Annual Report, two of the current auditors were former directors. In addition there were four Statutory Auditors, including Takhito Tsuyuno, who was part of MMC International Car Operations as well as a director; Yasutoshi Shizukawa, who was part of the MMC Services Part Division as well as a director; and Tsuneo Wakai, who was a senior advisor of the Bank of Tokyo Mitsubishi.

Ron Bevacqua, chief economist at Commerz Securities in Tokyo, was quoted in the *China Daily* (2000) as saying that the scandal appeared to "highlight Japanese management's ingrained tendency to give short shrift to the interests of outsiders, whether shareholders or consumers."

Gaston (2001) draws attention to the resistance by self-interested groups of "insiders" as a key force in explaining the slow pace of change in the structure of Japanese corporate governance.

Firm	Percent
Mitsubishi Heavy Industries	23.85
Mitusbishi Ltd	8.39
Bank of Tokyo-Mitsubishi Ltd	4.67
Mitsubishi Trust and Banking Corp.	3.16
Mitsubishi Jiko Employees Shareholding Assoc.	2.20
Pension Fund, Mitsubishi Trust and Banking	1.94
Mitsubishi Jiko Torihiksaki Shareholding Assoc.	1.09
Mitsubishi Materials Corp.	0.98
Mitsubishi Estate Co. Ltd	0.76
Mitsubishi Electric Corp.	0.76
Mitsubishi Chemical Co.	0.71

Table 1. Firms aligned with Mitsubishi Motors Company that hold shares of the company, and the percentage held.

MMC's internal report on the crisis raised four areas in which improvement is needed: corporate ethics, compliance, corporate governance, and the insular way in which the company was run. Kawasoe said in August 2000 that "There was an atmosphere in which employees felt that to issue a recall would be embarrassing." There was no recognition that the defects concealed would give consumers a poor experience with the motor vehicles concerned.

With Mitsubishi Motors we do believe the explanation comes down to a peculiarly Japanese characteristic, the issue of losing face. This apparently stemmed from an older view of corporate responsibility, that the company's own interests were paramount. However, it is also true that the strategy maintained the company's profitability. It is possible to argue that this case really stems from a corporate culture that had not changed in twenty years and that the system of corporate governance also dated from that period.

The weighing in of the board and its committees of internal representation made it hard for outside influences to generate change.

Conclusion

To answer the three questions posed at the beginning of this paper, in all three cases there is evidence of "disaster myopia"; that is, failure to recognize the signs of impending disaster because the probability of a big shock from the source was considered minimal. Second, there is evidence of cognitive dissonance in the consistent manner in which early warning signs were ignored. Third, only the Mitsubishi case exhibits the "loss of face" issue as a key player in the scenario. As the cover-up began more than twenty years earlier, it is possible to argue that this case belongs to an era where Japanese corporate governance may well have been distinctive. The Sumitomo and Daiwa cases are indistinguishable from cases in Western economies and suggest that the problems of corporate governance exposed by these cases are universal.

References

Abegglen, James C. 2001. Japan's Industries and Companies: Economic Dynamism and Social Continuity," in Freedman 2001.

Atkins, David H. 1995. "Corporate Governance: Lessons from Abroad." *Canadian Business Review* (September 22), http://static.highbeam.com/c/canadianbusinessreview.

Burgett, P., and T. Furukawa. 1996. "Sumitomo's Copper Crisis Deals Aftershocks." *American Metal Market* (June 17): 1.

Charkham, J. 1998. *Keeping Good Company*. Oxford: Oxford University Press.

China Daily. 2000. "Mitsubishi Motors Promises Clean-Up" (August 28): 5.

Chua-Eoan, H., and E. W. Desmond. 1995. "Lending a Hand to Godzilla." *Time* 146(18) (October 30).

Economist, The. 1996. "Sumitomo's Metal Fatigue." *Economist* 339(7971) (June 22).

Freedman, Craig, ed. 2001. *Economic Reform in Japan: Can the Japanese Change?* Cheltenham: Edward Elgar Publishing.

Fukao, Mitsuhiro. 1998. "Japanese Financial Instability and Weaknesses in the Corporate Governance Structure." *Seoul Journal of Economics* (Winter): 381–422.

Futatsugi, Y. 1990. "What Cross Shareholdings Mean for Corporate Management." *Economic Eye*, 17–18.

Gaston, Noel. 2001. "Comment on 'Can the Japanese Change?': Organizational, Psychological and Evolutionary Perspectives," in Freedman 2001.

Gilson, R., and M. Roe. 1993. "Understanding the Japanese *Keiretsu*: Overlaps between Corporate Governance and Industrial Organization." *Yale Law Journal* 102: 871–906.

Goldstein, Marc. 1998. "Pressure for Shareholder Returns Sparks Change in Japanese Governance." *Directorship* (July/August): 11–14.

Hamada, Koichi. 2001. "Can the Japanese Change? Organisational, Psychological and Evolutionary Perspectives," in Freedman 2001.

Jones, Randall S., and Kotaro Tsuru. 1997. "Japanese Corporate Governance: A System in Evolution." *The OECD Observer* (February/March).

Kim, Kenneth A., and P. Limpaphayom. 1998. "A Test of the Two-Tier Corporate Governance Structure: The Case of Japanese Keiretsu." *The Journal of Financial Research* 21 (Spring): 37–51.

Miles, Lilian. 1998. "Corporate Governance in Japan: An Overview and Evaluation." *Business Law Review* (March).

Murasawa, Yoshihisa. 1998. Changing Corporate Japan." *Far Eastern Economic Review* (May 7): 29.

Prowse, Stephen D. 1996. "Corporate Finance in International Perspective: Legal and Regulatory Influences on Financial System Development." *Federal Reserve Bank of Dallas Economic Review* (third quarter): 2–15.

Sakaiya, Taichi. 1996. *Isoshiki no Seisui (The Rise and Fall of Organisations: What Determines the Destiny of Corporations?)* PHP; Bunko.

Sheard, P. 1989. "The Main Bank System and Corporate Monitoring and Control in Japan." *Journal of Economic Bahaviour and Organisation* 11: 399–422.

Shuichi, Ito. 2000. "The Changing Corporate Climate in Japan." *Japan Economic Foundation Journal* (March–April).

Tsuru, Kotaro. 2000. "Japanese Corporate Governance in Transition." *Seoul Journal of Economics* (Fall).

Weston, Rae. 2003. "The Sumitomo Copper Fraud: Were There Signs?" *Academy of Legal, Ethical and Regulatory Issues Proceedings* (April).

———. 2004. "The NAB Foreign Currency Option Losses in the Context of a Disaster Myopia Model." Second Emerging Markets and Services in Asia-Pacific Conference, Sydney, May.

Yasui, T. 1998. "Corporate Governance in Japan." *OECD Conference on Corporate Governance in Asia: A Comparative Perspective*. Seoul (March 3–5).

The Author

Rae Weston is Professor of Management at the Graduate School of Management, Macquarie University, Sydney, New South Wales 2109, Australia. E-mail: rae.weston@mq.edu.au.

THE PETROLEUM INDUSTRY AND REPUTATION: DEVELOPMENTS IN CORPORATE REPUTATION OVER THE PERIOD 1990–2002

Susanne van de Wateringen
University of Amsterdam, Netherlands

Abstract

A good reputation is one of the most valuable assets a company can have. A problematic reputation can hinder companies in their performance. In competitive markets where products differ little in price, technology, or availability, reputation can make a difference. Petroleum companies are frequently associated with environmental issues such as oil spills and climate change. Since environmental performance rankings remain inconclusive due to methodological shortcomings, those issues may affect the sector's reputation. This paper examines whether the observation of a problematic reputation for multinationals in the petroleum sector is sustained by empirical data for the period 1990–2002. Taking in account methodological limitations, the analysis shows two downward trends for all companies, indicating a common reputation effect. The effect of catalyst events is observed for individual companies. However, the contribution of the paper is not only empirical. Conceptually, the results show the complexity of measuring the multidimensional concept of reputation, as well as the importance of the reputation commons, catalyst events, and a reputation mechanism.

Introduction

Most companies consider a good reputation a valuable asset.[1] A good reputation attracts investors and highly qualified employees; it lowers access barriers to resources and assures continuation of operations in times of difficulty. A good reputation can make the difference in competitive markets when products are hardly differentiable in price, technology or availability. A problematic reputation can hinder companies in their market performance. Petroleum multinationals are frequently associated with environmental issues that may affect their reputation negatively. Examples of topics that have gained negative media attention are oil spills and specific environmental issues such as climate change. The ultimate theme around which those topics revolve is environmental performance. However, methodological shortcomings hinder conclusive rankings, and data from sector initiatives are kept confidential. Performance results therefore cannot provide a definite answer to the perceived reputation debate.

 pp. 119–144

This paper therefore examines whether empirical data sustain the observation of a problematic reputation for the petroleum sector in the period 1990–2002. It presents a review of the reputation literature and discusses the availability and quality of a range of reputation rankings. Subsequently, the empirical data of a selection of rankings are analysed and discussed; suggestions for further research are formulated.

The Petroleum Industry and Issues of Reputation

Petroleum companies are frequently associated with negative media attention on environmental issues, such as oil spills and the debate on climate change. The occurrence of oil spills during tanker transport may be the issue that is most familiar to the general public.

Table 1 presents an overview of twenty major accidental oil spills since 1967.

Table 1. Twenty major accidental oil spills (ranked by volume)

Year	Ship name	Location	Spill*
1979	*Atlantic Empress*	Off Tobago, West Indies	287000
1991	*ABT Summer*	700 nautical miles off Angola	260000
1983	*Castillo de Bellver*	Off Saldanha Bay, South Africa	252000
1978	*Amoco Cadiz*	Off Brittany, France	223000
1991	*Haven*	Genoa, Italy	144000
1988	*Odyssey*	700 nautical miles off Novia Scotia, Canada	132000
1967	*Torrey Canyon*	Scilly Isles, UK	119000
1972	*Sea Star*	Gulf of Oman	115000
1980	*Irenes Serenade*	Navarino Bay, Greece	100000
1976	*Urquiola*	La Coruna, Spain	100000
1977	*Hawaiian Patriot*	300 nautical miles off Honolulu	95000
1979	*Independenta*	Bosphorus, Turkey	95000
1975	*Jakob Maersk*	Oporto, Portugal	88000
1993	*Braer*	Shetland Islands, UK	85000
1989	*Khark 5*	120 nautical miles off Atlantic Coast of Morocco	80000
2002	*Prestige*	Off the Spanish Coast	77000
1992	*Aegean Sea*	La Coruna, Spain	74000
1996	*Sea Empress*	Milford Haven, UK	72000
1992	*Katina P.*	Off Maputo, Mozambique	72000
1989	*Exxon Valdez*	Prince William Sound, Alaska, USA	37000

*tonnes.
Source: International Tanker Owners Pollution Federation 2003.

Some of the spills in the list caused little or no environmental damage, which is probably why their names are less familiar to the general public. The *Exxon Valdez* spill[2] is very well known but ranks only about number thirty-five on the list (ITOPF 2003). The accident involving the tanker *Erica* (December 1999) does not rank in a list of top spills; its release was 20,000 tonnes, which is considerably less than the large spills. However, this does not necessarily mean that its environmental impact was small. The spill from the tanker *Jessica*, which was stranded near the Galapagos Islands (January 2001), received a lot of media attention because of its location, but the spill was "only" ninety tonnes. In this case, favourable wind and currents prevented the spill from having graver consequences (Moss 2001).

The second example concerns climate change, or global warming.[3] Climate change is a direct impact of the petroleum industry because the most important greenhouse gas (carbon dioxide) is predominantly generated by burning fossil fuels, the industry's primary product. The American Petroleum Institute (API) categorized the technical issues of climate change into seven themes relevant for the sector: emissions estimating and reporting, operational processing techniques, participation in government programs, carbon sequestration, research and development, automotive partnerships, and renewable fuels and alternative energy supplies (American Petroleum Institute 1999). According to CERES, at least fourteen governance actions may be required before companies address climate change in a pragmatic and profitable way (CERES 2003). Although academic research shows that companies have made considerable shifts in their strategic position on climate change (see, e.g., Levy and Kolk 2002), the industry is heavily criticized for its response; some NGOs summarize it in five D's: deny, delay, divide, dump, and dupe (see TRAC 1999).

Environmental performance is the theme around which the above issues revolve. Unfortunately, environmental performance measurement still suffers from a range of methodological shortcomings. The most important difficulties result from an inconsistency in indicators—a lack of agreement on what should be measured. Limited access to data, its availability, and the specific interests of researchers result in further limitations. This makes comparison of conclusions between rankings hard (for a complete discussion, see Mauser 2001 and Bennet and James 1999).

Environmental performance rankings for the petroleum sector provide valuable insights, such as the fact that European companies seem to outperform US companies (Oekom Research 2003), and the conclusion that companies could lose up to 6 percent of their shareholder value as a result of environmental risks (Austin and Sauer 2002). However, those rankings also suffer from the limitations already mentioned. Oekom Research, for example, has experience in the analysis of investment risk analysis and emphasizes the use of double-hull tankers and investments in renewables (Oekom Research 2003). The World Resources Institute quantifies the financial impact of two issues that are signaled as the greatest challenges to the industry in the coming decade: climate change policies and access to reserves (Austin and Sauer 2002).[4] *Management & Excellence*, to take another example, did not release information on its methodology, which makes it hardly possible to interpret the results (*Management & Excellence* 2003). The ultimate illustration of the methodological difficulties is found in the overview of environmental performance rankings made by Ilinitch, Soderstrom and Thomas; they compare eight rankings, showing that the results are dependent on focus (Ilinitch, Soderstrom, and Thomas 1998).[5]

In addition, rankings that are made on basis of a range of criteria (as investment companies usually do it) are not often available in the public domain; they are often kept confidential because of commercial use (e.g., rankings by *Financial Times* Business or by the Energy Intelligence Group). According to Elkington, Fennell, and Stibbard, the industry's group of five (ARCO, BP, Conoco, Shell E&P, and Statoil) have been working on benchmarking techniques in this area for several years; Royal Dutch Shell has already developed core sets of key performance indicators and has been involved in setting the GRI guidelines (Elkington, Fennell and Stibbard, 1999). In 2002, the industry lobby group OGP published a summary of sector performance for the first time.[6] The aim of OGP's reporting system is to increase transparency concerning its operations, in response to shareholders and other stakeholders' wishes. However, the data represent only participating companies and OGP membership, except for a summary of cumulative absolute figures for 2001. Furthermore, OGP declares that reports contain gaps of information in many cases (as the average of only seven countries per company illustrates); data are mentioned to be non-representative of global OGP member performance (OGP 2002). Comparison over years and regions is thus impossible. As of yet, therefore, OGP does not increase transparency with its initiative; the status quo is a lack of comparability between company reported data.

A consequence of the present inadequacy of performance rankings is that improvements in performance are hard to prove. The lack of a definite answer keeps the reputation debate alive. Although companies consistently claim to have made changes in their environmental management efforts, allegations of "greenwash" and "window dressing" continue to be made.[7] Some CEOs address this kind of negative publicity and opinions quite explicitly in their annual and environmental reports; they speak of poetry, trust, and long-lasting commitment (Fig. 1). As there is not yet a definite resolution of the performance debate, it is important to examine the developments in reputation for the petroleum sector, with a focus on the period 1990–2002.

Reputation: A Multidimensional Construct

According to Hall, reputation is an increasingly important intangible asset (Hall 1993; Hall 1992). It can make the difference between buying a product from one company and another. Especially when product differences in terms of price, availability, and technology are small, reputation can be pivotal in decision-making. As Fombrun puts it, it seems unchallenged that a positive reputation is an unalloyed asset for performance: "reputations . . . matter because they create value" (Fombrun 2001: 293). But what exactly is a reputation?

A reputation accumulates over time and need not reflect a company's competence. According to Davies, corporate reputation consists of knowledge and feelings of individuals about the performance of a corporation in a particular field. A clear reputation means that an entity is expected to behave consistently and therefore predictably in certain circumstances (Davies et al. 2003:75). According to Hall (1992), reputation consists of two aspects: fame, which can be bought by advertising spending in the short term; and esteem, which has to be earned, usually over a longer period of time. Image is how the company is perceived by the public, while reputation is the sum of all of the images owned by its stakeholders (Brady 2002b). Furthermore, one should distinguish between corporate brand image (the name and logo of a company) and corporate reputation itself.

Fombrun, Gardberg, and Sever made an integrative definition of corporate reputation as "a collective representation of a firm's past behavior and outcomes that depicts the firm's ability to render valued results to multiple stakeholders" (Fombrun, Gardberg, and Sever 2000: 242). According to Brady, key characteristics consist of seven elements, which together represent a "useful, stand-alone hitlist" but cannot necessarily be measured (Brady 2002a, b):[8] (1) knowledge and skills; (2) emotional connections; (3) leadership, vision, and desire; (4) quality; (5) financial credibility; (6) social credibility; and (7) environmental credibility. According to Brady, reputa-

Figure 1. Overview of company statements related to window dressing.

Repsol (1) "All public debates on the environmental effect of human activity should be based on information and trust. With its 1997 Environmental Report, Repsol wishes to contribute in strengthening both these principles."	Conoco (2) "Vision without reality, of course, is not a sustainable proposition. And in today's increasingly interconnected world, there are many complex and even conflicting realities that Conoco must be responsive to in order to meet the expectations of its stakeholders."	Chevron (3): "In everything we do at Chevron, we strive to be "Better than the Best." This is not just a slogan but the basis for a detailed and deeply held operating philosophy."
Total (4) "People are often unfamiliar with our challenging front-line initiatives, which may sometimes have been overshadowed by such distressing events as the sinking of the *Erika* and the AZF disaster in Toulouse, France. However, a careful review . . . reveals that we were committed to sustainable development well before the concept began garnering broad media coverage. But we cannot afford to sit on our laurels."	Statoil (5): "Some dismiss our statement of corporate responsibility and contribution to sustainable development as cheap window dressing, aimed more at changing perceptions than at improving reality. But any substantial gap between words and deeds is not sustainable for long. There is no place to hide in today's interconnected world. A good reputation can only be created and maintained by results. Corporations must walk the talk. Otherwise they will have to pay."	Petrobras (6) "When we say that social responsibility today is part of our business, we are not merely poetic, and even less romantic."
ExxonMobil (7) "Our commitment to this value is not motivated by simple altruism or an effort to 'look good' in the public eye. It stems from sound business reasons and is backed by a significant investment of time, money and planning."	Exxon (8) "Our performance, consistently among the best in the industry, was obscured by the accidental grounding of the Exxon Valdez. This event, caused by human error, led many to forget the extent of Exxon's environmental commitment."	Shell (9) "Our commitment to contribute to sustainable development is not a cosmetic public relations exercise. We believe that sustainable development is good for business and business is good for sustainable development."
RepsolYPF (10) "A permanent attitude of cooperation and transparency in its dealings with public administrations and local communities. In this way, the oil and gas business constitutes a source of opportunity rather than conflict."	Texaco (11) "While this review is new, Texaco's commitment to dealing responsibly with environment, health and safety issues is not."	BP (12) "During 2002, the business world remained under intense scrutiny. . . . While such scrutiny can help to build greater trust in businesses, I believe that the lasting guarantees of corporate probity lie within a company rather than outside it: in its people, values, and behaviour. This Review therefore reiterates 'what we stand for.'"
Shell (13) "We had looked in the mirror and we neither recognised nor liked what we saw. We have set about putting it right, and this report is a small manifestation of widespread action taking place across the Group."	ARCO (14) "Many people have their doubts about oil companies' commitment to protecting the global environment. . . . If there were any doubts about ARCO's commitments in this area, I'm pleased to welcome you to this important publication by noting that, quite simply, our vision is to be a leader in providing clean energy. . . . We at ARCO are confident that we can make that vision a reality."	

(1) A. Cortina, Chairman and CEO (1997), "Environmental Report"; (2) Conoco (2002), "Conoco Sustainable Growth Report," p. 6; (3) Kenneth T. Derr, CEO in Chevron (1996), "Protecting People and the Environment: The Chevron Way"; (4) T. Desmarest, Chairman and CEO (2002), "Total: Sharing Our Energies. Corporate Social Responsibility Report 2002"; (5) Olav Fjell, CEO, in Statoil (2001), "The Future Is Now. Statoil and Sustainable Development"; (6) P. Reichstuhl, President, in Petrobras (2000), "Social Report"; (7) L. Raymond, President and Chairman, and L. Noto, Vice-Chariman, in ExxonMobil (2000), "Safety, Health, and Environment Progress Report: The People Behind the Commitment"; (8) L. Raymond, President, and L. Rawl, Chairman, in Exxon (1990), "HSE Progress Report"; (9) Sir P. Watts, Chairman of the Committee of Managing Directors (2002), "Meeting the Energy Challenge: The Shell Report 2002"; (10) A. Cortina, Chairman and CEO (2001), "Environmental Report 2001"; (11) J. W. Kinnear, President and CEO (1990), "Environment, Health, and Safety Review"; (12) Lord Browne of Madingley, Group Chief Executive (2002), "Environmental and Social Review 2002"; (13) Shell (1998), "Introduction in Profits and Principles: Does There Have to Be a Choice?" p. 2; (14) M. R. Bowlin, Chariman and CEO (1998), "ARCO Environment Health and Safety Report."

tion builds on performance, transparency, and trust, as perceived by both internal as well as external stakeholders. Brady adds that only the financial credibility element seems to be tangible, although such elements as environmental and social performance have the potential to have a significant impact on overall reputation. This tangibility barrier is reflected in the complexity of empirical operationalization, which is discussed later.

Reputation is the sum of images, that is, of perceptions of diverse (stakeholder) groups, and builds on a diversity of elements. Each stakeholder group (e.g., end consumers, shareholders, business to business, government, and employees) or market (capital, consumer, labor) has its own interest in a specific aspect of reputation. Reputation is a therefore a multidimensional construct. This multidimensionality is also reflected in the literature concerning reputation. Besides its relation with financial performance (e.g., Davies et al. 2003; Heugens 2001; Koch and Cebula 1994), reputation is frequently treated as an outcome variable, perceived from a legal or economic perspective (see, e.g., Jones and Rubin 2001; Karpoff, Lott, and Rankine 1998). Other topics are the relationship with the decision to enter into a joint venture (e.g., Dollinger, Golden, and Saxton 1997), intense media exposure (e.g., Wartick 1992; Fombrun and Shanley 1990), crisis (e.g., Zyglidopoulos 2001), corporate strategy (e.g., Fombrun 2001; Fombrun and Shanley 1990), studies from a corporate social responsibility perspective (e.g., Bowen, 2000; Fombrun, Gardberg, and Barnett 2000), and studies on reputation and issues management (Davies et al. 2003; Van Tulder and Van der Zwart 2003; King, Lenox, and Barnett 2002; Heugens 2001; Hoffman and Ocasio 2001).

Several of these results are important for the present study. To start with, the effect of media exposure on reputation has been found to be of a complex nature. Fombrun and Shanley (1990) found that more media exposure negatively affected corporate reputation, independent from the (positive or negative) tone of the media exposure. Wartick (1992) found that intense media exposure is significantly associated with changes in corporate reputation. He states that generalizations about the relationship should be tempered. The amount, tone, and recentness of the exposure appear to be associated with different dimensions of changes in corporate reputation. In addition, the relationships seem to vary depending on the initial level of corporate reputation. His results show that only companies with "poor" reputations show significant associations between positive media exposure and changes in corporate reputation. Companies with "good" and "average" reputations do well to devote resources toward an increase of exposure without the intention to influence the tone of the exposure (Wartick 1992).

With regard to reputation management, several observations are important. According to Davies et al. (2003), the secret to success (loosely defined as effective reputation management) lies in the linkage of the internal, employee view of the company and the external, customer view of the company. Reputation management involves harmonizing the emotional attachment of those two stakeholder groups, and that harmony produces the financial value. In other words, an understanding of corporate reputation means linking image and identity (Davies et al. 2003; see also Heugens 2001).

This perspective can be extended to the unit of analysis and to the stakeholder group involved. The unit of analysis for reputation management is not only the firm itself but also the sector of the industry in which it operates. King, Lenox, and Barnett point to the reputation commons problem, meaning that firms within an industry often find themselves "tarred by the same brush": in case of accidents or events, the whole industry is held responsible (King, Lenox, and Barnett 2002). Accident severity with respect to environmental damage has a significant negative impact on a firm's reputation (Zyglidopoulos 2001). Hoffman and Ocasio define an event as a critical trigger of institutional transformation and industry evolution, which must become the focus of public attention to have this effect. Whether an event receives industry-level attention depends on either outsiders holding the industry accountable for the event, or insiders' internal concerns with the industry image. Furthermore, an event can be transformed into a critical issue for an industry if outsiders contest the accountability for the event and its enactment, or if there are internal contradictions and challenges to an industry's identity (Hoffman and Ocasio 2001).

Ferguson, Deephouse, and Ferguson point to the importance of strategic groups, which can have different reputations (Ferguson, Deephouse, and Ferguson 2000). This concept seems related to the reputation commons concept. According to King, Lenox, and Barnett, a "reputation commons" is likely to occur when stakeholders have difficulty differentiating firms but have the ability to sanction them. They propose that firms may solve the reputation commons problem by reducing that sanctioning ability and by "privatizing reputation." Providing information, though costly, would be a means of differentiating from other firms (King, Lenox, and Barnett 2002). However, the way firms provide information can also lead to the creation of an issue. An example is the change of the name of British Petroleum to Beyond Petroleum, which was met by fierce campaigning.

Thus, if a company crosses a certain limit, this can lead to demonstrable damage and, as a consequence, to corrective measures by which stakeholders judge the company and that can affect its reputation. Disciplinary activities of the company to act on issues are self-initiatives such as voluntary reporting. The dynamics of corrective measures taken by stakeholders and the disciplinary activities of companies form the reputation mechanism. This mechanism indicates the limits of corporate responsibility (Van Tulder and Van der Zwart 2003).

Van Tulder and Van der Zwart discern several factors that influence the size of the impact of the reputation mechanism: the interest of the media, the strength of the NGO, the relation of a company to its government, the political agenda and economic importance of the countries where the issues are raised and played out, the complexity and maturity of the issue, the ethical position of stakeholders, the chance of a domino effect, and the first reaction and cleanness of the company involved (Van Tulder and Van der Zwart 2003). They find a differentiated response for a range of stakeholder groups (grouped by the capital market, labor market, and consumer market on which they operate): this represents a hierarchy in the reputation mechanism. The results show that corrective measures have a stronger effect on the consumer market and the capital market.

In the *consumer market*, the effect depends on specific market segments and specific stakeholder groups. The effect is mainly indirect, takes effect through large stakeholders, and persists for a long time. Demonstrable damage is suffered by companies with *icon-value* that produce corporate brands for business-to-customer markets, especially when they focus on a lifestyle image. The *capital market* turned out to be most sensitive for reputation damage in the short term. In general, prices drop more in reaction to negative publicity than they rise as a consequence of a company's action. An interesting phenomenon occurs when issues recur. On the one hand, recurrence can lead to a smaller reaction from stockholders, because the company's response was found satisfactory the first time and a reservoir of goodwill has built up. On the other hand, recurrence can result in a negative effect; it can be perceived as evidence of "guilt," leading to a drop in prices. The change in the stockholder configuration that resulted from the first conflict can also lead to a reversed effect. Less ethical stockholders may not appreciate giving way to societal pressure and respond negatively when a company does so, resulting in a large impact on the capital market. More ethical stockholders may have used their exit- or voice-option at the time of the event and can no longer react by selling their shares, resulting in a small effect upon recurrence. The *labor market* seems to be affected the least; there is little evidence that employees take collective action (Van Tulder and Van der Zwart 2003).

Review of Existing Measures

The measurement of reputation is a difficult task: questions of measurement, validity and causality are likely to dominate reputation research in the coming years (Fombrun 2001). This section first presents an overview of eight surveys on reputation in general. Subsequently, it gives attention to surveys oriented specifically to corporate reputation with regard to social and environmental issues. In both discussions, attention is given to pros and cons of the different rankings and their methodologies. Furthermore, suggestions are made for further analysis.

Overall Reputation

Fombrun, Gardberg, and Sever (2000) reviewed eight survey instruments on basis of the date of their first publication, the sample of companies, the respondents, and the number and content of criteria used. A summary of their conclusions appears in Table 2. According to Fombrun, Gardberg, and Sever, academics "routinely acknowledge many limitations to the data." Inconsistent findings are blamed on methodological shortcomings attributable to measurement issues. The difficulty, however, of developing a more valid database of corporate reputational ratings is also recognized (Fombrun, Gardberg, and Sever 2000: 242).[9]

Fryxell and Wang also indicate that measurement is a vexing problem, especially in research streams such as corporate social responsibility. Their criticism of the Fortune reputation index is that a single dominant factor underlies the database: financial

Table 2. Survey instruments most commonly used (ordered by date of first publication).

Survey	Date	Sample of firms	Mailing list	Criteria
Fortune America's Most Admired Companies (AMAC)	1984	Before 1995, Fortune 500 largest US manufacturers. 1995 and after, 1000 largest US service and manufacturing firms by revenue.	Expanded from 3000 to 10,000 corporate executives, directors and securities analysts. Climbed from 32 (1990) to 57 (2000) industry groups.	Respondents rate companies in own sector on eight criteria and "all stars," voting across industry lines.
Manager Magazine (MM)	1987	100 largest German manufacturing and service firms.	2000 managers from two levels of corporate hierarchy.	Rate overall reputation and rank on five attributes.
Management Today (MT)	1991	Britain's ten largest public companies in each of 26 sectors.	Boards of directors of >250 top companies and expert analysts at 10 leading investment banks.	Nine criteria.
Asian Business (AB)	1992	50 largest (turnover) companies from country of respondent, and high profile Macs in the region.	8600 senior executives, CEOs, and corporate brand managers randomly selected from subscribers.	Nine criteria, and ranking of nine attributes in order of importance.
		Company lists are divided into lists of 30 to be surveyed in 9 Asian countries.*		
Far Eastern Economic Review (FEER)	1993	Across 11 countries, 90 top-ranking non-Asian MNCs Ten largest Asian-based, as ranked in home markets.	6000 business executives randomly selected from subscribers in 11 Asian countries** and from five leading Asian business magazines in local languages.	Six criteria; 60% response rate.
Financial Times (FT)	1994	Before1998, Europe's Most Respected Companies. 1998 and after, World's Most Respected Companies. Based on FT 500 and other databases.	3500 CEOs from publicly traded, state-owned enterprises and subsidiaries, and private companies in 53 countries in 1998; 4000/70 in 2000. Survey by FT and PWC.	Nominations on the basis of eight criteria. Ranking by expected future attributes, and whether expected to be most respected in future. Response rates vary per sector, averaging 18%.
		Responses weighted by GDP of respondent's home country.		
Industry Week (IW)	1996 (1st) 2000 (last)	100 Best Managed Companies on basis of IW 1000 list; world's largest manufacturers based on turnover.	40–95 international expert panelists involved and own editors.	12 performance criteria. Multi stage nomination and voting process.
Fortune Global Most Admired Companies (GMAC)	1997	Basis in Fortune Global 500. Largest companies world revenue based, from 26 industries (2000), eliminating one country dominated companies.	Senior executives and outside directors each industry and financial analysts. Survey by Fortune and Hay group.	Nine criteria. Questions similar to Fortune's AMAC.

Source: Adapted from Fombrun, Gardberg, and Sever 2000. Original source contained some fallacies that have been adjusted and updated in the present overview.
*Hong Kong, Indonesia, Japan, Malaysia, Philippines, Singapore, South Korea, Taiwan and Thailand
**Australia, Hong Kong, India, Indonesia, Japan, Malaysia, Philippines, Singapore, South Korea, Taiwan and Thailand.

performance. All items (except for corporate environmental responsibility) appear to be directly influenced by the respondent's perception of the financial potential of the firm. According to Fryxell and Wang, it is unlikely that a firm's specific capabilities can be sufficiently discriminated from its reputation for financial prowess to be usable. Their conclusion is that reputation as measured by the Fortune index speaks most directly to reputation as a good investment. Non-investment-related implications drawn from the data would be beyond the domain of measurement. Furthermore, Fryxell and Wang indicate that this limitation also influences the survey item that relates to corporate environmental responsibility: "We believe this limitation also extends to the single CER [corporate environmental responsibility] item in the Fortune index, as the evidence presented here shows that it is also subject to a combination of mono-method bias and financial distraction" (Fryxell and Wang 1994: 11).

In addition to those measurement problems, Fombrun, Gardberg, and Sever conclude that similarities across the surveys far outweigh the differences among them. Financial and management items are leading, which confirms the investor bias of the surveys. Social and employee items appear less frequently, and ethics appears only once. They find two keys biases: (a) "They lack content validity by focusing on the perceptions of a limited respondent pool of corporate leaders and financial analysts," and (b) "Survey items do not capture the perceptions of multiple stakeholder groups that are necessary for a valid measure of corporate reputation" (Fombrun, Gardberg, and Sever 2000: 248).

The importance of this conclusion is underlined by the empirical case-based observations of the reputation mechanism described above. They indicate that the consumer market shows the most enduring impact on reputation, while the impact of issues on the capital market is short-lived and, in addition, subject to reconfiguration in the shareholder population. However, the ratings are derived from a population of respondents consisting mainly of individuals selected on basis of their responsibilities in/to the capital market and not their individual consumer status. This may bias the conclusions in that the observed effects are smaller than they would be, following the dynamics of the reputation mechanism, if the general (consumer) public were involved in the survey,

Three of the rankings were selected for further analysis. These are the *Financial Times* ranking and both the Fortune rankings: America's Most Admired Companies (AMAC) and Global Most Admired Companies (GMAC). They were selected for two reasons. Firstly, their basis sample includes the large international companies based in the US and Europe, which are the focus of this study (large MNCs). Secondly, the data are available over the longer period of time covered by this study. Data from other rankings were considered but are less applicable because of methodology and sampling.

For the general rankings, data are analyzed for the period 1990–2002, but the precise period differs across rankings: AMAC 1990–2002, GMAC 1997–2001, and 1994–2002 for *Financial Times*. The sample for both the Fortune rankings consist of the companies included in the Fortune 500 list for 1995 under the sector code "petroleum refining." The *Financial Times* survey uses a category named "energy/chemicals" or "oil, gas, and mining." It includes an extended but similar group of companies.

Companies engaged in petroleum refining activities but not included in the graph are usually not named in the ranking. One of the reasons for not being ranked is of course that a company has a reputation that, in comparison with other companies, is not good enough and results in exclusion. Another reason may be that the company has other activities that comprise most of its business. Merged companies continue under their new name, or adopt the name of the acquiring company. Graphs are presented for the rankings studied, showing company development over the years. All of the surveys in the selected sample generated several lists, including for example a sector ranking, an overall ranking, and a specific issue ranking. The disadvantage of these rankings is the lack of information on how close non-listed companies were to being ranked in the top ten, twenty-five, or fifty.

Environmental Reputation

Notwithstanding the remark of Dollinger, Golden, and Saxton (1997) that "if reputation is indeed multidimensional, researchers should be able to manipulate dimensions independently in a decision-making framework," measurement of environmental/social reputation proves to be a difficult process as well. Three ratings or indexes of some scale have been found.[10] Those are considered to be the most objective and come closest to the goal of measuring the perception of environmental reputation. They are listed in Table 3, which indicates their date of first publication, sample of firms, mailing list characteristics, and selection criteria.

The first and oldest rating, the Domini 400 Social Index or KLD, was "created to serve as a benchmark for socially and environmentally conscious investors. The index attempts to track the performance of primarily large-cap US companies broadly representative of the market in which the typical socially responsible investor would invest." The purpose of the second rating, the Dow Jones Group Sustainability Index (DJGSI), is "to provide a benchmark for financial products based on the concept of corporate sustainability and to measure the performance of fund managers." The third index presented, FTSE4Good, aims to be an "objective global standard for socially responsible investment." The indexes are composed of several dimensions that are selected as representative elements of sustainability. Unfortunately, this may lead to a bias in the results discussed later.

Brown and Perry adjusted the Fortune reputation index. They statistically removed the financial performance halo from Fortune's (America's) Most Admired Companies in order to produce a measure of reputation for corporate social performance (Brown and Perry 1994, 1995). The calculations (which required access to large data sets and computer resources) were performed on the first issue reporting data for 1982 through 1991. This leads to an interesting new data source on corporate social performance. Unfortunately the data are of a different period than those studied here. Time constraints, lack of data access, and other complications (for comments, see Baucus 1995; Logsdon and Wartick 1995; Sodeman 1995) prevent a repetition of the study; preference is therefore given to comparing the other methods. Single-issue ratings of Fortune are not particularly informative because of the halo effect.

Table 3. "Environmental" reputation/sustainability indexes (ordered by date of first publication).

Survey	Date	Sample	Mailing list	Criteria
Domini 400 Social Index (DSI 400) (KLD)	1990 first of its kind	Compiled by Kinder, Lydenberg and Domini & Co Ltd. (KLD). S&P 500 filtered through a number of traditional social screens, plus 150 non S&P 500. US firms only. Published several times a year.	Created by KLD. All dimensions equal weight. Some industries excluded from participation (alcohol, tobacco, gambling, nuclear power and weapons industry).	Community relations, employee relations, environment, product, treatment of women and minorities, military contracts, nuclear power and South Africa involvement (until 1993).
Dow Jones Sustainability Group Index (DJSGI)	1999 and 2001 (Eur. version)	300 companies, represent the top 10% of the leading sustainability companies in 59 industry groups in 33 countries covered by the biggest 2500 companies in the Dow Jones Global Index. Reviewed annually and quarterly.	Created by DJ. One composite index (DJSI World) and five narrower indices, excluding alcohol, gambling, tobacco, armaments and firearms, or all of those. Plus a European set.	Economic, social-ethic and ecological performance. Review process: (1) Industry group classification, (2) corporate sustainability assessment, (3) ranking within industry groups, (4) Eligible industry groups, (5) eligible companies, (6) component selection, (7) market capital coverage.
FTSE4Good	July 2001 Adj. Sept. 2002	To qualify for consideration, company must be constituent of the FTSE Developed Index or the FTSE All-Share Index. Continuous updating.	Created by FTSE. 4 benchmark indices: FTSE4Good UK, Europe, US and global index. Some industries (tobacco producers, conventional or nuclear weapon manufacturers/ operators) are excluded from access to those indexes.	Criteria to include constituents focus on the positive efforts of companies in three areas: environmental sustainability, social issues and stakeholder relations, human rights. Assessed against a variety of indicators.
		Only companies identified as operating in businesses of strategic importance in countries with the poorest human rights records are assessed for the human rights issue. Extractive industries (mining, oil and gas) operating in developing countries are considered highly strategic.		

Sources: www.domini.com/DSEF.html, www.sustainability-indexes.com, www.ftse4good.com. All consulted November 2002.

All three indices were studied as part of the empirical analysis. Unfortunately, these data have limitations, due to the sampling method and the short time series. For example, the oldest index of its kind is the KLD/DSI 400 ranking, but unfortunately it is oriented at US firms only. Furthermore, it must be said that the indexes are not exclusively oriented to environmental reputation. For one thing, they include several dimensions outside the environmental field, and secondly, they are based on perceptions as well as numerical data. This disturbs the perception-based construction of reputation used in the other rankings and in this study.

For these reasons, an additional survey from *Financial Times* (FT) was added. This survey was conducted along with FT's usual reputation survey and distinguished two groups of respondents. Data were available for two years only, 2001 and 2002.

Empirical Results: Overall Reputation and Environmental Reputation

This section presents an analysis of the reputation survey results of petroleum companies over the period 1990–2002. Both general reputation and the issue-specific environmental reputation are considered for companies in the petroleum sector. The analysis gives attention to the impact and/or occurrence of a reputation commons effect, the effect of catalyst events, company-specific issues, and the reputation mechanism.

Overall Reputation

The first results discussed here are those of the oldest ranking, America's Most Admired Companies (AMAC), which focuses on American companies. It is based on a sample from the Fortune 500 and the Fortune Service 500. Two graphs are presented, a graph of the top ten within the sector (Fig. 2) and a graph of the position of the petroleum companies in the whole sample (Fig. 3). A higher score in Figure 2 represents a better reputation. Some general observations are worth making. Firstly, all lines move in the same direction over the period: stability is observed in the relative positions of most companies. Secondly, two waves of downward trends are noted for most of the companies during the period: the first improvement is observed about 1994 and, after a decline in 1995/1996, again at the end of the period beginning in 2000. Company-specific observations include the new entries Tosco and Unocal, the speedy rise of BP America, and the disappearance of USX from the top ten. Further-

American Petroleum Companies (AMAC)
Sector of Industry Position 1990–2001

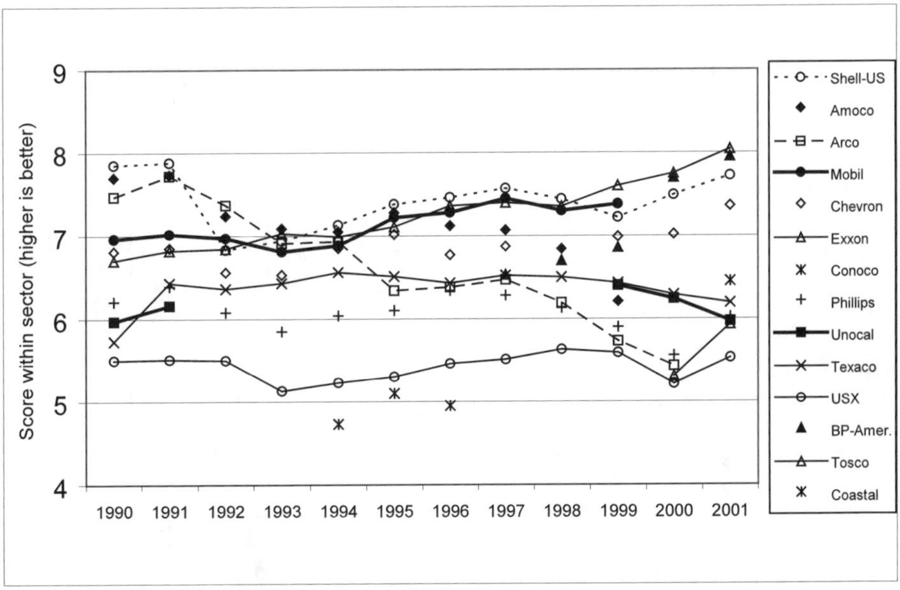

Figure 2. American Petroleum Companies: industry sector scores (AMAC)

more, ExxonMobil climbed back to a first position in the sector, after its fall in the beginning of the 1990s after the *Exxon Valdez* spill.

In the second AMAC-based graph, a company's reputation gets better as it gets closer to the horizontal axis. The graph shows the position of selected petroleum companies in the total sample of about 450 companies over the period 1990–2001. The listing for the years 1998–2001 has been put together on basis of the indexes published; for the other years Fortune did publish the overall positions. The most important overall observation here is that the companies tend to score better at the beginning of the period than at the end, although they fall into two groups: one group that continued to score rather high on reputation (including Shell Oil US, Exxon, BP America, and Chevron), and another group that steadily declined. The generally negative trend in rankings means that even although the companies stick together in respect of their scores (within-sector stability, as shown in the previous graph), companies from other industries started to "interfere" with the overall ranking. The company-specific results mentioned earlier are even more strongly evident in this graph: ExxonMobil fell from sixth position in 1989 (not shown) to 110th position in 1990 because of the ExxonValdex spill. It climbed back to the tenth position in 2001. Some companies lost much of their position in the ranking over the years, for example Atlantic Richfield (Arco), Occidental Petroleum (Oxy) and USX, which moved from 29 to 386, 271 to 443, and 252 to 360, respectively.

Fortune's other ranking (from 1997 onward) is the Global Most Admired Companies (GMAC).[11] It is based on a sample of the Global 500. Figure 4 shows company positions within the sector. In this graph, the higher the score, the better the reputation of the company. An overview of the reputation ranking of the global petroleum companies again shows the stability of the within-sector ranking. Only a few lines

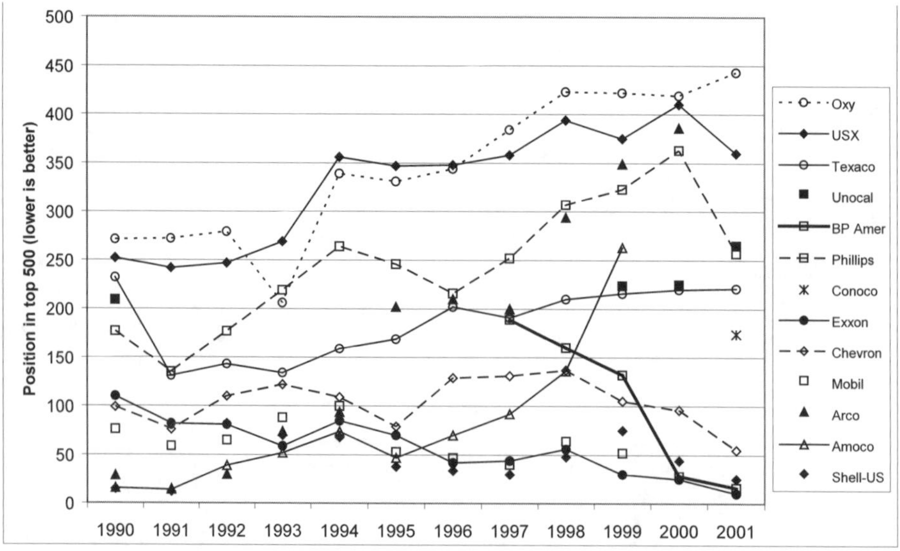

Figure 3. Overall ranking of American petroleum companies (AMAC 1990–2001)

cross one another. Three groups can be observed: one continuing the upward trend that started in 1999 (including Shell Group, ExxonMobil, BPAmoco, and Chevron), a second staying in the middle (TotalFinaElf, Conoco), and a third going down. Company-specific observations include the entrance of Asian companies such as Sinopec and SK. Indian Oil and Ssangyong both have a one-time appearance during the period. It is interesting to observe that Chevron climbed steadily following the merger of Chevron and Texaco, while Texaco was steadily decreased in the rating. Other rankings made by Fortune on the basis of this global sample show that petroleum companies are sometimes the best in a certain category, such as ExxonMobil for financial soundness in 2002, but are more often mentioned as national champions. In the "All Stars" top twenty-five or fifty list of Fortune, which is based on voting across sectors, the petroleum companies rarely come forward.[12]

A third ranking generated by the *Financial Times* analyzed Europe's most respected companies prior to1998, and the World's most respected companies from 1998 onward. The basis of the ranking is a sample consisting of the top twenty-five companies from six to nine countries, beginning with the FT 500 list of largest publicly quoted companies and including other databases. Two graphs are presented: one showing the sector position, and one showing the overall position of the companies in the top twenty-five to fifty of the sample.

The lower the score in the first graph, the better the company's reputation. The large MNCs engaged in petroleum refining and thus important for this study were included in two categories, as constructed by *Financial Times*: "Energy/Chemicals" and "Oil, Gas and Mining." The graph shows the results for companies categorized by Fortune as petroleum refining (standard industry code=31) on basis of the majority of their activities, which results in only a few data. A top three were presented by

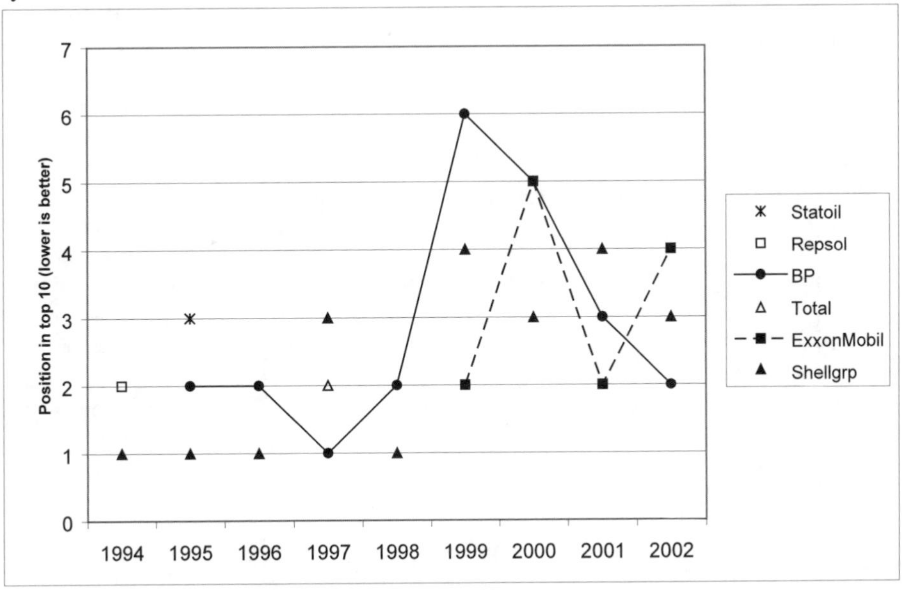

Figure 4. Oil company ranking in sector top 10 (FT, 1994–2002)

Financial Times until 1998, a top fifteen from 1998 onward (only a top ten for 2002). The most important observations are that after the inclusion of non-European companies, ExxonMobil entered the listing in the highest position, losing it to Shell Group in 2000, regaining it in 2001, and losing it again in 2002. BP climbs steadily on the sector list. Shell fell after the Brent Spar/Nigeria incident in 1995 to a third position in 1997 (which measures reputation over the previous year) and steadily declined in the ranking (overall and sector specific). Further, petroleum refining companies take only three positions of the top fifteen when combined with chemical companies, indicating worse (though stable) positions of the sector under study here.

Figure 6 is a second graph based on the *Financial Times* data. It shows the position of the petroleum companies within the overall top twenty-five, thirty, fifty, or sixty, depending on what is shown by FT. The lower the score, the better the company's reputation. What is striking is the relatively small amount of petroleum companies present in this group. A common trend of declining ranks in the AMAC after 1995 can be observed here as well (with the exception of BP), but this is based on only a few observations. The Shell Group shows a downward trend in the overall listing but seems to improve its position after 2001, as do BP and ExxonMobil.

Financial Times comments in 1995 that the financial performance of companies in this top group displays extreme variety (not shown). This suggests, according to FT, that European managers' perceptions of business excellence are far from identical to those of investors. The FT also notes that Shell ranked fifth in the top thirty and had nearly twice as many appearances in the list as second place company BP (in

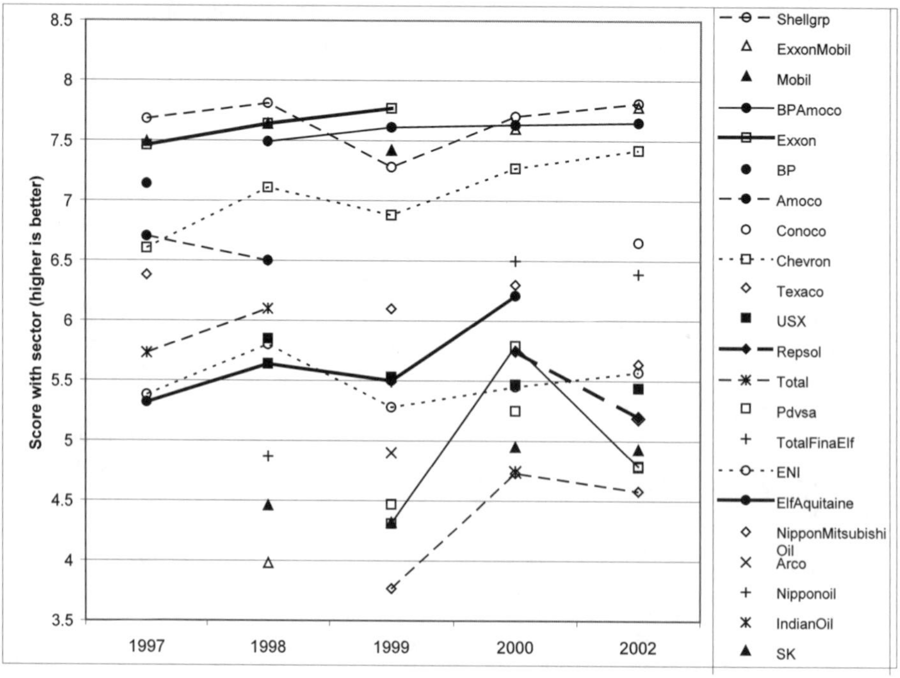

Figure 5. World petroleum companies: industry sector scores (GMAC 1997–2002)

fifteenth position). In 1996, the FT comments that the findings suggest that reputation rankings seem to depend on the ability to achieve sustained success by adopting long-term strategies, while adjusting quickly to changing market conditions: "The findings suggest that companies which score well on these criteria can ride out short-term reverses or blemishes to their reputation." The striking finding in this context is that Shell was named as the company dealing best with environmental issues, despite the controversy over the disposal of its Brent Spar oil rig. In 1997 however, Shell came in eleventh, which may be explained as a delayed reaction to the controversy. FT finds an explanation in the continuous bad publicity for Shell involving the Brent Spar environmental controversy and human rights in Nigeria, while BP has improved its reputation, has a so-called "visionary" leader,[13] and has dramatically improved its performance (FT 1997). However, BP disappeared from the list the following year, returning to a much lower position in 1998. All together, a declining reputation is signalled for the sector in comparison to companies from other sectors. A slight improvement can be observed after 1999.

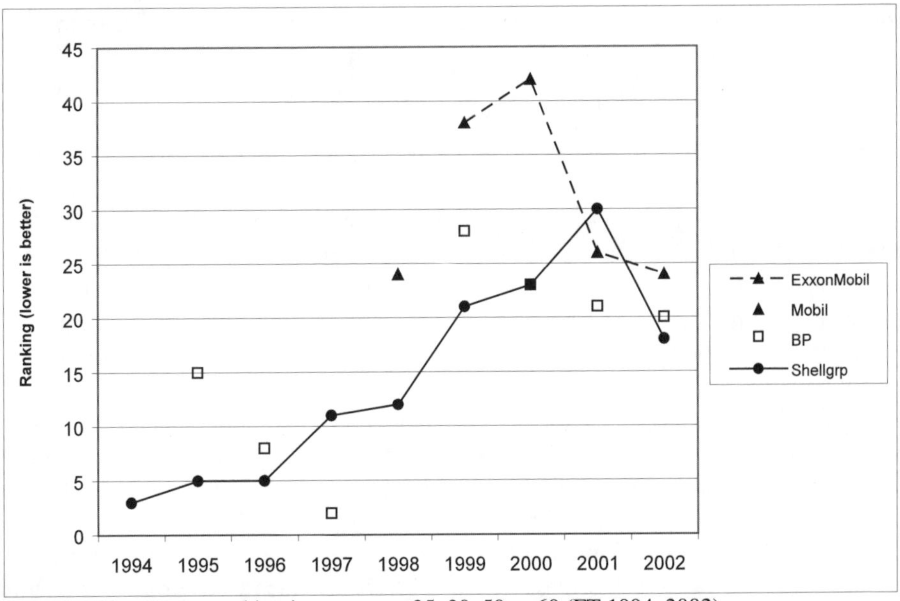

Figure 6. Oil company ranking in sector top 25, 30, 50 or 60 (FT 1994–2002)

Petroleum Companies and "Environmental" Reputation

The most important result from the KLD/DSI 400 ranking included in the 2002 list on the World Wide Web (as of October 2002) is that no single company of the ones ranked[14] is part of the Fortune sample. The original S&P 500 sample of US firms on which the index is based includes twenty-three energy companies, of which ChevronTexaco, ConcocoPhillips, ExxonMobil, Marathon Oil (formerly known as USX), Occidental Petroleum, and Unocal are part (S&P500, December 2002). Some of them make it to the other environmental rankings. However, none of them made it into the

Domini social/environmental ranking (Domini 400 Social Index, October 2002); it seems they were outperformed by other companies.

The FTSE4Good consists of several rankings: a European-based, US-based, and global ranking. The European top fifty list of June 2001 includes two oil and gas companies that "have passed the selection criteria with regards to environmental sustainability, relationships with stakeholders and supporting universal human rights." Those two are BP and Royal Dutch petroleum. The US top fifty list mentions no petroleum company, while the FTSE4Good Global's Top 100 (as published October 30, 2002) includes BP (sixth), Totalfinaelf (fifteenth), and Royal Dutch Shell Group (seventeenth)[15] (FTSE4Good Index Series 2002).

The third ranking, the Dow Jones Sustainability Index, lists the Shell Group as the leader of its sector for both the European and the World list published in 2002. The energy group mentioned in the index comprises several aspects of the energy chain: gas utilities, pipelines, oil drilling equipment and services, and oil, gas, and coal companies. Among the fourteen companies mentioned for the World Index (2002) are BP, Norsk Hydro, Shell Group, Shell Canada, Statoil, Suncor Energy Inc., Nexen, and Woodside Petroleum, which is waiting in line. BP and the Shell Group may be found in the European list (Dow Jones Sustainability Indexes 2002).

Some final, interesting results can be derived from an additional survey conducted by *Financial Times*. In 2001 and 2002, the *Financial Times* included out an issue-specific item on environmental reputation alongside its reputation survey, the results of which can be added to the three previous rankings. The survey distinguished two groups of respondents: CEOs, and media commentators and NGOs (Fig. 7). Only a few petroleum companies are included in both years and both groups. The list is much longer for CEOs, for which a top thirty and top forty-seven are presented, than for media commentators and NGOs: a top twenty and top eight, respectively. FT elaborates neither on this nor on the choice to combine NGOs and media commentators in one group.

For 2001, a remarkable consensus is observed on BP's number one position, with Shell ranking second for the CEOs and fifth for the NGOs. For 2002, BP is ranked third by the NGO group but still first by the CEOs. It is equally remarkable that Exxon is not ranked by NGOs, and is ranked seventeenth (2001) and ninth (2002) by the CEOs. For 2002, the NGO/media group includes the same companies as for 2001, although they are ranked slightly lower. The CEOs include more companies than in the previous year; TotalFinaElf and Petrobras are new on their list. An extraordinary entry in both lists is Greenpeace, which now appears next to its direct opponents. This NGO is ranked fourth by the NGOs and fifth by the CEOs.

Financial Times comments that the media and NGOs would choose less internationally known companies (*Financial Times* 2001). The empirical data from Van Tulder and Van der Zwart (2003) confirm this observation: the reputation mechanism is stronger for icon-companies, leaving the non-icon companies the better reputation scores. Other FT comments are:

> The general public thinks ExxonMobil did well for its consumers, they liked ExxonMobil even though it is a favourite target of the environmental move-

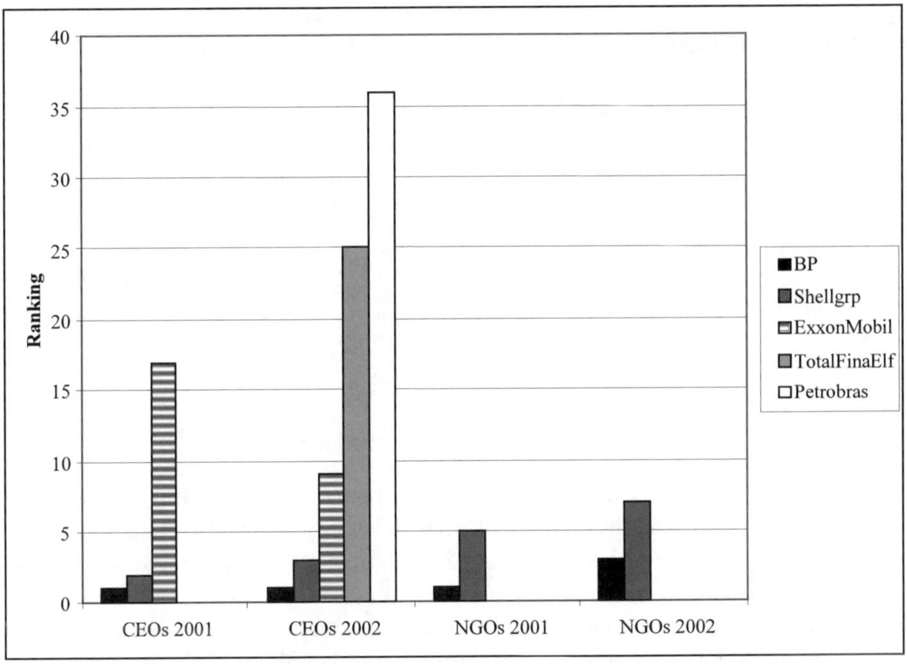

Figure 7. Environmental ranking of oil companies in top 40 by CEOs and top 10–20 by NGOs (FT 2001, 2002)

> ment. The environmentalists do not dislike all oil companies. The media and NGOs put BP at the top of their list of companies best managing environmental resources. Shell is in fifth position. Exxon did not make it into their top 20. The chief executives polled also put BP first. They put Shell 2nd and ExxonMobil 17th. The greens oppose ExxonMobil because of what they see as its unwillingness to help confront global warming. The CEOs, on the other hand, respect ExxonMobil for the practical steps it has taken since the *Exxon Valdez* disaster (*Financial Times* 2001).

FT concludes that the chief executives may occasionally have a better feel for public opinion than the NGOs. Other explanations are that NGOs chose to take a more extreme political stance to achieve their goals, or that the public just does not consider environmental issues to be a part of the consumer value it places on ExxonMobil.

Another company-specific conclusion the *Financial Times* draws is that BP is successful in its reputation management on environmental issues: "BP has definitely got its message across. The oil group, a leader in one of the most potentially harmful industries, has been voted not only by chief executives but also by activist groups and the media as the company that does the most to protect the environment." With regard to the sector, *Financial Times* observes that thirteen companies, of the top twenty most-respected companies overall, fail to appear in the chief executives' list of the most environmentally friendly companies. This casts doubt on whether the business world yet regards environmental performance as crucial to evaluating corporate success and reputation. For 2002, the difference is smaller; fifteen of the top twenty companies appear in the CEO environmental ranking. In 2001, the most commonly cited criteria of what constitutes good environmental management are (1) The development of and investment in cleaner greener products and processes (both CEO and NGO polls), (2) clearly defined environmental strategy/code, (3) external communication about ethical behavior/services and products (*Financial Times* 2001). In 2002, developments in environmental technology are again an important factor in explaining company nominations. This may also be the reason why the 2002 ranking is again dominated by engineering, energy, and chemical companies, which are responsible for the majority of the environmental impact. The cynical explanation is that those companies have developed the most sophisticated communication techniques on environmental performance. Another explanation is that some companies have been justly praised for improving performance.

Concluding Remarks and Further Research

In view of the frequent negative association of the petroleum sector with environmental issues, and inconclusive environmental performance rankings, this paper examines the developments in reputation for the petroleum sector in the period 1990–2002. The contribution of the paper is both conceptual as well as empirical. Its conceptual contribution consists of a review of the reputation literature, which shows the multidimensionality of the concept for diverse groups of stakeholders. This, in combination with the intangibility of certain components of reputation, lies behind the methodological complexity of measurement. Other important findings are the reputation commons effect, catalyst events, strategic groups, and the reputation mechanism; these are reflected in the empirical findings as well. The empirical contribution further shows the developments in corporate reputation for the petroleum industry over the period 1990–2002. Attention is given to both "overall reputation" and "environmental reputation"; a total of seven sets of data were analyzed.

With respect to overall reputation, the relative positions amongst companies in the sector appear to be relatively stable. The analysis shows two downward trends for all companies, indicating a reputation commons effect. Companies seem to have scored better at the beginning of the period than at the end, resulting in two strategic groups: one that continued to score high, the other steadily declining. In the case of Exxon and Shell, catalyst events affected company-specific reputations. Although a slight improvement is observed in 1999, a declining reputation is seen for the sector as a whole in comparison to other sectors.

With respect to environmental reputation, fewer data were available, and methodological issues remain. The ratings are not oriented solely toward environmental issues, and some of them include numerical data; this means they are not purely perception-based as the overall rankings were. Considering the economic and political importance of the sector, relatively few companies, primarily European, are present in the ratings. The additional *Financial Times* survey was administered only in 2001 and 2002; its main contribution lies in tracking the effect of different opinions among different groups of stakeholders. NGOs make different lists than CEOs. Another remarkable result is the large difference in how CEOs rank companies environmentally and overall. This might indicate that the former is not perceived as crucial in the evaluation of corporate success.

The most important comment on the results is that measurement difficulty hinders reliable operationalization. Present methods are biased toward financial indicators. In addition, different stakeholder groups are not well represented. The results for environmental reputation show the difference in opinion between different groups of respondents. Considering the hierarchy in the reputation mechanism, this may have affected the results. Moreover, only few and mixed data were available on environmental reputation, for which indexes were only recently developed. A second comment is that companies' reputation results may suffer or benefit from a reputation commons problem. If one company meets with an incident, all companies are blamed for a long time. Since some companies did not improve their operations as much as others, incidents and stories will remain and influence the reputation of all companies in the sector. Furthermore, operations are difficult, and even with high standards it is hard to keep incidents to a zero level. A third comment is that reputation change may suffer from a time lag. It takes a split-second to cause long-lasting damage to a reputation but years to build one.

Considering the methodological limitations, the empirical results confirm that both the overall and environmental reputations of the sector are indeed problematic. Changes in reputation are observed for the same period in which the changes in environmental management are. This means that a correlation between changes in environmental management and reputation is possible. However, further research is needed, firstly, to gain more insights into what lies behind a company's changes in reputation among various groups, and secondly, to examine the relationship between reputation and strategic environmental management. To achieve the latter, changes in environmental management at both the sector and the company-specific level must be examined. If one takes into integrative approaches to reputation management (see Davies et al. 2003), this requires a systematic examination of strategic and structural elements of environmental management. These include codes of conduct, publication of environmental reports, implementation of international standards and environmental management systems, and aspects of monitoring.

Notes

1. This paper has appeared, in an adjusted format, in the dissertation "The Greening of Black Gold: Towards International Environmental Alignment in the Petroleum Industry." For more information, please examine the author's website: www.vandewateringen.com.

2. The *Exxon Valdez* tanker ran aground March 24, 1989, in Alaska's ecologically sensitive area of Prince William Sound. The company was not prepared for the crisis, and its perceived arrogance resulted in public outrage. Lawrence Rawl, the company's chairman at the time, left subordinates to manage the crisis. So far the company has spent \$3.5 billion on cleanup, rehabilitation, and compensation. More than 11,000 Alaskans received \$300 million totally from the company,

voluntarily and immediately after the accident. However, compensation on punitive damage has not been settled to this day [September 2003](McNulty, 2003).

3. The Intergovernmental Panel on Climate Change (IPCC) estimates that a doubling of effective carbon dioxide levels could lead to an increase of temperature of 1.7 to 4.2 degrees Celsius. Scientific uncertainty exists with regard to the precise whereabouts of ocean circulation, behaviour of clouds and regional impacts of global warming (IPCC 2001). Notwithstanding, it is acknowledged by more than 180 countries that precautionary action is needed. They worked together in drafting the Kyoto protocol, which commits developed countries to reduce their greenhouse gas (GHG) emissions to 5.2 percent below 1990 levels by 2010. The Protocol will likely go into force; but probably without the participation of the United States.

4. The methodology of the study defined access to reserves by the proportion of reserves falling into environmentally sensitive areas (partly defined by the World Wildlife Fund). The methodology for the impact of climate change made use of five scenarios with changing variables for, e.g., quantities sold, production prices, and carbon permits. Some companies show competitive advantage in scenarios with increased emphasis on natural gas (Austin and Sauer 2002).

5. The rankings are: (1) The Council on Economic Priorities Corporate Environmental Data Clearing House Reports (CEP-CEDC), a within-industry ranking based on TRI emissions; (2) CEP-TRISIZ, which is CEP's CEDC within-industry ranking based on TRI emissions standardised by total sales; (3) Investor Responsibility Research Center's (IRRC) Spill Index, which is based on total number of oil and chemical spills; (4) IRRC Compliance Index, which is based on total penalties assessed under various environmental and regulatory acts; (5) IRRCs Efficiency Index, which is based on total TRI emissions; (6) Binary Scores, the mean of five binary process variables, including whether the company uses TQEM, has a written environmental policy, includes environmental factors in executive compensation formulas, performs internal environmental audits, and the reporting level of the company's top environmental officer; (7) Frank R&D, Franklin Research and Development Corporation's Rating; and (8) CEP Shop, CEP's *Shopping for a better world* (1990) rating (Ilinitch, Soderstrom, and Thomas 1998: 397).

6. Five indicators are used in the OGP project: emissions to air, aqueous discharges, discharges of oil-based and synthetic drilling fluids on cuttings, accidental spills, and energy consumption. Data have been collected on an annual basis over four years using common definitions; twenty-six companies participate and submitted data for an average of seven countries each.

7. Some NGOs, for example, mimic a company's annual report layout to address their concerns on company's practices. Examples are "Failing the Challenge. The Other Shell Report 2002" by (amongst others) Friends of the Earth (FOE) and "BP Annual Report 2002" by London Rising Tide, a UK-based network against climate change. Examples of their biting criticism: "We congratulated Shell eight years ago for committing itself to sustainable development. But the shocking reality is that for many communities . . . little has changed." "What matters to these communities is not what the company says in glossy brochures" (Friends of the Earth 2003: 3). And: "Please accept our sincere apologies if you detect at any time an absence of the smooth, reassuring tone that is usually a trademark of our style." "Our desire to deliver outstanding performance is matched only by a determination to give the impression of taking positive action. This demonstrates that BP is a sophisticated operator that knows how to balance our core investors' wish for a long-term commitment to oil extraction with the simple petrol consumer's need for guilt soothing clichés" (London Rising Tide 2003).

8. The list is the result of both a combination and an extension of the Fortune list and the Reputation Quotient, which are discussed later.

9. Fombrun, Gardberg, and Sever (2000) themselves developed the Reputation Quotient, a reputation construct that puts emphasis on its multidimensionality in a combination of two factors: emotional and rational appeal. A second study that developed a new reputation measure is found in Deephouse (2000). He developed a more theoretically informed version of the concept, by integration of mass communication and resource-based theories. The result is Media Reputation, defined as the

overall evaluation of a firm represented in the media (Deephouse 2000). A third recently developed tool to measure corporate reputation is the Corporate Personality Index. It measures customers as well as employees' perspectives of reputation and claims to be applicable on other stakeholders as well. It builds on seven dimensions: agreeableness, enterprise, competence, chic, ruthlessness, machismo, informality (Davies et al. 2003: 150). Socially responsibility is an aspect of integrity, which is categorized under agreeableness. Data are not available for the period this study examines.

10. Other indexes are often performance-based, such as the two indexes set up in the Netherlands: the ASN Trouw Index and the Triodos Sustainability Index (Van Tulder and Van der Zwart 2003). Some concentrate on one moment of observation such as the Better World Investment Guide published by the Council on Economic Priorities in 1991 (Prentice Hall) or on philanthropic activities instead of on environmental issues (e.g., Corporate 500 Directory of Corporate Philanthropy published by the Public Management Institute San Francisco). Again others, such as the Green Oscars are part of NGO campaigns to "show the world how hard business is working to achieve sustainable development." "Oscars" are awarded for "Best Director: the greenest-acting CEO," "Best Make-Up: to the company that makes up facts," and so on (www.earthsummit.biz, consulted August, 2002).

11. GMAC was not published in 2001. The change was made so that the list would coincide with AMAC publication.

12. Fortune shows its critical stance by its reflections on the position of Enron in this list: "Speaking of falling from grace, Enron, no. 25 last time [2001], also disappeared from the All-Stars list [2002]. . . . 'No company illustrates the transformative power of innovation more dramatically than Enron,' we wrote last year. Never mind. We meant 'fiction,' not 'innovation'" (Fortune 2002).

13. In the FT survey, John Browne, CEO of BP, has been among the top ten most respected business leaders for several years in a row. In that top thirty, he is the only CEO leading a petroleum company. The automotive sector, in contrast, has five companies in the 2001 list.

14. Ranked are Anadarko Petroleum Corporation, Apache Corporation, Devon Energy Corporation, EOG Resources Inc., Equitable Resources Inc., Noble Affiliates Inc., and Sunoco Inc.

15. Shell Transport & Trading Co. is an independent company but related to the energy sector. It turns up in several of the environmental rankings: in both the FTSE4Good Europe and global and also in the DJSGI.

References

American Petroleum Institute. 1999. *Climate Change. Voluntary Actions by the Oil and Gas Industry,* A conference on industry best practices to improve energy efficiency and to reduce greenhouse gas emissions, Houston, December 1–2, 1999.

Austin, D., and A. Sauer. 2002. *Changing Oil. Emerging Environmental Risks and Stakeholder Value in the Oil and Gas Industry*. Washington: World Resources Institute.

Baucus, M. S. 1995. "Commentary: Halo-Adjusted Residuals: Prolonging the Life of a Terminally Ill Measure of Corporate Social Performance," *Business and Society* 34(2) (August): 227–235.

Bennett, M., and P. James. 1999. "Key Themes in Environmental, Social, and Sustainability Performance Evaluation and Reporting," in *Sustainable Measures, Evaluation and Reporting of Environmental and Social Performance*, ed. M. Bennett and P. James. Sheffield: Greenleaf Publishing, 29–74.

Bowen, F. 2000. "Environmental Visibility: A Trigger of Green Organizational Response?" *Business Strategy and the Environment* 9: 92–107.

Brady, A. K. O. 2002a. "Corporate Reputation and Sustainability: Creating Value by Unifying Two Disciplines," *Ethical Corporation Magazine* (September), 26–27.

———. 2002b, *Profiling Corporate Imagery: A Sustainability Perspective*, research paper, Judge Institute of Management, University of Cambridge.

Brown, B., and S. Perry. 1994. "Removing the Financial Performance Halo from Fortune's 'Most Admired' Companies," *Academy of Management Journal* 37(5) (October): 1347–1359.

———. 1995. "Halo-Removed Residuals of Fortune's 'Responsibility to the Community and Environment—A Decade of Data,'" *Business and Society* 34(2) (August): 199–215.

CERES. 2003. *Corporate Governance and Climate Change: Making the Connection*, A CERES Sustainable Governance Project Report, Investor Responsibility Research Center, Boston (June).

Davies, G., R. Chun, R. Vinhas da Silva, and S. Roper. 2003. *Corporate Reputation and Competitiveness*. London: Routledge.

Deephouse, D. L. 2000. "Media Reputation as a Strategic Resource: An Integration of Mass Communication and Resource-Based Theories," *Journal of Management* 26(6): 1091–1112.

Dollinger, M. J., P. A. Golden, and T. Saxton. 1997. "The Effect of Reputation on the Decision to Joint Venture," *Strategic Management Journal* 18(2): 127–140.

Domini 400 Social Index. 2002. www.domini.com (October).

Dow Jones Sustainability Indexes. 2002. www.sustainability-indexes.com (October).

Elkington, J., S. Fennell, and H. Stibbard. 1999. "Oil Explorers," in *Tomorrow* 9(5) (September).

Ferguson, T. D., D. L. Deephouse, and W. L. Ferguson. 2000. "Do Strategic Groups Differ in Reputation?" *Strategic Management Journal* 21: 1195–1214.

Financial Times. 1994. "Europe's Most Respected Companies" (June 27).

———. 1995. "Europe's Most Respected Companies" (September 19).

———. 1996. "Europe's Most Respected Companies" (September 18).

———. 1997. "Europe's Most Respected Companies" (September 24).

———. 1998. "World's Most Respected Companies" (November 30).

———. 1999. "World's Most Respected Companies" (December 7).

———. 2000. "World's Most Respected Companies" (December 15).

———. 2001. "World's Most Respected Companies" (December 17).

———. 2002. "World's Most Respected Companies."

Friends of the Earth and Other Groups. 2003. *Failing the Challenge. The Other Shell Report 2002*, London.

Fombrun, C. J. 2001. "Corporate Reputations as Economic Assets," in *The Blackwell Handbook of Strategic Management*, ed. M. A. Hitt, R. E. Freeman, and J. S. Harrisson. Oxford: Blackwell Publishers Ltd, chap. 10.

Fombrun, C. J., N. A. Gardberg, and M. L. Barnett. 2000. "Opportunity Platforms and Safety Nets: Corporate Reputation and Reputational Risk," *Business Society Review* 105(1): 85–106.

Fombrun, C. J., N. A. Gardberg, and J. M. Sever. 2000. "The Reputation Quotient: A Multi-Stakeholder Measure of Corporate Reputation," *The Journal of Brand Management* 7(4): 241–255.

Fombrun, C. J., and M. Shanley. 1990. "What's in a Name? Reputation Building and Corporate Strategy," *The Academy of Management Journal* 33(2) (June): 233–258.
Fortune. 1990. "America's Most Admired Companies" (February).
________. 1991. "America's Most Admired Companies" (February 11).
________. 1992. "America's Most Admired Companies" (February 10).
________. 1993. "America's Most Admired Companies" (February 8).
________. 1994. "America's Most Admired Companies" (February 7).
________. 1995. "America's Most Admired Companies" (March 6).
________. 1996. "America's Most Admired Companies" (March 4).
________. 1997a. "America's Most Admired Companies" (March 3).
________. 1997b. "Global Most Admired Companies" (October 27).
________. 1998a. "America's Most Admired Companies" (March 2).
________. 1998b. "Global Most Admired Companies" (October 26).
________. 1999a. "America's Most Admired Companies" (March 1).
________. 1999b. "Global Most Admired Companies" (October 11).
________. 2000a. "America's Most Admired Companies" (February 21).
________. 2000b. "Global Most Admired Companies" (October 2).
________. 2001a. "America's Most Admired Companies" (February 19).
________. 2001b. "Global Most Admired Companies."
________. 2002. "Global Most Admired Companies" (March 4).
Fryxell, G. E., and J. Wang. 1994. "The Fortune Corporate 'Reputation' Index: Reputation for What?" *Journal of Management* 20(1): 1–14.
FTSE4Good Index Series. 2002. www.ftse4good.com (October).
Hall, R. 1992. "The Strategic Analysis of Intangible Resources," *Strategic Management Journal* 13(2) (February): 135–144.
________. 1993. "A Framework Linking Intangible Resources and Capabilities to Sustainable Competitive Advantage," *Strategic Management Journal* 14(8) (November): 607–618.
Heugens, P. P. M. A. R. 2001. *Strategic Issues Management: Implications for Corporate Performance*, ERIM Ph.D. Series Research in Management. Rotterdam: Erasmus University.
Hoffman, A., and W. Ocasio. 2001. "Not All Events are Attended Equally: Toward a Middle-Range Theory of Industry Attention to External Events," *Organization Science* 12(4) (July–August): 414–434.
Ilinitch, A. Y., N. S. Soderstrom, and T. E. Thomas. 1998. "Measuring Corporate Environmental Performance," *Journal of Accounting and Public Policy* 17 (1998): 383–408.
Industry Week. 1996. "The World's Best Managed Companies" (August 19).
________. 1997. "The World's Best Managed Companies" (August 18).
________. 1998. "The World's Best Managed Companies" (August 17).
________. 1999. "The World's Best Managed Companies" (August 16).
________. 2000. "The World's Best Managed Companies" (August 21).
International Tanker Owners Pollution Federation (ITOPF). 2003. *Oil Tanker Spill Statistics*.
IPCC. 2001. *Climate Change 2001, Synthesis Report*. Cambridge: Cambridge University Press.

Jones, K., and P. H. Rubin. 2001. "Effects of Harmful Environmental Events on Reputation of Firms," in *Advances in Financial Economics*, vol. 6, ed. M. Hirschey, K. John, and A. Makhija. Greenwich, Conn.: JAI Press, 161–182.

Karpoff, J. M., J. R. Lott, Jr., and G. Rankine. 1998. "Environmental Violations, Legal Penalties, and Reputation Costs," unpublished working paper, University of Washington Business School.

King, A. A., M. J. Lenox, and M. L. Barnett. 2002. "Strategic Responses to the Reputation Commons Problem," in *Organizations, Policy, and the Natural Environment: Institutional and Strategic Perspectives*, ed. A. J. Hoffman and M. J. Ventresca. Palo Alto, Calif.: Stanford University Press, chap. 17.

Koch, J. V., and R. J. Cebula. 1994. "In Search of Excellent Management," *Journal of Management Studies* 31(5) (September): 681–699.

Levy, D., and A. Kolk. 2002. "Strategic Responses to Global Climate Change: Conflicting Pressures on Multinationals in the Oil Industry," *Business and Politics* 4(3).

Logsdon, J. M., and S. L. Wartick. 1995. "Commentary: Theoretically Based Applications and Implications for Using the Brown and Perry Database," *Business and Society* 34(2) (August): 222–226.

London Rising Tide. 2003. *BP Annual Report 2002*. www.risingtide.org.uk.

Management & Excellence. 2003. "*Management & Excellence* Says Good Ethics Pay Off for Oil Companies," press summary (August).

Mauser, A. 2001. "The Greening of Business. Environmental Management and Performance Evaluation: an Empirical Study in the Dutch Dairy Industry," Ph.D. thesis, University of Amsterdam, Eburon, Delft.

Moss, N. 2001. "Galapagos Rue Lucky Escape," *Financial Times* (January 27/28).

Oekom Research. 2003. *Corporate Responsibility Industry Report, Oil and Gas*. München.

OGP. 2002. Summary of environmental performance indicators, paper 2001 data, London.

Sodeman, W. A. 1995. "Commentary: Advantages and Disadvantages of Using the Brown and Perry Database," *Business and Society* 34(2) (August): 216–221.

Transnational Resource Action Center (TRAC). 1999. *Greenhouse Gangsters versus Climate Justice*. San Francisco: TRAC.

Van Tulder, R., and A. Van der Zwart. 2003. *Reputaties op het Spel. Maatschappelijk Verantwoord Ondernemen in de Onderhandelingssamenleving*. Utrecht: Het Spectrum.

Wartick, S. L. 1992. "The Relationship between Intense Media Exposure and Change in Corporate Reputation," *Business and Society* 31(1) (Spring): 33–50.

Zyglidopoulos, S. C. 2001. "The Impact of Accidents on Firms' Reputation for Social Performance," *Business and Society* 40(4) (December): 416–441.

The Author

Susanne van de Wateringen is a Ph.D. candidate, Amsterdam Graduate Business School, University of Amsterdam, Roetersstraat 11, 1018 WB Amsterdam, Netherlands. E-mail: s.l.vandewateringen@uva.nl.

CORPORATE RESPONSIBILITY IN ADVERSE PECUNIARY EXTERNALITIES: THE CASE OF INTERNATIONAL AGRICULTURAL SUBSIDIES

Albino Barrera
Providence College, Providence, USA

Abstract

The United States, Europe and Japan provide farm subsidies at a rate of one billion USD per day. The bulk of this is captured by large corporate entities. Damage to less developed countries is extensive and deep. Besides the farmers who are harmed because of the resulting lower agricultural prices, these negative effects ripple through the rest of the economy, due to the central importance of the agricultural sector for developing nations. Besides being direct beneficiaries of these subsidies, farming corporations, including their ancillary support industries, have lobbied heavily to resist the growing international clamor to remove or at least substantially alter these subsidies. This paper examines the economics and ethics of international corporate responsibility on the issue of farm subsidies.

Industrialized nations have long insulated their agricultural sector from international competition through a variety of means such as quotas, tariffs, loans, guaranteed prices and subsidies. First World farmers would have otherwise been driven out of the production of certain crops in which developing countries have a comparative advantage. Moreover, industrialized country farmers have been spared from the vagaries of wild price swings in global food markets. However, such assistance to beleaguered farmers has come at the expense of Third World populations. The object of this paper is to use economic theory and moral philosophy together in assessing not only the nature but also the extent of corporate liability for the ill effects of international farm subsidies. After all, industrial and wealthy farmers have lobbied heavily for such farm support; they have been the biggest and the primary beneficiaries of such governmental assistance.

Ubiquity of Pecuniary Externalities

The notion of pecuniary externalities from economic theory and moral philosophy's principle of double effect can be effectively used together to ascertain the nature of corporate culpability for the ill effects of global farm subsidies. Pecuniary externalities are unintended consequences inflicted on third parties through the attendant price and

 pp. 145–156

quantity adjustments precipitated by exchanges in the marketplace. These inadvertent effects can be either positive (as in the case of cheap imports serving as a de facto increase in consumers' real incomes) or negative (as in the case of laid-off workers due to outsourcing or the flight of capital to overseas factories). Needless to say, the latter attracts more attention than the former because of the sudden and even catastrophic changes they can inflict on people's livelihoods and lifestyles. These market ripple effects do not arise solely because of globalization, or international trade for that matter. They are intrinsic to market exchange itself as we see in the impact of the Industrial Revolution on the Luddites in nineteenth-century England.

The unfettered market's principal strength is its much-vaunted approximation of allocative efficiency. No other social institution has thus far been able to replicate the market's unique capacity to allocate scarce resources to their most valued uses. Of course, at the heart of this process is the ability of price to convey enormous amounts of information efficiently and in a timely fashion across a wide variety of economic decision-makers. It is price that precipitates marginal but constant readjustments in economic agents' disposition of their goods or services. Consequently, the marketplace can be described to be in a never-ending state of flux as it moves toward the point of allocative efficiency that is itself continually shifting given unceasing changes in technology, organization and market characteristics.

Unfortunately, these unrelenting and unavoidable price and quantity adjustments produce both winners and losers, even in the most optimistic, but unlikely, scenario of an absolute improvement in the welfare of all parties in the exchange. International trade is paradigmatic of market operations, and it is best to illustrate this peculiar characteristic of market exchange using the Heckscher-Ohlin theorem of international trade theory. Countries (and, by extension, people) find it in their interest to trade if they are able to procure their needs from cheaper sources or to sell their produce for a better price. Such differentials in pre-trade prices are the proximate causes for gains from trade. Autarkic prices for the same good or service converge toward a single, uniform post-trade price given the unfettered market's "law of one price." Naturally, high-cost producers prior to trade will be hurt as they see a drop not only in prices but also a severe diminution, perhaps even complete loss, of their market share. Of course, the mirror image of these losses are the gains of low-cost producers who will see an increase both in their prices and customer base. An eloquent formulation of this attendant income redistribution to international trade can be found in the Stolper-Samuelson theorem, which concludes that in the post-trade regime, there is a real relative increase in the returns of the more abundant factor and a real relative decrease in the earnings of the scarce factor. Thus, there are winners and losers even in the most optimistic scenario of an absolute increase in the welfare of all trade participants because of concomitant changes in their relative standing. The overall size of the proverbial economic pie may be increasing with everyone getting a bigger share; nevertheless, the relative shares of the various slices of the pie are changing. In other words, there are always positive and negative collateral effects to any and all market exchange.

Nature of Corporate Liability

Applied to our current case, unfettered trade in global markets would ultimately drive out First World farmers from many agricultural activities since less developed countries enjoy a natural comparative advantage for most crops. It is precisely out of a desire to protect their farming sector from such adverse pecuniary externalities that many OECD nations have sought to provide governmental assistance to their distressed farmers; such farm support is extensive. As a group, the Organisation for Economic Development Co-operation and Development[1] (OECD) provides nearly $1 billion per day ($320 billion, 2000) to support agriculture (OECD 2003, Table III.12, 229). As a percentage of gross domestic product (GDP), this assistance amounts to approximately 1.2 to 1.3% for OECD. The European Union, Japan and the United States are among the biggest and the most aggressive in shielding their agricultural sectors. As a proportion of their GDP, their support runs to 1.3% (EU), 1.4% (Japan) and 0.9% (US).[2]

An alternative indicator of the extent of farm support is the extent to which farmers are dependent on governmental assistance in the form of higher prices and transfer payments. In 2000–2002, this public aid constitutes 35% (EU), 59% (Japan), 21% (US), and 31% (OECD) of farmers' total gross farm receipts (OECD 2003, Table III.3). Disparities between domestic and international food prices are another indicator of the degree to which governments intervene in markets. The ratio of the average protected domestic prices received by producers relative to the border (international) prices for the period 2000–2002 are as follows: 2.37 (Japan), 1.33 (EU), 1.13 (US), and 1.32 (OECD).[3] (Unfettered markets are subject to the "law of one price," producing an ideal ratio of one.) By whatever measure used, OECD public assistance to farmers is substantial.

Unfortunately, these protective measures precipitate their own set of harmful pecuniary externalities, borne principally by Third World farmers.[4] We will examine these injurious subsidiary effects in greater depth in the following sections. For now, it is sufficient to note that the industrialized countries' efforts to rectify the adverse ripple effects from the global food markets have themselves inflicted unintended costs on third parties, poor nations in particular.

Are these farm supports ethically permissible despite their ill effects since developed countries, or any country for that matter, owe primary responsibility to promoting the welfare of their own citizens? The principle of double effect provides an excellent framework within which to examine the ethics of this chain of unintended consequences.

The principle of double effect says that it is morally permissible to perform an act that has a bad effect under the following conditions:

> 1. *The act to be done must be good in itself or at least indifferent. . . .*
> 2. *The good intended must not be obtained by means of the evil effect. . . .*
> 3. *The evil must not be intended for itself but only permitted. . . .*
> 4. *There must be a proportionately grave reason for permitting the evil effect.*
>
> (Fagothey 1972: 32–33, original emphasis)

OECD agricultural farm subsidies satisfy the first three conditions. After all, providing assistance to their farmers is in itself not an evil act (condition #1), nor are the policy instruments employed to effect such farm support considered immoral per se (condition #2). Moreover, the harmful effects on Third World populations are not directly intended but are merely permitted as an unfortunate foreseen side effect of agricultural polices (condition #3). The last condition requires further examination and will be treated in greater depth for the rest of the paper. Ascertaining the proportion of good and ill effects of farm support relative to each other requires a set of standards itself. In what follows, I employ a non-exhaustive list of four criteria for examining such proportionality, to wit: justice as mutual advantage, justice as equal treatment, A. K. Sen's (1981, 1984) "functionings and capabilities," and the obligation to be efficient.

Justice as Mutual Advantage

Two standards can be used for this criterion. First, at the heart of market exchange is an unspoken but implicit understanding that people trade in order to provide mutual advantages for all parties concerned. This is implicit in the notion of pareto optimality itself, where a move toward a new position can indeed be considered to be an improvement only to the extent that somebody benefits without making anybody else worse off. Thus, at a minimum, trade should not lead to a worsening of people's autarkic position. Second, we can use John Rawls's (1971) notion of "justice as fairness." In particular his maximin rule of permitting inequalities only to the extent that the most disadvantaged benefit sheds much light on our case. Empirical evidence conclusively shows the violation of these two standards; agricultural trade is neither mutually advantageous, nor does it favor the most disadvantaged. In fact, it is the wealthy that reap the most benefits.

Landowners are the primary beneficiaries of farm support in industrialized countries. Thus, small farming households benefit from OECD public agricultural assistance only to the extent they own the land they till. This pattern is persistent across different studies, and even more alarming, this maldistribution still prevails despite reforms that have been specifically designed to maximize the increase of household farm incomes with minimal impact on international food markets (OECD 2001: 8; Piccinini and Loseby 2001: 15–16). Citing the US Government (1987), Tyers and Anderson (1992: 81) note that the wealthiest 20% of farmers are able to capture the majority of transfers from consumers. Gundersen et al. (2000: 1) conclude that for the year 1997, less than 20% of very small farms received US government direct payments compared to 75% for large farms and 60% for very large farms (Gunderson et al. 2000: Tables 9, 19).[5] According to the OECD, the top 25% of farmers have increasingly secured most of the public assistance in the last decade: as much as 70% of the subsidies in Europe and even 90% in the case of the US. Moreover, according to the Environmental Working Group, a nonprofit environmental research and watchdog organization, the top 10% of US farmers secured 65% of subsidies in 2002, up from 55% in 1995 (Becker 2003).

This regressive pattern is replicated in developing countries as well. OECD farm support benefits LDC urban populations, taxpayers and consumers by providing cheaper food—a positive transfer of around $15 to $33 billion per year—but at the expense of LDC farmers to the tune of $26 to $35 billion a year (Tyers and Anderson 1992: 214–215). LDC farmers in effect bear a hidden tax and subsidize their relatively wealthier urban fellow citizens.

By any social or economic measure, less developed countries (LDCs) are clearly disadvantaged relative to the OECD nations. For the year 2001, average per capita income in LDCs is $430 compared to $26,710 for high income countries. The human development index of the latter is twice that of the former.[6] One would consequently expect a preferential treatment of less developed countries. This, however, is not the case. Agriculture, on which LDCs are greatly dependent, is heavily taxed relative to manufactures, the primary source of earnings for industrialized nations. Observe, for example, the disparity in the average ad valorem tariffs imposed on imports coming from developing countries:

1. European Union: 20% for agricultural products compared to only 4.5% for manufactures
2. Japan: 21.9% for agricultural goods compared to 2.5% for manufactures
3. US: 12.7% for agricultural goods compared to 3.6% for manufactures
4. OECD: 32.5% for agricultural imports compared to 7.4% for manufactures

On the basis of average ad valorem tariffs alone, restrictions to trade in agricultural goods are anywhere from four- to ten-fold relative to that imposed on manufactures. Recall that these are precisely the very goods in which LDCs enjoy a comparative advantage.

Whether measured in terms of mutual advantages or of Rawls's maximin rule, international trade in agricultural goods is not for the benefit of the disadvantaged. In fact, additional burdens are imposed on the poorest populations—rural and farming households.

Justice as Equal Treatment

Justice can also be defined as like treatment for like cases. Industrialized countries can once again be seen in gross violation of this criterion. The major OECD countries have long pushed for liberalization of trade in goods and services. And indeed, the spectacular growth in the post–World War II era has been in part due to the relatively freer flow of goods and services across borders under the aegis of the General Agreement on Tariffs and Trade (GATT) (van der Wee 1987). The replacement of GATT with the World Trade Organization (WTO) has accelerated the liberalization of markets. In particular, industrialized countries have largely been successful in opening global markets in goods, services and capital—areas in which developed countries have a commanding comparative advantage and in which they reap the most benefits. The success of the developed countries in lobbying for a stricter enforcement of intellectual property rights (TRIPS) is likewise a boon for industrialized countries even as this imposes extra costs that many developing countries can ill afford. Even the multilateral agencies such as the World Bank and the International Monetary Fund have been effective instruments in promoting such liberalization in Third World nations through the packaging of loans and the conditions appended to structural assistance provided by the former to the latter.

Unfortunately, such liberalization is not uniform across all sectors. The ill effects of closed agricultural markets are widely known and studied; less developed countries have long been pushing OECD nations to open their farm market—areas in which less developed countries are acknowledged to have a comparative advantage and in which they can reap the largest gains. To this day, however, the major industrialized countries that heavily protect their agricultural sectors have balked at liberalizing these markets. Thus, there is an operative double standard. Developed countries enjoy the enormous benefits from open markets in manufactures, services, capital and intellectual property (areas in which they have a strong and distinct comparative advantage) while they simultaneously obstruct less developed countries from reaping benefits from freer agricultural trade (market segments in which OECD nations have a pronounced comparative disadvantage). The criterion of justice as like treatment is violated as industrialized countries push for market liberalization only in those areas in which they have a comparative advantage.

Justice as like treatment is also violated in the face of OECD nations' insulation of their agricultural sectors from the necessary price adjustments called for in market exchange. As noted earlier, economic life is a dynamic environment in which people continually readjust the disposition of their resources in response to price signals from the marketplace. These ceaseless marginal redispositions of resources move the community toward allocative efficiency. Recall that this requires constant price and quantity changes on the part of all economic agents in an unfettered market. By shielding their farmers from international prices, OECD nations in effect save their farming sectors from having to make the necessary painful price and quantity adjustments that are critical to equilibrating demand and supply in global food markets. This unresponsiveness to price signals introduces even greater distortions into the marketplace, thereby adding even greater burdens on the rest of the international economy, particularly on LDC farmers whose impoverished nations neither have the financial resources nor the social infrastructure to shelter their own citizens from the resulting larger price fluctuations. OECD nations are in effect passing on their share of price and quantity adjustments to other nations that are unable to take defensive measures of their own and are therefore subject to the vagaries of the market. To make matters worse, in the absence of price signals, OECD farmers overproduce, and their overproduction is then dumped in international food markets through governmental export subsidies. Not only does this depress prices, but it also increases the amplitude of price fluctuations. These domestic disequilibria are in effect transmitted to the rest of the global market. Tyers and Anderson (1992: 305) note that OECD farm policies in the early 1980s increased price volatility by as much as 50% and depressed it by as much as 14%. OECD nations and multilateral institutions like the World Bank and the IMF have been adamant about less developed countries making the necessary painful structural adjustments that would make their (LDCs) economies more responsive to price signals. Like treatment is not forthcoming for the agricultural sectors of developed countries.

Functionings and Capabilities

A. K. Sen (1981, 1984) has proposed substituting "functionings and capabilities" as alternatives to preference satisfaction as a measure of welfare in economic theory. After all, the whole point of economic life is to procure the means to exercise one's personal agency effectively. I propose that such a notion of "functionings and capabilities" can be extended to a macroeconomic level in describing the capacity of a nation for collective agency.

The literature in economic development is emphatic on the central importance of agriculture in the economic well-being of developing nations. In the early stages of development, it is agriculture that produces the necessary surplus to finance the subsequent industrialization of the nation. It is also a vibrant rural sector that furnishes the necessary labor pool and the consumer market for a nascent industrial base. Furthermore, since it is the dominant sector in terms of GDP share and employment, agriculture is the engine that pulls the rest of an emerging economy. Consequently, it is essential to maintain the vigor of the farming sector for less developed countries (Lewis 1954; Fei and Ranis 1964).

OECD agricultural protectionism has impeded LDCs' economic development by preventing them from earning much-needed foreign exchange through their farming sector, in which they have their greatest comparative advantage. Moreover, as already mentioned, OECD farm supports depress global food prices, thereby discouraging technological change and innovation in LDC farms. The extent of the damage is clearly seen in the paradox that despite their comparative advantage in agricultural produce, LDCs as a group are net food importers, when they should have been net food exporters (Tyers and Anderson 1992: 215). What makes this deeply disturbing is the great dependence of LDCs on agriculture, which represented 27% of their GDP and exports and 50% of their employment in 2001 (Lankes 2002: 10).

It is paradoxical that the major industrialized countries, whose average share of agriculture to GDP is less than1%, should be so protective of their farming sector at the expense of low-income countries, for whom farming accounts for 23% of their GDP. In the case of the poorest nations, this share rises to as much as 60%.[7] Far from supporting the development of poor countries, OECD nations have raised even greater hurdles and imposed heavier burdens on LDCs through distortionary agricultural policies.

Obligation to Be Efficient

Unimpeded international trade can provide enormous static and dynamic gains for all nations. In the first place, there are the consumption gains where it is now possible to consume outside one's production possibilities frontier. In buying cheaper goods and services from trading partners and selling one's resources and output at better prices, nations in effect see an increase in their real incomes. Second, there are production gains that come with shifting the nations' production toward their comparative advantage. Scarce resources are put to their most valued uses. Third, there are dynamic gains from trade through the resultant technological change precipitated by better prices and specialization. This represents an outward shift in the production possibilities of nations and augurs well for the welfare of subsequent generations.

All these gains are dissipated to the extent that international trade is impeded or distorted, as in the case of OECD agricultural farm support. In terms of forgone static consumption and production gains, the global welfare loss is estimated at $120 billion (1997 dollars); LDCs bear 20% of this loss (Lankes 2002, 10). Tyers and Anderson (1992, 210) estimate developing countries' net economic welfare losses in 1990 at US $11.2 billion (1985 dollars). And this is not even to count the forgone dynamic gains from trade-induced technological advances. Besides these inefficiencies, it is also essential to account for the undue degradation of water and land resources due to overproduction from OECD farm support.

Material Cooperation

Given the aforesaid criteria of justice as mutual advantage, justice as like treatment, efficiency and "functionings and capabilities," I argue that OECD agricultural protectionism cannot be justified because of the proportionately greater harms it produces in its wake. The fourth condition of the principle of double effect is violated. Wherein lies the role of corporate responsibility in this issue?

Corporate farms that lobby and receive a substantial part of these governmental subsidies cannot be held to be in formal cooperation with the ill effects inflicted on less developed countries. After all, pecuniary externalities are by their nature *unintended* consequences inflicted on third parties. OECD governments and even the special interests that lobby so heavily for such public assistance do not intend to harm LDC populations, but only permit such a foreseen injurious collateral effect in the course of providing relief and protection for OECD farmers. Nevertheless, there is significant material cooperation involved, both proximate and remote.

Proximate material cooperation stems from two sources. In the first place, OECD agricultural protectionism is a product of a political expediency and intense lobbying (Tyers and Anderson 1992: 80–122). Such lobbyists are key to keeping such harmful farm policies in place all these years despite the formidable literature that have unambiguously shown their deleterious impact on poorer populations. Second, in availing of and, indeed, capturing the bulk of public assistance that had been originally intended for small farm households, wealthy farmers and corporate growers have in effect enlarged these farm support programs more than should have been the case, thereby making them even more distortionary of global food markets. In other words, these large, wealthy and unintended beneficiaries of OECD farm support are adding even larger burdens on poor LDC populations. This proximate material cooperation is the most serious breach of ethical corporate behavior when it comes to international food trade.

Remote material cooperation comes from the notion of bounded rationality. Markets are undergirded by longstanding conventions and rule-creating institutions. Economic agents reinforce these informal standards and customs further through their participation in market exchange. After all, the market has properties of a network externality; its value and strength increases the more people use it.[8] Remote material cooperation also comes from the path dependency that stems from earlier rounds of economic activity. Opportunities or impediments in subsequent rounds of economic activity are partly a function of the outcomes and processes set in the earlier rounds of market exchanges. It is in this sense that lobbyists and corporate beneficiaries of OECD farm support in preceding years are liable for remote material cooperation from the indirect, lingering ripple effects of earlier rounds of OECD protectionism. This, of course, is in addition to the direct injurious collateral effects of OECD farm support in the current economic period.

Summary and Conclusions

The ethical dimensions of international farm subsidies provide compelling reasons for the exercise of corporate responsibility. *Justice as mutual advantage* is violated. Note the regressive incidence of the burdens imposed by these farm subsidies. The bulk of the benefits accrue to the large corporate farms and affluent farmers in developed countries, while the burdens are disproportionately borne by rural populations, who, in many cases, live on less than US $1 a day. Whether we use John Rawls's justice as fairness and its attendant lexical rules or A. K. Sen's "functionings and capabilities," there are strong philosophical arguments on the absence of mutual advantage in global agricultural markets that warrant corrective action. These remedial measures need not be governmental alone, but can also be private and corporate. The latter, of course, is the venue by which subsidized corporate farms and wealthy farmers are able to take responsibility for the ill effects of their government entitlements.

The view of *justice as equal treatment* likewise calls for ameliorative corporate responsibility. It is true that sovereign nations (such as Europe, Japan and the US) owe primary responsibility to their own citizens' welfare. However, one must remember that participation in international trade, not to mention membership in the World Trade Organization, entails an implicit acceptance of the rule of uniform trading rules for all. There is an asymmetric and selective compliance with the spirit of fair international trade. Developed countries have successfully pushed less developed countries into enforcing intellectual property rights and into liberalizing their markets for capital movements and industrial manufactures; at the same time, however, they have been unresponsive to the longstanding pleas from less developed countries for OECD openness in agricultural trade. The norms of justice as like treatment for like cases are violated with this lopsided pursuit of free trade.

Besides these two notions of justice, we can also invoke the obligations and ethics of allocative efficiency. There is a broad consensus among economists that international trade is not a zero-sum phenomenon because of the expansive gains that flow from division of labor, specialization and economic exchange. There are static and dynamic gains reaped from an increase in real incomes, an alignment of production consistent with comparative advantage and faster technological innovation. Farm subsidies distort prices and thus impose large welfare losses on the rest of the economic community. Such inefficiencies have inimical intertemporal effects on future generations as well.

Thus, the social costs imposed by subsidized farms are not only extensive, but they can also be long-lasting, especially in the face of hysteresis (path dependency) in the evolution of the marketplace.

Pecuniary externalities are unintended consequences that are mediated through the market. For example, OECD farm subsidies precipitate a global decline in agricultural prices, harming non-OECD farmers in the process. These adverse pecuniary externalities function just like technical externalities, because subsidized corporate farms do not internalize the social cost of their economic decisions—such as the perennial overproduction of subsidized crops that inflict severe harm on Third-World farmers. Left on their own, these subsidized entities have no incentive to change their behavior or to move into other crops in which they enjoy a natural comparative advantage without the need for government subsidies. Herein lies a critical venue for international corporate responsibility.

Given the lack of European, American and Japanese political resolve to cease these deleterious farm subsidies, it remains for the major corporate beneficiaries of these government grants *voluntarily* to do their share in changing the status quo and provide relief to millions of small farmers worldwide. Viewing these farm subsidies not only as pecuniary externalities but as technical externalities (inequality between private and social cost) provides compelling economic arguments for the urgent need for some measure of international corporate responsibility on this issue. Subsidized entities could choose not to internalize the social cost of their economic decisions and get away with it, or they can choose to take responsibility for their actions. Of course, this is not to mention their heavy lobbying for such preferential governmental assistance. In their capacity both as major recipients and as special interest lobbyists for agricultural protectionism, wealthy farmers and corporate growers are liable for their proximate material cooperation with the adverse pecuniary externalities of OECD farm support. In effect, subsidized corporate farms that lobby so heavily to preserve OECD farm assistance share complicity and accountability for sustaining, preserving and further reinforcing prevailing market practices that inflict such extensive harm. The principle of double effect cannot be invoked to justify such public assistance to OECD farms, given the disproportionate harms they occasion relative to whatever good they are able to produce—which is minuscule to begin with, in view of the ability of landowners and corporate growers to capture the bulk of such assistance.

In conclusion, the contentious, longstanding issue over OECD farm subsidies is a fertile area for international corporate responsibility. Non-governmental societal institutions, including firms, complement both market and governmental activities. These institutions can and do make up for the deficiencies of both the market and governments through their voluntary, non-market ameliorative actions. I submit that beneficiaries of OECD subsidies—the corporate farms, the wealthiest farmers and their ancillary support industries—have just such an opportunity. Given the lack of OECD political will to put an end to distortionary practices in global agricultural trade, it now remains for corporate responsibility to pick up where the government and the markets have failed. Indeed, farm subsidies paradoxically provide signal occasions for a burnished international corporate responsibility.

Notes

1. The OECD nations are: Australia, Austria, Belgium, Canada, Czech Republic, Denmark, Finland, France, Germany, Greece, Hungary, Iceland, Ireland, Italy, Japan, Korea, Luxembourg, Mexico, Netherlands, New Zealand, Norway, Poland, Portugal, Slovak Republic, Spain, Sweden, Switzerland, Turkey, United Kingdom, and the United States.

2. Data are drawn from OECD 2003.

3. These nominal protection coefficients (NPC) are drawn from OECD 2003: 213–214, Table III.3.

4. This is not even to mention the costs inflicted on First-World consumers and taxpayers.

5. "Very small farms" are defined as "limited resource farms" with a gross sales of less than $100,000 and a total household income of less than $20,000. Large farms, on the other hand, are defined as operations having sales between one-quarter million and one-half million dollars. Very large farms have sales exceeding half a million US dollars (Gundersen et al. 2000: 5).

6. World Bank 2003: 234–235, Table 1. See World Bank 2003: 243 for a listing of these low- and high-income countries. The human development index is a composite of achievements in life and health outcomes, knowledge and standard of living. See United Nations Development Programme (UNDP) 2001: 144, Table 1.

7. Data are from World Bank 2003: 238–239, Table 3.

8. This is an example of a non-pecuniary non-technical externality. Another example of network externalities is a new currency whose value and acceptability as a medium of exchange and a store of value are a function of the extent to which people use it.

Bibliography

Becker, Elizabeth. 2003. "Western Farmers Fear Third-World Challenge to Subsidies." *New York Times* (September 9).

Fagothey, Austin. 1972. *Right and Reason: Ethics in Theory and Practice*, fifth edition. St. Louis: C. V. Mosby Company.

Fei, John, and Gustav Ranis. 1964. *Development of the Labor Surplus Economy: Theory and Policy*. Homewood, Ill.: Richard Irwin.

Gundersen, C., M. Morehart, L. Whitener, L. Ghelfi, J. Johnson, K. Kassel, B. Kuhn, A. Mishra, S. Offutt, and L. Tiehen. 2000. "A Safety Net for Farm Households. U.S. Department of Agriculture." *Economic Research Service, US Department of Agriculture, Agricultural Economic Report 788*. Washington: USDA.

Lankes, Hans Peter. 2002. "Market Access for Developing Countries." *Finance and Development* 39: 8–13.

Lewis, W. Arthur. 1954. "Economic Development with Unlimited Supplies of Labor." *Manchester School* 22 (May): 139–191.

OECD (Organization for Economic Cooperation and Development). 2001. *Market Effects of Crop Support*. Paris: OECD.

________. 2003. *Agricultural Policies in OECD Countries: Monitoring and Evaluation 2003*. Paris: OECD.

Piccinini, Antonio, and Margaret Loseby. 2001. *Agricultural Policies in Europe and the USA: Farmers Between Subsidies and the Market*. New York: Palgrave.

Rawls, John. 1971. *A Theory of Justice*. Cambridge, Mass.: Harvard University Press.

Sen, Amartya. 1981. "Rights and Agency." *Philosophy and Public Affairs* 11(1): 3–39.

———. 1984. "Rights and Capabilities," in *Resources, Values and Development*. Cambridge, Mass.: Harvard University Press.

Tyers, Rod, and Kym Anderson. 1992. *Disarray in World Food Markets: A Quantitative Assessment*. Cambridge and New York: Cambridge University Press.

United Nations Development Programme (UNDP). 2001. *Human Development Report 2001*. New York: Oxford University Press.

United States Government. 1987. *Economic Report of the President, 1987*. Washington: Government of the United States.

van der Wee, Herman. 1987. *Prosperity and Upheaval: The World Economy 1945–1980*, trans. Robin Hogg and Max R. Hall. Berkeley: University of California Press.

The Author

Albino Barrera is Professor of Humanities, teaching economics and theology at Providence College, Providence, RI, 02918-0001, USA; e-mail: abarrera@providence.edu.

HOW INVOLVED SHOULD THE WORLD BANK BE IN INTERNATIONAL CORPORATE RESPONSIBILITY PROGRAMS?
A QUALITATIVE EXPLORATION OF OPTIMAL PROGRAM PROVISION

Bryane Michael
Linacre College, Oxford, United Kingdom

Abstract

The growth of popularity of International Corporate Responsibility (ICR) has brought several international organizations into the ICR "industry"—notably the World Bank. The World Bank sees its ICR activities as public goods which make up for under-provision by the market due to market externalities. Yet, ICR also benefits the Bank. The optimal level of World Bank involvement will depend on the degree to which it provides public goods and increases the quality of non-perfectly competitive markets where ICR activities may be under-provided. The optimal level of World Bank ICR project provision is discussed and policy issues are raised.

Introduction

International Corporate Responsibility (ICR)—or corporate social responsibility applied at the international level—has been seen as important for international economic development.[1] The value of ICR in international development has been discussed in the business literature (Bendell 2000; Schwartz and Gibb 1999; Hopkins 1998) and the development literature (Fox, Ward, and Howard 2002).[2] Inspired by the potential welfare gains of participating in ICR programs, the World Bank (2003) has attempted to assess the degree to which it should be involved in the issue of international corporate social responsibility. The World Bank (2004b) has generally concluded that ICR activity can help reduce poverty while promoting private sector development in developing countries.

Yet, choices about the *level* of activity or *types* of ICR activities which the Bank should engage in must be made. The Bank—with limited resources—must explore the extent to which it adds value while not crowding out potentially more effective private organizations. It should help develop the market for ICR activities while not overly profiting from that development. The first section of this paper will look at the Bank's involvement in ICR and the reasons for that involvement. The second section will look at the optimisation problem the Bank should be trying to solve through

 pp. 157–173

a discussion of "ICR activity creation" and "ICR activity diversion." The Bank is trying to expand markets and provide public goods while avoiding crowding out private firms. The third section will look at the extent to which the Bank should be involved—even if ICR activities were only private goods (and have no public goods attributes). This section will also explore the Bank's incentives to engage in ICR for self-interested reasons rather than public oriented ones. The fourth section tackles the Bank's potential level of involvement, while the final section concludes.

Before embarking on the main argument, several points should be noted. First, as previously noted, throughout this paper, I use "International Corporate Responsibility" to refer to Corporate Social Responsibility (CSR) practiced at the international level—and specifically to refer to concrete ICR projects. Second, I do not provide comprehensive literature surveys in order to keep focused on the paper's main argument. I recognize that ICR is a contested and multi-faceted topic and readers interested in ICR may consult Hooker and Madsen (2003).[3] Third, this paper has been written for the non-economist interested in exploring some of the economic reasoning behind Bank involvement in ICR. Economists will be uncomfortable as I do not derive optimal levels with rigorously defined parameters.[4] Non-economists will be uncomfortable with my treatment of ICR as a "product" like cars or widgets. I would urge both groups to come to this project with an open mind—taking what they find useful and leaving what they do not. Finally, there are a number of international organizations which work directly or indirectly with ICR—including the United Nations, the OECD and others. I chose the World Bank because it is more directly involved in project work, it is an institution I know something about, and the paper focuses on the decision problem rather than the institutions involved in ICR.

World Bank Work in ICR

The World Bank (2004c) asserts that the Bank's work in ICR was launched by World Bank President James Wolfensohn at the World Economic Forum in Davos, Switzerland, in January 2000.[5] Despite a host of policy objectives outlined in various World Bank documents, the Bank appears to be aiming to provide ICR as a "public good" which is underprovided by private sector firms and many developing country governments.[6] The Bank rarely uses the term "public good." Instead, the Bank (2004a) notes that these activities "strengthen national investment climates by enhancing sustainable development strategies, helping firms compete for [foreign direct investment] FDI inflows and helping position their exports globally." While the Bank does not specifically specify how ICR helps achieve these goals, the presence of Bank involvement clearly indicates that the Bank considers the public goods nature of ICR. In a policy document authored by Fox, Ward, and Howard (2002) for the World Bank, they note the role of ICR and some of the activities which they claim can be undertaken are listed in Table 1.

While all of these activities are "public goods" provided by governments, the Bank sees itself as providing the public goods needed for governments to provide these public goods (!). The Bank does not directly engage in providing tax incentives for

Table 1: Some Public Sector Activities in ICR

Defining minimum standards	Stock exchange regulations
Tax incentives and penalties	Loan guarantees
Ensuring access to information	Guidelines for public investment
Working with international organizations to build capacity	Endorsing metrics and indicators
Legislation promoting voluntary action	Tax incentives
Forum for debating public policy proposals	Mandating corporate contributions
Involving business representatives in public arenas	Licensing requirements for stakeholder consultation
Multi-stakeholder code development	Business advisory services
Reforming political financing	Education and awareness raising
	Pro-CSR public procurement

Source: Adapted from Fox, Ward, and Howard (2002).

businesses in member countries. Instead the Bank advises governments about ways that tax incentives might be used. Such public goods are usually in the form of Bank projects and activities—direct advice is given through its Private Sector Development Unit and training through its World Bank Institute.[7]

The World Bank Institute provides mostly information as its public good. The Institute claims to have delivered training on corporate responsibility to over 12,000 people—directly and through the Internet. Table 2 represents a list of Institute activities. The activities convey the impression that the Institute appears to still be defining its role in corporate responsibility training. The wide range of topics and locations suggests the Bank has not decided on a clear strategy for such training. The July 2002 event looking at the role of the World Bank in CSR appears to have produced very little concrete information or tangible recommendations. The program also focuses heavily on dialogue with students in US business schools who presumably are already receiving training in issues of corporate ethics and responsibility. The Internet training program itself provides the rationale for corporate responsibility without going to great detail about the concrete activities which can be undertaken to promote corporate responsibility.

Unlike the World Bank Institute, the CSR Practice advises developing country governments "on public policy roles and instruments they can most usefully deploy to encourage corporate social responsibility . . . [through] building public sector understanding of CSR incentives and pressure points, and on improving strategic interactions" (World Bank 2004c). While the Practice's strategy and limits of activity appear poorly defined, the team does provide a country-specific diagnostic "tool" for businesses and government officials. The team has also worked with the Bank's Foreign Investment Advisory Service (FIAS) to advise on country-wide CSR frameworks in Angola for oil sector, El Salvador for general education, the Philippines for mining and Vietnam for athletic footwear.

How Much Bank Involvement: A Public Goods Perspective

International Corporate Responsibility is a rubric under which thinking about the wider economic, political and social effects of corporate activity undertaken by firms working in more than one country are discussed. Given the international element of

Table 2: World Bank Institute Activities Oriented toward Corporate Responsibility

Date	Title	Description*
July 2004	Junior Enterprise in Brazil	World Bank visits several Brazilian universities and institutions to facilitate training sessions and discussions on corporate social responsibility and competitiveness
12–15 May 2004	Voluntary Codes of Conduct for Multinational Corporations Conference	Makes presentation at conference which brought together over 400 people globally from business and academia.
26–27 October 2003	Inter-American Conference on CSR	Presentation made on the positive effects on a company's reputation engendered by adopting CSR into core business strategy.
24–27 September 2003	Developing International Business Leaders for the New Millennium	Presentations made at an event bringing together businesspersons, government officials and academics from a number of countries.
24 September 2003	Redefining the Role of Business Leadership in Relation to Poverty and Development	Organized international video-conference exploring the role of future business leaders in promoting international development and reducing poverty for people from eight countries across the Americas.
22 September 2003	Is There A Role For Business In Promoting Building Peace and Democracy?	Make presentation asserting that corporations can make positive contributions to society through their involvement in building peace and democracy.
26 June 2003	Corporate Social Responsibility: Best Practices in Kenya	500 Kenyans attend a workshop which highlights CSR values and principles in Kenyan society.
26 June 2003	Business in Society Workshop for Kenya	60 participants from the University of Nairobi, Kenyatta University and United States International University meet to discuss how to integrate CSR into the university curriculum.
26 June 2003	Corporate Governance in Southeast Europe	Participants from Bosnia and Serbia and Montenegro discuss training programs.
18 June 2003	"Rebuilding Trust Through Corporate Responsibility" Conference	Moderated panel on ethical relations between business NGOs and government.
16 June 2003	Videoconference with International MBA Students, Boston College	Video-conference discussion between Bank staff and students from Boston College about how companies should interact with NGOs and governmental agencies to promote corporate responsibility.
11–13 June 2003	World Bank Staff Exchange Program	Bank staff set up a booth in headquarters to share CSR conference reports to other Bank staff.
9 June 2003	CSR Videoconference for Training of Trainers in Africa	Participants from Tanzania, Uganda, Ghana, and Ethiopia discuss by videoconference sustainable private sector development in Africa
25–27 May 2003	Philippines CSR Course	Approximately 1,000 Filipinos complete web-based CSR course
23 April 2003	Conversation on Resources, Conflict and Corporate Responsibility	Bank staff meet other multilateral institution, academia, nongovernmental organization, and other staff to discuss multi-stakeholder dialogue on business practices in conflict situations and to explore approaches to risk mitigation in zones of conflict.

6 December 2002	CSR in Russia Conference: Corporate Responsibility and Sustainable Competitiveness in Russia	Video-conference between Philadelphia, Washington, and Russia. Participants discuss corporate responsibility in Russia.
24 July 2002	Video-conference on Corporate Social Responsibility and Business Ethics	Video-dialogue between World Bank headquarters and the University of Cape Town's Graduate School of Business.
23 April 2002	Recommendations from "Successful Public-Private Partnerships: Perspectives of the Private Sector"	Mainly young professionals and graduate students from Washington DC are equipped with (the Bank claims) "knowledge and tools to design, implement and manage successful public-private partnerships."
19 April 2002	Workshop on "CSR and the Role of the World Bank"	Unclear who was at this event or its purpose.
2 April 2002	Roundtable discussion on CSR E-conference	Student recommendations from the Wharton School of Business revolving around increased Bank activity aimed at encouraging corporations to comply with the UN's Global Compact.
19–21 November 2001	Corporate Governance and Social Responsibility	Presented framework for improving the competitiveness of localized industrial clusters and for implementing appropriate governance structures.
13–16 November 2001	Third APEC Future Leaders Forum: "Corporate Citizenship: Doing Well by Doing Good"	Delegates from Asia discuss business and sustainable development, corporate volunteerism, and shaping a culture for corporate citizenship.
14–15 November 2001	National Solidarity Conference	Approximately 50 sectors and professional groups discuss social responsibility.

Source: Adapted from WBI Program Events (World Bank 2004a).

*Due to the highly ambiguous and jargon-laden descriptions offered by the Bank, I have tried to simplify and clarify their descriptions. See the Source for the original descriptions.

Note: A June 2003 meeting on "Portfolio Preferences of Foreign Institutional Investors," a September 2003 meeting "Toward the Millennium Development Goals: Children's Perspectives" and a November 2003 EconCrime conference were omitted due to the seemingly tangential nature of the meeting for corporate responsibility.

ICR, discussion tends to focus on multi-national enterprises or on national enterprises working abroad.[8] Much of the academic discussion tends to focus on the implementation of specific projects aimed at the adoption of codes of conduct (Kolk, Tulder, and Welters 1999; Jenkins 2001). Yet, a number of specific projects have also been elaborated to incorporate elements of corporate responsibility into the activities of these organizations. For example, GlaxoSmithKline established a Corporate Social Responsibility Committee to advise its Board on issues affecting corporate responsibility while ABB employees in Brazil work with slum children, the under-nourished, and AIDS victims.

Many of the ICR initiatives are the result of "products" marketed by organizations which specialise in offering advice on ICR for an economic return. For example, the group Business for Social Responsibility (BSR) conducts an annual conference that for 2004 cost non-members registering a month away from the conference $1850. The BSR also has an Advisory Service which addresses Assessment and Policy Development, CSR Strategy and Structure, CSR Supply Chain Management, CSR Convening, and Transparency and Stakeholder Relations. Principal areas covered by BSR include Consumer Goods, Information and Communication Technologies, Extractive Industries, Pharmaceuticals and Biotechnology, Food and Agriculture, and Transportation.[9] An EthicalCorp conference on "How to Make Corporate Responsibility Work in China" costs $1495.[10] CSR Europe offers a fifty-four-page book entitled "CSR and the Role of Investor Relations: From Switchboard to Catalyst" for €60.[11]

These ICR products are examples of "private goods." Private goods are rival goods in that consumption by one person or group of people reduces the amount available for others. They are also excludable in that certain groups of people who do not pay for these goods can be excluded from consuming them. In contrast, "public goods" are goods which all can use—they are non-rival and non-excludable. Many ICR products are purposely put into the public domain as public goods. All the organizations mentioned previously—BSR, CSR Europe, and EthicalCorp—offer some publications and meetings for free. The World Bank offers most of its ICR activities for free.

The rationale for putting ICR products into the public domain and making them public goods is different for the Bank than for the other organizations.[12] Organizations like Net Impact offer some free resources, but most of the resources require membership.[13] The World Business Council for Sustainable Development offers some resources, such as book chapters, for free while charging for the rest.[14] In the case of these organizations, public goods are distributed as a way of increasing demand for the private goods on sale.[15] The World Bank, though, as a public organization, aims to promote international development and increase overall welfare. Public ICR goods are provided in the hopes of increasing social rather than individual returns to the Bank.[16]

Despite the nature of the organization, the basic economic logic of ICR projects remains the same—their long-run, risk-adjusted return must exceed their long-run, risk-adjusted cost. Even for the World Bank, if it uses more resources on ICR projects

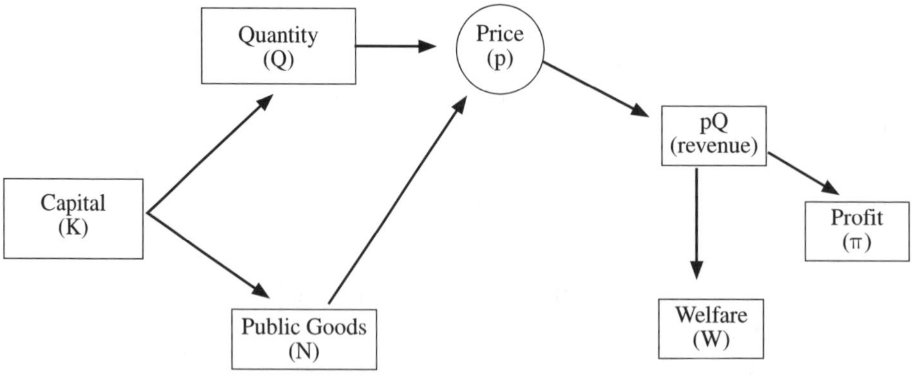

Figure 1. Investment in public and private ICR goods.

than they contribute to long-run welfare, then the Bank is wasting resources. For the consulting companies which advise international companies, ICR projects (such as training, publications, and conferences) have a direct return in the price of the services. They also have costs in the form of marketing, staffing, accounting, managerial attention, and research and development. The problem firms engaged in ICR have is to use their pre-existing resources to either develop products which either earn an immediate return or to invest in activities which expand interest in corporate responsibility. Figure 1 shows the self-explanatory investment decision to be taken by the ICR firm.

Organizations such as CSR Europe or BSR want primarily to maximize profit for themselves and their members. Contributions to public goods will be made to expand demand for private ICR projects. As with regular goods, increased demand (generally) raises both quantity demanded and thus price. Such investment in public goods affects the return to private goods investments through price and quantity effects.[17] However, investments in public goods (N) are less efficient at producing returns than normal projects (Q). They might raise the price slightly and the quantity demand, but have little other effect.[18] Indeed, investments in N would be expected to suffer from the under-production as other public goods. [19] Under-production would be expected as the cost of N is borne directly by a few but the benefits accrue to all. As incentives abound to free-ride, few organizations would have an incentive to provide these goods. Given these problems, there is an argument for a public organization like the World Bank to provide these public goods.

For a public organization like the World Bank, the "price" may not be directly paid by the consumers of the ICR activity. Instead, returns may come through increased budgetary allocations to the Bank by member governments who want to see increased levels of ICR activity given free-rider problems affecting private sector provision. Member governments would represent the interests of their electorates—including their national firms—in the Bank. Thus, the Bank has the objective (in theory) of maximising the welfare impact of its activities to obtain the highest "price" (or returns).

Figure 2 shows the effects of investing in public and private ICR goods for both private firms and the Bank.[20] In the figure, the total initial size of the ICR market can be represented as x^2 (squared).[21] Of the total market, the World Bank has a certain proportion which can be labelled as a^2—for a total proportion of a^2/x^2. Once the Bank makes an investment in ICR activities, a part of those activities will displace activities which might have been undertaken by a private company and another part will be a public good which no private firm would want to invest in. The expansion of the total market can be represented by b. Such a "market creation effect" increases the market to a total size of $(x + b)^2$. The effect of the Bank's relative share of the market is ambiguous. If the Bank's share grows less than proportionately, then it has facilitated the activity of other ICR organizations. If the Bank's share grows an additional amount, c, which represents a more than proportional growth, then it crowds out other players.

There are a number of reasons why Bank provision of private goods might expand more than proportionally. First, such expansion may be accidental. For ICR public good provision in the form of conferences, advice, or publications will always have

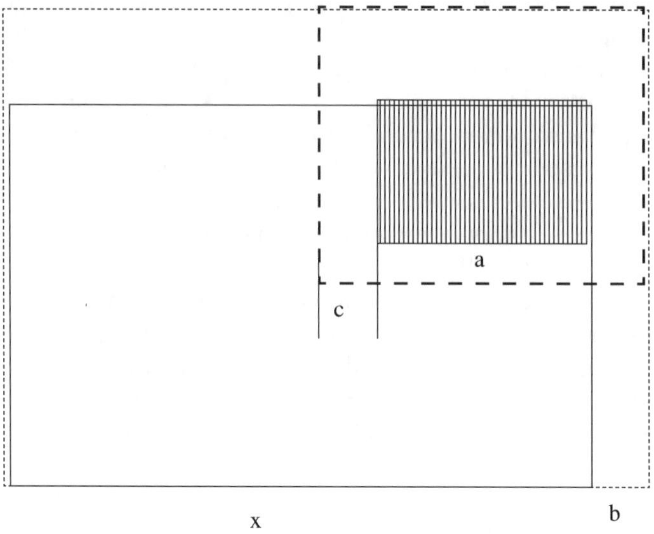

Figure 2. Market expansion and market diversion.

some degree of rival and excludability. Over the program life-cycle which consists of a number if ICR projects, some may have more private goods attributes at some points in time while others have more public goods attributes at other points in time. Second, the Bank may be more efficient at providing certain types of ICR activities—either due to competencies gained in other parts of its corporate governance work or through its high-level connections with government officials. Private good provision may have a lower cost than a private company or may be specifically requested during other work. Third, Bank staff may be self-serving and have career objectives which promote program expansion. The Bank, seeking to maximize its returns, would target activities with the highest *political returns*, which would then translate into financial returns.[22] Bank staff directly interested in reputation may use "means testing" or "market demand testing" as rationale for conducting self-financing programs in which participants pay the full cost of the activity.

How Much World Bank Involvement: Private Goods Perspective

Private provision of ICR projects by the Bank may or may not be optimal, but will almost certainly be undertaken. The decision to engage in the provision of private versus public goods will depend on the returns to the Bank. The return to ICR activities (R) is shown by equation (1) as the political return (r) per activity times the amount of activity undertaken (Q_B) minus the costs of those activities (c).[23]

$$R = (r - c)Q_B \qquad (1)$$

Using this simple equation, the optimal provision maximizes the Bank's political returns subject to costs. To find the returns on welfare (W), an "adjusting term" can be added such that s_B representing social returns or returns to the wider community for the Bank and s_o for other organizations—leading to equation (2). Evaluating the effects of Bank work vis-à-vis other organizations, s_o are the social returns to non-Bank work, r_o are the private returns to non-Bank work, and Q_o represents the quantity of non-Bank work.

$$W = s_B(r_B Q_B) + s_o(r_o Q_o) - (c_B Q_B + c_o Q_o) \quad (2)$$

From the simple equation (2), a number of implications can be derived as shown in Table 3. The table assesses the cases when private returns to the Bank are greater and less than the returns to other organizations, when Bank costs are higher and lower than other organization costs, when the social benefits of both Bank and non-Bank work are greater and less than zero, and where the private returns are greater than, less than and equal to the social returns for the Bank. For each of these cases, the positive implication (what the Bank has the incentive to do) is discussed as is the normative implication (what the Bank should do to maximize welfare). For example, if the returns to the Bank are higher than the returns to private organizations, the Bank will certainly compete on ICR projects. However, the effect for society is ambiguous and depends on whether the social returns are positive or not.

Having determined the conditions under which the Bank will compete in the private provision of ICR products, the question remains whether such provision is optimal. Table 4 summarizes a number of interesting cases. First, if $r_B + r_o = s_B + s_o$, or the social returns equal the private returns, then ICR programs are optimally

Table 3: Should the Bank engage in private ICR goods provision?

Implications	Condition 1		Condition 2	
Positive Normative	$r_B > r_o$	Bank will compete Ambiguous whether should	$r_B < r_o$	Bank won't compete Clearly shouldn't compete
Positive Normative	$c_B < c_o$	Bank may compete depending on returns Should compete	$c_B > c_o$	Bank may compete depending on returns Should not compete
Positive Normative	$s_B > 0$	Ambiguous, depends on returns Bank should compete	$s_B < 0$	Ambiguous, depends on returns Bank should not compete
Positive Normative	$s_o > 0$	Ambiguous Should reduce crowding out	$s_o < 0$	Ambiguous Should try to crowd out private activity
Positive Normative	$s_B > s_o$	Ambiguous, depends on returns Should reduce crowding out	$s_B < s_o$	Ambiguous, depends on returns Should reduce crowding out
Positive Normative	$r_B > s_B$	Will engage in activity If $s_B > 0$, should compete	$r_B < s_B$	Will not compete Should compete if $s_B > 0$.
Positive Normative	$r_B = s_B$	Will engage in ICR Should engage in ICR		

Note: the comparison of rB with ro is not done, as the Bank does not (or is not supposed to) compete directly with private firms for financial returns.

provided by the Bank and others. The Bank "internalizes"—or receives the full social return—of its work. Second, if $r_B > s_B$, then programs are overprovided. There are other institutions competing for these economic (and political) returns and there may be over-provision. The private returns exceed the social returns and there is excess competition—especially if each organizations esteems it can successfully compete against the others. Finally, if $r_B < s_B$, then programs are underprovided because of the free-riding problems referred to previously.

However, other reasons may exist—besides the free-riding problem or the problem of externalities—which may cause the under-provision of ICR goods. A simple argument would note that, as with other firms, market power derived from a lack for competition can lead to a case where imperfect competitors increase the price of services well beyond their costs.

A more complicated argument refers to the potential lack of co-ordination between organizations. In this simple model, each actor must decide how much ICR activity to provide. The World Bank can become fully committed to ICR and assume most of the ICR work by engaging in consulting and ICR-related conditionality. Other organizations can become heavily involved through extensive donations of staff time and financial contributions to ICR programs. Realistically though, each actor knows it can not cover the entire range of ICR activities and so must "share" ICR activity. The Bank must decide *at the same time* as other ICR organizations the level of ICR activity it will provide. Other organizations must also decide at the same time their level of ICR project provision. If each organization worries that it may over-provide activities (and thus receive no returns on excess projects), then they may under-provide projects.[24]

As Table 4 shows, the level of ICR provision depends on the level of information ICR project providers have about each other's activities. When each actor pursues its ICR activity without centralized co-ordination, one would expect *over-provision* of ICR activity. Excess competition occurs as each organization tries to capture its share of the overall market given an accurate assessment of the other organizations. If there is not enough information, even though each actor tries to cover a certain proportion of ICR activity, overall there is *under-provision* of ICR activities due to their strategic interaction. Each actor over-estimates the amount of ICR activity to be provided by other actors and so under-provides its own share of ICR activity due to lack of public-private partnership. If the World Bank exercises a leadership role, then such over and under-provision may not occur and optimal provision is attained.

Table 4: Level of World Bank ICR project provision

Provision Level	Social and Private Returns	Information Level
Socially optimal	Simple political returns maximisation (r = s)	Bank exercises leadership (optimal information)
Over-provision	Competition for political rents (r < s)	Too much information
Under-provision	Competition with imperfect information (r > s)	Too little information

The Best Level of World Bank Involvement in ICR

Having derived the optimal *level* of activities, the Bank must still choose the *types* of activities to undertake. The World Bank's possible involvement in ICR activities can be portrayed along a continuum of commitment from lowest to highest as shown in Table 5.[25] The lowest level of commitment is information dissemination while the highest comprises including ICR provisions in loan conditionality. Integrating the previous discussion, the table also assesses whether returns are mostly public or private and the probably cost to the Bank. Given the returns and costs, the table assesses the probability of Bank involvement in that level of ICR good provision.

The lowest level of World Bank involvement in ICR would be to provide information about ICR. Much of such information would probably be a public good given the sparse incentives for other firms to conduct unbiased research on the economic impacts of ICR programs. The Bank currently provides such public goods in the form of information on investment, economic statistics, and studies in a wide range of development issues. A number of other information providers—such as Eldis, Business for Social Responsibility, CSR Wire and others—exist and thus Bank activity in this area could be seen as

Table 5: Levels of Bank involvement in CSR

World Bank commitment (from lowest to highest)	Private returns	Public returns	Mostly public or private?	Cost to Bank	Probable commit-ment
Information dissemination	Promotes visibility	Makes up for under-provided information "knowledge goods"	Public	Low	High
Advocacy	Promotes adoption of wider WB agenda	Solves collective action problems	Public	Low	High
Monitoring	Increases WB influence in member private sectors	Monitoring is public good and so under-provided	Neutral	Medium	Medium
Consulting	Increases Bank revenue	Increases provision of ICR products	Private	High	Medium
Debt and equity participation	Increases Bank revenue and diversifies portfolio	Deepens markets and sets their "strategic direction"	Private	High	Low
Conditionality	Improves probability of conditionality's success	Provided public sectors with incentives	Private	Medium	Medium

Source: Adapted from discussions held during the World Bank's e-conference on Public Policy and Corporate Social Responsibility (World Bank, 2003). Figure 1, Investment in public and private ICR goods.

"crowding out" these businesses and NGOs.[26] However, these information dissemination programs appear to be complementary to private organizations' commercial interests and the World Bank provides a medium to disseminate some of this information.

The second level of commitment would consist of Bank advocacy of ICR programs to both firms and governments. The Bank would actively generate its own data and conduct research illustrating the potential benefits and harms of increased expenditure on "corporate responsibility." The Bank already acts as an advocate claiming in its publications and public speeches that ICR promotes international development. However, there is a potential interaction with the Bank portfolio which may affect the quality of advice. If the Bank suggests activities which are best for the country, it may decrease returns on its investments. Such advice might also contradict advice on reducing large firm expenditure on social goods which distort price signals and resource allocation.[27] Moreover, given the wide-spread popularity of CSR, the Bank does not appear to be providing a good the private sector can not produce itself.

A third level of Bank commitment to corporate responsibility consists of active monitoring of ICR activities conducted by firms and governments. Either the Bank would collect systematic and impartial data in the form of ratings, or would monitor on an *ad hoc* basis instances in which egregious violations of corporate responsibility occur. The public goods rationale for monitoring would be higher than simple advocacy given the increased expense and co-ordination problems inherent in monitoring.[28] Moreover, the Bank has diplomatic and economic clout which could lower the cost of monitoring potentially below the costs of private firms such as Moody's.[29] Such monitoring would also be a valuable asset which private sector firms would potentially pay for. Such a practice, however, would represent a shift in Bank policy away from working with governments and more toward working with the private sector—a practice which has questionable status in its Articles of Agreement. Monitoring would give the Bank a great deal of political clout and visibility—just as the Transparency International Index has given that organization a great deal of political capital.

The Bank could offer consulting services to firms in developing countries as a fourth and greater level of commitment to corporate responsibility. The Bank could send experts to help firms and governments design and implement corporate responsibility programs—possibly using the diagnostic instrument it has already developed. The Bank would have enormous private incentives to engage in such work as the return could be quite lucrative if the Bank could charge for such advice. Bank consulting would also greatly expand the overall market of ICR as the Bank engages consultants and forms co-operative agreements with other ICR providers. However, such consulting would probably call into question the mandate of the Bank as the Bank would become just another consulting firm. Moreover, the Bank—as a public institution—must represent the interests of the government rather than any firm or its own profit maximisation. Thus, if Bank advice could be politically influenced, its advice could decrease welfare and possibly long-term corporate responsibility. Such political influence would not be mitigated by profit motive as the Bank would not see financial returns directly tied to the quality of its advice irregardless of whether it charged market prices for its advice or not.

Taking equity or debt positions in the companies it advises would help increase the incentive to give high quality advice. Such positions, especially if profitable, could help generate the funds which would increase the Bank's gross return on outstanding loans (which was about 5 percent in 2003).[30] Bank leadership in taking positions and promoting ICR would be influential enough to shape national regulatory and business practices in many member countries—thereby offering a useful public service. However, such a proposal would encourage business as well as government to become financially committed to the World Bank—expanding the already large influence of the Bank in many countries. If such investment is politicized, the encouragement of soft budget constraints in borrowing enterprises may work against lending packages which advocate the removal of market distortions.

Tie-in with lending conditionality represents the highest form of World Bank commitment to corporate responsibility. Along with the other macroeconomic, firm-level and public sector reform conditions, the Bank could request specific regulations to be passed promoting worker, environmental or consumer welfare. Conditionality would increase the likelihood of ICR programs being implemented and would offer a fertile ground of experimental results upon which to evaluate the effectiveness of ICR activities. Corporate responsibility conditionality, if designed correctly, could also bolster macroeconomic and public sector conditions. Such a commitment, however, would give the Bank almost complete economic and political power in developing countries and potentially destabilize pre-existing power relations.[31] Conditionality encouraging firms to make public investments could also distort prices and other signals.

In practice, the Bank will probably choose a mix of the above activities. The Bank will expand its information dissemination as part of its new mandate to become a "knowledge bank" (Wolfensohn 1996). It will continue its almost completely uncritical advocacy of ICR projects despite the potentially welfare-increasing value of offering more objective advice. The Bank will also probably expand its consulting services in co-operation with external partners. The Bank will probably continue to operate in the short-term under a vague ICR strategy so as to maintain its flexibility to maximize its political returns given the still nascent ICR market.

Conclusions

The World Bank should engage in ICR programs both as a public actor and as a private participant. Public involvement increases the size and return to ICR projects. Private involvement provided competition needed to encourage private actors to increase the scale of their operations. However, unlike a private market organization, the Bank will need to worry about over-extending its mandate. Given its size, it could crowd out rather than encourage private participation in ICR.

The Bank can avoid crowding out other actors' ICR by offering a clearer strategy about when it will participate in ICR projects. These projects should be more focused on concrete results rather than dialogues with US students. These projects should also seek to increase the returns of ICR projects to companies rather than to the consulting companies which sell this advice.

Notes

1. The author would like to thank the participants of the World Bank's e-conference on Public Policy and Corporate Social Responsibility whose deliberations inspired this paper. This paper has been significantly modified to incorporate the feedback of the participants of the Second Conference on International Corporate Responsibility held in Amsterdam on 18–20 June.

2. For an interesting historical perspective on international corporate responsibility (or the lack thereof), see Litvin (2003).

3. Michael (2003) also covers the pros and cons of engaging in corporate responsibility activities.

4. In my defense, the economics is so simple I would not see why an economist would need such definition which stems from the basic equation for profit.

5. Despite the assertion, I was unable to find further information about the launch or the deliberations surrounding the launch.

6. Distilling the objectives of Bank work from documents has been difficult due to the highly ambiguous and jargon-laden language employed by Bank documents. World Bank (2004a) notes that "the objective of this program is to develop an integrated approach to action-learning and capacity-building for institutional change in the field of corporate social responsibility and sustainable competitiveness. At the country level, this integrated approach can be used in the design and implementation of appropriate policy measures and initiatives aimed at creating an environment supportive of sound corporate social responsibility practices. . . . The approach also helps companies use the concept of corporate social responsibility as an important element for developing sustainable competitive advantages and to address the interests of key stakeholders, including the communities in which they operate, in a more systematic way." World Bank (2004c) helpfully notes "while CSR business drivers are market-based, there are clear opportunities for the public sector in our client countries to support and promote CSR. These efforts need to be rooted in an understanding of the market-based drivers and of businesses' CSR implementation challenges." The lack of concrete direction highlights the importance of this paper for Bank work.

7. However, the mandate of both entities is vague. The CSR Practice educates through a number of toolkits and analytic reports while the World Bank Institute asserts that it works with governments to "design and implementation of appropriate policy measures and initiatives aimed at creating an environment supportive of sound corporate social responsibility practices" (World Bank, 2004a).

8. In the international business literature, multi-national enterprises (MNEs) differ from international enterprises in that they operate in a number of countries and lose their "home country" affiliation (Rugman and Hodgetts, 2000). As this paper focuses on an international organization working on corporate responsibility in an international context, I will not address the role of MNEs specifically.

9. For more, see http://www.bsr.org/AdvisoryServices/index.cfm.

10. See http://www.ethicalcorp.com/usa2004/ for the conference announcement.

11. http://www.csreurope.org/publications/roleofinvestor_page23.aspx.

12. In this case, public goods are being put into the public domain. Private goods may also be put into the public domain but, for reasons of simplicity, I will not discuss the public domain here.

13. For more information, see http://www.net-impact.org/. By quoting prices of ICR products, I am making a positive rather than normative evaluation of these activities.

14. For example, see Fussler, Cramer, and van der Vegt 2004, which offers some chapters on-line but not others.

15. Information is unusual product to sell as it is an "experience good" or a good which must be experienced in an attempt to assess the quality of the product being purchased. While I will not

address the economics of information goods, for information goods, it is often wise to offer free samples (Shapiro and Varian 1998). Public goods might also be provided by private actors, see Ley (1993) for a diagrammatic representation.

16. For a discussion of the Bank and its work, see Gilbert, Powell, and Vines 1999.

17. Economists may find it useful to think analytically about such investment as a stock of advertising whose cost per unit should yield an equivalent return per unit minus any returns obtained from having a better society (Schmalensee 1972).

18. These organizations might be altruistic and interested in maximising social welfare or may have a wider and longer profit function. Based on my experience, I am skeptical about these organizations being strongly altruistic and refer readers to Simon (1993) for the academic discussion.

19. For more on public goods, see Hardin (1982).

20. See Coates (1996) for another exposition.

21. To increase the rigor of the figure, the horizontal axis can be thought of as areas of ICR work and the vertical as "varieties" of activities undertaken. For simplicity, we will assume that the programs have the same number of varieties as types and label that "x." The figure is illustrative rather than an attempt to quantify the ICR market.

22. The reader may consider increased returns to the organization as weak incentives. As ICR project budgets expand, salaries and non-salary benefits increase through the increased potential for promotion and increased budgets for hiring extra staff.

23. Costs may be decomposed in political risk (σ), direct budgetary costs (c), and the opportunity cost (o) of using resources for activities which could increase the Bank's political returns elsewhere. I ignore any complicated discussion of costs for simplicity of exposition—though the political risks of projects are ever-present. An example of "political risk" is the OECD's support of the Multi-lateral Agreement on Investment (MAI).

24. In an earlier version of this paper, I argued for under-provision using the logic of the Cournot model. However, the discussion of imperfectly competitive pricing was complex for non-economists and therefore I have omitted this discussion.

25. The reader may ask why the World Bank should be assuming the role of promoting ICR and how it relates to its charter. Given that the Bank is already engaged in this work, I will not address this issue.

26. For interesting data on the effect of public spending on volunteering, see Day and Devlin (1996) which find that such spending influences the degree of altruistic volunteering activity.

27. A core element of Bank advice is the reduction of public expenditure which distorts the functioning of the price system. Motivated by "neo-liberal" economic theory, a free and functioning price system guarantees the optimal allocation of economic resources. See Stiglitz (1998) for an overview and critique.

28. Monitoring costs may significantly affect investment. For a rather complex treatment and empirical results, see Aizenman and Spiegel (2002).

29. One examples of such an index includes the Business in the Community Index (http://www.bitc.org.uk/docs/CR_Index_Execsummary.pdf).

30. Source: ttp://treasury.worldbank.org/web/PDF/2003_Info_Statement.PDF.

31. For more on the effects of Bank conditionality on borrower's internal political arrangements, see Bienen and Gersovitz (1985).

References

Aizenman, J., and M. Spiegel. 2002. "Institutional Efficiency, Monitoring Costs, and the Investment Share of FDI." NBER Working Paper 9324.

Bendell J. 2000. "Terms for Endearment: Business, NGOs and Sustainable Development." Sheffield: Greenleaf Publishing.

Bienen, H., and M. Gersovitz. 1985. "Economic Stabilization, Conditionality, and Political Stability." *International Organization* 39(4): 729–754.

Coates, D. 1996. "A Diagrammatic Demonstration of Public Crowding-Out of Private Contributions to Public Goods." *Journal of Economic Education* 27(1): 49–58.

Day, K., and R. Devlin. 1996. "Volunteerism and Crowding out: Canadian Econometric Evidence." *Canadian Journal of Economics* 29(1): 37–53.

Fox, T., H. Ward, and B. Howard. 2002. "Public Sector Roles in Strengthening Corporate Social Responsibility: A Baseline Study." Washington: The World Bank.

Fussler, C., A. Cramer, and S. van der Vegt, eds. 2004. *Raising the Bar: Creating Value with the United Nations Global Compact*. Sheffield, U.K.: Greenleaf.

Gilbert, C., A. Powell, and D. Vines. 1999. "Positioning the World Bank." *The Economic Journal* 109(459): 598–633.

Hardin, R. 1982. *Collective Action*. Baltimore: Johns Hopkins

Harila, H., and K. Petrini. 2003. "Incorporating Corporate Social Responsibility." Available at http://epubl.luth.se/1404-5508/2003/064/LTU-SHU-EX-03064-SE.pdf.

Hooker, J., and P. Madsen, eds. 2003. *International Corporate Responsibility: Exploring the Issues*. Pittsburgh: Carnegie Mellon University Press.

Hopkins M. 1998. *The Planetary Bargain: Corporate Social Responsibility Comes of Age*. London: Macmillan.

Jenkins, R. 2001. *Corporate Codes of Conduct: Self Regulation in a Global Economy*. Geneva: UNRISD.

Kolk, Ans, Rob van Tulder, and Carlijn Welters. 1999. "International Codes of Conduct and Corporate Social Responsibility: Can Transnational Corporations Regulate Themselves?" *Transnational Corporations* 8(1): 143–180.

Ley, E. 1993. *On the Private Provision of Public Goods: A Diagrammatic Exposition*. Papers 93-27. Ann Arbor, Mich.: Center for Research on Economic and Social Theory.

Litvin, D. 2003. *Empires of Profit: Commerce, Conquest and Corporate Responsibility*. New York: Texere.

Michael, B. 2003. "Corporate Social Responsibility in International Development: An Overview and Critique." *Journal of Corporate Social Responsibility and Environmental Responsibility* 10(3).

Rugman, A., and R. Hodgetts. 2000. *International Business: A Strategic Management Approach*, 2nd edition. London: Financial Times/Prentice Hall-Pearson.

Schmalensee, R. 1972. *The Economics of Advertising*. Amsterdam: North Holland.

Schwartz P., and B. Gibb. 1999. *When Good Companies Do Bad Things: Responsibility and Risk in an Age of Globalization*. New York: Wiley.

Shapiro, C., and H. Varian. 1998. *Information Rules: A Strategic Guide to the Network Economy*. Cambridge, Mass.: Harvard Business School Press.

Simon, H. 1993. "Altruism and Economics." *American Economic Review* 83(2) (May): 156–161.

Stiglitz, J. 1998. "More Instruments and Broader Goals: Moving Toward the Post-Washington Consensus." WIDER Annual Lectures No. 2. Helsinki: United Nations University.

Utting, P. 2000. *Business Responsibility for Sustainable Development.* Geneva: UNRISD Occasional Paper 2.

Wolfensohn, J. 1996. "People and Development." Annual Meetings Address on October 1, 1996. Available at http://web.worldbank.org/WBSITE/EXTERNAL/NEWS/0,,contentMDK:20025269%7EmenuPK:34474%7EpagePK:34370%7EpiPK:34424%7EtheSitePK:4607,00.html.

World Bank. 2003. "Public Policy for Corporate Social Responsibility." World Bank Institute and Private Sector Development Vice Presidency E-Conference. Available at http://info.worldbank.org/etools/docs/library/57434/publicpolicy_econference.pdf.

_______. 2004a. "About Corporate Social Responsibility and Sustainable Competitiveness." Available at http://web/worldbank.org/WBSITE/EXTERNAL/WBI/WBIPROGRAMS/CGCSRLP/0,,contentMDK:20244656~menuPK:460868~pagePK:64156158~piPK:64152884~theSitePK:460861,00.html.

_______. 2004b. "CSR and Poverty." http://www.worldbank.org/wbi/corpgov/csr/pdf/csr_poverty.pdf (link no longer accessible).

_______. 2004c. "The World Bank Corporate Social Responsibility Practice: A Note for Staff." http://www.worldbank.org/privatesector/csr/doc/March_flyer_revised194.pdf (link no longer accessible).

The Author

Bryane Michael is a postgraduate student in Development Studies, Lineacre College, Oxford University, Oxford OX1 3JP, United Kingdom. E-mail: bryane.michael@linacre.ox.ac.uk.

THE EVOLUTION OF MULTINATIONALS' RESPONSES TO CLIMATE CHANGE

Ans Kolk and Jonatan Pinkse
University of Amsterdam, The Netherlands

Abstract

Climate change is one of the environmental issues that has increasingly attracted business attention in the course of the 1990s. Multinationals have developed different strategies over the years, initially more political, non-market in nature, but currently also market-oriented. This article examines the evolution of multinationals' responses to climate change, paying attention to both market and non-market components. It first gives an overview of the main policy developments, followed by a characterisation of non-market and market responses, based on a survey among the largest multinationals worldwide. The chapter also reflects on overall corporate responses to climate change, paying attention to the influence of the policy contexts on emergent market strategies, and taking respondent characteristics regarding country of origin and sector into account.

Introduction

Climate change is one of the issues that have increasingly attracted business attention in the course of the 1990s. While public and policy interest started already in the late 1980s, leading to a first international agreement at the Rio Conference in 1992, the main driver for corporate strategic change was the adoption of the Kyoto Protocol in 1997 (Grubb, Vrolijk, and Brack 1999). This event spurred the development of regulation, and increased the pressure from non-governmental organisations (NGOs) on governments to ensure ratification of the Protocol, and on multinational corporations (MNCs), which were urged to take appropriate steps to address global warming.

In the period leading to the Kyoto meeting, a considerable number of large multinationals in particular had started to spend much time and effort in trying to influence, both individually and through a range of business associations, their government's stance on an international climate treaty and emission reduction policies (Ikwue and Skea 1994; Kolk 2000; Levy 1997; Newell and Paterson 1998). With only some exceptions, companies initially opposed the adoption of such measures and regulation. Uncertainties about the economic, technological and strategic impact of an international climate policy led many of them to stress the threats to their business and the negative consequences for the economy as a whole. Especially in the USA, the

 pp. 175–190

unresolved scientific nature of the global warming debate was often used as further argument.

When government support for Kyoto turned out to be more widespread than expected, however, the picture started to change slowly but surely, and an increasing number of MNCs stopped their opposition. Some openly adhered to the precautionary principle and emphasised the opportunities that a more proactive approach would bring. Others followed rather reluctantly, merely preparing to comply with expected regulation (Kolk 2000; Packard and Reinhardt 2000). The timing and pace of these shifts varied by industry and country of origin. Early proponents could be found in those sectors where market chances were quickly discovered, or where the risks of climate change prevailed. In the automotive and oil industries, MNCs from European countries changed positions much earlier than their US counterparts (Kolk and Levy 2004; Levy and Kolk 2002; Levy and Rothenberg 2002). As the climate issue matured, however, more companies adopted proactive climate strategies. Corporate support for climate measures became evident in the wave of activities and initiatives to reduce emissions, through product and process improvements, cooperation with other companies, government agencies and NGOs to exchange technologies and expertise, and the exploration of options such as emissions trading (e.g., Dunn 2002; Rosenzweig, Varilek, and Janssen 2002; Whittaker, Kiernan, and Dickinson 2003).

A decade of business interest in climate change has thus led to a clear shift in the strategies adopted. While political, non-market, strategies predominated in the first half of the 1990s, the market component is clearly increasing in importance (Baron 1995; Levy and Kolk 2002). At the same time, however, the fact that MNCs operate in a range of countries with sometimes different climate policies (Hamilton et al. 2003; Schreurs 2003) means that the more multi-domestic non-market strategies (Baron 1997) continue to have an impact. But in the firm-specific blend of market and non-market strategies in the field of climate change, the former is currently receiving more attention, although political strategies continue to play a role as part of companies' overall strategic positioning (Baron 1995; Kolk and Levy 2004).

This chapter examines the evolution of MNCs' responses to climate change, paying attention to both market and non-market components, and referring to a survey among the largest multinationals worldwide. Corporate strategies have developed against the background of regulatory activities, at the international, regional and national levels. The next section will first examine the main policy developments. The two subsequent sections analyse how respectively non-market and market responses can be characterised. Finally, we reflect on overall corporate responses to climate change, paying attention to the influence of the policy contexts on emergent market strategies, and taking respondent characteristics regarding country of origin and sector into account.

Policy Developments on Climate Change

International policy on climate change started with the adoption of the United Nations Framework Convention on Climate Change (UNFCCC) at the United Nations

Conference on Environment and Development in Rio de Janeiro in 1992. This agreement marked the beginnings of a long process of international policy developments on climate change, as shown in table 1. UNFCCC was a broad plan for action, but did not set clear targets for the reduction of greenhouse gas (GHG) emissions other than the objective for a stabilisation in 2000 at the 1990 level. While there were international discussions about the issue in subsequent years, it was not until 1997 that countries agreed upon more detailed, differentiated reduction targets under the Kyoto Protocol (Grubb, Vrolijk, and Brack 1999). In the years following Kyoto, the negotiations about the exact rules for implementation of the Protocol have been very turbulent, however. This has created great complexity for MNCs since the specific shape of their home country governments' climate policies continues to be uncertain. As subsequent sections will show, corporate reactions have shown considerable variety, as part of a dynamic process marked by antagonism and opposition, but also agreement and cooperation.

Table 1. Overview of policy developments on climate change

Year	Policy/event	Elaboration
1992	Framework Convention on Climate Change	Adopted at the United Nations Conference on Environment and Development (Rio de Janeiro); expression of intent by industrialised countries to stabilise emissions at 1990 levels by the year 2000; no mandatory emission curbs.
1992 and 1995	EU carbon tax proposal	The European Commission proposed in 1992 a carbon tax that would raise prices of fossil and nuclear energy by 50%. The proposal was conditional on the introduction of a similar tax by the US and Japan. In 1995 a carbon tax was proposed without this condition. Both proposals failed because several EU countries refused to accept the tax.
1997	Kyoto Protocol (COP 3)	Agreement on reduction targets for greenhouse gases compared to 1990 levels, to be reached in 2008–2012. Differentiated targets per country/region, e.g., Australia +8%; Canada -6%; Japan -6%; Russia 0%; US -7%; EU -8%. EU overall target translated into specific ones for each member country, e.g., Germany -21%, France 0%, Italy -6.5%, Spain +15%, UK -12.5%.
1998	COP 4 in Buenos Aires	First Conference of Parties after Kyoto. Confirmation of the Kyoto agreement and adoption of a 'Plan of Action' to implement the Protocol.
1999	COP 5 in Bonn	A 'process meeting' which showed different views. Discussion points were targets for developing countries (China and India refused to accept targets) and the EU-US disagreement on restrictions on the use of the Flexible Mechanisms. Agreement to conclude final negotiations on global greenhouse gas emissions by November 2000.
2000	EU renewable energy proposal	Proposal of the European Commission to set 'indicative' national targets for renewable energy production with the aim to double energy consumption from renewables to 12% by 2010.
2000	COP 6 in The Hague	Failure to achieve agreement between the US and EU. Main issues concerned rules for emissions trading and the Clean Development Mechanism. The issue on which the negotiations ultimately failed was the use of forests and farmlands as carbon sinks, which was favoured by the US, but contested by the EU.

Year	Policy/event	Elaboration
2001	IPCC 3rd Assessment Report	Third report by the Intergovernmental Panel on Climate Change (IPCC), released in January. It contained expectations that the consequences of climate change will be greater than expressed in earlier assessments.
2001	US rejection of Kyoto Protocol	In March 2001 the Bush administration declared that it would not implement the Kyoto Protocol and intended to withdraw the US signature.
2001	Launch of US alternative 'science-based' climate plan	Some 'softening' of the US stance in June , shown in the proposal of an alternative 'science-based' response to climate change. Main elements were increased research expenditure for energy efficiency improvements and voluntary measures for industry.
2001	Bonn Agreement on Kyoto implementation	Agreement by the EU, Japan, Canada, Australia, Russia, and a number of developing countries on the rules for the reduction of GHG emissions as laid down in the Kyoto Protocol. Concessions of the EU included allowing emissions trading, and the limited use of forests and agricultural land as carbon sinks, which enabled Japan to meet its targets.
2001	EU emissions trading scheme proposal	Proposal by the European Commission to set up an emissions trading scheme to come into effect in 2005.
2001	COP 7 in Marrakech	2001 Bonn Agreement turned into a legal text. Further concessions won by Russia and Japan on the use of carbon sinks and the ability to sell surplus emission credits.
2002	EU ratification of Kyoto	EU agreement to ratify the Kyoto Protocol by the end of May 2002.
2002	Launch of UK emissions trading scheme	The UK government opened a national emissions trading scheme in April. Under the scheme, companies received a limited amount of emission allowances that served as a 'cap' on their carbon emissions, which they are allowed to trade.
2002	COP 8 in New Delhi	The eighth Conference of Parties put the position and vulnerability of developing countries central. India criticised calls for emission targets for developing countries and stressed the growing tension between the developed and developing world on climate change.
2003	McCain-Lieberman plan	Senators McCain and Lieberman propose a bipartisan plan to introduce industry-wide caps on GHG emissions and to set up an emissions trading scheme. The bill failed to pass US Congress by 12 votes, which was commonly viewed as a positive sign.
2003	Opposition of US states to federal government climate policy	Twelve US states file a lawsuit against the Environmental Protection Agency for denying responsibility for GHG emissions. The lawsuit reflected the opposition of states to the US federal government environmental policy.
2003	COP 9 in Milan	No clear results (mostly discussion on Russian ratification).
2004	Announcement of Russian intention to ratify Kyoto Protocol	President Putin announced that Russia will accelerate the process towards ratification of the Kyoto Protocol (as a 'quid pro quo' for EU's acceptance of Russian WTO admission). Russian ratification puts the Protocol into force.

The negotiations about the implementation of the Kyoto Protocol most obviously took place at the so-called Conference of Parties (COP) meetings. The first COP after Kyoto was held in Buenos Aires in 1998, where parties reaffirmed their commitment to the Protocol. In 1999, at the COP in Bonn, some fundamental disagreements between countries emerged, however. First, the US pushed for the inclusion of, and thus targets for, developing countries, which was opposed by India and China in particular. Second, the EU called for a restriction on the use of emissions trading, offset projects and carbon sinks, whereas the US favoured an approach with maximum flexibility and no limits on the use of these mechanisms.

These differences had already been visible in the years leading up to the Kyoto Protocol. The policy measure originally put forward in the EU in these years was some form of carbon tax. However, two proposals (in 1992 and 1995) to implement an EU-wide carbon tax failed due to lack of agreement between the member states. By contrast, the US introduced the option of GHG emissions trading in the discussion, because it had good experiences with a similar trading scheme for the reduction of sulphur (Grubb, Vrolijk, and Brack 1999). It was the conflict between the US and the EU that led to the failure of the climate talks at the sixth COP in The Hague in November 2000. The use of forests and farmlands as carbon sinks formed the central issue on which the negotiations collapsed. In March 2001, hopes that the Kyoto Protocol would enter into force soon were blown when US President Bush decided to reject it altogether, out of the belief that ratification would harm the US economy and its international competitiveness.

In the course of 2001, however, the US government experienced considerable pressure to reconsider its position towards the Kyoto Protocol. As a result, the negative stance was alleviated somewhat and an alternative, "science-based," climate change plan was presented. The main elements consisted of increased expenditures on climate research and incentives for industry to adopt voluntary GHG reduction targets. The plan emphasised a technology-based solution to global warming that would not harm competitiveness.

One month after the launch of this US proposal, negotiations in Bonn, which aimed to 'save' the Kyoto Protocol and move on without the US, resulted in an agreement between the EU, Japan, Russia, Australia, Canada and a large number of developing countries. The EU made concessions to Japan and Russia by allowing unrestricted use of the flexible mechanisms (emissions trading, Clean Development Mechanism and Joint Implementation), and to Canada and Australia by allowing (limited) use of forests and farmlands as carbon sinks. The 2001 Bonn agreement put the US in an isolated position. Shortly afterwards, the European Commission adopted a proposal to start a European emissions trading scheme in 2005. Looking back at the negotiations preceding the Bonn agreement, it is remarkable that the EU had become the main advocate of the policy measure they rejected for years: emissions trading. At the next COP in Marrakech, the political agreement of Bonn was turned into a legal text that enabled the ratification of the Kyoto Protocol. Most parties, including the EU, Japan, and Canada, have ratified the Protocol, while the US and Australia have not.

The period after Marrakech has been characterised by three developments in climate policy. First, the discussion about emission reduction targets for developing countries after the first commitment period (2008–2012) came to the forefront again. At COP 8 in New Delhi, held in 2002, India repeated its refusal to impose targets, based on the argument that industrialised countries have traditionally been the main contributors to global warming and are thus responsible for its solution.

Second, a growing tension could be noted in the US regarding the government's position on climate change. Senators McCain and Lieberman launched a bipartisan plan to set industry-wide caps and create an emissions trading scheme; this proposal failed to pass Congress by 12 votes. Moreover, differences emerged between the federal and some state governments. A number of US states implemented stricter policy measures to combat climate change than required by the federal government; others are preparing for emissions trading and a decreased reliance on fossil fuels. In addition, the Environmental Protection Agency was sued by 12 states for its neglect to take responsibility for the problem of global warming. US companies also faced increased pressure from shareholder groups who asked them to take climate change seriously, and from institutional investors who called for disclosure requirements on climate risks. This movement built on unease that had been growing in some US companies after Bush's rejection of the Kyoto Protocol, and who started to take steps, such as the creation of a pilot project for carbon emissions trading (the Chicago Climate Exchange).

Finally, for the Kyoto Protocol to come into effect in the absence of US support, Russian ratification is necessary. Signals from the Russian government about whether it will ratify or not were mixed. Most recently, however, President Putin declared that Russia would accelerate the ratification process. This signal was a consequence of the negotiations with the EU about the speedy admission of Russia to the WTO.

It can be concluded that the international policy context on climate change can hardly be characterised as a "level playing field" in the post-Kyoto period. It is not only difficult to keep track of the exact details of climate policy on an international level, but also on a national level. Even though many countries have ratified the Kyoto Protocol, it is still not evident how national governments intend to meet their targets. The EU will go ahead with its emissions trading scheme, but whether Japan will set up a similar scheme that is compatible with the European scheme remains to be seen. The responses of companies, both in the political process and the market place, will be addressed in the remainder of this paper. The success or failure of the proposed policy measures under the Kyoto Protocol will depend to a great extent on whether the business community, and particularly large international companies, support the measures. The following sections will examine the interaction between governments and MNCs and investigate the corporate strategies that have been emerging.

Characterising Non-Market Responses to Climate Change

With the emergence of climate change as business concern, attempts have been made to characterise corporate strategic responses, in which the reaction to regulation played a large role. In line with the broader literature on environmental management, particularly continuum models and, to a lesser extent, typologies have been used (Doty and Glick 1994; Kolk and Mauser 2002; Rugman and Verbeke 1998). An example of a continuum is the RDAP-scale (Clarkson 1995), adapted from a well-known classification in research on corporate social responsibility. On this continuum, responses range from a reactive stance, which denies responsibility, at the one end, to proactivity at the other, where managers anticipate developments. In between these two extremes, defensive and accommodative postures can be seen, characterised by, respectively, reluctant admission and acceptance of responsibility.

In view of the difficulties in distinguishing the last two categories, a three-step continuum (defensive, opportunistic/hesitant, and offensive) has been used to classify the evolution of corporate climate change strategies since the mid-1990s (Kolk 2000). The defensive posture involves active opposition to an international climate treaty, with emphasis on the costs involved and the lack of scientific evidence for global warming. In an opportunistic/hesitant strategy, companies prepare themselves for regulatory and market changes, but take a cautious approach in public. They see no need to be a first mover and to take risks, but, at the same time, preparations are being made to change sides if necessary. Finally, companies that follow an offensive approach point at their own responsibility and the need to take the first step themselves, not only for environmental reasons but also because it will offer market opportunities or improve their image. Moreover, the potential consequences and risks of climate change are seen as so serious that a precautionary approach should be taken. In the description of the categories, elements of other environmental management typologies can be recognised. This involves particularly perceptions of environmental impact and its scientific significance (Roome, 1992), the risks involved (Rondinelli and Vastag 1996) and the market opportunities offered through environmental protection (Steger 1993).

Especially in the 1990s, corporate responses could be typified by using this classification. Initially, when opposition to climate policy prevailed, the main channel for expressing views was sector-wise, by trade and industry associations or broader national and international coalitions. Objections to drastic or quick measures used to be raised by energy-intensive sectors such as coal, oil, steel and aluminium, chemicals, automobiles, and paper and pulp. Particularly many US MNCs joined lobby organisations, which included the Global Climate Coalition and the Coalition for Vehicle Choice. More offensive voices could be found in those sectors where this position appeared to offer new market chances or where the risks of climate change predominated. These included solar and wind energy, gas, environmental technology, telecommunications, nuclear energy, insurance and banks. Their views were represented by organisations such as the Business Council for Sustainable Energy and the Pew Center on Global Climate Change. After the adoption of the Kyoto Protocol, the opponents lost momentum, and an increasing number of MNCs left defensive organisations, sometimes even joining offensive associations. Remarkable in particular were MNCs that first broke away from more traditional sector behaviour, such as BP, Shell, General Motors and Toyota.

It should be noted that the defensive-opportunistic-offensive continuum involves broad categories, and that companies can move from one strategy to another in whatever direction. Moreover, they can adhere to one strategy openly (for example, resisting an international treaty—defensive) while simultaneously preparing for change (research into new technologies—opportunistic). This was the case for most companies that lobbied actively against climate measures. The one-dimensional climate model also suffers from another well-known caveat, that is its inability to take internal differences into account. Especially inside large multinational companies, divergent views, for example between European and US locations, have been observed.

Hence, while this continuum had value in the period when corporate reactions to climate policy started to change, and when these positions more than their actual activities mattered since the latter were just emerging, more differentiation became needed when the issue matured. A response to the limitations is the typology developed out of Gladwin and Walter (1980), and applied to the development of climate change responses by US and European oil multinationals (Levy and Kolk 2002; see Fig. 1).

Figure 1. Corporate responses to climate change by oil multinationals*

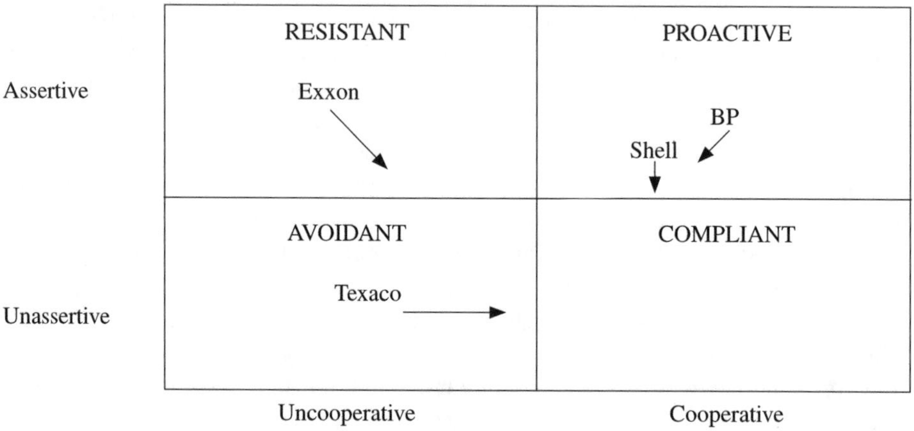

* Positions as of 1998; arrows indicate subsequent movement.
Source: Levy and Kolk (2002: 289).

This two-by-two matrix identifies whether companies are cooperative, through support for mandatory emission controls and climate investments (in this oil case, involving renewable energy technologies) or not. The second dimension relates to the assertiveness of companies' public position, identifying their support for or opposition to attempts at regulation. The different climate strategies of large oil companies in the US and Europe can be seen in Fig. 1, which pictures the development over time, showing a certain degree of convergence.

Although this typology addresses some of the deficiencies of the continuum model, it still focuses more on their approach towards public policy than on the actual market activities undertaken by companies. In view of the fact that a considerable number is currently involved in such market strategies for climate change, committing resources to reduce emissions, there seemed to be a need for a classification that reflects these realities appropriately.

Characterising Market Responses to Climate Change

To characterise the much more recent market responses to climate change that have emerged since the adoption of the Kyoto Protocol, Fig. 2 gives an overview of current activities. It is based on a survey carried out among 500 large multinationals (part of the 2002 FT500 list), which were requested to answer questions on their greenhouse gas emission policies (for more details and the full analysis, see Kolk and Pinkse 2004).

Figure 2. Corporate actions on climate change (N = 111)

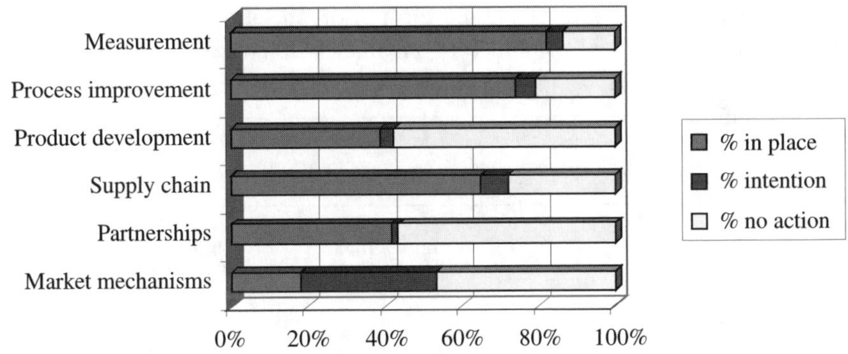

Source: Kolk and Pinkse (2004: 309).

The figure shows that measurement of greenhouse gases is most common. For the majority of MNCs, an inventory of emissions seems a first step towards more sophisticated action on climate change. If greenhouse gas emissions are measured, then most companies have used this information to draw up environmental programmes that include targets for emission reduction or stabilisation. A focus on internal measures appears to be the most common route currently taken. This frequently consists of changes in the production process enabled by new technologies. Other measures include new product development, improved products with higher energy efficiency or a switch to other types of energy sources (for example from fossil fuels to renewables).

Various MNCs have also started to consider emissions of their supply chain (upstream and/or downstream), with some of them translating their responsibility in this regard in a life-cycle analysis of the major products, and others considering the emissions of their suppliers. The intensity of supplier engagement differs, ranging from sampled monitoring of only large suppliers to detailed emission targets and guidelines. Some companies do not monitor their suppliers' emissions directly, but select suppliers based on their environmental programmes and sometimes require ISO 14001 certification. There are also companies that expect their suppliers to have the same environmental standards or cooperate actively with them to increase understanding of the supply chain.

To address climate change, a number of companies engage in partnerships other than their suppliers: with governments, NGOs or other companies, for example through a strategic alliance. While the latter usually focuses on innovation, other forms of interaction with third parties frequently aim to compensate for a company's emissions. Almost half of the companies in the sample mentions the importance of market mechanisms (by trading emissions credits or partnering in offset projects) to reduce emissions.

The evidence presented in Fig. 2 points at the existence of a typology of market strategies towards climate change. Companies differ on two important dimensions: the main aim (strategic intent) and the form of organisation (degree of interaction). These two dimensions are combined in one matrix in table 2.

Table 2. Strategic options for climate change

Organisation	*Main aim*	
	Improvements in business activities	*Compensatory approaches*
Internal (company)	Process improvement (1)	Internal targets, control and trading (2)
Vertical (supply chain)	Product development (3)	Supply chain targets, control and trading (4)
Horizontal (beyond the supply chain)	New product/market combinations (5)	External market mechanisms (6)

Source: Kolk and Pinkse (2004: 311).

The table shows that, on the one hand, the main aim of companies differs. They can focus either on *improvements in business activities* (thus reducing emissions through improvements in processes, products, product or product/market combinations) or *compensatory approaches* (external or internal emission trading, and other forms of offsets through for example the Clean Development Mechanism or Joint Implementation). On the other hand, there is a clear variation in the degree of interaction and form of organisation that companies choose to reach their objectives. This can be done at the individual company level (*internal*), through companies' own supply chain (*vertical*), or by interaction with other companies (competitors or companies in different sectors—*horizontal*).

The main focus of the strategies shown in table 2 reflects the extent to which a company wants to develop firm-level green resources and capabilities (Hart 1995; Rugman and Verbeke 1998), reach such competitive advantages through its supply chain, or cooperate through the formation of alliances in which knowledge is combined (cf. Contractor and Lorange 2002; Ruigrok and van Tulder 1995). And it refers to the type of control and coordination mechanisms needed to reach targets in companies' internal operations, its value chain and network, or on the market (cf. Husted 2003; Martinez and Jarillo 1989).

It must be noted, however, that companies can follow more than one strategy simultaneously, and that different profiles exist, which combine the options to varying degrees. A follow-up cluster analysis of the companies in the sample resulted in six groups with different characteristics (Kolk and Pinkse 2005):

- Cautious planners, which score relatively low on all the dimensions represented by the boxes of table 2 (31 percent of the companies can be classified as having this profile).
- Emergent planners, consisting of companies that have set a target for reductions, but are only in the early stages with regard to implementing organisational change to realise this; in their case, particularly box 2 stands out (this characterises 36 percent of the companies).
- Internal explorers have a strong internal focus, which involves a combination of targets, control and improvements in the production process (particularly boxes 1, 2, 4 and 6) (14 percent).
- Vertical explorers are characterised by a strong focus on measures within the supply chain, and score particularly high in boxes 3 and 4 (10 percent).
- Horizontal explorers focus on the exploration of opportunities in markets outside the current business scope, sometimes in cooperation with partners (box 5) (5 percent).
- Emissions traders stand out for their high score on the engagement in emission markets and the participation in offset projects, and the accompanying internal control and target-setting (boxes 2 and 6) (4 percent).

With these strategic options and profiles, it seems possible to characterise market responses to climate change in a useful way.

Reflecting on Corporate Responses and Respondents

Market strategies currently receive much more attention than when climate change first started to become a corporate concern. However, these are not the only strategies followed by companies. There is still a considerable number that takes a more defensive, "wait-and-see" approach towards the Kyoto Protocol and emission reduction measures in general; in these cases, a concomitant higher dominance of non-market strategies can be observed. Others follow a mix of responses. Even in the case of what can be assumed to be the most active companies, the multinationals that completed the questionnaire in the survey mentioned in the preceding section, the regulatory environment shapes their market activities. The overwhelming majority of the respondents start from the position that government regulation is a reality they have to cope with. About one third of the MNCs in the sample mentioned upcoming regulation as one of the main drivers for action to reduce emissions. Their perceptions on whether regulation is a threat or an opportunity differed considerably however.

It is notable that many companies that have already taken steps to address climate change also try to influence the contents and strictness of the forthcoming EU emission-trading scheme, either individually or through business associations, and engage in partnerships with governments. Their market activities are thus influenced by the regulatory context. Taken more broadly, the nationality (country of origin) of the multinationals also plays a considerable role in determining whether they responded to the survey or not. This conclusion can be drawn from the examination of the sample peculiarities.

For this analysis, the dependent variable "Response" was measured on a dichotomous scale, indicating the presence ('1') or absence ('0') of a fully answered questionnaire. A categorical variable 'Region' was used to indicate the origin of the MNCs from one of the Triad regions—the US, Japan, and the EU, with respectively 233, 50, and 133 multinationals. To assess the relative influence of sector as well, a variable 'Sector' was added. In view of the dichotomous nature of the dependent variable, OLS regression could not be used. Instead, Logistic Regression (LR) was applied (Hair et al. 1998). LR calculates the logistic coefficient, or the odds ratio, by comparing the probability of an event occurring with the probability of an event not occurring. Such an odds ratio for a category should be interpreted as the change in the odds of an event occurring for a company in a particular category vis-à-vis the odds of this event occurring when a company would be in a reference category.

To assess the overall model fit, the Hosmer-Lemeshow test was conducted. Since the Chi-square value (7.14) is not significant, this indicates that there is a good model fit. The analysis (see table 3) shows that the Region variable has a significant Wald statistic, while the Wald statistic of the Sector variable is not significant. This thus leads to the conclusion that the country-of-origin effect is more important than the sector effect in determining the probability that a company would respond to the questionnaire. In addition, the estimated odds ratios (Exp(B) in table 3) of the Region variable show that a company from the EU is 7 times more likely to respond to the questionnaire than a US multinational. Japanese companies are in between EU and US companies; they are almost 2 times less likely to respond than European multinationals and more than 4 times more likely to respond than US MNCs.

The likelihood to respond to the questionnaire gives an indication of the overall posture of large multinationals towards the issue of climate change. The results clearly correspond to the position that their home-country governments have taken towards the Kyoto Protocol in recent years. The refutation of the protocol by the US government appears to have had its effect on the majority of US multinationals. By contrast, the EU ratified the protocol at an early stage, leading to a more positive stance on the part of European companies. The Japanese government only ratified after some hesitation and has been less outspoken on the subject than the EU, resulting in a more modest position of Japanese multinationals.

Table 3. Variables for region and industry for the full sample

	B	*S.E.*	*Wald*	*df*	*Sig.*	*Exp(B)*
REGION			62.38	2	0.000	
European Union	1.99	0.26	58.10	1	0.000	7.32
Japan	1.45	0.36	16.57	1	0.000	4.26
SECTOR			19.95	16	0.222	
Automotive	–0.89	0.82	1.18	1	0.277	0.41
Chemicals and synthetics	–1.20	0.71	2.84	1	0.092	0.30
Communications and media	–1.79	0.65	7.56	1	0.006	0.17
Electronics and computers	–0.91	0.56	2.70	1	0.100	0.40
Finance and securities	–1.50	0.55	7.46	1	0.006	0.22
Food and beverages	–1.09	0.69	2.51	1	0.113	0.34
Insurance	–1.69	0.65	6.70	1	0.010	0.19
Metals and manufacturing	–1.73	0.76	5.11	1	0.024	0.18
Mining	–0.43	1.29	0.11	1	0.737	1.54
Oil and gas	–0.84	0.86	0.93	1	0.334	0.43
Pharmaceuticals	–1.32	0.68	3.74	1	0.053	0.27
Constant	0.35	0.48	0.54	1	0.461	1.42

The reference group for region is US, and for sector utilities.

While country of origin clearly affected the response rates, the content analysis of the responses showed that industry peculiarities play a role in shaping the type of debate on climate change, particularly regarding the perceived risks, threats and opportunities. It also influences the room of manoeuvre that companies have in target setting and the type of internal measures available. On the whole, however, the analysis of the concrete actions reveals a much less pronounced industry effect. Within each sector, companies turn out to follow rather distinctive approaches and have different strategic profiles on climate change, reflecting considerable managerial discretion. The policy context, however, continues to be an important factor in this regard, even though current climate change policies are mostly flexible and rely on market mechanisms such as emissions trading.

Concluding Remarks

This paper examined and characterised the non-market and market response of multinational corporations to developments in the international policy context on climate change. It turned out that the type of responses of MNCs has changed considerably over time, and has reflected the high degree of turbulence of the international policy debate. In the period leading up to the 1997 Kyoto Protocol, the majority of companies from 'traditional' sectors opposed any policy measure to reduce GHG emissions and their strategy could be characterised as a defensive posture. As a result of the broadly based adoption of national targets for emission reduction under the Kyoto Protocol, many companies changed their position to a more opportunistic or offensive posture. These last two positions implied that companies started to implement measures to actually reduce GHG emissions themselves.

At the time of Kyoto, there appeared to be international agreement among governments on the necessity to set reduction targets to combat climate change. However, in subsequent years the policy debate became fragmented again, as national governments could not agree upon the rules for implementation of the Kyoto Protocol. A failure to solve an US-EU conflict about the use of emissions trading and carbon sinks to meet their national targets, and the US rejection to ratify, put the Protocol at serious risk. Nevertheless, many companies already shifted their behaviour from merely taking position in a political debate and following a non-market strategy to actually making progress in reducing emissions and develop market strategies. Corporate climate strategies thus started to become more differentiated and complex than captured by classifications introduced when the issue first emerged.

The government position on Kyoto did not induce all US companies to abandon their efforts. The Bush decision actually revealed a divide between those companies that were 'relieved' and those that were disappointed, reflecting differences between corporate expectations to either gain a competitive advantage or suffer a loss of competitiveness (Houlder 2001). Moreover, other countries reached agreement to move on without US participation and to allow emissions trading and the use of carbon sinks, which created new incentives for European and Japanese companies to develop climate strategies. Especially for US MNCs with considerable activities in these regions, these developments continue to be important to consider.

To characterise the market strategies for climate change, we developed a typology of the strategic options of MNCs to mitigate climate change. A distinction was made between strategies with respect to the strategic aim and the organizational scope. A further analysis showed that corporate climate strategies differ considerably, and companies can be clustered in six groups based on the combination of the strategic options implemented. While especially the policy context and companies' country of origin, plays a role in shaping corporate responses, further research on the determinants (country, industry, and especially firm-specific factors) is necessary. It would also be interesting to see how strategic responses develop over time, since policies continue to evolve as well.

References

Baron, D. P. 1995. "Integrated Strategy: Market and Nonmarket Components." *California Management Review* 37(2): 47–65.

———. 1997. "Integrated Strategy, Trade Policy, and Global Competition." *California Management Review* 39(2): 145–169.

Clarkson, M. E. 1995. "A Stakeholder Framework for Analyzing and Evaluating Corporate Social Performance. *Academy of Management Review* 20: 92–117.

Contractor, F. J., and P. Lorange, eds. 2002. *Cooperative Strategies and Alliances*. Amsterdam: Pergamon.

Doty, D. H., and W. H. Glick. 1994. "Typologies as a Unique Form of Theory Building: Toward Improved Understanding and Modelling." *Academy of Management Review* 19: 230–251.

Dunn, S. 2002. "Down to Business on Climate Change." *Greener Management International* 39 (Autumn): 27–41.

Gladwin, T. N., and I. Walter. 1980. "How Multinationals Can Manage Social and Political Forces." *Journal of Business Strategy* 1 (Summer): 54–68.

Grubb, M., C. Vrolijk, and D. Brack. 1999. *The Kyoto Protocol: A Guide and Assessment*. London: RIIA/Earthscan.

Hair, J. F., R. E. Anderson, R. L. Tatham, and W. Black. 1998. *Multivariate Data Analysis*. Englewood Cliffs, N.J.: Prentice Hall.

Hamilton, K., T. L. Brewer, T. Aiba, T. Sugiyama, and J. Drexhage. 2003. *Corporate Engagement in US, Canada, the EU and Japan and the Influence of Domestic and International Policy*. London: RIIA.

Hart, S. L. 1995. "A Natural-Resource-Based View of the Firm." *Academy of Management Review* 20: 986–1014.

Houlder, V. 2001. "Raising the Temperature: President Bush's Rejection of the Kyoto Protocol Has Created a Deep Divide among Businesses about the Urgency of Addressing Global Warming." *Financial Times* (18 April).

Husted, B. W. 2003. "Governance Choices for Corporate Social Responsibility: To Contribute, Collaborate or Internalize?" *Long Range Planning* 36: 481–498.

Ikwue, T., and J. Skea. 1994. "Business and the Genesis of the European Community Carbon Tax Proposal." *Business Strategy and the Environment* 3: 3–10.

Kolk, A. 2000. *Economics of Environmental Management*. Harlow: Financial Times Prentice Hall.

Kolk, A., and D. Levy. 2004. "Multinationals and Global Climate Change: Issues for the Automotive and Oil Industries." In *Multinationals, Environment and Global Competition*, ed. S. Lundan. Oxford: Elsevier, 171–193.

Kolk, A., and A. Mauser. 2002. "The Evolution of Environmental Management: From Stage Models to Performance Evaluation." *Business Strategy and the Environment* 11(1): 14–31.

Kolk, A., and J. Pinkse. 2004. "Market Strategies for Climate Change." *European Management Journal* 22(3): 304–314.

———. 2005. "Business Responses to Climate Change: Identifying Emergent Strategies." *California Management Review* 47(3): 6–20.

Levy, D. L. 1997. "Business and International Environmental Treaties: Ozone Depletion and Climate Change." *California Management Review* 39(3): 54–71.

Levy, D. L., and A. Kolk. 2002. "Strategic Response to Global Climate Change: Conflicting Pressures in the Oil Industry." *Business and Politics* 4(3): 275–300.

Levy, D. L., and S. Rothenberg. 2002. "Heterogeneity and Change in Environmental Strategy: Technological and Political Responses to Climate Change in the Global Automobile Industry." In *Organizations, Policy, and the Natural Environment. Institutional and Strategic Perspectives*, ed. A. J. Hoffman and M. J. Ventresca. Stanford, Calif.: Stanford University Press, 173–193.

Martinez, J. I., and J. C. Jarillo. 1989. "The Evolution of Research on Coordination Mechanisms in Multinational Corporations." *Journal of International Business Studies* 20(3): 489–514.

Newell, P., and M. Paterson. 1998. "A Climate for Business: Global Warming, the State and Capital." *Review of International Political Economy* 5: 679–703.

Packard, K. O., and F. L. Reinhardt. 2000. "What Every Executive Needs to Know about Global Warming." *Harvard Business Review* (July–August): 29–135.

Rondinelli, D. A., and G. Vastag. 1996. "International Environmental Standards: An Integrative Framework." *California Management Review* 39(1): 106–122.

Roome, N. 1992. "Developing Environmental Management Strategies." *Business Strategy and the Environment* 1(1): 11–24.

Rosenzweig, R., M. Varilek, and J. Janssen. 2002. *The Emerging International Greenhouse Gas Market*. Arlington, Va.: Pew Center on Global Climate Change.

Rugman, A. M., and A. Verbeke. 1998. "Corporate Strategies and Environmental Regulations: An Organizing Framework." *Strategic Management Journal* 19: 363–375.

Ruigrok, W., and R. van Tulder. 1995. *The Logic of International Restructuring*. London and New York: Routledge.

Schreurs, M. A. 2003. "Divergent Paths: Environmental Policy in Germany, the United States, and Japan." *Environment* 45(8): 8–17.

Steger, U. 1993. "The Greening of the Board Room: How German Companies are Dealing with Environmental Issues." In *Environmental Strategies for Industry. International Perspectives on Research Needs and Policy Implications*, ed. K. Fischer and J. Schot. Washington: Island Press, 147–166.

Whittaker, M., M. Kiernan, and P. Dickinson. 2003. *Carbon Finance and the Global Equity Markets*. Richomnd Hill/London: Innovest/Carbon Disclosure Project.

The Authors

Ans Kolk is Professor of Sustainable Management, Amsterdam Graduate Business School, University of Amsterdam, Roetersstraat 11, 1018 WB Amsterdam, The Netherlands. E-mail: akolk@uva.nl.

Jonatan Pinkse is a graduate student at the Amsterdam Graduate Business School. E-mail: J.M.Pinkse@uva.nl.

ENVIRONMENTAL INITIATIVES AT TATA STEEL: GREEN-WASHING OR REALITY? A CASE STUDY OF CORPORATE ENVIRONMENTAL BEHAVIOR

Runa Sarkar
Indian Institute of Management, Calcutta (Kolkata), India

Abstract

The firm has an overwhelming role in sustainable development, and this paper identifies what influences a firm's management of the business-environment interface. This is done through an in-depth case study of the environmental behavior of Tata Steel, India's largest and oldest integrated steel plant. The Indian regulatory environment is one of strict (and sometimes contradictory) laws and slack enforcement. This paper examines the inclination of a firm in this context to commit to pollution abatement and honor its commitment by achieving long-run improvement in its environmental performance. Environmental responses studied include compliance with existing norms, involvement in voluntary schemes, and implementation of environmental management programs. Other responses examined are investment in pollution prevention strategies, adoption of cleaner technologies, taking adversarial positions against regulators vs. working with them to develop regulations, influencing environmental policy, and meeting and/or exceeding stakeholder expectations. This paper analyzes Tata Steel's reactive and proactive responses and generalizes some of its conclusions to firms in developing countries.

Introduction

The business and management literature has addressed corporate environmental behavior and corporate social responsibility from many angles. A large fraction of the literature uses a normative approach, prescribing (from a policy-maker's perspective) what a firm should do, or what is optimal for a firm to do, to benefit the environment. However, it is important to recognize that the approach chosen by a firm to handle an environmental issue is often context-specific—it depends on existing regulatory frameworks, market conditions, competence levels, public awareness, and so forth. In this paper, we address context specificity by looking at environmental issues facing the Tata Iron and Steel Company Ltd., India's largest and oldest iron and steel company, and analyzing its responses. In the Indian regulatory environment of strict (and sometimes contradictory) laws and slack enforcement, this paper

 pp. 191–215

examines the inclination of the firm to commit to pollution abatement and honor its commitment—that is, it assesses whether there is actually a long-run improvement in the firm's environmental performance. Although this is an Indian case study, its findings could be generalized in the developing country context, where firms often operate in a similar regulatory ambience.

The objective of this study is to identify what motivates or de-motivates a firm's management of the business-environment interface in a relatively lax regulatory environment. We also identify some of the accelerating and retarding factors that aid or hinder environmentally responsible behavior. Different environmental practices used by the company are studied and assessed with the ultimate objective of identifying what drives environmental behavior, and how to ensure that the environmental behavior is conducive to the goal of sustainable development, through policy and non-policy measures. Thus, we use a positivist approach to identify factors that encourage a firm to honor its social commitments to the environment, with the goal of finding ways and means to strengthen these factors and ensure that corporate responsibility evolves from a being a publicity buzzword to playing an integral role in business as usual.

The paper is organized as follows. We first provide a brief company profile, followed by a short description of the process of steel making, highlighting the pollution aspects. Next, the regulatory ambience in which Tata Steel operates is briefly covered. We then chart the progress of environmental management in Tata Iron and Steel Company, beginning in 1902, when its first blueprints were prepared. We thereby summarize the company's achievements in a longitudinal perspective and address general environmental management issues. Two specific management thrust areas, management of solid wastes and the process of obtaining ISO 14001 certification, are discussed in greater detail. We draw from these discussions to contribute to the debate on whether pollution abatement and prevention really is "good" company strategy. Finally, we briefly consider the ambiguities in Tata Steel's environmental management program, identify drivers for such a program, and conclude by deriving some practical lessons in environmental management for firms in other developing countries.

Tata Iron and Steel Company: A Company Profile

The Tata Iron and Steel Company (henceforth called Tata Steel) is India's largest and oldest integrated steel producer in the private sector. It was established in 1907 at Jamshedpur, currently in the state of Jharkhand in the eastern part of India. While the plant had an installed capacity of 0.1 million ton per annum (mtpa) of crude steel when it commenced operation, its current installed capacity is 3.5 mtpa of crude steel. The plant has undergone four phases of modernization in its ninety-seven years of existence, which have witnessed the phasing out of old, energy intensive, inefficient, and pollution-prone technologies, the installation of pollution control equipment, and an increase in installed plant capacity.

Over the years, Tata Steel has diversified to manufacture, apart from saleable steel, welded-steel tubes, cold-rolled strips, seamless tubes, carbon and alloy steel bearing rings, alloy steel ball bearing rings, bearings, ferro-manganese, ferro-chrome, metallurgical machinery, and so on. Their product range includes branded products like Tiscor, Tiscrom, Tistrong I, Tistrong II and Tiscon CRS reinforcing bars. Saleable steels include semi-killed micro alloyed steel sheet, R-43 grade steel, Si-Mn spring steels, grip bars, EDD (extra deep drawn) quality steel strips, low carbon high strength low alloy steels, creep resistant steel and forging quality ingots. Having successfully commissioned (in record time) and operated a new cold rolling mill complex in its works, the company is among the lowest-cost steel companies in the world, and it has been identified as the only world-class steel plant in India (Tata Steel 2003).

Tata Steel is now poised for the next phase of modernization, which involves the augmentation of plant capacity further to five million tonnes within the limited area of the plant at Jamshedpur itself. The objective of this brown-field expansion is to make optimum use of the existing facilities and to install balancing facilities at minimal cost. The project is likely to cost around 20,000 million INR and is likely to be completed by March 2005. Through this process of continuous modernization, Tata Steel is the oldest yet most modern steel plant in India, with its cold rolling mill, galvanizing line, steel melting shops and blast furnaces having state of the art technology at a par with its western counterparts, even though its capacity is much smaller than theirs.

Tata Steel has several unique advantages vis-à-vis other Indian steel makers. First, through continuous modernization, cost rationalization, and leveraging of its strategic advantage in having captive sources of raw materials, it has ensured low manufacturing costs. To further reduce steel cost per ton, it has identified and is working on many parameters. Such sustained focus on cost minimization has ensured profits even when steel markets are down and steel plants around the world are sustaining losses.

Second, Tata Steel has moved up the value chain and increased its earnings from value-added products. To begin with, it reduced the contribution from ingots and semis in favor of long (wires, rods, etc.) and HR (hot rolled) products. Then it increased the contribution from HR by expanding its HR mill in 2000. After that, it commissioned its CR (cold rolled) mill, followed by its galvanizing mill, thereby substituting CR products for HR, and converting CR steel into import substitute GP/GC (galvanized plain/galvanized corrugated) products. Thus for the same level of production tonnage, it is able to fetch higher realization and earn more from value addition (i.e., higher profit margins). Also, Tata Steel has been transforming itself into a solution provider for the customer by providing products suited to the customer's needs, rather than being a commodity provider. It also plans to further increase the share of branded products in its total sales. Incidentally, the realizations are about 10 percent higher for branded products. In fact, the company aims to achieve 25 percent of its sales volume from branded products in the next two to three years.

Third, Tata Steel has undergone substantial restructuring. It got out of its non-core assets, sold unrelated business units, shut down nonviable units, and right-sized its human resources. Hence, it has become a more focused and lean organization, although its manpower strength is still high by international standards.

With its progressive outlook, Tata Steel did exceptionally well during the financial year 2002–03, when the domestic economy looked up and steel exports rose, with record production, sales, and profitability. Its exports increased by 126 percent; its PAT was up by about 400 percent. This was not only on account of an upturn in realizations, but also due to an improved product mix, tremendous cost cutting, improvements in working capital, and reduction in staff costs.

Tata Steel is located in Jamshedpur, a burgeoning township and India's first planned industrial city, named in tribute to its founder. It is a model for the harmonious co-existence of industry and environment. Acres of verdant parks and gardens dot the city and provide bucolic sanctuaries from the pressures of everyday life.

Responsibility for maintaining most of the parks and places of interest lie with the industries operating in and around Jamshedpur, with Tata Steel taking the lead. Several other industries have grown up in Jamshedpur, many under the Tata name. Some of the bigger names include TELCO, Tinplate, and BOC India. Other industries include Indian Steel & Wire Products, Incab Industries, Tata Timken, TRF Ltd, Tata Electric Cos, TAYO, Tata Cummins, Jemco, Usha Martin Industries, Tata Pigments, Tata Ryerson, Jamipol and Fusion Engineering.

Process Description

Tata Steel produces steel using the blast furnace—the basic oxygen furnace route. Among the key raw materials, coal and iron ore are brought to Jamshedpur from the company's captive mines, while limestone is purchased from outside. There are over forty-four operating and service departments in Tata Steel, with over 30,000 people working inside the plant premises at a given time.

One could break the steel making process at Tata Steel into four different stages:[1] the iron-making stage, consisting of seven coke oven batteries, seven blast furnaces and two sinter plants, the steel-making stage, consisting of two steel melting shops with three LD furnaces; the rolling and finishing stage, with primary rolling mills and finishing mills for diverse finished products (five in number), including the recently commissioned cold rolling mill and galvanizing complex; and finally, the production support sector, including six lime kilns for refractory production and other ancillaries. These include maintenance services, material handling services, power and utilities like steam, water, compressed air and industrial gases.

The coke ovens generate waste water, which is cleaned in an effluent treatment plant in the coke oven complex, emit dust from their stacks, and generate fugitive emissions during charging and pushing operations. The blast furnaces and sinter plants emit flue gas through their stacks, and dust emissions from the sinter plant are quite high without pollution control devices. The blast furnaces are also a source of blast furnace slag (BF slag), which is essentially a solid waste. The steel melting operations generate air pollution and also result in large quantities of sold waste, primarily LD slag.

Tata Steel generates around two kilograms of suspended particulate matter per tonne of crude steel, produced as stack emissions from a total of forty-three stacks. All of its stacks meet the 150mg/Nm^3 norm of the CPCB. It has four channels through which effluent is discharged: the Ram Mandir Nallah[2] and Jugsalai Nallah, which discharge effluents into a river called Kharkai, as well as Garam Nallah and Susungaria

Nallah, which discharge effluents into a river named Subarnekha after its confluence with Kharkai. Of these, the Ram Mandir Nallah is only a storm water drain and does not discharge any waste water from the plant. The total amount of water pollutants discharged is of the order of 0.2 kgs per tonne of crude steel. The total amount of solid wastes generated from steel making activity is around 2.7 million tonnes per annum, from which a little over 73 percent is sold or reused within the plant. Most of the remaining waste in dumped in landfills, and proper utilization of this remaining 27 percent is a major thrust area of Tata Steel's environmental strategy. While Tata Steel also measures and reduces noise, radioactivity, and similar parameters, we limit our attention in this study to solid wastes, and air and water pollution.

The Regulatory Environment of the Iron and Steel Industry

India began to develop distinctive forms of environmental laws and regulations in the 1970s. The very first act, the Water Act, established a framework for implementation by establishing a Central Pollution Control Board (CPCB), whose mandate was to set environmental standards for all plants in India, lay down ambient standards, and coordinate the activities of State Pollution Control Boards (SPCBs). The SPCBs were present in every state and were responsible for monitoring the compliance of firms to the prescribed standards. However, this regulatory framework has not proved very effective. Decentralization of enforcement has led to lack of accountability; the capability of SPCB officers leaves much to be desired; the judicial process is very slow; and the system is enmeshed in corruption. Given the above limitations, we proceed to give a very brief overview of the environmental legislation applicable to the Indian steel industry. We also discuss some specific regulatory limits for the iron and steel industry to demonstrate the command-and-control nature of these regulations.

Some of the major pollution regulations are listed and summarized below.

- The Water (Prevention and Control of Pollution) Act, 1974, and its amendments, which prohibits the discharge of any polluted effluent into a body of water or onto land unless it meets discharge norms specified in the act.

- The Water (Prevention and Control of Pollution) Cess Act, 1974, and its amendments, which levy a cess (fee) on the quantity of water consumed by industrial units, primarily as a means of augmenting resources of SPCBs. The rate of cess depends on the industry type as well as the purpose for which water is used, and the maximum amount of water to be withdrawn per industry is specified.

- The Air (Prevention and Control of Pollution) Act, 1981, and its amendments limit the extent to which industries can pollute the air by setting specific standards for stack emissions and ambient air quality. The act empowers SPCBs/governments to specify specific control equipment to abate air pollution where required.

- The Environment (Prevention) Act, 1986, and its amendments. This is an umbrella legislation that ties together the previous legislations and introduces legislation for handling and disposal of hazardous wastes. Strict liability for accidents while handling hazardous substances was enacted through the National Environmental Tribunal Act of 1995, and the National Environmental Appellate Authority Act of 1997 provided a means for industries to appeal decisions of legislative authorities.
- Hazardous Waste (Management and Handling) Rules, July 1989, were released to ensure proper handling, transportation, storage, and disposal of solid wastes.
- The Public Liability Insurance Act, 1991, gave some teeth to the above regulations by holding the owner of a unit liable for deaths or accidents in his unit due to noncompliance with environmental regulations.
- Each act usually has a set of rules which specify emission limits and other pollution-related information, such as standards for storing, handling, and disposing solid wastes. For the iron and steel industry, most of the standards were formulated with the concurrence of major integrated steel plants in India, including Tata Steel, and a National Task Force was formed to develop detailed time lines for complying with the norms, depending on the nature of investment required to bring the subsystem to compliance. Some of the standards prescribed by the CPCB applicable for iron and steel plants are summarized in Table 1.

Table 1. Regulatory limits applicable to the steel industry

Parameter	Standard	Monitoring Frequency
Air quality—stack emissions		
SPM	150 mg/Nm^3	Frequency of monitoring dependent on which subsystem emission takes place from
SO2, NOx	No standard, stack height specified	
Air quality—ambient air		
SPM	500 μg/m^3	8 air quality stations, 4 inside and 4 outside the plant to be monitored once in 8 days for 24 hours
SO2	20 μg/m^3	
NOx	120 μg/m^3	
Work area		
Dust concentration	10 mg/Nm^3	
Water quality—consumption		
Quantity	20 m^3/tss	"Suggested Norm"
Water quality—pollution		
TSS	100 mg/l	
Cyanide	02 mg/l	
Ammonia (as N)	50 mg/l	
BOD	20 mg/l	Once a week for coke oven and plant outfall

As is evident from the above summary, industry in India is subject to a command and control type legislation. There are some elements of a market based instrument in the water cess rules, but they are diluted due to the abysmally low tariffs charged on water usage. This is clearly demonstrated in Table 5, which displays the amount of water cess Tata Steel has been paying over the last few years.

In addition to these, there is a requirement for companies to submit monthly compliance reports to the SPCB and obtain consent certificates from them each year for continuing production. Also the SPCB is empowered to conduct site inspections and take independent samples for monitoring at any time. Hence the implementation of regulations is left entirely to the SPCBs, while the CPCB in conjunction with the Ministry of Environment and Forests frame the regulations.

Tata Steel's Approach to Environmental Management

The role of Tata Steel as a socially responsible organization was defined by its founder, J. N. Tata, when he envisaged the city around the steel plant as a green and shady place with wide roads, plenty of trees, and lots of gardens. A more formal approach to environmental management can be traced from the time when Tata Steel established its Environment Management Division (EMD) in 1986, in response to a spate of legislation. The primary duty of this division at that time was to monitor pollution levels and report them to the concerned legislative authorities. It was involved in liaison activities with statutory authorities to negotiate and develop environmental standards and determine a timeframe for enforcement so that impact on the company's bottom line was minimal. Since generation of solid wastes was over 1.2 tonnes per tonne crude steel, which made disposal difficult, this was also an area of attention. This section traces the evolution of environmental management at Tata Steel, through this process, identifies many of the factors that were responsible for their green response. We will evaluate the relative importance of these drivers in a later section.

The journey toward becoming a green plant started with the modernization of Tata Steel. As it began to introduce newer, more efficient, and cleaner steel making technology in a phased manner in the 1980s and 1990s, its efforts ushered in a cleaner environment as a by-product. Since the first phase of modernization was over before the inception of the EMD, the EMD was actively involved in formulating modernization projects along with other team members from the second phase. From successive Environmental Performance Reports it is evident that the EMD was continuously involved in looking for new and appropriate technologies for pollution reduction, both within the process and as an end of pipe measure. The approach was always two pronged—to improve environmental quality on one hand and increase production efficiency of the other. In 1996, after the installation of an electrostatic precipitator (ESP), a manager commented "The successful operation of the ESP (in the stock house area of G Blast furnace) has also helped in the recovery and recycling of nearly fifty to sixty tonnes per day of fine material which would otherwise become airborne leading to major pollution problems in the area" (Basu et al. 1996). While advocating process changes and the use of newer technologies the environmental managers were pragmatic enough to realize that there are situations like in the case of raw material transfer where "end of pipe" measures seem to be the only option and have to be employed. In their words, "process modifications, change of layout etc. may be effective, but they have to be in tandem with end of pipe measures" (Sarkar et al. 1996).

Since its inception, the EMD has used several environmental tools to comply with environmental legislation and pressure from other stakeholders while causing minimal disruption in the day-to-day production process. The first systematized tool perhaps was that of *performance audits* of existing pollution control systems, which was employed before it was made mandatory by legislation. As per the mandate of the Ministry of Environment and Forests, Tata Steel started *characterizing its waste streams* and quantifying the extent of pollution from them in 1991 to reduce the information asymmetry between the centre and the industry. *Environmental Impact Assessments* (EIA) for new projects as well as a regional EIA of the Jamshedpur Township were commenced in 1992, even though EIAs were not mandatory at this point. The regional EIA study was extended to assess the *carrying capacity* of the Jamshedpur region, given its burgeoning industrial activity, to ensure sustainable development in the region. More detailed *environmental audits*, tailored to the needs of the ministry, were undertaken each year, starting in1992. Another management tool used was that of *reporting environmental parameters* to all stakeholders through an Environmental Performance Report, starting in 1990. Once a commitment toward an environmental goal or past pollution figures appeared in writing, the EMD was accountable and had to achieve the goal and maintain/ improve upon the pollution figure provided to ensure that the Performance Reports had some credibility. By releasing an *Environmental Manual* in 1991, and by organizing numerous training sessions, awareness camps, and competitions, the EMD increased awareness about environmental damage, its legal implications, and means of reducing pollution levels. It was hoped that such actions in the long run would bring about an attitudinal change in the employees.

As environment management evolved in Tata Steel, a need was felt to make environment management a line function for all managers rather than restrict it to the purview of a single department. Involvement of the EMD in *departmental review meetings* was a step in this direction, taken in 1992. Further, an environmental policy was formulated and released to give credence to and share with stakeholders the approach of Tata Steel in managing its business-environment interface. Toward gaining a competitive edge through environmental management, resource inventories and specific resource-use tracking were taken up seriously with respect to water, power, and solid wastes. Solid waste management has been a thrust area for Tata Steel and will be discussed in a separate section; the primary factor responsible for added attention to solid waste is its volume, consequent difficulty to dispose it, and stricter legislation governing disposal.

The nineties brought with them new challenges, primarily due to liberalization. For the company, "One perceptible outcome of liberalization was intensified competition" (Chatterjee 2000). "It was evident that with growing environmental awareness, stricter environmental legislation and its enforcement, tougher competition in the global market, and increasing environmental demands from the customer, companies have to incorporate environmental issues in their decision making process" (Prasad, Sarkar, and Prasad 1997). In its quest to rise above local competition, Tata Steel embarked on a *benchmarking* strategy for key parameters. This involved identifying the best in the world for a particular parameter and attempting to emulate the process followed by the best to achieve the same parameter. In the environmental management area, three projects were identified for benchmarking in 1998. These included optimizing the water treatment system inside Tata Steel, implementing environmental management systems, and improving the operating performance of the biological treatment plant (BOD Plant) for the treatment of waste water from the coke oven.

A visible shift in approach is evident when *pollution control equipment data*[3] were made available in the environmental performance report. This represents a shift in the approach of Tata Steel from "initial compliance" to "continuous compliance," which demonstrates that compliance with statutory norms was internalized into the system rather than being considered a distraction from production. In due course, the operating cost of complying with environmental regulations and going beyond compliance was computed on an annual basis and reported. Around the same time, there was a palpable effort by the EMD to identify, compute, and circulate all fiscal benefits possible from pollution control efforts. This could be due to intensified competition for scarce resources—a means of justifying (unprofitable) investments in pollution control measures that crowd out other, more attractive investments.

Toward the late nineties there was an increased focus on "*technovation*," or technical innovation, as a means of reducing pollution. This amounted to identifying and giving recognition to workers and officers who took the initiative to make small modifications to the steel making process and met the objective of a cleaner environment as a result. Such measures ensured optimal utilization of both *operating and design expertise*.

A watershed event in the efforts to internalize environmental management in mainstream operations was the implementation of a structured environmental management system (EMS), in line with the internationally accepted environmental standard, *ISO 14001*. Implementing and maintaining these globally accepted environmental standards have not been an easy task for Tata Steel; some of the hurdles, and how they were overcome, will be discussed in another section.

Tata Steel just completed a *life cycle assessment* study carried out in conjunction with the Indian Ministry of Environment and Forests (MoEF) and the International Iron and Steel Institute (IISI) in Brussels, where it is a partner institution with two other Indian steel plants. While serving as a quantitative baseline for producers to assess the environmental consequences of potential process changes, it also provides pointers for methods to reduce energy consumption and guide technology choices compatible with plant- and region-specific factors. Improving the work area environment became another area of thrust for the EMD, as occupational safety issues were brought under its purview. This could be partly due to a new set of legislation that focused on improving the environment around coke ovens, blast furnaces, and steel melting shops for the steel plant workers. Currently, the EMD is firmly on its way to obtaining OSHAS certification for its steel plant at Jamshedpur.

As is evident through the endeavors described above, Tata Steel has attempted to go beyond mere legal compliance to becoming an environmentally responsible company. While some of this may be due to the culture and founding values of Tata Steel, there is also a distinct desire to be recognized as a "leader" in all fields, on a par with global excellence standards. Quoting from its website, Tata Steel "has joined the Green Club by committing itself to follow the global Environment Management Practices" (Tata Steel 2004).

Table 2 presents a snapshot of milestones in environmental management at Tata Steel. Following this, we discuss in some detail, Tata Steel's approach to solid waste management and obtaining ISO 14001 certification.

Table 2. Historical milestones in environmental management at Tata Steel

Date	Achievement
1902	J. N. Tata, founder, advises his son, Sir Dorabji Tata: "Be sure to lay wide streets planted with shady trees, every other of a quick growing variety. Be sure there is plenty of space for lawns and gardens."
1911	December—1st Blast Furnace blown in
1939	Tata Steel regarded as the largest steel plant in the British Empire, with a capacity of 800,000 tonnes of saleable steel
1944	4 MGD Sewage Treatment Plant installed in India for the first time
1940s	Production of 1 million tonne of hot metal Solid waste amounted to 1500–2000kg/tcs (Basu, Sharma, and Dhillon 2002)
1951	The Jubilee Park and Jubilee Lake dedicated to the people of Jamshedpur
1959	A sintering plant was installed in the works to "not only utilize the hitherto wasted iron ore fines" but also materially improve blast furnace efficiency. (Chatterjee 2000)—It is important to note the emphasis on using up wasted resources in addition to improving process efficiency. Productivity increase by using sinter in the blast furnaces was of the order of 10%.
1960s	Production of 2 million tones of ingot steel
1962	New Merchant Mill #2 commissioned—cleaner technology
1971	Pelletizing plant set up in Joda iron ore mines to utilize blue fine dust (Lonial 2000)
1972–73	Coal fines washeries constructed at Jamadoba and Bokaro collieries for Tata Steel
1980	Modernization program launched to include state of the art technologies for environment control.
1980–84	Modernization Phase I - LD shop with two LD converters installed, continuous casting of steel (higher yields, lower energy consumption)
1985–89	Modernization Phase 2 - Bar and rod mill installed with closed circuit water recirculation, raw material blending yard set up for servicing the sinter plant (consistent quality, better use of fines), second sinter plant commissioned to use up to 50% of "blue dust" and other solid wastes, coal injection in blast furnaces introduced (Chatterjee 2000), stamp-charged coke oven batteries to use low grade coal (Lonial 2000)
1986	Environment Management Division established
1989	A coke oven battery using stamp charging was commissioned—can produce coke of improved strength, while having the flexibility of using medium grade coking coal as feed (Lonial 2000), Rail and structural mill shut down due to energy inefficiency (among other things)
1991	Environment Manual released in August

1989–94	Modernization Phase 3—More efficient G blast furnace with state of the art environmental control facilities, LD shop 2 with 2 LD converters, complete with a fume extraction system (with LD gas recovery) to replace open hearth furnaces, semi continuous hot strip mill with close circuit water system, another set of stamp charged coke ovens added and new by product plant with minimum pollution with incinerator for excess ammonia; also coal tar charging in blast furnace, replace dolomite by dunite, and use lime fines as well, regenerative type shaft kilns—increase productivity of sinter plant, while reducing coke consumption as well.
1993	40% utilization of solid wastes
1994, Jun	5th June—First Environmental Policy Released
1994, Oct	Secondary Products Profit Centre set up
1995–98	Modernization Phase 4—Double capacity of hot strip mill with state of the art equipment, new bar and rod mill, add 3rd LD converter to LD shop 2, continuous casting machine for 100% continuous casting, connect open hearth furnaces to old energy optimizing furnace Gas Cleaning Plant (EOF GCP) (Jayaraman, Agarwal, and Chatterjee 2003).
1995, Mar	4 Open Hearth Furnaces shut down
1995, Nov	Open Hearth Furnaces shut down, Last two connected to EOF GCP
1997	Environment Management System Initiatives begin Billet mill # 1 shut down due to energy inefficiencies, among other things November—Core group for implementing EMS decide to scrap the existing system of EMS and restart the process after identifying a benchmark. Nov 10th—Revised environmental policy released
1998	Jan 99—ISO 14001 certification for Sukinda Chromite mine, Joda East Iron mines, Noamundi Iron mines (Tata Steel 2001) Nucleus formed for implementing EMS, with Hoogovens as benchmarking partner at Tata Steel Works. The last two furnaces of Steel Melting Shop 3 (with seven open hearth furnaces), commissioned in 1959, were shut down Sheet bar and billet mill shut down due to energy inefficiencies, among other causes
1999	Tata Steel Works get ISO 14001 (Tata Steel 2001) 70.2% solid waste utilization Cold Rolling Mill complex added to Tata Steel
2002	Continuous Galvanizing Line Commissioned
2003	31 Jan—Environment, Occupational Health and Safety Policy Issued—integrating environment with health and safety—march toward OSHAS standards

Solid Waste Management

Waste recycling and reuse rates of Indian plants are abysmally low compared to their counterparts in the developed world. Although creative use of solid waste has been accepted as a business challenge in similar plants abroad, Tata Steel has an abysmally poor record in this respect. The EMD came up with five key causes:

- Inferior quality of raw materials due to lack of beneficiation at pit heads,[4]
- Use of energy intensive and less productive technologies,
- Less recycle and reuse due to technological and economic reasons,
- Dumping sites available in abundance, and
- *No strict legislation for solid waste management.* (Basu et al. 1997, emphasis added)

Over the years, however, legislation has become more stringent, as is evident from Basu, Sharma, and Dhillon (2002), who cite "increased pressures from legislative authorities" as one of the reasons for reducing the quantum of solid wastes. In addition, there is "public pressure on steel industries from world over," as well as an increasing shortage of waste disposal sites. Coupled with these factors, the escalating costs of treating surface runoff and developing dumping sites with polymer linings to prevent groundwater contamination (partly to correct the reckless disposal practices of the past) have made solid waste management a key focus area of the EMD.

On paper, at least, solid waste management has been a thrust area for the EMD as early as the late 1980s, when a cross-functional Waste Utilization Committee was set up to focus firstly on efficient resource use, hence avoiding the generating of waste, secondly on recycling and reusing waste, and thirdly on minimizing the adverse environmental impact of waste yet to be disposed (Basu et al. 1997). To start with, a Waste Recycling Plant (WRP) was set up in 1985 to recover and recycle iron-bearing materials from steel melting slags. The next watershed event was the establishment in 1994 of a profit center for "Secondary Products" as a separate division of the company. The primary objective of this center was to "market all byproducts and wastes" and ensure that their sales generated profits for the company. An increased focus on segregation of scrap and identification of suitable customers led to a rise in total sales realization from 3275.3 million to 5266.6 million INR between 1994–95 and 1996–97, although 80 percent of this came from the selling of scrap (Mathias 1997). While the division was very successful in disposing of scrap, it was not very effective at coping with other wastes, since substantial investment was needed before they could be converted into a saleable form. While a large fraction of BF slag was used for cement making after granulation, slag from steel making was not utilized despite its potential uses as soil conditioner or railway ballast. The prevalent practice for disposing oily/tarry wastes was to deposit them in landfills without adequate leachate collection systems and polymer lining, owing to the prohibitive cost, paucity of adequate space, and lax regulations.

Solid waste utilization therefore hovered around the 40 percent mark until 1977, when a task force for solid waste management was set up. At this point around 450 kgs of wastes per tonne of crude steel produced were not reused and had to be disposed of (Prasad, Sarkar, and Prasad 1997). A benchmarking exercise was taken up to identify the best-in-class solid waste recycling practices worldwide. With increased efforts, the utilization of blast furnace slag witnessed a sudden jump from 50 percent in 1994–95 to 65 percent in 1997–98, with the slag being primarily used for cement making. Also, a quantity of lump blast furnace (BF) slag and steel-making slag was used in road and railway track construction. Although the generation of lime fines is much higher in Tata Steel than other comparable plants, most (98 percent) of the fines were reused either in the sinter plant, briquetted and used for steelmaking, or sold (Basu et al. 1997). A benchmarking exercise for better use of mill scale resulted in a 95 percent increase in its reuse, primarily in sintering (Roy and Das 1999).

When Tata Steel becoming an ISO 14001 certified company, disposal and sales of wastes became even more difficult, since the stringent regulations on hazardous wastes had to be complied with. Government certified recyclers and re-processors were very selective of the types of wastes they purchased, which further motivated the EMD to find more solutions for their waste problem. A use for steel-making slag had been found in cement making, and bench scale trials were giving favorable results. A task force was set up to tackle the disposal of oily and tarry wastes, which was becoming a cause of concern. The task force administered measures to reduce lubricant consumption and institutionalized a system of sorting and collecting wastes for easier reuse or sale (Basu et al. 2003). Most commendably, they devised a technical solution for reusing oily wastes as fuel in the blast furnace, saving substantial fuel costs.

Table 3. Solid waste utilization in Tata Steel, and world benchmarks

Waste	Percent Utilization 1996–97	1998–99	2000–01	World Benchmark	End Use
Blast furnace slag	58.6	73.2	78.54	100	Cement manufacture Construction Industry
LD slag	57	49.6	49.81	100	In ladle furnace and blast furnace as fluidizer/flux Cement making Soil conditioning
BF sludge	nil	62.8	67.73	97	Sinter making (after de-alkalification) Domestic fuel
LD sludge	nil	100	97.71	97	Sinter plant
Flue dust	28	37.2	37.53	97	Sinter making (after de-alkalification) Domestic fuel
Lime fines	100	100	100	100	Sinter plant Brick and aggregate manufacture
Mill scale	45	100	100	100	Sinter plant

Source: Basu, Sharma, and Dhillon (2002), Solid Waste Management in Steel Plants: Challenges and Opportunities, Tata Search, Jamshedpur.

In spite of the drastic increase in waste usage from as low as 40 percent in 1997 to around 70 percent (Basu, Sharma, and Dhillon 2002) in 2001, Tata Steel has a long way to go to reach the global benchmark of almost 100 percent utilization (see Table 3). Notwithstanding its marketability, Tata Steel cannot achieve a 100 percent utilization of BF slag because of a lack of granulation facilities in the old blast furnaces. Not only is the higher capital outlay for granulation facilities a deterrent, but also the layout of the furnaces is such that there is too little space to install cast house granulation plants. The BF sludge and flue dust have excessively high levels of phosphorus and alkali, which make them unsuitable for direct use in the sinter plant, and appropriate commercially viable technology for alkali removal and/or separation of magnetite from the sludge and dust is not available yet. Regulatory issues—such as excise duty on the sale of LD slag (until very recently), and unwillingness of the Indian Railways to use LD slag as railway ballast—have inhibited the search for alternative options for using LD slag. As the markets open up and plants get more competitive, it is hoped that better solutions for solid wastes will be found.

Implementation of ISO 14001 at Tata Steel

Tata Steel initiated the implementation of a comprehensive structured environmental management system (EMS) conforming to the international standard ISO-14001-1996. It did so in order to "facilitate progress toward increased competitiveness through measurement and innovation leading to increased profits, more efficient processes, reduced costs and a more creditable image" (Basu et al. 2003). The successful implementation of ISO 14001 has not only led to the these benefits, but it also let loose a process of cultural transformation at all levels in the organization.

The process of implementing an EMS commenced as early as November 1997, when a cross-functional core group was formed. A consultant was also appointed to train the workforce and facilitate the implementation process. By May 1998 the EMD had designed the EMS and released the EMS manual, objectives, targets and all operating procedures to all the departments within Tata Steel. However, it was clear in subsequent internal audits by the EMD that, while the documentation was thorough, targets were not being met. There was no sense of ownership at the managerial or worker level, and this resulted in poor deployment. The pervasive feeling was that achieving ISO 14001 was the responsibility of the environmental management division, thus defeating the purpose of establishing an EMS.

Meanwhile, some of Tata Steel's associated mines were well on their way to getting certification. Hence the current approach for implementing EMS was abandoned, and a management cell was formed to trouble-shoot and redesign the implementation process. By benchmarking with M/s Hoogovens BV (Netherlands), the task was broken up into several subtasks, each with a time schedule. Workers, officers, and executives were nominated from each department for different posts, in order to liaison with the central cell and the EMD, and to ensure complete involvement of the department. Comprehensive training was provided to all the departments to assist them in developing their own set of objectives and targets based on significant environmental issues. After these were compiled and ratified, each department developed its own environmental management plan. This sort of methodological micro-planning yielded fruit, and Tata Steel was awarded an ISO 14001 certificate in May 2000, which has since been revalidated.

The role of the EMD was limited to measuring and reporting to the concerned division pollution parameters for legal purposes. Compliance tracking was the responsibility of the department. Hence the EMD played a facilitating and monitoring role, but compliance with legal requirements became a line function. Each department met this target along with other production targets. The same held for resource consumption targets set by each department. Even waste management practices were integrated with EMS procedures and decentralized to the department level.

The reason EMS has been so successful is that there is a sense of ownership of procedures and functions under ISO 14000, all the way from the executives to the workers at the shop floor level. This was achieved by integrating the whole process with the Joint Departmental Council (JDC). The JDC is the mechanism through which joint consultations between management and labor unions takes place. The machinery of JDCs was chosen to spread EMS awareness at all levels of the company and to enlist everyone's participation in EMS activities. Each departmental JDC formed a Safety, Health and Environment (SHE) committee consisting of an EMS Coordinator, an assistant EMS Coordinator, and a Safety and Environment Inspector. The SHE committee is responsible for periodic inspections and generates non conformity reports for preventive and corrective action, which are reviewed in monthly JDC meetings.

Visible improvements in both environmental ambience and safety are evident after the implementation of ISO 14001. In addition, the EMS ensured sustained legal compliance and an enhanced public image, which led to Tata Steel's classification among the top ten green companies in India by Tata Energy Research Institute, a leading environmental and energy think tank in New Delhi. There is a discernible cultural transformation in the workforce, whose concern for the environment has increased manifold. The workforce is more amenable to change and have begun to value the improvements in the workplace, so much so that the EMD is now progressing toward OSHAS compliance for a safe and healthy workplace. ISO 14001 has led to significant cost reductions as well. Quantifiable gains from waste and resource management activities, due to the adoption of EMS, have been posted for the first year after achieving ISO 14000, directly demonstrating that pollution prevention pays. Table 4, adapted from Basu et al. (2003), displays some steel-related data from the company's Annual Report to shareholders.

Table 4. Cost savings achieved in the year 1999–2000 from implementation of ISO 14001 through departmental activities and targets

	Quantity	Unit cost reduction (INR)	Total savings (INR millions)
Cost savings from waste management activities			
Additional melting scrap collected above AOP target	15360 T	753	11.6
Additional scrap sold above AOP target	56345 T	2477	139.6
Used oil collected (barrels)	1100 bbl	2000	2.2
Rejected conveyor belt collected	270 T	20000	5.4
Rejected wood collected	1350 T	701	0.9
Additional slag granulated	70026 T	169	11.9
Use of waste refractories	95%		20.0
Total savings			191.6
Less: expenditure for collection, clean up, bin and pit construction			–10.6
Net savings			181.0
Cost savings from resource conservation activities			
Reduction in coal consumption at Power House 3	23756 T	657	15.6
Reduction in hydraulic oil, lubricant and diesel consumption			6.3
Reduction in wooden sleeper consumption	1664	794	1.3
Net savings			23.2
Total savings due to implementing ISO 14001			204.2
Total Profits after tax for Tata Steel in 1999–2000			4225.9
Contribution of Environment Management to the bottom line			4.8%

Is Paying Attention to the Environment Profitable?

Tata Steel is one of India's best known symbols of industrial growth. A blue chip company, Tata Steel has a market share of around 13 percent and is looked upon as a professional and responsible corporation. Besides producing steel, it is also responsible for the upkeep (including provision of municipal services) of most of the areas where its employees reside. Tata Steel's strategic philanthropy[5] encompasses the provision of educational and training services, medical facilities, rural improvement programs, developing wastelands, and so on. Judging by the extent of social and environmental involvement of Tata Steel, a cursory glance at its balance sheet tempts us to state unequivocally that pollution prevention and social responsibility pays. While social responsibility in its holistic sense is beyond the scope of this paper, the environmental responsibility of Tata Steel has been rated as among the highest in the country, and there has been a simultaneous increase in both the profitability of and the number of green initiatives taken at Tata Steel. This would tend to indicate that environmental responsibility and profitability go hand in hand, but the direction of causation is rather unclear.

In depth discussions with managers at the EMD seem to suggest that increased profitability could lead to environmental responsibility, but not vice versa. However, this conjecture also appears rather simplistic, as reality is far more convoluted. More often than not, the return on investments from environmentally related projects are lower that the normal corporate hurdle rates for investment. In fact, during the "compliance era" in the late 1980s and early 1990s, most environmental projects could not compete with other projects and had to be approved under the threat of legal consequences. These were primarily pollution abatement projects that involved treating the effluent before release—an end of pipe solution—rather than involving changes in the production process.

Table 5 summarizes the operating and capital costs incurred for pollution control during seven years, starting 1995–1996. It is evident that the operating costs went up 1.6 times in seven years in spite of higher capital expenditure, which reflects the installation of more modern, clean, cost-effective, and energy efficient equipment. In the company's own words, "the increase in cost is mainly due to increase in numbers of pollution abatement facilities and better availability of these equipment" (Tata Steel 1999, 2000), which clearly demonstrates that environmental compliance was viewed as a cost to the company even in 2002. The spurt in capital investment in 1995–1996 and 1997–1999 is a reflection of modernization phase III and IV of the company, when several types of end-of-pipe equipment, such as electrostatic precipitators, were installed. The expenses in 2000–2002 are due to the addition of the cold rolling mill complex and the continuous galvanizing line.

Of late, however, employees with adequate training and experience have learned to identify environmental solutions that are truly win-win in nature—the environment is cleaner, and there are cost savings. As an example, we can look at the benefits obtained from re-utilizing oily and tarry wastes, which were previously being sold or dumped in landfills. To begin with, waste generation was reduced by cutting back on

Table 5. Operating costs and capital investments related to pollution control

	95–96	96–97	97–98	98–99	99–00	00–01	01–02
Operating Costs (INR millions)							
Power consumption	98	143	199	235	238	254	268
Consumables	91	48	40	43	213	345	263
Revenue expenses	4.5	5	6	6	6.9	7.8	8
Water cess and other charges	6.5	7	7	6.3	6.5	7	7.6
Total operating costs	200	203	252	290	465	614	647
Crude steel production (million tonnes)	3.02	3.1	3.23	3.26	3.43	3.57	3.75
Specific operating costs (INR/tcs)	66.1	65.5	78	89.0	135	172.1	173
Capital investments (INR millions)	410	60	80	350	400	115	145

lubricant consumption. This was achieved by using technologically advanced grades of lubricant and installing in-situ filtration systems for hydraulic oil installations. This generated annual savings to the tune of 24 million INR. In addition, the establishment of a centralized reclamation facility for selective recycling and reusing of oils generated annual savings of 6 million INR. Further, the usage of waste oil in blast furnaces as fuel resulted in coke savings, which translates to a benefit of 3 million INR per annum (Basu et al. 2003).

However, even in these cases, complete accounting for environmental benefits is lacking. This means that projected return on investments are lower than they would be if benefits such as a clean workplace, lower fugitive emissions, and so forth, could be quantified. In addition, it is not easy to identify win-win cases in the context of steel manufacturing. In most projects, it is very difficult to separate gains due to environmental improvements from those achieved by other process improvements, and a systematic reporting of gains attributable to specific projects is lacking. Even win-win opportunities that can be documented are seldom identified by employees, until there are regulatory pressures which compel them to look for business opportunities in areas which are considered as extraneous to the manufacturing process.

To generalize our findings, this study of Tata Steel provides anecdotal evidence to support the hypothesis that pollution prevention projects usually make more business sense than pollution abatement projects, which cost the company money. So far, however, pollution prevention projects are few compared to the large number of pollution abatement projects undertaken to meet regulatory norms. Hence the net contribution of the EMD to the bottom line at Tata Steel is still negative—it is a cost centre that ensures legal compliance and strives to build and maintain a green image for Tata Steel. Of course, if one evaluated the EMD in terms of the noncompliance penalties averted, it would make a very positive contribution to the company's profits.

In conclusion, as long as such resources such as wastelands and lowlands (to use as landfills) and clean air (to use as a pollution sink) are inadequately valued, environmental management issues will not make business sense in most cases. They will always be looked upon as burdens forced upon the company by legislative or public pressure rather than as a means to gain a competitive edge.

Ambiguities in Tata Steel's Environmental Management Approach

So far, it appears that Tata Steel is the complete antithesis to the general environmental irresponsibility we attribute to the corporate world. Not only has no public interest litigation been filed against them, but they also have a very green image world over. On the other hand, NGOs in and around Tata Steel have confessed that while they did not have any complaints against the company at present, they would think twice before filing a public interest litigation for a grievance, since they felt powerless against such a giant.

Tata Steel appears to have used all the textbook environmental management tools to improve and streamline its environmental management practices, and their beyond-compliance results are evident from their annual environment performance reports. More recently, they have been publishing a Corporate Sustainability Report that is accessible on their website.

A closer look at their environmental initiatives, however, demonstrates that most of the "voluntary" environmental initiatives—those that are unnecessary for meeting regulatory norms—are undertaken only when they make clear business sense, or when they are useful to pre-empt further legislation. Most of their green initiatives are a direct result of legislation. Again, some of their environmental initiatives appear to be more rhetoric than action. We discuss some of these contradictions in this section, while trying to understand the factors responsible for such contradictory behavior.

Green Supply Chain Management: Rhetoric or Reality?

Green supply chain management (Green SCM) in Tata Steel is limited to training the vendors and urging them to obtain ISO 14001 certification. There is no evidence that Tata Steel insists on ISO 14001 certification as a criterion for inclusion in the approved vendor list. This is true even in 2004, despite the fact they started green supply chain management as early as 2000. In addition to encouraging and training vendors, the initiatives listed under Green SCM include increased involvement of the materials management group at the design stage, and rationalization of suppliers. While these measures would improve SCM, their environmental implications are not clear. The initiatives listed also include integrating environmental requirements with purchase specifications, a procedure that has to be followed regardless of adoption of green SCM to ensure legal compliance for the firm.

Hence it is not clear why or how "Tata Steel has adopted the concept of 'Greening of Supply Chain' in its operations" (Tata Steel 2002). Given the guidelines of ISO 14000 and the Global Reporting Initiative, as well as the number of environmental awards for which the company competes, one wonders whether these would be reasons for the company to advertise that they have adopted green SCM even though they have done precious little in this area. This is definitely an instance where business interests have prevailed over environmental concerns. Tata Steel is practical enough to realize that many of their smaller but cost-effective vendors would be in no position to conform to the requirements of ISO 14001 without raising their input costs. The cost of conforming to norms is evident in Table 5 above, and it is possible that Tata Steel prefers to overlook environmental deficiencies in its suppliers to ensure its own cost effective production. Small wonder then, that the world's least-cost producer (Tata Steel) is also recognized as among the top ten greenest companies in India!

Sustained Commitment, or Spurts of Commitment

With respect to solid waste management, Tata Steel is committed to reducing waste generation and reusing or recycling as much waste as is feasible. This has been reiterated time and again from as early as 1989. Yet we see several lacunae in the practices employed to utilize LD slag.

Several uses have been identified for LD slag. It can be used as railway track ballast or material for road construction. Given its lime content, the slag has much potential as a soil conditioner. Another potential use is as a sweetener for cement. Tata Steel has taken several initiatives for the utilization of LD slag, but perhaps many of them were not seen through till the end. The use of LD slag as railway ballast has two problems: first, the Indian Railway authorities are very conservative and would not prefer to experiment with alternative ballasts, and second, the slag must be seasoned before it is suitable as ballast material, which requires large storage yards that Tata Steel does not have. While Tata Steel uses LD slag for its own road making, it has not been able to obtain end users in the highway construction industry. Interestingly, even the SPCB had expressed concern over Tata Steel's use of LD slag for road making alongside the banks of the river Kharkai, although this misapprehension was later cleared (Tata Steel 2002).

Tata Steel extensively explored the alternative of using LD slag as a soil conditioner, and for some time LD slag was being sold under the brand name Growell. However, this effort was abandoned due to tax issues, and because the market response to Growell was lukewarm. Later, when the tax issues were resolved, Tata Steel put all its efforts into developing LD slag cement and abandoned "Project Growell." While the option of LD slag cement would generate more returns than Growell, not all slag can be used for cement making, and another use must be found for the remaining slag. Even in March 2004, when the LD slag cement project ran into roadblocks, the managers did not really consider reviving the Growell alternative. Perhaps the extension services that are required to popularize and develop a customer base for Growell were too demanding for Tata Steel to pursue this option aggressively. Currently a large fraction of LD slag continues to be dumped, even though there are uses for the slag, perhaps because it is more cost-effective to procure landfills and dump indiscriminately than to find an environmentally friendly solution.

Acting Responsibly, or Acting Defensively

Whenever new or more stringent legislation is passed, there is always a tendency to oppose the legislation with a view to diluting its stringency or at least delay its implementation. One would expect that Tata Steel would not respond in such a passive and environmentally irresponsible manner. Nevertheless, we find instances of such behavior in Tata Steel, as revealed in the anecdote below. This is especially surprising considering that Tata Steel was consulted before these regulations were finalized.

In the recent past, new legislation has been passed with respect to work area norms for coke ovens, which must be complied with within a stipulated timeframe. Since most coke ovens in integrated steel plants are "top-charged' recovery-type ovens, the norms were devised with them in mind. The basic thrust of these new regulations is to improve the working areas in and around the coke oven by minimizing the quantity of fugitive emissions. The norms are rather stringent and require significant modernization or modification to the existing coke ovens in India's integrated steel plants. A very suitable timeframe was provided for firms to meet these norms.

Tata Steel uses a superior stamp-charged technology for coke ovens, which means that these ovens cannot technically be classified as top-charged. Due to this better technology, fugitive emissions from the coke ovens are lower than those from top-charged ovens. However, they exceed the fugitive emission norms that are mandated in the new legislation. A significant amount of investment is required to bring these coke ovens into compliance with the new norms. Interestingly, Tata Steel is actively lobbying to exempt their coke ovens from the purview of this new legislation, or delay its implementation, rather than formulate strategies to meet these norms. Its only defense is that the norms are for top-charged batteries, and that their batteries are, strictly speaking, not top-charged.

Thus, we see that even an exemplary socially responsible corporation has a long way to go before changing its mindset enough to give the same importance to environmental and social issues as to the typical shareholder objectives of increasing profits or market share. One must keep in mind, however, that by staying profitable or increasing market share, the company meets one of its primary social objectives of providing stable employment to a wide variety of people. Also, in a system plagued by corruption and incompetence, Tata Steel has consistently met and even exceeded legal norms and won accolades in India and around the world, which in itself is commendable.

Notwithstanding the debate on rhetoric or reality, there are some general lessons in corporate environmental responsibility that can be learned from the Tata Steel case. These are relevant for other businesses in developing countries, especially those that may not have linkages with transnational corporations with established internal codes of conduct.

Determinants of Environmental Behavior

Before generalizing observations of Tata Steel to lessons for firms in developing countries as a whole, it is useful to identify the drivers of Tata Steel's environmental behavior and evaluate their relative importance. Factors that drive corporate environmental responses could be internal to the firm or the result of external pressures. Through detailed interactions with Tata Steel personnel and from the data made available, some drivers of environmental behavior have been identified and are presented in Table 6. We now discuss the role of these factors in determining Tata Steel's responses. It must be noted, however, that often it is not a single factor, but the interplay of several factors that causes a firm to respond and determines the timing and nature of the response.

Table 6. Causal variables determining responses and response strategies.

External	Internal
Regulation	Strategic Attitude
• Stringency and application	• Long-term vision
• Implementation	• Competitiveness
• Penalty	• R & D rivalry
Policy	Organizational culture
• Taxes, duties, financial incentives	• Sense of Ownership at all levels
• Property rights issues	• Individual Recognition
Voluntary schemes	• Managerial Support
• Public disclosure programs	Resources and costs
Trade links	• Infrastructural resources
Stakeholder concerns	• Availability of appropriate technology
• (Consumer preferences)	• Corporate hurdle rate
• Judicial activism	• Production costs
• Company image	Competence
	Enlightened self-interest

External Factors

Among all the external determinants, perhaps the most potent ones for green responses are regulatory pressures, trade links, and the need to maintain a clean and green company image. Tata Steel, along with other publicly held steel plants, is always consulted before the introduction of any environmental legislation. Hence it is not entirely surprising that many environmental initiatives are taken even before legislation is passed to require them. Although the implementation of legislation and the levy of penalties leave much be desired, the establishment of norms results in investments in pollution prevention or reduction that bring the plant in compliance. The command-and-control nature of the regulations, and their bias toward end-of-pipe measures, explain why Tata Steel's environmental management approach has been biased toward pollution control equipment and processes rather than pollution prevention.

Coupled with regulatory pressures, the opening up of the economy and trade with the developed world put added pressures on the company to adopt ISO 14001 practices, and as a result, it had to record 100 percent compliance with legal obligations. The decision to comply regardless of monitoring or imposition of penalties, to obtain ISO 14001 certification, be a part of the global reporting initiative, and to publicize widely the company's green image, all came from the company's desire to project a clean and green image. This has always been a stakeholder expectation from Tata Steel, hence it had to oblige.

Other governmental policies have played a less important role. For example, the abysmally low water cess (See Table 5 for annual expenditure on this account) has provided no incentive to reduce water consumption. Conflicting policies sometimes discourage positive environmental actions, as in the case of the tax on sales of LD slag. Whereas such public disclosure programs as the global reporting initiative have provided Tata Steel a publicity platform, their impact on actual environmental responses appears to be minimal. As discussed earlier, judicial activism is not a great concern for Tata Steel, and consumer preferences are not developed to the point that they would determine the demand for a commodity like steel, although a substantial fraction of Tata Steel's production is branded.

Internal Factors

Most of the environmental improvements in Tata Steel appear to be the (un)intended result of modernization, cost reduction exercises, and production process changes. The company's strategy of being an industry leader in low-cost production, technology, and management is perhaps the most important driver in this regard. Thus, such managerial tools as performance audits, benchmarking, and "technovation" have been used just as effectively at the EMD as in the rest of the company. Managerial competence is essential for effective use of these tools, and it was not lacking in the EMD. In addition, the "sense of process ownership" was identified as the key factor that led to the implementation of systematic environment management practices. Another key factor responsible for all the positive environmental developments at Tata Steel has been the availability of infrastructural as well as monetary resources to ensure that the company image is maintained. Very few companies in India can match the resources spent for disseminating information about small successes in environmental management within the plant. At the same time, however, the lack of such infrastructure as cast houses for several blast furnaces (which cannot be constructed due to paucity of space) has resulted in less that 100 percent use of blast furnace slag.

We cannot totally discount the role of enlightened self interest in shaping Tata Steel's environmental responses. One must realize that in the regulatory environment in which Tata Steel operates, it could have got by without many of the investments in pollution abatement. However, the role of enlightened self interest seems dwarfed by the modernization, technological advancement, and managerial prowess that transformed environment management systems in Tata Steel.

Factors such as R&D rivalry with other integrated steel plants in India and abroad did not appear to play a major role in determining environmental responses, although this could well become an important driver in the future. The ability to think out of the box and come up with innovative solutions is nurtured by a management policy of providing individual recognition for useful ideas and giving subordinates sufficient space to explore them. Several small but effective pollution prevention schemes originated in employee suggestions. Although corporate hurdle rates were cited as a deterrent against environmental investments, no such instances were observed.

Having discussed the relative importance of some variables in determining environmental response at Tata Steel, we now generalize our findings in the context of developing countries.

Lessons for Corporations in Developing Countries

Of the many firm-specific and external drivers of environmental responses, perhaps the most important is environmental regulation—its stringency, application, implementation, and penalties for noncompliance. In most developing countries, not only are regulations insufficiently stringent, there are also serious flaws in their application and implementation. A holistic approach to governmental legislation is often missing. Regulations and guidelines issued by different ministries are in conflict and send confusing signals to the firm. Implementation is faulty, primarily because the regulatory agencies are staffed by under-qualified people who do not understand the regulations or the environmental implications of noncompliance. Imposition of penalties for noncompliance is rare, and where penalties are imposed, they are given minimal publicity. Corruption is a pervasive problem. While financial incentives are provided through tax breaks, reduced duties, or other subsidies, these measures are given too little publicity and remain accessible only to larger firms that have "contacts" with the government. Property rights issues often come up in such environmental initiatives as restoring wastelands used as solid waste dumps. Most of these factors are tremendous disincentives for proactive environmental behavior. Firms want to play it safe and will at best comply with regulatory norms, which are usually biased toward end-of-pipe controls. There is little incentive to experiment with novel production processes or go beyond compliance.

This is where Tata Steel teaches us valuable lessons on how vital trade links are for bringing environmental management systems up to a par with firms operating in developing countries. While consumer preferences in developing countries have not evolved to the extent that there is a marked preference for green products, particularly at a higher price, companies that are outward-looking tend to keep their foreign customer preferences in mind when framing environmental policies. A connected world indeed has benefits for developing countries.

Participation in voluntary public disclosure programs, such as the global reporting initiative, has made Tata Steel accountable to its shareholders, and that has gone a long way toward making the company more environmentally responsible. By adopting such voluntary measures, Tata Steel has kept judicial activism at bay at a time when it is emerging as the most formidable environmental threat to a firm in developing countries. Bad publicity and unnecessary harassment thus emerge as very potent drivers for good environmental management practices.

Besides these external factors, internal drivers such as the long-term vision of company leadership, competitiveness with acknowledged industry leaders, and organizational culture strongly influence environmental reactions. When a firm can look beyond its short-term problems and regulatory hurdles and position itself in a strategic niche for the future, it is bound to be more forward-looking and develop long-term cost-effective solutions for its environmental problems. This is a highly desirable quality, especially since most firms in developing countries take a firefighting approach to environmental regulations. Any decisions on modernization or capacity expansion in Tata Steel are taken in conjunction with professionals trained in environment management, to ensure that the choice of technology addresses environmental issues in the process stage and minimizes end-of-pipe measures. Other corporations should similarly involve their environment management departments in production and planning, rather than restrict their roles to mere coordinators and liaison agents with regulatory bodies.

As is evident in the way Tata Steel implemented its environmental management system, there is a tremendous need for a sense of process ownership at all levels. Individual recognition for good environmental initiatives tend to motivate the work force and send them signals that these initiatives are just as important as production targets. In addition, managerial support and basic competence building is essential. Another useful initiative is to publicize cost savings achieved by each environmental initiative. Such knowledge-sharing exercises drive home the point that there are real monetary benefits to "going green," and they motivate employees to look for other pollution prevention opportunities.

Another interesting observation is that environmental improvements are often the result of cost-saving drives by Tata Steel (for example, energy conservation measures) or stem from more productive operational practices. These are definitely win-win measures that any corporation can employ with minimal investment of time and other resources.

As we trace the evolution of environmental management at Tata Steel, we see that while the department was established predominantly for liaison and lobbying purposes, it has evolved to perform a very different role. The company moved from a position of primarily lobbying to reduce the impact of environmental legislation in the mid 1980s, to 100 percent compliance with statutory norms in the mid 1990s. Furthermore, it moved beyond compliance through such measures as adopting ISO 14000 standards and subscribing to global reporting standards. On examining its pollution prevention projects we find examples of unconventional thinking about how to create value from waste, for instance by using the calorific value of oily and tarry wastes. However, this transition from compliance-based management to strategic management is still nascent in Tata Steel. Despite wholehearted managerial support and high business profits, the process is neither quick nor easy to implement. This is a valuable lesson for other firms with high expectations: implementing environmental management systems can completely change the nature of business. Whereas implementing an EMS acts as a catalyst for better environmental management, a firm has much further to go before it can truly be called a green value-creating organization.

To conclude, this paper attempts to put forward a practical application of corporate environmental responsibility through a case study of a respected Indian steel company. Specific stumbling blocks faced by the firm when implementing environmental projects were identified, and in the course of the study, several motivating and de-motivating factors for responsible environmental management were identified. It is hoped that insights from this paper can assist corporate environmental decision making in the developing world, where business environments tend to be similar.

Notes

I would like to thank the management of Tata Steel for allowing me to conduct this study and share the results. I also acknowledge the guidance of my thesis advisors, Professors Anindya Sen and Ramprasad Sengupta.

1. We do not look at the captive power plants in Tata Steel. We try to concentrate on only the "steelmaking process." Mining operations, transport of ores or finished steel, etc., are also outside the purview of this case study.
2. "*Nallah*," when translated into English, means "drain."
3. This refers to the fraction of time that the pollution control equipment was functioning effectively and was not shut down due to malfunctioning and/or maintenance.
4. Owing to a poorer quality of coal and iron ore, solid waste generation is of the order of 1000–1200 kg per tonne of crude steel produced (Prasad, Sarkar, and Prasad 1997).
5. The reader can refer to Porter and Kramer (2002) for a detailed discussion of the implications of the term "strategic philanthropy."

References

Basu, G. S., S. M. R. Prasad, D. N. Jha, R. P. Sharma, and V. Balasubramaniam. 1996. "Environmental Control in Raw Materials Handling at G Blast Furnace," *Tata Search 1996*, Jamshedpur, 106–108.

Basu, G. S., R. P. Sharma, and A. S. Dhillon. 2002. "Solid Waste Management in Steel Plants: Challenges and Opportunities," *Tata Search 2002*, Jamshedpur, 39–42.

Basu, G. S., R. P. Sharma, M. Jegannathan, and A. S. Dhillon. 1997. "Recycling and Reuse of Solid Waste at Tata Steel," *Tata Search 1997*, Jamshedpur, 31–34.

Basu, G. S., R. P. Sharma, J. P. N. Singh, M. Mashiruddin, and M. D. Maheshwari. 2003. "Utilisation of Oily and Tarry Wastes in an Integrated Steel Plant," *Tata Search 2003*, Jamshedpur, 119–124.

Chatterjee, A. 2000. "Evolution of Technical Facilities and Technologies at Tata Steel," *Tata Search 2000*, Jamshedpur, sec. SC2.

Jayaraman, R., R. K. Agarwal, and A. Chatterjee. 2003. "The Transformation of Tata Steel," *Tata Search 2003*, Jamshedpur, 33–40.

Lonial, S. K. 2000. "Evolution of Raw Materials at Tata Steel," *Tata Search 2000*, Jamshedpur, sec. SC1.

Mathias, A. 1997. "Wealth from Waste," *Tata Tech* 27, Jamshedpur, 31–36.

Porter, M. E., and M. R. Kramer 2002. "The Competitive Advantage of Corporate Philanthropy," *Harvard Business Review* (December): 5–16.

Prasad, A. S., P. K. Sarkar, and S. M. R. Prasad. 1997. "Environment Friendly Production of Iron and Steel: The Case of Tata Steel," *Tata Search 1997*, Jamshedpur, 113–117.

Roy, T. K., and A. K. Das. 1999. "Optimising Specific Raw Materials Consumption through Benchmarking." *Tata Search 1999*, Jamshedpur, 31–34.

Sarkar, P. K., A. Ahmad, N. Krishnaswami, and A. S. Dhillon. 1996. "Water Conservation, Recycling and Reuse in Tata Steel," *Tata Search 1996*, Jamshedpur, 116–123.

Sripriya, R. S., P. V. T. Rao, and R. P. Sharma. 2000. "LCA Study for Steel Sector: Analysis for Blast Furnace Operations." *Tata Search 2000*, Jamshedpur, 97–101.

Tata Steel. 1999. *Environmental Performance Report, 1998–1999*, Environmental Management, Tata Steel, Jamshedpur.

________. 2001. *Environmental Performance Report, 2000–2001*, Environmental Management, Tata Steel, Jamshedpur.

________. 2002a. *Corporate Sustainability Report, 2001–2002*, Environmental Management, Tata Steel, Jamshedpur, http://www.tatasteel.com/corporatesustainability/GRI%2001-02.doc, last accessed 8 June 2004.

________. 2002b. *Environmental Performance Report, 2001–2002*, Environmental Management, Tata Steel, Jamshedpur.

________. 2003. Tata Steel: An organisational profile, http://www.tatasteel.com/corporateprofile/organisation.htm, last accessed 7 June 2004.

________. 2004. Corporate website, http://www.tatasteel.com, last accessed 7 June 2004.

The Author

Runa Sarkar is a Ph.D. student in the Fellow Program, Indian Institute of Management Calcutta, Diamond Harbour Road, Joka, Kolkata 700104, India, runa@email.iimcal.ac.in.

FOREIGN INVESTMENT IN THE MENA REGION: ANALYZING NONTRADITIONAL DETERMINANTS

Nada Kobeissi
Long Island University–C. W. Post, Brookville, New York, USA

Abstract

Although there is substantial literature examining the flow of foreign investments into various regions of the world, there is still a lack of research about joint ventures and foreign investment activities in the Middle East and North Africa (MENA). One objective of this paper is to remedy this neglect and extend previous empirical work by focusing on foreign investments in the MENA region. The second objective is to focus on non-traditional determinants that have tended to be overlooked or underestimated in previous research. The increasing globalization has led to a reconfiguration of the ways in which multinationals pursue various types of foreign investments, and changed the motives for and the determinants of FDI. This has prompted some to suggest that non traditional determinants have become more important. In view of that, the paper will focus on factors such as governance, legal environment, and economic freedom and examine their impact on foreign investment activities in the MENA region.

Introduction

The objective of this paper is to focus on two significant research questions that have not yet been thoroughly examined in the literature on foreign investment. Over the last fifteen years, the flows of foreign investment around the world have been growing spectacularly. While international trade has doubled, the flow of foreign direct investment (FDI) has increased by a factor of ten (Levy-Yeyati, Panizza, and Stein 2003). Within the various regional growth of foreign investment, FDI flowing to developing countries has accounted for about 40 percent of global FDI (Erdal and Tatoglu 2002). Although there is substantial literature examining the flow of foreign investments into various regions of the world, unfortunately the majority of this research has focused on U.S. foreign investment activities in Europe, NAFTA Signatory nations, Asia and Pacific Rim nations, and economies in transition (Kingsley and Crumbley 1997). There is a paucity of information and studies relating to joint ventures and foreign investment activities in the Middle East and North Africa (MENA) region. The first objective of this paper is to remedy this neglect and extend previous empirical work by focusing on foreign investment in the MENA region.

 pp. 217–233

Looking at foreign investment data within the MENA region, one cannot help but notice the wide variability in the flow of foreign investment and joint venture activities, and wonder why some countries are more attractive to foreign investments than others. In trying to determine some of the factors that impact foreign investment flow, it is important to distinguish between three categories of foreign investment, these are: (1) market seeking; (2) resource seeking; and (3) efficiency seeking investments (Dunning 1993). A 1998 UNCTAD report argued that globalization has led to a reconfiguration of the ways in which multinationals pursue these various types of foreign investments, and changed the motives for and the determinants of FDI (Dunning 1999). For example, in recent years, foreign investment in developing countries has shifted from market and resource seeking investments, to more of efficiency seeking investment (Dunning 2002). This has prompted some to argue that the relative importance of some of the traditional market related factors (relative wage costs, infrastructure, macroeconomic policy) no longer hold (Loree and Guisinger 1995) and to suggest that less traditional determinants have become more important (Noorbakhsh, Poloni, and Youssef 2001; Addison and Heshmati 2003).

The need to examine less traditional determinants is particularly relevant within the MENA region. The majority of the countries in that region are neither big enough to attract significant number of market seeking foreign investment, nor resource rich enough to attract resource seeking foreign investment. Therefore, in analyzing foreign investment in the MENA region the second objective of this paper is to focus on some of the non-traditional factors that have tended to be overlooked or underestimated in previous research on foreign investment. In light of this focus, the paper will thus consider factors such as governance, legal environment, and economic freedom and examine their impact on foreign investment in the MENA region.

Hypotheses

Foreign investment and the MENA region

Foreign investment has numerous effects on the economy of the recipient country. It influences labor market, income, prices, export and import (Erdal and Tatoglu 2002). It is an important vehicle for the transfer of technology and a positive contributor to economic growth (Lim 2001). Unfortunately however, the recent unprecedented growth in foreign investment activities has largely bypassed the Arab world (UNCTAD 1999). Compared with other developing countries, the capital inflow in the Arab world remained constant at about $10 billion in the last two decades, whereas it has increased four times to reach $300 billion in other developing countries, mainly in East Asia, Latin America, and, increasingly, in Central Europe. Recent analysis revealed that the Arab world received on average 1 percent of global FDI in the 1990s compared to 2 percent of their share in world GDP. Most of these FDIs were concentrated in six Arab countries, namely Egypt, Jordan, Morocco, Oman, Saudi Arabia and Tunisia and were mostly undertaken in the oil, petrochemical, and manufacturing industries, especially textiles, metals and minerals (Sadik and Bolbol 2001).

Comparing inward FDI performance with potential for the same region produces a matrix representing *front runners, below potential, above potential and under performers* respectively (Table 1).

Table 1. FDI potential and performance of MENA countries.

	High FDI Performance	Low FDI performance
High FDI potential	Front Runners: Bahrain, Jordan, Israel	Below Potential: Egypt, Kuwait, Lebanon, Libya, Oman, Qatar, Saudi Arabia, UAE
Low FDI potential	Above Potential: Morocco, Sudan	Under-Performers: Algeria, Iran, Syria, Tunisia, Turkey, Yemen

Source UNCTAD: Inward FDI performance and potential 1999–2001.

Further examination of some of the countries in this matrix, reveals some interesting information. For example, although it is the largest economy in Eastern Europe, the European Union's sixth biggest trading partner, and the world's seventh largest emerging economy, Turkey is an under-performer. FDI flows into Turkey is only a fraction of the level of FDI attracted to countries of comparable size and development like Argentina and Mexico, and only one-quarter the level of FDI attracted into Poland (Loewendahl and Ertugal-Loewendahl 2000). On the other hand, the significantly smaller country, Bahrain has managed to be a front runner. The country has been able to attract foreign investment through significant incentives such as labor subsidies, electricity and land rental rebates, 100 percent rebate on customs duties for major equipment/raw materials, export credit facilities and tariff protection. Many investors cited the country's tax structure as their key motivation to invest. Bahrain imposes virtually, no personal tax, no restriction on capital or profit repatriation and most significantly no corporate taxation. (Gilmore et al. 2003).

It is important to note that the recent shift from markets and resources seeking investments, toward more of an efficiency seeking investment could—if properly exploited—be advantageous to the MENA countries due to their relatively small market sizes and limited natural resources. The main objective of market-seeking investment is to meet the demand in the domestic market. In resource-seeking investment, the objective is to make use of the host country resources to produce goods but for sale outside the local market (Asiedu 2002). Demands and resources however, are less relevant in efficiency seeking investment, where the emphasis is more on the efficiency with which foreign investors can operate, network, sell and export their products to other countries. Therefore, in striving to attract foreign investment, the most viable among the alternatives for the MENA region, would be a focus on efficiency seeking investors. Such notion reinforces the importance of examining efficiency enhancing elements such as governance, legal system and economic freedom and their impact on foreign investment.

Governance

Globerman and Shapiro (2002) suggested that governance represents the public institutions and policies created by governments as a framework for economic and social relations. Kaufmann, Kraay, and Zoido-Lobaton (2000) defined governance as the traditions and institutions that determine how authority is exercised in a particular country. Good governance infrastructure is a complex, multifaceted concept generally manifested in a country's accountability, government effectiveness, regulatory burden, political stability, rule of law and control of corruption (Kaufmann, Kraay, and Zoido-Lobaton 1999a, and 1999b). It contributes to the effective implementation of economic policies and helps to determine whether or not there is a sound, attractive business environment for investment. It provides the mechanism to minimize policy distortions, reduces information asymmetries and uncertainties, increases the flexibility of a country to respond to economic shocks and makes it easier to start, run and expand new businesses (World Bank 2003).

Globerman and Shapiro (2003) found governance infrastructure to be an important direct determinants of location choice by U.S. investors. The presence or lack of the various elements of governance has a potential to affect host country's attractiveness to foreign investment. One particular element that has been widely related to governance and associated with foreign investment is transparency. Lack of transparency or opacity—a term largely associated with bribery and corruption—is a particular and common sign of lack of good governance (World Bank 2003). Davis and Ruhe (2003) found a highly significant relationship between corruption and foreign investment. Nowadays prospective investors are paying attention to the realities of corruption in some foreign countries (Conklin 2002). Corruption has been a significant obstacle for U.S. investors due to the United States' Foreign Corrupt Practices Act, which has outlawed foreign bribery. In theory a firm will be less likely to enter a non-transparent country because of the increased risks, uncertainty and costs of doing business. On the other hand, a country that takes steps to increase the degree of transparency and reduce corruption could expect a significant increase in the level of foreign investment. On average, a country could expect 40 percent increase in FDI from one point increase in their transparency ranking (Drabek and Payne 2001).

Beyond U.S. investor, Globerman and Shapiro (2002) also found governance infrastructure to be an important determinant of both FDI inflows and outflows in most countries; however they found that FDI will be more strongly affected by improvements in governance in developing countries than in developed countries. The returns to investments in good governance were greater for developing and transition economies. Unfortunately, the quality of governance in MENA region is very poor. When compared with countries that have similar incomes and characteristics—the main competitors in the global marketplace—the MENA region ranks at the bottom on the index of overall governance quality (World Bank 2003). Consequently, in 1999–2001, six out of the bottom ten countries in inward FDI performance from various regions in the world were from the MENA region, namely Iran, Kuwait, Libya, Saudi Arabia, UAE, and Yemen. The remaining countries were Malawi, Indonesia, Gabon and Suriname (UNCTAD 2002). Looking back at the above matrix, these six MENA countries were categorized as either below potential or under performer in terms of their performance in foreign investment.

Hypothesis 1: There is a positive relationship between the level of governance and the flow of foreign investment in MENA countries.

Legal System

Several papers have argued that the legal system can play a key role in attracting foreign investments or encouraging financial and economic development (LaPorta et al. 1998a, 1998b; Globerman and Shapiro 2003; Chan-Lee and Ahn 2001). Generally, the legal system around the world can be classified according to whether its origins is primarily in pure common law based on the English system, or pure civil law based on the Roman system—with specific categories in French, Spanish, German, Scandinavian, or Socialist. Other classifications include countries with customary or religious laws (Muslim, Talmudic etc.), or mixture of two or more systems (LaPorta et al. 1998b; Globerman and Shapiro 2003; Chan-Lee and Ahn 2001).

A legal environment that protects investors can be significant in investors' decision making (LaPorta et al. 1999). For example, in Common Law countries managers have less flexibility in exercising discretion over reported earning. Hence, the relation between reported earnings in the financial statements and "economic value" of the firm is expected to be stronger. Such factors might persuade joint venture investors to favour Common Law countries, as they can feel more secured about their investments. This is not true in Code Law (another classification based on an all inclusive system of written rules) countries where the law tolerates more latitude in accounting practices to smooth earning. More latitude implies that the financial figures in Code Law countries are to be perceived as less a reflection of economic reality (Guenther and Young 2000).

Countries whose commercial legal systems are rooted in English Common Law have less market regulations and are better at protecting shareholders and creditors, and at preserving property rights (LaPorta et al. 1998a, 1999, 2001; Djankov et al. 2002). They also have low cost of contracting because the legal system interprets the spirit rather than the letter of the contract (Lang and So 2002). Common Law facilitates the development of capital markets and investment opportunities and as a result attracts more foreign investment (Globerman and Shapiro 2003; Reese and Weisbach 2002). Analysing the relationship between U.S. foreign direct investment and legal system researchers found a clear indication that countries whose legal systems are rooted in English Common Law are more likely to be a recipient of U.S. FDI flows (Globerman and Shapiro 2003). According to the authors, Civil law regimes are expected to attract less foreign investment because they are likely to be associated with higher durations of judicial proceedings, more corruption, less honesty and fairness and inferior access to justice.

Within the MENA region, the legal system is rooted in various origins. If we are to spread the countries across a spectrum, at one end would be situated those countries that observe the sharia, and at the other end, would be those whose legal system have developed far from it (Shaaban 1999). When it comes to commercial transaction it is possible to group MENA countries into three categories: first are those that followed the Western system such as Lebanon, Syria, and Egypt. Second are those that have codified their laws but drew mostly from sharia such as Saudi Arabia, Oman, and Yemen. Third are countries that went both ways. They Westernised their commercial laws but still draw from Islamic law in such areas as contracts. These countries include Iraq, Jordan, and Libya (Shaaban 1999). To date there has been no academic research examining the impact of the legal system on foreign investment in the MENA region, however, Globerman and Shapiro (2003) suggested that countries that adopt a legal system that mixes common law with customary or religious law are less likely to receive FDI.

Hypothesis 2: There is a positive relationship between countries whose legal systems are rooted in Common Law and the level of foreign investment in MENA countries.

Economic Freedom

Beyond governance and legal system, another element that could have an impact on foreign investment is economic freedom, specially with regards to aspects of a country's trade policy, its banking and finance services and its property right protection (Drabek and Payne 2001; Globerman and Shapiro 2003). Gwartney, Lawson, and Emerick (2003) suggested that key ingredients to economic freedom include freedom to compete, voluntary exchange, and protection of person and property. O'Doriscoll, Holmes, and Kirkpatrick (2001: 43) defined economic freedom as "the absence of government coercion or constraint on the production, distribution or consumption of goods and services beyond the extent necessary for citizens to protect and maintain liberty itself."

Open trade and investment regimes are particularly powerful instruments to attract investments in general and foreign investments in particular (Drabek and Payne 2001). There is a strong empirical evidence about the positive contribution of trade liberalization on FDI inflows (Selowsky and Martin 1997). Countries open to international trade provide a good platform for global business operations and reflect their competitiveness (Habib and Zurawicki 2002). Unfortunately however, responding to protectionist and special interest politics, virtually all countries adopt trade barriers of various types (Gwartney, Lawson, and Emerick 2003). Trade barriers lower productive efficiency by reducing competition and raising transaction costs (Harms and Ursprung 2002). The extent of the host country tariff and non-tariff barrier, import and export limitations, licensing requirements can have a direct bearing on foreign actors' ability to pursue economic goals and present roadblocks that limit international trade and restrict the flow of foreign investment (Drabek and Payne 2001).

In the area of banking and finance, heavy bank regulations and absence of an independent oversight of financial services, lack of safe and sound financial sector, inadequate financial system that meet basic fiduciary responsibilities can restrict economic freedom (O'Doriscoll, Holmes, and Kirkpatrick 2001). This, in addition to weak enforcement of contract and protection against fraud can interfere with market provision of financial services and create disincentive for foreign actors to invest in the host country (Beck, Levine, and Loayza 2000).

Finally, economic freedom would be meaningless if individuals do not have secure rights to property. Poor protection of property rights is sure to deter investment and undermine the operation of a market-exchange system (Gwartney, Lawson, and Emerick 2003). It determines the legal rights of foreign firms and limitation on foreign ownership (De Mello 1997). Protecting privately held assets from arbitrary direct or indirect appropriation encourages sunk cost investments by multinational corporations (Globerman and Shapiro 2003). The protection of property rights is vital for firms to pursue new investments and ensure that they will see profit from their endeavors. Without this profit incentive there is little motivation to take risks and invest (Drabek and Payne 2001).

Within MENA countries, enhancing economic freedom in terms of trade, financial sector and property rights is of absolute importance if the region is to attract more foreign investments. According to a World Bank report (World Bank 2003), foreign investment could be five to six times what they are today, if exports other than oil were higher and were in a better investment climates. Inefficient and costly services, provided mostly by the public sector, raise the cost of MENA merchandise export and limit attractiveness to investment (World Bank 2003). The financial sector is controlled by state owned banks which dominate banking activities (up to 95 percent of assets in several countries in the MENA region) resulting in poor services, high costs, and weak financing of new investments and trade (World Bank 2003). Due to a complete lack of faith in its domestic economic infrastructure, the Middle East holds the largest share of wealth abroad in the world, with $350 billion currently collecting interest abroad, rather than in local financial institutions.[1]

Finally, although property rights are protected by the constitution in many countries, the legal system creates a lot of delays and obstacles. Dispute resolution can be difficult and uncertain, enforcement of judgments is not always easy, and judicial proceedings could go on for several years. In Egypt, it can take six years for a commercial case to be decided, and with appeal it might extend beyond fifteen. In Qatar, the legal system is biased in favor of citizens and the government. In Saudi Arabia, the U.S. Department of State reported that in several cases disputes have caused serious problems for foreign investors by preventing their departure from the country, blocking their access to exit visas, or imposing restraint of personal property pending the adjudication of a commercial dispute. In the end, trade policies that impose inefficiencies and foreign investment restrictions, heavy bank regulation, in addition to expropriation of property, are signs of weak economic freedom and can be an obstacle to foreign investment as it can be indicative of the various ways in which a government may take away potential profits (Conklin 2002).

Hypothesis 3. There is a positive relationship between economic freedom and the level of foreign investment in the MENA countries.

Methods

Model Specification

Foreign Investment = Constant + $\beta_1 \cdot$ Governance + $\beta_2 \cdot$ Legal System + $\beta_3 \cdot$ Economic Freedom + [$\beta_{4-11} \cdot$ Control Variables] + [$\beta_{12} \cdot$ Time Trend, or $\beta_{12-23} \cdot$ Year Dummies] + Error Term

That is:

Foreign Investment = Constant + $\beta_1 \cdot$ Governance + $\beta_2 \cdot$ Legal System + $\beta_3 \cdot$ Economic Freedom + [$\beta_4 \cdot$ Inflation Level + $\beta_5 \cdot$ Wage Rate + $\beta_6 \cdot$ Technological Infrastructure + $\beta_7 \cdot$ Economic Growth + $\beta_8 \cdot$ Education Level + $\beta_9 \cdot$ Composite Risk + β_{10} $\cdot$ Market Size (Population) + $\beta_{11} \cdot$ Fuel Economy Dummy] + $\beta_{12} \cdot$ Time Trend (or β_{12-23}Year Dummies) + Error Term

where Foreign Investment is the ratio of total joint venture and foreign direct investment to gross domestic product, (JV + FDI)/GDP.

Sample and Data

The paper analyzed both joint venture and FDI activities in the MENA region using data from 1990–2001 time period. The idea was to start with a sample representing all the countries in the MENA region. However, I had to eliminate some of the countries due to lack of consistent data for all the variables over the twelve-year period. In the end, the sample size consisted of the following twelve countries: Egypt, Islamic Republic of Iran, Israel, Jordan, Kuwait, Lebanon, Morocco, Oman, Sudan, Tunisia, Turkey, and Yemen.

Measures

Dependent Variable

The dependent variable foreign investment is a combination of total foreign inflow of funds in a given country in a given year as a percentage of GDP of respective countries. The inflow of funds is composed of two components: total joint venture (JV) related inflow of funds and the foreign direct investment (FDI) associated with each of the sample countries. The traditional literature uses FDI using the UNCTAD or World Bank Development Indicators which do not explicitly include the joint venture activities undertaken in each by countries. The JV data was collected from the "Joint Venture" component of the Security Data Corporations (SDC) database of the Thompson Financial Corporation. It is an aggregate dollar amount of the total joint venture deals signed by individuals and companies by each of the sample countries with other foreign companies and nationals. The other component of the dependent variable, the net flow of net Foreign Direct Investment, was collected from the World Bank's Development Indicators (data was also confirmed by checking the UNCTAD source on FDI).[2] I have estimated alternative regressions using JV and FDI as dependent variables separately and given that the results of alternative definitions do not change the economic or statistical significance of our three focus variables, I only report the estimations based on the broader definition of Foreign Investment, i.e., the combination of JV+FDI.

Independent Variables

Governance. The governance variable is based on an index developed by Kaufmann, Kraay, and Zoido-Lobaton (1999a, 1999b, 2003). The index is an aggregate of the following six constructs: rule of law, corruption, voice and accountability, government effectiveness, political instability and violence, and regulatory burden. The governance score lies between -2.5 and 2.5, with higher scores corresponding to better governance.

Legal system. The legal system data was collected from different published sources on the legal practice followed in each of the sample countries, e.g., Egypt follows a common law structure relative to Lebanon which follows French or civil code of law. Two papers that have used these scores extensively are (LaPorta et al. 1998b, 1999).

Economic freedom. The data for economic freedom was based on the economic freedom indicators developed by the Wall Street Journal and Heritage Foundation in the U.S. I used an index developed from an average aggregate combination of each country's *trade policy* (openness to export and import); *banking and finance* (relative openness and deregulatory environment in the banking and financial sectors, the extent of government's intervention in monetary policy, and the economic and financial policy making issues of the country); and finally the relative score given to a country based on its ranking of *property rights* (degree to which private property rights are protected, and the degree to which the government enforces laws that protect private property). The scale on the index of economic freedom runs from 1 to 5. A score of 1 on the index signifies an institutional or consistent set of policies that are most conducive to economic freedom, while a score of 5 signifies a set of policies that are least conducive (for more details see O'Doriscoll, Holmes, and Kirkpatrick 2001 and different issues of *Index of Economic Freedom*).

Control Variables

Among the control variables are Inflation Level (consumer price index; wage rate—which is wages and salaries as a percent of total national expenditure), Economic Growth (annual GDP growth is taken from IMF's International Financial Statistics), Technological Infrastructure (telephone lines per 10,000 population), Educational Level (percentage of children enrolled in secondary school—taken from the World Bank's Development Indicators), Composite Risk (a variable with a combination of Economic, Financial, and Political Risk, taken from the PRS Group reports on Composite Risk). The dummy variable Fuel takes a value of 1 if the sample country is an oil-producing country (Iran, Kuwait, Oman, and Yemen) and a value of zero for other sample countries. I also used a time trend variable to see whether there is a trend in FDI over the years in addition to a more direct measure of time fixed effect by using time dummies for sample years.

Analysis

I used Ordinary least square (OLS) regressions to estimate the relative importance of the independent variables in the model. Data were pooled from twelve years of data to increase the degrees of freedom. All the regressions reported in the various tables were computed using White's (1980) heteroskedasticity-adjusted t-statistics which adjusts for any biasness due to heteroskedasticity. I had a total of 144 observations.[3]

Results

Table 2 represents overall descriptive statistics of the sample observations. In summary, the statistics shows that my sample consists of a wide range of experience ideal for a robust empirical analysis. For example, foreign investment to GDP ratio varied from a significant positive number of a net outflow to a negative number in a given sample year. Almost 40 percent of the countries are mostly rooted in a common law legal system. About

Table 2. Descriptive Statistics

Variables	Mean	Standard Deviation	Minimum	Maximum
Foreign Investment to GDP (FI)	0.999	2.476	–5.423	19.158
Governance Index (KKZ)	0.164	0.443	–0.330	1.170
Common Law (LEGAL) Dummy	0.417	0.495	0	1.000
Economic Freedom (EFREEDOM)	4.058	1.470	2.500	4.650
Inflation Level (INFLAT)	19.406	29.402	–1.272	132.824
Wages Rate (WAGES)	29.741	11.690	12.521	61.177
Technological Infrastructure (INFRAS)	117.876	116.521	2.400	471.000
GDP Per Capita (GDPPC)	3732.52	4189.35	123.600	17018.40
Education (EDUCAT)	57.418	19.978	14.400	88.400
Composite Risk (RISK)	62.406	13.908	23.000	80.500
Population (POP)	22.814	23.073	1.420	67.380
Time Trend (TREND)	26.194	2.936	21.000	30.000
Energy Dummy (FUEL)	0.250	0.435	0	1.000

Table 3. Mean Values 1990–2001

Country Name	FI	GVRNANCE	LEGAL	EFREEDOM
EGYPT	1.254	–0.150	0	3.550
IRAN	–0.026	–0.290	0	4.650
ISRAEL	1.334	0.680	1.000	2.820
JORDAN	1.493	0.330	1.000	2.090
KUWAIT	0.192	0.340	0	2.500
LEBANON	0.559	–0.090	0	3.050
MOROCCO	0.624	0.190	0	2.950
OMAN	. 0.798	0.520	1.000	2.780
SUDAN	1.333	–0.200	1.000	3.150
TUNISIA	2.163	1.170	0	2.900
TURKEY	0.455	–0.330	0	2.800
YEMEN	1.821	–0.200	1.000	3.800

25 percent of the observations are from countries with energy-based economies. Table 3 provides further details of key variables by individual countries establishing additional support for the varied experience and environment existing among the sample observations. Tunisia has the highest governance score of 1.17 while Turkey has the lowest score of -0.33. With regards to economic freedom, Iran is the country with the lowest economic freedom with a score of 4.65 (on a scale of 1 to 5. Note that the higher the score the less is the economic freedom), while Jordan is the highest with a score of 2.09.

Table 4. Correlation Coefficients

Variable/Ratio	1	2	3	4	5	6	7	8	9	10	11	12	13
1. FI	1.00												
2. GVRNANCE	0.118	1.00											
3. LEGAL	0.122	0.118	1.00										
4. EFREEDOM	0.026	0.383	0.289	1.00									
5. INFLAT	0.041	-0.486	0.073	-0.349	1.00								
6. WAGES	0.157	-0.108	-0.073	-0.236	-0.122	1.00							
7. INFRAS	-0.048	0.252	-0.013	0.269	-0.057	-0.343	1.00						
8. GDPPC	-0.040	0.371	0.021	0.297	-0.279	-0.262	0.735	1.00					
9. EDUCAT	-0.078	0.250	-0.299	0.412	-0.389	-0.214	0.634	0.453	1.00				
10. RISK	0.001	0.426	-0.133	0.306	-0.569	0.230	0.227	0.399	0.427	1.00			
11. POP	-0.088	-0.262	-0.342	-0.348	0.464	0.008	-0.155	-0.429	0.007	-0.161	1.00		
12. TREND	-0.049	0.007	-0.017	0.016	-0.169	-0.015	0.186	0.158	0.132	0.408	0.059	1.00	
13. FUEL	-0.158	0.034	-0.097	0.216	-0.221	0.139	0.077	0.385	0.225	0.307	-0.040	0.038	1.00

Note: All correlation coefficients greater than 0.14 in magnitude are statistically significant at least at 10 percent confidence level.

Table 4 provides a correlation coefficient of all variables used in the analysis. Except in few specific cases, e.g., per capita GDP (GDPPC) and Technological Infrastructure (INFRA) (0.735); education (EDUCAT) and Technological Infrastructure (0.634); and finally inflation (INFLAT) and composite risk (RISK) (0.569), the correlations coefficients do not show any systematic bias or problems. To check for the robustness of the result, I re-estimated the basic model by deleting variables that are highly correlated. In fact, these estimates provide more significant-statistics for my key independent variables.

Table 5A provides the regression analysis by reporting six different estimates.[4] The first estimate simply focuses on the key three independent variables followed by a similar regression that includes time fixed affect by adding time dummy variables. Then I gradually added the other key relevant independent variables (regression 3). I added the time trend variable (regression 4). I added the fuel dummy variable (regression 5). Finally, I used a time fixed affect using year dummy variables instead of time trend in regression 6. The model statistics show relatively low adjusted r-squared ranging from 2 percent to 6 percent however the goodness-of-fit statistics of these estimates is somewhat consistent with the various FDI literatures (De Mello 1997).[5] Overall, the evidence indicates a strong positive and statistically significant impact of governance, legal system, and economic freedom influencing the variability of the inflow of foreign investment. Better governance, legal system with higher protection to stockholders, and countries with higher economic freedom (score 1 represents highest therefore showing a negative coefficient) are significantly associated with higher foreign investment inflow in sample countries.

The overall statistical significance in table 5A is best for the coefficients of governance variable supporting the hypotheses at 1 percent (regression 4), 5 percent (regressions 1, 2, and 3) and 10 percent (regressions 5 and 6) levels respectively. The coefficients are less significant however for legal system with 1 percent (regression 4), 5 percent (regression 3) and 10 percent (regressions 1, 2, 5 and 6) levels. Finally, they are marginally significant for economic freedom, with 5 percent (regression 4) and 10 percent (regression 3) supports only. In general the key results remained relatively the same—except for a loss of statistical significance for economic freedom—even after the year fixed effect and control variables were added. A number of additional estimates were also performed, including regression with country fixed effect variable and regression where highly correlated variables were deleted from the estimate. The tables for these regressions are not included given that the overall results did not change significantly.

Table 5A. Key Factors Explaining the Foreign Investment (All Sample Countries)

	1 FDI	2 FDI	3 FDI	4 FDI	5 FDI	6 FDI
Intercept	2.118 (2.50)**	1.724 (1.79)*	2.179 (1.32)	5.946 (1.99)**	2.43 (0.71)	-1.459 (0.35)
GVRNANCE	1.657 (2.20)**	1.658 (2.19)**	3.757 (2.81)**	4.573 (3.19)***	3.031 (1.88)*	2.824 (1.71)*
LEGAL	0.799 (1.82)*	0.800 (1.81)*	2.111 (2.57)**	2.731 (2.99)***	2.031 (2.10)**	1.882 (1.87)*
EFREEDOM	−0.424 (1.80)*	−0.425 (1.79)*	−1.160 (2.10)**	−1.682 (2.59)**	−0.825 (1.07)	−0.629 (0.76)
INFLATION	-	-	−0.012 (1.08)	−0.015 (1.37)	−0.013 (1.18)	−0.016 (1.23)
WAGES	-	-	0.051 (2.41)**	0.045 (2.12)**	0.067 (2.82)**	0.074 (2.83)**
INFRAS	-	-	0.001 (0.38)	0.003 (0.84)	−0.004 (0.83)	−0.005 (−1.00)
GDPPC	-	-	0.001 (1.51)	0.002 (1.86)*	−0.001 (2.62)**	0.003 (2.65)**
EDUCAT	-	-	0.014 (0.73)	0.017 (0.88)	0.020 (0.99)	0.020 (0.96)
RISK	-	-	−0.027 (1.20)	−0.007 (0.29)	−0.029 (1.01)	−0.046 (1.25)
POP	-	-	0.034 (1.87)*	0.042 (2.22)**	0.047 (2.46)**	0.049 (2.48)**
TREND	-	-	-	−0.144 (1.51)	−0.077 (0.77)	-
FUEL	-	-	-	-	−1.789 (2.01)**	−1.949 (2.14)**
Adj-R^2	0.0170	0.0274	0.0386	0.0477	0.0610	0.0692
F-Statistics	1.91*	2.35**	1.68*	1.69*	1.89*	1.92*
Number	144	144	144	144	144	144

Note: ***, **, and * indicate statistical significance of the parameters at 1, 5, and 10 percent significance level respectively. White-corrected t-statistics are in the parenthesis. Column 2 and 6 include time or year dummy variables for each of the sample year as independent variables. For brevity, I do not report them in the table. In summary, there is an increasing trend of foreign investment over the sample years.

Finally, considering that among the sample countries, Israel may be an outlier as it represents one of the most economically developed country with stronger ability to attract foreign investment; I therefore performed additional estimations of the same model excluding Israel from the estimations. These results are presented in table 5B. In almost all cases, these results are consistent with the results listed in table 5A where Israel was included in the regression estimates. Therefore, the relative importance of governance, legal system and economic freedom in affecting foreign investment suggests a consistent and robust finding in the MENA sample countries.

Table 5B. Key Factors Explaining the Foreign Investment (Excluding Israel)

	1 FDI	2 FDI	3 FDI	4 FDI	5 FDI	6 FDI
Intercept	2.376 (2.32)**	1.948 (1.70)*	2.267 (1.76)*	7.583 (2.08)**	3.864 (0.95)	−0.230 (0.05)
GVRNANCE	1.742 (2.17)**	1.742 (2.16)**	3.814 (2.29)**	5.572 (2.83)**	4.160 (2.02)**	3.939 (1.87)*
LEGAL	0.753 (1.61)	0.753 (1.61)	2.111 (1.82)*	3.696 (2.47)**	3.075 (2.04)**	2.926 (1.89)*
EFREEDOM	−0.497 (1.74)*	−0.497 (1.73)*	−1.191 (1.78)*	−2.058 (2.44)**	−1.241 (1.33)	−1.049 (1.08)
INFLATION	-	-	−0.012 (0.95)	−0.022 (1.57)	−0.021 (1.47)	−0.023 (1.46)
WAGES	-	-	0.052 (2.30)**	0.039 (1.63)	0.064 (2.39)**	0.069 (2.41)
INFRAS	-	-	0.001 (0.15)	0.008 (1.15)	0.001 (0.09)	−0.001 (0.01)
GDPPC	-	-	0.001 (1.35)	0.002 (1.62)	0.002 (2.43)**	0.001 (2.40)*
EDUCAT	-	-	0.015 (0.70)	0.021 (0.99)	0.025 (1.16)	0.024 (1.10)
RISK	-	-	−0.028 (1.14)	−0.004 (0.15)	−0.029 (0.92)	−0.045 (1.14)
POP	-	-	0.035 (1.58)	0.054 (2.17)**	0.062 (2.47)**	0.063 (2.42)**
TREND	-	-	-	−0.205 (1.66)*	−0.127 (0.99)	-
FUEL	-	-	-	-	−1.895 (1.99)*	−2.037 (2.08)*
Adj-R^2	0.0260	0.0287	0.0272	0.0402	0.0634	0.0701
F-Statistics	2.17*	2.19*	2.28*	1.99*	2.15*	2.31*
Number	132	132	132	132	132	132

Note: ***, **, and * indicate statistical significance of the parameters at 1, 5, and 10 percent significance level respectively. White-corrected t-statistics are in the parenthesis. Column 2 and 6 include time or year dummy variables for each of the sample year as independent variables. For brevity, I do not report them in the table. In summary, there is an increasing trend of foreign investment over the sample years.

Conclusion

While many regional, bilateral, and unilateral efforts have led to a remarkably favorable government policy towards foreign investment activities around the world, differences still exist in the scope and depth of the free flow of foreign investments and the operations of MNCs (Fatouros 1990). Foreign investment activities can play a significant role in the development process of host economies. In addition to capital inflows, foreign investment activities can be a vehicle for obtaining foreign technology, knowledge, managerial skills, and improving the international competitiveness of firms and the economic performance of countries (UNCTAD). Foreign activities in terms of direct investment are probably one of the most significant factors leading to the globalization of the international economy (Erdal and Tatoglu 2002).

As the MENA region competes for economic benefits for its citizens in the new global economy, it is important that the policy makers in these countries evaluate their comparative advantage and relative strength (weakness) in attracting foreign investment in their respective countries. Given the recent shift toward efficiency seeking investments in developing countries (Dunning 2002), it is imperative for the market and resource limited MENA countries to improve their quality of governance and transparency; to promote a legal system that protects shareholders and creditors rights; and enhance their economic freedom with more open trade and better protection of property rights.

Beside country-based improvement a significant increase in FDI inflow could also be achieved if the entire MENA region is promoted as an integrated field of investment. Not only foreign investors will be able to see increased efficiency but also an integrated regional market would enlarge capacity and ensure scale effect in relatively small national markets. If these elements are ignored, not only foreign investors will not invest, it is likely that even local investors will take their investments abroad (Reese and Weisbach 2002).

Notes

1. The Middle East Forum Website: http://www.meforum.org/.

2. Following Asiedu (2002) I do not distinguish between local market and non-local market seeking FDI. There are other definitions of FDI, see World Development Indicator Report on FDI for more details.

3. I attempt some robustness check of our estimations by using a one year lag variable for all independent variables. Although our key variables—Governance, Legal System, and Economic Freedom—still show a strong and statistically significant impact on the dependent variable, as shown in my reported result, my over all model statistics, R-squared and F-statistics, showed a weaker impact especially in estimations that do not use Israel as a sample country. These results are available upon request.

4. As mentioned earlier that I have estimated alternative regressions using JV and FDI as dependent variables separately. In both cases, the result came out to be similar to the reported results except the regressions using FDI only as a dependent variable had provided stronger statistical

significance of parameters and higher adjusted R-squared relative to the estimations using JV only as the dependent variable. These results are available upon request.

5. The sample size of twelve countries may be a cause of the relatively low adjusted R-squared.

References

Addison T., and A. Heshmati. 2003. "Democratization and New Communication Technologies as Determinants of Foreign Direct Investment in Developing Countries." *Research In Banking and Finance* 4: 102–128.

Asiedu, E. 2002. "On the Determinants of Foreign Direct Investment to Developing Countries: Is Africa Different?" *World Development* 30(1): 107–119.

Beck, T., R. Levine, and N. Loayza. 2000. "Financial Intermediation and Growth: Causality and Causes." *Journal of Monetary Economics* 46(1): 31–77.

Chan-Lee, J., and S. Ahn. 2001. "Informational Quality of Financial Systems (IQFS) and Economic Development: An Indicators Approach for East Asia." *Asian Development Bank Institute* Working Paper 20.

Conklin, D. 2002. "Analyzing and Managing Country Risks." *Ivey Business Journal* 66(3): 36–41.

Culem, C. G. 1988. "The Locational Determinants of Direct Investments among Industrialized Countries." *European Economic Review* 32: 885–904.

Davis, J., and J. Ruhe. 2003. "Perceptions of Country Corruption: Antecedents and Outcomes." *Journal of Business Ethics* 43(4): 275.

De Mello, L. 1997. "Foreign Direct Investment in Developing Countries and Growth: A Selective Survey." *The Journal of Development Studies* 34(1): 1–34.

Djankov, S., R. LaPorta, F. Lopez-de-Silanes, and A. Shleifer. 2002. "Courts: The Lex Mundi Project." Washington: The World Bank, mimeo.

Drabek, Z., and W. Payne. 2001. "The Impact of Transparency On Foreign Direct Investment." *World Trade Organization, Economic Research and Analysis Division* Working Paper #ERAD-99-02.

Dunning, J. 1993. "Multinational Enterprises and the Global Economy." Workingham: Addison-Wesley.

________. 1999. "Globalization and the Theory of MNE Activity." University of Reading, Discussion Papers in International Investment and Management, 264 Reading.

________. 2002. "Determinants of Foreign Direct Investment Globalization Induced Changes and the Roles of FDI Policies." Paper presented at the Annual Bank Conference on Development Economists in Europe, Oslo, mimeo.

Edwards, S. 1990. "Capital Flows, Foreign Direct Investment, and Debt-Equity Swaps in Developing Countries." Working Paper Series. Cambridge, Mass.: National Bureau of Economic Research.

Erdal, F., and E. Tatoglu. 2002. "Locational Determinants of Foreign Direct Investment in an Emerging Market Economy: Evidence from Turkey." *Multinational Business Review* 10(1).

Fatouros, A. 1990. "The Code and the Uruguay Round Negotiation on Trade in Services." *Centre Reporter* 29: 7–15.

Gilmore, A., A. O'Donnell, D. Carson, and D. Cummins. 2003. "Factors Influencing Foreign Direct Investment and International Joint Ventures: A Comparative Study of Northern Ireland and Bahrain." *International Marketing Review* 20(2): 195–215.

Globerman, S,. and D. Shapiro. 2002. "Global Foreign Direct Investment Flows: The Role of Governance Infrastructure." *Working Paper*.

———. 2003. "Governance Infrastructure and U.S. Foreign Direct Investment." *Journal of International Business Studies* 34: 19–39.

Guenther, D., and D. Young. 2000. "The Association between Financial Accounting Measures and Real Economic Activity: A Multinational Study." *Journal of Accounting & Economics* 29(1): 53–72.

Gwartney, J., R. Lawson, and N. Emerick. 2003. *Economic Freedom of the World: 2003 Annual Report*.

Habib, M., and L. Zurawicki. 2002. "Corruption and Foreign Direct Investment." *Journal of International Business Studies* 33(2): 291–308.

Harms, P., and H. Ursprung. 2002. "Do Civil and Political Repression Really Boost Foreign Direct Investments?" *Economic Inquiry* 40(4): 651–664.

Hewko, J. 2002. "Foreign Direct Investment in Transitional Economies: Does the Rule of Law Matter?" *East European Constitutional Review* (Fall 2002/Winter 2003): 71–79.

Kaufmann, D., A. Kraay, and P. Zoido-Lobaton. 1999a. "Aggregating Governance Indicators." *World Bank*, Working Paper #2195.

———. 1999b. "Governance Matters." *World Bank*, Working Paper #2196.

———. 2000. "Governance Matters: From Measurement to Action." *Finance & Development* 37(2).

———. 2003. "Governance Matters III: Updated Indicators 1996–2002." *World Bank*, Working Paper.

Kingsley, O., and L. Crumbley. 1997. "Determinants of U.S. Private Foreign Direct Investments in OPEC Nations: From Public and Non-Public Policy Perspectives." *Journal of Public Budgeting, Accounting & Financial Management* 9(2): 331–355.

Kravis, I. B., and R. E. Lipsey. 1982. "The Location of Overseas Production and Production for Export by U.S. Multinational Firms." *Journal of International Economics* 12: 201–223.

Lang, L. H. P., and R. W. So. 2002. "Ownership Structure and Economic Performance." Working Paper.

LaPorta, R., F. Lopez-de-Silanes, A. Shleifer, and R. Vishny. 1998a. "Legal Determinants of External Finance." *Journal of Political Economy* 106: 1113–1155.

———. 1998b. "The Quality of Government." *NBER Working Paper 6727*, Cambridge, Mass.: National Bureau of Economic Research, mimeo.

———. 1999. "Investor Protection and Corporate Valuation." *NBER Working Paper 7403*, Cambridge, Mass.: NBER, mimeo.

———. 2001. "Investor Protection and Corporate Governance." Cambridge, Mass.: Harvard University, mimeo.

Levy-Yeyati, E., U. Panizza, and E. Stein. 2003. *The Cyclical Nature of North-South FDI Flows*. World Bank.

Lim, E. 2001. "Determinants of, and the Relation Between, Foreign Direct Investment and Growth: A Summary of the Recent Literature." Working paper WP/01/175.

Loewendahl, H., and E. Ertugal-Loewendahl. 2000. "Turkey's Performance in Attracting Foreign Direct Investment: Implications of EU Enlargement." *CEPS Working Document No. 157.*

Loree, D. W., and S. E. Guisinger. 1995. "Policy and Non-Policy Determinants of U.S. Equity Foreign Direct Investment." *Journal of International Business Studies* 26(2): 281–300.

Noorbakhsh, F., A. Poloni, and A. Youssef. 2001. "Human Capital and FDI Inflows to Developing Countries: New Empirical Evidence." *World Development* 29(9): 1593–1610.

O'Doriscoll, P., K. Holmes, and M. Kirkpatrick. 2001. *Index of Economic Freedom.* Washington: Heritage Foundation and Wall Street Journal.

Onyeiwu, S. 2003. "Analysis of FDI Flows to Developing Countries: Is the MENA Region Different?" Working paper presented at the *Economic Research Forum 10th Annual Conference.*

Perry, A. 2001. *Legal Systems as a Determinant of FDI: Lessons from Sri Lanka.* The Hague, Boston: Kluwer Law International.

Reese, Jr., W. A., and M. S. Weisbach. 2002. "Protection of Minority Shareholder Interest, Cross Listings in the United States and Subsequent Equity Offerings." *Journal of Financial Economics* 66: 65–104.

Sadik, A., and A. Bolbol. 2001. "Capital Flow, FDI, and Technology Spillovers: Evidence from Arab Countries." *World Development* 29(12): 2111–2125.

Selowsky, M., and R. Martin. 1997. "Policy Performance and Output Growth in the Transition Economies." Paper presented at the *Annual Meeting of the American Economic Association.*

Shaaban, H. S. 1999. "Commercial Transactions in the Middle East: What Law Governs." *Law and Policy in International Business* 31(1): 157–173.

Srinivasan, T. G. 2002. "Globalization in MENA: A Long-Term Perspective." Paper Presented at *The Fourth Mediterranean Forum.*

UNCTAD. 1999. *World Investment Report.* New York: United Nations.

_______. 2002. *The Development Dimension of Foreign Direct Investment: Policies to Enhance the Role of FDI in the National and International Context: Policy Issues to Consider.* Note by the UNCTAD Secretariat.

White, H. 1980. "A Heteroskedasticity-Consistent Covariance Matrix Estimator and a Direct Test of Heteroskedasticity." *Econometrica* 48(4): 817–838.

World Bank. 2003. *MENA Development Report: Trade, Investment and Development in the Middle East and North Africa: Engaging with the World.* Washington: The World Bank.

The Author

Nada Kobeissi has a PhD and an MBA in organizational management from Rutgers University and a Master of International Management from Baylor University. She is currently an assistant professor in the Department of Management, Long Island University–C. W. Post. Before joining Long Island University, Dr. Kobeissi worked as a consultant at the United Nations Development Programme. E-mail: Nada.Kobeissi@liu.edu.

EXPLORING ORGANIZATIONAL DETERMINANTS AND CONSEQUENCES OF CONTINGENT EMPLOYMENT IN THE PHILIPPINES

Vivien T. Supangco
University of the Philippines, Quezon City, Philippines

Abstract

This study looks into the factors that foster the use of contingent employment in the Philippines, and its consequences. It also explores the relationship between corporate social performance and the nature of contingent employment. Results indicate an inverse relationship between levels of social performance and utilization of contingent employment. There is a direct relationship between the size and intensity of utilization of temporary employees and the combined effects of unionization and total employment size. Publicly listed companies exhibit higher utilization of temporary employees. However, factors that foster the use of project employees need to be explored further. Benefits are influenced by the intensity of utilization of contingent employees. Formalization of the use of contingent employees tends to blur the difference between casual and regular employees. The use of subcontracting positively influences the number of benefits provided and diminishes the differential benefits between regular and project employees. Unionization, however, tends to increase the differential benefits between regular employees and project employees.

The debt crisis in the 1980s triggered a period of industrial restructuring in many countries, the Philippines included. As part of the structural adjustment program recommended by the World Bank, borrowers were encouraged to relax rules on minimum wages and lift constraints on firing workers to pave the way for labor-market flexibility, which was thought to increase profits, stimulate investment, and substitute labor for capital. These were coupled with measures to focus on export, devaluate currency, and weaken barriers to free trade (Lloyd and Weismann 2001). These and other developments in the industrialized countries, which triggered search for new markets as well as low-cost production localities, hastened the process of globalization.

Globalization has introduced tremendous impact on the ways organizations conduct business. This has far-reaching implications on the employment structures of organizations. Industrialized countries are able to make use of their capital advantage by locating in countries where wages are low. With the deregulation of markets, however, even a traditional low wage country like the Philippines, faces real threat of a growing loss of employment in the formal sector because of the even lower wage rates

 pp. 235–258

prevailing in its Asian neighbors. Meanwhile, changing consumer demand and the frenetic pace of development in technology also increase the need for organizations to be more flexible especially in their use of labor. Labor flexibility has come in many forms. With each type of labor-flexibility objectives come different labor-utilization arrangements: multi-skilling, work team designs, downsizing, subcontracting, and increased use of contingent workers, among others.

The importance of contingent employment cannot be overemphasized. The use of contingent workers has enabled firms to deal with temporary fluctuations in workload. It has likewise enabled firms to reduce labor cost because contingent workers need not be provided training, health insurance, pensions, and other benefits (Allan and Sienko 1998; Coolidge 1996, Wysocki 1996 cited in Matusik and Hill 1998). However, greater labor-market flexibility, the use of contingent workers in particular, does not come in free. Some sectors, most likely the public sector, are left with retraining, health care, and other forgone worker benefits (Deetz 1995; Dau-Schmidt 1995). The latter concern is of utmost importance to developing countries like the Philippines whose public sector may not even be in a strong enough position to undertake such tasks.

This study is important for several reasons. It explores the nature of contingent employment in the Philippines using a cross section of organizations thus providing an empirical scenario of the nature of contingent employment and its consequences. It also attempts to explore the neglected link between corporate social responsibility and the utilization of contingent employment—which is associated with short-term employment, low wages, and absence of training and advancement opportunities.

Specifically, this study aims to answer the following research questions:

1. What organizational factors foster the use of contingent employment?
2. What are the effects of the use of contingent employment on benefits?
3. What happens to the character of contingent employment when corporations exhibit social responsibility?

Labor-Market Flexibility and Contingent Work

Contingent work is associated with jobs in the secondary sector—characterized by short-term employment, absence of advancement opportunities, and low wages. Included in the secondary sector are unskilled, manual labor jobs; blue-collar jobs; and low or unskilled service and white-collar positions. Workers in the secondary sector are mostly migrants who work on a seasonal or part-time basis (Milgrom and Roberts 1992). As such, contingent workers have fewer benefits and cannot expect promotion and long-term employment relations (Cappelli 1995, cited in Van Dyne and Ang 1998). In the Philippines, contingent workers are paid less than the regular workers, but larger firms pay contingent workers more than smaller firms (Torres 1993). The growth of contingent workers is a result of the prescription for making labor market more flexible. This is because unemployment has been partly attributed to rigidities in the labor market (Lagos 1994; Di Tella and McCulloch 1999; Lazear 1990). Such rigidities are traced to institutional constraints, which include minimum wage, mandated benefits, and hiring and firing restrictions such as severance pay and notice of termination. These factors introduce disincentive for utilizing labor, and difficulty in adapting to technological changes, and more intense price and non-price competition.

Labor-market flexibility takes on several forms: labor-cost flexibility, functional flexibility, and numerical flexibility (Lagos 1994). Labor-cost flexibility involves the relaxation of minimum wage and other non-wage rules. Such is expected to bring down costs and increase labor absorption by encouraging the substitution of labor for capital and increasing profits that stimulate investment.

Functional flexibility, on the other hand, pertains to the ability of the firm to vary the work performed by its employees as a response to changes in technology and workload. This form of flexibility requires that workers have the capacity to carry out different tasks with different levels of complexity. In addition, this entails that the firm invest in training and retraining of workers, provide a system of job rotation, and have a structure that is fluid (Lagos 1994). In the Philippines some indications of a movement toward functional flexibility exist. These are evidenced by practices such as organizing around teams, multi-skilling, flexible compensation, and a move toward cooperative labor-management relations through heightened labor-management communication and establishment of labor-management councils (Aganon 1995; Amante 1997; Erickson et al. 2003; Ofreneo and Ortiz 1998).

Numerical flexibility is of two kinds: external and internal. The former pertains to the ability of the firm to increase or decrease the number of employees; the latter pertains to the extent to which the firm can maintain the number of employees by modifying the number of working hours (Lagos 1994). Thus the flexibility afforded by the relaxation of restrictions on dismissals encourages the substitution of labor for capital. In the Philippines external flexibility is practiced through layoffs and reliance on contingent workers, specifically casual and contractual labor, as well as subcontracting and labor-only contracting (Aguilar 1990; Amante 1995; Barranco-Fernando 1995).

External flexibility has varying appeal due to its degree of externalization. Three types of externalization may obtain: place, administrative control, and employment duration (Uzzi and Barsness 1998). Examples of externalization in terms of place include home-based and freelance workers. In the Philippines, the practice of hiring home-based workers is prevalent in the service sectors as well as in manufacturing, particularly in the garments sector (Macaraya and Ofreneo 1992, cited in Aganon 1995). Externalization of administrative control may be found in agency-provided workers and independent contractors. Agency-provided workers that fall under labor-only contracting have been made illegal in the Philippines since 1974. An arrangement is considered labor only contracting when the contractor does not have the necessary and substantial capital to undertake the job and hence does not have the capability to independently perform the subcontracted work. In effect it only supplies employees to a principal to perform activities that are regularly done and directly related to the principal's business. Because of some confusion in what constitutes labor-only contracting, the prohibition in utilizing this form of arrangement was reiterated in 2001.

Yet several firms resort to labor-only contracting—extensively used in department stores, hotels, and restaurants. Externalization in terms of employment duration is realized in hiring temporary workers. External numerical flexibility in its various forms, however, has become a controversial approach to labor-market adjustment in the Philippines as more companies are downsizing and have increasingly relied heavily on contingent labor (Esguerra 1996). On the other hand, internal flexibility in the form of hiring part-time workers is the least utilized form of numerical flexibility in the Philippines (Torres 1993).

Utilization of Contingent Workers

One of the most often cited reasons for hiring contingent workers is to enjoy cost flexibility. Cost flexibility addresses payroll, exit, and other hidden costs.

Inasmuch as contingent workers are not necessarily given fringe benefits and training, payroll costs are supposed to decrease. However, empirical studies present mixed results. For example, Mangum, Mayall, and Nelson (1985) reported that hiring more call-ins and temporary service employees was directly related to firms providing fringe benefits, but fringe benefits had no relationship with the use of temporary workers when they are hired and managed by the firm. A parallel result was reported by Davis-Blake and Uzzi (1993) where the degree of firm-specific training was negatively associated with the use of temporary workers but was positively associated with the use of independent contractors. These studies imply that different forms of contingent employment have different characteristics.

In addition to payroll costs, firms may incur exit costs. When workers are hired during high labor demand and routinely let go during low demand, firms will incur additional expenses in terms of severance pay (Matusik and Hill 1998). More importantly, firms will incur other indirect costs such as negative reputation as employer, reduced morale, overtly damaging behavior, and decreased motivation among surviving employees (Matusik and Hill 1998; Brockner 1987; Parks and Kidder 1994). These may be mitigated when firms hire contingent workers—specifically fixed-term workers—because then there are no promises of long-term employment. Such arrangement may be highly attractive for firms facing fluctuating demand for their products.

Thus another reason for hiring contingent workers is to enable firms to respond to variability in the demand for their products. Indeed, firms facing fluctuating employment levels hired more temporary workers (Mangum, Mayall, and Nelson 1985; Davis-Blake and Uzzi 1993) and independent contractors (Abraham and Taylor 1996; Davis-Blake and Uzzi 1993). One rationale for hiring contingent workers when firms face fluctuations in manpower demand is that it is costly for firms to base their employment at high demand because they will incur excess capacity (Davis-Blake and Uzzi 1993). Thus hiring contingent workers provides firms numerical flexibility to respond to fluctuations in demand for their products or services and, hence, employment levels.

Increasingly, firms utilize contingent workers because of the benefits of functional flexibility derived from getting specialists whose skills may take time to develop in-house or expensive to retain when such expertise is used only occasionally. For example some skill-intensive services, such as computer support, require a full range of services, which may be costly when provided from within (Abraham and Taylor 1996). In addition, contingent workers contribute to a firm's performance by introducing knowledge into the firm (Matusik and Hill 1998).

The above reasons for the use of contingent workers are parallel with the reasons for outsourcing given by selected firms in the Philippines: cost consideration, specialization of service provider, reduced administrative load, and other reasons, including practicality and urgency (Supangco 2000).

Organizational Factors and Utilization of Contingent Workers

Several studies have been made on contingent workers in the Philippines; however these are based on either macro data or case studies of a limited number of firms. This study will therefore examine the patterns of utilization of contingent workers across several firms in different industries. While the above discussions provide an overview of why firms employ contingent workers, this study brings analysis further to understanding why the use of contingent workers differs across firms. Thus this study focuses on organizational factors that foster the use of contingent workers. To provide continuity and comparison with other studies on contingent employment, the following organizational-level factors will be looked into: unionization, organizational size, age of the organization, policy on the use of contingent workers, whether or not the organization is a multinational corporation, the extent to which goods and services are sold in domestic market, and industry sector.

It is argued that labor flexibility is a euphemism for diminishing union power (European Trade Union Institute 1985, cited in Lagos 1994). Subcontracting and the use of casual labor were found to coincide with a decrease in the number of regular workers and union membership (Barranco-Fernando 1995). Thus, one way to diminish union power is to hire contingent workers who may be beyond union's reach. Abraham and Taylor (1996) reported higher utilization of independent contractor for trucking services, but unionization did not explain the use of independent contractors in the other types of services studied. On the other hand, unions will resist the employment of contingent workers inasmuch as their tenure is not secured and, thus, they are difficult to organize (Pfeffer and Baron 1988, cited in Davis-Blake and Uzzi 1993). Abraham (1988, cited in Davis-Blake and Uzzi 1993) found that the higher the percentage of unionized workers, the lower the firm's utilization of temporary workers. Uzzi and Barsness (1998) reported a nonlinear relationship between the degree of unionization and the utilization of contingent workers.

The influence of organization size on the utilization of contingent workers has been widely studied. On the one hand, large firms possess large slack compared to small firms, and are less likely to hire temporary workers (Davis-Blake and Uzzi 1993). On the other hand, large firms with more diversified product lines require that they have access to different specialized skills, which are more costly to develop within the firm but may easily be provided by independent contractors. However, the results of empirical studies on the relationship between the hiring of temporary workers and organization size were mixed. The negative relationship between utilization of temporary workers and organization size was reported by Davis-Blake and Uzzi (1993) and Abraham (1988, cited in Davis-Blake and Uzzi 1993). However, organizational size was positively related with the use of temporary workers, (Mangum, Mayall, and Nelson 1985; Uzzi and Barsness 1998), independent contractors, (Uzzi and Barsness 1998; Davis-Blake and Uzzi 1993), and temporary and contract workers (Torres 1993).

Another factor of interest is age of organization. To the extent that older firms were designed for stable environments (Rousseau and Libuser 1997) and job routines become resistant to change over the long run (Hannan and Freeman 1989, cited in Uzzi and Barsness 1998), older organizations are less likely to utilize contingent workers. It appears that the relationship between organization age and the use of contingent workers depends on the type of contingent worker involved. The relationship was negative for independent contractors but positive for part-time workers (Uzzi and Barsness 1998).

Fluctuations in demand for labor make the employment of contingent workers attractive. Export firms face more complex environments compared to those that produce solely for the local market. In the Philippines, firms producing for exports have greater proportion of contingent workers (Soriano 1993). On the other hand, while multinational corporations similarly face more complex environments compared to domestic firms, its sheer global presence provides them the potential of enjoying economies of scale (Gupta and Govindarajan 2001). Such economies of scale are possible in the provision of training (Black, Noel, and Wang 1999) and perhaps in the provision of other benefits.

Consequences of Utilization of Contingent Workers

It has been argued that relaxing the institutional restrictions on hiring and firing workers—such as minimum wage, severance pay, and requirements for notice of termination, among others—increases flexibility and employment. However, empirical support for this contention is mixed. While positive results were reported in studies made in Europe (Di Tella and McCulloch 1999; Lazear 1990) and India and Zimbabwe (Fallon and Lucas 1991), negative results were reported, where employment is merely moved from formal sector to informal sector, in the cases of the Philippines (Erickson et al. 2003) and Latin America (Lagos 1994). At the firm level, increased use of part-time workers at Air Canada resulted in lower opportunities of women to gain access to secure full-time white-collar jobs in the organization (Shalla 2003).

Studies on the consequences of contingent employment were made at the individual level of analysis. Such also reported mixed results. Contingent workers had higher motivation potential scores and knowledge of results and strength of growth need, but regular workers had higher satisfaction with job security (Allan and Sienko 1998). Pearce (1993) reported higher levels of extra role behavior among contingent workers compared to regular employees. However, several studies found no differences in the behavior of contingent workers compared to regular employees (Porter 1995 and Kidder 1995, cited in Van Dyne and Ang 1998). Van Dyne and Ang argued that the differences in behavior depend to a great extent on whether or not the contingent worker status was voluntary. Contingent workers who would rather have regular jobs may have more positive attitude and higher performance, hoping to be absorbed into the regular workforce. On the other hand, workers who voluntarily choose contingent work, have the tendency to exhibit less organizational citizenship behavior, expectation from their employers, and affective commitment. Empirical evidence shows that contingent workers with high commitment to their organizations and positive attitude towards their psychological contracts with their organizations have high levels of organizational citizenship behavior (Van Dyne and Ang 1998).

The above studies looked at the consequences of contingent employment for macro-level employment and individual worker behavior. This study looks into the consequences of contingent employment at the firm level in terms of provision of benefits.

Contingent Employment and Social Initiatives

Corporations are a significant entity in modern life. We deal with them directly or indirectly through the goods and services they provide or as part of the processes that provide such. Corporate decisions affect us in more ways than we can imagine. Decisions on goods and services to produce influence the skills required and hence the concomitant production of education. Decisions on employment structure may extend into how we arrange our own time and define even child rearing practices, values—including those that determine how we treat the environment and the community in general—and lifestyles, including those that center on the perpetuation of the corporation (Deetz 1995).

No decision is value free. In modern corporations, where ownership is separate from control, decisions often reflect the values of corporate leaders, and not necessarily of those who also have stake in them. Corporate leaders have insulated themselves from corporate decision mistakes. They have protected themselves with golden parachutes, they may not have even set foot on public schools or transportation, and they may have utterly removed themselves from the plight of the unemployed on the streets (Deetz 1995). It is the workers and communities, whose lives and general well-being are invested in the corporation, who have become vulnerable and have more to lose from poor corporate decisions.

Utilization of contingent workers by corporations, primarily to reap benefits from lower costs, passes the responsibility of retraining, providing health care, etc., to the government and sectors other than themselves. Yet, damage to health, skills, and morale of individuals tossed from one low-paying job to another make for an unattractive market—either as a source of labor or consumption—that can have unimaginable consequences: strategic considerations could point to closing down plants and locating elsewhere not because such have become unprofitable, but because profit is greater (Morgan 1996).

Thus corporate decisions on employment may be made based on short-term gains, or on a genuine objective of providing jobs and quality life. Companies may concern themselves with short-run profits or consider social initiatives as solutions to problems to which they are responsible as well as from which they potentially benefit (Margolis and Walsh 2001). Several studies have demonstrated that corporate social performance is associated with financial performance (McGuire, Sundgern, and Schneeweis 1988; Russo and Fouts 1997; Berman et al. 1999). Indeed in a review of ninety-five studies, 53 percent reported positive relationships between corporate social performance and financial performance (Margolis and Walsh 2001).

Variables

In the Philippines, the most extensively utilized contingent workers are casual or temporary workers and contractual or project employees. Analyses will therefore focus on these two types of contingent workers.

Dependent Variables

The first research question deals with organizational factors that foster the use of contingent employment. Contingent employment is measured four ways: number of temporary or casual workers, proportion of temporary workers, number of project employees, and proportion of project employees. The absolute number of casual or project employees measures the size of the specific contingent employment while the proportion of casual or project employees measures the intensity of use of the specific contingent employment. Casual or temporary employees are hired to do work other than those necessary for the usual business of the employer while project or contractual employees are hired for a fixed period and for a specific undertaking (Foz 2001).

The second research question deals with the consequences of contingent employment, the focus of which is on benefits. Benefits are measured as percentage of benefits given to casual and project employees based on a list of possible benefits, the details of which are listed in Appendix A. Four measures of benefits are: benefits index for casual employees, the difference between the index for regular and casual employees, benefits index for project employees, and the difference between the index for regular and project employees. Differential benefits are computed as the difference between the proportion of benefits given to regular employees and the proportion given to casual or project employees.

Independent Variables

The third research question pertains to the impact of social performance on the character of contingent employment. The interest is in how the independent variable, social performance, affects the dependent variables discussed above, namely: number of temporary or casual workers, proportion of temporary workers, number of project employees, proportion of project employees, benefits index for casual employees, the difference between the index for regular and casual employees, benefits index for project employees, and the difference between the index for regular and project employees. The measure of social performance is discussed below.

In addition to social performance, several variables were examined to determine their effects on the dependent variables.

1. Social Performance Index: This measures the organization's concern with its stakeholders. The list of social issues was adapted from Clarkson (1995), with special focus on stakeholder consultation, corporate philanthropy, ethics, and concern for employees. The index was computed as the percentage of social practices present in the organization.

2. Absolute Change in Employment of Regular Employees: This is measured in terms of the average change in the number of regular employees in the last three years.

3. Proportion of Produce Sold in Local Market: This is measured in terms of the proportion of goods and services sold in the local market.

4. Proportion of Unionized Employees: This is measured in terms of the proportion of employees who are members of the union.

5. Employment Size: Total number of employees in year 2003.

6. Organization Age: This is measured in terms of the difference between the year the organization was established in the Philippines and the year 2003.

7. Formalization of Stakeholder Concern Index: This measures the degree to which stakeholder interests are formalized in any of the following documents: mission statement, vision, and company policies. The index was computed as the percentage of mention of possible stakeholders in the above documents.

8. Interaction between Union Status and Employment Size: This is measured as the product of employment size and a binary variable, unionization status.

9. Interaction between Age and Market Growth: This is measured as the product of organization age and a binary variable, market growth.

10. Written Policy on Use of Contingent Workers: This is a binary variable, the value of which is one when the organization has written policy on the use of contingent employment; otherwise the value is zero.

11. Downsizing Experience: This is a binary variable, the value of which is one when the organization has engaged in downsizing activities; otherwise the value is zero.

12. Subcontracting Experience: This is a binary variable, the value of which is one when the organization engages in subcontracting otherwise the value is zero.

13. Unionization Status: This is a binary variable, the value of which is one when the organization has a union; otherwise the value is zero.

14. Public Listing: This is a binary variable, the value of which is one when the organization is publicly listed; otherwise the value is zero.

15. Multinational Status: This is a binary variable, the value of which is one when the organization is a multinational corporation; otherwise the value is zero.

16. Market Growth: This is a binary variable the value of which is one when the organization is facing a growing market otherwise the value is zero.

17. The concern in the second research question is the impact of contingent employment on benefits. Thus in addition to the above independent variables, the following variables—which were the dependent variables in addressing the first research question—were used as independent variables. Measurement of these variables was described earlier.
    - Number of Casual Employees
    - Proportion of Casual Employees
    - Number of Project Employees
    - Proportion of Project Employees

Method

This study is based on a convenience sample of fifty-one human resource officers in the greater Manila Area. A structured questionnaire was sent through e-mail to 841 member organizations of the Personnel Management Association of the Philippines. Because convenience sampling was resorted to, results can be generalized only to participating organizations.

To determine the factors that foster the use of contingent employment, several steps were undertaken. The first step determined which among the independent variables contributed to explaining the different measures of contingent employment. For this phase, a stepwise regression analysis was used. Those with at least an interval measure were introduced first. Once significant variables were selected, qualitative variables were introduced into the model using multiple regression analysis. Only significant variables were retained in the final model.

Profile of the Sample

The respondent companies have been in existence for the past 23.06 years. About 36.2 percent of them are publicly listed, 60.8 percent are engaged in services, and 74.5 percent face a growing market. While 48.0 percent are multinational corporations, still 73.21 percent of the total organizations' outputs or services are sold in the local market. These organizations employ an average of 1,222.51 workers, 44.4 percent of whom are female. About 82.4 percent of these companies hire casual or temporary workers and some 76.5 percent hire project or contractual workers. On the average

16.74 percent of an organization's workforce are casual workers while 11.61 percent are project employees. While the difference in the proportion of casual and project employees are not statistically significant, work assignments of the two types of contingent workers differ. Casual employees are mostly found in services such as janitorial, messengerial, etc.; professional/technical work such as accounting, finance and engineering; and in the "others" category. On the other hand, project employees are hired to do mostly professional, technical, and clerical work. In addition to employing casual and project employees, 87.2 percent of the organizations subcontract some of their activities and 54.2 percent of them have engaged in downsizing activities. About a third of the organizations (32.7 percent) are unionized, with some 19.2 percent of employees belonging to a union.

Results and Discussions

Appendix B presents the means and standard deviations and Appendix C presents the correlation matrix of the variables used in the study. The following sections present the results of analyses addressing the three research questions.

Organizational Factors that Foster Utilization of Contingent Workers

Table 1 presents results of regression analyses on the four measures used in analyzing contingent workers: number of casual employees, proportion of casual employees, number of project employees, and proportion of casual employees.

Model 1 explains the number of casual employees. The number of casual employees is positively associated with joint effect of unionization status and employment size (significant at $p < 0.000$ [almost zero]) and negatively associated with the main effect of unionization status (significant at $p < 0.007$). The overall model fit is significant at $p < 0.000$ (almost zero), and 91.6 percent of the variation in the number of casual employees is accounted for by the model.

Because of a significant interaction effect between unionization and employment size the effect of unionization cannot be seen independently from the effect of employment size. Model 1 implies that unionized organizations have more casual employees,

Table 1. Factors explaining the use of contingent workers

	Model 1 Number of casual employees	Model 2 Proportion of casual employees	Model 3 Number of project employees	Model 4 Proportion of project employees
Social performance index		-0.246[b]	-2.521[b]	-0.195[b]
Interaction of size and union Status	0.398[a]	0.004891[a]		
Public listing		11.908[c]		
Union status	-183.037[b]			
Employment size			0.02860[d]	
Constant	62.097[a]	29.196[a]	288.817[b]	22.010[b]
F	239.156[a]	4.080[b]	3.755[b]	4.765[b]
R^2	0.916	0.244	0.158	0.104

[a]p<.010 [b]p<.05 [c]p<.10 [d]p<.11

and as the employment size gets bigger unionized organizations employ more casual workers. When larger organizations are unionized, there is more at stake in the sense that larger organizations have concomitantly more union members and such could be a source of union strength. Thus from the perspective of power, the tendency for unionized organization to hire more casual workers as its size increases is consistent with the argument that externalization is a move by employers to weaken union influence inasmuch as casual workers are not qualified to join unions (Pfeffer and Baron 1988, cited in Uzzi and Barsness 1998). The results also point to supporting the cost argument. Inasmuch as the union has the right to bargain collectively, wages and benefits are higher in unionized firms (Mondy, Noe, and Premeaux 2002). Thus as the size of a unionized organization increases, labor costs also increase. Organizations mitigate this situation by hiring casual workers.

Model 2 explains the intensity of use of casual employees. The proportion of casual employees is negatively associated with social performance (significant at $p < 0.031$), positively related with the interaction of union status and size (significant at $p < 0.008$), and also positively related with public listing of corporations (significant at $p < 0.055$). The overall model fit is significant at $p < 0.000$ (almost zero), and 24.4 percent of the variation in the proportion of casual employees is explained by the model.

Model 2 implies that organizations with higher sense of social responsibility have lower proportion of casual workers in their ranks. In addition, the effect of unionization is dependent on employment size. Unionized organizations have higher intensity of utilization of causal employees and as employment increases in unionized organizations, the proportion of casual employees increases. Higher proportion of casual employees is also found in publicly listed companies compared to those that are not publicly listed. Theorizing on the impact of social performance is discussed in the section on contingent employment and social responsibility. On the other hand, the joint effect of unionization and employment size is consistent with both the power and cost arguments discussed above. Meanwhile, the positive relationship between publicly listed organizations and the proportion of casual employees may be consistent with institutional theory. Publicly listed corporations operate in a network of social relationships. Concern for legitimacy is important because it affects chances of survival. Legitimacy is gained when an organization is accepted in its network (Di Maggio and Powell 1983). The argument that the attention large organizations invite from media, government, and other actors in the network increases need for legitimacy may be extended to publicly listed corporations (Oliver 1991). Publicly listed corporations attract the attention of shareholders, government, media, etc. and such increases pressure for them to engage in actions that enhance legitimacy. To the extent that the use of contingent employment increases flexibility to adjust to market fluctuations even as it decreases labor cost make for it an action that enhances legitimacy. Thus publicly listed corporations are more likely to have higher intensity of utilization of casual employees.

Model 3 explains the size of project employees. The number of project employees is negatively associated with social performance (significant at $p < 0.016$), and negatively associated with employment size (marginally significant at $p < 0.108$).

The overall model fit is significant at $p < 0.032$, and 15.8 percent of the variation of the number of project employees is explained by the model.

Model 3 implies that organizations with higher sense of social responsibility have a smaller number of project employees. Social responsibility and the use of contingent employment will be discussed in more detail below. On the other hand, the larger the organization, the more it hires project employees. This is consistent with the cost argument. Larger organizations have broader product lines and hence a higher need for various specialized skills which may be costly to develop in-house but may very well be provided by independent contractors (Uzzi and Barsness 1998). Hence the greater utilization of project employees as employment size increases.

Model 4 explains the intensity of use of project employees. The proportion of project employees is negatively associated with social performance (significant at $p < 0.035$). The overall model fit is significant at $p < 0.035$, and 10.4 percent of the variation in the proportion of project employees is explained by the model. This is discussed further in the section on social responsibility and utilization of contingent employment.

Consequences of Contingent Employment

This section discusses the results of exploration of patterns of relationships that explain the effects of contingent employment on benefits. While the benefits of casual and project employees do not significantly differ, they differ from the benefits of regular and probationary employees. Table 2 presents results of regression analyses on the effects of contingent employment on benefits.

Model 5 explains benefits of casual employees. Benefits index for casual employees is positively associated with the proportion of casual employees (significant at $p < 0.043$) as well as on the presence of policies on the use of contingent workers

Table 2. Effects of utilization of contingent workers on benefits

	Model 5 Benefits index for casual employees	**Model 6 Differential benefits index of casual and regular employees**	**Model 7 Benefits index for project employees**	**Model 8 Differential benefits index of project and regular employees**
Proportion of casual employees	0.362^{b}	$.361^{c}$		
Written policy on use of contingent workers	16.853^{b}	-13.854^{c}		
Proportion of project employees			0.720^{a}	$-.457^{c}$
Social performance index			0.357^{b}	
Subcontracting experience			20.896^{c}	-29.388^{b}
Union status				17.628^{c}
Constant	18.042^{a}	72.259^{a}	-23.128	88.315^{a}
F	5.895^{a}	3.741^{b}	4.505^{a}	4.936^{a}
R^2	0.201	0.148	0.268	0.27

$^{a}p<.010$ $^{b}p<.05$ $^{c}p<.10$

(significant at $p < 0.016$). The overall model fit is significant at $p < 0.008$, and the model explains 20.1 percent of the variation in benefits index.

Model 5 implies that benefits given casual employees increase as its proportion increases. This result is consistent with the cost argument. The more intensive use of casual employees implies lower cost structure of organizations; thus it is possible to give casual employees higher benefits and still remain competitive in the product market. On the other hand, when the high proportion of casual employees is an indication of an organization's need for numerical flexibility, the implication is that organizations that have high need for numerical flexibility have to provide more benefits to attract and retain the right casual workers to their organization in a timely fashion. Meanwhile, organizations with written policies or formal statements on the use of contingent workers have higher benefits index. This result is understood by extending the concept of commitment. Accordingly, individuals are bound to actions when they are voluntary, visible and public, irrevocable, and explicit (Salancik 1977, cited in Pfeffer 1992). In formalizing and publicizing the use of contingent workers, the organization binds itself to treating them positively and one of its manifestations is in providing them more benefits.

Model 6 explains the differential benefits of casual and regular employees. Recall that the differential benefits index measures the degree to which benefits given to casual employees approximate those given regular employees. The smaller the difference the better is the arrangement for contingent employees. Differential benefits index for casual employees is negatively associated with the proportion of casual employees (significant at $p < 0.060$) as well as on the presence of policies on the use of contingent workers (significant at $p < 0.061$). The overall model fit is significant at $p < 0.032$, and the model explains 14.8 percent of the variation in benefits index.

Model 6 implies that as the proportion of casual employees increases, benefits given to casual employees get closer to the benefits given regular employees. Similar to reasons advanced in model 1, the result is consistent with cost perspective. As the percentage of casual employees increases, organizations carry a lower cost structure such that they are able to afford benefits closer to what they give regular employees and still be competitive in the product market. Another interpretation of the result is that high proportion of casual workers indicates high need for numerical flexibility and thus such organizations offer benefits close to what they offer regular employees to attract and retain the right casual workers in a timely manner. Organizations with formalized statements on the utilization of contingent workers give benefits that approximate those given the regular employees. Again this result is understood by extending the concept of commitment. Accordingly, individuals are bound to actions when they are voluntary, visible and public, irrevocable, and explicit (Salancik 1977, cited in Pfeffer 1992). In formalizing and publicizing the use of contingent workers the organization binds itself to treating them positively and one of its manifestations is providing them benefits that blur the difference between casual and regular employees.

Model 7 explains benefits of project employees. Benefits index of project employees is positively associated with the proportion of project employees, (significant at $p < 0.008$), social performance (significant at $p < 0.027$), and subcontracting experience (significant at $p< 0.096$). The overall model fit is significant at $p< 0.009$, and 26.8 percent of variation in benefits index for project employees is explained by the model.

Model 7 implies that higher benefits are observed as the proportion of project employees increases. This result is similar to that observed in benefits of casual employees. Taking a cost perspective, organizations with a greater proportion of project employees have a lower cost structure, which enables them to afford more benefits to project employees. On the other hand, high intensity of use of project employees implies high need for numerical flexibility, which is enjoyed at higher cost such that organizations provide higher benefits to attract and retain the right project employees. Results also show that organizations with higher social responsibility provide more benefits to project employees. This will be discussed further in the next section. Moreover, organizations that likewise engage in subcontracting provide more benefits to project employees. This result is consistent with cost perspective. Organizations that engage in subcontracting, in addition to hiring project employees, enjoy lower cost structure which enables them to provide more benefits to project employees. However, because regression does not imply causation, the direction of relationship may be the reverse. Organizations faced with high labor cost indicated with more benefits given project employees try to mitigate this by engaging in another form of contingent arrangement—subcontracting of activities.

Model 8 explains the differential benefits of project and regular employees. Differential benefits index for project employees is negatively associated with the proportion of project employees (significant at $p < 0.081$) and subcontracting experience (significant at $p < 0.033$), and positively associated with unionization (significant at $p < 0.058$). The overall model fit is significant at $p < 0.005$, and 27.0 percent of variation in differential benefits of project employees is explained by the model. Recall that the differential benefits index measures the degree to which benefits given to project employees approximate those given regular employees. The smaller the difference the better is the arrangement.

Model 8 implies that, as the proportion of project employees increases, benefits given to project employees get closer to the benefits given regular employees. This result is consistent with the cost perspective. The more intensive use of project employees implies lower cost structure of organizations thus it is possible to give project employees higher benefits and remain competitive in the product market. Another interpretation of the result is that high proportion of project workers indicates high need for numerical flexibility and thus such organizations offer benefits close to what they offer regular employees to attract and retain the right project workers in a timely manner. In addition, organizations that engage in subcontracting, apart from hiring project employees, also have smaller benefits gap. The result is consistent with the cost as well as the need for numerical flexibility arguments advanced earlier. On the other hand, when the relationship is reversed, organizations whose benefits given to project employees is almost similar to those given to regular employees may face high labor cost structure such that these companies also engage in other contingent arrangements such as subcontracting.

In contrast to the above factors, which negatively influence benefits gap, unionization contributes positively to benefits gap. Unionized organizations have wider benefits gap between project and regular employees. This is consistent with the power view. The importance of the union—where membership is mostly limited to regular employees—to its members lies in its ability to provide them security of tenure and superior wages and benefits. Thus regular employees have much higher benefits than project employees in unionized firms, hence the higher differential benefits.

Contingent Employment and Corporate Social Responsibility

One of the reasons for the utilization of contingent workers is cost flexibility in terms of both retaining and separating workers. However, concerns have been raised in the aspect of the responsibility of providing benefits necessary to maintain workers' health and well-being as well as in providing training opportunities to enhance their productivity and continued employability. This study addresses such concern and looks into the character of contingent employment when corporations exhibit social responsibility.

Table 1 shows the regression results of factors that foster the use of contingent employees. In three of the four models, social performance index shows consistently negative and significant impact on the use of contingent employment. The results imply that as an organization's degree of social responsibility increases, its use of contingent workers, whether in terms of size or intensity decreases. This result is understood by extending the concepts of commitment and consistency. One of the means in which commitment is generated is through the process of consistency where past actions guide attitudes and behavior (Pfeffer 1992). To the extent that contingent employment is associated with labor insecurity, absence of promotion and training opportunities, and low wages, such conditions are inconsistent with the concept of social responsibility to employees. Thus there is a tendency for socially responsible firms to hire fewer contingent workers or utilize them less intensively. On the other hand, the result may also be understood from the cost perspective; however, the direction of relationship may be reversed. Socially responsible actions entail additional costs to the organization (Aupperle, Carroll, and Hatfield 1985), such that firms saving on labor cost, by hiring contingent workers, are less likely to engage in socially responsible activities.

On the other hand, Table 2 shows that the result of regression analyses of effects of social responsibility of organizations on benefits of contingent workers is significant only for project employees. In model 7, it is shown that the higher the degree of social responsibility of organizations, the more benefits are provided to project employees. This result is consistent with the concept of consistency. Organizations that are socially responsible strive to satisfy not only stockholders but also those that have a stake in it including employees, among others. Thus one of the means to satisfy employees is to provide them with more benefits, and such is applied consistently to both regular and contingent workers.

Summary and Conclusions

This research looked into the organizational factors that explain the utilization of contingent workers and its impact on benefits. It also explored the role of social responsibility in determining utilization of contingent workers and benefits.

Several patterns of relationships emerged. Results show that the only factor that is generally significant in explaining the different measures of utilization of contingent employment is social performance. Organizations with greater sense of social responsibility tend to utilize less contingent workers. It appears that social responsibility is inconsistent with what contingent employment is associated with: labor insecurity, low wages, and absence of promotion and training opportunities.

However, there are factors that explain the utilization of contingent employment that are unique to each type of contingent worker. This may be understood better when job assignments are taken into consideration. Casual or temporary employees are located in services—such as janitorial, messengerial, and so forth—while project employees are mostly assigned to professional and technical work. A significant determinant of employment of casual workers, both in terms of number and intensity, is the interaction of employment size and unionization. The effect of unionization cannot be taken independently from the effect of size and vice versa. As organizational size increases there is a tendency for unionized firms to increase the number and intensity of utilization of casual employees. This reinforces the argument that utilization of contingent employment is management's response to increasing labor cost or increasing union power. In addition, utilization of casual employees is also affected by public listing status of the organization. To the extent that utilization of casual employees increases flexibility even as it decreases labor cost, publicly listed corporations engage in such activities more than those that are not publicly listed. Such action appeals to them inasmuch as they have higher need for legitimacy because of the attention they attract from stockholders, government, and the media among others.

On the other hand, the utilization of project employees in terms of numbers is influenced by the size of the organization. Inasmuch as project employees mostly take on professional and technical work, such pattern seems to point to the argument that large organizations with broader product offerings have greater need of specialized skills, which may be expensive when developed in-house, but which may be provided at a lower cost by project employees.

Intensity of utilization of contingent employees does impact on benefits received. Benefits for casual workers are influenced by the intensity of use of casual workers while benefits given to project employees are influenced by the intensity of use of casual employees. Such patterns are explained by cost considerations. More intensive utilization of contingent workers produces lower cost structure that allows organizations to provide more benefits. However, when intensity is interpreted as an indicator of the need to be numerically flexible, the higher benefits given are taken as indicative of the premium paid by the organization to be flexible. It is a means through which organizations are able to attract and retain the right contingent employees to the organization.

There are other factors that influence benefits given contingent employees and these are unique to each type of contingent worker. Benefits given casual employees or the degree to which benefits of casual employees differ from regular employees is also influenced by formalization of the utilization of contingent workers. Such serves to bind the organization's action to giving contingent workers more benefits—benefits that blur the difference between casual and regular employees. Meanwhile, benefits given project employees are influenced by the utilization of another flexibility measure, subcontracting. When organizations engage in subcontracting, their lower cost structure allows them to provide more benefits—at levels that blur the distinction between project and regular employees. However, because regression does not necessarily signify causation, the relationships could be taken in reverse. When benefits given project employees are high, the organization will tend to substitute utilization of project employees with other means of flexibility and engage in subcontracting activities.

Benefits given project employees are positively influenced by the degree of social performance. This reinforces the notion of consistency to the argument that socially responsible organizations provide project workers more benefits. Again, if the direction of relationship is reversed, organizations engaged in the utilization of contingent employees to reduce labor costs are less likely to be socially responsible because being socially responsible can also be costly. On the other hand, differential benefits relate to unionization. Consistent with the view of power, the union must be able to protect wages and benefits of union members to the exclusion of those beyond its reach.

Directions for Future Research

This study has uncovered the relationship between social responsibility and utilization of contingent employment both in terms of size and intensity. The results show that socially responsible organizations have fewer and less intensive utilization of contingent employees. There is also an indication that socially responsible organizations provide better benefits to project employees. These relationships need to be explored further and validated in future studies. Cost considerations have been identified as motivations in the utilization of contingent employment. This study also uncovered possible institutional considerations particularly in the intensity of use of casual employees. Again, this aspect may be further explored and validated. Unionization is significant in the utilization of casual employees, who are mostly assigned to low-level service work, but is significant in influencing benefits only of project employees. Its role in the provision of benefits to casual employees may be further explored.

This study focused only on the impact of utilization of contingent employees on benefits. The low coefficient of determination of the analyses on project employees may point to further exploration of this type of contingent employment. Other variables of interest may also be looked into.

References

Abraham, K. 1988. "Flexible Staffing and Employers' Short-Term Adjustment Strategies," in *Employment, Unemployment, and Labour Utilization*, ed. R. A. Hart. London: Unwin/Hyman.

Abraham, K., and S. Taylor. 1996. "Firms' Use of Outside Contractors: Theory and Evidence." *Journal of Labor Economics* 14(3): 394–424.

Aganon, M. 1995. "Sink or Swim: HRM Strategies in a Borderless Economy and Trade Union Response." *Philippine Journal of Labor and Industrial Relations* 16(1&2): 6–30.

Aguilar, V. 1990. *Subcontracting, Employment and Industrial Relations in Selected Philippine Export Manufacturing Establishments*. Working Paper, School of Labor and Industrial Relations. University of the Philippines.

Allan, P., and S. Sienko. 1998. "Job Motivation of Professional and Technical Contingent Workers: Are They Different from Permanent Workers?" *Journal of Employment Counseling* 35(4): 69–178.

Amante, M. 1995. "Labor Relations and Enterprise Competitiveness in the Philippines." *Philippine Journal of Labor and Industrial Relations* 16(1&2): 31–49.

———. 1997. "Converging and Diverging Trends in HRM: The Philippine 'Halo-Halo' Approach." *Asia Pacific Business Review* 3(4): 111–132.

Aupperle, K., A. Carroll, and J. Hatfield. 1985. "An Empirical Examination of the Relationship between Corporate Social Responsibility and Profitability." *Academy of Management Journal* 28(2): 446–463.

Barranco-Fernando, N. 1995. "Globalization and Its Impact on the Philippine Labor Market." *Philippine Journal of Labor and Industrial Relations* 16(1&2): 69–98.

Berman, S., A. Wicks, S. Kotha, and T. Jones. 1999. "Does Stakeholder Orientation Matter? The Relationship between Stakeholder Management Models and Firm Financial Performance." *Academy of Management Journal* 42(5): 488–506.

Black, D., B. Noel, and Z. Wang. 1999. "On-the-Job Training, Establishment Size, and Firm Size: Evidence for Economies of Scale in the Production of Human Capital." *Southern Economic Journal* 66(1): 82–100.

Brockner, J. 1987. "Survivors' Reaction to Layoff: We Get by with a Little Help from Our Friends." *Administrative Science Quarterly* 32: 526–547.

Cappelli, P. 1995. "Rethinking Employment." *British Journal of Industrial Relations* 33: 563–602.

Clarkson, M. 1995. "A Stakeholder Framework for Analyzing and Evaluating Corporate Social Performance." *Academy of Management Review* 20(1): 92–117.

Coolidge, S. D. 1996. "'Temping' Is Now a Career—With an Upside for Workers." *Christian Science Monitor* (October 7): 1.

Cooper, C. L., and D. Rousseau, eds. 1994. *Trends in Organizational Behavior*, vol.1. New York: John Wiley and Sons.

Dau-Schmidt, K. G. 1995. "The Labor Market Transformed: Adapting Labor and Employment Law to the Rise of the Contingent Workforce." *Washington and Lee Review* 52(3): 879–885.

Davis-Blake, A., and B. Uzzi. 1993. "Determinants of Employment Externalization: A Study of Temporary Workers and Independent Contractors." *Administrative Science Quarterly* 38: 195–223.

Deetz, S. 1995. *Transforming Communication, Transforming Business: Stimulating Value Negotiation for More Responsive and Responsible Workplaces*. Cresskill, N.J.: Hampton Press.

Di Maggio, P., and W. W. Powell. 1983. "The Iron Cage Revisited: Institutional Isomorphism and Collective Rationality in Organizational Fields." *American Sociological Review* 48: 147–160.

Di Tella R., and R. McCulloch. 1999. "The Consequences of Labor Market Flexibility: Panel Evidence Based on Survey Data." Retrieved October 27, 2003, from http://www.zei.de/download/zei_wp/B99-0z.pdf.

Erickson, C. L., S. Kuruvilla, R. Ofreneo, and M. A. Ortiz. 2003. "From Core to Periphery? Recent Developments in Employment Relations in the Philippines." *Industrial Relations: A Journal of Economy and Society* 42(3): 368–395.

Esguerra, E. 1996. "Flexible Labor Arrangements in the Philippines: Trends, Theory, Implications," in Esguerra and Ito 1996.

Esguerra, E., and K. Ito, eds. 1996. *Employment, Human Resource Capital and Job Security: Recent Perspectives on the Philippine Labor Market*. Tokyo: ASEAN Economic Development Project, Institute for Developing Economies.

European Trade Union Institute. 1985. *Flexibility and Employment: Myths and Realities*. Brussels: European Trade Union Institute.

Fallon, P., and R. Lucas. 1991. "The Impact of Changes in Job Security Regulations in India and Zimbabwe." *World Bank Economic Review* 5(3): 395–413.

Foz, V., ed. 2001. *The Labor Code of the Philippines*. Quezon City: Philippine Law Gazette.

Gupta, A., and V. Govindarajan. 2001. "Converting Global Presence into Global Competitive Advantage." *The Academy of Management Executive* 15(2): 45–58.

Hannan, M., and J. Freeman. 1989. *Organizational Ecology*. Boston: Harvard University Press.

Kidder, D. L. 1995. "On Call or Answering a Calling? Temporary Nurses and Extra Role Behaviors." Vancouver: Paper presented at the annual meeting of the Academy of Management.

Lagos, R. 1994. "Labour Market Flexibility: What Does it Really Mean?" *CEPAL Review* 54: 81–95.

Lazear, E. 1990. "Job Security Provisions and Employment." *Quarterly Journal of Economics* 105: 699–726.

Lloyd, V., and R. Weismann. 2001. "Against the Workers: How IMF and the World Bank Policies Undermine Labor Power and Rights." *Multinational Monitor* 22(9). Retrieved October 27, 2003, from http://www.hartford-hwp.com/archives/25/077.html.

Macaraya, B., and R. Ofreneo. 1992. "Structural Adjustments and Industrial Relations." Sydney: Proceedings of the International Conference on Labour and Management (October).

Mangum, G., D. Mayall, and K. Nelson. 1985. "The Temporary Help Industry: A Response to the Dual Internal Labor-Market." *Industrial and labor Relations Review* 38(4): 599–611.

Margolis, J., and J. Walsh. 2001. *People and Profits? The Search for a Link Between a Company's Social and Financial Performance*. Mahwah, N.J.: Lawrence Erlbaum Associates, Inc.

Matusik, S. F., and C. W. L. Hill. 1998. "The Utilization of Contingent Work, Knowledge Creation, and Competitive Advantage." *Academy of Management Review* 23(4): 680–697.

McGuire, J., A. Sundgern, and T. Schneeweis. 1988. "Corporate Social Responsibility and Firm Performance." *Academy of Management Journal* 31(4): 854–872.

Milgrom, P., and J. Roberts. 1992. *Economics, Organization and Management*. New York: Prentice Hall.

Mondy, R., R. Noe, and S. Premeaux . 2002. *Human Resource Management*, 8th ed. Upper Saddle River, N.J.: Prentice Hall.

Morgan, G. 1996. *Images of Organizations*, 2nd ed. Thousand Oaks, Calif.: Sage Publications.

Ofreneo, R., and I. Ortiz. 1998. *Globalization and Employment Relations in the Philippines*. Working Paper, School of Labor and Industrial Relations, University of the Philippines.

Oliver, C. 1991. "Strategic Responses to Institutional Pressure." *Academy of Management Review* 16(1): 145–179.

Parks, J., and D. Kidder. 1994. "Till Death Us Do Part: Changing Work Relationships in the 1990s," in Cooper and Rousseau 1994.

Pearce, J. 1993. "Toward an Organizational Behavior of Contract Laborers: Their Psychological Involvement and Effects on Employee Co-Workers." *Academy of Management Journal* 36: 1082–1096.

Pfeffer, J. 1992. *Managing with Power: Politics and Influences in Organizations*. Boston: Harvard Business School Press.

Pfeffer, J., and J. N. Barron. 1988. "Taking the Workers Back Out: Recent Trends in the Structuring of Employment," in *Trends in Organizational Behavior*, vol. 10, ed. B. Straw and L. L. Cummings. Greenwich, Conn.: JAI Press.

Porter, G. 1995. "Attitude Differences Between Regulat and Contract Employees of Nursing Departments." Vancouver: Paper presented at the annual meeting of the Academy of Management.

Rousseau, D., and C. Libuser. 1997. "Contingent Workers in High-Risk Environments." *California Management Review* 39(2): 103–123.

Russo, M., and P. Fouts. 1997. "A Resource-Based Perspective on Corporate Environmental Performance and Profitability." *Academy of Management Journal* 40(3): 534–559.

Salancik, G. 1977. "Commitment and Control of Organizational Behavior and Belief," in *New Directions in Organizational Behavior*, ed. B. Straw and G. Salancik. Chicago: St. Clair Press.

Shalla, V. 2003. "Part-Time Shift: The Struggle over the Casualization of Airline Customer Sales and Service Agent Work." *The Canadian Review of Sociology and Anthropology* 40(1): 93–109.

Soriano, M. 1993. "The Implications of Flexible Employment Arrangements in the Philippines." Unpublished master's thesis, University of the Philippines, Quezon City.

Supangco, V. 2000. "Outsourcing: An Exploratory Study." *Philippine Management Review* 8(1): 84–95.

Torres, C. 1993. "External Labor Flexibility: The Philippine Experience." *Philippine Journal of Labor and Industrial Relations* 15(1–2): 97–130.

Uzzi, B., and Z. Barsness. 1998. "Contingent Employment in British Establishments: Organizational Determinants of the Use of Fixed-Term Hires and Part-Time Workers." *Social Forces* 76(3): 967–1005.

Van Dyne, L., and S. Ang. 1998. "Organizational Citizenship Behavior of Contingent Workers in Singapore." *Academy of Management Journal* 41(6): 692–703.

Wysocki, B. 1996. "Flying Solo: High-Tech Nomads Write New Program for Future of Work." *Wall Street Journal* (August 19): Sec. A1.

Appendix A. Checklist of Common Benefits

- Training
- Bonuses
- Overtime Pay
- Holiday Pay
- Paid Vacation Leave
- Paid Sick Leave
- Social Security System/Government Service Insurance System
- Philhealth
- Employee Compensation
- Pag-ibig
- Life Insurance
- Accident Insurance
- Health Plans
- Separation Benefits
- Free Medicines and Consultations

Appendix B. Means and Standard Deviations of Variables Used in the Study

	Mean	Standard deviation	N
Proportion of casual employees	16.739	18.9809	49
Number of casual employees	222.8367	591.4649	49
Proportion of project employees	11.6131	20.1778	49
Number of project employees	69.1837	229.6949	49
Proportion of female employees	44.4487	20.3339	
Proportion of female casual employees	31.1812	30.8687	49
Proportion of female project employees	20.5031	30.9391	49
Differential proportion of female casual employees and total female employees	-12.7461	24.3226	49
Differential proportion of female project employees and total female employees	-23.4242	30.6058	49
Benefits index for casual employees	34.2667	23.6762	50
Benefits index for project employees	30.533	30.2998	50
Differential benefits index of project and regular employees	8.7	3.7212	50
Differential benefits index of project and regular employees	9.26	4.6896	50
Proportion of produce sold in local market	73.2120	40.2754	46
Absolute change in regular employment	12	78.8072	47
Proportion of unionized employees	19.1652	29.3846	48
Social performance index	74.6475	26.5532	45
Formalization of stakeholder	39.3802	20.1828	49
Organization age	23.06212	21.5304	49
Total number of female employees	648.9	1482.4685	50
Employment size	1222.5098	2323.0444	51
Interaction between union status and employment size	558.4286	1523.4987	49
Interaction between age and market growth	15.3696	17.8006	46

The Author

Vivien T. Supangco is Associate Professor of Human Resource Management and Organization Development, College of Business Administration, University of the Philippines, Diliman, Quezon City, Philippines, vivien.supangco@up.edu.ph.

Appendix C. Correlation Matrix of Variables Used in the Study

	1	2	3	4	5	6	7	8	9	10	11	12	13	14	15	16	17
1. Proportion of casual employees	1																
2. Number of casual employees	.47	1															
3. Proportion of project employees	-.22	-.16	1														
4. Number of project employees	-.10	.05	.65	1													
5. Benefits index for casual employees	.27	.08	-.03	.00	1												
6. Differential benefits for casual employees	-.26	-.00	.03	-.01	-.87	1											
7. Benefits index for project employees	-.06	-.04	.54	.17	.34	-.27	1										
8. Differential benefits for project employees	.06	.10	-.52	-.18	-.27	.39	-.92	1									
9. Absolute change in regular employment	-.08	-.07	-.04	-.08	.03	-.065	.09	-.11	1								
10. Total employment size	.14	.71	-.12	.15	-.03	.14	-.08	.12	.00	1							
11. Proportion of goods sold in the local market	.05	-.16	.17	.11	-.05	-.03	.19	-.25	-.24	-.38	1						
12. Proportion of unionized employees	.16	.23	-.21	-.08	.14	-.03	-.13	.21	-.31	.05	.19	1					
13. Social performance index	-.18	.12	-.32	-.32	.04	.11	.15	-.01	.09	.29	-.32	-.05	1				
14. Index of formalization of stakeholder concerns	-.00	.29	-.26	-.14	.23	-.01	.03	.15	.11	.32	-.30	.06	.52	1			
15. Company age	.08	.28	-.17	.12	.05	.10	-.04	.16	-.30	.18	.21	.60	.05	.22	1		
16. Interaction of unionization and employment size	.32	.95	-.15	.04	.08	.03	-.01	.09	-.09	.53	-.07	.37	.15	.30	.42	1	
17. Interaction of company age and market growth	.11	.21	-.08	-.05	-.09	.22	.06	.05	-.23	.10	.01	.25	.15	.17	.45	.18	1

CULTURAL PERSPECTIVES OF CSR OPPORTUNITIES FOR GERMAN FIRMS IN POLAND

Roy W. Smolens, Jr., and Nicolaas Tempelhof
Aalen University of Applied Sciences, Aalen, Germany

Abstract

This chapter examines cultural issues related to corporate social responsibility (CSR) as practiced by German firms operating in Poland. Recognizing the interdependence of a corporation's social and financial performance, the chapter attempts to analyze how German firms can increase profit through good social performance. However, implementing CSR measures requires detailed knowledge of Polish society and culture. Behavior and attitudes must be considered to understand a company's CSR target group and achieve the desired financial return from investments in CSR. The authors characterize the most profitable types of CSR initiatives available to firms operating in Poland.

Introduction

Our first source of inspiration when approaching the issue of Corporate Social Responsibility (CSR) in Poland is the economic potential we find in Eastern European countries. Poland was the largest of the ten countries that joined the European Union in March 2004. Its accession was not a result of "lucky coincidence" but of hard work and improvements in the country, as well as political and social changes since 1989.

A process of transformation began with Poland's transition from a Communist regime to a democratic state. It is the basis for Poland's market economy today. Poland opened its market and began to develop international relationships, especially within the EU zone. "The rapidly growing Polish market was beneficial for all: for employers as well as for employees, consumers, and the local communities" (CSR Europe 2003).

However, during this period nobody paid attention to social duties of the business sector and new responsibilities arising with the change. Our second source of inspiration is therefore the country's lack of experience in CSR. CSR still is a relatively new issue even in Germany, and it is even less familiar in Poland. Society's expectations of business increased only near the end of the 1990s, when the number of business scandals was growing.

 pp. 259–283

In Polish society the spotlight is on the need for experience in the fields of corporate culture and corporate responsibility. The CCG (Centrale für Coorganisation, an organization that sets standards for German consumer industries) considers this a challenge for German companies dealing with CSR. Corporations can profit from the same CSR measures they undertake to meet society's needs and improve the natural environment.

We argue that CSR increases a company's competitiveness and is linked with financial performance. Results of previous studies confirm this. Ninety-four percent of company executives believe that "the development of a CSR strategy can deliver real business benefits" (Ernst & Young survey 2002). "Companies with a public commitment to ethics perform better on three out four financial measures than those without. These companies also have 18 [percent] higher profits on average" (Institute of Business Ethics 2003).

In order to implement CSR measures successfully in Poland, German companies should be aware of areas in which CSR is required. This leads us to the purpose of our study. We first discuss the issue of CSR in general. We examine Carroll's four-part CSR classification, introduce our concept of CSR, and discuss the implementation of CSR in corporations. We then present an overview of the Republic of Poland and analyze Polish economy and culture. Finally, we focus on CSR in Poland, and in particular on the challenges and opportunities German companies face when implementing CSR measures. We conclude by identifying the most profitable types of internal and external CSR initiatives available to firms operating in Poland.

Corporate Social Responsibility

Definition of CSR

The concept of CSR has a very wide range of interpretations and meanings. For most companies it is an issue that goes beyond personnel management, workplace morale, and business relations. It is often view as "the wider social role" of business. Yet what does it mean for a corporation to be socially responsible? Academics and business practitioners have been trying to agree on a definition of this concept for thirty years, but even today there are a variety of terms to describe CSR: business ethics, human rights, social and environmental engagement, sustainability.

The EU Commission (2002) defines CSR as "a concept that is considered as a basis for companies to integrate voluntary social and ecological issues in their business activities and in their interrelation with stakeholders." This definition refers to the need to act responsibly toward the whole community, whether it be local or global, and toward our environment. It assumes that a corporation's goal is to have a positive effect on the greater community rather than a harmful and self-serving one.

James Wolfensohn, president of the World Bank, defines CSR in another way: "CSR is not a question of charity; it's a question of enlightened self-interest. It's an issue of how we're going to keep our planet stable so that your businesses survive." This definition emphasizes a new aspect of CSR: self-interest. It is connected to a company's purpose of making a profit or being the best. Companies therefore have an incentive to define and integrate CSR into all aspects of their business, because it has a positive impact on economic performance.

CCG defines CSR as long-term activities of a company to assume responsibility for its impact on all those who are affected by its activities. CSR measures lead to a win-win situation; companies not only satisfy all those affected but are recognized for creating social responsibility as well. This brings key benefits to the company. Viewed in this sense, CSR is a comprehensive set of policies, practices, and programs that are integrated into business operations, supply chains, and decision-making processes. CSR includes responsibility for current and past actions of a company as well as for its future impact.

Carroll's Four-Part CSR Classification

As part of our research we reviewed and analyzed A. Carroll's four-part classification of CSR. Carroll, one of the most prolific authors on the subject, divided CSR into four categories:

- economic responsibility
- legal responsibility
- ethical responsibility
- philanthropic responsibility.

CCG agrees with his view that "a corporation has not only economic and legal obligations, but ethical and philanthropic responsibilities as well" (Carroll 1979: para. 7). "Historically, businesses were created as economic entities" (Carroll 1979: para. 7). Their principal role consisted in the production of goods or services that consumers needed, with the aim of making a good profit in the process. However, the restriction of a company's role to its economic aspect is obsolete. Nowadays, social and ethical aspects play a major role as well.

Economic responsibility includes profitability for both shareholders and stakeholders. Thus a corporation should assume responsibility for carrying out five requirements:

- Its activities must be consistent with maximizing earnings per share.
- It must commit to being as profitable as possible.
- It must achieve and maintain a strong competitive position.
- It must attach importance to a high level of operating efficiency.
- To be a successful corporation, it must be continuously profitable.

The implementation of these requirements leads to "being profitable for shareholders, while providing economic benefits to other corporate stakeholders, such as fair-paying jobs for employees and good quality, fairly priced products for customers" (Lantos 2002).

Business is also expected to comply with government laws and regulations. Corporations must be legally responsible and carry out their economic activities while respecting these basic rules, which provide the framework for their actions. Therefore, a company must comply with the following five requirements:

- Its activities must be consistent with the expectations of the government and its laws.
- It must comply with various federal, state and local regulations.

- It must be a law-abiding corporate citizen.
- To be a successful corporation, it must fulfill its legal obligations.
- Its goods and services should at least meet the minimal legal requirements.

Although Carroll's economic and legal responsibilities include such ethical norms as fairness and justice, he created a third component of responsibility: ethical responsibility. It embraces all activities that society expects and are not part of the law. This category focuses on the expectations of consumers, employees, and community with the aim of respecting "people's moral rights; and doing what is right, just and fair" (Smith and Quelch 1993, cited by Lantos 2002: para. 3). In order to meet these expectations, businesses may have to go beyond what is currently required by law. Ethical responsibility affects includes responsibility but at the same time requires business to accomplish more than what the law requires. Specifically, a corporation is expected to meet five requirements:

- Its activities must be consistent with meeting the expectations of society and ethical norms.
- It must recognize and respect new ethical norms as they are adopted by society.
- It must not compromise ethical norms in order to achieve corporate goals.
- To be a successful corporation, it must deliver what is expected ethically.
- To be a successful corporation, it must acknowledge that ethical behavior goes beyond the requirements of laws and regulations.

Carroll's fourth component of CSR concerns philanthropic responsibility, which includes voluntary financial giving and service. The focus is on "alleviating various social ills within a community or society" (Lantos 2002). These "social ills" can be alleviated by improving human welfare, supporting educational institutions, reducing urban blight, fighting illiteracy, and building infrastructure, among other measures. Philanthropic responsibility should be distinguished from ethical responsibility. Communities may ask companies to support humanitarian programs with their money, employees' time or facilities. However, a company is not unethical because it fails to provide the desired support. Philanthropic responsibility therefore has more of a voluntary character, even though society expects it. The five philanthropic requirements of a corporation are:

- Its activities should be consistent with meeting the philanthropic and charitable expectations of society.
- It should support fine arts and performing arts.
- Its managers and employees should take part in voluntary and charitable activities in their local community.
- It should support private and public educational institutions.
- It should assist in voluntarily projects to improve a community's quality of life.

Our Concept of CSR

Using this background as framework, CCG suggests four categories of CSR: non-profit, for-profit, internal, and external. Non-profit CSR pertains to private individuals or private charitable service organizations that support social and environmental causes. Their goals for CSR activities are altruistic rather than PR- or profit-oriented. One might mention the Red Cross and Greenpeace as examples. Non-profit CSR corresponds to Carroll's philanthropic responsibility.

Non-profit CSR is not part of a business corporations' activities. Businesses do not donate money for purely altruistic reasons; they expect a return on their "investment" in charity. The upward trend in corporate giving is a result of better calculation rather than an act of generosity.

This leads us to our next category, which is the most common type of corporate CSR: for-profit CSR. It is part of strategic CSR because it accomplishes strategic business goals that focus on profit maximization and the improvement of reputation and image. We view it as legitimate because it contributes to a company's goals on the one hand while supporting all stakeholders on the other. It can be described as a "win-win situation that benefits both the firm and its constituencies" (Lantos 2002).

We also distinguish two kinds of for-profit CSR: internal and external. We make this distinction because of its importance for understanding the groups to which CSR is targeted. Without a clear delineation of the target group, CSR measures will not achieve the desired success. "The mainstreaming of CSR activity in the region [Poland] requires a dual shift in thinking not just on the part of businesses, but on the part of potential partners from other sectors" (CSR Campaign 2003). Internal CSR concerns measures taken within companies. It focuses mainly on employees and suppliers. External CSR includes measures taken outside companies and is directed to society in general. Consumers, among others, are part of this group.

Carroll includes legal responsibility as one of his four CSR categories. However, we argue that laws are there to be obeyed and not voluntary. Legal responsibility is a prerequisite of conducting business. CSR is voluntary, and law is therefore not part of CSR as we conceive it.

We can now develop our concept of CSR on the basis of the four types of CSR outlined above as well as the "three bottom lines"—people, planet and profit. CSR "is about integrating the issues of the workplace, human rights, the community and the marketplace into core business strategies" (CSR Campaign, n.d.). We divide CSR more finely into social, environmental, and economic responsibility, corresponding to people, planet and profit.

People are affected by social aspects of business policies, which include the social environment, safety, employability, and human rights, among others. Two groups of people can be distinguished: internal and external. The internal group consists of those who are part of a company's workplace, primarily employees. Corporations undertake numerous measures in this area. Most realize that employees are their most important resource. Manufacturing firms see safety as one their top priorities. Guidelines must be observed, appropriate machines and clothes provided, and various kinds of training and seminars conducted. Some companies even offer a kindergarten for employees' children in order to support working women.

Customers and society belong to the external group. A company's commitment to external issues is multiple. A pharmaceutical company may donate drugs to poor people in Africa, a bank may make micro loans with very low interest rates, a car company may support a museum financially. A chemical company may donate chemicals to schools so that teachers can incorporate more experiments in their lessons to help students understand things better. Some of the companies we investigated form partnerships with such charity organizations as UNICEF. The list could be extended with numerous examples. Both "people"-groups deserve fair and right treatment.

The second bottom line, which we call *planet*, covers ecological aspects of business policy, such as the protection of the environment and nature, global warming, sustainable construction, energy conservation, and so forth. Companies try to provide products and packaging that are easy to recycle or dispose. The impact of humankind on the environment should be minimized by using thoughtful means of production, transportation, and sale.

The third bottom line of our circle considers profit, the economic side of CSR. It focuses on profitability, continuity, long-term expansion, sustainable investment, business processes, and corporate governance. Most companies have financial incentives to practice CSR and to show social and environmental commitment. We deduce that CSR makes a business more competitive as well as more attractive to employees and consumers. This is confirmed by three surveys, conducted in 2002, that examined the relationship between social responsibility and financial performance.

PricewaterhouseCoopers's annual CEO survey found that 79 percent of CEOs believe that sustainability, meaning such long-term programs as the implementation of CSR, is "vital to any company" (PricewaterhouseCoopers 2003). Seventy-one percent of them would exchange short-term profitability for long-term values when implementing CSR. Other surveys come to the same result. "[Ninety-four percent] of companies' executives believe the development of a CSR strategy can deliver real business benefits" (Ernst & Young survey 2002). Brand value and reputation are increasingly seen as one of the most valuable assets of a company. Interbrand estimated in 2000 that 96 percent of Coca Cola's values are intangibles; for Kellogg's the figure is 97 percent, and for American Express 84 percent. Some companies feel that CSR is a significant part of their risk management and reputation strategy because CSR-activities can build loyalty and trust for a sustainable future.

CCG concludes that most research points to a positive relationship between CSR and financial performance. By integrating CSR into business strategy, corporations not only make a significant contribution to society or environment, but are also recognized for doing so. This has obvious benefits for the company.

CSR Implementation

Each company differs how it implements CSR. The differences depend on such factors as company size, sector, culture and the engagement of its management. While investigating the websites of German companies investing in Poland, we found out that some show no awareness of CSR on their website, some focus on a single area (such as the environment), and others integrate CSR into all aspects of their business activities. It is obvious that the implementation of CSR follows no single pattern. Each company must design a suitable CSR structure for its own mission, size, culture, geographic location, and level of CSR commitment. Three factors should be considered:

Communication, education and training. All companies must recognize that their employees are unlikely to behave responsibly if they are unaware of the company's responsibility. Employees should be provided with necessary information and tools to act appropriately when carrying out their duties.

The company environment. CSR cannot be implemented in an environment where innovation and independent thinking are not welcome. Such multinationals (MNCs) as BASF, Siemens, and Bayer are aware of this and try to encourage innovation, above-average commitment, and transparency in CSR activities. An ongoing process of CSR requires a company's willingness to adopt non-traditional ways of handling social problems.

Stakeholder analysis. Before implementing CSR measures, a stakeholder analysis should be done in order to understand the target audience. Stakeholder analysis has "become more important than issue management in the generation of policy. Issues like health and safety, human rights and business ethics . . . do not necessarily take up a central position at the beginning of it" (CSR Europe n.d.).

The field of CSR has been influenced by several additional factors over the last decade. Stakeholder activism has grown, along with society's expectations of business. The Polish people have reacted to the growing number of business scandals, including corruption, financial scandals, violations of employees' rights, and pollution from production plants, and they have shown a growing interest in the principles of CSR.

Government interest and action have also grown. CSR has become an important issue for both business and policy agenda in Europe generally. The European Commission sees CSR "as a main point of European competition strategy" and issued a Green Paper (a discussion paper on CSR). Apart from defining CSR, this paper outlines steps that companies, governments, and society can undertake to strengthen their commitment to CSR.

During the last decade, companies have faced increasing demands for transparency and haven been asked to measure, report, and improve their social, environmental, and economic performance. "Companies are now expected to provide access to information on impacts of their business activities and to engage stakeholders in meaningful dialogue about issues of concern" (Business for Social Responsibility 2003). Leading companies investigate different types of audit and verification in order to increase their transparency and the credibility of their reports. As part of this trend many companies try to live up to external standards created by both governmental and non-governmental organizations. While many of these standards consider only single issues, such as environmental or social performance, others address a wider range of CSR issues. The standards listed below cover a wide range and encompass multiple CSR issues.

Social Accountability 8000. This standard specifies requirements for social accountability and covers programs for child labor, wages and benefits, working hours, health and safety, and freedom of association.

The Global Reporting Initiative (GRI). This is a reporting standard, established in 1997, with the mission of designing globally applicable guidelines for the preparation of social and environmental reports.

United Nations Global Compact was launched in September 2000. UN Secretary-General Kofi Annan called on leading companies to incorporate nine principles into their company practices and to support public initiatives.

Organization for Economic Cooperation and Development (OECD) Guidelines for Multinational Enterprises. These guidelines are addressed to multinational companies and include voluntary principles and standards. Companies are encouraged to observe these guidelines wherever they operate worldwide.

Benefits of CSR

"Corporate Social Responsibility is a business strategy that works" (CSR campaign 2003). In a business world where brand value, image, and reputation are becoming more important, CSR can be seen as a competitive advantage that creates loyalty and trust and ensures a sustainable future. Companies are becoming increasingly visible. They are not only judged by their results but by their behavior, too. Socially responsible behavior affects their activities in at leas three ways:

Reduction of operating costs. External CSR measures, particularly environmental initiatives, "can reduce operating costs dramatically by cutting waste and inefficiencies or improving productivity."

Increased sales and customers' loyalty. External CSR commitment is increasingly recognized by society because of the rise of the new media. Consumers' purchase decisions are influenced by a company's positive or negative reputation for CSR. More and more consumers are critical of products and the companies that make them and are willing to "punish" companies with a bad social or environmental record. "One in five consumers would be very willing to pay more for products that are socially and environmentally responsible" (MORI 2000).

Increased productivity. Internal measures, such as employee benefit programs, can boost worker commitment, reduce costs related to absenteeism, disability, and turnover, and improve worker motivation and efficiency (CSR Europe n.d.). These factors raise productivity and reduce hiring and dismissal costs. Companies with strong CSR commitments often find it easier to recruit employees, who increasingly want to feel proud of the company they work for. Star employees have a choice. They work for companies that are in accord with their own value systems. If they do not want to work for a polluter, they will not. After all, people want to hold their heads up when they are with their peers. They do not want an embarrassed silence when they announce whom they work for (GE's Jack Welch, cited by CSR Europe n.d.).

An integration of CSR into corporate business policy contributes to sustainable success. Demonstrated social responsibility can "secure continued success for an organization through building a more secure environment in which that business operates" (Osmond 2002: 1). However, companies must know how to implement CSR before they can enjoy its benefits.

Research Aims

CCG argues that there is a link between a company's financial performance and its corporate social performance. An integration of all relevant aspects, namely the three bottom lines, into corporate policy contributes to sustainable success. We claim that win-win situations exist; companies can make a profit through good corporate social performance.

Country Profile of Poland

The Republic of Poland (*Rzeczpospolita Polska*) is situated in central Europe, where it is surrounded by Germany, the Czech Republic, Slovakia, Ukraine, Byelorussia, Lithuania, and Russia, and covers an area slightly larger than Italy.

Figure 1. Polish position analysis

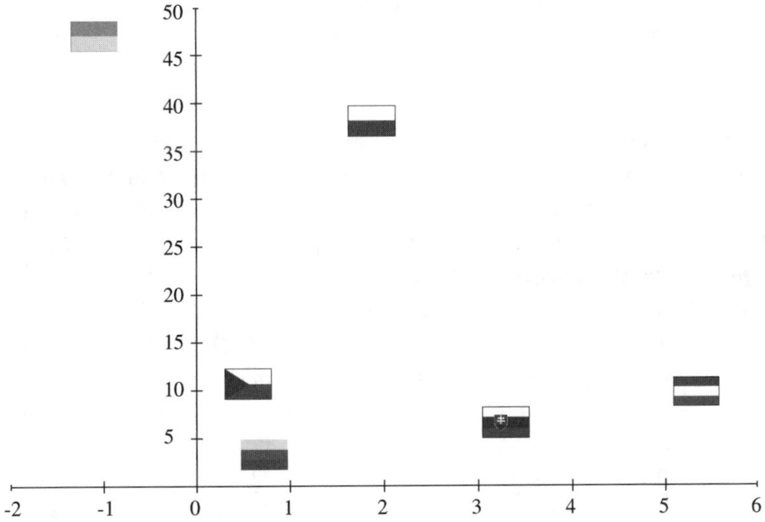

		population (millions)	inflation rate, %
Czechia (CZ)		10.2	0.6
Hungary (HU)		10.0	5.3
Lithuania (LI)		3.6	0.8
Poland (PL)		38.6	1.9
Slovakia (SL)		5.4	3.3
Ukraine (UK)		48.1	−1.2

Source: World Factbook (2003).

Poland is the ninth-largest country in Europe and is divided into sixteen provinces (*Województwa*), and subdivided into counties (*Powiaty*) and municipalities (*Gminy*). The capital, Warsaw (*Warszawa*), has more than 1.6 million citizens (Economy of Poland 2003).

Population

Poland's population of 38.6 million is the eighth-largest in Europe and therefore offers new market potential. Poland ranks twenty-sixth worldwide in its growth rate and "is one of the youngest countries on the continent—35 [percent] of the Polish society is under the age of 25 years" (PAIZ 2003). Today's Poland is almost homogenous ethnically, consisting of 98 percent Poles, in contrast to the pre–World War II period, when there were significant ethnic minorities: "4.5 million Ukrainians, 3 million Jews, 1 million Belorussians, and 800,000 Germans" (Nation by Nation n.d.).

Despite Poland's economic recovery since its political transformation, unemployment is relatively high at 18.8 percent (February 2003), especially in rural areas. The unemployment rate among women is even higher.

Economy

Beginning with the process of transformation that started in 1989, Poland has undertaken a number of reforms in tax and law policy, health care, and education, among others. These reforms, along with strict budgetary and monetary discipline, improved Poland's market situation substantially. Companies were released from price controls, and the Polish market was opened for international competition.

The privatization of state-owned companies and a liberal law that governs the establishment of new firms have contributed to the development of the private sector, which is "responsible for 70 [percent] of economic activity" (Photius 1999) and employs about 63.4 percent of the work force (Blazyca 1999: 803, cited by Abdelgadir N. Abdelhafiz Elbadri 2001: 69). Today, "Poland stands out as one of the most successful and open transition economies" (Photius 1999).

The Polish inflation rate fell from almost 60 percent in 1991 to 1.9 percent in 2002. "Poland could now capitalise on the benefits of lower inflationary expectations" (World Markets Research Centre 2002). The inflation rate is expected to remain broadly stable in both 2003 and 2004. Keeping the inflation rate below 2 percent was a requirement for Poland's EU accession in May 2004. The government's decision to join the EU affected all aspects of the Polish economy. Improving Poland's foreign trade and internal budget deficits is now a top priority.

Due to the development of its market, Poland has become much more attractive to foreign investors. Western European models were established in Poland, and German companies saw a new opportunity.

The growth rate of the Polish gross domestic product (GDP), which has remained positive over the last decade and increased steadily until 1997, also attracted German companies (Figure 2). A return to domestic investment, followed by lower consumption, caused a slowdown after 1997. Economic contraction, particularly in Germany, also contributed to the declining rate of development, because of the interdependences between the two countries. The Russian collapse and high oil prices also had downstream effects. An upward trend of the GDP growth rate began in 2003, and the rate is projected to reach approximately 3 percent in 2004.

Figure 2. Annual GDP growth rates in Poland

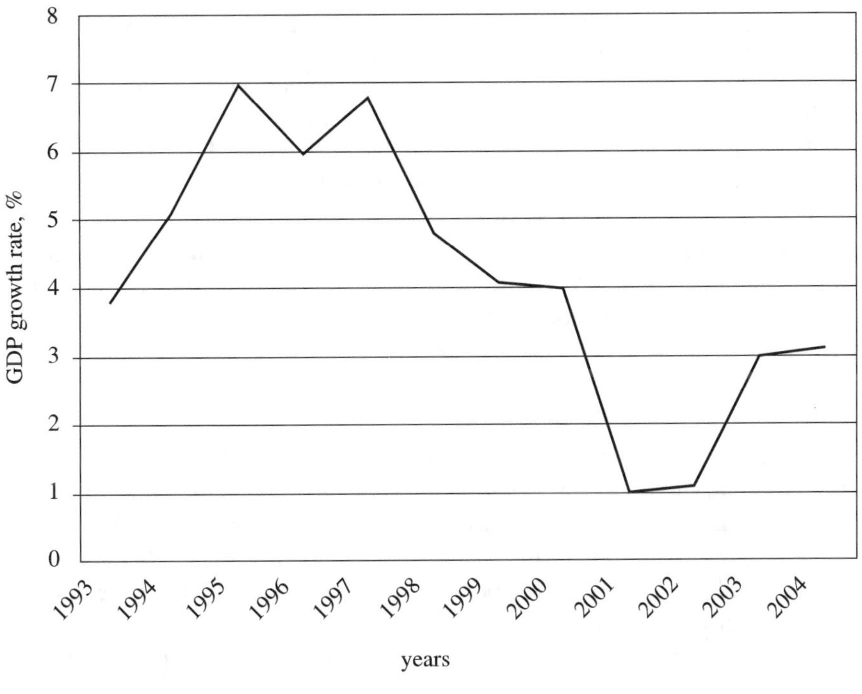

Apart from Poland's stable inflation rate and promising GDP, one of the most important factors attracting German companies are low labor costs, despite a high level of education. "Workers in Central and Eastern Europe have a lower wage level and are willing to work a greater number of days per year than workers in Western Europe" (World Markets Research Centre 2002). The average wage amounts to approximately 510 EUR monthly, and the minimum wage is currently about 180 EUR (World Market Research Centre 2002).

Poland is one of the most promising Eastern European countries, offering a skilled workforce, a large labor pool, high technical capability, and well-trained engineers and computer experts—all factors that contribute to a company's competitiveness and the development of its products. Other benefits for German companies in Poland are investment incentives and subsidies offered by the Polish Ministry of Economy. They include subventions for job creations, investments, and environmental involvement, as well as subsidies for the employment of handicapped persons and tax breaks in special economic zones (SEZ), which are structurally underdeveloped regions.

Poland's EU accession in 2004 was an opportunity for German companies investing in the country. In order to join the EU, Poland had to comply with rules, standards, and policies imposed by EU law. It must the inflation rate under 2 percent, meet the conditions for a stable democracy, and respect human rights and the rule of law.

The EU accession significantly affected German companies, since Germany is Poland's largest trading partner and accounts for 34.3 percent of Polish exports (CIA World Factbook 2003). German companies are among the most important business partners and foreign investors in Poland. "EU enlargement will therefore have a direct impact on all businesses in the current EU member states" (Ian Glogoski and Joachim Sohn 2003). Poland's EU accession offers them the opportunity to build up and extend their position in common markets. Poland's duty adjustment to EU standard enhances trade with other EU countries. Most products now enter Poland duty-free, and the transportation of goods is becoming much easier. Fewer border controls result in greater quantities products exported and imported. A common EU currency simplifies trade. Previous additions to the EU have shown that accession countries become economically and politically more stable, and foreign companies experience less investment risk.

Culture

After the abolition of Communism, German companies set up business in Poland and found the country to be worth operating in. They have begun to realize the potential of its markets and people. Yet they may face conflicts when different cultural systems interact, if they are unaware of the specific characteristics of the other culture (Fink 2002). Cultural differences should be understood and used to advantage in building successful cooperation with the Polish people.

During the initial years of their presence in Poland, German companies found some aspects of German business structure and strategy to be inapplicable and were obliged to adapt to the Polish cultural situation to make business profitable. The same challenge applies to implementing CSR. Whereas CSR is already established in Western European countries, it is only now being implemented in Eastern Europe.

Profit-minded German companies expect to benefit from effective CSR decisions. CSR must be seen as an investment in a more efficient workforce and not as a pure act of charity, without any return on the investment. The focus in recent times has shifted from shareholders to stakeholders. "The success of a company is mainly considered to be determined through its stakeholders" (Jackson and Schuler 2003: 16), and institutions aim for a closer interaction with them. In times when products and services are easier to imitate, commercial enterprises look for other sources of differentiation, such as CSR programs, to create competitive advantage. "The increasing role of business also leads to higher social expectation to serve society as a reflection of cultural values" (Rogovsky 2000).

Knowledge of the national culture is indispensable for understanding social expectations. Culture can be characterized as "group-specific cognitive organization or world view comprised of the mosaic elements of meanings" (Szalay and Maday 1973, cited by Mroczkowski and Linowes 1999). According to Triandis and Vassilou, there is a close relationship between people's subjective interpretations and their behavior (Triandis and Vassilou 1967, cited by Mroczkowski and Linowes 1999). Culture is primarily a system of symbolic communication created by humans, who "communicate it and express themselves in it; they enter into various dependencies or interactions; people communicate, they are interrelated with one another in various ways and form specific social systems, called also social groups or structures" (Dyczewski n.d.).

According to Hofstede's cultural model, values lie at the core and are surrounded by concentric circles of attitudes, beliefs, and opinions (Hofstede 1984; Hofstede, Neuijen, Ohayv, and Sanders 1990, cited by Mroczkowski and Linowes 1999). Hofstede, as well as Kluckhohn and Strodtbeck, sees a national culture as the result of society's answers to fundamental problems related to human nature and human existence (Todeva 1999). Cultural studies (Schwartz 2003; Smith, Dugan, and Trompenaars 1996, cited by Mroczkowski and Linowes 1999) have explained and stressed the connection between culture and values (Mroczkowski and Linowes 1999), which are its major determinant. Basic values build the foundation of culture. They express "what people believe is good or bad, what they think should and should not be done, what they hold to be desirable or undesirable" (Schwartz and Bardi 1997). A person's behavior in society is mainly determined by his or her set of values. They form the basis of all decisions a person makes and establish "standards for us to evaluate our own and others' actions" (Chen and Starosta 1998).

Poland, which was associated with the former Communist bloc for over half a century, still exhibits a collectivistic culture. According to Paliwoda (1997, cited by Mehta, Dubinsky, and Anderson 2001), even though Poland is currently attempting to change to a capitalistic economy, it is difficult to replace the old planned economic system in such a short period of time. Since Poland is still in a process of reform, its history and culture, as well as its experience with reforms, must be considered (Kemme 1991, cited by Giffin 1994). Yet Poland is probably the most Western nation of the former Communist countries, and its transition from a former Communist society to a market economy serves as a model for the new democracies of Eastern Europe.

An examination of Polish traditions and society reveals the effects of other cultures on Polish culture. "Polish culture was always enhanced when it opened towards other cultures" (Bárkányi 2002). From this background Poland's opening to the West and the EU may be favorable. The difference today, however, is that Poland has no alternative but to join the EU while preserving its sovereignty, national identity, and culture (Bárkányi 2002). The question arises, can Poles accept the cultural change this implies? They may to some extent, since capitalism is accompanied by a tendency for people to give up their collectivistic and feminine values and adopt more individualistic and masculine ones (Hofstede 1984). On the other hand, Polish people protect such values as language, history, traditions, religion, and national independence, and they resist penetration of these values.

It remains unclear to what extent the incentives of wealth and money may lead Polish society to weaken or sacrifice certain of its core values. Developments so far show a persistence of old cultural habits in the new system. Poles have been relatively successful at making the new institutions conform to old habits, rather than vice versa. One may assume that many Poles will continue to prefer some aspects the home culture to cultural diversity even in the post-accession period (Kochanowicz and Marody 2003).

Polish culture can be characterized as both open and closed. It is open to elements of other cultures, but it is closed to threats to its coherence and persistence. This sense of caution derives from strong cultural ties among the Polish people (Dyczewski n.d.).

It is possible to point to specific characteristics of Polish culture: importance of the family, anarchic collectivism, national identity and independence, religiosity, a weak work ethic, a short-term orientation, and ambiguous attitudes toward wealth (Kochanowicz and Marody 2003). Family, family values, and home are precious in Polish culture. Commitment to home and relatives, and a sense of belonging to a family, are still strong. They seek aid within the family in crises and difficult situations. The nuclear family model of many Western countries is unpopular in Poland, where the extended family survives, and the idea of a multigenerational family living under one roof persists. Grandparents, parents and children may live in separate domiciles, and yet they reside in the neighborhood and remain in constant touch, visiting and offering spiritual and material help to each other when there is need (Dyczewski and Jedynak n.d.).

There is a clear division between the world outside and a close circle of relatives and friends. Poles appreciate the small collectivistic world of family and friends, whereas the outside world is generally marked by individualism (Kochanowicz and Marody 2003). In that world, individuals are responsible for their actions and seek their own profit. Failure is not seen as failure of the group but of the individual. Hofstede's findings on Polish culture place Poland in a middle position between individualism and collectivism. This may represent an equilibrium between native collectivism and outsides pressures toward individualism.

Patriotism and sovereignty are deeply impressed on Polish consciousness. The insistence on maintaining Polish identity is remarkable but understandable when one considers their long-term struggle for an independent state. A commitment to independence after two centuries of occupation, suppression, and annexation by other nations has strengthened their patriotism. Surrounded by the two powerful states of Russia and Germany, Poland has always been in a difficult situation (Jablonska-Deptula n.d.).

Nearly 97 percent of Poles are Roman Catholics. The Catholic Church played an important role in people's lives during the struggle for freedom. It supported the fight for independence and opposed the suppressive regimes. Throughout the years the Church has earned people's trust by helping, assisting, and advising them, and by not trying to dictate their lives. The Church opposed the communist regime (1945–1989), kept citizens "critical towards socialist propaganda and interested in the political situation in the country" (Hirvonen 1998), and supported the establishment of the first workers' union Solidarity (*Solidarnosc*) at the beginning of the 1980s.

Another cultural trait is a weak work ethic. If the workplace is perceived as an alien place, then people will not identify with it (Kochanowicz and Marody 2003). Communism played a crucial role in shaping such behavior, as we will see below.

One can find a mix of individualism and collectivism in Poland. On the one hand, a stereotypical Pole seems to be highly individualistic. People do not like it when other people or institutions (including the Church) invade their privacy. They do not like to obey authority, particularly the state, and they have difficulty reaching compromise in discussions. On the other hand, there is a high level of expectation as to what the community owes the individual, and Poles stress their rights more than their responsibilities (Kochanowicz and Marody 2003).

Elbieta Tarkowska (1999, cited by Kochanowicz and Marody 2003) noted that the Polish sense of time focuses much more on the present than on the future. In that sense Poles are short-term oriented, and they see whatever lies further ahead as "blurred and vague" (Tarkowska 1999). Thus everyday punctuality is not a problem, but people have difficulty planning their activities over a longer time horizon. Historical instability and wars have made it difficult to plan one's future and make long-term commitments (Hirvonen 1998).

The Polish attitude toward conspicuous consumption and wealth is ambiguous. Money obviously counts and is important for life. People are sensitive to prices, calculate their earnings and spending; at the same time, they are not good at financial planning and are prone to irresponsible spending from time to time (Kochanowicz and Marody 2003).

Influence of Communism

Stereotypical thinking in the West, as well as the distance separating the West from former Communist countries, has led to the impression of a homogenous Eastern bloc in which one country is indistinguishable from another. Cultural influences are diverse, however, and the combination of influencing factors varies from country to country.

Residents of Eastern Europe were educated in Communist ideology for years prior to the fall of the Communist regime (Avis 1987; Roskin 1991, cited by Schwartz and Bardi 1997), but they accept it only partially. Communism often "produced reaction against the regime and its symbols" (Barghoorn and Remington 1986, cited by Schwartz and Bardi 1997) and it remained an imposed but not an accepted ideology (e.g., Rupnik 1988a,b; Vajda 1988, cited by Schwartz and Bardi 1997). At the beginning of the 1990s, East Europeans were not really different from West Europeans in certain values, such as those related to politics, religion, and primary relations, but they allocated less importance to initiative, achievement, and work responsibilities (van den Broek and de Moor 1994: 226, cited by Schwartz and Bardi 1997).

The Communist regime did have some fundamental impacts on values. Adaptation to life circumstances is important for value formation (e.g., Almagor 1994; Inkeles and Smith 1974; Kohn and Schooler 1983; Rokeach 1973). Adapting to ideologically imposed conditions did not imply acceptance, but was a matter of adjusting effectively to opportunities offered by the circumstances, and even figuring out ways to circumvent an unwanted system (Schwartz and Bardi 1997).

A survey conducted between 1988 and 1993 among professors and students from twenty Eastern and Western European countries supports Schwartz's hypothesis that the Communist influence led to a greater emphasis on conservatism and hierarchy, and a lesser emphasis on intellectual autonomy, affective autonomy, egalitarianism, and mastery values. However, this survey suggests that Communism penetration in Poland was lower than in other Communist countries. It was found that, under Communism, all Eastern European countries upgraded the importance of values that were already achieved and downgraded the importance of values that were impossible to achieve or dangerous to pursue. This phenomenon affected business life in Poland, and especially the work ethic, by reducing appreciation for such values as initiative and personal achievement, but by enhancing the ability to get accustomed to these values more rapidly. Certain suppressed values, especially toward wealth and material well-being, are now appreciated more than ever. This is what Maslow (1959) called "deficit needs." "Deprivation increases the strengths of such needs" (Schwartz and Bardi 1997). This effect was evident when many people, after the fall of Communism, purchased expensive goods they had never been able to buy. Polish values change as life conditions shift. Values that become attainable are strengthened, and those that are no longer required are weakened (Schwartz and Bardi 1997).

Attitude toward Work

The major influence on Polish business culture has been forty years of Communist rule, which severely damaged the work ethic. During this time it was only possible to reach a higher status by being a member of the party and having the right connections, not by qualification and skills. As a consequence there was no need to be enthusiastic about work. People showed little initiative and commitment but only did what they were told to do or was otherwise necessary (Todeva 1999). This legacy remains, especially among the generation that endured communism in business life.

Another difficult aspect facing German employers in Poland is the language barrier. Under the Communist regime, Western languages were not taught in school. Those who can speak German or English today are young entrepreneurs or people living close to the German border. Communication with expatriates from international firms can therefore be problematic.

A third force that has shaped Polish business culture is Catholicism. The church was very efficient in shaping social consciousness and sensitivity to the value of labor.

The transition from Communism to Western values meant that Polish managers had to adopt Western management styles. The rapid changeover led to a collective culture shock (Feichtinger and Fink 1998), which tends to last longer than individual culture shock and may inspire an even harsher judgment of the present situation than the old one. The extent of culture shock depends on the individual's ability to cope with the new cultural circumstances (Chen and Starosta 1998). The better people adapt, the lesser are feelings of frustration, alienation, and stress. The ability to adapt and change values probably depends on age and life stage. Whereas adults are more likely to resist or to oppose social changes to preserve their value priorities, younger people may adapt more quickly to changing life circumstances (Schwartz and Bardi 1997).

Polish youth has established its own value priorities. Due to the systemic changes and new post-Communist lifestyle, Western values have affected young people's surroundings and contributed to a shift in values. However, the new Western influences have not completely penetrated the value system of young Poles. Due to the close family ties, young people remain under the influence of the family, especially parents, and consequently their values.

Nonetheless life and work in Poland have changed considerably, as have young people. A study of work entrants in 1989 and 1997 reflects these shifts. The business themes that have risen most in importance to the employee are training, competition, work groups, and security. The ones which have lost most significantly are duty, order, consultation, power, and seniority (Mroczkowski and Linowes 1999).

These young people must be the objects of business focus in Poland. They are the future managerial elite of society, and since the opening of Eastern Europe, the new generation of workers are most receptive to global influences. The new workforce entrants were not part of Communist organizations and are likely to replace the old business culture with new ideas (Mroczkowski and Linowes 1999).

CSR in Poland

Following globalization, the opening of markets, and the road to EU accession, "standards of corporate behavior are becoming universal even when applied to the transitioning countries of the former Soviet bloc" (CSR campaign, n.d.: para. 1). However, CSR activities are still in a process of development in Poland. During the transition, companies had to tackle many social challenges. The opening of markets lead to high social costs: a high level of unemployment, insufficient health care, and social marginalisation. In particular there was a lack of adequate training "to prepare a new generation of businesspeople and public administrators" (CSR campaign, n.d.: para. 5). Today, businesses are called on to take on a more active role in society in order to meet social challenges.

Our research shows that some multinational German companies already have become more active in Poland by investing in educational programs or "green" initiatives. Three multinationals will serve as examples.

The Bertelsmann Foundation undertook an educational project in 2002 with the name "Library Program." The Foundation donated 2.2 million EUR to public libraries in Breslau and Bielsko-Biala over a five-year period starting in 2002. The aim is to give young Poles the opportunity to improve their education through reading and study. Bertelsmann focused in particular on young Poles of ages thirteen to twenty-five because they are the future of modern Polish society and represent a large segment of today's population. "Initiatives like community education can serve to create the foundations for a valuable future workforce and a more prosperous market place" (Osmond 2002: 1)

Bayer Corporation supports environmental programs and created its own "eco-class" in 2001, a program for schools and universities. It is a joint effort of Polish teachers and Bayer to provide students an informative, clear, and practical approach to environmental issues. In particular, the program focuses on environmental requirements and standards, to which Poland must adapt now that it is a member of the EU.

Apart from supporting young professionals in Poland, Hungary, Slovakia, and the Czech Republic, the Robert Bosch Foundation is engaged in a Polish-German editing program. This program supports the cooperation of German and Polish newspaper editors who report on each other's country, in order to dispel myths and prejudices about the two countries.

Additional initiatives have been undertaken to support and popularize CSR. The Academy for the Development of Philanthropy is one of them. Established in 1998, it started a campaign that addresses business people and organizations under the motto, "Good Deeds All Year Through." It offers Polish foundations and associations the opportunity to nominate donors or partners who have supported them through financial, material, or other kinds of aid. In an annual contest, called *Dobroczynca Roku* or "Benefactor of the year, " the most engaged and involved donors or partners receive awards.

Another initiative, with the name "Fair Play," was put in place by the Institute for Private Enterprise and Democracy, a foundation established by the Polish Chamber of Commerce in 1993. The program was implemented under the auspices of the Ministry of Economy, and the underlying idea is supported by Polish President Aleksander Kwasniewski and Prime Minister Leszek Miller. The title "Fair Play Company" as well as trophy are awarded to a company that manifests ethical principles in its business relations with other parties, customers, and employees. The purpose of this initiative is "to promote ethics in business activities, understood as a set of standards of behavior in the mutual relations of entrepreneurs with business partners, customers, employees, and shareholders, as well as the local community, local government, and state authorities" (Fair Play 2005).

It is interesting to note how these two organizations measure CSR commitment. The basis for assessment is a questionnaire that includes questions about a company's behavior in certain fields, such as employee motivation, behavior in conflict situations, commitment to charitable activities, and payment of liabilities or employee wages. The first step of the evaluation process is to ask regional commissions to award points to the answers supplied. The commissions are composed of representatives of banks, employers' organizations, labor offices, tax bureaus, and the Social Insurance Institution. In the second step, the organizers of the initiatives scrutinize the information they obtained during visits to all companies participating in the program.

The advantages of participating in such programs are multiple. They offer a company the opportunity to prove its credibility and reliability. Reliability leads to more trust from business partners and customers. Participation and the announcement of the awards contribute to the company's public relations efforts, as well as involving and motivating employees.

CSR: A New Opportunity for German Companies in Poland?

CSR can be seen as a challenge and an opportunity for German companies investing in Poland. During the last decade German companies, as well as other foreign investors, have led the CSR movement there. They applied their tradition of community engagement to the Polish situation and created ways to solve problems in the new environment (CSR campaign: 2003: para. 7). They should now compare their present and previous position with respect to profitability, performance, and reputation.

Models of good CSR practice are needed in Poland. German companies can take this opportunity to create a climate of learning that leads to sustainable CSR. Achieving sustainability is a way to ensure the future of their business activities. Sustainable CSR measures lead to a "return on investment" in several areas (see the section on Benefits of CSR).

How to Create Profit through CSR

Effective CSR implementation has a positive effect on community and corporations and leads to win-win situations.

Internal CSR pertains to social responsibility programs undertaken inside a company. Although many books and articles describe internal programs, apparently no field research has been conducted on Polish employees' response to such programs as a result of cultural factors. Consideration of such factors should play an important role. The return on investment in such initiatives correlates positively with the efficiency of internal CSR programs, which in turn depends on employees' response to the programs. German companies should focus on designing the most efficient CSR programs to maintain a high return on investment.

German CSR activities in Poland are likely to result in high benefits when employees put more into their work, as this results in increased output for the company. Worker input is highly influenced by motivation. Whether Polish employees see internal CSR programs as useful and are willing to accept them are determinants of job motivation.

McClelland (1961, 1975, cited by Riggio 2000: 186, 187) characterizes motivation in his Achievement-Motivation Theory. He states that motivation stems from individual needs and is enhanced by their fulfillment. His theory recognizes three key needs: achievement, power, and affiliation. German companies should direct their CSR activities to meeting these needs in order to build a motivated workforce.

Affiliation and group achievement were emphasized during the Communism era. In this system career advancement depended on personal connections and membership in the Communist party rather than on individual achievement, skills, and abilities (Todeva 1999). A lack of motivation was seen among those who could not benefit from individual achievement. Those with personal connections had no need to achieve. The socialist system contributed even more to these effects, since the job security it provided allowed people to remain unwilling to work efficiently. The situation is different in the new market-driven economy. Companies require individual achievement, initiative, and responsibility, and they offer possibilities for career advancement.

It is not easy, however, to identify the needs of the Polish people today. It is likely that they will rediscover a need for achievement and responsibility. Under Communism these needs could not be met and were therefore downgraded. Now that they can be met, they are likely to be picked up again (Schwartz and Bardi 1997). Investment in CRS programs that accommodate a need for achievement and power are therefore promising. The present situation in Poland reveals a desire to catch up with the West and accept working long hours.

Polish opposition to the Communist regime, as well as unionization (especially through Solidarity) may indicate that the old system did not meet worker needs that failed to coincide with Communist values. This suggests that Poles are rediscovering their need for achievement rather than simply adapting to pressure to achieve. Poland is perhaps the most Western of the formerly Communist countries, and it is progressing quicker than others. One might predict that the Polish people will develop Western needs faster than those in other post-Communist countries. Companies should provide future-oriented training and career development programs when investing in CSR measures. The results, however, will probably not be obvious immediately but will be optimal only after a few years have passed and much money is spent.

Companies should take into account the cultural diversity of their employees. In Poland two groups can be distinguished, and for best results CSR measures should address them separately. The first group consists of those who worked during the Communist era and were influenced by socialism. It can be assumed that the longer an individual was exposed to Communism at work, the longer it will take to adapt to the requirements of a market economy and German companies. The second group are young people who were educated in Poland and started work after Communism. They already show Western values and attitudes toward work.

Some CSR programs offer immediate benefits to both groups and promise a rapid positive response from employees. Employee Assistance Programs (EAPs), for example, are a valuable CSR measure in Poland. The requirements of the new market economy can induce a high level of stress, especially among employees who worked under the socialist system. According to Leiter and Harvie (1998: 253), organizational change, which is obvious enough in Poland, can cause additional stress. Employees who feel that they cannot adapt in a way they themselves believe to be necessary are subject to stress. Problems, illness, and suffering within the family are particularly stressful in Poland, since strong family ties are deeply rooted in Polish culture and family loyalty is a core value.

Another program to be recommended is performance-based pay. The Polish attitude toward wealth and money could overcome a weak work ethic. Money has a high value in Polish society and plays an important role in everyday life. When people realize the benefits of working hard on their pay slip, they will probably get over their longstanding lack of motivation.

Company-supported child care can also contribute to higher motivation among Polish employees, especially young entrepreneurs with new ideas and no experience with Communism. Almost 35 percent of the young Polish people are less than twenty-five years old (PAIZ 2003). Child care reduces turnover and creates good relations between employer and employee. It provides the company a larger pool from which to recruit its workforce.

"Of all the new corporate challenges that have arisen since the early 1970s, the environment is now the best defined in terms of developing bodies of national and international law" (CSR Forum 2001). Companies are under increasing pressure to adopt environmentally responsible practices. If companies fail to act responsibly, tighter rules must be introduced. Secretary-General Kofi Annan proposed a Global Compact between the UN and business at the World Economic Forum in Davos on 31 January 1999. Its purpose is to establish core values in the area of environmental practice.

Recalling Wolfensohn's definition of CSR, which emphasizes that "CSR is a question of self-interest" and "an issue of how we're going to keep our planet stable," environmental protection can be viewed as one of the most profitable CSR opportunities in Poland. The landscape in southern Poland revives dark memories of the costs of Communist industrial planning. It is one of the most polluted regions in Europe. Although much has changed since 1989, when there were no environmental regulations at all, Poland has yet to meet EU requirements. Consumerism, which has been steadily growing since 1989, has unfortunately brought new problems. Plastic packaging has created a new challenge for waste management. The number of cars in Prague has skyrocketed from 40,000 in 1989 to 300,000 in 2000. (CSR Europe 1999)

In view of these problems, German companies must be aware that such matters as improved health care and a better quality of life are concerns of high-income countries but not Poland. The expectations of Polish "communities enduring the legacies of the centrally planned, industrial eco-disasters in the former Soviet Union and economies in transition, cannot be ignored by companies aspiring to build truly global markets" (CSR Web 2003). Environmental initiatives receive top priority in Poland, particularly in connection with EU accession. Poland was determined to follow the advice of Margot Wallstrom (European commissioner for environment) as it prepared to join the EU in 2004: "Clean up, or stay out."

German companies investing in Poland should keep this warning in mind and contribute to environmental improvement, since it benefits them as well. "The environment, once considered purely a bottom line cost, is fast becoming a commercial opportunity, as this aspect of corporate performance becomes a core competitive issue at the heart of reputation management" (CSR web 2003).

Companies operating in Poland have a significant impact on the natural environment through their daily business activities, including consumption of energy and other resources and indirectly through the supply chain. By supporting such initiatives such as reduced gas emissions, reduced use of agrochemicals, and recycling, companies can lower operating costs and create an environment in which businesses will survive.

Conclusion

Although CSR activity has increased in Poland and is supported by national organizations, it is only beginning to gain popularity. More support and improvement are needed. Jarostaw Pietras, Undersecretary of State at the Office of the Committee for European Integration, states that "For most Polish companies, profit is the only priority at the moment, while thinking about the welfare of employees, consumers or environmental protection is a rare practice" (Domańska 2002). Private business is only beginning to become aware of their responsibility toward the entire community.

The ongoing CSR development process therefore requires steady support. German companies can play a major role in sustainable CSR development, and in particular in such areas as education and training, due to their knowledge and experience. "CSR is for many companies in the West an element of their practical everyday operations" (Domańska 2002). By supporting these efforts they can increase their own profitability, performance, and reputation and establish a strong position in the market.

Spreading the idea of CSR is a significant issue for the Republic of Poland, especially after of its EU accession in 2004. Jaroslaw Pietras, Undersecretary of State at the Office of the Committee for European Integration (UKIE), argues that "it is very important to refer to the models and standards set in the Green Paper, . . . and to show that Poland as a future EU member is guided by the same ideals as the current EU member countries."

Implementing CSR measures in Poland contributes to the development of the Republic while simultaneously enhancing brand recognition and corporate profit.

References

Almagor, R. 1994. "Value Structure and Importance in the Kibbutz: Impacts of Industrialization and Occupational Experience." Unpublished doctoral dissertation, The Hebrew University, Jerusalem.

Avis, G. 1987. "The Making of the Soviet Citizen: Character Formation and Civic Training in Soviet Education." London: Croon Helm.

Barghoorn, Frederick C., and Thomas F. Remington. 1986. *Politics in the USSR*, 3rd ed. Boston: Little, Brown and Company.

Bárkányi, P. 2002. "The Influence of Globalisation on Polish Consumer Attitudes." *European Integration Studies* 1(2): 85–89. Retrieved October 22, 2003, from http://www.uni-miskolc.hu/uni/res/kozlemenyek/2003/pdf/barkanyipeter.pdf.

Blazyca, George. 1999. "Polish Socioeconomic Development in the 1990s and Scenarios For EU Accession." *Europe-Asia Studies* 51: 799–819.

van den Broek, A., and R. de Moor. 1994. "Eastern Europe After 1989." In *Socialization After Childhood*, ed. O. Brim, Jr., and S. Wheeler. Chicago: University of Chicago Press, 11–55.

Business for Social Responsibility. 2003. Retrieved October 20, 2003, from http://www.bsr.org/BSRResources/HumanRights/index.cfm.

Carroll, Archie B. 1979. "A Three-Dimensional Model of Corporate Social Performance." *Academy of Management Review* 4: 497–505.

———. 1991. "The Pyramid of Corporate Social Responsibility: Toward the Moral Management of Organizational Stakeholders." *Business Horizons* (July–August); retrieved October 30, 2003, from http://www.oldredlion.here2stay.org.uk/ethics/carroll%20model.ppt.

Chen, G., and W. J. Starosta. 1998. *Foundations of Intercultural Communication*. Boston: Allyn & Bacon.

CIA World Fact Book. 2003. Retrieved October 20, 2003, from http://www.cia.gov/cia/publications/factbook/geos/pl.html.

CSR Campaign. 2003. "Corporate Social Responsibility: The European Business Campaign." http://www.csrcampaign.org/why/default.aspx.

CSR Europe. 1999. "Clean Up or Clean Out." http://www.csreurope.org/news/_page2126.aspx.

_______. 2002. "World Bank President Urges Greater Social Responsibility." http://www.csreurope.org/news/_page1999.aspx.

_______. N.D. "CSR Facts and Figures." Retrieved November 15, 2003 from http://www.csreurope.org/aboutus/CSRfactsandfigures_page397.aspx.

CSR Forum. 2001. "Environment: Framing the Issue." http://www.iblf.org/csr/csrwebassist.nsf/webprintview/a1a2g3a4.html.

_______. 2003. "Environment." http://www.iblf.org/csr/csrwebassist.nsf/content/a1a2g3.html.

Domańska, Agnieszka. 2002. "A Matter of Ethics." *The Warsaw Voice*. http://www.warsawvoice.pl/archiwum.phtml/5308/.

Dyczewski, L. N.D. "Values and Polish Identity." Retrieved October 22, 2003, from www.crvp.org/book/Series04/IVA-19/chapter_i.htm.

Dyczewski, L., and B. Jedynak. N.D. "Family, Family Values and Home." Retrieved October 22, 2003, from www.crvp.org/book/Series04/IVA-19/chapter_ii.htm.

East-West-Information-Service. 2003. Retrieved October 21, 2003, from http://www.ewis.de.

Economy of Poland. 2003. Retrieved November 3, 2003, from http://en.wikipedia.org/wiki/Economy_of_Poland.

Elbadri, Abdelgadir N. Abdelhafiz. 2001. "Training Practices of Polish Companies: An Appraisal and Agenda for Improvement." *Journal of European Industrial Training* 25: 69–79.

Ernst and Young. 2002. "Corporate Social Responsibility: Unlocking the Value." Retrieved August 27, 2002, from http://www.ey.com/Global/content.nsf/Australia/News_Release_-_Corporate_Social_Responsibility_26Aug02.

EU Commission. 2002. "Corporate Social Responsibility." http://europa.eu.int/comm/trade/csr/index_en.htm.

Fair Play. 2005. "Fair Play: Edition 2005." http://sss.fairplay.pl/fairplay/edycja2005/edycja2005_eng.php.

Feichtinger, C., and G. Fink. 1998. "The Collective Culture Shock in Transition Countries: Theoretical and Empirical Implications." *Leadership & Organization Development Journal* 19(6): 302–08.

Fink, G. 2002. "Intercultural Knowledge Research and Intercultural Knowledge Management." Retrieved November 26, 2003, from http://fgr.wu-wien.ac.at/institut/ef/inteknow.pdf.

Giffin, P. E. 1994. "Institutional Development in a Transition Economy: The Case of Poland." *International Journal of Social Economics* 21(7): 35–55.

Glogoski, Ian, and Joachim Sohn. 2003. "EU Accession." Pricewaterhouse-Coopers (April). http://www.pwc.com/extweb/service.nsf/docid/7DD93E93A418383780256D1E0051796A.

Hirvonen, K. 1998. "Doing Business in Poland." Retrieved October 22, 2003, from http://www.hut.fi/~akhirvon/Polccb98.htm.

Hofstede, G. 1984. *Culture's Consequences*. Newbury Park, Calif.: Sage Publications.

Hofstede, G., B. Neuijen, D. D. Ohayv, and G. Sanders. 1990. "Measuring Organizational Cultures: A Qualitative and Quantitative Study across Twenty Cases." *Administrative Science Quarterly* 35(2): 286–316.

Inkeles, A., and D. H. Smith. 1974. *Becoming Modern*. Cambridge, Mass.: Harvard University Press.

Institute of Business Ethics. 2003. "Does Business Ethics Pay?" Retrieved December 3, 2003, from http://www.ibe.org.uk.

Jablonska-Deptula, E. N.D. "Patriotism and Sovereignty." Retrieved October 22, 2003, from www.crvp.org/book/Series04/IVA-19/chapter_vi.htm.

Jackson, S. E., and R. S. Schuler. 2003. *Managing Human Resources through Strategic Partnerships*, 8th ed. Mason: South-Western, 16.

Keane, J., ed. 1988. *Civil Society and the State: New European Perspectives*. London: Verso.

Kemme, D. M. 1991. *Economic Transition in Eastern Europe and the Soviet Union: Issues and Strategies*. Boulder, Colo. Institute for East-West Security.

Kochanowicz, J., and M. Marody. 2003. "Towards Understanding the Polish Economic Culture." Retrieved October 22, 2003, from http://politikon.politik.uni-halle.de/postsozges/Tagung2003/Kochanowicz2.pdf.

Kohn, M. L., and Schooler, C. 1983. *Work and Personality*. Norwood, N.J.: Ablex.

Lantos, G. 2002. "The Ethicality of Altruistic Corporate Social Responsibility." *Emerald* 19(3) (2002): 205–208, 211–213, 222–226.

Leiter, M. P., and P. Harvie. 1998. "Conditions for Staff Acceptance of Organizational Change: Burnout as a Mediating Construct." *Anxiety, Stress and Coping* 11: 1–25.

Maslow, A. H. 1959. *New Knowledge in Human Values*. New York: Harper.

McClelland, D. C. 1961. *The Achieving Society*. New York : Van Nostrand Reinhold.

———. 1975. *Power: The Inner Experience*. New York : Irvington.

Mehta, R. A., J. Dubinsky, and R. E. Anderson. 2001. "Leadership Style, Motivation and Performance in International Marketing Channels." *European Journal of Marketing* 37(1/2): 56–58, 60–64, 71–77.

MORI. 2000. "The First Ever European Survey of Consumers' Attitudes Towards Corporate Social Responsibility." Cited by CSR Europe, http://www.csreurope.org/whatwedo/stakeholderdialogue/consumerattitudes.

Mroczkowski, T., and R. G. Linowes. 1999. "Differing Interpretations of Key Management Terms: Old Versus New Poland." Copenhagen Business School. Unpublished working paper; accessed November 2004.

Nation by Nation. N.D. Retrieved December 5, 2003, from http://www.nationbynation.com/Poland/Population.html.

Osmond, Margy. 2002. "CSR: A Vital Element for Sustainability." http://thechamber.com; last accessed on November 23, 2004.

PAIZ (Polish Agency for Foreign Investment). 2003. Retrieved December 17, 2003, from http://www.paiz.gov.pl/oldpaiz/index.php?action=why1_3&where=Why%20Poland%20>>%20Human%20Capital.

Paliwoda, S. J. 1997. "Capitalising on the Emerging Markets of Central and Eastern Europe." *European Business Journal* 9(1): 27–36.

Photius. 1999. "Polish Economy." Retrieved December 5, 2003, from http://www.photius.com/wfb1999/poland/poland_economy.html.

PricewaterhouseCoopers. 2003. Retrieved October 20, 2003, from http://www.pwcglobal.com/extweb/newcoweb.nsf/docid/4C8958D52000A27385256DB8005875A3.

Riggio, R. E. 2000. *Introduction to Industrial/Organizational Psychology*. Englewood Cliffs, N.J.: Prentice Hall.

Rogovsky, N. 2000. *Corporate Community Involvement Programmes: Partnerships for Jobs and Development*. Geneva: International Institute for Labour Studies.

Rokeach, M. 1973. *The Nature of Human Values*. New York: Free Press.

Roskin, M. G. 1991. *The Rebirth of East Europe*. Englewood Cliffs, N.J.: Prentice Hall.

Rupnik, J. 1988a. *The Other Europe*. London: Weidenfeld and Nicholson.

________. 1988b. "Totalitarianism Revisited." In Keane 1988: 263–89.

Schwartz, S. H. 2003. Personal communication.

Schwartz, S. H., and A. Bardi. 1997. "Influences of Adaptation to Communist Rule on Value Priorities in Eastern Europe." *Political Psychology* 18(2): 385–410.

Smith, N. C., and J. A. Quelch. 1993. *Ethics in Marketing*. Homewood, Ill.: Irwin.

Smith, P. B., S. Dugan, and F. Trompenaars. 1996. "National Culture and the Values of Organizational Employees." *Journal of Cross-Cultural Psychology* 27(2): 231–64.

Szalay, L. B., and B. C. Maday. 1973. "Verbal Associations in the Analysis of Subjective Culture." *Current Anthropology* 14 (February–April): 151–173.

Tarkowska, E. 1999. "On Social Time in Poland." *Framtider International* 9(4).

Todeva, E. 1999. "Models for Comparative Analysis of Culture: The Case of Poland. Retrieved November 26, 2003, from http://www.som.surrey.ac.uk/SoM/StaffDirectory/Profiles/Academic/ETPDFs/Culpol.pdf.

Triandis, H., and V. Vassiliou. 1967. *Componential Analysis of Subjective Culture*. Urbana: University of Illinois Press.

Vajda, M. 1988. "East-Central European Perspectives." In Keane 1988: 333–360.

World Factbook. 2003. Retrieved December 17, 2003, from http://www.cia.gov/cia/publications/factbook/.

World Markets Research Centre. 2002. Global Insight, www.worldmarketsanalysis.com.

The Authors

Roy W. Smolens, Jr., is Professor in the School of Management and Business Sciences, Aalen University of Applied Sciences (Fachhochschule Aalen), Beethovenstraße 1, 73430 Aalen, Germany. E-mail: rsmole@rz.fh-aalen.de.

Nicolaas Tempelhof is a postgraduate student in the School of Management and Business Sciences, Aalen University of Applied Sciences.

NEW GLOBAL BUSINESS MORAL ORDER AND BUSINESS ACTIVITIES IN DEVELOPING COUNTRIES: THE NIGERIAN EXPERIENCE

A. Adewole Asolo-Adeyeye
Federal Polytechnic, Ilaro, Ogun State, Nigeria

Abstract

Given the overwhelming expansion of globalization that has reduced the entire globe to a small village, especially in international business activities, there is a pressing need to design a new paradigm of moral rules for global business, in order to take care of emerging moral exigencies in corporate activities—especially multinational activities, which have grave cross-cultural moral implications. While the international business arena has addressed this new reality by fashioning various moral orders to guide activities in the international business scene, this paper observes that the developing countries of the world have been at the receiving end of the moral configuration of global business. This is why the responses of most developing countries to the global business moral order is predicated on resolving the apparent conflicts generated by this moral order vis-à-vis the value systems of individual countries. Specifically, the paper examines the issue of a global business moral order with particular focus on how it is faring in developing countries. It notes that in these countries, the moral order is merely a paper tiger due to its weak implementation framework, whence its inability to make any meaningful impact in developing countries. After a critical survey of the Nigerian business terrain, this paper concludes that the global business moral order barely impacts the Nigerian situation despite the promise of better, honest, fair, and sustainable business practices implied by corporate social responsibility.

Introduction

It is no longer in doubt that increased globalization has reduced the entire globe to a small village, especially with respect to international business transactions. We are indeed confronted with the stark reality of today's conventional wisdom, which stipulates that the only condition for corporate success is to go global.[1] This situation is accentuated by an unimaginable explosion of modern superhighways, global e-commerce, and activities of multinational firms, coupled with increasing transactional free flow of capital, goods, and services, giving rise to a new pattern of business

 pp. 285–302

thought.[2] The end result is that the whole world becomes encapsulated into a new unified market in which people across nations engage and interact in the production of goods and services, resulting in massive cross-border movements of products.

Against the backdrop of this emerging global business conflagration and perceived tendency for unruly behavior in the global marketplace,[3] there has arisen a need to design a new paradigm for the moral rules of global business, in order to take care of emerging moral exigencies in corporate activities—especially the activities of multinationals, since they have grave cross-cultural moral implications.[4] The international business arena has addressed this new reality by fashioning various moral orders to guide activities on the international business scene.[5]

The developing counties of the world, however, have been at the receiving end of this new global system of business morals. Apart from the fact that the new morals were foisted on developing countries, which accepted them due to pressure to survive in an ongoing global economic configuration that permits no other option,[6] it appears that the global business moral order is "moral[ly] outlandish" when judged by the cultural sensibilities of most developing countries.[7] From their perspectives, the evolution, installation, implementation, and monitoring of the global business moral architecture are fraught with obvious contradictions. While most global business rules are byproducts of Western cultural expediencies, a fact that seems to justify the much-talked-about cultural imperialism, the same rules were foisted on developing countries that lack an enabling framework to ensure effective implementation and monitoring.[8] The activities of multinationals operating in developing countries have continued to show very clearly that the global business moral order is a detestable travesty.

It is little wonder that the responses of most developing countries to the global business moral order have been predicated on resolving its apparent conflicts with their individual value systems. It is also predicated on confusion arising from efforts to implement the global business moral order in the absence of an enabling capacity for its full implementation, even in the face of constant moral harassment by multinationals.

In this paper, the issue of a global business moral order is examined with particular focus on how it is faring in developing countries. The paper notes that the global moral order presents developing countries with a dilemma, partly because it is, strictly speaking, incongruent with cultural realities in the host countries,[9] and more specifically because it has remained a paper tiger due to a weak implementation framework.

The phenomenon of the global business moral order has not made a meaningful impact in developing countries because of this precarious situation. In Nigeria, for instance, despite the promise of better, honest, fair, and sustainable business, the new moral order has barely affected ethical practices in the Nigerian business terrain. There is an unstable business situation in Nigeria, due to activities of multinationals that expose the global business order as a mere imperialistic lullaby—packaged, arranged, and chorused to perpetuate business relationships which from a corporate social responsibility viewpoint are battered, beaten, and strained!

Globalization, Global Business, and the Problems of Global Business Morality

Globalization denotes a phenomenon of emerging international cooperation that is gradually transforming the entire world into one network, one character, one mission, and one vision. It is indeed a new deal in which the whole world is interlinked in one way or another. Gone are the days when various barriers narrowed horizons by limiting access to activities. With globalization, the entire globe is now under the firm grip of interconnectivity. The major fallout of the globalization train is that every individual, institution, and nation is transiting into a system of global reckonings, interdependencies and international networks.

The globalization phenomenon has become an octopus. It bestrides activities in our modern-day world like a colossus, so much so that such globalization jargon as "universalism," "multinationalism," "unipolarism," and so forth have become the most frequently used terminology of recent times. Globalization is not just a vague phenomenon but depicts the rapidly emerging global metamorphosis into the pervading clutch of interconnectedness, inter-linkages, and integration among persons and institutions, with concomitant effects on the massive international flow of finance, goods, and services.[10] In essence, globalization has become the energizing force of a gradual metamorphosis toward one world and one humanity, even in the face of existing prima facie global political, economic, linguistic, religious, physical, cultural, and technological diversities.

The implication of the globalization phenomenon is an expansive, broadening, and deepening interjection of national economics into a worldwide market characterized by the free flow of goods, services, and capital.[11] The result of globalization is that erstwhile barriers to a global reach, such as communication bottlenecks, language differences, and cultural divergences that once hindered free global interaction, are broken down daily under the grip of interconnectivity. The linkages established by globalization have reached a level at which it is increasingly difficult to define what constitute national boundaries, especially in an economic and business sense.[12]

Be that as it may, considerable efforts are underway to determine the relative benefits and drawbacks of globalization. The whole idea of globalization has been attacked as completely overambitious and overwhelmingly destructive, especially when viewed against the backdrop of its unfair treatment of the poor nations of the world.[13] The apparent advantages of globalization include a beautiful interlocking of nations, individuals and institutions across the world, the free flow of resources from one region to another, an increase in global productive capacity, and systematic global redistribution of wealth.[14] The globalization phenomenon has had an increasing impact on basic human activities, especially business.

Due to the globalization imperative, all facets of a business are constrained to acquire a global outlook. The advance of humanity toward globalization is based primarily on the desires of the private sector, especially the multinationals. The implication is that business activities, as propelled by the multinationals, have become the main driver of globalization. It is little wonder that the increasing spate of globalization is inextricably tied to the increasing activities of multinationals in global business.

Global business refers to a number of interrelated features in the world economy, which include the expanding geographical scope of business activities of private corporations and financial institutions, market interactions across national boundaries, and a tendency toward a higher degree of uniformity in policy and institutional environments. Global business is an emerging economic pattern in which people across nations engage and interact in the production of goods and services, and that races toward a unified global marketplace. With global business it is possible for the multiplicity of daring multinationals increasingly to spread their tentacles into any part of the world. The slogan of global business is "produce for the global marketplace,"[15] while the motto is "global competitiveness."[16] Global business is playing itself out in the global marketplace. The key players are multinationals and other businesses roaming the entire world in search of cheap resources, cheap labour, and a large market to which to sell their products.[17]

Interestingly, global business is not restricted to multinationals alone. In recent times, small and medium enterprises (SMEs) have embarked on the global voyage. To underscore the increasing ascendancy of SMEs in global business, the World Bank Institute sponsored conferences January 19–24, 2004, to discuss the emerging global trends in SMEs, while international conferences on SMEs in global business were held in Malaysia and Australia in July 2004. The implication is that global business is now very pervasive, ubiquitous, and all-embracing in the emerging international business configuration. The reality of global business continues to undermine any business and entrepreneurial textbook that assumes an entirely national[18] or indigenous[19] philosophy.

Be that as it may, the horizon of global business has been remarkably widened by the activities of multinationals. The multinationals are global business units, or corporations that have subsidiaries around the world.[20] Evidence of the scope of multinational corporations are the household brand names that are familiar across the length and breadth of the globe. Global corporations have access to large resources as a consequence of their international business activities. They also operate across cultures by daring to ignore politico-religious and social divergences. From north to south, west to east, goods and services are interchanged, while transactional volumes increase every second. Investments across borders are growing bigger and larger, as the entire world becomes one "straitjacket" marketplace.[21] The unparalleled success of this effort is brought about by the sheer determination of transnational corporations to promote a new economic and business order based on total business universalism.[22]

Since the 1960s there has been a phenomenal increase in corporate international activities. The greatest impetus to multinational activities includes availability of cheap labour, as well as expanding markets for products (goods and services) all over the globe. Multinationals, both citizens and non-citizens, launch themselves into business activities in any region of the planet. In both developed and developing countries, the interdependence of business activities has become so complex that it is increasingly difficult to pin down a product to a particular country.[23] In actual fact, products now have their production and supply chains scattered across different countries, while products manufactured in one country depend on other countries for their market and commercial sustainability.

There is no denying the fact that global business has entered the center stage of global activities with quantum leaps and bounds.[24] It continues to facilitate the spread of high-level industrialization and worldwide mobility. Cotton contends that multinational activities propelled by global business lead to cheaper and better products, bring in much needed resources, deploy expertise, and generate employment worldwide.[25] S. K. Rogolf asserts that a major unsung benefit of global business is that it has been able to promote global disinflation in a strict economic sense.[26]

Nevertheless, the activities of global business concerns have posed a serious moral challenge, one that raises the question of the moral status of global business multinationals. This challenge cannot be ignored simply because the exploits of the multinationals have attracted increasing moral scrutiny over time. Studies have confirmed the many dimensions of the moral challenge presented by global business. It starts with the fundamental question of what ethical values are being pursed by global business concerns, especially in view of the conflicting moral undertones often exhibited by different firms.[27] For instance, there are provable instances of immoral behavior on the part of multinationals, particularly in the context of international business transactions. Other specific ethical challenges continue to rear their ugly heads as multinationals operate worldwide! One would expect multinationals to share resources across boundaries in a manner that benefits humanity and promotes fairness, equity, and responsibility, given the vast network and large resources at their disposal. Yet the multinationals have long been accused of unfair trade practices. The reported cases include dumping as well as the sale and distribution of expired, adulterated, and substandard products. Other unethical practices include irresponsible product marketing, involvement in bribery, and corruption. Cases abound in which multinationals have been caught neck-deep in corporate scandals. The Enron and WorldCom cases are the most recent examples. Multinationals have also been entangled in a serious moral quagmire due to charges of large scale involvement in environmental degradation, especially those in energy, fuel, and extractive industries, thereby putting the world ecosystem under serious threat of water, air, and land pollution.[28]

Another moral critique of multinational corporations hinges on their penchant for human rights abuses. They have been accused of being blinded by selfish profit motives to the point that they engage in gross violations of human rights. They encourage, promote, and prosecute unethical child labor policies. Records abound of their despicable human rights violations. Multinationals exploit workers and violate their rights with impunity worldwide, due to their insatiable appetite for cheap labor. Even where they profess commitment to improved working conditions, it is rather cosmetic.

Artful evasions of legitimate responsibilities are also major moral challenges that confront global multinational business corporations. They are increasingly guilty of tax evasion, involvement in corporate crimes, transfer pricing, money laundering, unauthorized capital flights, and so forth. Other critical moral challenges highlighted by various experts and authors include international currency speculation, arms trading, exacerbating the level of unemployment due to work and production restructuring across national boundaries, promotion of unsustainable and conspicuous levels of consumption, resource depletion, lack of support for emerging democratic institutions, global warming, degradation of communities for selfish motives, and casual attitudes toward global problems such as famine, AIDS, and genocide.

There are also charges of inconsistent human resource management (HRM) practices, including the continued split between core and peripheral employees,[29] improper use of political influence, worker exposure to toxic chemicals, and high-level exploitative practices without adequate compensation, the effect of which is the denial of societal legitimate resources for their development efforts. UNDP reports attack multinationals for undermining the resource base, exacerbating inequality, and contributing to the dynamics of the consumption-poverty-inequality-environment nexus.[30] Thomas Pogge asserts that the major fallout of unfair international business activities of multinationals is the promotion of extreme poverty worldwide.[31]

Given the increasing level of high-level immorality, unruly behavior, and ethically questionable practices of multinationals in the global business terrain, there is much concern about the urgent need to address the problem. For instance, the World Parliament of Religion echoed in 1993 the urgent need to insert values into global business.[32] The American people, according to a survey conducted by Americans Talk Issues Foundation in 1994, believe that international regulation of every sector of the global economy, especially business, is indispensable.[33] Participants in an international conference on business dimensions in 2000 pointed out the need to instill decorum in international business, while the global e-conference on business ethics standards in October 2001 concurred that the rise in international trade, globalization, and instant communication has led to increasing pressures from various groups for the formation of a global moral standard for business.[34] This is against the backdrop of a critical observation by Anup Shah that "as the entire world globalizes, especially in business realm, with corporations becoming larger and multinational, their influence and interests go further than the choices that corporations take to make profit, but affect the people all over the world, sometimes fatally."[35]

The totality of the moral challenge to global business is encapsulated in what Baird and Shetty called Millennium Development Goals for businesses, which they aptly described as urgent business imperatives to work assiduously toward environmental sustainability and to commit to maintaining an open, rule-based, and ethical trading, financial, and business system.[36] The implication of this is that a major price of the transformation of local business into global business, with its attendant consequences for instability and unsalutary effects, is a redefinition of the character, structure, scope, and dimensions of business dealings from a local moral orientation to a global moral world view.[37]

The Emerging Global Business Moral Order

The rapid and accelerating deterioration of human value systems occasioned by the activities of multinationals is a critical—perhaps the most critical—challenge of our day.[38] It is a matter of fact that humanity must be protected from environmental degradation. There should be a right to self-determination with respect to job and income security. People must not suffer corporate harassments and arbitrariness. It is therefore out of expediency that global business has responded to the challenge by putting in place appropriate global ethical principles to regulate multinational activities. The existing global business moral order can be broadly categorized as having two parts. There are the *fundamental global business values* and *international norms*.

The fundamental values for global business are a collection of core ethical principles upon which there is universal consensus. These values are expected to provide the basis for global transactions due to their overriding nature. Examples of fundamental values are human rights, keeping promises, fairness, equity, honesty, and avoidance of harm. These values are considered legitimate ethical principles because they appeal directly to humanity. For instance, in the discussion of human rights as a form of fundamental value, Donaldson regards fundamental values as part of the minimal set of rights that provides the basis for consensus in evaluating international conduct in general, and particularly in business.[39] The implication of this is that the fundamental values for the global business moral order are core expectations of humanity in the modern world. They summarize business practices that can be considered right or wrong from the perspective of humanity.

International norms, which make up a second aspect of the global business moral order, are derivatives of such international bodies as the United Nations, OECD, UNCTAD, UNEP, GATT, and other international stakeholders such as NGOs. The efforts of these bodies have led to enactment of various codes, conventions, and statutes that are aimed at regulating activities in the business world for sustainability and development. Ans Kolk and Rob Van Tulder showcased in their monumental work the trends and effectiveness of international codes of conduct in the global business terrain.[40] Some of the norms include the U.N. Human Rights principles and Responsibilities for Transnational Corporations,[41] the ILO tripartite declaration of principles concerning multinational enterprise and social policy,[42] and OECD guidelines for multinational Enterprises.[43] Apart from specific guides, the global business scene is also replete with an array of codes, as well as management and reporting standards. These codes include the U.N. Global compact, various ISOs (ISO14001, ISO9000), SA800, the Global Reporting Initiative, AA1000, and so on.

Nonetheless, the global business moral order has been branded as promoting a moral nihilism because it tends to overwhelm local value systems,[44] thereby giving credence to ethical relativism.[45] The beauty of the global business moral order, however, lies in its capacity to rise above the multiplicity of cultures. It promotes universal moral value based on a consensus that is being reached within the context of an ongoing business moral paradigm. Essentially, the existence of a business moral order has put paid to the problems raised by ethical/cultural conflicts and diversity. In a sense, the moral power of a unified world acting in the form of a global moral community provides the needed succor against the apparent absurdity of multiculturalism.[46] Against all odds, global business moral standards have become popular because they rest on a universal approach to behaviour.[47] The essence of the global business moral order is to promote sanity in the global business scene, with a focus on the enhancement of sustainability and human dignity. Abiding by the standards of the global business moral order is often referred to as corporate social Responsibility (CSR) or corporate citizenship.[48]

In the international business scene, unilateral and multilateral institutions strive to promote corporate citizenship, which is hinged on the need for corporate entities to imbibe the culture of global business standards in their operations. Countries all over the world are providing necessary support to global business standards, one way or the other. Much of the burden must be assumed by the companies themselves. Companies, particularly multinationals, must be committed to the global business moral order. Indeed, some have embarked on programs to develop a clearer understanding of corporate social responsibility practices, while others have gone so far as to develop a body of management principles to regulate their activities. It is also worthy of note that some multinationals have either not endorsed the global business moral order or have completely failed to respect its standards. Some of the reasons that have been identified as to why companies fail to endorse the moral order include outright denial of corporate social responsibility, ignorance of the challenge of ethical business practices, lack of understanding of principles, conflicts between global rules and local value systems, and other limiting factors in an operational context.

It is worthwhile, at this juncture, to highlight the basic problems that has encumbered the global business moral order, some of which have make it totally impossible for the moral order to achieve its objectives. There is the problem of enforceability, which has greatly restricted the efficacy of the moral order. Compliance is inherently voluntary in nature, thereby lacking the weight of legal force to enforce its standards; the whole exercise has been reduced to mere gentlemanly regulations.[49] There is also the dilemma of whether to adhere to global standards or acknowledge the practicality of conforming to local value systems.[50] In addition, there are problems in establishing an audit mechanism. Audit is essential not only to determine the level of compliance to global standards but also to assess the benefits of compliance.

Despite all the above inadequacies, the global business moral order—through its avalanche of standards, codes, norms, and ethical principles—remains the major human effort in this century to respond to the growing concern for moral values in the international business arena. If nothing else, it has challenged business to operate on the basis of the triple bottom line—economic growth, environmental regeneration, people friendliness—as a way of addressing the embarrassing behavior of too many multinationals, the challenge of poverty eradication, and popular concern for sustainable development.[51] The essence of the global business moral order is to transform and reorient global business away from blind profiteering, so that companies can adopt the posture of responsible corporate citizenship. Global business envisions an order in which destructive selfish tendencies of individual businesses cancel each other in the long run, making it possible to maintain a moral order despite the arbitrary behavior, harassments, and unfair practices of some corporations. It is hoped that society can be protected from constant disruption and destruction due to the activities of multinationals. This stands in perfect conformity with the United Nations' strategy of trying to forestall international inhumanity to man.

The Global Business Moral Order and Business Activities in Developing Countries

The developing countries are the emerging nations of the world. They have not reached a more advanced stage of economic development because their growth is characterized by an absence of sustainability.[52] The developing countries are also victims of imperialistic machination.[53] Other characteristics of developing countries include political instability, a monolithic economic system, widespread poverty, illiteracy, a high level of ignorance, unchecked population growth, low life expectancy, and general suffering under the yoke of excruciating poverty.[54] The developing counties are scattered across Asia, Latin America, and Africa. Because of their development problems, they adopt various policies and actions aimed at pushing themselves up the development ladder. Most have taken on globalization as a developmental stratagem. They ride the globalization train so as to extend their development horizon. As a result they have allowed rapid global investment in their countries. For instance, foreign direct investments (FDI) in developing countries totaled 205 billion USD in 2001, compared to a paltry 5 billion in 1980. A World Bank report indicates that FDI to developing countries was stable in the face of a sharp fall in global FDI from 1.3 trillion USD in 2000 to 0.8 trillion in 2001.[55] Global activities in developing countries are expected to increase in the foreseeable future. This is because many multinationals see developing countries as an important source of future profitability by providing large markets for goods and services. In addition there are vast resources in most developing countries. They provide an attractive opportunity for investment, especially by oil, mineral, and other natural resource companies.

Apart from the fact that OECD economists see business deriving from globalization efforts as a window of opportunity,[56] the 2001 World Investment Report describes multinationals as the main vehicles for achieving economic stability and prosperity in developing nations. The report further states that global business stimulates economic growth and improves the international competitiveness of recipient countries. In the past few years, jobs have been created and poverty alleviated, with the attendant increase in demand for goods and services, coupled with improved social conditions. Subsequent reports indicate that many emerging nations have indeed benefited immensely from globalization, especially from the point of view of redistribution of income from the first to the third world.

Nevertheless, there is a potential for harmful consequences when multinationals do business in less developed countries. These include possible human right abuses, intentional harm, dumping of hazardous waste, outright sales of toxic products, support for oppressive regimes in the name of a stable business environment, damage from mining, and deforestation.[57] There is an absolute lack of social and environmental responsibility on the part of multinationals, thereby exposing current trends toward globalization, neo-liberalization, free trade, and open markets to intense criticisms. It is a pathetic situation when the interests of powerful nations and corporations shape the terms of world trade due to structural defects in world economy. There have been worldwide protests against inequalities in the global business system. For instance, the Seattle protest of November 1991, Devo's 2000 protest in Switzerland, and similar protests were targeted against global inequality. Due to the activities of multinationals, it is obvious that the developing countries come to the bargaining table as unequal partners in the emerging international trade configuration. As a result they are susceptible to exploitation by multinationals. Even the much-touted global business moral standards have been faulted because their concepts, theories, and methods were taken from Western industrial nations and applied elsewhere without adequate consideration of salient local issues. The implication of this is that the situation in developing countries appears problematic when measured against a rationalized conception of world order extrapolated from Western culture.[58]

The resultant effect of this anomaly is that while multinationals find it easy to conduct themselves in an obviously responsible manner in developed countries, they find it much more difficult to behave morally in developing countries. It is little wonder that the activities of multinationals in developing countries are saddled with negative reports of untoward practices, in which developing countries are forced to tolerate social injustices that may not be permitted in developed countries. It is a reality that the developing countries are at the receiving end of the grave consequences of multinational activities. The multinationals are becoming too powerful for a local government to control. Their activities in developing countries are determined thousands of miles away, and they are grossly insensitive to the feelings of their host communities.

There is a high incidence of multinational involvement in anti-competitive activities, poor labour policies, bribery and corruption, exploitation of the people's resources with impunity, and local currency destabilization. Another dimension of multinational unethical practices is the purchase of national resources from corrupt regimes that use the proceeds for personal benefit, in the face of pervasive and ravaging poverty around them.[59] These problems have, of course, been blamed on both the multinationals and the local governments.

Multinationals have been accused of failing to self-regulate in the absence of an international enforcement agency. The governments of developing countries have been accused of failing to put in place an appropriate and effective state regulatory mechanism to check the excesses of multinationals. Whichever way one may look at it, the multinational issue has become a phenomenon in developing countries. It continues to raise a thick dust, due to the unwholesome activities that trail multinational business activities in developing countries.

The Global Business Moral Order, Multinational Activities, and the Nigerian Business Terrain

The nexus consisting of the Nigerian business terrain, multinational activities, and the global business moral order provides a classic case study for an analysis of the impact of multinational activities on developing countries against the backdrop of the "gentlemanly regulatory role"[60] that characterizes the global system. The Nigerian business situation provides clear evidence of what multinationals are doing but should not do, and what they should do but are not doing. Such an analysis can also evince the apparent conflict between the global value system and local cultural sensibilities. In essence, it will show how this particular business terrain has put the global business moral order to trial, especially from the perspective of what the global business moral order should address and how to go about it.

Nigeria is a very large African nation. The country has a population of about 120 million people. It obtained independence from Great Britain in 1960 after a prolonged colonial rule. Since her independence, Nigeria has maintained a mixed socio-political and economic identity that derives from traditional aggregates of her multiple ethnic groups. Politically, the country has not been lucky enough to evolve a long-standing culture of democratic governance. Economically speaking, Nigeria has an abundance of natural resources, especially hydrocarbons. It is Africa's fifth-largest economy and most prolific oil producer. Its economy is largely dependent on the oil sector, which supplies 95 percent of foreign exchange earnings.[61] In spite of this enviable profile, the economic situation in Nigeria is ironically characterized by woes, such as resource waste, a low standard of living, inflation, and excruciating poverty in the midst of plentiful human and natural resources.[62] Either by accident or design, the pervasive influence of globalization has penetrated and established itself on the Nigerian terrain. The economy has opened up to permit the free flow of goods and services. Multinationals have increased their activities, especially in the last five years. Key globalization business policy instruments are now in place, such as market deregulation, liberalization, removal of controls, dismantling of tariffs and non-tariff barriers, and the creation of avenues for resource allocation across borders.

One attempt to survey the history of ethical practices in Nigerian business led to a categorization of business ethical practices into four regimes: traditional Nigerian society, the colonial era, the formative years after independence, and the present time.[63] One lesson highlighted by this effort is the impact of traditional Nigerian business values, particularly in traditional society and during the colonial era. The study also unearths the hard fact that Nigerians practiced and witnessed an enviable tradition of business ethics in the past, which is a good lesson to teach!

Nonetheless, the Nigerian formative years, up to the contemporary period, have opened up an entirely new dimension in the practice of business ethics. This can be easily attributed to the increasing complexity of business activities. When analyzed from the perspective of corporate social responsibility, contemporary Nigerian business is on its own. The principle that business has responsibilities to its stakeholders is a farce in the Nigerian situation, since there are collusion and lack of competition in many areas of business.

There is a total lack of customer service, and customers are usually at the mercy of businesses. There is absolutely nothing on the ground to suggest that the average Nigerian company appreciates the need to respond to societal expectations. There is flagrant air, land, and water pollution. Other common untoward business practices include unfair practices in all their ramifications. For instance, in the banking industry there is fraud, poaching, and seduction, while pharmaceutical industries sell harmful products. Firms evade taxes at will, disregard laid-down rules and procedures, and engage freely in bribery and corruption.[64] Favoritism, egoism, ethnic ties, and personal connections have significant impact on managerial decisions.

It is interesting to note that, although multinationals can bring to bear their extensive networks, foresight, and hands-on experience when formulating social responsibility policies, multinationals in Nigeria indulge in unruly and immoral behavioral, or at best refuse to do anything to help the situation.[65] Their activities are dotted by incidents of palpable callousness. There is absolutely no sector of multinational activities in Nigeria that is free of despicable moral laxity. A general report card of most multinationals indicates that there is no regard for law. There is a total lack of transparency and accountability. Available reports indicate that the Nigerian business scene is fraught with lack of discipline, immorality, and corruption.[66] The Corruption Perception Index published by Transparency International fingered Nigeria as the most corrupt country to do business for the years 1995 through 1997.[67] The World Bank and IMF are reported to have threatened to cut off Nigeria from their assistance programs on account of corruption.[68] In 1998, Nigeria ranked as the fourth most corrupt country in the world. Other reports indicate that multinationals engage in false reports and corporate misappropriation, while consumer rip-offs and unethical labour practices are a common phenomenon.[69] Most manufacturing companies in Nigeria in the year 2004 are yet to convert from the 1994 industrial standards certification.[70] The average multinational in Nigeria routinely sidetracks insurance law[71] by colluding with the underwriting firms and allocating them some percentage in exchange for allowing the corporation to circumvent the law in pursuit of their wicked profit motives. At a conference on corporate governance, the Director General of the Nigerian Security and Exchange commission, Dr. Sulayman Ndanusa, acknowledged the weak and ineffective regulatory framework in Nigeria but berated the multinationals and other Nigerian businesses for executive over-indulgences, noncompliance with regulations, and unethical practices.[72]

The immoral activities of businesses in Nigeria, especially those of multinationals in the extractive sectors, are a tale of woes. Multinationals in the extractive industry are notorious for human right violations, environmental degradation, and shameless neglect of their responsibilities. In the Niger delta area, which is their major place of operation, they maintain a near-permanent posture of an army of occupation. This region hosts the multinational oil and gas companies and supplies about 90 percent of the country's crude oil and gas resources. The mainstay of people in the Niger delta area is subsistence family fishing and petty trading. The ecosystem is susceptible to seasonal change. Apart from the fact that the region is often awash with such natural phenomena as devastating floods, organic pollution, overgrowth of water hyacinths, and oceanifications, the multinational oil companies in the region have added to the ecological dislocation with gas flaring and frequent oil spillage. The oil belt is a picture of instability occasioned by pervasive neglect, starvation, environmental degradation, and criminal abandonment.[73]

The Niger delta region of Nigeria is under a severe threat, due to pressure from the extractive activities of oil and gas industries. It suffers from mounting social and ecological debt, due to reckless exploitation of resources through an unchecked and near-permanent degradation of the environment. The multinationals in Nigeria have taken advantage of weak environmental regulation. They have caused massive damage to the Nigerian air, water, and land environment through reckless emissions of poisonous substances.

Multinationals in the Niger delta also display flagrant disregard for international business decorum in the area of human rights. Most multinationals operating in Nigeria are complicit with human right violations. They exploit and amass the resources of the people without giving anything back, except terrorism. The failure of oil companies to share their wealth equitably with the people from whose land they extract it has led to a cycle of violence throughout the Niger delta. Residents enraged over the continued exploitation often kidnap oil company employees, occupy oil facilities, and stage protests to bring attention to their plight, especially in regard to poverty and environmental degradation.[74] Such legitimate actions are often countered with brutal military repression that allows companies to continue their operation without disturbance. Friends of the Earth charges that Shell is a careless and wicked multinational company that has no milk of human kindness; it collaborates with government forces to perpetrate evil against legitimate agitation by the people of the Niger delta. The situation is so bad in the Niger delta that soldiers and mobile force units are deployed at will, military men harass people and extort money, and people are detained on flimsy excuses only to be released after paying huge sums of money, which in turn gives rise to sporadic clashes. The situation is worsened by an obvious conspiracy between the government and the multinationals to maintain a policy of cracking down.[75] For instance, it is asserted that there is conspiratorial connivance between Exxon Mobil and the state apparatus to protect the oil company.

More generally, the activities of all categories of multinationals in Nigeria can be regarded as a multinational display of the highest forms of corporate irresponsibility. It is very rare to see a Nigerian daily that does not regularly report mind-boggling stories about multinationals in both the extractive and other sectors of the economy. The Nigerian encounter with multinational activities is anything but fair, with the Nigerian side losing out when it comes to corporate social responsibility. The situation is nothing less than tragic. It is ironic that, given the extensive exposure and background of multinationals in modern corporate governance, the multinationals in Nigeria have bluntly refused to bring their CSR pedigree to bear in their transactional activities!

Many reasons have been cited for their abysmally poor ethics record. These include their overbearing posture; lack of an effective regulatory agency in the host country; the cosmetic nature of global business rules; the apparent conflicts between the Nigerian local value system and global business standards, such as with respect to bribery; ineptitude on the part of the government as an institution as well as dereliction of duty on the part of officials; and ravaging poverty among the Nigerian people.

Recently, however, due to overwhelming pressure from within and without the business community, efforts are being intensified to institute good corporate practices, especially among Nigerian multinationals. The multinationals themselves are being vigorously challenged to respect and uphold global business standards. They are enjoined to respect human rights and the environment, with the latter especially relevant to extractive industries, and to maintain accepted standards in all their business transactions. The Nigerian government is also under intense pressure to establish a better and more effective regulatory framework that can check the unwholesome activities of multinationals. This has led to the establishment of new ombudsman institutions and the overhaul of existing regulatory agencies. The commitment of the Nigerian people and government to democratic governance and a liberalized economy are also said to add impetus to efforts toward good corporate governance. Non-governmental organizations and multilateral agencies are working hard to see that moral standards are promoted in Nigeria, and that good corporate governance becomes part of the modus operandi of multinationals and other businesses. Transparency International, UNDP, and the West African Network on Business Ethics fall into this category. Their efforts in organizing workshops, symposia, and other business ethics projects are designed to spur companies to live up to their social responsibilities.

The multinationals themselves are being challenged to meet the CSR challenge. Yet apart from recent efforts to establish a Convention on Business Integrity, in which they profess commitment to ethical business practices, there is absolutely no practical action on the ground to suggest their seriousness.

Agenda for an Effective Global Business Moral Order in Nigeria and Other Parts of the World

The challenge of CSR in Nigeria is daunting. There is urgent need for companies to comply with global business principles and show more commitment to the standards they define. The present situation calls for general and urgent rededication to CSR practices by all stakeholders, not only in Nigeria but across the developing world. The peculiar problems associated with CSR practices in Nigeria and other developing countries clearly indicate that the old approach to the prosecution of the CSR agenda requires immediate review. The exigencies of the moment call for a more proactive strategy, renewed commitments, and radical action plans in which stakeholders, consumers, shareholders, management, society, government, and multilateral agencies have roles to play. The new approach should encompass the following action plans.

First, an international organ within the United Nations system should be set up without delay to ensure the enforceability, or at the least the monitoring, of global business moral standards. As observed by David Cotton and by Tom Campbell and Sheena Smith, the currently unenforceable nature of global standards lies behind the "gentlemanly regulator" or "soft law" and does not promote CSR practices among multinationals, in Nigeria or elsewhere. The proposed institution might be called the *United Nations Global Business Regulatory Agency* (UNGBRA). This suggestion is in perfect conformity with UNCED Agenda 21, which calls for multilateral agencies to monitor, analyze, and regulate the activities of multinationals.[76]

As a corollary to the above, a global tax on wealth can oblige multinationals to bear their share of the impact of their activities. The tax should take the form of an institutionalized redistributive scheme to recompense apparent harm due to a corporation's failure to do what it is supposed to do. I wish to propose the establishment of a *Global Business Negative Impact Reduction Fund* (GBNIRF) that would collect taxes internationally from multinationals. The proposed GBNIRF is similar to Tom Campbell's Global Humanitarian Levy.[77] The fund should be administered by the U.N. so as to ameliorate the effects of multinational activities in Nigeria, other developing countries, and the world at large.

In addition, multinational corporations worldwide should dedicate themselves to CSR by taking the tenets of corporate citizenship more seriously. The idea of CSR should be internalized and incorporated into all firm activities. The practice of CSR by multinationals both in developed and developing countries should be a matter of policy. Multinationals should rigidly follow a CSR ideology in all parts of the world.

Efforts should also be made to accelerate the global trend toward overhauling the regulatory framework in developing countries. The principles of democratic governance should be supported, along with such attendant benefits as openness, transparency, and accountability. This is addition to national adoption of economic policies of liberalization and competition. The ripple effect of these efforts can enhance the capability of multinational firms to practice CSR effectively.

Conclusion

The negative effects of global business, especially on developing countries, are catastrophic. They are comparable to the HIV/AIDS pandemic. The recent multinational scandals involving Enron and WorldCom in developed countries indicates that unethical practices are not restricted to any particular region of the world. They are a multidimensional global scourge. The matter of international business moral standards is too critical to be left entirely in the hands of multinationals, through self-regulation and soft laws. Global agencies regulate other key aspects of human endeavor, such as health, agriculture, population, and drugs. It is appropriate, as a matter of expediency, to have a regulatory agency to check the unwholesome activities of businesses worldwide.

Notes

1. Michael J. Mazarr, "The Five Paradoxes: Business Competition in the Knowledge Era" (Center for Strategic and International Studies 2002), http://www.csis.org/gt2005/2002bus.pdf.

2. Cynthia D. Churchwell, "Globalization: The New Global Business Manager" (Harvard Business School Working Knowledge 2003), http://hbswk.hbs.edu.

3. K. M. Leisinger, "Corporate Ethics and International Business: Some Basic Issues" (Novartis Foundation for Sustainable Development, 2004), http://www.novartisfoundation.com.

4. The international business scene has fashioned few codes, standards, and ethical guidelines through such multilateral agencies as UN, UNCTAD, ILO, WTO, OECD, etc., to regulate business activities globally.

5. Ans Kolk and Rob Van Tulder, *International Codes of Conduct: Trends, Sectors, Issues and Effectiveness* (Erasmus University Rotterdam, 2002), http://www.eur.nl/fbk/dep/dep8/publications/codesofconduct.

6. Mansoob Murshed, *Globalization, Marginalization and Development* (London: Routledge, 2002).

7. E. Tsahuridu, and A. Adewole Asolo-Adeyeye. "Business Ethics and Socio-Cultural Interface," working paper, University of Greenwich and Federal Polytechnic Ilaro.

8. Harris S. Mule, "Institutions and their Impact in Addressing Rural Poverty in Africa" (International Fund for Agricultural Development, 2001), http://www.ifad.org/poverty/mule.pdf.

9. Giorgio Barba Navaretti and Anthony J. Venables, with Frank G. Barry, Karolina Ekholm, Anna M. Falzoni, Jan I. Haaland, Karen Helene Midelfart, and Alessandro Turrini, *Multinational Firms in the World Economy* (Princeton, N.J.: Princeton University Press, 2004), http://www.pupress.princeton.edu/titles/7832.html.

10. Fons Trompenaars, *Riding the Waves of Culture* (London: Nicholas Brady Publishing, 1993); Deepak Nayyar, "Globalization: The Game, the Player and the Rules," in *The Political Economy of Globalization*, ed. Ngaire Woods (London: Kluwer Academic Publishers, 2000).

11. John F. E. Ohiorhenuan, "The South in an Era of Globalization," *The Cooperation South Journal*, United Nations Development Programme, Issue no. 2 (1998).

12. The NISER policy brief on "Globalization and Nigeria development" depicts how globalization is predicated on an unequal balance.

13. Most textbooks that assume a rigid national outlook in their economic and business analysis are now being challenged, especially on the need to acknowledge the overwhelming influence of globalization forces.

14. Angus Deaton, "Is World Poverty Falling?" *Finance and Development* 39 (2002), International Monetary Fund, http://www.imf.org/external/pubs/ft/fandd/2002/06/deaton.htm.

15. A. Adewole Asolo-Adeyeye, "Internationalization of Asian SMEs and the Challenge of Global Business Moral Order," International Conference on SMEs in Global Economy, Malaysia, July 6–7, 2004.

16. Ibid.

17. David Cotton, *International Business Topics* (London: Evans Publishers, 1984).

18. S. A. Adebayo, *Economics: A Simplified Approach* (Lagos: African International Publishing Company, 1998).

19. B. A. Alawe-Tijani, *Entrepreneurship Process and Small Business Management* (Lagos: Industrial Science Center Publishers, 2004).

20. Op. cit.

21. Ibid.

22. Jabulani Sithole, http://www.afrol.com/news/2001.

23. Churchwell, "Globalization."

24. Christopher Farrell, "Riding the Global Business Cycle," *Business Week* (March 29, 2002).

25. Cotton, *International Business Topics*.

26. S. K. Rogoff, "Disinflation: An Unsung Benefit of Globalization," *Finance and Development*, International Monetary Fund (December 2003), pp 54–55.

27. Adewole A. A. Asolo, "Internationalization of Asian SMEs."

28. Anup Shah, "Corporations" (2001), http://www.globalissues.org/TradeRelated/Corporations.asp.

29. Michelle R. Greenwood, "Questioning 'Ethical' HRM," Centre for International Corporate Governance Research, Monash University (2002), http://www.businessandlaw.vu.edu.au/cicgr/Refereed%20Papers/Greenwood_ref.doc.

30. United Nations Development Programme, *Human Development Report: Overview* (1998).

31. Thomas Pogge, "Severe Poverty as a Human Rights Violation" (2003), http://www.law.utoronto.ca/documents/globalization/Pogge_Sept%2030th_04.pdf.

32. The World Parliament of Religion, which was held in Chicago in 1993, hammered on the need to establish a global moral order to check and reorder the activities of global business.

33. Americans Talk Issues Foundation, *Perceptions of Globalization, World Structures, and Security*, Survey Report No. 17 (1991), http://www.publicinterestpolling.com/atisurveys.htm.

34. Reports of a conference on global business ethics standards in October 2001.

35. Anup Shah, "Corporations."

36. Mark Baird and Sudhir Shetty, "Getting There: How to Accelerate Progress Toward the Millennium Development Goals," *Finance and Development* (December 2003), http://www.imf.org/external/pubs/ft/fandd/2003/12/pdf/baird.pdf.

37. Mazarr, "The Five Paradoxes."

38. Inge Kaul, "A New Global Ethics for Global Human Security," *Development*, Society for International Development, 1994.

39. Thomas Donaldson, "Multicultural Perspectives, Fundamentals of International Rights," in *Perspectives in Business Ethics*, ed. Laura Hartman (Boston: Irwin McGraw-Hill, 1994).

40. Kolk and Van Tulder, *International Codes of Conduct*. The work is monumental in its treatment of international codes of conduct as they relate to business practices in a global sense.

41. International Labor Organization. *Codes of Conduct for Multinationals*, http://www.itcilo.it/actrav/actrav-english/telearn/global/ilo/guide/main.htm.

42. Ibid.

43. Ibid.

44. Gerald L. Rowles, "The New Moral Order—Nihilism," Toogood Reports (2001), http://www.tysknews.com/Depts/society/new_moral_order.htm.

45. Edward Stevens, *Business Ethics* (New York: Paulist Press, 1979).

46. Michael White, "Let Us Reorder this World," *The Guardian* (October 3, 2001).

47. Ghislain Pastre, "Introducing the Global Compact," United Nations Development Programme, http://www.undp.bg/en/gc_launch_pastre_opening.php.

48. Philip Stiles, "Corporate Governance and Ethics," in *Current Issues in Business Ethics*, ed. Peter Davies (London: Routledge, 1997).

49. Cotton, *International Business Topics*.

50. Novartis Foundation for Sustainable Development, "Globalization, *Minima Moralia*, and the Responsibilities of Multinational Companies" (n.d.), http://www.novartisfoundation.com/en/articles/business/globalization_multinational_companies.htm.

51. Leisinger, "Corporate Ethics and International Business."

52. John Toye, *Dilemmas of Development*, 2nd ed. (Oxford: Blackwell Publishers, 1993).

53. Edward G. Stockwell and Karen G. Laidlaw, *Third World Development* (Chicago: Nelson-Hall, 1981).

54. A. Adewole Asolo-Adeyeye, *Principles of Development Administration: A Developing Country Perspective* (Ibadan: IB Publishers, 2002).

55. William Shaw, "FDI to Developing Countries is Resilient," in *Global Development Finance 2002*, slides, World Bank (2002), http://www.worldbank.org/prospects/gdf2002/slideshow/slideshow/sld011.htm.

56. Office of Economic Cooperation and Development, *The World in 2020: Towards a New Global Age* (1997), http://www.fedpubs.com/subject/international/world2020.htm.

57. Richard T. De George, *Competing with Integrity in International Business* (Oxford: Oxford University Press, 1993).

58. Everett M. Rogers and Lynne Svenning, *Modernization among Peasants: The Impact of Communication* (New York: Holt, Rinehart, and Winston, 1969).

59. Tom Campbell and Sheena Smith, "Global Justice, Human Rights and Multinational Corporations," *Proceedings, Australian Association for Professional and Applied Ethics (AAPAE 2003)* (Melbourne: Victoria University, 2003.

60. Cotton, *International Business Topics*.

61. Mbendi Information for Africa, "Africa: Oil and Gas Industry" (n.d.), http://www.mbendi.co.za/indy/oilg/af/ng/poo5.htm.

62. A. Adewole Asolo-Adeyeye, "Nigerian Development and the Challenge of NGOs in the New Millennium," in *Perspectives of National Development*, ed. O. A. Jiboku, A. B. Ajayi, B. A. Tijani-Alawe, A. A. Asolo-Adeyeye, and B. O. Ifenowo (Ibadan: Marvel Books, 1998).

63. A. Adewole Asolo-Adeyeye, "History of Ethical Business Practice in Nigerian Business Terrain," prepared for Nigerian Business Ethics Project (Washington: International Business Ethics Institute, 2001).

64. A. Adewole Asolo-Adeyeye, "Ethics in Business: How Much do Nigerian Businessmen Know?" *African Journal of Business and Economic Research*, vol. 2, nos. 1 & 2 (2000).

65. Elfrida Taylor, Interview with A. Adewole Asolo-Adeyeye, Interview reports on Nigerian business ethics (Washington: International Business Ethics Institute, 2001).

66. Peter Eigen, "Nigeria No Longer the Most Corrupt Country in the World," *Candor*, vol. 1, no. 4 (1998).

67. Gbenga Agbana, "Corporate Governance in Nigeria," *The Guardian* (March 26, 2004).

68. K. Fagbemi, "419 and Business Ethics," *The Nigerian Economist*, vol. 5, no. 11 (1992).

69. Dixon, "Renewed Search for Transparency in Corporate Nigeria" (Lagos: The Guardian Publishers, 1987).

70. Babatola Adeyemi, "Standards Organization May Axe 99 Firms in Nigeria," *The Guardian* (June 8, 2004).

71. Joshua Nze, "Multinationals Sidetrack Insurance Law," *The Guardian* (June 8, 2004).

72. This observation was made by Dr. Ndanusa during the 2003 Conference of the Institute of Chartered Secretaries and Administrators.

73. Nengi James, "Campaign against Oceanification and Ecological Hazards in the Niger Delta Region of Nigeria" (2003), www.nigerdeltacongress.com/carticles/ campaign_against_oceanification.htm.

74. Asad Ismi, "Nigeria's Corporate Killers," *Canadian Center for Policy Alternatives Monitor* (November 2003), www.policyalternatives.ca.

75. Environmental Rights Action and Friends of the Earth, "NO to Corporate Rule: Support the Kyoyo Protocol," press release, Benin City, Nigeria (July 11, 2001).

76. The UNCED Agenda 21 actually called for immediate institution of a multilateral agency to monitor, analyze, and regulate activities of multinationals.

77. Campbell and Smith, "Global Justice."

The Author

A. Adewole Asolo-Adeyeye is Senior Lecturer, Department of Business Administration and Management, Federal Polytechnic, Ilaro, Ogun State, Nigeria, asoloaaa@yaho.co.uk. He is also Executive Secretary of the West African Network on Business Ethics (WANETHICS) and Executive Director, Centre for Organizational and Professional Ethics (COPE-NIGERIA).

EFFECTS OF CORPORATE SOCIAL RESPONSIBILITY IN LATIN AMERICAN COMMUNITIES: A COMPARISON OF EXPERIENCES

Roberto Gutiérrez
Universidad de los Andes, Bogotá, Colombia

Audra Jones
Inter-American Foundation, Arlington, Virginia, USA

Abstract

Five different Latin American experiences help us to understand the impacts of corporate social responsibility on communities. We focus on communities composed of low-income populations to compare types of interventions, their main characteristics, spaces for community participation, and some results and impacts. Some of the findings indicate that (a) a company's enlightened self-interest in its CSR program ensures its commitment to the program and the program's sustainability; (b) community involvement from the outset in defining a project increases the probability of success, since corporations cannot assume they understand the needs of a community by taking them at face value; (c) projects do not create untenable expectations in local communities when they consider the whole life cycle and the sustainability of the investment after an appropriate exit strategy is executed; and (d) financial resources are only part of the equation because corporations can have enormous impacts with limited financing if programs are well defined and supported.

Introduction

This section concentrates on five case studies of corporate social responsibility (CSR) in the Latin American context, in order to understand the resulting impact on communities. After a review of the research and practice of CSR in Latin America, it highlights successful and unsuccessful experiences in community development as a result of CSR activities. The focus is on communities composed of low-income populations, and on deriving lessons from their experience.

Latin America is a region in which enormous gaps exist between social groups. Joint endeavors between the haves and the have-nots are a constant challenge. They have always been linked in one way or another: through exploitative relations, paternalism, charity, or solidarity. Yet exclusion and distance between groups have created

 pp. 303–328

distrust. It is not surprising that socially responsible activities, aimed at improving living conditions in a surrounding community, are not a common corporate practice in Latin America. It is important to explore when and why business and community decide to work side by side, and the effects of such efforts. Great opportunities lie ahead.

An Overview of CSR in Latin America

Ethical questions have been raised about philanthropy at someone else's expense. Friedman's (1962) arguments keep coming back in one way or another. While managers are entrusted with the care of assets belonging to the firm's shareholders, "[s]upporting good causes out of their own generous salaries, bonuses, deferred compensation, options packages and incentive schemes would be admirable; doing it out of income that would otherwise be paid to shareholders is a more dubious proposition" (*The Economist* 2004). Other questions can be asked about why, in a democracy, managers should decide social-policy priorities when this is a job for voters and elected politicians.

In Latin America, where there is a highly skewed distribution of income and opportunities, these questions are not at the forefront of the debate. The interests of communities, rather than shareholders, frequently dominate the discussion. A move towards a "compassionate capitalism" comes as no surprise.

Multilateral agencies have been turning to the private sector to further the development agenda. States have lost part of the preeminent role assigned to them in pushing the carts of development. To face diverse social problems, all sectors of society are asked to contribute their share. On the one hand, a vibrant third sector is evolving in many societies. On the other hand, expectations as to what private companies can do as corporate citizens have increased. Multilateral agencies are providing various kinds of support to the private sector so that it can fulfill these expectations.

In the meantime, distance and distrust make it difficult for businesses to assess community needs, to develop plans to address these needs, and to learn from the process. Attitudes of community leaders differ significantly from those of corporate leaders, not only in Latin America but in other regions of the world (for an example of these differences in Israel, see Boehm 2002). Since "attitudes toward supporting collaborative dimensions are influenced by the expected profitability of the collaboration," community leaders are more supportive of CSR because "the expected costs to the community are lower and their interests are more evident" (Boehm 2002: 188–189). Sometimes a humble and direct approach gets community and corporate leaders to work together; other times an intermediary brings together a business with its surrounding communities.

There are several frameworks available for understanding why a business might decide to work for the improvement of living conditions in a community. Carroll (1999) describes the evolution of the CSR construct since the 1950s, along with such alternative frameworks as corporate social performance, stakeholder theory, and the theory of business ethics. Considerable attention has been given to the reasons behind business engagement, and to classifying the different approaches. However, what drives a corporation to engage in socially responsible activities, and what are the expected benefits of such engagement, are two different questions.

The Argentine and Peruvian economic crises, as well as the Brazilian and Colombian social crises, have elicited responses from the private sector. Many more businessmen and women have come to understand that "there is no healthy business in a sick society." They have joined philanthropic traditions that in the past were rooted in religious beliefs and today respond to civic obligations. For example, Thompson and Landim (1997) describe philanthropy and volunteerism introduced by Spanish and Portuguese colonial authorities in close coordination with the Catholic Church. A special issue of *Revista* (Spring 2002) traced such practices into modern days and described it as the evolution "from charity to solidarity."

One approach to understanding motivations behind CSR is Martin's virtue matrix. The virtue matrix is a tool for understanding what generates socially responsible corporate conduct. It considers a civil foundation (the norms, customs, and laws that govern corporate practice) and an innovation frontier where benefits for shareholders and society can be accrued. Widespread imitation of a successful innovator or government mandate will increase the civil foundation; abandonment of a socially responsible practice by a critical mass of firms will diminish the civil foundation.

The virtue matrix is helpful to address such questions as what creates public demand for greater corporate responsibility, what are the barriers to increasing responsible corporate behavior, and what forces can add to the supply of corporate responsibility. Martin argues that "the most significant impediment to the growth of corporate virtue is a dearth of vision among business leaders," and that "the most effective weapon against inertia is collective action, either on the part of governments, nongovernmental organizations (NGOs), or corporate leaders themselves" (Martin 2002: 10).

The Role of Legislation

Although motivations help explain the evolution of CSR practices, one point little researched is how the evolution of CSR itself is different in developed and developing countries, and how this affects the trends defining CSR at any given time. One can hypothesize that business responses to legislation or to organized pressure depend heavily on local context. Compare, for example, the evolution of CSR in Latin America to that in the United States. The origins of CSR in both regions are philanthropic, resulting from a few rich industrial families such as the Rockefellers and Packards in the U.S. and the Mendozas and Fortabats in Latin America. However, the axes of CSR activities in each region are distinct and have much to do with the role government played or did not play in creating a framework for enabling and fostering CSR activities.

CSR in the U.S. has grown through regulation and was initially driven by *responsible business operations* rather than by community investment. As a result of the great industrial boom in the late 1960s and early 1970s, the U.S. government established the "Big Four" regulatory agencies that shaped much of the baseline for responsible corporate business operations: OSHA (Occupational Safety and Health Administration), EEOC (Equal Employment Opportunity Commission), CPSC (Consumer Product Safety Commission), and the EPA (Environmental Protection

Agency). These agencies created and continue to maintain standards for responsible corporate business practices that have become thresholds for CSR behavior with respect to daily operations of business. The U.S. government has continued to innovate on ways to influence responsible business practices. In 1994, the U.S. Department of Commerce's Bureau of Economic Analysis took the first steps in calculating a "green" gross domestic product, a move that, over time, could produce a widespread impact on how the government sets tax policy. More recent examples of industry-specific and sector-wide regulation include the Community Reinvestment Act in the banking sector, the Clean Air Act, the Foreign Corrupt Practices Act and, post-Enron, the Public Company Accounting Reform and Investor Protection Act.

In Latin America, regulation of corporate operations is less common, particularly outside of the Mexican and Mercosur markets, where U.S. and European foreign direct investment has influenced some requirements. There has been little government movement towards regulatory standards for business. In part, this is a result of weaker formal organizations of workers, such as trade unions, or weaker social groups, such as women or ethnic populations, which greatly influenced U.S. labor and business practices in the twentieth century. Without pressure from society, governments are less likely to create standards that incur a cost to corporations, which often enjoy more wealth and power than government itself. Even in those cases where standards are in place, such environmental regulations along the U.S.-Mexican border, or the environment ministries that exist in several countries, the question becomes one of enforcement. While NAFTA envisioned creating California-like environmental standards for the border region, the resources on the Mexican side initially were not adequate to manage its enforcement. The other missing factor in promoting a culture of responsible business practices in Latin America is consumer or public consciousness. Absent pressure or kudos from consumers, a traditional corporation without idealistic leadership is unlikely to operate responsibly at a cost it cannot recuperate through social marketing (Jones 2004).

With little government support for or enforcement of responsible business practices, those Latin American corporations that have an interest in creating a common baseline for responsible practices have taken it upon themselves to create standards. For example, the Abrinq Foundation, a non-profit organization in Brazil, offers a logo to companies that are committed to fight the use of child labor. Corporations are certified through Arbinq's Child Friendly Companies Program once they pass a series of social audits conducted by unions, employees, and NGOs. Companies use the logo to market their corporate value to the youth community (Grayson and Hodges 2002).

In contrast, the evolution of CSR through *community investment* has been, arguably, more relevant in Latin America than that of CSR through business operations. Given that more than 60 percent of Latin America lives on less than one dollar a day, it is evident that governments in the region often do not the basic needs of their communities. Although corporations in Latin American are not well rewarded through tax-breaks, as are their North American counterparts, the private sector has stepped in to supplement and sometimes to replace government as a way to foster social stability, create jobs, and ensure an enabling environment that allows businesses to operate effectively. Corporations in Latin America are investing in communities in order to have a stable society where they can produce and sell their products. Community investment has a direct positive impact on their bottom line no less than on improving the lives of those in these communities. Doing good beyond legal requirements is more important where legal frameworks are limited and enforcement is weak.

There are even some cases in Latin America where corporations have influenced government regulation in order to enhance the impact of CSR activities on local communities. In 1990, after a flood devastated the state of Chihuahua in Mexico, the business community approached the state government with a plan to get assistance to those most in need: a special tax of 0.2 percent of earnings to be paid by each of the 29,000 business enterprises in the region, on the condition that members of the business community themselves would manage the funds generated. The overwhelming success of this effort in providing disaster relief and rebuilding the community prompted the business community to ratify a "Community Investment" tax permanently into state law. In 1994, the Chihuahuan Business Foundation (FECHAC) was established to administer these funds. Its creation was indicative that business leaders had come to two important decisions. First, the flood aid, though successful, was reactive in nature. To respond adequately to Chihuahua's social and economic inequalities, a more proactive strategy was needed. Second, corporations recognized that the complexities of implementing community development programs lay outside their own core business functions and areas of expertise. A separate entity was needed if these programs were to develop the successful methodology and strategies to make them effective.[1]

Legislation influences the type of CSR practices companies adopt in a particular context. However, governments can reduce their dependence on the contingencies of legislative action. Some roads have been opened: public-private partnerships (PPP) are particularly attractive because they pool different resources and involve practitioners from different walks in life.

Typologies for CSR Practices

In an article in which Jones (2004) emphasized CSR as a process, he defined CSR as "the notion that corporations have an obligation to constituent groups in society other than stockholders and beyond that prescribed by law and union contract." He views both stakeholders and scope as critical: "the obligation is a broad one, extending beyond the traditional duty to shareholders to other societal groups such as customers, employees, suppliers, and neighboring communities"; furthermore, "the obligation must be voluntarily adopted" (1980). Carroll identified "four kinds of social responsibilities [that] constitute total CSR: economic, legal, ethical, and philanthropic." (1991) He also describes a philosophy of responsiveness based on reactive, defensive, accommodative and proactive categories. Wood (1991) elaborates on the processes of corporate social responsiveness, including environmental assessment, stakeholder management and issues management.

A good portion of the CSR literature is devoted to the classification of responsible practices. Several typologies are based on the dimensions of CSR practices. These dimensions are related to basic questions such as:

- What activities are completed to fulfill social expectations?
- How are these activities carried out?
- What is the scope of these activities?
- Who is the target of these activities?

Different forms of intervention can be classified by examining what activities have been carried out by a company (strategic or unrelated to the core business) and how these activities were carried out (by the company itself or in alliance with another organization) (see Gutiérrez 2003). Another possible typology rests on the fact that the social responsibility of a business encompasses economic, legal, ethical, and philanthropic expectations (Carroll 1999).

The combination of Martin's virtue matrix and stakeholder theory provides yet another way of classifying company activities (Fig. 1). The horizontal axis accounts for the scope an activity can have within the four quadrants outlined by Martin (2002): the first two within the scope of the social foundation, and the last two extending the innovation frontier. The vertical axis lists the stakeholders that participate in CSR activities, ranging from those directly linked to the business to society in general (Freeman 1984; Epstein 1987; Blair 1995; Carroll 1995; Donaldson and Preston 1995; Jensen 2000).

Figure 1. A Typology for CSR Practices

Scope / Stakeholders	Compliance with law	Observe social norms by choice	Direct integration into business	Social investment
Groups with direct link to business	OSH/EEO Consumer Protection	Fair trade		
Other groups with ties to business	Antitrust regulation	Cluster competitiveness		
Local community	Local content	Local culture		
Society	Environmental protection	Social inclusion		

The first two columns for Fig. 1 list some of the issues through which a company might comply with the formal and informal expectations of a society. In Martin's virtue matrix, these activities lie within the social foundation: those norms, customs, and laws that govern corporate practice. The last two columns represent the space within which companies may innovate through their social programs. In Latin America, large businesses have realized that their stakeholders consist of more than vendors and customers. As for scope, the tendency is to cluster towards the left of the continuum. It is important to understand the characteristics of businesses that are socially involved, because they hold the promise of addressing the region's social injustices. The experiences of some of these organizations are described below.

CSR Interventions

Communities can be identified as communities of geography, communities of identity and/or communities of interest. The community of geography could be the community closest to the corporation, or the community most affected by the primary function of the business. These communities are interested in the benefits associated with being a company's neighbor: access to education, infrastructure, less crime, jobs, etc. Communities of identity are those that define themselves through race, heritage, creed or age group. Finally, communities of interest are those that define themselves through topics of common interest, such as environmentalism or human rights (Burke and Gilmartin 1999). The communities discussed in this section represent a range of interests but are similar in that they consist of low-income populations.

The existence of a company in a community does not go unnoticed. From the moment it establishes itself, relations are forged, and they evolve hopefully beyond dependency into interdependency. Sometimes the moment of truth arrives when the company leaves a community. At that moment one can examine how much stronger and healthier a community is. A comparison of life conditions before the arrival of a company and after its departure is the ultimate test of its impact. An approximation to this ideal situation can be found in a few cases where some information has been gathered (Lozano 2003; Gutiérrez, Barragán, and Uribe 2004).

Changing Perspectives on Development

The first step toward understanding the impacts of CSR practices is to define what a strong and healthy community is. Around the middle of the twentieth century, philanthropy was the CSR practice of choice, and it created dependency relationships between donors and recipients. During the 1960s, the practice of giving things to poor people was criticized: it was said that people needed the ability to procure things for themselves. In the 1990s, these ideas changed even more: knowing how to get things is a limited ability; it is key to know how to organize. Poverty is no longer regarded as the lack of things, but as the inability to control circumstances. Poverty is equated with lack of organization. It is more a matter of empowerment than income.

In this conception, underdevelopment means waiting for others to solve one's problems, while development is the capacity to shape one's future through self-sustaining economic, political and social processes. It took decades for the notion of citizenship to replace paternalistic and dependent relationships. A citizen is someone capable of working with others to create or modify a social order. Therefore, according to Flores d'Arcais (1992), democracy is the possibility of legitimately transforming oneself. A strong and healthy community is one made up of citizens; that is, people who organize themselves to define their own future. Participation, organization, and interdependency characterize such communities. We will look for these characteristics in the cases where companies intervene and change community life.

Types of Interventions

Life changes when a company arrives in a community. A relationship begins, one in which participation and autonomy are key elements. The matters in which community members are invited to participate, or the way in which their participation is elicited and maintained, are important aspects in understanding of the relationship between business and community. From the corporate standpoint, at least two types of intervention can lead to a strengthened community: companies can concentrate internally on their business or they can focus externally and develop social investments that support community projects.

A company can develop internal CSR strategies and pay attention to social issues within its *operations*. In order for a business to develop, all stakeholders are asked to pitch in, and they expect benefits from their participation. To concentrate solely on providing benefits to shareholders runs the risk of ignoring the needs of other stakeholders. Since this affects the sustainability of the whole enterprise, many companies read their environments to consider the needs of their stakeholders.

Alternatively or as a complement, corporations contribute to society by focusing externally and developing *social investments*. A company is willing to make such investments for several reasons: to satisfy various needs of the communities where it is located, to improve its public image, to increase its control over the resources it gives to government through taxes, to increase worker morale, to attract better employees, and—last but not least—to obtain favorable responses from investors and public officials. Social investments primary involve stakeholders who are beyond company boundaries. Although these investments are not directly related to the core of the business, companies benefit from them, and they help to alleviate certain social problems.

External CSR programs lie on a continuum that connects three discrete points: traditional philanthropy, social investment and business integration. Philanthropy is the oldest form of corporate social responsibility and is characterized by a limited dialogue between donor and recipient. Social investment represents the evolution of traditional philanthropy from a top-down approach to a more responsive approach based on social needs. When making a social investment, corporations view their CSR activity as an investment with a social return. Finally and most recently, corporations are beginning to integrate vulnerable populations directly into their regular business practice. This is what we mean by business integration.

Philanthropy

While some would argue that philanthropy is outdated and often takes a top-down approach, there are instances where philanthropy is appropriate and even necessary. In areas such at the arts where it is important to preserve the creativity of the beneficiary, philanthropic giving allows for a less involved type of giving. It is a reasonable option when a corporation is unable to involve itself more deeply in external CSR. Also, on the receiving end, incipient and/or grassroots organizations may not be ready to "partner" with a corporation. For these organizations, reliance on philanthropy is a necessary first-step in their evolutionary process.

Social Investment

The second level of external CSR, social investment, is a phenomenon that appeared midway through the twentieth century in response to heavy regulation and social lobbying. Corporations felt they needed to direct charitable giving in response to social pressures. As a result, external CSR became less top down in many corporations and more participatory by responding needs expressed by the community. Many of these early programs were related to social marketing and public awareness campaigns in which corporations would improve their image by discussing social issues relevant at the time.

In the late 1980s and 1990s, the concept of social investment became prevalent in discussions of external CSR programs. Social investments funded through the technology boom in particular were analyzed from a business perspective, and the program's "social return" was discussed. While one could argue that defining "social investment" is largely a matter of semantics, the results have been more sustained and have involved more corporate levels than those of philanthropy. The "investment" approach to giving is now becoming widely used in many external CSR initiatives.

A network of corporate foundations, RedEAmérica, promotes two types of social investments to transform life conditions in a community: the strengthening of community-based organizations, and the development of public interest institutions that support community development. Programs to strengthen community-based organizations adopt financial and operational strategies that aid the creation and development of community-based organizations and their networks. Programs that develop public interest institutions use several strategies that support community development, ranging from the creation and financing of non-profit organizations, to the establishment of public-private partnerships, to the dissemination efforts of good practices and public debates. Each one of RedEAmérica's 49 members in 12 countries has projects in these areas and is moving ahead to understand the impact of their interventions (Villar 2003).

Direct Integration

On the forefront of CSR evolution, particularly in lesser-developed countries, companies are integrating vulnerable populations into their business processes by developing relationships through trainers, suppliers, distributors and even market competitors. These programs are often hotly debated as external CSR initiatives, since they are directly tied to the companies' business interest. However, the direct integration model is enticing in the context of the developing world, since many countries rely heavily on foreign direct investment rather than creating value-added, second-tier industries. Without value-added industry, the poorest echelon of a society will never have true economic opportunity, since the necessary enabling environment will remain undeveloped.

Value-added business often provides the multiplier that creates the necessary enabling environment for economic development. Examples include an educational system capable of training future employees, open financial markets that allow small- and medium-sized business to participate in the supply chain, and a peaceful society that prospers economically and socially by allowing the poor equal representation.

Business integration seeks to fill the socioeconomic gaps that are a feature in countries where the economy is dominated by first-tier industry, as is commonly the case in less developed countries.

Reports of corporate social responsibility tend to emphasize social investments; it is less common to report a social impact by concentrating on the business at hand. One challenge for management is to eliminate, at the source, any factor that feeds problems that will later require intervention. In this way, businesses act responsibly and avoid creating social problems.

It is important to examine the effect of corporate intervention. Comparison of success stories and difficult experiences answers several questions: When does empowerment occur and how does it happen? What makes a community investment more likely to be sustainable? What are suitable policy environments for sustainable company-community interaction?

Interventions at Work

There is a wide array of occasions on which a company has had a lasting impact on a community. In this section we look at several cases that highlight the achievements and shortcomings of CSR practices with regard to improving the life conditions in a community. In each case we analyze the characteristics of the community, the process in which they engage, and the effects of the intervention. Some of these experiences involve the *direct integration* of low-income populations into business processes; others exemplify *corporate social investment*. Some include community members as active participants and others continue to exclude them. A road map is beginning to emerge from lessons learned, and an examination of these cases will highlight the issues.

Participation throughout All Stages

Twenty miles off the north coast of Honduras is a group of islets and keys known as Cayos Cochinos (Hog Keys). Though small and geographically unprotected from the storms coming through the Caribbean Sea, the keys are an important economic hub for three Garifuna artesanal fishing communities. The Garifuna, descendants of survivors of a wrecked slave ship and local Arawak Indians, have been designated by the United Nations as a World Heritage Culture and maintain a distinct identity in their language, traditions, and livelihood. Unfortunately, the Garifuna are faced with the challenges of extreme poverty, lacking access to healthcare and education, as well as with the complexities of being a racial minority.

Beginning in the early 1990s, there has been significant interest in the keys because the surrounding coral reefs exhibit some of the best biodiversity in Central America. In 1992, the Smithsonian Institute completed a study that found threats to the local environment and concluded that a proactive management plan restricting human activity would eventually repair the damage. The study did not contemplate, however, a specific strategy for limiting local human activity or, more importantly, the needs of the Garifuna. Interest in the area converged to create a strategy of collective action for its long-term environmental sustainability. The Cayos Cochinos Foundation was established as a nonprofit organization and was capitalized jointly by members of the private sector, including multinational corporations and a dozen representatives of national Honduran businesses. Why did corporations in Honduras, a country with little CSR culture, commit to such a long-term, complicated undertaking? First, the international attention and support that Cayos Cochinos has received from the Inter-American Foundation, Texaco, Avina Foundation, and World Wildlife Fund, created a level of prestige in being associated with the project. Second, members of the Foundation's Board all have an individual interest and dedication to the preservation of the environment, and as a result the Foundation becoming fully operational within a very short time frame.

Today, the Cayos Cochinos Foundation represents a model of companies bringing together resources, community input, political will, and scientific study. As originally conceived, the Foundation dedicated itself solely to the scientific study and environmental preservation of the area by restricting human activity. Its neglect of the interdependency between the ecosystem and human activity resulted in friction with local communities, which subsist on fishing. The Foundation learned that the socio-economic welfare of the Garifuna is critical to successful of management of the reserve, and that local buy-in was at risk if the community was not involved in the Foundation's planning process.

The Foundation's philosophy today reflects the intrinsic role of community in its projects. The Foundation learned a valuable tool in managing community development programs: participation. This transition occurred in several of the programs managed by the Foundation. For example, in a scientific research and observation station on Cayo Menor, only Foundation staff, scientists, and members of the Honduran Navy originally lodged there to patrol the waters of Cayos Cochinos and ensure compliance with fishing controls. Today, Garifuna fishermen are employed as park rangers and reside at the station along with Foundation and naval staff. Their job is to monitor activities in the protected zones, educate people about policies protecting the keys, and lend their unique expertise of the area to assist in the management of the reserve. Educational programs are jointly developed and taught by the Foundation and Garifuna educators to local school children. One such program is the involvement of the students in raising and eventually releasing endangered species of sea turtles. Other initiatives include capacity building exercises such as micro-enterprise development, exchange visits with artesanal fishermen in other countries, and grassroots lobbying efforts with the national government.

Cayos Cochinos teaches many lessons on how community engagement must be participatory to be successful. Corporations that wish to support community development often find themselves acting in concert with other international and national donor organizations, all pursuing development from many angles. This can be a double-edged sword if project goals and coordination are not managed well and the community is an afterthought. Corporations should carefully consider the motives of an intermediary organization when working with it to make a community investment. Communities are complex systems. CSR programs must be clearly articulated to fit local communities, commit for the long term, and have a feedback mechanism from all involved partners. Personnel who are dedicated to the program are key for stability, both from the company's perspective and the community's (James 2004a).

The Learning Curve during the Life Cycle of CSR Programs

The Department of Oruro houses 5 percent of Bolivia's eight million inhabitants. The richness of the native Aymara Indian culture contrasts with the economic poverty resulting from the region's precarious agricultural system. In the early 1990s, more than 70 percent of the families in Oruro were officially categorized as living in poverty, 84 percent did not have access to potable water and/or latrines, and 55 percent could not reach the nearest community health center for lack of adequate transportation. The Inti Raymi gold mine is located in this region, and it is responsible for over 60 percent of the gold production in Bolivia. It has created 700 jobs, filled by Bolivian citizens who collect 8.2 million USD per year in salaries and benefits. The mine also spends eighteen million USD annually on local goods and services and pays four million USD in taxes. The Newmont Mining Corporation, a company that became the world's largest gold producer in early 2002, is the majority owner of the Inti Raymi mine. The company exemplifies how a company can contribute to worker welfare by concentrating on its business. One of its proud achievements is a much higher worker salary level than local and national averages. According to their figures for 2001, Oruro's villagers annual income averaged 300 USD, while their annual average salary was 10,500 USD (the annual income per capita in Bolivia averaged 1,021 USD). The company also provides its employees training, education, and full access to medical care. The Inti Raymi mine has one of the best reputations in Bolivia, a strong safety and health record, and good relations with the union representing the mine workers.

Inti Raymi also engages with the community. Mario Mercado, a former company president, established in 1991 the Inti Raymi Foundation to promote sustainable development through alliances between the public, private, and civil society sectors. Today, grassroots development is one of the foundation's key objectives, and it takes the form of social and productivity investments in the Oruro communities. Social investments include health and education programs, while a small business program, grants, and a loan program contribute to productivity. These were developed in partnerships with the municipal governments and the Inter-American Foundation. By 2003 the Foundation had invested more than ten million USD in rural development projects for twenty-five communities and the city of Oruro. Living conditions, according to community members, have changed: "Our lives have improved, as we now have water, electricity, and latrines in our communities." The project has brought these services to more than 200 families in the region. Once dependent on potato farming, they now have access to a small fund that has made more than fifty credits to local community members for micro-enterprise development.

Whenever a large corporation has physical presence in a specific location, expectations rise in the surrounding community. This is particularly true in regions where residents have little or no means of economic security other than the company. An extractive industry is in the commodity business and, like the local community, depends on the available natural resources. There is one significant distinction between the industry and the community, however; the mining corporation will eventually close operations and move on, while the community cannot. Since the life of the mine is finite, community, corporation, and foundation have worked together to develop a strategic plan to assure a smooth transition once the mining concession is over. Their overarching goal is to achieve continuity in the design, funding and implementation of social programs, so that even after the mine shuts down the foundation can continue.

To that end, the foundation is exploring an endowment fund with seed capital from the company. As a first step, Inti Raymi created a U.S.-based foundation for the purpose of fundraising. Different sources of funding have been explored, such as the Bolivian expatriate community. Beyond organizational self-sufficiency, Inti Raymi is considering sustainability for specific projects like its micro-credit program. Another important factor in long-term planning is the development of sustainable leadership. Attracting visionary leaders to run the foundation could become more difficult once the business interest is no longer behind it. In response, Inti Raymi expects to open its Board of Directors to both community members as well as nationally known leaders, thereby increasing both the talent pool and the visibility of the foundation's management. Finally, certain procedural issues have already been planned in conjunction with community input, such as ownership of land and payment/compensation for land use. Due to the presence of the mine for so many years, the region enjoys good infrastructure such as roads, electricity, airport, etc. This could open the door for new productive land use. Possible replacement institutions, once the mine shuts down, are an industrial park, a university, or a wildlife habitat.

Early in its timeline of community involvement, the Inti Raymi Foundation carried out a number of programs that included such health initiatives as the construction of a hospital and such economic development initiatives as a sheep-raising project. Some of the projects were primarily intended for the mineworkers but were made available to the wider community as well. Others, such as the sheep-raising and marketing projects, did not include miners at all and were targeted towards other segments of the population. Though the programs were described as successful and well-received overall, the foundation managed a top-down model of program funding, with ideas and implementation of projects generated by Inti Raymi. The communities did not take part in the planning process.

To capitalize on corporate-sponsored social programs, communities must be able to participate fully and equally in this and other aspects of the operations. When local people are equal stakeholders, sensitive issues such as land tenure and usage rights can be resolved in a transparent manner. Inti Raymi has discovered that if communities are part of the negotiation process, agreements necessary for the mine's existence are resolved much more quickly and profits increase. The agreements have a certain legitimacy in the eyes of the people, and the mine's daily operations are less likely to be interrupted by civil unrest.

This case presents two valuable lessons for other corporate foundations involved in CSR programs with local communities. There is a learning curve that can be accelerated by partnerships with institutions experienced in community engagement. Though an obvious issue for a mining company, a well-planned exit strategy should be a part of every company's community engagement efforts, since it actively commits both the company and the community to avoid traditional dependency programs. Finally, intangible benefits to the community, such as an increase in individuals self-esteem (2,300 community members indicated this in an evaluation process), are more valuable than an increase in income, since they represent a change in mindset—particularly one from dependency to independence, which lies at the root of participation (James 2004c).

Strategic Initiatives that Promote Citizenship

Rural communities in Huila, a southern department in Colombia, made a living from cattle ranching for more than two centuries. Government presence was rare for these dispersed and isolated communities, and the arrival of an oil company in the 1950s was an important event. Roads were built to start oil production in the 1960s, and the international oil crisis of the 1970s boosted the oil industry in this neglected region. Communities then had someone to ask for basic social infrastructure. Hocol, one of the companies there, responded by providing the resources to build schools and health centers.

Until the beginning of the 1990s, Hocol subcontracted organizations that would work with the communities in which they had operations. In 1992, some of the community leaders who had been supported by Hocol through its micro-enterprise program organized a strike against the company. The oil industry was blamed for a painful drought, which in fact was due to specific weather patterns and cattle raising conditions. Hocol's production was halted, and guerrillas blew up some of the production infrastructure several days after the strike began. It was evident for Hocol that the community did not view the company as beneficial to them. Hocol therefore decided to stop subcontracting its social initiatives. From then on, its own foundation (established five years earlier) developed the micro-enterprise program and started an environmental education program. The latter became crucial for community members to understand the reasons behind the drought and develop projects that would protect and recuperate water sources.

Another turning point occurred in 1994: due to financial difficulties, the company slashed its budget for social initiatives by half. Hocol Foundation had promised the communities projects that required twice the resources that were now available. Hocol's people in the field decided to keep the current year's plan intact by raising funds within the communities and the government. The question came up: why had education and health become Hocol's responsibility? From then on, government organizations were summoned to participate in every program, and all programs were funded by several partners. Between 2001 and 2003, social initiatives costing two million USD were developed; 46 percent of the funds came from Hocol, 19 percent from communities, 16 percent from government, and 19 percent from other sources such as multilateral agencies.

As the relationship between the communities and Hocol evolved, the meaning of community development changed for all parties. The Hocol Foundation opened programs for community development and institutional strengthening. One program created a School for Democracy and a Rural School for Community and Citizen

Participation. Hocol wanted to learn, with its communities, how to take advantage of a shift to a participatory democracy within the framework of the new Colombian Constitution enacted in 1991. According to a Hocol executive, "the best we can do is to teach people the value of being leaders of their own life." The "School for Democracy" is now a formal offering in the state university and teaches how to participate in order to decide; community members are given tools to diagnose their needs, set priorities, and develop projects that are funded by different partners. Similar to the expansion of this school, other projects became regional initiatives. For example, in the institutional strengthening program, Hocol started by inviting the government to participate in community projects. In 2004 the company participated in eight different coordinating and decision-making committees at the regional level.

Strengthened communities have been key to the development of Hocol as a business. Oil companies explore vast and remote territories and produce with expensive machinery. As part of the armed conflict in Colombia during 2003, there were 753 attacks on the oil infrastructure. None of these affected Hocol's infrastructure. One of Hocol's main competitive advantages nowadays is its capacity to operate in any part of Colombia. This capacity, very much appreciated in the oil industry, has been instrumental to Hocol's expansion. The company has been invited to become a partner in various projects sponsored the main oil companies. It has become the third largest operator in the country, and its overseas shareholders have decided to close operations elsewhere and concentrate their investments in Hocol, and to expand its operations to other Andean countries. The numbers related to any of its projects are impressive: they set record time for one of the largest private seismic initiatives in recent years in Colombia, logged 2,350,000 working hours without any disabling accident in forty-eight rural communities of five municipalities, created jobs for 1,430 local workers, and invested 5.7 million USD for social development in the region. An award-winning communications program was responsible for clear, transparent and timely information that paved the way to reaching consensus with the communities on such issues as wages, local workforce hiring, and payments for land usage, all within a moderate budget relative by industry standards.

Hocol has learned that it needs long-term relationships with communities. Communication, participation, consensus building, and feedback are all characteristics of these relationships. From their interaction with Hocol, communities have learned to work together to change their life conditions. Not only are they able to solve their internal conflicts, but they can apply pressure externally for their rights to be honored. The communities quitted by Hocol pulled have continued to improve on their own. As Hocol's employees like to state it, "A public good has strengthened the social fabric" (Gutiérrez, Barragán, and Uribe 2004).

Economic Benefits through Adequate Responses to Legal Requirements

Pará is the second largest state in Brazil. While the state can cite significant indicators of industrial development, few benefits trickle down to local communities: the average annual income is 2,200 USD, whereas the national average is 7,600. Communities in the Amazonian basin are further removed from the larger economy due to their geographic isolation. Despite having rich and plentiful natural resources, community-based agro-industries in the region face obstacles in their efforts to market products and engage in sustainable resource management. In terms of commercialization, these producers often have limited organizational capacity, as well as limited access to technologies needed to tap into the larger markets. POEMAR, a non-profit organization located in the state of Pará, offers training in all aspects of product development, with a focus on low cost technologies that add value. POEMAR works with producers to diversify their products, to acquire information on market demand and quality standards, and to establish relationships with corporations that seek local sourcing agents. POEMAR provides support in a way that helps local agro-industrialists preserve their natural environment for future generations.

POEMAR is part of the larger "POEMA system" within the Environmental Center at the Federal University of Pará. POEMAR capitalizes on the university's laboratories to study the natural products of the region, as well as to develop processing and quality control technologies. POEMAR's competitive advantage is its ability to establish market relationships between the different actors. An example is the link POEMAR has forged between buyers and suppliers in Pará's coconut fiber industry. POEMAR approached Daimler-Chrysler (at the time Daimler-Benz AG) to conduct research on substituting natural fibers for synthetic materials in interior car parts. Daimler-Chrysler agreed in 1992 to make an initial investment of 1.4 million USD to research viable natural fiber products and the role local communities could play as suppliers. The result of three years of research was a pilot project to produce headrests and other interior car parts in the community of Praia Grande. Initially the manufacturing was done manually. Eventually Daimler-Chrysler donated equipment to allow for more efficient processing of fibers. Additional investments in the project were then financed by Amazonian Bank BASA. POEMAR trained community members in technology, administration, marketing, and innovative agro-forestry practices. Coconut production increased from nine to forty coconuts per tree.

Two major challenges were identified in the pilot project: transporting the car parts from the remote community, and meeting production deadlines that were not customary in rural community production. With help from POEMAR these obstacles were removed, and in March 2001 the first fiber processing plant was inaugurated. POEMATEC, a business in the POEMA system, undertook management of the plant and assured that quality and quantity were consistent with market requirements. The plant was financed by the State of Pará, the municipal government of Ananindeua, the Amazonian Bank, Daimler-Chrysler, and DEG, a German Investment and Development Company. Specifically, Daimler-Chrysler financed four million USD worth of imported machinery and provided training in the use of the equipment.

Today the plant has a production capacity of 80,000 tons per month. Some 25 percent of its production is dedicated to interior car parts for Daimler-Chrysler. The plant is rapidly expanding to meet demand from General Motors and Honda. It is also adding such product lines as gardening pots and mattresses. It is easy to get lost in the plethora of cutting-edge plant and technological developments. One success story relates to benefits enjoyed by rural community organizations in eight districts that supply coconut fiber to POEMATEC. POEMACOOP, a cooperative of small producers and specialized technicians, purchases inputs in bulk to allow small producers to benefit from the associated economies of scale. All this translates into approximately 4,000 new jobs in coconut fiber production, including agricultural producers, processing plant workers, and plant workers. The project has allowed this community of agricultural producers to participate in the global economy along with a Fortune 100 company.

The project also has measurable benefits to Daimler-Chrysler's business. The company meets its local content requirements by sourcing its interior car parts from the coconut fiber plant. This also ensures that the company's vehicle production meets the high environmental and recycling standards in Germany. Finally, natural fibers are as economically viable as synthetic ones, if not more so.

The key lessons learned from this case, from the corporation's perspective, are two-fold. The first is that corporate self-interest can be a powerful motivator in establishing sustainable, successful CSR programs. Daimler Chrysler has tied many business objectives to this program, as well as local content and environmental content compliance, making it one of the most successful economic development programs in the region. Secondly, innovative commercial relationships can be mutually beneficial for a company and local communities, while also adhering to environmentally sound principles of sustainable development. Communities must identify their indigenous comparative advantage when engaging with a corporation. The environment is often the organizing issue for communities of interest, whether these communities are represented by NGOs or governments. There is enormous support for sustainable resource management in the Amazon basin. The Daimler-Chrysler project addressed the concerns of communities of interest that are focused on the environment (Menucci 2004).

Community Investment through Partnerships

The Delegación of Iztapalapa, located on the periphery of Mexico City, houses one of Mexico's most marginalized populations. Over 90 percent of its inhabitants live in poverty. Annual family incomes range from 1800 to 3600 USD. Prospects for future generations are bleak, since only 50 percent of the children finish elementary school. Iztapalapa attracts immigrants from Mexico's thirty-five states, who come in search of economic opportunity. For most, the stark reality of Latin America's biggest city sets in, and families begin to search for ways to sustain themselves as micro-entrepreneurs in the new urban setting.

In contrast, a well-known Mexican industrialist family, the Servitjes, founded Grupo Bimbo S.A., the eighth-largest baked goods corporation in the world, with operations in sixty countries. In 2001 the group employed 70,000 worldwide and boasted net sales of 3686 million USD. Today, it ties its community investment directly into its core business by making loans available to micro-entrepreneurs who want to participate in its distribution system. The loans are provided through an innovative partnership with FinComún, a Mexican financial services business dedicated to serving low-income people. FinComún is widely recognized as Mexico's premier micro-finance institution. It is a pioneer on several fronts, including the capture of capital through savings accounts, customer service, use of technology, and the testing of new ideas and innovative partnerships. These savings programs support FinComún's micro-lending program. Loans are made to low-income individuals, for small business and productive activities, at the prevailing market rate for a period of sixteen weeks. As of 2001, 11,576 loans totaling twelve million USD had been made, with a default rate of 0.1 percent. FinComún uses its reputation and ties to the private sector to achieve recognition from the Mexican government, including management responsibility for a three million-dollar government micro-credit fund, and rather deep involvement in shaping national regulation of micro-finance activities.

FinComún presented an innovative opportunity to Grupo Bimbo, as it undertook to tie its community investment strategy directly into core business activities. The partnership allows Bimbo to take advantage of FinComún's expertise in providing micro-loans, while FinComún taps into Bimbo's distribution network and product delivery systems. For instance, FinComún's loan advisors accompany Bimbo delivery drivers on their daily routes. Because loan amounts are small (from fifty USD up), with an average of 750 USD per client, financial sustainability depends upon volume. As a way to increase its customer base, FinComún goes physically into the low-income neighborhoods to identify new clients rather than depending exclusively on branch offices to attract business. The partnership with Bimbo allows this and, since the Bimbo brand is strongly associated with quality, it gives FinComún instant credibility as well as potential clients.

Grupo Bimbo was concerned about the bottom line. The company derives 80 percent of its income from small "mom and pop" stores, and 20 percent of these clients regularly ask for credit. Previously Bimbo had an informal program to provide credit services to these stores. As a result of the partnership with FinComún, Bimbo expects to reduce bad debt, reduce the amount of time in which loans are repaid, and achieve its goal of providing credit to 22–30 percent of its clients.

Initial results of a small-scale pilot program showed that 20 percent of Bimbo clients received credit, and they expressed overall satisfaction with the customer service provided by FinComún. The next stage of the plan involves the donation of a Bimbo van that will be customized as a mobile FinComún branch office. If neighborhood conditions are favorable to micro-credit operations, the van will be a precursor to a permanent branch office. With this new method, FinComún expects new branch offices to break even in six months, rather than in one year as currently. Additional collaborative plans are in the pipeline. A pre-authorized credit program is possible, once Grupo Bimbo's customer database can be merged with FinComún's credit analysis and client/industry profiles. FinComún is looking at managing some of Bimbo's liquid assets. The possibilities for these community investments seem limitless.

The impact of this project is being evaluated. The issue is to what extent access to credit has allowed small- and medium-sized enterprises in Mexico City to grow their business, create employment, and generate capital in their local communities. More than 50 percent of the FinComún's loan recipients are low-income women who engage in commercial activities, ranging from fruit and vegetable stands to seamstress hops and grocery convenience stores. Access to credit also allows entrepreneurs to develop a credit record that will be invaluable to them as they attempt to grow their business and acquire more capital (James 2004b).

The community affected by Grupo Bimbo is less tightly knit than others discussed in this section, since it is comprised of individuals in an urban setting. They are a community of micro-entrepreneurs who relate to each other at arms length to drive the local economy forward and recycle loan money that helps to capitalize their businesses. The process of engagement relies on a bank, FinComún, as an intermediary to meet a very specific need of the community of micro-entrepreneurs in Iztapalapa: access to capital. Urban community interventions are arguably harder to assess in a collective sense, since people act more independently in defining and responding to their needs.

A Continuum of Results from CSR Interventions

A company's impact on a community can be placed on a continuum that stretches from one end at which environmental degradation, corruption and social unrest are the norm, to an opposite end at which conservation and citizenship practices are institutionalized. A company with clean production that fails to promote citizenship lies in the middle. Movement towards the desirable end requires democratic efforts that increasingly empower community members.

Since no previous study has determined the main factors that govern the community impact of CSR, we chose to concentrate on five cases (summarized in Table 1). We identify only some of the characteristics of the relationships between types of intervention, processes, and impacts. At most we can state hypotheses about these relationships.

Table 1. Main Characteristics of Five Case Studies

Cases	Initial life conditions in community	Type of intervention	Spaces for community participation	Link to operations	Distinctive characteristic of the intervention	Results and impacts
Cayos Cochinos	Low access to health and education for racial minority	Corporations invest through foundation	Foundation programs and community education programs	Innovation not related to businesses	Community integration into foundation	Organized grassroots lobbying
Inti Raymi	84% with no access to potable water and latrines	Corporate investment by foundation	Negotiation processes and foundation board	Innovation sometimes related to business	Foundation's learning curve	Social services, 700 jobs, 10 million USD invested
Hocol	Fragmented and isolated rural communities	Foundation's business strategy	Foundation and community development programs	Strategic innovation for business	Social initiatives become sources of competitive advantage	Organized citizens; in one project alone, 1430 jobs and 5.7 million USD invested
Daimler Chrysler	Fragmented and isolated rural communities	Strengthen community suppliers through NGO	Small producers cooperative	Strategic innovation for business	Compliance with local content and environmental standards	4000 jobs, 5.4 million USD invested
Grupo Bimbo	Fragmented urban interest communities	Services to customers through NGO		Strategic innovation for business	Strategic partnership with NGO	12 million USD in loans

The five cases show different ways in which direct integration of communities into business processes and corporate social investment can take place. Daimler Chrysler and Grupo Bimbo were able to directly integrate a community investment program into their core business practices. The Inti Raymi Foundation and the Cayos Cochinos Foundation exemplify two different types of corporate social investments: a corporate foundation invested in the community, and a foundation established by several corporations to pursue a common interest. Hocol started by investing in social initiatives and, in time, found those initiatives to be one of their main sources of competitive advantage.

The Business Integration Approach

Corporations increasingly see the value of incorporating low-income communities directly into their supply chain through training relationships, supplier relationships, distribution relationships, and even market competitor relationships. Business integration can fill the socioeconomic gaps common in less economically developed countries. It involves some transfer of technology, capital, and business process from the corporation to the community: Daimler Chrysler invested in industrializing an indigenous technology and capitalized its development; Grupo Bimbo increased access to financial services to better serve its distribution system; and Hocol worked in partnerships to improve life conditions in the society where it operates (see Fig. 2).

Figure 2. Examples of CSR Practices

Scope Stakeholders	Compliance with law	Observe social norms by choice	Direct integration into business	Social investment
Groups with direct link to business	OSH/EEO Consumer Protection	Fair trade	Daimler Chrysler	
Other groups with ties to business	Antitrust regulation	Cluster competitiveness		Grupo Bimbo
Local community	Local content	Local culture		Inti Raymi Found. Cayos Cochinos F.
Society	Environmental protection	Social inclusion	Hocol	

Various factors motivate multinationals in developing countries to engage in the business integration model of CSR: compliance regulation, profit from market opportunities, competitive advantage, stronger appeal to consumers and employees, or the advantages of creating wealth in poverty-stricken contexts. Locally based companies are also concerned that governments are not investing in the local resources required to keep their businesses going (Jones 2004).

The effects of corporations on communities are unique to each experience. Interventions that directly tie communities into business practices provide local groups with an opportunity to participate in the global economy. Sometimes, however, this opportunity is not available because corporations do not want to share their privileges. This happened when, in 2003, Bogotá's garbage collection system was renegotiated and this metropolis of 7.5 million people was divided into six geographic zones. Around 70,000 recycling workers, organized in twenty-three cooperatives, wanted to participate in the bidding process for garbage collection. It was far from an equal opportunity process. Despite their efforts, recycling workers were unfairly excluded—according to the Colombian Supreme Court of Justice—and the six zones were assigned to large corporations. For none of these companies did CSR mean working with the recycling employees.

The Social Investment Approach

Dialogue and community participation, rather than top-down programs, are required when corporate foundations undertake social investments for which corporate and community needs are less closely linked than for direct business integration. In three of the cases described above, an initial top-down approach resulted in loosing sight of the community. The strikes and lack of organizational effectiveness disappeared when the foundations went beyond information exchange and consultation and opened up spaces for community participation in the design, funding, and execution of programs. Without community input into program development, well-meaning corporate foundations can create projects that have no positive long-term effect on local communities, and there is an increased risk of treating the symptoms of social problems rather than their root cause.

When are corporate foundations the best vehicle for CSR investment in a community? In Latin America, corporate foundations offer companies a vehicle to administer social programs under its brand name, with specialized staff that can design, implement, and evaluate programs effectively. The corporate foundation is also, at times, a helpful intermediary between the community and the corporation. The foundation deals directly with the community and the corporation can focus on day-to-day business. On occasion, however, corporate foundations get in the way of community development.

Some examples of the potential shortcomings of corporate foundations can be found among the micro-credit programs of the past couple of decades in Colombia. An evaluation of the National Plan of Micro-Enterprise Development concluded that employment was not generated and people were not pulled out of poverty (Departamento Nacional de Planeación, Fundación Corona y Corporación para el Desarrollo de las Microempresas 1998). Rojas examined the National Plan and focused on the role corporate foundations played in it. He concluded that "while [contact] with corporate philanthropy increases economic resources and provides innovative solutions to social ills, it has not similarly contributed to the democratization of the decision making process nor the strengthening of state legitimacy. Programs in the hands of foundations are not accountable to citizens nor do they increase the capacity of the state to act as an intermediary of powerful interests" (Rojas 2002: 28). Corporate foundations, for example, resisted the creation of an organization of micro-entrepreneurs that would participate in the decision making processes. According to Villar (1999), political empowerment was not part of the agenda of corporate foundations in their work with micro-entrepreneurs.

A Necessary Intermediary Role

Despite their shortcomings, corporate foundations have a role to play. Applying a well known principle in chaos theory, companies are high-energy systems that can distort or destroy a low-energy system like a community unless an intermediary exists. In the cases mentioned above, the relationship with the community is not direct: nonprofit organizations served as intermediaries between the company and the community. These intermediaries have been the catalysts to engage the communities with the corporation, articulate the potential for a partnership, and bridge corporate requirements with community capacity. Nonprofit organizations can play an important role in the inclusion of disadvantaged populations within social, political, and economic circles. Through service or advocacy, these organizations can make a difference.

Interaction between a company and an intermediary organization is not easy, and one must also ask about the effect of this intermediary on the community. The Social Enterprise Knowledge Network (SEKN) research team studied the interactions between private and social sector organizations in twenty-four cases throughout Latin America. They discovered six barriers to collaboration:

- The search for an interlocutor: "Sometimes, choosing an interlocutor is almost as important as choosing the message" (Austin et al. 2004: 27).
- The power of pre-existing relations: social networks are a critical organizational resource, and prior links to an individual or a cause can influence the unfolding dialogue in different ways.
- Imbalances among partners' institutional capabilities: the greater the institutional capacity, the smaller the barriers to cross-sector collaboration. A community without an organizational structure exhibits the least institutional capacity, and this capacity increases as a community leader attempts organizing efforts. A greater capacity exists when an individual or a group is backed by an established organization, and the greatest capacity is achieved when a mature organization exists, one with executive leadership and specialized staff.
- Differences in organizational cultures: lack of a common language, negative stereotypes, clashes between a culture of austerity and a culture of opulence, and different time frameworks.
- Communicating effectively: "An effective message demands a skilled communicator" (Austin et al. 2004: 42).
- The importance of being proactive and persistent: "Connecting successfully with another organization entails an alignment of several factors" (Austin et al. 2004: 43).

The development of alliances takes time and encounters difficulties. Holly Wise, one of the leaders from USAID in its alliance with Procter & Gamble, says: "true partnership involves shared problem definition and joint design of solutions; partners want to be involved at the front end, not invited to join after major decisions have been made; and alliances require special outreach and messaging which we are not accustomed to doing" (Gutiérrez 2003: 7).

However difficult the collaboration between companies and intermediary organizations is, and however varied the impacts of the latter on communities, these organizations are key to increasing social well-being. For example, they persuade governments and communities to increase common goods, help protect some rights, promote self-control and, on occasion, promote citizenship.

In the past decade, cross-sector alliances have dealt with every type of social problem, and these collaborations are expected to increase even more (Sagawa and Segal 2000). As an alternative path to development, alliances are particularly important in Third World countries. In Latin America, collaborative work has been enabled by three trends that have changed relations throughout the entire social landscape: democratization, decentralization, and "growth through the market" (Fizbein and Lowden 1999; Googins and Rochlin 2000). Tackling social problems is now a shared responsibility. As Trist recognizes, important social issues belong to an inter-organizational domain and cannot be solved by an organization acting alone (Huxham and Vangen 2001).

Lessons Drawn from a Comparative Perspective

Both success stories and difficult experiences help one understand some of the important characteristics of the relationships between corporations and communities. Some of the lessons are the following:

- A company's enlightened self-interest in its CSR program ensures its commitment to the program and the program's sustainability;
- Communities involved from the onset in the definition of a project make it successful; corporations cannot assume that they understand the needs of a community by taking them at face value;
- Partnerships last when both institutional and individual relationships exist throughout. Partnering for the sake of it is not enough; alliances involve alignment and value generation and have to be managed;
- Projects do not create untenable expectations in local communities when they consider the whole life cycle and the sustainability of the investment after an appropriate exit strategy is executed;
- Financial resources are only part of the equation. Corporations can have enormous impacts with limited financing if programs are well defined and well accompanied.

All sectors of society are asked to contribute their share, since social problems have increased and states have lost part of the preeminent role assigned to them in pushing the carts of development. Expectations related to what private companies can do as corporate citizens have increased, and a support system is being developed so that the private sector can fulfill these expectations: multilateral agencies are investing more resources in the private than in the public sector, universities offer new programs for social enterprises, coalitions of civil sector organizations are forged, volunteerism is on the rise, and mass media gives increasing attention to social initiatives.

Following in the footsteps of corporations in economically developed countries, current trends in Latin America include the deepening of CSR models, the extension of CSR practices to small- and medium-sized suppliers, an increase in cross-sector alliances, and the building of relational capital through the development of grassroots organizations. All these paths depend on leaders who search for consistency between strategy definition and implementation. They are paths in which profits, power, and prestige are combined, and that pose critical challenges to the firm and its stakeholders. On the one hand, companies need inclusive dialogues despite the lack of shared understandings; and firms better avoid legitimizing and de-legitimizing fragmented stakeholders. On the other hand, stakeholders need to dialogue, even though trust does not exist, and must learn to deal with contradictory views within the firms. There are challenges right and left.

Note

1. A similar scheme was developed in Colombia when some companies in Department of Antioquia gave some money to their workers with families and the lowest income during the mid-1950s. This example prompted the national government to enact a 4 percent wage tax in 1957. Regional nonprofit organizations were created to manage these funds and distribute it to the workers with the lowest income. In time, a smaller percentage of the collected funds were distributed and more were dedicated to different social services.

References

Austin, J. E., E. Reficco, G. Berger, R. M. Fischer, R. Gutierrez, M. Koljatic, G. Lozano, and E. Ogliastri. 2004. *Social Partnering in Latin America: Lessons Drawn from Collaboration of Businesses and Civil Society Organizations*. Boston: David Rockefeller Center for Latin American Studies.

Blair, M. M. 1995. *Ownership and Control: Rethinking Corporate Governance for the Twenty-First Century*. Washington: Brookings Institution.

Boehm, A. 2002. "Corporate Social Responsibility: A Complementary Perspective of Community and Corporate Leaders." *Business and Society Review* 107(2): 171–194.

Brammer, S., and A. Millington. 2003. "The Effect of Stakeholder Preferences, Organizational Structure and Industry Type on Corporate Community Involvement." *Journal of Business Ethics* 45(3): 213–226.

Burke, E. M., and R. V. Gilmartin. 1999. *Corporate Community Relations: The Principle of the Neighbor of Choice*. Westport, Conn.: Greenwood Publishing Group.

Carroll, A. B. 1991. "The Pyramid of Corporate Social Responsibility: Toward the Moral Management of Organizational Stakeholders." *Business Horizons* 34(4): 39–48.

———. 1995. "Stakeholder Thinking in Three Models of Management Morality: A Perspective with Strategic Implications." In *Understanding Stakeholder Thinking*, ed. J. Näsi. Helsinki: LSR-Publications, 47–74.

———. 1999. "Corporate Social Responsibility: Evolution of a Definitional Construct." *Business & Society* 38(3): 268–295.

Davis, K. 1967. "Understanding the Social Responsibility Puzzle: What Does the Businessman Owe to Society?" *Business Horizons* 10 (Winter): 45–50.

Departamento Nacional de Planeación, Fundación Corona y Corporación para el Desarrollo de las Microempresas. 1998. *Evaluación de los Programas de Apoyo a la Microempresa, 1997–1998*. Bogotá: Departamento Nacional de Planeación.

Donaldson, T., and L. E. Preston. 1995. "The Stakeholder Theory of the Corporation." *Academy of Management Review* 20: 65–91.

Economist, The. 2004. "Two-Faced Capitalism." (January 22). Available at www.economist.com, accessed on February 21, 2004.

Epstein, E. M. 1987. "The Corporate Social Policy Process: Beyond Business Ethics, Corporate Social Responsibility, and Corporate Social Responsiveness." *California Management Review* 29: 99–114.

Fizbein, A., and P. Lowden. 1999. *Trabajando unidos para un cambio: las alianzas público-privadas para la reducción de la pobreza en América Latina y el Caribe*. México, D.F.: Mundiprensa.

Flores d'Arcais, P. 1992. *Etica senza fede*. Rome: Einaudi.

Freeman, R. E. 1984. *Strategic Management: A Stakeholder Approach*. Boston: Pitman.

Friedman, M. 1962. *Capitalism and Freedom*. Chicago: University of Chicago Press.

Googins, B., and S. Rochlin. 2000. "Creating the Partnership Society: Understanding the Rhetoric and Reality of Cross-Sectoral Partnerships." *Business and Society Review* 105(1): 127–144.

Grayson, D., and A. Hodges. 2002. *Everybody's Business: Managing Risks and Opportunities in Today's Global Society*. New York: DK Publishing, Inc.

Gutiérrez, R. 2003. "Partnerships in Local Economic and Community Development." In Vives and Heinecke 2003: 5–7.

Gutiérrez, R., A. Barragán, and E. M. Uribe. 2004. "La transformación de las comunidades en el área de influencia de Hocol." Bogotá: Mimeo.

Huxham, C., and S. Vangen. 2001. "Leadership in the Shaping and Implementation of Collaboration Agendas: How Things Happen in a (Not Quite) Joined-Up World." *The Academy of Management Journal* 43(6): 1159–1175.

James, K. 2004a. "CSR in Environmental Protection and Human Development: Two Different but Complementary Objectives." www.iaf.gov/grants/community_outreach, accessed on March 15, 2004.

_______. 2004b. "The Evolution of a Company's Commitment to CSR From Philanthropy, to Investment, and Beyond." www.iaf.gov/grants/community_outreach, accessed on March 15, 2004.

_______. 2004c. "The Lifecycle of CSR Programs: Inti Raymi Gold Mine." www.iaf.gov/grants/community_outreach, accessed on March 15, 2004.

Jensen, M. C. 2000. "Value Maximization and the Corporate Objective Function. In *Breaking the Code of Change*, ed. M. Beer and N. Nohria. Boston: Harvard Business School Press, 37–57.

Johnson, H. L. 1971. *Business in Contemporary Society: Framework and Issues*. Belmont, Calif.: Wadsworth.

Jones, A. 2003. "Partnerships with NGOs and Civil Society." In Vives and Heinecke 2003: 8–13.

_______. 2004. "Making Sense of Corporate Social Responsibility." www.iaf.gov/grants/community_outreach, accessed on February 12, 2004.

Jones, T. M. 1980. "Corporate Social Responsibility Revisited, Redefined." *California Management Review* (Spring): 59–67.

Lozano, J. M. 2003. "*Danone en Ultzama*." Barcelona: ESADE.

Martin, R. L. 2002. "The Virtue Matrix: Calculating the Return on Corporate Responsibility." *Harvard Business Review* (March): 5–11.

McGuire, J. W. 1963. *Business and Society*. New York: McGraw-Hill.

Menucci, J. 2004. "Innovative Supply Chain Management in the Amazon Basin." www.iaf.gov/grants/community_outreach, accessed on March 15, 2004.

Revista: Harvard Review of Latin America. 2002. "Giving and Volunteering in the Americas: From Charity to Solidarity." Spring: 1–87.

Rochlin, S., and J. Boguslaw. 2000. *Making the Business Case: Determining the Value of Corporate Community Involvement*. Newton, Mass.: The Center for Corporate Citizenship at Boston College.

———. 2001. *Business and Community Development*. Newton, Mass.: The Center for Corporate Citizenship at Boston College.

Rojas, C. 2002. "Corporate Philanthropy: A Reflection Based on the Colombian Experience." *Revista: Harvard Review of Latin America* (Spring): 27–29.

Sagawa, S., and E. Segal. 2000. *Common Interest, Common Good: Creating Value through Business and Social Sector Partnerships*. Boston: Harvard Business School Press.

Thompson, A., and L. Landim. 1997. "Non-Governmental Organizations and Philanthropy in Latin America: An Overview." *Voluntas* 8(4) (December): 337–350.

Villar, R. 1999. "La influencia de las ONG en la política para las microempresas en Colombia." Bogotá: Mimeo.

———. 2003. "Marco sobre el desarrollo de base y el papel de los miembros de RedeAmérica en su apoyo y promoción." Washington: Mimeo.

Vives, A., and A. Heinecke, eds. 2003. *Alliances for Development: Proceedings of the Americas Conference on Corporate Social Responsibility*. Washington: IDB.

Wood, D. J. 1991. "Corporate Social Performance Revisited." *Academy of Management Review* 16: 691–718.

The Authors

Roberto Gutiérrez is Associate Professor in the School of Administration, University of the Andes, Bogota, Colombia. E-mail: robgutie@uniandes.edu.co.

Audra Jones is Foundation Representative, Inter-American Foundation, 901 N. Stuart Street, Arlington, VA 22203 USA. E-mail: ajones@iaf.gov.

MARKETING OF HARMFUL PRODUCTS

Laura Radulian
University of Economics (VSE), Prague, Czech Republic

Abstract

The paper focuses on the rapidly evolving concept of "harmful products" and its connection with marketing practices. It examines (a) products generally recognized as harmful, and (b) innocuous products that are sometimes (unintentionally) transformed into harmful ones by marketing activities. We indicate how the effects of these activities depend on individual perceptions as well as the norms of social and business ethics. We advocate the creation of marketing codes of ethics for particular product categories, as well as the dissemination of product information that can link the ethical codes with individual values. We illustrate these concepts with a case study of the fragrance industry and olfactory marketing.

Introduction

We live in a rapidly developing world in which consumer demands multiply, producers strive to keep up with the trends, and time-pressed shoppers rely increasingly on information provided through advertising. We buy products to satisfy our wants and needs, but our purchases are influenced by external factors as well as our internal structure and values. We buy in a global market, perhaps without being aware of it, since we tend to think only about the demands of the moment. Companies caught up in the globalization process offer more and more products to meet the needs of their customers—and to create new needs (false or real). It is an environment in which we buy every day but only occasionally reflect on our buying decisions. Did we purchase the right product? Is it useful? Is it healthy? Is it fresh? Is it the best? Is it the right product for our budget? Is it *harmful*?

"Harmful" is a word we hear more frequently nowadays, as we become more concerned about the content of the ready-made meal, cakes, or soap we use daily. We think about what might be harmful to ourselves and to the environment. We involve ourselves in campaigns and take positions in the fight against harmful products featured in the media. We might be for or against McDonald's, for instance, in the debate about the effects of McMeals on health and obesity, but does this mean that if we are against, we will never eat at McDonald's?

The concept of harmfulness in the public mind relates to a number of subjective or *internal factors* such as learning, perception, personality, and emotions, as well as

pp. 329–357

such *external factors* as culture, values, demographics, social status, and reference groups. It is therefore important to try to understand how people perceive harmfulness in products and advertising.

Everyone is familiar with the idea of "harmful products." The media are full of campaigns against them. Our response is to interpret them in our own subjective way. We may learn something from many of the campaigns but fail to change our behavior accordingly, while other campaigns may teach lessons that become part of our lives. Either case presents an interesting subject of analysis.

The issue should be addressed at a social level as well as the level of an individual purchase decision. Societies can be more or less developed with respect to whether they provide consumers the necessary information to judge a product as harmful or good. In a less developed society, for instance, we may be unable to compare products but may be obliged to buy what we find on the market without regard to our health or the environment.

Theoretical Background

Definition of Harmful Products

A brief and general definition of harmful products might be "products that can damage, physically or morally, the life of the consumer or the lives of people around the consumer, or that can have negative effects on the environment."

In view of the current importance of the harmful products issue, we conducted research with the help of students at the Academy of Economic Studies in Prague and Bucharest. A questionnaire[1] dealing with harmful products was completed by about sixty students from these schools. When requested to define "harmful products," all of the students gave the definition just cited, which is not surprising, since harmful products are precisely the products that damage the person (physically or mentally) and the environment.

It is interesting to analyze the categories of products the students considered harmful. Figures 1 and 2 show the breakdown of all responses (three responses per questionnaire) by food category. In answer to the question, "Which products do you consider harmful?" respondents in both countries mentioned food[2] products most often (32 percent of responses given by Czech students, 61 percent for Romanian students). Chemicals and gasoline station products (a threat to the environment) tied for the second most often mentioned by Czech students. Some cosmetic products and cigarettes were the second and third most often mentioned by the Romanians. The least mentioned categories in both countries were medicines and candy.

The definition of harmful products is clearly connected with education and state of mind (individual factors) as well as the cultural environment and economic development (external factors). This was borne out by the results of our research. Different categories of harmful products were mentioned by Romanian and Czech students in the questionnaire.

The list of harmful products varies from person to person, and from one time period to another. At the beginning of the questionnaire students were asked to mention

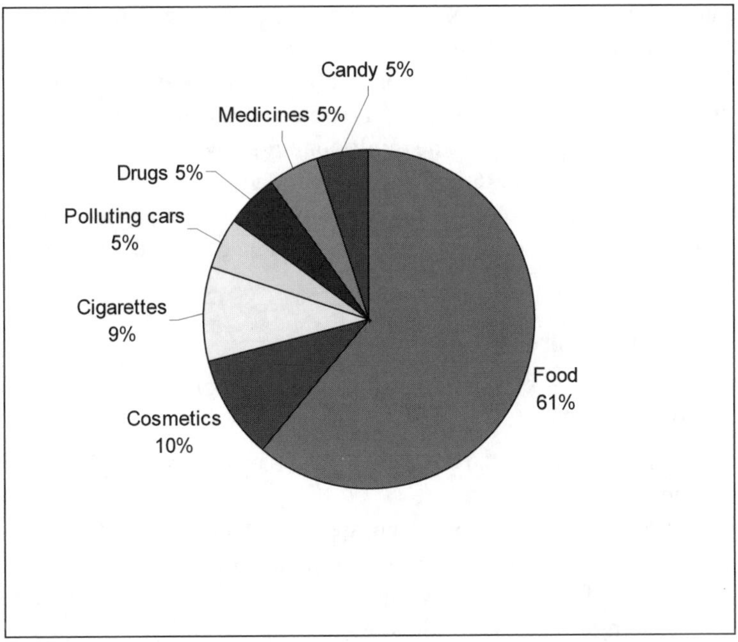

Figure 1. Categories of products considered harmful by Romanian students.

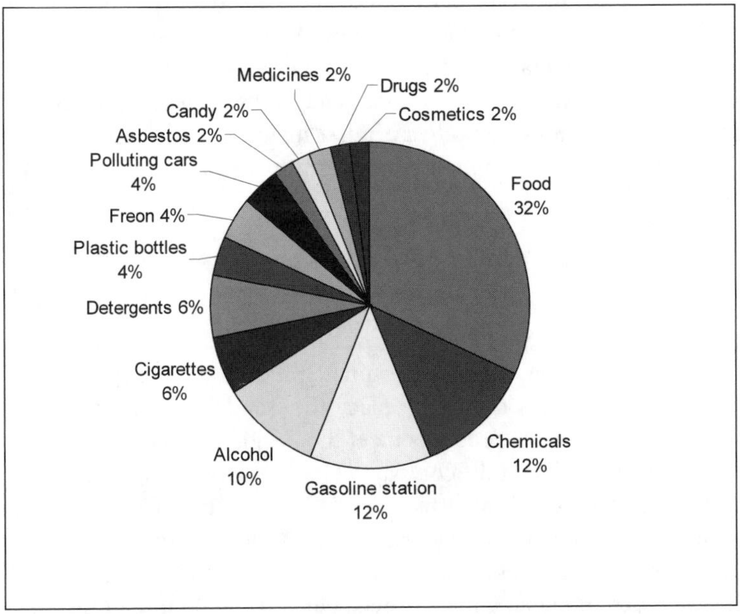

Figure 2. Categories of products considered harmful by Czech students.

three products they consider harmful and, at the end of the questionnaire, they were given a list of five products and asked to characterize them. These five were products that had been the subject of legislation or identified in the literature as harmful (e.g., Nestlé's infant milk formula, polyester attire, etc.).[3] Students sometimes mentioned these products at the beginning of the questionnaire as well.

The respondents therefore define harmful products broadly to include not only such items as alcohol and cigarettes that are conventionally regarded as harmful, but a number of other products on the market that can a negative effect on the consumer or the environment.

Classification of Harmful Products

Harmful products can be classified as illegal (e.g., illicit drugs) and legal. In the second category we include:

- harmful products that can be legally sold if they bear warnings (e.g.: cigarettes, alcohol);
- "good and useful" products that are transformed to harmful ones (or are revealed as harmful) by some additional factor, such as
  - failure of users to follow the instructions on the label (e.g., household cleaning products, Nestlé's Infant Milk Formula);
  - subsequent scientific research that discovers harmful effects (e.g.: anti-bacterial cleaning substances, cosmetic chemicals);
  - poor quality (e.g., food in restaurants).

We must not forget that the concept of harmfulness can receive many interpretations. For example, a successful and widely-used product can be perceived as harmful by some people. As seen by many consumers, a polyester dress is a garment that is easy to clean, requires little ironing, feels good, and looks perfect after being worn five hours, but people who are averse to artificial materials may regard it as harmful. Conversely, a product widely regarded as harmful can meet a real need for some people (e.g., smoking).

General Considerations about Harmful Products

There is no shortage of campaigns and social activism against harmful products that are illegal, such as drugs. Society in general fights against them. A question mark appears, however, when we consider legitimate products that may be harmful.

Thousands of companies nowadays place thousands of products on the market. It may be assumed that these products meet thousands of needs, so long as they are purchased and make profits for the company. The companies employ a wide variety of marketing strategies, of which advertising and the company image are very important elements. Some of these marketing activities may transform innocuous products into harmful ones, a process that has subjective as well as objective aspects. We will analyze this process and explore what a marketing specialist can do to minimize its effects.

At this point numerous questions arise. Do such products as cigarettes and alcohol respond to real or false needs? Is the trade in these products ethical or not? When is it the consumer's fault that he or she is harmed by such products as anti-bacterial agents, and when is it due to a lack of information? Should we go back in time and use traditional cleaning methods, such as scrubbing the tile with vinegar and water rather than powerful chemical products, or is it just a question of providing more information?

These questions have social, moral and ethical aspects that should be analyzed in order to give complete and coherent answers. Legislation and the ethical norms vary from country to country. But the main common element is a concern for providing information about the possible harmful effects of the product.

Given that we live in an information society, it should not be a problem to provide everyone the relevant facts. Access to information is normal and routine, and we are exposed to it in great quantity. Yet do we have the time and concentration to pay attention to and understand each piece of information?

The Marketing Mix and Harmful Products

Marketing, which focuses on consumer demand and people's needs (Kotler 2002), should be distinguished from *selling*, which focuses only on the company's results (the financial aspect) without regard to consumers and their needs. Marketing is commonly viewed as consisting of four components, known as the *marketing mix*: product, price, place (distribution), and promotion.

When discussing the marketing of legal products, we should take into consideration two aspects: on the one hand, the possible influence of different parts of the marketing mix on the process of transformation of an innocuous product into a harmful one and, on the other hand, how companies can react to this process and reverse it.

We classify legitimate harmful products as follows:

- inherently harmful products that can be legitimately sold with proper notification of the dangers, and
- inherently innocuous products that can be transformed into harmful ones by various elements of the marketing mix.

We follow this classification from here out, in order to cover the entire range of harmful products, to understand the differences existing between them at the marketing mix level, and to try to find solutions in either category.

The Marketing Mix and Harmful Products that Can Be Sold with Proper Warning

Legal and social rules determine the selection of harmful products that are available on the market when accompanied by proper warnings. People in general already regard these products as harmful, and the restrictions are nothing new. Everyone knows, for example, that certain products must bear a warning (tobacco/alcohol "is dangerous to your health"), that such products cannot be distributed to minors, and that the price includes special taxes in order to discourage use.

At the advertising level, however, some questions can arise. The legal framework may restrict tobacco companies from showing cigarette smoking in their advertisements, which is why the advertisements have begun promoting positive images and stereotypes of product users. Marlboro, for example, advertises its products by using images of tough cowboys who ride freely in the mountains. In this case, the use of such an image-based technique proves its deceptiveness. Does smoking actually give you freedom? Do you become a "tough American cowboy" by smoking Marlboros? In another case, according to Smith and Cooper-Martin, "R. J. Reynolds Tobacco Company (RJR) was accused of marketing its product, Uptown, to African-American smokers. RJR later introduced Dakota brand cigarettes. This product was aimed at young, poorly educated, blue collar, white females" (Smith and Cooper-Martin 1997). Both of these commercials were denounced for targeting a vulnerable group of consumers.

Elements of the Marketing Mix that Can Transform a Product into a Harmful One

We live in a society of marketing messages and images. Marketing strategies and their tools are used to promote products on the market, survive intense competition, attract the interest of consumers, and convince them to buy.

However, the various elements of the marketing mix can transform a product into a harmful one, without anyone's intending to do so. This assertion is supported by our research. The students who responded to our questionnaire collectively saw all

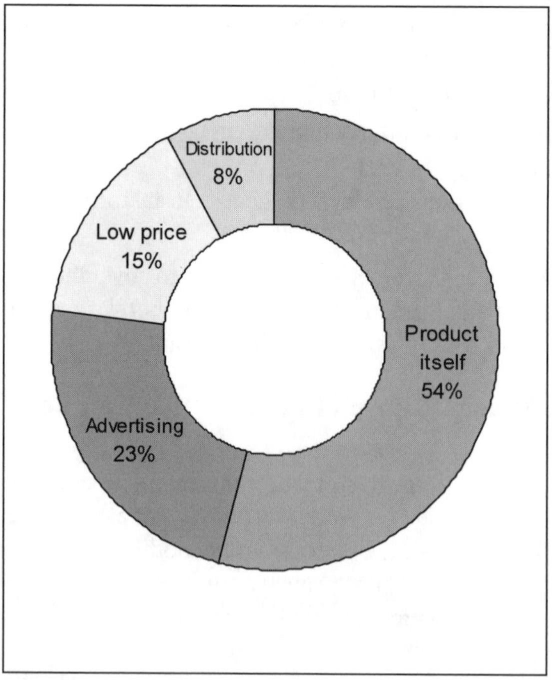

Figure 3. Elements of marketing mix that can transform products into harmful ones, according to Romanian students.

four components of the marketing mix as negatively influencing a product's effect (Figs. 3 and 4).

The largest number of students found the source of the harmful effects in the *product itself* (composition, shape, expiration date, etc). Twenty-six percent of the Czech respondents versus 23 percent of the Romanians attributed the harmful effects to *advertising*, while the Czech students did not consider *price* (specifically, a low price) to be a harmful indicator. In order to better understand how different elements can influence the "four P's" of the marketing mix, we analyze them in detail.

Product

When we buy something, we actually buy a complex package: a product, a service, information concerning the product, a formula (for chemicals and food), and a mode of use. Are we sure that this package provides us with the necessary information to be sure that the product is not somehow harmful? Even if so, does the information attract our attention?

A product is the sum of its utilities that consumers attach to it. Even if people, when asked, can cite a large number of attributes that would induce them to buy a product, it has been shown that, in reality, they consider three or at most four attributes, and no

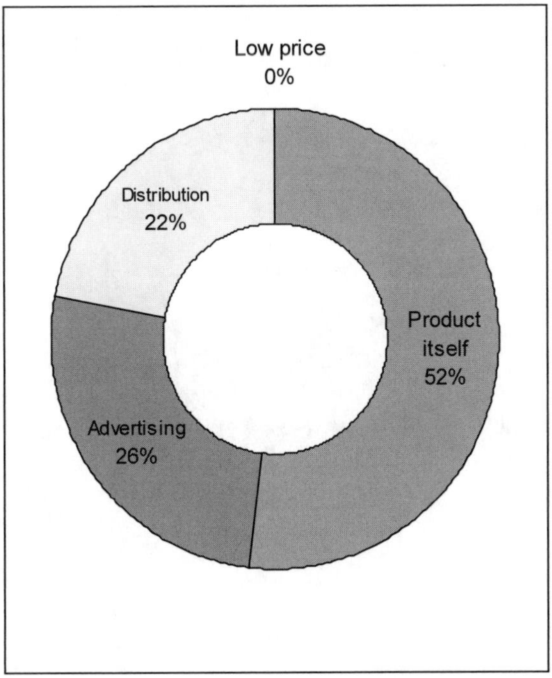

Figure 4. Elements of marketing mix that can transform products into harmful ones, according to Czech students.

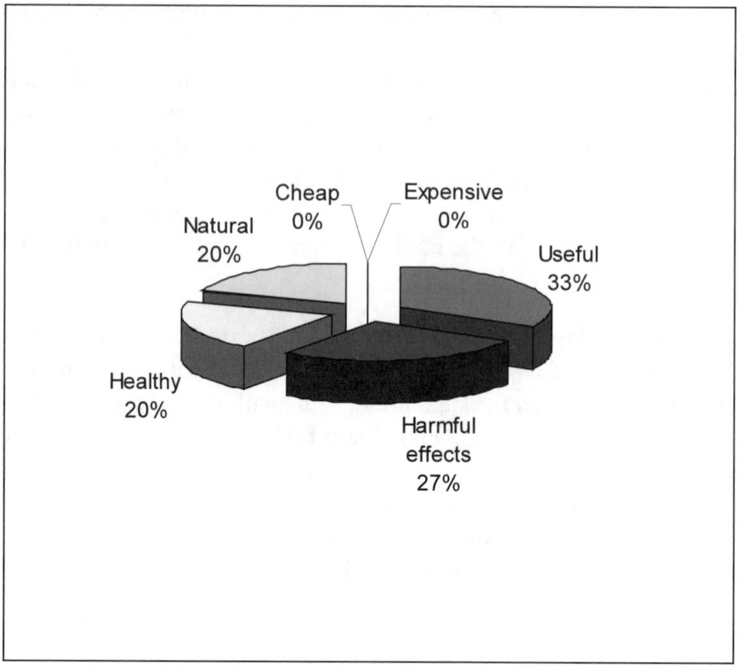

Figure 5. Product attributes that Romanian respondents consider when making purchase decisions.

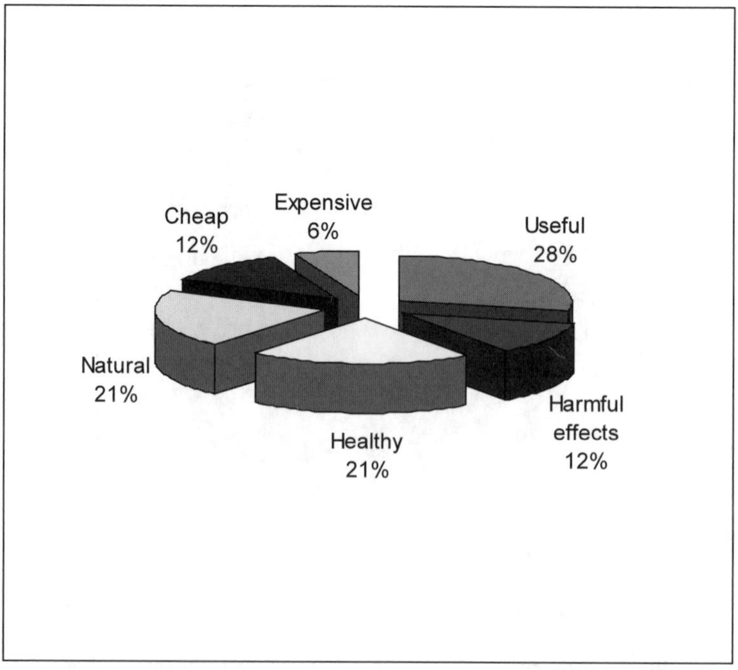

Figure 6. Product attributes that Czech respondents consider when making purchase decisions.

more, when buying the product. By way of example, we present in Figs. 5 and 6 the attributes that our respondents take into consideration when they buy a product.

In the modern world, any company that wishes to launch a product develops a wide range of studies of market characteristics, people's needs, the evolution of potential demand, and so forth. People sometimes buy products without checking the contents or even the expiration date. We need milk and we just decide quickly among low fat milk, chocolate milk, or one and one-half liter cartons, on the assumption that the shop is responsible for checking the expiration date. Some product characteristics that can transform an innocuous product into a harmful one are considered below.

Expiration date. A customer who buys a product that is past its expiration date can contact the local office for consumer protection to register a complaint about the supermarket where he/she bought the product, throw it away, and never buy that particular product again. The product's brand image will suffer because injured customers do not have the time to think about who actually bears the responsibility. They just know that they paid a certain price for a defective product and had to throw it away. In a developed economy, customer satisfaction is the rule. Bad management of stock can damage the producer's image (halo effect). This is why the producer should closely collaborate with the distributor.

In the Czech Republic there are supermarkets where food products with an imminent expiration date (within one or two days) are sold from special shelves with a price discount. In this case consumers are alerted to the condition of the product. They can decide whether they want to buy it and use it before the expiration date.

Packaging. Sometimes a product that is safe and popular with consumers comes in packaging that can damage the environment if not correctly recycled. Is this a harmful product? Not at all, in the customer's opinion. The customer buys the product and enjoys using it, since it answers to his needs completely. But suppose the plastic packaging is incinerated by mistake and pollutes the air that the buyer and others breathe. If the damage is discovered, responsibility probably will not be assigned to those who burned the trash but to the producer, since the packaging will always wear its logo.

Composition. Product content, especially in the case of food products, is always an important consideration for avoiding harm. Such additives[4] as E330 (citric acid) and E123 (amaranth-based dye, known as Red No. 2 in the U.S., where it is banned) tend to be noticed only by people who are very concerned about nutrition. Even if they are noticed, they are not necessarily avoided, since we do not know exactly how much harm they can do or what are the long term consequences. Some people simply avoid certain "E"s that various articles on the Internet have singled out as the most dangerous. But they do not know why these foods are dangerous. Whose fault is this? A consumer with little free time to cook may select instant mashed potatoes or instant soup. Even if the advertising says that the product is made of fresh vegetables, attentively selected and full of vitamins, it is obvious that it probably includes chemical additives that may harm any organism that consumes it over an extended period of time.

The questions surrounding the composition of just one product are quite complicated. On the one hand, scientific research tends to replace additives with new ones that are considered healthier or more appropriate, while on the other hand, research can prove that substances once considered safe are harmful (e.g., antibacterial products). Researchers for St. Jude Children's Research Hospital report that using antibacterial products may actually make drug-resistant strains of bacteria more prevalent.[5] These products introduce into the environment an antibacterial compound called triclosan, which interacts with bacteria and causes them to develop a resistance to the compound. Thus, the accumulation of triclosan in the environment could lead to the emergence of drug-resistant bacteria.

A briefing[6] promulgated by the American Medical Association stressed that people should not only stop overusing antibiotics, but they should also stop buying anti-bacterial soaps and detergents, which can also build up bacterial resistance. The Canadian government currently prohibits the use of three substances: chloroform, estrogenic compounds, and mercury. It also requires products to be "safe for their intended usage."

Improper use. The consumer, as well as the company, can transform a product into a harmful one—by using it improperly. For example, an iron made by a reputable manufacturer becomes a harmful product if it is not used with the proper quantity of water and at the right temperature. It will not only fail to work properly but will destroy clothing.

Quality. Fluctuation in quality is an important factor that can easily transform a good product into a harmful one. This is especially true for food products. If the quality of one single ingredient used to prepare a meal in a restaurant is lower than normal, the quality of the meal itself will be poor and may adversely affect the health of patrons.

Quantity. Sometimes using a product (especially food) in excessive quantities can harm one's health. In a January 2004 court case, U.S. District Judge Robert Sweet said: "Don't blame McDonald's that your children are fat." Judge Sweet claimed that "the plaintiffs, including a fourteen-year-old girl who stands 125 centimeters and weighs 82 kilograms, failed to show that customers were unaware that eating too many Big Macs, Chicken McNuggets, and Egg McMuffins could be unhealthy."

According to Richard Berman, executive director of the Center for Consumer Freedom, "anyone with an IQ higher than room temperature understands that the best way to stay healthy is to enjoy a variety of foods in moderation—and, of course, to exercise regularly." The McDonald's food chain presented evidence that it has provided nutrition information to customers for more than thirty years. According to statistics cited by Judge Sweet, Americans spend more than $110 billion on fast food each year, and studies show that on any given day in the United States, almost one in four adults visits a fast-food restaurant. The situation is beginning to be the same in European countries.

In similar fashion, chocolate or sweets can have negative effects on the health if consumed in large quantities. We must stress that the chocolate in itself is not a harmful product; quite the opposite! Information on the ill effects of huge quantities of chocolate, coffee, Coca-Cola, and so forth, is available everywhere. The consumer simply must be willing to access and understand this information. Not all consumers can be excused from responsibility on the ground that they honestly do not understand the dangers of the products they are consuming or using.[7]

Scientific research, product changes, consumer experience, and one's state of mind and knowledge all influence what is placed in the category of "harmful products." We should stress once again the subjective character of this classification. For example, cigarettes represent a need for some people and a genuinely harmful product for others.

In order to reduce the controversy around certain products and find a new source of income, businesses have begun to offer product substitutes and complements that can diminish or eliminate the harmful effect of the originals. Smoke-eating candles reportedly reduce the effects of second-hand cigarette smoke, sugar substitutes reduce calories, plastic gloves and special creams diminish the effect of washing powder on skin, and solid deodorants avoid damage inflicted by aerosol sprays on both the skin and the environment. The list goes on and on. However, the creation of substitutes and complements doesn't mean that the original "harmful" products disappear. Figure 7

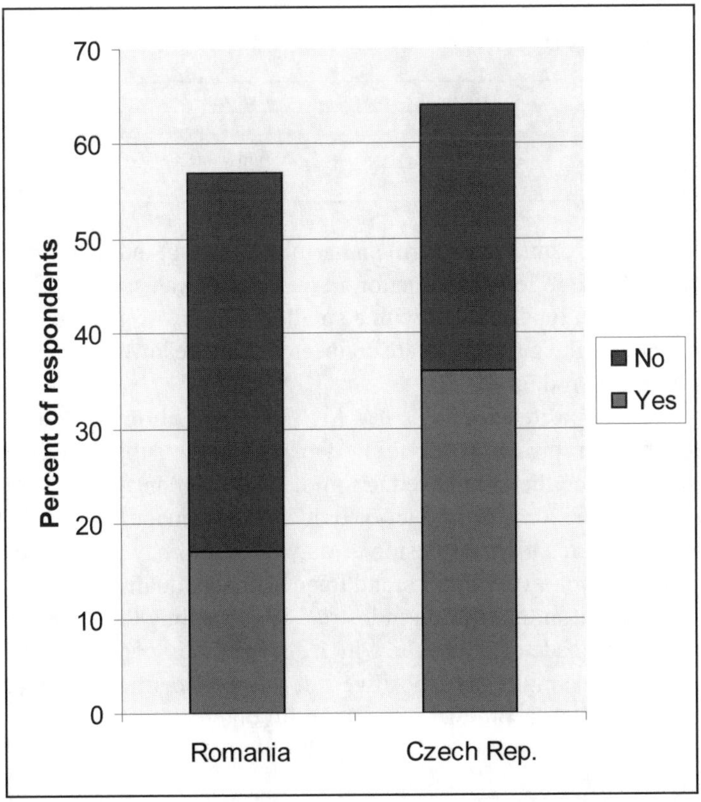

Figure 7. Can a product's harmful effects be neutralized by using another product?

indicates the opinion of respondents as to whether a product's harmful effects can be neutralized by using another product.

Price

Figures 8 and 9 display some factors that students (from the analyzed groups) take into consideration when they buy a product. Price is mentioned most often. When discussing price, it is again important to distinguish products viewed as inherently harmful (cigarettes, alcohol) from normal products that can become harmful for various reasons.

In many countries the price of alcohol and cigarettes is high in order to discourage consumption, usually due to special taxes. This raises the question as to whether the higher prices do not simply reposition the product on the market, since high prices are normally connected with luxury products.

The question of price is much more important for products that are not viewed as inherently harmful. Companies may try to beat the competition by reducing the quality of the product, so as to lower costs and offer it at competitive prices. In this case we might say that price is the reason for the transformation of a normal product into a harmful one, since a low-quality product may be harmful. There are nine quality-price strategies from which a company may choose (Kotler 2002):

Table 1. Quality-price strategies.

Quality/price	High	Medium	Low
High	1. premium	2. high value	3. super value
Medium	4. overcharging	5. mid value	6. good value
Low	7. rip-off	8. false economy	9. economy

The price in itself cannot transform an harmless product into a harmful one. But if a reduction of price follows a reduction in quality, we can speak about a possible harmful effect (e.g., a food product with a smaller quantity of nutritional elements). The last three price strategies, which are connected with the lowest quality,[8] can result in possibly harmful products.

Moving to the opposite extreme, can a high-quality/high-price strategy result in harmful products? In this case everything depends on the subjective interpretation of the consumer, since there is no reduction of quality in an objective sense. Here we must introduce the idea of product or brand-name "image," which is the based on the consumer's perception.[9] A customer may decide to pay high price for a YSL dress on the strength of a very good brand image (image, quality and innovation are particularly important in the fashion industry). She may buy the dress even if it includes an accessory made of polyester, which she normally considers harmful. This may be an extreme example, but a positive image can nonetheless increase the risk of transforming a harmless product into a harmful one.

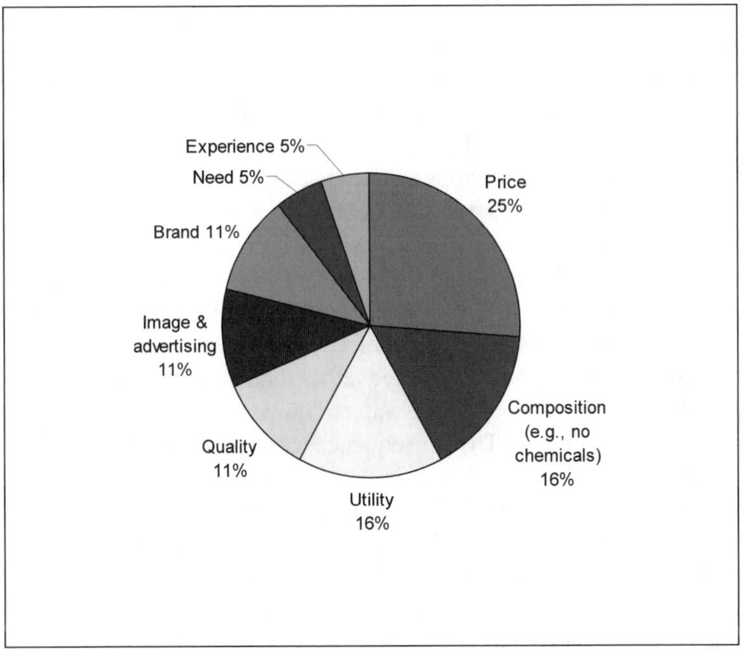

Figure 8. Factors that Romanian respondents consider when making purchase decisions.

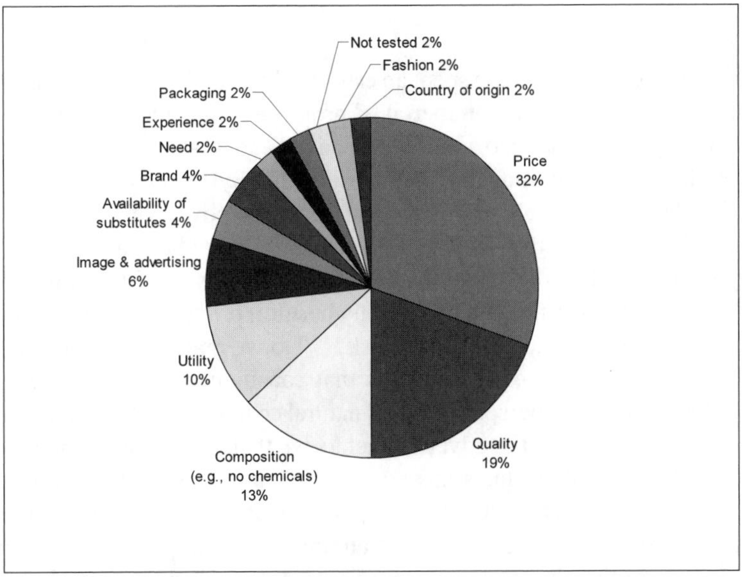

Figure 9. Factors that Czech respondents consider when making purchase decisions.

Place (Distribution)

There have been studies of mothers' complaints about the positioning of sweets near the cashier's counter, where children see them at the end of an exhausting shopping experience with Mom and want to buy them (LSA 2002). Sweets in themselves are not harmful. They become harmful for mothers who must refuse their children's wants or buy sweets for them at an inappropriate time (e.g., before lunch). Where should one sell sweets? Where should one sell alcohol or cigarettes?

Another well-known case concerns Nestlé, which distributed samples of its new infant milk formula in hospitals and maternity wards, where it could make direct contact with mothers, and where the specialized medical environment suggested that doctors approve of the formula and considered it useful and correct for babies. Mothers sometimes used the product out of choice rather than necessity, as a replacement for their own milk (as it was easier). Some watered down the milk because they could not afford to use it in full strength. The consequence was that some babies died. Nestlé was accused of causing the deaths and "manipulating" mothers to use Nestlé's milk instead of breast milk through an immoral marketing scheme that took advantage of their emotional state of mind just after giving birth, when they are easily influenced.

The method of distribution can also transform a safe product into a harmful one. For example, food products transported in the wrong way (inadequate refrigeration, beyond the expiration date, etc.) could transform them into harmful products, since the ultimate consumers could be harmed.

Distribution therefore raises questions of both business ethics (products should be transported under appropriate conditions) and social ethics (products should be positioned in shops so as not to harm children or others). The next major section will deal with ethics and in particular the equilibrium between business and social ethics.

Promotion and Advertising

"By the time we die, we will have spent an estimated one and a half years just watching TV commercials. Exposed to commercials' promises, consumers not only lose their decision making rights, but also are being deceived and misled with chimeras offered to them by the advertising industry" (Sutherland and Sylvester 1993).

We often hear people talk about the manipulative power of promotion and the media, and about the fact that they feel "obliged" to buy when sales people "make" them buy with a "pushy" presentation of the product or brand. Therefore we can ask ourselves: "Are we manipulated when we buy harmful products, or do we know about possible harmful effects and assume the risk?" "Do we really have a choice?" "How exposed are we to promotional strategies that can induce us to consume harmful products?" For example, a person who uses natural cosmetic products may start to use synthetic products because the advertisement says that they hydrate the face during winter, while the natural products meet only the vitamin needs of the skin.

Another question: "When should we speak about harmful products as opposed to harmful advertising?" McDonald's restaurants, for example, tend to be crowded in countries where they have recently been introduced. They are fun, fast, open all day, provide good service, and become part of social and cultural activities (such as birthday parties for children). Despite all this, some articles accuse McDonald's food of being unhealthy and leading to obesity. McDonald's uses both traditional and non-traditional advertising. Does its advertising manipulate people to consume its products in excess?

The power and influence of the media should be considered in any examination of the role of advertising in transforming innocuous products into harmful ones. With respect to the *power* of the media, much rides on the good will of those who write the articles. Public opinion is sensitive to what the articles say, since people usually believe what they read. If a newspaper, for example, spreads the information that a certain product or brand is harmful, it will be very difficult for the producer to regain public trust and rebuild the product image.

The *influence* of media is very strong, especially on children. Beginning at a very young age, we get most of our information from the media, which include television, movies, magazines, the Internet, videos, and all forms of advertising. While the media offer many opportunities for learning and entertainment, media images and messages can contribute to a variety of public health concerns. Research has shown that, among children and adolescents, key areas of concern include aggressive behavior and violence; substance abuse; nutrition, obesity and dieting; and body image and self-concept. All of these directly affect their behavior and are influenced by products they consume—whether properly or improperly, as in the case of drugs.

Another important factor in advertising is the association of a product or brand with a celebrity. The celebrity image may overshadow the harmful character of the product. For example, an actress who appears in an advertisement for L'Oreal may promote a positive image for a product that is generally high quality but is harmful to some users whose skin is sensitive to a substance it contains. A celebrity image can also transform a good product into a negative (harmful) one by falsely raising consumer expectations about their own image if they use the product.

Deceptive advertising is generally understood as advertising that makes false or misleading statements about the product advertised. Advertisers may claim that misleading statements encourage consumers to act in ways harmful to themselves, without actually causing them to do so. Misleading statements nonetheless result in harmful behavior.

Advertising can be deceptive about matters other than the product, and in so doing they can cause depression and psychological stress. Even when promoting health products that can enhance the consumer's well being, advertisers have no right to lie to consumers in other ways, such as through image manipulation. According to Sutherland and Sylvester, when a certain image is used in a commercial message, "what changes is not so much our perception, or image, of the product, as our perception of the *user-stereotype*—the kind of person who typically uses the brand, or the situation in which the brand is typically used." It is true that such advertising can be useful to consumers, even while interfering with their autonomy, for example by making them realize whether a product is suitable for their age. But image-based advertising can have negative effects as well. As Sutherland and Sylvester put it, "if the user image resembles us, or the type of person we aspire to be," such advertising might convince us to buy a certain product. Purchasing the product is not the problem. The actual deception comes with the image to which one might aspire or dream about having for oneself (e.g., that of the movie star who appears in an advertisement for an anti-cellulite cream).

Vulnerable consumers, such as young girls, for example, are exposed to perfect female images on television, in the press, and in their favorite magazines. These consumers do not understand the power of Photoshop, or the miracles that can be done by the right combination of light and makeup. Even if they recognize a professional photograph, or a perfectly air-brushed picture, they are deprived of their autonomy, since such commercials discourage them from using their cognitive skills to make a rational purchasing decision. Such consumers are in danger, since they compare the real, wrinkled, blemished world with the perfect porcelain images on magazine pages, and they try to resemble them.

Calvin Klein's commercials, for example, use the image of the female model Kate Moss, whose body weight is between 40 and 45 kilograms. According to Laurence Levy,[10] "with the great success of fashion model Kate Moss, anorexia is becoming trendy, and with the media advertising anorexia as a 'product,' more than half of the women are on a slimming diet or are planning to do so."[11]

The cases mentioned above, and all the commissions on health care and cosmetic trades, show only one side of the coin. Reasonable persons would ask themselves: Do people who claim to be harmed by commercials and indirectly by the products advertised (especially by cosmetics that may not have the same results as on the face of Catherine Zeta Jones), actually act in good faith and really fail to understand the nature of the products they have been using?

Whatever means of communication is chosen for advertisement, it is very important to transmit genuine information that is understandable and can be easy remembered.

Marketing of Harmful Products

Marketing is a science that analyses the market in all its aspects. It is goes far beyond the simple desire to sell. Marketing and image have become key strengths of a company, and this is not just a temporary fashion. Consumers and their needs have become so sophisticated that marketing is nowadays much more than the simple marketing mix. Consumer behavior, psychology, sociology, and motivational analysis are only a few aspects of the field.

In this environment, the company image is naturally connected with its products and marketing strategy, but it can also be judged from the viewpoint of ethics or morals. The difference between the two terms is important, as sometimes it is unclear which one applies. Actually they have the same meaning but come from different roots. *Ethics* comes from the Greek *ethos*, and *morals* comes from the Latin *mores*—the word used by Cicero to translate the Greek *ethos*. Nowadays, morals tend to be associated with social and individual values, and *ethics* is a term widely used in business, as in "business ethics" (Donaldson 1989).

What is the place of ethics in the business world? Ethics should understand economics and economics should understand ethics.

In the broadest sense, the responsibilities of business are economic, legal, and ethical in nature. If legal and economic norms are spelled out in official rulebooks and legal statutes, ethical responsibility is defined in a more general way. It depends on individual as well as social values, it is created and developed by and for society, and it is the foundation for the existence of any business. Here we must stress the difference between *ethics* and *etiquette* (Heiderich 2003), the first term referring to true values, understood as such and observed by the company in good faith, and the second term referring only to company actions that maintain a positive image in the public mind, without any real concern for the values themselves.

Why should companies observe such social rules as discharging their economic responsibilities, obeying the law, behaving ethically, and voluntarily attempting to meet social expectations? (Hay 1989). They do it in the first place because they want to survive in the market and make a profit. The social value of its activity also creates a positive image for the company, which is very important in today's image-based culture. We may therefore say that there is a positive correlation between ethics and profitability. But if ethical values are not understood and followed consistently, there is a significant risk of destroying the company image and transforming its products into harmful ones.

In order to show their commitment to ethical behavior and social values, companies have begun to create ethical codes. These codes set general moral principles on which rational people can agree. They provide incentives for compliance, with the aim of becoming a self-enforcing system of norms. Business ethics has been a very fashionable term since the 1980s, and corporate ethical codes have become the main tool for implementing ethics within firms. In the U.S. there has been a rapid dissemination of documents that are clearly recognizable as ethical codes, despite their differences in form and structure. According to some empirical surveys, only 8 percent of the largest American companies had ethical codes in 1980, but by 1990 the number had reached 85 percent.

Ethical codes are highly relevant to the concerns of this paper. They can become part of the solution when innocuous products are transformed into harmful ones. We have seen that this kind of transformation is difficult to define objectively, which suggests a need for ethical codes that pertain to particular products or categories of products (not only at the company level). Of course the wide range of products that companies offer nowadays will not make things easy, but maybe one can start a trend!

This paper has tried to demonstrate the importance of marketing as a factor in the consumption of harmful products. The rapid development of the marketing field will probably lead to the creation of a subfield that deals specifically with harmful effects, a subfield that will certainly require its own rules and norms. We will perhaps speak of the marketing of harmful products as a science in itself and therefore about the ethics of this type of marketing.

There are three approaches to business ethics (Ulrich 1999): corrective business ethics (ethics is seen as an antidote against too much economic rationality), functional business ethics (ethics as a lubricant for more economic rationality), and integrative economic ethics (ethics as a sound basis for a different, value-based economic rationality). Where should one place the ethics of marketing harmful products? Probably in a fourth category!

Ethics for the Marketing for Harmful Products

When it comes to harmful products, business ethics is a must. Accepted norms of business conduct can induce companies that sell such harmful products as cigarettes to acknowledge the effects of these products on consumer health and the environment.

As mentioned earlier, innocuous products can be "harmful" for certain categories of people (e.g., chocolate for persons who are allergic to it, polyester clothes for those with sensitive skin, and synthetic food for those who want a completely natural diet). To be sure, companies do not wish to target these categories of persons. However, they should communicate information about product contents to the general public, including those who are not in the targeted segment—if only to ensure that consumers for whom the product is unsuitable do not spread an unjustly negative reputation for it. At the same time, even information that is correct, understandable, and widely available may attract customers who would normally view the product as harmful. For example, a convinced naturist may start to buy chocolate if it contains no sugar, whereas if the sugar were replaced by honey rather than synthetic sweeteners, the product would again be good from the naturist's point of view.

Knowing and understanding the complaints of people who consider a product "harmful" can be of real benefit to the company that offers the product. This kind of information can form the basis for the creation of a new product and, at the same time, for a future communication campaign. Ethics includes the obligation to communicate, to send correct information to the public about a product, including rules for proper use.

How Do Companies React to Rules of Business Ethics?

Product sales are certainly a company's main objective (the rule of existence). The question is what will be sold, and how it will be sold (the marketing approach).

Business in the present global environment should be carried out responsibly. It should take a deeply global view in a world of political, social and cultural differences. In some cases there is a thin line between harmful products and harmless products, and an equally thin line between the ethical and the unethical.

Philip Morris, which produces Marlboro cigarettes and other leading brands, has taken steps to alert their customers of the dangers of smoking. The company has faced a number of major legal actions in the United States, the most recent being a ten billion USD damages settlement related to its marketing of "light" cigarettes. The company has taken out advertisements in major newspapers to advise customers that "light" cigarettes offer no significant health benefits over any other type of cigarette. The company website is littered with advice on how to quit smoking. The site relates what measures the company is taking to reduce the prevalence of smoking and in particular to discourage young people from taking up of the habit.[12] The company changed its name in 2003 to Altria Group, Inc. The group also includes Kraft foods, which boast such well-known brand names as Nabisco cereals, Oreo cookies, Philadelphia cream cheese, and Maxwell House coffee. The move was viewed with suspicion by anti-smoking groups, one of whom published a web article suggesting that lung cancer could be renamed "Philip Morris," since this name was more universally recognized as being associated with lung cancer than the name "lung cancer" itself! Others have suggested that Altrea advertisements in the British press are designed to head off any potential legal action in the U.K., where litigation has been significant in its absence. Others have suggested that there are enough people in less developed countries to fill any gap left by Europeans who give up smoking or do not start.

Many are asking the logical question: why would a company that makes its money from cigarette sales want to reduce sales and discourage potential customers from taking up the habit? This question is addressed by the company's mission statement. The company recognizes that it must meet the needs of its customers if it is to be successful. If responding to such needs means reduced sales in the future, then the company says, "So be it!" Is this anything more than image-polishing?

Governments and trade commissions have imposed rules and norms that limit the distribution of products generally recognized as harmful, in order to reduce the negative effects, or if that is not possible, at least to inform consumers about effects that can change their lives. These rules limit the type of advertising that producers can use (e.g., they are not allowed to show cigarettes in advertisements). As a result producers are moving in new promotional directions, the most popular of which is BTL (below the line) advertising. Companies that sell alcohol and cigarettes involve themselves in cultural and social activities, which are generally acceptable to society and provide a means to promote the products indirectly. For example, the companies sponsor social, sporting, and cultural events. It is unclear, incidentally, whether this form of promotion is sufficient for their purposes. Their products are directed toward certain needs that are perhaps rooted in human nature, but a person will not start to drink just because he saw the brand-name of a brand on a banner announcing a cultural event.

We might conclude that the same authorities that restrict advertising of harmful products tolerate a different kind of promotion of these same products, since they permit cigarette and alcohol companies to divert money from advertising to social and cultural events. During the past fifty years, R. J. Reynolds Tobacco built a legacy of caring and corporate responsibility by giving millions of dollars to support education, economic development, tobacco agricultural programs at land-grant universities, and many more worthy causes. Notable contributions include those to the North Carolina Zoo; the North Carolina Aquarium; Old Salem, Inc.; the United Way of Forsyth County; the Arts Council of Forsyth County; Forsyth County schools; Yadkin County schools; Winston-Salem State University; and Wake Forest University Medical School.

In addition, RJRT employees have the opportunity to direct funds to nonprofit organizations through plans sponsored by the R. J. Reynolds Foundation.

The actions certainly do not diminish the effects of cigarettes and alcohol, but they substantially enhance the image of companies that distribute and sell these products. BTL advertising has a strong impact by creating an image of a company that helps society, supports the cultural environment, and so forth. Does image-building neutralize the harmful effects of the product? Certainly not. The image does change the product itself but only turns attention away from it.

Kraft, maker of such favorites as Oreo cookies, has announced plans to fight rising obesity in America (Barboza 2003). The food giant said it would eliminate in-school marketing to children, introduce smaller portion sizes, and develop healthier and more nutritious products. Obesity puts many people at risk for heart disease and increased health care costs. But let's remember that what seems so need not be so. Kraft is not just looking out for our midriffs, but is trying to avoid an increasing number of lawsuits against food companies that market products that contribute to health problems. In other words, they want to avoid getting into the same hot water that burned tobacco companies. In any case, it is welcome news that major food companies are moving to a healthier line of products. If one goes into health/natural foods stores today, the price is ridiculously high compared to the likes of Kraft foods.

We cannot go back in time by renouncing useful products we now regard as harmful. Society must move ahead. Even if a product is discovered to contain harmful substances, research can help replace these substances with new ones. This is itself a form of social progress.

The survey respondents, when asked about the marketing of products they considered harmful, said that marketing practices are not good, but they welcome the economic development of which these practices are a part. People fear "harmful products" but probably fear the term more than the products themselves, since they often pay little attention to what they are buying. They are uncomfortable when they lack full information. They are nervous about seeing "E's" in the ingredients list on a package of biscuits, but they are not sure what "E" means! The harmful products issue in the food industry has generated much controversy. After reading articles on the Internet about which is the more dangerous type of E, and after learning them by heart (without knowing what exactly they mean), consumers where surprised to find Es disappearing from food packaging. Regulators in Romania had decided to oblige producers to print the full name of an additive rather than the E code, on the theory that this would better equip consumers to defend themselves from harmful substances. As a result the situation became even worse. Since consumers have little knowledge of the relevant chemical compounds, they can no longer tell whether a pack of biscuits contains any harmful substances. Even the small amount of information they had is now lost!

In conclusion, companies that offer good products on the market are exposed to the risk that they may be transformed into harmful products. To manage a wide range of products and minimize this risk, companies should consider creating ethical codes for harmful products. The variety of products on the market will certainly make this initiative difficult, but it is necessary nonetheless. Communication between regulatory bodies and consumers is also very important. The subjective character of a good vs. a harmful product can be confusing if this kind of dialogue does not exist. Communication in turn requires appropriate infrastructure and education. People should be educated about business ethics and social ethics, good vs. harmful products, compounds often found in products, and institutions that can offer help when needed. Another dimension of the debate is terminology. Regulatory bodies, companies, and consumers should speak the same language when discussing harmful products.

Marketing of Harmful Products in Some Ex-Communist Countries

Harmful products that are legally available with notification, along with good products that can be transformed into harmful ones by different elements of the marketing mix, can be found in any economy. A shampoo component that recent research has shown harmful has the same effect on consumers in any country. But even though the effects are the same, the problem should be dealt with differently, depending on the level of economic development, as well as the perceptions and knowledge of the population. Neither a closed economy nor a subsistence economy allows its members the possibility of comparison shopping, or the luxury of thinking about possible harmful effects.

The purpose of this chapter is not to discuss general marketing ethics in ex-Communist countries, but to examine how their marketing and concepts of harmful products have evolved since the introduction of a market economy. It is important to see how these concepts have been perceived and have developed.

Harmful Products Available on the Market with Notification

Legislation regarding such products as cigarettes and alcohol are the same in ex-Communist countries as in EU countries, since many of them are already members of the EU or will become so in the near future.

Innocuous Products that Can Be Transformed into Harmful Ones

A marketing mix for these products necessarily developed quickly during the transition to a market economy. However, the product itself, the distribution, and the price did not create so many problems as the advertising.

Below are some examples of promotion and advertising techniques in Romania immediately after 1989.[13]

- Advertisements talked exaggeratedly about the qualities of the product (it was difficult to tell the difference between products).
- Consumer behavior was not properly studied (it was difficult to discover what consumers viewed as harmful).
- Products were advertised mainly on TV and radio. Later on, interest developed in outdoor advertising, etc.
- Advertising was created simultaneously with the market penetration of new foreign brands.
- The product guarantee, contents, and instructions for proper use were not considered important.

All these elements represented sources of risk for the transformation of a good product into a harmful one. The lack of instructions for proper use could harm the user, the exaggeration of product qualities in advertisements could lead to misunderstanding about the product, and so forth.

Aside from these, some additional factors led to the creation of harmful products in ex-Communist countries. First there was the technology of production.[14] High-quality ingredients for chocolate, for example, are useless if the mixing machines are made of low-quality metal. The final product can be harmful to the consumer. Other problems included hygienic norms, industrial reorganization, and the management of scientific research. Scientific research is both the source of harmful product identification and the antidote for harmful effects, since science can discover new substances to replace the harmful ingredients.

The marketing environment evolved rapidly. Marketing in general, and marketing of harmful products in particular, are now common ideas that public institutions in these countries deal with regularly. In their rush toward international marketing norms, these countries were able to escape some of the developmental stages, which is a good thing. For example, when a shampoo compound on the market elsewhere was discovered to be harmful, the ex-Communist country was in a position to develop a substitute before the shampoo entered its own market. This saved time and money and provided occasions to develop new products.

We discussed the necessity of introducing a marketing code of ethics at the national and international level for harmful products. The fact that some ex-Communist countries escaped some developmental stages can call for different codes, depending on the evolution of marketing practices in each country.

Case Study: The Fragrance Industry and Olfactory Marketing

The Fragrance Industry

Perfume is one of the oldest products in the world. Originally made from natural flower petals, fragrances developed gradually into the major industry they are today. Fragrances are bought all over the world, in different quantities, at different kinds of shops, for different personalities.

Beauty products and fragrances present the marketing specialist with a greater challenge than mass-produced products. They play more with senses and feelings; they are more connected to people's psychological structure, to the image that people want to have about themselves. And if we add to these a new shopping concept and a new formula for the distribution of luxury beauty products, we have a general image of what the fragrance industry is all about today.

The philosophy of modern fragrance marketing is based on new ideas of freedom (the client may walk freely in a wide sales area, smelling and touching new fragrances, and letting herself be guided by her feelings and mood), beauty (an impressive number of products to enhance the entire body and its equilibrium), and pleasure (skin tests for choosing the right fragrance, etc).

New fragrances and new concepts of shopping and promotion open a world of "good" beauty-enhancing products.

However, there are people and organizations that view fragrances as harmful. For example, Mary Lamielle, president of the National Center for Environmental Health Strategies lists in a 1990 press release[15] the following symptoms induced by fragrances: "watery eyes, double vision, sneezing, stuffiness, allergic rhinitis, sinusitis, tinnitus, dizziness, vertigo, coughing, bronchitis, difficulty breathing, chest tightness, asthma, anaphylaxis, headache, migraine, cluster headaches, seizures, convulsions, fatigue, confusion, disorientation, incoherence, short term memory loss, anxiety, irritability, depression, mood swings, rashes, hives, eczema, flushing, muscle and joint inflammation, pain and weakness, irregular or rapid heartbeat hypertension." The recent history of two products used by the fragrance industry may help explain some of these symptoms and raise some additional concerns.

Case 1. Musk AETT (musk tetralin) was commonly used until the late 1970s.[16] In 1977, it was shown that Musk AETT caused permanent brain damage in laboratory animals, and further research disclosed additional adverse health effects, including vascular degeneration of the brain, spinal cord, and peripheral nerves; hyperactivity and irritability; weakness; foot drop; and irreversible degradation of the central nervous system. It was voluntarily withdrawn by the fragrance industry after twenty-one years of use.

Case 2. In 1994, Musk Ambrette was identified as causing "central and peripheral nervous system damage." It was voluntarily withdrawn from the market by the fragrance industry.

Since the industry withdrew these products voluntarily, no government regulation was enacted to require their removal. Unfortunately, tests by the U.S. Food and Drug Administration for the presence of Musk Ambrette in 1989, 1990, and 1992 found products in the marketplace still containing this substance. This raises serious questions about the effectiveness of the industry's self-imposed withdrawal.

At the present time there is no requirement for the testing of scented products for chronic neurotoxic effects. There is also no way to predict how many of the chemicals are dangerous, or how long they will damage health before the hazards are identified. In a study on Musk AETT, Dr. Peter Spencer concluded that many other widely used aromatic hydrocarbons have properties similar to Musk AETT and should be tested for possible neurotoxic properties. Unfortunately such testing is not yet required. "Perfumes and their constituent chemicals are subjected to relatively little legislative control, apart from that imposed on all chemicals" (Cooke 1994). The voluntary withdrawal of known hazards does not appear to be working. In one instance it took twenty-one years of use before the health hazards of a product were proven conclusively enough for it to be voluntarily withdrawn.

Yet fragrances exist and will continue to exist, since they are part of our lives and help us build an image for ourselves. Scientists will continue to do research, but solutions must be found for the survival of fragrance industry.

Olfactory Marketing

In addition to the existence of harmful fragrances, one must consider the practice of *olfactory marketing*. Why? Because this is a new trend in marketing, a new technique for attracting clients in a selling area by wafting a scent that can be identified with a particular brand. This new technique imposes on the shopper the very products that we found can be harmful: fragrances. Is this ethical?

Marketing nowadays must compete with talent and tenacity. Its power increases as we witness the creation of a kind of marketing underworld. We can speak, even if without total confidence, about the marketing of image, the marketing of senses, and in this last category, olfactory marketing, which has become very fashionable.

Today consumers are more sophisticated than those of yesterday. They are in a hurry, demand more, and are more influenced by the world around them. Consequently, they become more refined, deeper, more cultivated . . . more *sensorial*. Why sensorial? It is because we are victims of the information society. We are constantly bombarded with information. The only remaining doors to our awareness are our senses, which are exploited more and more, to the point that we can neither resist nor escape their manipulation.

Marketing in general already uses images, sounds, tastes, and touch to direct the public's attention to a product or service. The fifth sense, smell, has lately become part of marketing activity and image-creating strategies. Olfactory marketing uses odors for marketing and commercial aims. We can speak today about the scent of a shop, the scent of a promotional object, the scent of the logo. Even the company itself may have a scent, perhaps the perfume that creates the company image and identifies it henceforth. The fragrance is in the product, advertising panels, promotional objects, and perfumes discreetly spread in the selling area.

It is certain that perfumes will continue to exist, and it will be difficult to convince consumers that they can be harmful. But given that they may contain harmful substances, is it not appropriate to ask if the use of fragrances in promotion is ethical? Advertisers connect the product with certain images—images that we associate with wearing a certain fragrance, as well as images we have about ourselves. The same effect is achieved when a fragrance is "worn" by a company. We live in a business world governed by marketing, communication, and image. The practice of associating fragrances with company names and logos was born as a natural consequence of the rapid development of marketing science. Is this use of fragrance ethical? At first glance, a fragrance that simply recalls a brand without having harmful effects on consumers seems ethical. But the debate is far more complicated than this.

Conclusions

We live, and buy to satisfy our needs, in a global business environment. Companies, in turn, try to deal with this reality by adapting their products and strategies to this new dimension of the business world.

Companies offer and consumers demand a vast array of products, which undergo constant modification and development. In this diversity of products we can identify some that are generally considered harmful, in that they pose a danger to the mental and physical health of the consumer, as well as to the well-being of society and the environment.

These products exist and are consumed by certain categories of people. But it is a delicate matter to offer them on the market when not everybody agrees with their use. The information transmitted to customers and potential customers should be correct, complete, detailed, understandable, and easily accessible by people using the product.

The marketing mix plays a special role in how harmful products are perceived.

The social ethics of "harmful" products stands in opposition to individual ethics. The element that can link the two concepts is *information* that permits an enlightened choice between using and not using a product. Information educates people and influences individual ethics. It can demonstrate that a product generally considered harmful is useful to a particular person. One might therefore say that providing information contributes to the evolution of society.

A society's ethical norms should determine whether harmful products are sold and how they are promoted. The norms should never result in damage to the life, health, or range of activities of anyone. They should be encoded as legal regulations.

In a global economy, ethical norms should be standardized. We may therefore ask whether we are on a path toward defining global norms. These norms should determine not only which products are ethical, but which means of promotion are ethical.

Notes

1. See Appendix.
2. Including soft drinks, ketchup, ready-made foods, etc.
3. For example, De George (1999).
4. Food additives approved by the European Union are given "E-numbers."
5. The researchers are Dr. Charles O. Rock and Dr. Richard J. Heath. See Heath et al. (1999).
6. Reuters.
7. http://www.gortbusters.org/forum/viewtopic.php?t=547.
8. A low-quality product is not necessarily a harmful product, since it may have no harmful effects on the consumer, as in the case of a handbag that disintegrates after the first day of use.
9. Image = image in the mind of consumer + reference groups + communication strategy of the company + physical image of the product or shop where it is sold.
10. M.D., endocrinologist-nutritionist.
11. Anorexia is characterized by low body weight, at least 25 percent below normal.
12. http://www.philipmorrisusa.com/responsible_marketing/marketing_practices.asp#advertising.
13. Victoria A. Seitz, Professor of Marketing, State University of California, Fulbright Professor in Cluj, Romania.
14. Radu Cristea, engineer, Habasit Corporation, Romania.
15. Cited in Barrett (1994–1995).
16. http://www.geocities.com/Athens/Aegean/9318/smells.html.

References

"The Advertisement of Harmful Products" (undated), http://www.uoguelph.ca/~mbateson/harmful.html.

"Alimentele romanesti sunt sanatoase?" *Despre Copii* (online forum), http://www.desprecopii.com/forum/topic.asp?TOPIC_ID=25942&whichpage=5.

"Antibacterial Products May Be Harmful in Long Run," *Memphis Business Journal* (April 9, 1999), http://www.bizjournals.com/memphis/stories/1999/04/05/daily16.html.

Barboza, David. 2003. "Food Giant Maps Steps to Fight Rising Obesity," *New York Times* (July 3), http://www.iht.com/articles/101578.html.

Barrett, Robin. 1994–1995. "The Harmful Effects of Scented Products," Nova Scotia Allergy and Environmental Health Association (Winter), http://www.environmentalhealth.ca/w9495harmful.html. See also http://nofragrance.org/.

Cooke, M. A. 1994. "Fragrance: Its biology and Pathology," *Journal of the Royal College of Physicians of London*, vol. 29, no. 2 (March/April): 133. Cited in Barrett 1994–1995.

Cristea, Radu. Undated. "Benzi transportoare alimentare pentru industria dulciurilor si a ciocolatei," *Revista Industriei Alimentare Romanesti*, http://www.globus.home.ro/articole/11_curele2.htm.

De George, Richard. 1999. *Business Ethics*, 5th ed. Upper Saddle River, N.J.: Prentice Hall.

Donaldson, John. 1989. *Key Issues in Business Ethics*. London: Academic Press.

Hay, Robert D. 1989. *Business & Society: Perspectives on Ethics and Social Responsibility*, 3rd ed. Southwestern Educational Publishing.

Heath, R. J., et al. 1999. "Mechanism of Triclosan Inhibition of Bacterial Fatty Acid Synthesis," *Journal of Biological Chemistry* 274 (April): 11110–11114.

Heiderich, Didier. 2003. "Marketing ethique ou simple changement d'etiquette?" http://visionarymarketing.com/articles/entrepriseethiqueccc.html (October).

Hoffman, W. Michael, Robert E. Frederick, and Mark Schwartz. 2000. *Business Ethics: Readings and Cases in Corporate Morality*. McGraw-Hill.

Koslowsky, Peter, ed. 1999. *Contemporary Economic Ethics and Business Ethics*. Springer.

Kotler, Philip. 2002. *Marketing Management*. Upper Saddle River, N.J.: Prentice Hall.

Lilien, Gary L., Philip Kotler, and K. Sidhar Moorthy. 1995. *Marketing Models*. Upper Saddle River, N.J.: Prentice Hall.

LSA (*Revue de la grande distribution*). 2002. http://www.lsa.fr.

Machipisa, Lewis. 2002. "Health Focus/Africa: Continent's Health Systems Collapsing" (December 1), http://phmovement.org/pha2000/media/media-1dec-3.html.

"Marketing Ethique," Centrale Ethique, Paris. 2003. http://www.centraliens.net/groupements-professionnels/centrale-ethique/Centrale%20Ethique-235.htm.

Memphis Business Journal. http://www.bizjournals.com/memphis.

Mercier, Samuel. 1999. *L'ethique dans les entreprises*. Paris: Editions Decouvertes & Syros.

Le Monde. http://www.lemonde.fr.

Moore, Charles W. 1999. "Scents to Die For—Literally," *Barquetine Ventures Online Journal*, http://www.geocities.com/Athens/Aegean/9318/smells.html.

Polonsky, Michael Jay. 1994. "An Introduction to Green Marketing," *Electronic Greeen Journal* 1(2) (November), http://egj.lib.uidaho.edu/egj02/polon01.html.

Smith, N. C., and E. Cooper-Martin. 1997. "Ethics and Target Marketing: The Role of Product Harm and Consumer Vulnerability, " *Journal of Marketing* 61 (July): 1–20.

Sutherland, Max, and Alice Sylvester. 1993. *Advertising and the Mind of the Consumer*. Allen & Unwin (Australia) Pty Ltd.

Ulrich, Peter. 1999. "Integrative Economic Ethics: Towards a Conception of Socio-Economic Rationality," in *Contemporary Economic Ethics and Business Ethics*, ed. Peter Koslowsky. Springer.

The Author

Laura Radulian is a postgraduate student at the University of Economics (Vysoká Škola Ekonomická), Prague, Czech Republic. E-mail: radulian@vse.cz.

Appendix

QUESTIONNAIRE

1. How would you characterize the products that you consume daily? (*multiple answers*)

   □ Healthy   □ Useful

   □ Natural   □ Expensive

   □ Partially harmful   □ Cheap

2. Please list three characteristics that you take into consideration when you buy a product.

   ____________________ ____________________ ____________________

3. How would you define "harmful products"?

   ____

4. What are the first three products that you think of when you hear the phrase "harmful products"?

   ____________________ ____________________ ____________________

5. Are you aware of a normal product that was transformed into a harmful product after scientific research, improper use, or aggressive advertising, etc.?

   □ yes

   □ no   If yes, please give an example ____________________________

6. Do you consider it ethical to distribute the products enumerated in question 4?

   □ Yes   □ No

7. Which of the following elements could transform, in your opinion, a normal product into harmful one:

   □ the product itself (composition, shape, smell, dimensions, etc.)

   □ the means of distribution

   □ excessive advertising

   □ price that is too low

   Please give examples for the chosen answer:

   ____

8. Are you for or against the development of new products, for progress, for civilization?

   □ for □ against

9. Characterize in a minimum of two words the following products

   honey ________________ polyester dress ________________

   chamomile soap ________________ lemon dishwashing liquid ________________

   powdered milk for babies ________________

10. Do you think that the effects of the use of a product that has some damaging effects (e.g., the effect of dishwashing liquid on the skin of the hands) can be neutralized by the use of other products (e.g., hand cream)?

    □ Yes □ No

    Why? ________________________________

11. Your hobbies

    ____

CODES OF BUSINESS CONDUCT: PHARMA MARKETING AT A CROSSROADS?

Jayraj Jadeja
The M. S. University of Baroda, Baroda, India

Bharat R. Shah
Unicure Remedies Pvt. Ltd. and The M. S. University of Baroda, India

Preshth Bhardwaj
Indian Institute of Management, Ahmedabad, India

Abstract

In a perfect world, physicians and drug producers would have only one goal: to advance the health of their patients. Unfortunately, ours is not a perfect world. While every physician's prime responsibility—by oath and by law—is to the patient, every pharmaceutical producer's first and foremost obligation, by design, is to shareholders and employees. Their ultimate objectives are diagonally diverse. This situation calls for a code of ethics to govern the marketing and prescription of pharmaceuticals. This paper attempts to identify the business practices prevailing in the Indian pharmaceutical industry, in order to provide a basis for constructing an appropriate code of ethics. The research is based on surveys or in-depth interviews of physicians, patients, retail pharmacists, and drug manufacturers.

Introduction

The World Health Organization made a summary observation: "There exists an inherent conflict between the legitimate business goals of manufacturers and the social, medical, and economic needs of providers and the public to select and use drugs in the most rational way."[1] The ethical dilemma of competitive marketing and health interests is real in the pharmaceutical industry. The underlying problem has a genesis in the conflict between the optimal use of medicines for the patient's benefit and the tremendous pressure the pharmaceutical companies are under continuously to expand product sales.

Although the Indian pharmaceutical industry contributes a mere 1 percent to the global pharmaceutical turnover, it is a vibrant industry manufacturing and marketing medicines, which are being accepted even by the developing countries for domestic use.

 pp. 359–374

The pharmaceutical industry has been called to task for its flamboyant outlook and dubious marketing practices. Drug prices have always been a controversial global issue. The U.S. Senate Labor and Human Resource Committee, chaired by Senator Edward Kennedy, expressed its misgivings at the extravagant marketing practices of the pharmaceutical industry in the USA. "Doctors who accept lavish industry gifts are jeopardizing their objectivity and compromising the trust of their patients," charged Mr. Kennedy (Fig.1). His deepest concern was that the consumer finances these marketing practices, which deliver no health benefit, through higher drug prices.

Figure 1: Ethics as an Antecedent to Trust[2]

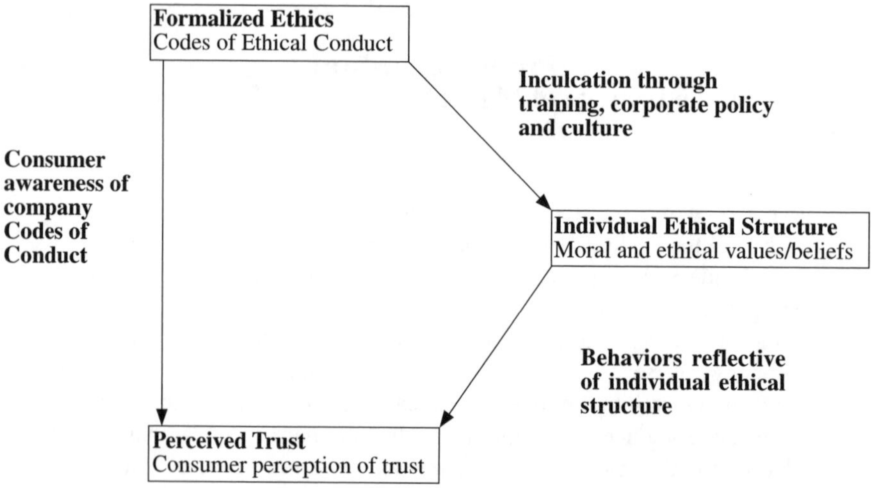

Following the WHO conference of experts on the rational use of drugs, held in Nairobi in November 1985, WHO prepared a revised drug strategy that was endorsed by the 39th World Health Assembly in May 1986 (resolution WHA39.27). This strategy included, among other components, the establishment of ethical criteria for drug promotion that are based on an update and extension of the ethical and scientific criteria established in 1968 by the 21st World Health Assembly (resolution WHA21.41). The main objective of ethical criteria for medicinal drug promotion is to support and encourage the improvement of health care through the rational use of medicinal drugs. These criteria do not constitute legal obligations. The Governments may adopt legislation or other measures based on these criteria as they deem fit.[3]

The Association of the British Pharmaceutical Industry voluntarily adopted a Code of Practice for the Pharmaceutical Industry in 1958. This code was purported to regulate the standards of conduct for the marketing of medicines intended for use under medical supervision. The code encompassed various facets of the marketing of medicines, viz., methods of promotion, grant of product license, nature and availability of information, printed promotional materials, issues pertaining to references of official bodies, medical representatives, samples, gifts and marketing research, and so forth.[4] The other operating international standard is the International Federation of Pharmaceutical Manufacturers' Association (IFPMA) Code of Conduct of Pharmaceutical Marketing Practices, developed in 1981 and revised in 1994. It describes itself as defining "universally applicable baseline standards of marketing practice."[5] The American Medical Association (AMA) adopted a chastity code titled *Guidelines for Gifts from Industry to Physicians*, which was prepared by the AMA's council on Ethical and Judicial Affairs during December 1990. The Pharmaceutical Manufacturers' Association (PMA) adopted this code immediately thereafter.

However, these voluntary industry self-regulatory codes lack any mechanism for active monitoring, effective sanctions, and clear procedures to correct violations. In the end they remain "more show than substance." The spirit of the codes is disregarded.

With this backdrop, this paper will attempt to identify the business practices prevailing in the Indian Pharmaceutical Industry. Although the Indian Pharmaceutical Industry contributes a mere 1 percent to the global pharmaceutical turnover, it is a vibrant industry manufacturing and marketing medicines, which are being accepted even by the developing countries for domestic use.

Global Pharmaceutical Marketing Practices: Codes of Conduct

Pharmaceutical Medicine is a discipline that involves the discovery, development, evaluation, registration, monitoring and ethical marketing of medicinal products, medical devices and diagnostics.[6]

The main objective of ethical criteria for medicinal drug promotion is to support and encourage the improvement of health care through the rational use of medicinal drugs (WHO Geneva, 1988).

Ethical criteria for drug promotion lay the foundation for proper behavior concerning the promotion of medicinal drugs, consistent with the truthfulness in the information provided. These criteria constitute general principles for ethical standards which could be adapted by governments to the national circumstances appropriate to their political, economical, cultural, social, educational, scientific and technical situation, laws and regulations, disease profile, therapeutic traditions and the level of development of their healthcare systems.

The current global pharmaceutical market is estimated to be more than $317 billion.[7] The major regions contributing to the global pharmaceutical market are the United States, Japan, and the European Union. GlaxoSmithKline, Pfizer and Merck are the top three companies in the global pharmaceutical market, with annual sales of $23.5, 22.6, and 20.2 billion, respectively.

Around the world, more than 4,000 new molecules are brought into the market. On an average, a global pharmaceutical company is likely to spend between $450 million and $800 million over the next twelve to fourteen years to launch a new molecule into the market. To maintain the present market growth rate, pharmaceutical companies would be under tremendous pressure to add new molecules into their existing pipeline. To tackle this, the use of new and current drug needs to be increased. This may raise a need to launch aggressive promotional campaigns to move their brands.

The commitment of pharmaceutical market is towards providing high quality effective medicines, which could bring major benefits to both the health of the nation and the country's economy.

Investment into researching and developing new molecules takes an average of ten to twelve years before it is authorized by the doctors, with no guarantee of commercial success. It is vital therefore that the pharmaceutical industry keeps the medical profession informed about its products and promotes their rational use.[8]

Pharmaceutical companies, through their advertising, promotion and contributions to medical journals, can also play an important role in keeping the medical practitioners informed about the latest information on the developments in pharmaceutical products, which in turn determines the demand for various prescription drugs.

Scope of the Codes of Conduct of Various Countries

Ethical Criteria for Medical Drug Promotion (WTO Geneva, 1988)

Promotion in the form of financial or material benefits should not be offered to healthcare practitioners for the prescription of drugs. Scientific and educational activities should not be deliberately used for the promotional purposes.

Advertisements should not take undue advantage of the public's concerns about health and must not be directed at children. Language that brings about fear or distress should not be used. Information on price to the consumer should be accurately and honestly projected.

Medical Representatives should be trained to present medical and technical information on drugs to healthcare professionals, to facilitate their prescription.

Free samples of legally available prescription drugs may be provided in modest quantities to healthcare professionals.

IFPMA Code of Pharmaceutical Marketing Practices

The promotional activities covered by the code related to direct-to-consumer advertising. Promotional materials used for the promotion of medicines should be accurate, fair and presented in a way that conforms not only to legal requirements but also to high ethical standards. They should be in the best interest of health professionals, public health officials and the general public.

The Association of the British Pharmaceutical Industry and its Code of Practice

The Association of the British Pharmaceutical Industry (ABPI) is the trade association representing manufacturers of prescription medicines. The ABPI encourages pharmaceutical companies to try to settle inter-company disputes between themselves before submitting complaints to the authority. The aim of the code of practice is to ensure that the promotion of medicines to members of health professions and to administrative staff is carried out in a responsible, ethical and professional manner.

The code incorporates the principles set out in:

- The International Federation of Pharmaceutical Manufacturers Associations' (IFPMA) Code of Pharmaceutical Marketing Practices,
- The European Federation of Pharmaceutical Industry's Associations' (EFPIA) European Code of Practice for the Promotion of Medicines,
- The European Directive on the Advertising of Medicinal Products for Human Use (92/28/EEC), and
- The World Health Organization's Ethical Criteria for Medicinal Drug Promotion.

This code applies to the promotion of medicines to the members of the UK health profession and to administrative staff, as well as to information available to the general public about the medicines.

A medicine must be promoted after marketing authorization is granted (clause 3). The prescribing information must be a part of the promotional material (clause 4). The prescribing information includes:

- The name of the medicine;
- A quantitative list of active ingredients;
- Information related to the dosage and the method of use;
- A statement of the side-effects, precautions and contra-indications;
- Warning issued by the Medicines Commission, the Committee on Safety of Medicines or the licensing authority, which is required to be included in advertisement;
- The cost of a specified package of medicines;
- The legal classification of the drug;
- The number of the relevant marketing authorization.

APMA Code

The APMA code sets the standard of conduct for companies engaged in the advertising and marketing of prescription drugs.

The APMA code covers the guidelines for the industry to:

- provide medicines that conform to the highest standards of safety, efficacy and quality;
- ensure that medicines are supported by comprehensive technical and informational services; and
- professionalism must be adopted in dealing with health care professionals, public health officials and the general public.

The Australian Pharmaceutical Manufacturers Association and its Code of Conduct

The Code of conduct administered by the Australian Pharmaceutical Manufacturers Association (APMA) represents the interest of those companies engaged in the research and development, manufacturing, marketing and export of pharmaceutical products that by regulation must be supplied under a prescription.

Australia holds a small share of the global pharmaceutical market. The global market is dominated by large multinational corporations that enjoy economies of scale in the development of research driven molecules. These developments involve considerable investment risk and thus need to be backed by patents.

The Australian government regulates the prices of prescription-based medicines by providing patients with drugs subsidized under the Pharmaceutical Benefits Scheme (PBC). This leads to the diversion of resources of pharmaceutical companies towards advertising and promotion of drugs. The conduct of pharmaceutical manufacturers in using advertisement and promotional activities for their drugs is the subject of the APMA Code of Conduct.

Canada's Research-Based Pharmaceutical Companies—Code of Marketing Practices

Canada's Research-Based Pharmaceutical Companies (Rx&D)[9] is a member of the International Federation of Pharmaceutical Manufacturers Association (IFPMA). The Rx&D strives to provide:

- Medicines of the highest standards of safety and efficacy;
- Adequate technical and general information regarding the efficacy of medicines (provided to health professionals);
- Honest dealings with the healthcare professionals, public health officials and the general public.

Rx&D follows the Code of Advertising Acceptance of the Pharmaceutical Advertising Advisory Board (PAAB), as well as the guidelines for general advertising, supplied advertising inserts, and Journal supplements of the Canadian Association of Medical Publishers (CAMP).

The Pharmaceutical Association of Malaysia (PhAMA): Code of Conduct for Prescription (Ethical) Drugs

The objective of the Code is to provide accurate and fair information to the medical professionals to assist in the rational prescription of medicines.[10] Medical professionals and the pharmaceutical industry are required to adopt high standards of conduct and professionalism in the marketing of medicines.

Promotional materials must conform to legal requirements and reflect high ethical standards.

Major Guidelines Mentioned in the Codes

Guidelines for Offering Samples

As per the ABPI, samples of a medicine may be provided only to a health professional qualified to prescribe that medicine (clause 17). Not more than ten samples of a particular medicine may be provided in a year. Samples may only be supplied in response to written requests that have been signed and dated. Companies must have adequate systems of control and accountability for samples.

As per IFPMA, samples must be supplied to the prescribing professionals to enable them to test the efficacy of the medication for its future use.

As per PhAMA code, samples provided for specific clinical trials should be modest both in terms of size and value, and clearly labelled as samples.

Guidelines for Gifts and Inducements

As per ABPI, gifts provided to the health professionals and appropriate administrative staff must be inexpensive and relevant to the practice of their profession (clause 18).

As per IFPMA, promotional items of insignificant value may be provided to the health professionals to facilitate their work and also provide benefit to the patients.

As per PhAMA code, inappropriate financial or material benefits should not be offered to the healthcare professional. No gifts or financial inducement should be offered for the purpose of sales promotion. Gifts designed as promotional aids may be distributed to healthcare professionals but must be of small value and relevant to the practice.

Guidelines for Meetings and Hospitality

As per ABPI, the level of hospitality provided to the members of the health professions and appropriate administrative staff must be in proportion to the occasion (clause19). Meetings sponsored by the pharmaceutical companies must be disclosed in any published proceedings.

As per IFPMA, inappropriate financial or material benefits should not be offered to the healthcare professionals to influence their preferences while prescribing.

As per PhAMA code, inappropriate hospitality must not be offered to the healthcare professionals to influence them in the prescription of medicines.

Guidelines for Relations with the General Public and the Media

As per ABPI, prescription-based medicines must not be advertised to the general public (clause 20). The introduction of a new medicine must be made known to the members of the medical profession before it is announced to the general public.

As per IFPMA, all information communicated to the patients regarding the prescription medicines must be accurate and fair.

As per PhAMA code, information regarding prescription medicines or matters related to the scientific discoveries or advances in treatment should not be available to the general public and the media.

Guidelines for Training Medical Representatives

As per ABPI, medical representatives must pass the appropriate ABPI representatives examination (clause 16), in order to receive training on how

- to call upon the doctors, and
- to promote the medicines on the basis of their particular therapeutic properties.

As per IFPMA, medical representatives must be adequately trained and possess sufficient medical and technical knowledge to present information to the healthcare professionals in an accurate and ethical manner.

As per PhAMA code, Medical Representatives must be adequately trained with medical and technical knowledge to present accurate information to the healthcare professionals. They should maintain high standard of ethical conduct in the discharge of their duties.

Indian Pharmaceutical Marketing Practices

With 2005 and a new product patent regime around the corner, most pharmaceutical companies are gearing up their R&D resources to build new molecules to tap future potential.

In India, drugs are imported, manufactured, promoted, and sold as per the guidelines laid down in the Drugs Act. The Central Government has the power to prohibit any drug that proved to be "irrational drug combinations."

Advertising and Sales Promotion

Advertisements of drugs and pharmaceuticals are prohibited in India. There are also laws that regulate advertisements of drugs and pharmaceuticals. The Drugs and Magic Remedies (Objectionable Advertisement) Act (1954) is designed to ensure that advertisements do not make unjustified claims. Guidelines regarding advertisements are published in the Code of the Advertising Standards Council of India (ASCI). ASCI is a voluntary association and not a government body.

The ASCI Code has several objectives: to ensure truthfulness and honesty of representations and claims, to safeguard against misleading advertising, and to ensure that advertisements do not lead to unfair competition. The manufacturers, advertisers, agencies and associations use the mechanism of ASCI, but these guidelines are not enforceable by courts of law.

Thus, there exists an urgent need to formulate and implement a Code to regulate the practices of manufacturers, trade channels and doctors to ensure better healthcare management in India.

Research Plan

Responses were collected from Physicians, retailers, and patients through a self-administered questionnaire. In-depth interviews were conducted to seek the views of drug manufacturers.

Sample Plan

The total sample selected for this paper is 200. The breakup of market segments and data collection tools appears in Table 1.

Table 1. Segment sizes and research tools used

	Physicians	*Retail Pharmacists*	*Patients*	*Drug Manufacturers*
Segments Size	60	60	60	20
Data Collection tools	Questionnaire	Questionnaire	Questionnaire	In-depth interviews

Data Analysis

Information about the belief constructs of doctors, patients and retailers with respect to marketing practices was solicited. They were asked to respond on a 5-point scale (5 for strongly agree, 4 for agree, 3 for neither agree nor disagree, 2 for disagree, 1 for strongly disagree).

Retailers

Retailers were asked attitudinal questions to know their belief constructs on various aspects.

Stock of medicine brands. Most retailers stock brands based on higher margins and keep common consumable items to increase the frequency of visits of patients. Their preference of brands is not based on the specialties and preferences of the doctors and keeps all standard brands for specific disease that are normally prescribed by doctors.

Sources of information for keeping medicine brands. For stocking specific range of medicine brands, retailers compare various brands of medicine for specific disease based on their fast or slow moving nature, promotional schemes, trade discounts and the trade margins provided by the company.

They also refer to the latest index of medicine brands, mentioned in the Chemist Association circulars, to decide on stocking the specific range of medicine brands.

Most retailers do not read trade journals and are normally not aware of drug advertisements and pamphlets shown by the Medical Representatives.

Stock preferences of medicine brands. Retailers while ordering medicine brands had given high preferences on certain factors:

- Cost comparison of different brands having the same efficacy;
- Frequency of prescription slips comes to their counter;
- Shelf life of specific medicine brand;
- Preservation standards required by the medicines and the storage capacity of the store;
- Gifts, promotional schemes, trade discounts, margins and the frequency of visits by Medical Representatives.

Caution about a fixed set of medicinal brands of doctors. Most retailers feel that the doctors do not have any fixed set of medicine brands for specific disease. They are strongly agreeing that doctors decide on their final choice of medicine brand for specific disease based on gifts, samples, promotional schemes and frequency of visits by the Medical Representatives.

Table 2. Results of retailer survey.

Belief Constructs	*Weighted Average*	*Standard Deviation*
1. Stock of Medicine Brands		
a) I normally stock brands that are prescribed by the doctors near my store	2.52	0.748
b) Selection of medicine brands is based on the specialties and preferences of the doctor	2.43	0.561
c) I visit doctors to fix the quantity of medicine brands to be prescribed by them for a period mutually decided	1.65	0.606
d) I stock medicines based on the margins provided by the drug manufacturer	4.50	0.537
e) I keep certain common consumable products, as these help in increasing the frequency of visits of patients	4.70	0.561
2. Sources of information for keeping medicine brands		
a) I normally look at what medicine brands are fast/slow-moving	4.55	0.565
b) Preferences of doctors near the store is the major reason to keep a specific set of medicine brands	1.45	0.594
c) Promotional schemes and trade discounts provided by the company help me in deciding specific range of medicine	4.73	0.446
d) Trade margins provided by the drug companies help me in deciding on a set of medicine brands	4.37	0.486
e) I regularly refer to the latest index of medicines listed in the Chemist Association circulars	4.90	0.303
f) I also read Medical trade journals to update myself of coming medicine brands	3.03	0.181
g) I also read drug advertisements while reading Medical trade journals	3.02	0.130
3. Stock preferences of medicine brands		
a) I compare costs of different medicine brands with same efficacy while ordering	4.53	0.596
b) I normally look at the frequency of prescription slips coming to my counter to decide on the stock of medicines	4.70	0.454
c) I look at the shelf life while deciding the stock level of medicines	4.62	0.527
d) I identify preservation standards required for medicines and the storage capacity of my store	4.50	0.537
e) Refrigerator is on during business hours except while repairing	4.70	0.561
f) I normally repair my refrigerator by next day	4.68	0.567
g) Gifts, promotional schemes, trade discounts, and margins are the major reasons in deciding on a set of medicine brands	4.63	0.581
h) My decision on final choice of medicine brands is based on the regular visits by Medical Representatives	4.47	0.596
4. Cautiousness about fixed set of medicinal brands of doctors		
a) I feel that the doctor prescribes the patient a pre-determined set of medicine brands for specific disease	2.58	0.619
b) Gifts, samples, promotional schemes, and frequent visits by MRs helps doctors in deciding their final choice of medicine brands for prescription	4.62	0.524
5. Awareness about the ethical criteria for drug promotion and codes of conduct		
a) I believe that ethical criteria for drug promotion can play a major role in establishing trust and reliability of new/existing drug	4.47	0.503
b) I am aware of the legal and moral obligations of my profession	4.80	0.403
c) I believe that drug promotion by ethical means will build trust between patients and drug companies	4.82	0.469
d) I am comfortable with the clauses mentioned in the Code of Business Conduct	4.33	0.705
e) I believe proper vigilance towards practices and the implementation of the clauses of Code of Conduct is necessary to safeguard the interests of various stakeholders	4.93	0.252

Awareness about the ethical criteria for drug promotion and the Code of Conduct. Retailers believe that following the ethical criteria for drug promotion plays a major role in establishing trust and reliability of new and existing drugs between patients and drug manufacturers.

They were cautious while responding to the aspects regarding their professional obligations and the awareness about the clauses mentioned in the published literature on the code of business conduct. But the facts drawn out of personal interactions with them are just opposite. They are not aware about the role of the code of business conduct and had never read the guidelines of the code in any literatures published.

Physicians

Physicians were asked attitudinal questions to know their belief constructs on various aspects (Table 3).

The process of consultation. Most physicians take history about the health of the patients and also elicit their personal health beliefs about the illness.

When a new drug is introduced, they mostly use the sample of these drugs on few patients and monitor their efficacy. They also seek information from published findings on the efficacy of new drugs.

Most physicians do not have fixed set of medicine brands for specific disease. Instead, their prescription primarily depends on the stage of the disease and the age of the patient.

Sources of information for prescribing medicines. Most physicians read medical journals and the drug advertisements in these journals to update themselves about the latest development in their field. They also read all promotional materials given by drug manufacturers.

Physicians do not seek information, of their own, about the promotional schemes and samples from medical representatives. Their confidence on the authenticity and efficacy of medicine brand does not depend on the frequency of visits by medical representatives. Instead, they try to judge the efficacy by testing medicines on patients and then monitoring their effect.

Prescribing behavior. While prescribing medicines, physicians always:

- compare costs of different medicine brands that have the same efficacy;
- check the medical literature when they are uncertain about any aspect of a drug treatment.

Most physicians agreed that the frequency of visits by the local retail pharmacist has a strong impact on their prescription of specific medicine brand.

Relationship with drug companies and retail pharmacist. Most of the physicians agreed that they prescribe medicine brands with which they are most comfortable.

Physicians do not rely on gifts, samples, promotional schemes, or visits by medical representatives. Instead, they have relationship with drug manufacturers based on their experience regarding the services offered by the company's sales force in building the trust on the efficacy of the medicine brand.

Table 3. Results of physician survey.

Belief Constructs	*Weighted Average*	*Standard Deviation*
1. The Process of consultation		
a) When a patient comes for treatment, I prescribe a fixed set of brands for a specific disease	1.43	0.500
b) When a new drug becomes available what I do most commonly is:		
i) use the drug on few patients and monitor	4.37	0.486
ii) seek information from published findings on the efficacy of new drug	4.40	0.494
iii) believe MR briefs on the information about the new drug	1.25	0.474
c) When I take a history of my patients, I elicit their personal health beliefs about their illness	4.88	0.324
2. Sources of information for prescribing medicines		
(a) My normal practice is to seek regular information of updates about the promotional schemes and samples from the MRs.	4.38	0.524
(b) Frequency of visits by MR provide me with confidence on the authenticity and efficacy of a specific medicine brand.	4.43	0.500
(c) Frequency of visits by MR helps me in deciding the preferred set of brands of medicine for a specific disease.	1.07	0.252
(d) When I receive written promotional material from drug companies, I read it thoroughly	4.37	0.486
(e) I refer to medical journals to update myself with the latest developments in my field.	4.90	0.279
(f) I read drug advertisements while reading medical journals.	4.27	0.607
3. Prescription Behavior		
a) When I prescribe, I compare the costs of different medicine brands that have the same efficacy.	4.85	0.360
b) When I am uncertain about an aspect of drug treatment, my first action, before I write a prescription, is to check the medical literature.	4.80	0.403
c) My decision on a final choice of brand is based on regular visits from local retail pharmacists to ask me to prescribe a certain set of brands.	4.63	0.486
d) I sometimes follow consultation from my known physicians in deciding the drug options for specific disease of my patients.	1.23	0.465
4. Caution about fixed set of medicinal brands		
(a) I normally prescribe my patients the pre-determined set of medicine brands for specific disease	1.07	0.252
(b) Gifts, samples, promotional schemes, and frequent visits by MRs help me to make my final choice of medicine brands for specific disease	1.32	0.537
5. Relationship with Drug companies and Retail pharmacists		
(a) I prescribe medicine brands of drug companies with which I am most comfortable.	4.47	0.503
(b) I feel that relationships with drug companies can be built based on the frequency of launch of promotional schemes, gifts, sample of new drugs, and visits from company's MR.	1.30	0.497
(c) Relationship with local retail pharmacist also plays major role in deciding final set of medicine brands for specific disease for my patients.	1.17	0.376
6. Awareness about the ethical criteria for drug promotion and Code of Conduct		
(a) I believe that ethical criteria for drug promotion can play a major role in establishing trust and reliability of new/existing drugs.	4.83	0.418
(b)I am aware of legal and moral obligations of my profession.	4.82	0.390
(c) I believe that the drug promotion by ethical means will build trust between patients and drug companies.	4.93	0.252
(d) I am aware of the published literatures related to the code of conduct for ethical drug promotion and rational use of drugs.	4.80	0.403
(e) I am comfortable with the clauses/conditions mentioned in the code of business conduct literatures.	4.87	0.343
(f) I believe that a proper vigilance towards the practices and the implementation of the clauses of code of business conduct is necessary in safeguarding the interests of various stakeholders.	4.97	0.181

Awareness about the ethical criteria for drug promotion and the Code of Conduct. Most physicians believe that following ethical criteria for drug promotion can build trust and reliability between patients and drug companies.

They believe that proper vigilance towards the practices and implementation of the clauses mentioned in the Code is required to safeguard the health standards of the patients.

Patients

Patients were asked attitudinal questions to know their belief constructs on various aspects (Table 4).

The prescribing behavior of the physician. Most patients believe that physicians do not always prescribe a fixed set of medicine brands. Instead, they seek information about the stage of disease for changing the medicines.

Table 4. Results of patient survey.

Belief Constructs	*Weighted Average*	*Standard Deviation*
1. Prescribing behavior of Physician		
a) While visiting the physician, do you normally feel that:		
(i) he/ she prescribe medicines for similar number of days	1.70	0.530
(ii) he/ she ask you to visit him/ her again	4.30	0.462
(iii) prescribes fixed set of medicine brands for specific illness	1.63	0.486
b) Do you feel that the prescribed medicine(s) will take few days in providing you relief but will not aggravate	4.43	0.500
c) Physician while listening to your brief about the illness and prescribing you medicines, shows his/ her moral and professional obligation in improving your health	4.17	0.418
d) When the physician is prescribing you medicines, you are mostly not aware about its effectiveness	1.75	0.654
2. Behavior of your local retail pharmacist		
a) Your local retail pharmacist tries to give you the substitute brand, in case the brand prescribed is not available	4.15	0.457
b) In that case, do you protest to provide the same brand mentioned in the prescription slip	3.98	0.701
3. Prescription Fees		
The prescription fees of the physician will be worth paying because:		
(i) Prescribed medicines are effective	3.95	0.565
(ii) Of the location and ambience	4.03	0.610
(iii) No other equally qualified and effective physician near-by	1.87	0.596
(iv) Maintains good relationship	4.18	0.537
(v) Trust of getting right prescription and guidelines	4.50	0.567
4. Medicine information regarding dosage and ingredients		
a) Does the doctor guides you how to take the dosage of medicines	4.37	0.486
b) Does the doctor tells you to take any precautions while taking the medicines	4.38	0.490
c) While buying medicines, when you ask the local retail pharmacist about the dosage of medicines, does he/she guides you	4.35	0.547
d) Do you normally read the information provided on the cover of the medicine	4.92	0.279
e) Does the cover of the medicine contains the details regarding ingredients and the precautions to be taken while consuming it	4.90	0.303

Patients believe that the prescribed medicines may not provide relief immediately, but will not allow the disease to aggravate.

Behavior of the local retail pharmacist. Most patients do not mind purchasing substitute medicine brand when the prescribed medicine brand is not available, provided that it has the same efficacy.

Prescription fees. Patients feel that the prescription fee charged by the physician is worth paying due to:

- their trust that they are getting right medicines;
- their desire to maintain the relationship;
- the location and ambience where the physician sits.

Information regarding dosage and ingredients. Patients mostly get guidelines from physician regarding the dosage of medicines. Sometimes, a local retail pharmacist also guides them about the dosage.

Patients seek information about the expiry date, ingredients and cost mentioned in the cover of the medicine.

Drug Manufacturers

Drug manufacturing companies are of the strong opinion that regular visits by their medical representatives, promotional schemes, gifts and samples can provide them the access to new markets.

Manufacturers strongly believe that physicians always seek costs and financial benefits as well as other promotional facilities to prescribe their medicine brands. Physicians are very cautious about the efficacy of a brand, as it has a direct impact on patient trust.

In order to hold shelf space in medicine stores, drug companies concentrate more on their promotional schemes and trade discounts than on passing the margins. These promotional activities are of greater interest to the retail pharmacist than the margins.

Manufacturers sponsor regular training sessions for their medical representatives and train them to present the technical and professional information to physicians and retail pharmacists.

Most drug manufacturers subscribe to medical journals and read regularly about the scientific advancements in their field around the world. They believe that sales promotions and public relations are the major options for them to get access to new physicians and retail pharmacists, as opposed to advertising in the medical journals and trade magazines.

Suggestions

Model of Code for Conduct for Indian Marketing Practices

Based on the insights drawn from various stakeholders of pharmaceutical market, it is clear that there is an urgent need for a proper Code of Business Conduct for the Indian pharmaceutical market.

The basic objective of the proposed Indian Code of Business Conduct (ICBC) should be to encourage practices that improve the health standards of the patients through the rational use of medicinal drugs.

The major clauses of the proposed Indian Code of Business Conduct (ICBC) would concern:

- Samples given to physicians;
- Gifts;
- Trade discounts to intermediaries;
- Holiday packages offered to Physicians;
- Financial packages;
- Training of medical representatives;
- Advertisements about hygiene conditions; and
- Education about various diseases and their possible prevention measures.

Who Should Draft the Code of Business Conduct?

The major participants in drafting the Code of Business Conduct would be:

- Drug Manufacturers;
- Doctors;
- Retail Pharmacists and other trade intermediaries;
- Representatives from customers; and
- Independent body of the Central Government.

Conclusions

The ethical dilemma of competitive marketing and health interests is real in the pharmaceutical industry.

In a perfect world, the physicians and drug producers would have only one goal: to advance the health of their patients. Unfortunately, ours is not a perfect world. While every physician's prime responsibility—by oath and by law—is to the patient, every pharmaceutical producer's first and foremost obligation, by design, is to shareholders and employees. Their ultimate objectives are diagonally diverse.

In India, healthcare professionals and retail pharmacists provide the main impetus for improving the health standards of the patients. There is a factor of trust and reliability involved in this profession. There exists a real gap that can only be filled by a proper Code to regulate practices in the market. Central government can form a panel of experts that, along with other stakeholders, would build a Code of Business Conduct suited for the Indian pharmaceutical market. This code should safeguard the interests of physicians, the trade channel, and the general public.

Notes

1. World Health Organization, *Clinical Pharmacological Evaluation in Drug Control*, EUR/ICP/DSE, 173 (Copenhagen: WHO, 1993).

2. Michael Callaghan and Robin N. Shaw, "Relationship Orientation: Towards an Antecedent Model of Trust in Marketing Relationships," presented at the Conference of the Australian and New Zealand Marketing Academy, 2001, http://130.195.95.71:8081/WWW/ANZMAC2001/anzmac/AUTHORS/pdfs/Callaghan2.pdf.

3. Ethical criteria for medicinal drug promotion, World Health Organization, Geneva, 1988.

5. Code of Practice for the Pharmaceutical Industry, 1984, Association of the British Pharmaceutical Industry, 12, Whitehall, London SW1A2DY.

5 International Federation of Pharmaceutical Manufacturers' Association, Code of Pharmaceutical Marketing Practices, Geneva, 1994.

6. International Code of Ethical Conduct for Pharmaceutical Physicians, 1e, April, 2003.

7. Sanjay K. Rao, "Pharmaceutical Marketing in a New Age," *Marketing Health Services* (Spring 2002): 7–12.

8. Code of Practice for the Pharmaceutical Industry, ABPI.

9. Australian Pharmaceutical Manufacturers Association (APMA) Code of Conduct, 108–123.

10. *The Indian Pharmaceutical Industry: Business, Legal and Tax Issues*, February 2004 edition (Mumbai: Nishith Desai Associates).

The Authors

Jayraj Jadeja is Reader in Marketing, Faculty of Management Studies, The Maharaja Sayajirao University of Baroda, Baroda, Gujarat, India. E-mail: jdjadeja@yahoo.co.uk.

Bharat R. Shah, M.D. (deceased), was associated with Unicure Remedies Pvt. Ltd. and a visiting faculty member at the Faculty of Management Studies, The M.S. University of Baroda.

Preshth Bhardwaj is a Research Associate, Indian Institute of Management, Ahmedabad, Gujarat, India.

"AIDS IS NOT A BUSINESS": A STUDY IN GLOBAL CORPORATE RESPONSIBILITY

William Flanagan
Queen's University, Kingston, Canada

Gail Whiteman
RSM Erasmus University, Rotterdam, Netherlands

Abstract

Most major pharmaceutical companies have corporate social responsibility policies that pledge their commitment to improving the health and quality of life of people around the world. Yet these same companies also have difficulty in ensuring that developing countries have access to affordable medications. In the late 1990s, Brazil engaged in a heated battle with large US-backed multinational pharmaceutical companies. Brazil was facing a growing HIV epidemic and was determined to provide treatment to those in need. This required massive price reductions on HIV medications. Although met with resistance, Brazil's campaign eventually resulted in the negotiation of significant price reductions. Our study examines how Brazil was able to secure these price concessions. We conclude that corporate social responsibility initiatives must be viewed as a dynamic interaction between multiple actors. Our study highlights the importance of governmental action, in both the national and international forums, to negotiate pro-actively with companies to ensure that CSR commitments are met.

Introduction

Multinational companies increasingly commit to appealing corporate social responsibility (CSR) policies.[1] For example, most major pharmaceutical companies have expansive corporate social responsibility policies that pledge their commitment to reducing the suffering and improving the health and quality of life of people around the world.[2] Yet many of these companies also have difficulty in ensuring that developing countries have access to affordable medications. For instance, beginning in the late 1990s, Brazil engaged in a heated battle with large US-backed multinational pharmaceutical companies. Brazil was facing a growing HIV epidemic and was determined to provide treatment to those in need. In a resource poor country, this required massive price reductions on HIV medications. Although the large multinational pharmaceutical companies were at first resistant, Brazil's campaign

pp. 375–391

eventually met with remarkable success resulting in the negotiation of significant price reductions.

Our study begins with an exploration of Brazil's negotiation strategy through in-depth interviews with key Brazilian policymakers, Brazilian pharmaceutical manufacturers, and civil society. How did Brazil succeed in negotiating price reductions? Notwithstanding stated international corporate responsibility commitments, why were the multinational corporations so reluctant to proceed and how was Brazil able to persuade them otherwise? What do these developments tell us about evolving mechanisms of global corporate governance and evolving norms of global corporate responsibility? We conclude that corporate social responsibility initiatives must be viewed as a dynamic interaction between multiple actors. Our study highlights not only the importance of corporate social responsibility commitments, but the equal importance of governmental action, in both the national and international forums, to negotiate pro-actively with companies to ensure that CSR commitments are met. Corporate responsibility initiatives are frequently framed as a debate between voluntary compliance by companies versus regulator enforcement by governments. Our story is more complex, with interesting implications for global corporate good governance.

Theory: Corporate Social Responsibility and Governance

As transnational corporations increasingly expand their activities in developing countries, a key challenge for developing country governments like Brazil is to ensure adequate local mechanisms of corporate governance. Since many developing countries lack wel! developed governance systems, they have the greatest potential for gaps in global governance.

The critical debate in corporate governance is the degree to which transnational companies are able to govern themselves effectively. Civil society actors typically argue that companies are too self-interested to govern themselves reliably, particularly in terms of social and environmental considerations. Thus, companies need to be forced to comply with society needs in terms of laws or regulations. On the other hand, corporations and business interest groups, like the World Business Council on Sustainable Development, argue that it is in the firm's best interest to voluntarily delivery on the "triple bottom line"—and perform well in terms of economic, social and environmental measures.[3] Thus, companies should be left to their own devices in order to develop their own CSR policies and programs.

Corporate governance involves

> a set of relationships between a company's management, its board, its shareholders and other stakeholders. Corporate governance also provides the structure through which the objectives of the company are set, and the means of attaining those objectives and monitoring performance are determined. Good corporate governance should provide proper incentives for the board and management to pursue objectives that are in the interests of the company and its shareholders and should facilitate effective monitoring.[4]

A corporate governance system has behavioural and normative dimensions.[5] The behavioural side of corporate governance "encompasses the relationships and ensuring patterns of behaviour between different agents in a limited liability corporation; the way managers and shareholders but also employees, creditors, key customers and communities interact with each other to form the strategy of the company."[6] The normative side "refers to the set of rules that frame these relationships and private behaviours, thus shaping corporate strategy formation."[7] These rules can be based in law or in self-regulation through corporate social responsibility initiatives. With self-regulation, companies are primarily responsible for their own governance.

Since at least the 1950s, the specific term "social responsibility" has been used to describe the firm's responsibilities to society.[8] Early definitions suggested that social responsibility begins where the law ends. However, this perspective is somewhat narrow. More broadly, Carroll[9] has argued that there are four basic social responsibilities—economic, legal, ethical and philanthropic—which, when taken together, form the basis of corporate social responsibility. These four domains (economic, legal, ethical, and philanthropic) can be linked to key corporate social performance processes which include environmental assessment, stakeholder management and issues management.[10] In turn, these processes relate to corporate social performance outcomes such as social impacts, programs, and policies. Thus, corporate social responsibility (CSR) and corporate social performance (CSP) are important non-regulatory governance mechanisms that have both normative (CSR policies) and behavioural (CSP processes and outcomes) dimensions.

Normative dimensions of corporate governance have been increasingly addressed by companies in terms of CSR strategy development. Most transnational corporations have voluntary codes of conduct and CSR policies.[11] Such codes often identify social impacts, particularly for local communities, as important issues for their operations. However, a typical weakness in normative governance is the lack of meaningful participation of external stakeholders in strategy development.

Behavioural dimensions of corporate governance are less well developed. Many companies lack effective processes for ensuring and measuring the implementation of their CSR policies. In a review of international codes of conduct, Kolk and van Tulder found that "monitoring and sanctions are the most important test for the seriousness of codes' implementations."[12] Yet they found that less than 25 percent of firms had clear monitoring systems and processes embedded in their codes, and very few agreed to independent third party external monitoring of performance. An OECD study also shows that while corporate codes are prevalent, they are typically weak in terms of identifying specific tools for implementation and management control.[13]

Consequently, the actions and policies of governments and external organizations have potentially important governance roles. In particular, governments are responsible for establishing the societal 'rules of the game' by which these companies must follow, both domestically and internationally through regulation, legislation, and more recently with the case in Brazil and HIV medication, through strategic negotiation. Optimally, if corporations adopt CSR as part of their 'core business operations,' self-regulation holds promise. Yet the delegation of public responsibilities to private firms (through self-regulation and voluntary CSR initiatives) raises challenges in developing countries where laws and governance mechanisms to monitor local corporate social responsibility may be poorly developed, particularly under conditions of bounded rationality and opportunism. Governance gaps can also exist when multinational companies, left to their own devices, are unwilling or unable to effectively address societal needs despite stated policies on CSR.

A better understanding of Brazil's success in turning around its HIV epidemic can make an important contribution to the CSR and corporate governance literatures by identifying the conditions under which government action is required to ensure effective governance, over and above voluntary initiatives undertaken by companies.

Research Study

Our research study utilized qualitative interviews and document analysis. Qualitative open-ended interviews with Brazilian government representatives and Brazilian pharmaceutical manufacturers were conducted in Brazil in July 2002 and April 2003. Our research followed an iterative research design[14] where choice of interviews and observation evolved while in the field. We also conducted document analysis of corporate and government documents, including relevant developments in international law and Brazilian domestic law. Our study examines how Brazil succeeded in negotiating significant price reductions on HIV medications. Notwithstanding stated international corporate responsibility commitments, why were the multinational corporations so reluctant to proceed and how was Brazil able to persuade them otherwise?

Background on Brazil, HIV, and TRIPS

By the end of the 1990s, Brazil was faced with a potentially explosive HIV/AIDS epidemic. As part of its national HIV/AIDS program, the government was determined to make HIV medications available to those in need free of charge. However, the multinational pharmaceutical industry that produced most of these patented medications refused to negotiate lower prices with Brazil. These companies continued to maintain global pricing levels, where the price of HIV medications was approximately US $12,000 per person per year: a strategy of "one world—one price." For developing countries like Brazil, with a per capita gross national income of only US $2,830 in 2002,[15] the costs of this medication were prohibitively expensive.

Through an innovative campaign, Brazil was able to negotiate lower prices from the multinational firms and develop its local capacity to produce HIV medications. The HIV epidemic has now stabilized, with approximately 660,000 HIV positive adults and a seroprevalence rate of 0.65 percent.[16] The Brazilian Ministry of Health currently covers the cost of antiretroviral treatment for over 135,000 Brazilians with HIV/AIDS.[17] Brazil has reduced HIV related mortality to half of what was predicted in the early 1990s. Hospital admissions related to HIV have decreased by 80 percent since 1996. The Brazilian Ministry of Health estimates that despite the high cost of treatment, there have been net savings of US $50 million, due to reduced illness.[18]

Brazil, as a member of the World Trade Organization, must comply with the provisions of the WTO agreements that deal with intellectual property, that is, the Agreement on Trade-Related Aspects of Intellectual Property Rights (TRIPS).[19] TRIPS has two primary objectives. The first is to improve the minimum levels of intellectual property protections already provided for in existing international agreements. The second is to link these new levels of protection to international trade laws, including access to the effective dispute settlement mechanism of the WTO, a mechanism that could ultimately lead to trade-related sanctions to enforce obligations under TRIPS.

TRIPS imposes a number of important obligations in the area of intellectual property. Article 27 of TRIPS requires that patents shall be available for any new inventions in all fields of technology without discrimination as to the place of invention or whether the products are imported or locally produced. Article 28 provides that the patent shall confer on its owner exclusive rights to prevent third parties from making or selling the patented product. The patent period shall be not less than twenty years from the filing date for the patent.[20]

As a result, member states must make twenty-year patents available for any new inventions including pharmaceutical chemicals. Prior to TRIPS, in order to reduce prices, many developing countries such as Brazil did not grant patents for pharmaceutical chemicals. TRIPS now requires member countries to grant patents for such treatments. Specifically, HIV medications that constitute an "invention" are subject to the TRIPS provisions. Pursuant to various transitional provisions, these rules did not have immediate effect in the developing world. Most developing nations such as Brazil were permitted to delay the application of these rules until January 1, 2000.[21] Least developed countries originally had until January 1, 2006, to comply with most TRIPS obligations, although this period was later extended to January 1, 2016.[22] Developing countries that did not provide patent protection for a particular area of technology, such as pharmaceuticals, prior to the entry into force of TRIPS have until January 1, 2005, to enforce patent rights in that area. This explains the present lack of pharmaceutical patents in India and the significant Indian generic manufacturing of low cost HIV medications.[23]

TRIPS includes certain exceptions to the general rule that states must make patents available for new inventions. One of the most important is found in Article 31 of TRIPS. Article 31 sets out the obligations relating to other uses of a patent "without the authorization of the patent holder," more commonly known as "compulsory licencing." Unlike other types of intellectual property protected in TRIPS, Article 31 permits the compulsory licencing of patents in certain circumstances. A compulsory licence is permission to produce and sell a patented product without the consent and likely over the objections of the patent holder. A member's patent law may provide for such compulsory licencing and where it does, certain obligations apply. Among other requirements, such use can only be permitted if the proposed user has first made efforts over a "reasonable period of time" to obtain authorization from the patent holder on "reasonable commercial terms."[24] In situations of a "national emergency or other circumstances of extreme urgency or in cases of public non-commercial use" this requirement to negotiate for a reasonable period of time with the patent holder can be waived.[25] The scope and duration of the compulsory licence must be limited to the purpose for which it was authorized and shall be non-exclusive.[26] The use can only be authorized "predominantly for supply of the domestic market."[27] The patent holder is entitled to be paid "adequate remuneration" taking into account the "economic value of the authorization."[28]

Compulsory licences are not a new concept.[29] But they have come under increasing scrutiny in the last few years in light of the impact of the HIV/AIDS epidemic in developing countries that cannot afford the HIV medications that can slow the progression of HIV/AIDS. A number of developing countries, notably Thailand, South Africa and Brazil have threatened to issue compulsory licences to local producers in order to produce generic copies of patented HIV medications at much lower costs. These efforts initially met with the fierce opposition of the United States and other developed countries with strong research-based pharmaceutical industries. However, one key feature of Article 31 is that it places no restrictions on the purposes for which a compulsory licence may be issued. In this regard, Article 31 was a significant achievement for developing countries.[30] During the TRIPS negotiations, the US had insisted that there should be only two grounds for the issuance of a compulsory licence: an adjudicated violation of competition laws or a declared national emergency. However, no such restrictions were included in the final draft of Article 31. This suggests that compulsory licences can be issued for any reason including matters as broad as the general public interest. Nonetheless, as is examined below, the US pursued a strategy that was determined to limit as much as possible the issuance of compulsory licences.

Findings

Based on interview data and document analysis, we identify and analyze a range of tactics used by the Brazilian government to negotiate price reductions and thereby set a global standard for corporate social responsibility from the multinational pharmaceutical industry.

Our results indicate that this strategy was multi-faceted. Key government actions included unwavering political leadership at the international level. Part of this strategy was Brazil's successful political campaign to clarify the TRIPS Agreement at the WTO Doha negotiations, culminating in the *Doha Declaration on TRIPS Agreement and Public Health*.[31] Another aspect of this strategy was Brazil's threatened use of the compulsory licencing provisions found in TRIPS. By offering multinational pharmaceuticals guided tours in Rio de Janeiro to review Brazil's manufacturing capabilities, Brazil was able to demonstrate not only its willingness to issue compulsory licences but also its *capacity* to produce generic versions of patented HIV medications. Despite a US government-initiated petition at the WTO level,[32] Brazil was able to pressure companies like Roche to negotiate price reductions. Brazil also launched a sophisticated international public relations campaign and by developing powerful strategic alliances with key NGOs like Oxfam and Medicin sans Frontiers (MSF).

Through its National STD/AIDS Program (NSAP), Brazil makes HIV medications available free of charge to all citizens who need them. NSAP was initiated in the early 1990s and the treatment of HIV/AIDS patients was made a legal obligation in 1996. NSAP supplies HIV medications to nearly 135,000 of the estimated 660,000 Brazilians living with HIV.[33] Only about 230,000 of the 6 million people needing HIV treatment in the developing world actually receive it, and about one half of those receiving this treatment are in Brazil.[34] Among developing countries, Brazil's achievement in treating people with HIV is remarkable. The total annual cost of NSAP is about US $500 million, out of a total health budget of $10 billion, and $300 million of that $500 million is spent on HIV medications.[35] The cost of acquiring these drugs has been greatly reduced for two reasons. First, Brazil has developed its domestic capacity to produce HIV medications that are not patented in Brazil, and second, backed with a credible threat of issuing a compulsory licence, Brazil has successfully negotiated lower prices for those medications that are patented. Far-Manguinhos (part of the Owsaldo Cruz Foundation—FIOCRUZ) is the main government producer and it has developed the technology that provides Brazil with low cost HIV medications.[36]

Far-Manguinhos currently produces seven of the anti-retrovirals used to treat HIV infection:

- Zidovudine (AZT)
- Lamivudine (3TC)
- Zidovudine + Lamivudine (AZT + 3TC)
- Didanosine (DDI)
- Stavudine (d4T)
- Indinavir (Crixivan)
- Nevirapine (Viramune).[37]

None of these medications is patented in Brazil because they were invented prior to the enactment of Brazil's 1996 patent legislation.[38] Prior to this legislation, patents for pharmaceutical products were not available in Brazil.[39] To bring Brazilian law into compliance with TRIPS, this was changed under the 1996 legislation.[40] Because these seven medications are not patented, Brazil did not need to issue a compulsory licence, or seek a voluntary licence, in order to reverse engineer and produce these medications. Brazil was able to produce these drugs because it has developed at Far-Manguinhos the capacity to reverse engineer and produce its own high quality generics. The prices of these drugs, when developed for local production, fell by an average of 72.5 percent between 1996 and 2000.[41]

Under Brazil's new patent legislation, patents are now available for all new HIV medications. For example, the following five more recent HIV medications have all been patented in Brazil:[42]

- Efavirenz (Sustiva)—Merck & Co.
- Nelfinavir (Viracept)—Roche
- Tenofovir (Viread)—Gilead Sciences
- Atazanavir (Reyataz)—Bristol-Myers Squibb
- Lopinavir (Kaletra)—Abbott Laboratories

Most of these companies have extensive corporate social responsibility policies. For example, Merck's mission statement provides that its "business is preserving and improving human life."[43] The company expects "profits, but only from work that satisfies customer needs and benefits humanity."[44] Its Chairman's message on the company's corporate responsibility web site, quotes the company's founder, George W. Merck, who said:

> We try never to forget that medicine is for the people. It is not for the profits. The profits follow, and if we have remembered that, they have never failed to appear.[45]

At Roche, the CEO's message states:

> We aim to reduce suffering and improve health and quality of life of people all around the world. At Roche, we have pursued this mission with patience, dedication, imagination and skill, for over a century. Our vision is to develop targeted medicines and diagnostic tools that combine to offer patients, physicians and payers better, safer, more cost-effective healthcare.[46]

In discussing the company's approach to corporate social responsibility, Roche chairman Franz B. Humer explains: "Good corporate citizenship at Roche is a multifaceted process of commitment and action in areas ranging from humanitarian aid, health promotion and education to environmental stewardship and support for the arts."[47] Likewise, Bristol-Myers Sqibb states, "Our company's mission is to extend and enhance human life by providing the highest-quality pharmaceutical and related health care products."[48]

But our findings suggest that despite a publicly stated commitment to society, these companies were not initially able or willing to address Brazil's public health concerns. Notwithstanding their public CSR statements, our interviews with key Brazilians indicated that all of these companies actively resisted Brazil's efforts to negotiate lower prices for these newly patented medications in Brazil. Our interviews indicated that Brazil first approached the foreign pharmaceutical companies that produced many of the HIV medications and requested reduced prices. Initially the pharmaceutical companies refused. While our findings cannot conclusively identify the motivations behind this refusal, interviews with Brazilian government officials indicated that they believed that the companies were more focused on profitability than on CSR performance which was not highlighted by the companies in these negotiations.

Nevertheless, Brazilian government officials were still searching for a means to access low-cost medications. In response, the Brazilian government undertook an active and multi-faceted strategy to address a potential public health disaster and address the HIV epidemic. In order to force further negotiations, Brazilian government officials argued that it had the legal system in place to permit the issuance of compulsory licences for these medications, the political will to do so, and the necessary domestic capacity among Brazilian pharmaceutical companies to produce these medications.

Although Brazil has never actually issued a compulsory licence for an HIV medication, Article 68 of the 1996 Brazilian patent law permits the issuance of compulsory licences.[49] Under Brazilian law, a compulsory licence can be issued in a variety of different cases, including cases where the patent has been "exercised in an abusive manner."[50] Brazilian law also permits the issuance of a compulsory licence in the event that there has been a failure to exploit or manufacture the subject matter of the patent in Brazil.[51]

To further add weight to these negotiations, Far-Manguinhos investigated the possible domestic production of these patented medications. Because Far-Manguinhos has the capacity to reverse engineer and manufacture many of these medications, it can accurately assess its production costs and use these figures in negotiations with patent holders for reduced prices. Interviews suggested that this domestic capacity added weight to the Brazilian government's negotiations with the pharmaceutical companies. Initially, the pharmaceutical executives did not believe that Brazil had the capacity to produce quality medications. To counter this skepticism, Brazilian government officials invited executives from the multinational pharmaceutical companies to tour the production facilities at Far-Manguinhos in Rio de Janeiro to verify Brazil's capacity to reverse engineer and produce these medications.. Executives thus had the first-hand opportunity to see that Brazil had both the domestic will (through the threat of compulsory licence) and domestic ability to produce low-cost HIV medications. In July 2000 the Brazilian Minister of Health visited India to secure an agreement to get India to supply the raw materials to assist Brazilian production of HIV medications.

However, Brazil's strategy was not without counter-attack. In February 2001, the US took action against Brazil at the World Trade Organization over the local working requirement found in Article 68. The US did not contest the more general provisions dealing with the issuance of a compulsory licence where the patent has been exercised in an "abusive manner." These more general provisions are likely TRIPS consistent because, as noted above, article 31 of TRIPS permits compulsory licencing and TRIPS does not limit the grounds under which such a licence can be issued. Instead the US contested only the Brazilian law that permits the issuance of a compulsory licence where there has been a failure to exploit or manufacture the subject matter of the patent in Brazil. The US took the position that the Brazilian provisions were among other things inconsistent with Article 27.1 of TRIPS because they permit the issuance of a compulsory licence where the goods are not being domestically produced.[52] Article 27.1 of TRIPS prohibits discrimination between imported and domestically produced products.[53] The US took the position that local working requirements in effect discriminated against imported goods and were thus inconsistent with Article 27.1. Although Brazil had not actually issued a compulsory licence under its local working provision, the US still decided to pursue the matter before the WTO.

Over the next few months the ground shifted quickly. The US position, as represented in the February 2001 WTO challenge, underwent significant change that ultimately resulted in the Doha Declaration on TRIPS completed less than nine months later in November 2001.

Our document analysis and interviews also suggests that there were three major world events that helped to move this policy along. First was the UNGASS conference on HIV/AIDS held in New York in June 2001, second the World Trade Centre terrorist attack on September 11, 2001, and the subsequent anthrax scare, and finally the need to launch a new round of trade negotiations in Doha in November 2001.[54] Also crucial to all these developments was the increasingly influential involvement of global NGOs in the policy debate.

The UNGASS conference served to highlight the growing pressure to address the HIV epidemic in the developing world. The US had come under increasing pressure to abandon its WTO challenge to Brazil's local working requirements. Just before the conference opened in New York, as public pressure mounted, the US announced that it would withdraw its request for a WTO panel to review Brazil's local working requirements.[55] The UNGASS final declaration also indirectly addressed the controversial Brazilian strategy and asserted the need to strengthen "pharmaceutical policies and practices, including those applicable to generic drugs and intellectual property regimes, in order further to promote innovation and the development of domestic industries consistent with international law."[56]

As part of its campaign to get the US to alter its position, Brazil ran two advertisements in the *New York Times*, displayed in Figs. 1 and 2.[57]

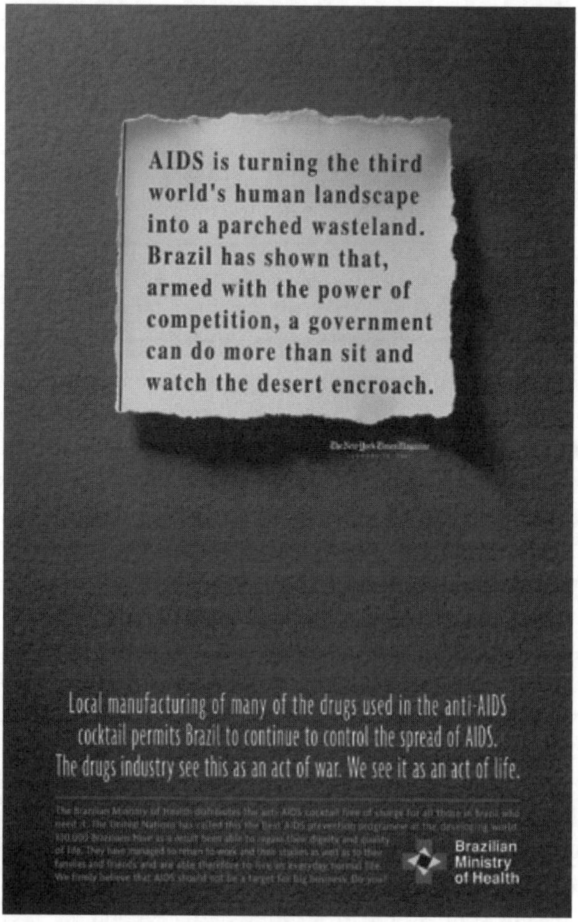

Figure 1

According to one senior Brazilian trade diplomat, it took three months to convince the *New York Times* to run the advertisements due to concerns about potential liability.[58] In compelling terms the advertisements outline Brazil's strategy is to build its local capacity to produce affordable HIV medications. The first notes that Brazil distributes HIV medications free of charge to over 100,000 Brazilians permitting them to return to work and live an "everyday normal life." It adds that local manufacturing is not an "act of war" but instead an "act of life" and that "AIDS should not be a target for big business."

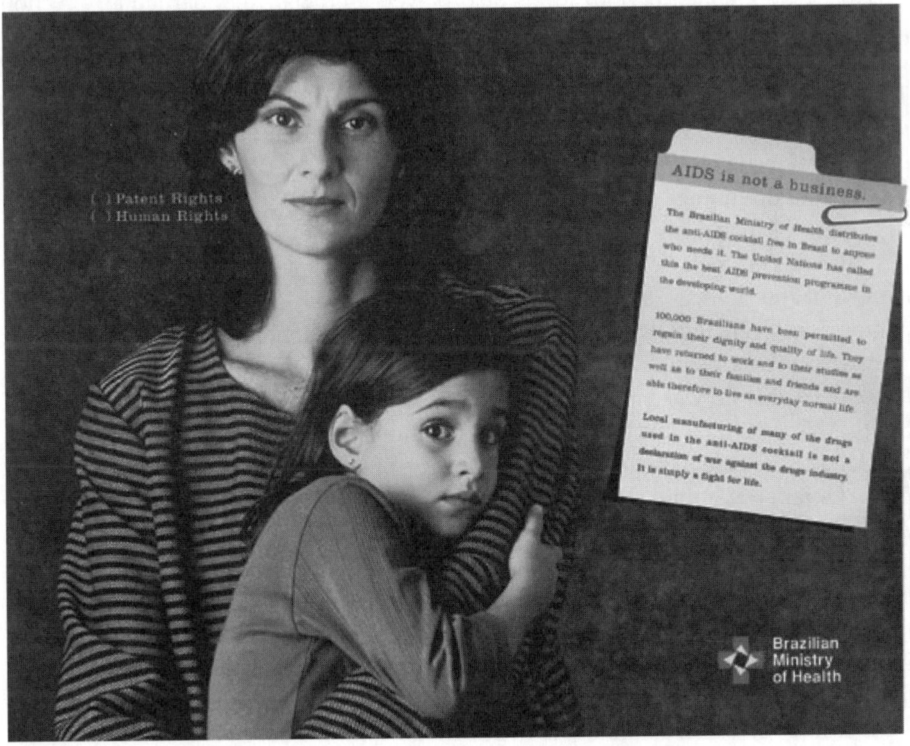

Figure 2

The second advertisement argues that "AIDS is not a business" and the local manufacturing of HIV medications is not a "declaration of war against the drug industry." The reader is given a choice between "patient rights" and "patent rights." The advertisements seem to focus on the local working requirements under which Brazil could issue a compulsory licence, thus the reference to "local manufacturing." But as our document analysis indicates, Brazilian law permits the issuance of a compulsory licence simply because the patent had been exercised in an "abusive manner" and it is not necessary to rely on any local working requirement. Nonetheless, the larger theme is that through the threat of a compulsory licence, Brazil was able both to negotiate lower prices and to develop its own domestic capacity to produce HIV medications.

The September 2001 terrorist attacks also fuelled this debate when both the US and Canada announced that they would investigate the possibility of permitting generic firms to produce copies of Cipro, the patented antibiotic used to treat anthrax.[59] Few observers missed the irony that countries like the US or Canada might set aside patent protection to produce Cipro, when only a handful of people had been affected by the anthrax attacks in the US following September 2001, yet simultaneously vigorously oppose similar measures to make HIV medications available in the developing world where HIV has killed tens of millions.

Non-governmental organizations also played a crucial role, particularly Action Aid, Medicins Sans Frontieres (MSF), Oxfam, Third World Network (TWN), Treatment Action Campaign (TAG), and the Consumer Project on Technology (CPT).[60] This debate represented an interesting example of global NGOs operating in concert with Brazil and other developing countries to increase the pressure on the US and other developed countries to modify their position. US pressure on South Africa and Thailand to discourage the use of compulsory licences in 1997 and 1998 marked the beginning of increasing NGO involvement in this issue. In one early example, the US HIV/AIDS advocacy group, ACT UP began disrupting Vice-president Gore's campaign appearances in 1999. Gore had been supportive of the US strategy to resist compulsory licencing in South Africa, however when banners began to appear at his campaign events reading "Gore's Greed Kills," his position quickly shifted and he announced that he was supportive of compulsory licencing and parallel imports in South Africa. At the same time, the Clinton administration withdrew its objections to the South African legislation authorizing the use of compulsory licences.[61] In October 2000, Oxfam UK got involved in the campaign and collaborated with MSF and CPT. All these NGOs collaborated in building public pressure to get the pharmaceutical companies to abandon their legal challenge of the South African legislation. The trial became a high profile event and a public relations disaster for pharmaceutical companies and the case was abandoned in April 2001. During the TRIPS negotiations, international NGOs were not significant players but in the post-TRIPS world, NGOs have become impressively engaged.

Pressure increased as the Doha negotiations approached. In November 2001 the members of the World Trade Organization met in Doha with the goal of launching a new round of trade negotiations. The previous meeting in Seattle in 1999 had ended in failure without an agreement to launch a new round, leading to enormous pressure on member countries to agree to a new round in the Doha negotiations. Access to HIV medications emerged as a deal breaker in these negotiations. Without some movement on this issue, it seemed most unlikely that leading developing countries such as India or Brazil would agree to the launch of a new round. And without a new round, the future of global trade was arguably at risk.

However, a new round of trade negotiations was successfully launched in Doha, a key part of which was the *Doha Declaration on the TRIPS Agreement and Public Health.*[62] This declaration represented a major success for the developing countries and their supporting coalition of non-governmental organizations. The *Doha Declaration* recognizes the "gravity of public health problems afflicting many developing and least-developed countries, especially those resulting from HIV/AIDS, tuberculosis, malaria and other epidemics."[63] Perhaps the most important provision in the *Declaration* is the recognition that each WTO member "has the right to grant compulsory licences and the freedom to determine the grounds on which such licences are granted."[64] As noted above, the US had consistently rejected this interpretation of TRIPS in its previous negotiations with Brazil, Thailand, and South Africa, taking the position that compulsory licences could only be issued where there was an adjudicated violation of competition laws or a declared national emergency. However, there is nothing in Article 31 of TRIPS that limits the grounds on which a compulsory licence can be granted, and the *Doha Declaration* simply states directly what is implicit in TRIPS itself: WTO members can determine for themselves the grounds on which they can issue a compulsory licence. Thus although the *Doha Declaration* did not alter TRIPS, it nonetheless had the very important result of legitimizing the successful Brazilian strategy by which it negotiated price reductions backed up by the threat of compulsory licencing.

Having confirmed its right to issue compulsory licences, Brazil has since been able to negotiate significant price reductions for HIV medications, including deep discounts from Roche, Abbott, Merck and Bristol-Myers Squibb ranging from 72 percent to 77 percent.[65] Even with the expected addition of 20,000 new patients to therapy and the introduction of two new medications (Tenofovir and Atazanavir), the Brazilian government has reduced by 37 percent the amount it will have to pay for HIV medications in 2004, the biggest price reductions on HIV medications that it has obtained in the last five years.[66] The average cost per patient of treatment will fall by more than half when compared with 1999.[67]

Discussion

This is an interesting story about the evolving mechanisms of corporate governance and corporate social responsibility, one that demonstrates the many levels and sites at which these mechanisms can operate. Our findings show that CSR action can be viewed as a dynamic negotiation—an interaction between multiple actors. Furthermore, our study highlights the importance of a strong role for national governments and international organizations, pressuring companies to perform better. This is an interesting finding because the CSR and corporate governance debate is often framed as a simple yet false dichotomy: that of voluntary compliance by companies versus regulatory enforcements by governments. The story here is more subtle.

First, the CSR policies (a normative dimension of corporate governance) of the pharmaceutical companies encourage companies to maximize health care and thus arguably to maximize the access of society to HIV medications. While the pharmaceutical companies have actively developed new medications to combat HIV/AIDS, the same companies are less active in developing new business approaches to dealing with developing countries which require low-cost medications. Such companies have developed appealing Corporate Social Responsibility (CSR) policies at the normative level, but our findings show that they were less active (in fact, most reluctant) in concretely addressing Brazil's public health concerns. Our study demonstrates that voluntary CSR initiatives were not sufficient to address Brazil's need for low cost HIV medications. Thus, there was a behavioural gap in corporate governance, whereby companies were not adequately addressing Brazil's HIV epidemic.

Secondly, our findings indicate that effective change required a national government, in this case Brazil, to push both the companies and the international community (e.g., via the WTO) to improve corporate governance at the normative and behavioural level in order to achieve low cost access to HIV medications in Brazil. Our findings thus demonstrate the necessity of active government participation in pressuring companies to engage meaningfully in CSR-related actions and provide low-cost HIV medications.

In summary, our study suggests that Brazil's success in turning around its HIV epidemic rests on the fact that the government did not rely only upon voluntary CSR initiatives. Instead, Brazil's success is linked to the government's active role in developing a strategy to pressure companies to make available affordable prices for HIV/AIDS medication, giving meaning to the pharmaceutical companies' declared policies on CSR.

Conclusion

Transnational corporations continue to be key drivers of development as many developing nations adopt policies and laws that favor liberalized trade and investment. For many countries in the developing world, the nation state is declining in importance, revealing a growing gap in international multi-level governance—a gap of particular significance for the (de)regulation of increasingly powerful transnational corporations. At the same time, the private transnational sector is moving to fill this gap through strategies of global corporate social responsibility, which may only partially address the governance issues of international trade and investment. Our research illuminates the need for governments to move beyond the passive acceptance of voluntary CSR initiatives and to consider active participation in CSR and corporate governance.

Notes

1. This research is sponsored with a grant from the Law Commission of Canada and the Social Sciences and Humanities Research Council of Canada. In addition, field research was supported by ERIM (Erasmus Research Institute of Management).

2. See the corporate social responsibility commitment of the CEO of Roche, infra note 46.

3. http://www.wbcsd.ch/templates/TemplateWBCSD5/layout.asp?MenuID=1.

4. OECD, "OECD Principles of Corporate Governance," 2004. http://www.oecd.org/pdf/M00015000015442.pdf.

5. S. Nestor, "International Efforts to Improve Corporate Governance: Why and How." Paris: OECD, 2001. www.oecd.org.

6. Ibid., p. 1.

7. Ibid.

8. A. Carroll, "Corporate Social Responsibility." *Business and Society* 38(3) (1999): 268–295.

9. A. Carroll, "The Pyramid of Corporate Social Responsibility: Toward the Moral Management of Organizational Stakeholders." *Business Horizons* 34 (1991): 39–48.

10. D. Wood, "Corporate Social Performance Revisited." *Academy of Management Review* 16(4) (1991): 691–718.

11. A. Kolk and R. van Tulder, *International Codes of Conduct: Trends, Sectors, Issues and Effectiveness*. Rotterdam: Erasmus University, 2002.

12. Kolk and van Tulder, *International Codes of Conduct*, p. 26.

13. OECD, "Making Codes of Corporate Conduct Work: Management Control Systems and Corporate Responsibility." Working papers on international investment, number 2001/3. Paris: OECD, 2001. http://www.oecd.org/dataoecd/45/29/1922806.pdf.

14. M. Hammersley and P. Atkinson, *Ethnography: Principles in Practice*, 2nd edition. London: Routledge, 1995.

15. World Bank. 2002. http://devdata.worldbank.org/external/CPProfile.asp?SelectedCountry=BRA&CCODE=BRA&CNAME=Brazil&PTYPE=CP.

16. UNAIDS, *2004 Report on the Global AIDS Epidemic*, Table of Country Specific HIV/AIDS Estimates and Data as of the end of 2003, http://www.unaids.org/bangkok2004/GAR2004_html/GAR2004_00_en.htm.

17. UNAIDS, http://www.unaids.org/EN/Geographical+Area/by+country/brazil.asp.

18. http://www.iprcommission.org (London: Commission on Intellectual Property Rights, 2002), at pp. 50–51.

19. The TRIPS Agreement is attached as Annex 1C to the WTO Agreement. http://www.wto.org/english/docs_e/legal_e/legal_e.htm. For a general discussion of TRIPS, see J. S. Thomas and M. A. Meyer, *The New Rules of Global Trade* (Toronto: Carswell, 1997); *Intellectual Property and International Trade: The TRIPS Agreement*, ed. C. M. Correa and A. A. Yusuf (London: Kluwer Law, 1998); and J. Watal, *Intellectual Property Rights in the WTO and Developing Countries* (The Hague: Kluwer Law, 2001).

20. Article 33.

21. Article 65(2)–(3).

22. Article 66(1). This period was later extended under Article 7 of the "Doha Declaration on the TRIPS Agreement and Public Health" (World Trade Organization [Geneva: WTO, 2001]). http://www.wto.org/english/thewto_e/minist_e/min01_e/mindecl_trips_e.htm.

23. India is able to produce HIV medications at a much lower cost than in developed countries. A UN study reports that 150 mg of the HIV drug fluconazole costs $55 in India and around $700 to $800 in countries where it is patented, such as Indonesia and the Philippines. Another HIV treatment, AZT, costs $48 a month in India compared to $239 a month in the United States, where it is patented: United Nations, Report of the High Commissioner of the Human Rights Commission on Economic, Social and Cultural Rights, The Impact of the Agreement on Trade-Related Aspects of Intellectual Property Rights on Human Rights, UN Doc E/CN.4/Sub.2/2001/13 at 14, para. 44 (2001) ("UNCHR Report"). Combination HIV therapy in the US costs about $10,000 to $15,000 a year. If sourced from the Indian pharmaceutical industry, the same therapy can cost as little as $200–$300 a year. World Bank, *Battling HIV/AIDS: A Decision Maker's Guide to the Procurement and of Medicines and Relates Supplies* (Washington: World Bank, 2004), at p. 80.

24. Article 31(b) TRIPS.

25. Article 31(b). "Public non-commercial use" would likely include situations where a government procurement authority is purchasing medications for distribution through public clinics and without seeking to make any commercial profit from such distribution: World Bank, *Battling HIV/AIDS: A Decision Maker's Guide to the Procurement and of Medicines and Related Supplies* (Washington: World Bank, 2004), at p. 121.

26. Article 31(c) and (d).

27. Article 31(f).

28. Article 31(h).

29. See S. M. Ford, "Compulsory Licensing Provisions Under TRIPS Agreement: Balancing Pills and Patents" (2000), 15 *Am. U. Int'l L. Rev.* 941; and A. O. Sykes, "TRIPS, Pharmaceuticals, Developing Countries and the Doha 'Solution'" (2002), 3 *Chi. J. Int'l L.* 47; Watal, *Intellectual Property Rights*, at pp. 318–329; and World Bank, *Battling HIV/AIDS*, pp. 119–125. For a review of the history of the use of compulsory licences by the US, UK, and Canada, see F. M. Scherer and Jayashree Watal, "Post-TRIPS Options for Access to Patented Medications in Developing Nations" (2002), 5 Oxford Univ. Press Journal of International Economic Law 913.

30. Watal, *Intellectual Property Rights*, p. 320.

31. World Trade Organization, Doha Declaration on TRIPS Agreement and Public Health.

32. J. M. N. Viana, "Intellectual Property Rights, the World Trade Organization and Public Health: The Brazilian Perspective" (2002), 17 *Conn. J. of Int'l Law* 311, at 312.

33. UNAIDS, http://www.unaids.org/EN/Geographical+Area/by+country/brazil.asp.

34. WHO Press Release (WHO/58), July 8, 2002, www.who.int/mediacentre/news/re/eases/who58/en/index.html.

35. http://www.iprcommission.org, at pp. 50–51.

36. Interviews were conducted with three members of the Brazilian Ministry of Health, Far-Manguinhos, Oswaldo Cruz Foundation (FIOCRUZ), on March 18, 2003: N. Boechat, Director; A. A. Soares, Manager of Development; and C. d'Almeida, Intellectual Property Adviser.

37. "Nossos Produtos" Far Manguinhos, http://www.far.fiocruz.br.

38. Interview with C. d'Almedia, March 18, 2003.

39. Prior to TRIPS, in many developing countries, particularly Latin America and South and East Asia, product and even process patents were excluded for inventions relating to food, agriculture, chemical, and pharmaceutical products. See Watal, *Intellectual Property Rights*, p. 109.

40. Article 27 of TRIPS provides that "patents shall be available for any inventions, whether products or processes, in all fields of technology, provided that they are new, involve an inventive step and are capable of industrial application."

41. http://www.iprcommission.org, at pp. 50–51.

42. Interview with C. d'Almedia, March 18, 2003. See also M. Jordan, "Brazil to Stir Up AIDS-Drug Battle," *Wall St. Journal* (September 5, 2003).

43. http://www.merck.com/about/mission.html.

44. Ibid.

45. http://www.merck.com/about/cr/.

46. http://www.roche.com/home/company/com_ceo/com_ceo_read.htm.

47. http://www.roche.com/home/company/com_soc_com_intro/com_soc_com_foreword.htm. Accessed 15 November 2004.

48. http://www.bms.com/aboutbms/content/data/ourple.html.

49. Article 68 of Brazil's patent law allows for compulsory licencing. See the "Lei da Propriedate Industrial," Decretp Mp/ 9.279, art. 68, 14 de maio de 1996, D.O. de 15.05.1996 (Braz.), translated in British Industrial Property Law 23 (1998): "A patent owner shall be subject to the grant of compulsory licence of his patent if the rights resulting therefrom are exercised in an abusive manner or if the patent is used in abuse of economic power, as proven by an administrative or judicial decision pursuant to the provisions of the law." See also J. M. N. Viana, "Intellectual Property Rights, the World Trade Organization and Public Health: The Brazilian Perspective," 17 *Conn. J. of Int'l Law* 311 (2002), p. 312.

50. Viana, "Intellectual Property Rights," p. 312.

51. Article 68, supra, provides that in addition to the issuance of a compulsory licence for abuse of "economic power," a compulsory licence may also be issued for the "non-exploitation of the object of the patent within the Brazilian territory for failure to manufacture the product of failure to fully use a patented process, except in cases of economic unfeasibility, in which case

importation shall be permitted." See P. Champ and A. Attaran, "Patent Rights and Local Working under the WTO TRIPS Agreement: An Analysis of the U.S.-Brazil Patent Dispute," 27 *Yale J. Int'l L.* 365 (2002), at note 97, p. 382.

52. Champ and Attaran, "Patent Rights."

53. Article 27.1 of TRIPS provides that "patent rights [shall be] enjoyable without discrimination as to . . . whether products are imported or locally produced."

54. United Nations General Assembly Special Session on HIV/AIDS (UNGASS), June 25–27, 2001, http://www.unaids.org/html/pub/publications/irc-pub03/aidsdeclaration_en_pdf.pdf; *Doha Declaration*, November 14, 2001: http://www.wto.org/english/thewto_e/minist_e/min01_e/mindecl_e.htm.

55. Viana, "Intellectual Property Rights." See Joint Communication Brazil-United States, June 25, 2001. The UN Commission of Human Rights (Resolution 2001/33, Access to Medication in the Context of Pandemics such as HIV/AIDS, 57th Sess. April 2001) had also been critical of the US actions against Brazil.

56. *United Nations Declaration of Commitment on HIV/AIDS*, June 27, 2001, para. 55.

57. Copies obtained from J. Viana in the July 19, 2002 interview.

58. J. Viana, interview, 19 July 2002.

59. Viana, "Intellectual Property Rights."

60. For a review of NGO involvement, see Ellen't Hoen, "TRIPS, Pharmaceutical Patents and Access to Essential Medicines: A Long Way from Seattle to Doha" (2002) 3 *Chi. J. Int'l L.* 27, at 31; S. K. Sell, "TRIPS and Access to Medicines Campaign" (2002) 20 *Wis. Int'l L. J.* 481, at 500; and F. M. Abbott, "The Doha Declaration on the TRIPS Agreement and Public Health: Lighting a Dark Corner at the WTO" (2002) 5(2) *Journal of Inter. Eco. Law* 469. at 478–79.

61. Sell, "TRIPS and Access to Medicines Campaign," p. 503.

62. WTO, *Declaration on the TRIPS Agreement and Public Health.* For commentary, see A. Lacayo, "Seeking a Balance: International Pharmaceutical Patent Protection, Public Health Crisis, and the Emerging Threat of Bio-Terrorism" (2002) 33 *U. Miami Inter-Am. L. Rev.* 295; A. O. Sykes, "TRIPS, Pharmaceuticals, Developing Countries, and the Doha 'Solution'" (2002) 3 *Chi. J. Int'l L.* 47; A. Attaran, "The Doha Declaration of the TRIPS Agreement and Public Health, Access to Pharmaceuticals, and Options under WTO Law" (2002) 12 *Fordham Intell. Prop. Media and Ent. L. J.* 859; and F. M. Abbott, "The Doha Declaration on the TRIPS Agreement and Public Health: Lighting a Dark Corner at the WTO" (2002) 5(2) *Journal of Inter. Eco. Law* 469.

63. Para. 1, *Doha Declaration*, supra.

64. Para. 5(b), *Doha Declaration*, supra.

65. M. Osava, "Lula Pressing for New Drug-Price Cuts in AIDS Fight" IPS-Inter Press Service (January 14, 2004). In September 2003, the President of Brazil issued a decree indicating the willingness of Brazil to issue a compulsory licence to permit the domestic production of generic versions of patented HIV medications: Miriam Jordan, "Brazil to Stir Up AIDS-Drug Battle" Wall St. Journal (September 5, 2003).

66. *Gazeta Mercantile Online* (Brazil) (January 16, 2004).

67. Ibid.

The Authors

William Flanagan is the Dean of Law of the Faculty of Law, Queen's University, Kingston, ON, Canada. E-mail: wflan@sympatico.ca.

Gail Whiteman is Assistant Professor, Department of Business and Society, Rotterdam School of Management, RSM Erasmus University, Netherlands. E-mail: gwhiteman@fbk.eur.nl.

THE USE OF INFORMATION AND COMMUNICATION TECHNOLOGIES FOR PROVIDING ACCESS TO HIV/AIDS INFORMATION MANAGEMENT IN A RESOURCE-POOR COUNTRY: NIGERIA, A CASE STUDY

Adedayo O. Adeyemi
M. H. Ayegboyin
Healthmatch International, Lagos, Nigeria

Abstract

We investigate the growing use of information and communication technology in Nigeria and its potential as a tool to combat the HIV/AIDS epidemic through information management. Potential applications include data gathering for research and disease tracking, knowledge sharing, and dissemination of information on research findings, prevention methods, available care and support, and patient rights. The research is based on 1450 responses to a widely distributed questionnaire.

Background

HIV/AIDS is the greatest challenge today to the healthcare delivery and surveillance systems of a resource-poor country like Nigeria. Information and communication technologies (ICT) can provide efficient and cost-effective access to HIV information management.[1] ICT can promote HIV/AIDS research and service delivery by providing health information to the public facilitating the collection of data.

The use of economical and reliable information and communication technologies such as the Internet, computers, CD-ROMs, and mobile phones is a necessity in the management and routine surveillance of HIV/AIDS. They can assist in collecting information on control, prevention, treatment, care and support, as well as in storing and retrieving information. ICT can make information available via e-mail or a mobile network of telecom providers.

Nigeria has a population of about 112 million (1999), with an HIV-positive incidence of 5.4 percent, or about 6 million people.[2] Due to the growing population and increasing risks of contracting HIV/AIDS, ICT is an information management tool that must be embraced in the fight against this disease. Poor information management[3] practices from the past, however, must be addressed and corrected with affordable, appropriate, and sustainable information systems that will work.[4]

 pp. 393–400

In Nigeria today there are a growing number of mobile phone operators, fixed wireless telephone operators, several registered and unregistered Internet service providers, and numerous cyber cafés. These provide an infrastructural opportunity for aggressive, sustainable, and far-reaching HIV/AIDS information management for control and prevention programs in the country. The introduction of reliable and cost effective ICT tools such as e-mail, websites, and mobile phone networks will go a long way toward providing access to HIV/AIDS information management in this resource-poor country.

Understanding the information needs of all the stakeholders in the country, including population at risk and people living with HIV/AIDS, is crucial to good design and implementation of an ICT program for information management for both service delivery and all forms of research.[5] HIV/AIDS directly and indirectly affects all of humanity, and combating the disease through information management is a challenge to the entire world.

The impact of HIV/AIDS on the Nigerian society and economy is felt at individual, family, community, and national levels, especially in the health sector. ICT tools must be employed to mitigate this effect, first through efficient information management, and subsequently by scaling up to HIV/AIDS prevention activities.

Hypothesis

Information and communication technology can facilitate HIV/AIDS information management in a resource-poor setting.

Objectives

- To assess ICT use in HIV/AIDS management in Nigeria.
- To promote wider ICT use in HIV/AIDS management.

Methodology

A survey of 1,450 people was conducted in September 2003 by distributing a questionnaire in six geopolitical zones. The aim was to examine access to preventive information, treatment information, care, and support, as well as government policies and patient rights relative to HIV/AIDS. The percentage of people with personal computers, handheld computers, access to the Internet, and mobile phones was also examined.

Results

Five percent (73) of the people in the survey had personal (desktop) computers, and none had a handheld or palmtop computer. Eight percent (116) had access to the Internet 24/7, while 65 percent (943) people had access to a mobile phone, 24 percent (348) had access to a land phone, and 72 percent (1044) had personal e-mail addresses (Fig. 1).

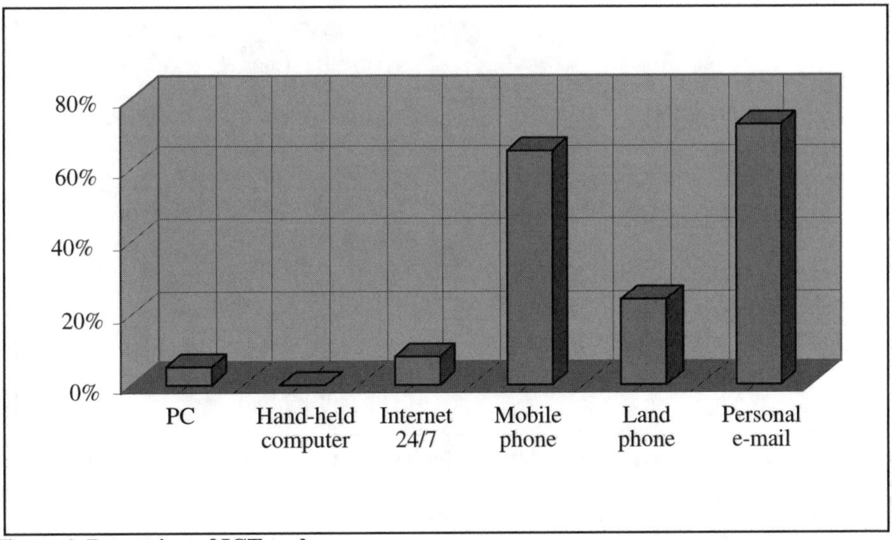

Figure 1. Possession of ICT tools

Only 2 percent (29) of the people surveyed had ever checked or searched the Internet for HIV/AIDS-related information, while the remaining 98 percent (1421) had never done so (Fig. 2).

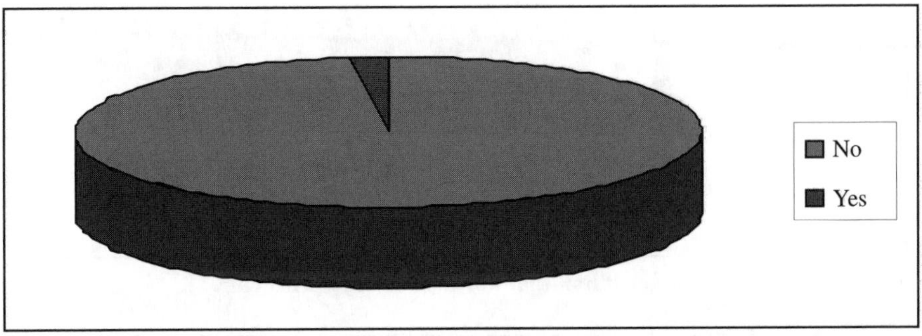

Figure 2. Have respondents searched for HIV/AIDS information on the Internet?

Seventy percent (1015) of the respondents had used the Internet for less than six months at the time of the survey, while 18 percent (261) had used the Internet for more than six months, but 12 percent (174) had never used the Internet before.

Of the 88 percent (1276) who had used the Internet before, 89 percent (1136) of them used it in a cyber café, 2 percent (26) used it at home, and 9 percent (115) used it at work.

Ninety-one percent (1320) of the people in the survey believed that there was a need for the creation of local HIV/AIDS websites to access preventive information, treatment information, care and support, government policies, or information about

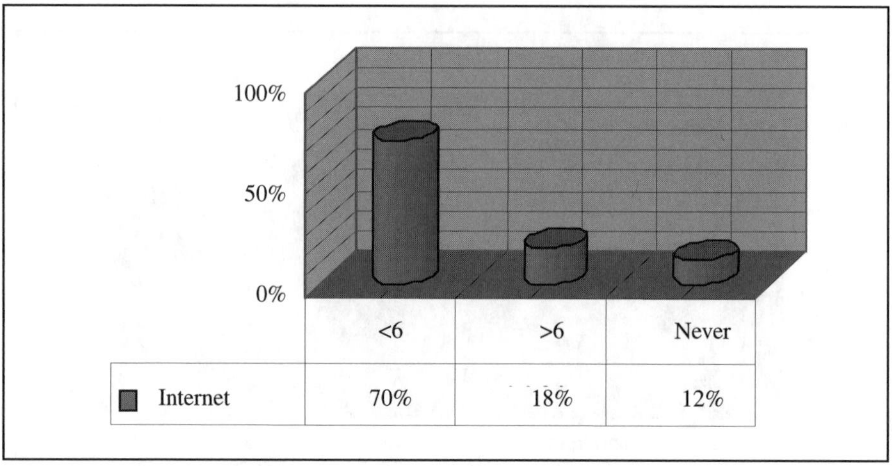

Figure 3. Respondents have used the Internet for less than six months, more than six months, or never.

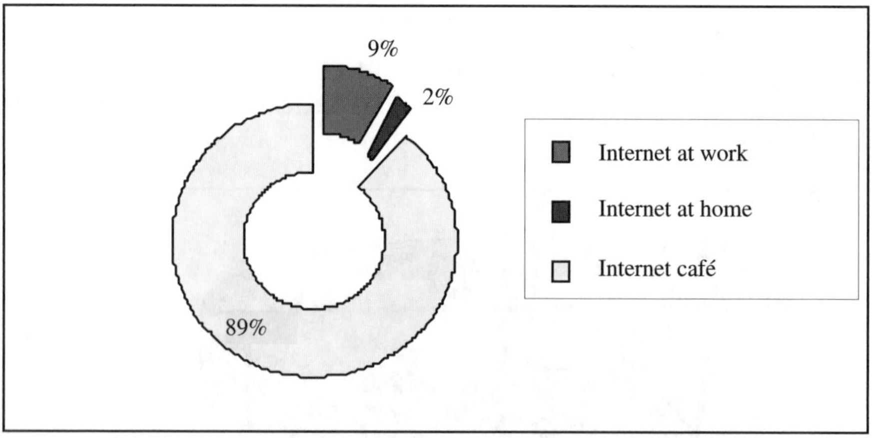

Figure 4. Use of the Internet at home, at work, or at an Internet cafe.

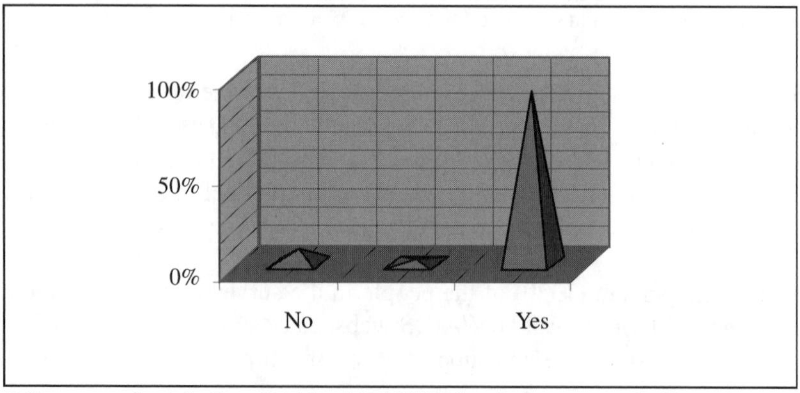

Figure 5. Do respondents believe that local HIV/AIDS websites are needed?

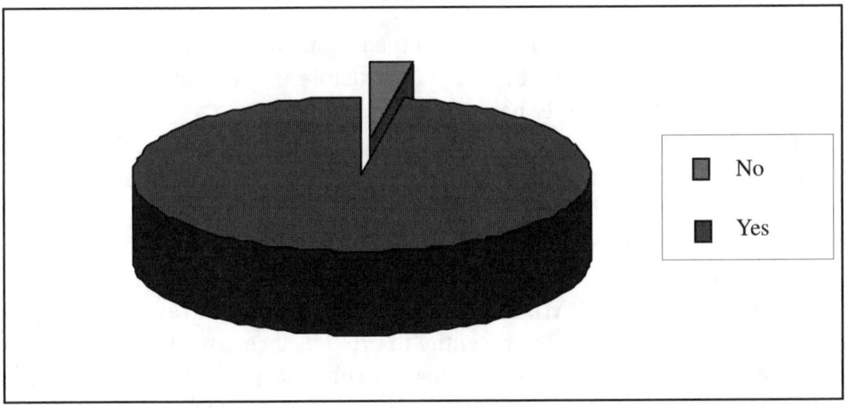

Figure 6. Do respondents believe HIV/AIDS-related ICT should be developed in Nigeria?

rights in HIV/AIDS management and research findings, while 7 percent (102) felt there was no need, and 2 percent (29) were undecided.

In addition, 97 percent (1407) advocated for effective development and use of ICT in HIV/AIDS information management in Nigeria, while 3 percent (44) felt there was no need for this.

Discussion

Information and communication technologies offer an excellent avenue for providing access to HIV/AIDS information. The results above show that ICT use affects HIV/AIDS information management in a resource-poor setting like Nigeria. Unfortunately, however, ICT use for this purpose is still very limited. There is a need for ICT development and, in particular, the creation of local HIV/AIDS websites for service delivery and information management.

In the past, improper information management has led to poor analysis of the HIV/AIDS situation and possible control measures. HIV/AIDS information management[6] in Nigeria should be thoroughly assessed and evaluated, so that the results of research can be applied to determining good policies for access to care. There is a similar need to study the potential usage of ICT[7] and its relevance[8] to managing and coordinating HIV/AIDS research projects. HIV/AIDS information management should harness the potential of the Internet, mobile phones, land phones, handheld computers, and e-mail addresses.

Nigeria should improve its information and knowledge management for HIV/AIDS control and prevention.[9] ICT can enhance information sharing among stakeholders, as well as information access, gathering, utilization, and dissemination. It can improve the quality of prevention, control, and health services delivery in the fight against HIV/AIDS.

Conclusion

The use of ICT in HIV/AIDS information management in Nigeria remains limited, despite the increasing potential of ICT infrastructure in the country. Unfortunately, this potential has yet to be fully harnessed.

There is a need to maximize the performance and usefulness of ICT in several aspects of HIV/AIDS information management. It can aid with research, decision making, health policy formulation, and advocacy based on research findings and available data. Appropriate policy and management structures should be developed to help realize the potential of ICT for HIV/AIDS prevention and control. Prevention is the first line of defense against HIV/AIDS, and it can readily be made available through ICT tools.[10] In particular, ICT has the potential to provide access to HIV/AIDS information through web-based discussion groups, e-mail, websites, CD-ROMs (especially for those without Internet access or full Internet connection), online discussions, telemedicine, database management, continuing medical education, virtual libraries, videoconferencing and networking.[11]

The HIV/AIDS epidemic has the potential to devastate Nigeria, rolling back years of progress toward a healthier and more prosperous tomorrow. More sustained and appropriate use of ICT is required, to enhance information management for the effective and coordinated control and prevention of HIV/AIDS.[12] The Nigerian government should issue an information technology policy with the aim of safeguarding the national healthcare system against devastation by the HIV/AIDS epidemic.[13] The health ministry and local NGOs should enhance their skills in CIT approaches.

Finally, HIV/AIDS is not a problem of the health sector alone but of all sectors in Nigeria. There should be full adoption of various forms of ICT, not only to strengthen efforts to manage the impacts of HIV/AIDS, but as a strategy against poverty.

Recommendations

- All Federal and State Ministries of Health and HIV/AIDS organizations should create elaborate websites with local content relating to HIV/AIDS prevention and control, treatment, government policies on HIV/AIDS, care and support, and the protection of rights of people living with HIV/AIDS.
- The government, working through the National Action Committee on AIDS (NACA), should encourage mobile telephone operators to send weekly HIV/AIDS information on prevention, control, treatment, and care and support through their networks to their subscribers, in the form of short message service (SMS) or text messages. More people use and have access to mobile phones than computers.
- There is a need to focus funding on ICT applications for HIV/AIDS research and information management in Nigeria.
- A national policy should be adopted to increase access to the Internet/ICT, so as to create a reasonable enabling environment for HIV/AIDS information management.

- There should be a national policy to provide computer and Internet training to all stakeholders involved in HIV/AIDS control and prevention, including people living with HIV/AIDS, so that the potential of the Internet can be fully harnessed in information management.
- The United Nations Development Program should assist in prevention programs by using their World Space Satellite System to help with information management in Nigeria.
- CD-ROM development should be promoted for areas with poor Internet access.
- An international organization or agency should create a Nigerian HIV/AIDS Information Management Center that will promote information management, policies, and networking.
- The use of handheld computers should be promoted in Nigeria in the healthcare delivery system, so as to provide access to HIV/AIDS information management even in rural areas.
- Databases should be established and funded by international donor agencies, together with knowledge sharing and information sharing networks. ICT is vital to the development of both.
- Online HIV/AIDS learning modules should be created for secondary and post secondary school students, as their reception to the use of the Internet is gradually increasing.

Notes

1. A. O. Adeyemi and M. H. Ayegboyin, "A Study on the Use of Information Systems to Prevent HIV/AIDS in Lagos State, Nigeria," Informedica 2004: 3rd Virtual Congress of Medical Informatics, 1–30 March 2004.

2. "HIV/Syphilis Sentinel Sero-Prevalence Survey in Nigeria," Technical Report, National AIDS Control Programme. Federal Ministry of Health, 1999.

3. I. Akinsete, "Situation Analysis Report on STD/HIV/AIDS in Nigeria," Technical Report, National AIDS/STD Control Programme, Federal Ministry of Health, March 2000.

4. M. Korpela, "Information Systems for Healthcare Management and Services: How to Ensure Their Impact, Appropriateness and Sustainable Development?" Invited presentation in World IT Forum / Health Commission, Vilnius, 27–28 August 2003.

5. A. O. Adeyemi, "The Role of Health Informatics in HIV/AIDS Control in Nigeria," HELINA 2003 Conference, Communication and Information Technology in the Global Fight against HIV/AIDS, Johannesburg, South Africa, 2003.

6. N. Stoops, "An Assessment and Evaluation of the Use of the HISP (Health Information System Programme) Computer Software Package in the Cape Metropole Region, Western Cape, South Africa," HELINA 1999: Third International Conference on Health Informatics in Africa, Harare, Zimbabwe, 29 Nov–2 Dec 1999, 26–29.

7. J. Braa, E. Macome, J. C. Mavimbe, J. L. Nhampossa, J. L. da Costa, B. José, A. Manave, and A. Sitói, "A Study of the Actual and Potential Usage of Information and Communication Technology at District and Provincial Levels in the Health Sector in Mozambique," HELINA 1999:

Third International Conference on Health Informatics in Africa, Harare, Zimbabwe, 29 Nov–2 Dec, 1999, 162–167.

8. A. Shamboul and A. Hasman, "The Relevance of Information Technology to Health Sector in Developing Countries—Baseline Study," HELINA 1999: Third International Conference on Health Informatics in Africa, Harare, Zimbabwe. 29 Nov–2 Dec, 1999, 149.

9. R. G. Wilson, "Strengthening Primary Health Care Programme Management through Informatics and Improved Management Information Systems," *Information Technology for Development* 4 (1989): 703–732. A. Mursu, H. A. Soriyan, and M. Korpela, "Risky Business: A Case Study on Information Systems Development in Nigeria," In *Information & Communication Technologies and Development: New Opportunities, Perspectives and Challenges*, ed. S. Krishna and S. Madon. Proceedings of the Seventh International Working Conference of IFIP WG 9.4, Bangalore, India, May 29–31, 2002, Bangalore: Indian Institute of Management, 385–401. M. Korpela, "Information Systems for Healthcare Management."

10. "Effectiveness of Condoms in Preventing Sexually Transmitted Infections including HIV," WHO and UNAIDS Information Note, 15 August 2001.

11. M. J. Kelly, "The Response of Information and Communications Technology to the Challenge of HIV/AIDS in Higher Education Institutions in Africa," *The African Symposium: An Online Educational Research Journal* 2(1) (2002), http://www.ncsu.edu/ncsu/aern/mjkelly.html.

12. Adeyemi, "The Role of Health Informatics."

13. *The National Health Policy and Strategy to Achieve Health for All Nigerians*, Lagos: Federal Government of Nigeria, 1996.

The Authors

Adedayo O. Adeyemi and M. H. Ayegboyin are affiliated with Healthmatch International, P.O. Box 123, Unilag Post Office, Akoka-Yaba, Lagos, Nigeria. Healthmatch is a research and outreach NGO concerned with HIV/AIDS control and developing health information systems. Mr. Adeyemi's e-mail address is dayo_bunmi@yahoo.com.

CORPORATE SOCIAL RESPONSIBILITY: AN INFORMATION STRATEGY

Pegram Harrison
European Business School, London

Abstract

Corporate Social Responsibility (CSR) continues to evolve as an important paradigm for business strategy. There is much disparate information about it available; evaluating that information and deciding what applies to any given organisation is thus becoming a more complicated task. With an idea to simplifying this process, the Sustainable Development Unit at the Royal Institute for International Affairs (RIIA) considered how it might position itself as an information filter for CSR generally. The research summarised here concludes that CSR is too large and vague a concept to be practical or applicable, and suggests that an international organisation such as RIIA should concentrate on creating opportunities for focusing the idea, rather than actually attempting to effect practical change. Whether these opportunities emerge out of discussion, analysis, research, policy briefings, or by other means, will depend on the nature and timing of any specific topic within the overall CSR context.

Introduction

> CSR has never been more prominent on the corporate agenda than it is today, its historical origins and the uncertainty about the societal obligations of business notwithstanding. (Smith 2003: 3)

There is an extremely large quantity of interest and publication in the area of Corporate Social Responsibility (CSR). Whatever CSR is—and it is notoriously difficult to define—it is an exploding phenomenon. Interest at the corporate, academic, governmental, and NGO policy levels, as well as in the media and financial communities, is emphasizing the topic now more than ever. Because of this, the likelihood that any one organisation will gain a comprehensive understanding of the field is constantly decreasing. The need for coordinating, consolidating, and condensing efforts is broadly felt. Whether the emerging supply of such efforts is adequate to the task, and whether the principles of selection and evaluation by which they operate are worthy or efficient, has also become of great import in turn. In effect, how can one evaluate the evaluators? Quis custodet custodes? In the effort to inculcate greater trust

 pp. 401–417

in corporations and commercial institutions generally, the importance of maintaining that trust in the facilitators of the debate is also crucial.

Definitions

Part of the problem is the definition of CSR. The concept can be said to have existed for a long time, with various names and in very many forms, and yet never really to have settled on a stable meaning. Possibly its roots are in the paternalism of Victorian social reformers who worked from within the managerial classes to improve and defend the living conditions of their employees—whether by ethical, religious, or even commercial motivations. Some might consider the increased social consciousness of the 1960s as a source of much systemic change in corporate practice. Recently, more explicit institutional attention has been paid to the study and practice of the idea, with increased attention following various environmental and public relations disasters in the oil and extraction industries, pension fund collapses (Equitable Life), political stalemates (Kyoto Protocol), and corporate accounting scandals (Enron, WorldCom, Marconi, Parmalat). The pressure to reconstruct the Balkans, Afghanistan, and Iraq through sensible engagement of entrepreneurial impulses and foreign direct investment; the continuing imbalances of interests and entitlements in Latin America and Africa; the pace of unsustainable development in the developing world—each of these current issues motivates debate on CSR. But thirty years ago this was not a new topic, and even at that time it was observed that the term was sufficiently catholic to mean all things to all people (Sethi 1975: n. 9). Throughout the span between the present day and the Industrial Revolution in Britain, as early as the 1830s, interest in the social responsibilities of commerce and the corporate entities that conduct it, has been evolving. Thus the term "CSR" is not a stable one, and to use it indiscriminately or injudiciously is counterproductive.

Each participant in the debate tries to operate according to some definition or another, but there are too many participants and too many definitions for the field to stabilize. Much stress is currently placed on CSR by global corporate bodies such as the World Economic Forum (WEF 2003), the World Business Council for Sustainable Development (WBCSD 1999), the International Business Leaders Forum, Business for Social Responsibility, Business in the Community. A massive quantity of publication on the topic, in mainstream as well as academic, management-oriented, and specific industry-related sources, further testifies to the accelerated interest in the idea of CSR. In Britain alone there are hundreds of organisations—think tanks, policy units, NGOs, conference organisers, university research units—that purport to monitor and comment upon CSR, each one of them producing outputs in various media: Ethical Corporation (2004), SustainAbility (2004), ResponsAbility (2004), Forum for the Future (2004). Perhaps most tellingly for our times, websites and portals and discussion groups are proliferating to provide dynamic information, analysis, online "solutions," comparisons of codes of practice, etc.: Global Ethics Monitor (2004), AccountAbility (2004), PCG Worldwide (Coorsh 2003), etc.

Additional complexity is added by the fact that CSR is a term applied with equal frequency to practice in governance, accounting, reporting, management, strategy, production-oriented, and environmental contexts—more or less anywhere along the supply-chain, and most of the way along the value chain as a whole. As a term, it is fast becoming a catch-all, like "value" or "leadership" that can be put at the service of almost any point or policy. As with other such "fads" there is a risk of the concept fading from acceptance or credibility, despite the vague general intuition that there is something important about it.

Figure 1 describes a "hype" curve, whereby too many elements converge on the concept without sufficient clarity of objective, eventually slowing progress toward general, innate understanding of the concept and how to accommodate into normal business practice.

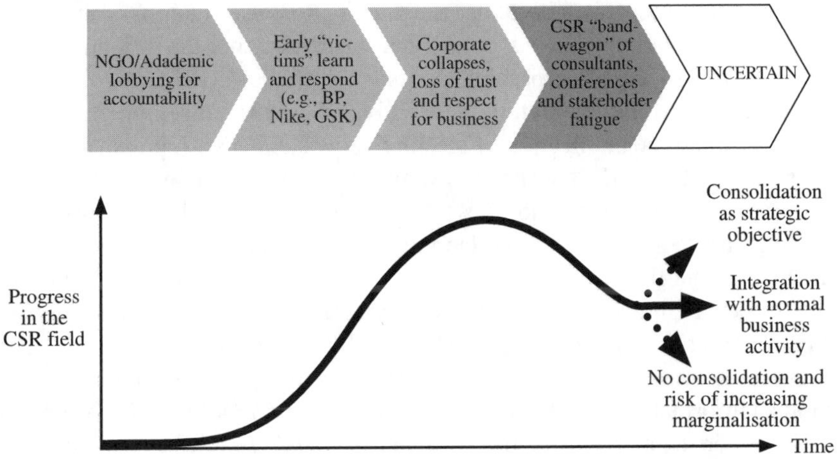

Figure 1. "Hype Curve"

There have been various attempts to change this pattern, or to establish terms of reference, or actually to assert a definition—all in the service of getting beyond debate and down to business in a responsible way. If the impulse behind these attempts is one of frustration, then that is only likely to mount as debate continues and focus dissipates. But no one organisation, or government, or legal code, or voluntary code of conduct, or normative impulse will satisfy all participants and create an uncomplicated atmosphere for practical change—and the search for such a utopian state seems an inappropriate use of resources.

Alternatives

While it is important to be aware of debate, it is equally import to focus that debate toward actionable outcomes: "a key question is whether [the CSR] agenda demands new approaches. . . . The challenge is to recognize the value of engaging in serious discussion on how to eradicate the most exploitative forms of business behaviour from the global economy" (Ward 2002: 1, 11). Here the focus is on change, and here the focus must stay if it is to be useful.

Organisations placed by circumstance somewhat near the centre of the debate (think tanks, universities, research institutes) have a role to play. To the extent that they can be neutral, or can facilitate the exchange of ideas between more polarised perspectives in the debate, they create opportunities wherein the actual exchange of ideas is productive, engaged and actionable—where debate is focused toward change.

Change at Chatham House

The Royal Institute of International Affairs (RIIA), also known as Chatham House, is one of the world's leading institutes for the analysis of international issues. RIIA works to stimulate debate and research on political, business, security and other key issues in the international arena. The Chatham House Rule, famous worldwide for facilitating free speech and confidentiality at meetings, originated here: "When a meeting, or part thereof, is held under the Chatham House Rule, participants are free to use the information received, but neither the identity nor the affiliation of the speaker(s), nor that of any other participant, may be revealed" (RIIA website 2003). The chief mechanisms for conducting these activities are the convening of seminars and discussions, and the publication of briefing papers and other reports.

In the spring of 2003 RIIA began to re-evaluate its own position in the CSR debate, aware of its resources and responsibilities to take a more focused role. The Sustainable Development Programme (SDP), in collaboration with the European Business School London (EBSL) and the London Business School (LBS), initiated a study into the feasibility of developing some sort of CSR information service at Chatham House.

The initial remit was very broad: how should RIIA best be involved in CSR? Subsequent questions emerged from this: should RIIA be simply a source of information, or should that information be enhanced or edited in some way? Should RIIA function as a venue for debate, and who should participate? Can these roles act as a force for change, and if so how? What are the resources available or procurable to achieve or expand these roles? Beginning with a survey of the "market" for RIIA's CSR activities and developing a set of four strategic options by which RIIA might supply the demands of that market, the process culminated in some clear recommendations. What follows presents those recommendations and demonstrates that RIIA is in a position to change its own involvement in the CSR debate. In so doing, it has the opportunity to effect more substantive change in international business practice generally.

Change beyond Chatham House

In the course of conducting the feasibility study, a clear pattern emerged from all sources of information: CSR can backfire or spin its wheels as much as any other vehicle for attempting social change. Should RIIA spend too much time and effort clarifying its own position or role, it will risk losing credibility in the field. But should it be able quickly to move the debate into areas where action is required and effective, then it will be an example to other "neutral" organisations that strive to contribute to the CSR debate in a practical way. Clarifying the mechanisms by which debate is first focused and then channelled efficiently is the aim of RIIA's feasibility study, and beyond that of the role of any other CSR research and information providers. So realised, an "information strategy" with this goal will help make CSR more of a reality.

Process

Some aspects of the feasibility study are worth describing in detail, although most of the process was mechanical. The general methodology is described below, and the more significant issues that arose are developed in more specific detail in the sections that follow.

Like any think tank or research institute or university, RIIA is a place replete with ideas that are not always realisable. Its current funding model requires a constant flow of project proposals in order to accommodate the likelihood that not all will be affordable; this is resource-draining. At the same time, by proposing a superabundance of projects, the organisation risks spreading itself too thinly, and this in turns threatens to reduce the quality of the work it does do—also menacing the ability to attract further funding. The risk of a vicious circle is always present, and the idea of adding a complex CSR information service to existing responsibilities must be carefully judged, as represented in Figure 2.

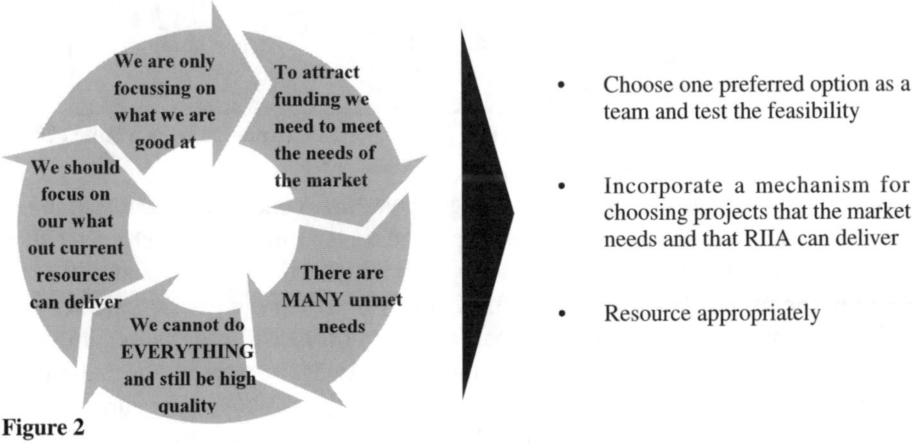

Figure 2

With the dual understanding that 1) a multitude of stakeholders needs to be satisfied, and 2) that a careful assessment of available resources ought to be made before anything else, the feasibility study began with a new model for making such assessments. While there are many models for conducting resource audits (Timmons and Spinelli 2003: 11, 12; Stevenson 1994), this new model (Mullins 2003) easily accommodates multiple domains of interest—even the diverse stakeholders that characterise the market for CSR information, and the constituency of RIIA.

Mullins identifies seven domains for the assessment of any market opportunity and for testing ideas as worthy of further planning: four external domains (market and industry attractiveness, benefits to target market and sustainable advantage within industry), and three internal ones (sense of mission, ability to execute on critical success factors, connectedness of value chain), as seen in Figure 3.

These domains were used to assess the resources available to Chatham House, either externally or internally. Without going into great detail about the resource audit, it is worth reporting that RIIA eventually defined its target market according to six product

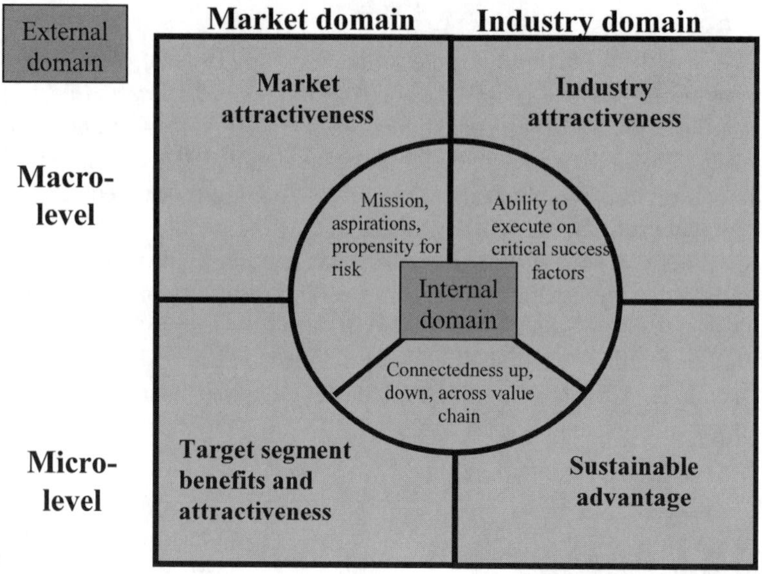

Figure 3

(Adapted from Mullins 2003)

characteristics that the CSR information might have, three concerning *quantity* of information and three concerning *quality*, and evaluated these according to ten characteristics of a potential CSR information "product"—as summarised in Tables 1 and 2.

With the resources more clearly understood, including the external market and industry environment as well as the market demand for CSR information, a matrix was drawn up showing nine possible options for entering the market. The axes of the matrix were determined by the six product characteristics above. The current position of RIIA within the market for providing CSR information was placed in the least evolved position (Figure 4).

Table 1. Quantity of Information

	Bespoke	*Wholesale*	*Retail*
Number of Customers	30–50	500	~10,000
Revenue Model	Sponsorship	Membership	Subscription Report Sales
Depth of Relationship	Regular Contact, personal service	Regular contact	Intermittent contact
Need for marketing skills	Helpful	Important	Very important
Internet capabilities	Helpful	Important	Very important
Fit with RIIA model	Major corporate partners	All corporate partners	New relationships required?

Table 2. Quality of Information

	Specialist	*Tailored*	*One-Stop Shop*
Breadth	Narrow focus on specific industry, geography or issue	Respond to client requests for deep, focussed research	Be the preferred source of a wise range of knowledge
Depth	In-depth	As required	High level
Skill set	Technical knowledge, specific experience and expertise	Client facing, project management	Collating extensive existing and developing knowledge
Initiation of contact	Proactive contacting of client with relevant issue/conclusions	As requested by client and/or proposed on 'as-needed' basis	Regular (time) based contact (e.g., monthly, 3x/year). General awareness of point of contact

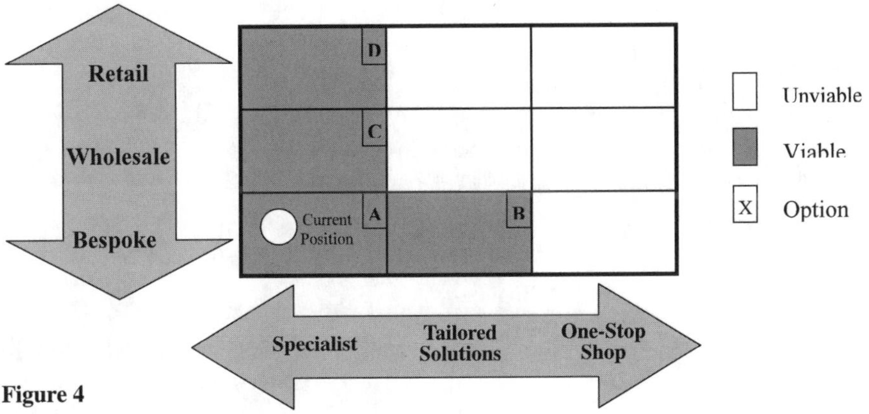

Figure 4

Five of these options were quickly eliminated as being obviously beyond RIIA's reach given available resources; the other four seemed more or less viable within a near timeframe:

A. Tailored Report Series
B. CSR Leaders Forum
C. Global Standards Bulletin
D. Broader Retail Roll-Out

These will be described in more detail under Option D below.

Next, in order to assess each of the four viable options, the ten evaluative characteristics were further narrowed down to the following six:

1. target market
2. breadth of content
3. depth of content
4. delivery mechanism
5. associated partners
6. the basic revenue model

These characteristics, as opposed to any others, were selected to match the normal structure of projects at RIIA: to be approved and initiated, projects must establish their credibility on each of these bases. Thus, mechanisms were already in place for assessing each of the four possible options, once those options had been selected from a larger pool. Evaluating against normal criteria for approving RIIA projects then created the basis for a fairly detailed and systematic view of the feasibility of each, as illustrated in Figures 5 and 6.

Target Market
- Relationship, wholesale, retail
- Level within corporation (CEO, Business Unit, CSR/policy director)

Breadth of Content
- Industry/sector focus
- Geography
- Issue (e.g. green labelling, AIDS, supply chain, etc.)

Depth of Content
- News – search / categorisation
- News plus implications (editorial)
- Implementation guidelines

Delivery Mechanism
- Frequency
- Newsletter
- Hardcopy vs. softcopy
- Internet vs. email

Partner
- Who?
- What resource/expertise gap do they fill?

Revenue Model
- Value added service for corporate members?
- Fee per report vs fee per year

Figure 5

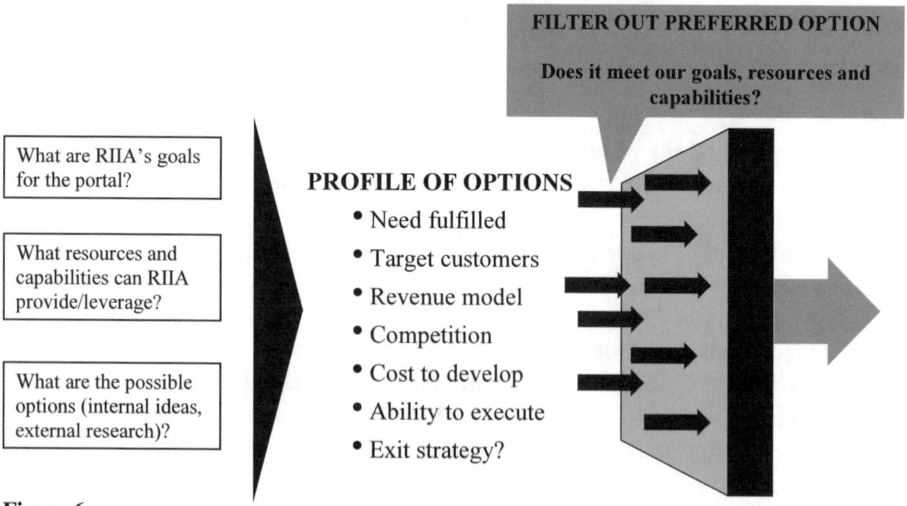

Figure 6

Initially, this filtering process was applied to the four viable options through the fairly superficial mechanism of consulting people inside RIIA and gauging their own resource capabilities. This suggested developing a complex operation with a self-sustaining revenue base, to provide information on may aspects of CSR to many segments of the market—in effect, Option D in Figure 4 above, and described in more detail in Section 3.4 below. This was the most ambitious option, and since it was in line with some of the original inspirations for the exercise as a whole, it seemed an encouraging sign that RIIA should start moving into CSR as a big player, and be able to fund the effort through its own operating revenues.

The next stage of the process involved testing these initial results against the opinions of other stakeholders: people and organisations outside RIIA itself with different interests. These tests were conducted mainly through confidential structured interviews with decision-makers in various areas of government, industry, NGO, media, and financial organisations. A brief summary of the key points from these confidential interviews is given in Table 3.

Table 3. Interview Results

General Perspectives	*Specific needs: Government*	*Specific needs: Corporate*
Focus and depth are very important	Capture examples of local community focussed initiatives of SMEs in UK to promote best practice for SMEs in developing countries	Strategic implications and opportunities of climate change regulations
More important to have input into which issues are analysed than input into analysis itself	Facilitate stakeholder engagement to alleviate "stakeholder fatigue"	Training and education task of general managers on the important and relevance of sustainable business principles
Risk of wasting energy and effort in trying to redefine CSR and develop codes of conduct	Reinforcing Government role in CSR	Implementation of community engagement plans and triple-bottom-line reporting process
Business managers could be discouraged by any addition process or structure to engagement: seen as "bureaucracy"		Training for non-executive directors
Improve neutrality and balanced perspective	*Specific need (NGOs)*	*Specific Needs (Investors)*
RIIA still a good non-threatening forum	Sustained change in companies	How to define stakeholders and incorporate their views
Don't position CSR-RIIA as 'competing,' rather be a catalyst for change on specific issues and themes	SME-SME dissemination of best CSR practice	Non-executives and materiality risks on CSR
Don't be too formalised; be forward-thinking as well as responsive to client needs	More local need/perspectives in roundtable discussion	Supply chain issues
RIIA completely changes as the staff changes – no consistency	Face-to-face stakeholder engagement (beware of facilitation!)	Climate change and CSR
	Gov't needs more opportunities to communicate with NGOs	Voluntary v. mandatory reporting

Final results of the interviews were somewhat surprising but very clear: in the very crowded and ill-defined CSR space almost everyone interviewed expressed the firm opinion that RIIA should not attempt to "compete" with other players in the market for information. Such a role was regarded as being inconsistent with RIIA's mission and beyond its current resource base—in a word, unfeasible. This realisation, while apparently negative, was also a strong vindication of the effectiveness of the Mullins (2003) model for "road-testing" an idea before sinking more resources into it. And, on a more positive note, these results did refine the viable options down to one or two that could be entirely actionable, with adjustments.

What follows from here is a more detailed description of the interview process and the elimination of several of the four options, as well as a discussion of where this leads RIIA next. This will form the basis for a larger discussion of where other stakeholders in the CSR debate can begin to take their places, and how they can start making a more positive impact through this important strategic paradigm.

Assessing the Options

To paraphrase the process described above, several decisions needed to be made in order to decide which was the best option:

1. Will customers/clients value the content, delivery and reputation of the product?
2. Can RIIA develop partnerships to make the project happen, if required? Can it make the *right* partnership?
3. Does RIIA have any advantage over its competitors?
4. Does an option meet RIIA's current goals?
5. Can RIIA afford to invest in the require time and resources?

Both internal and external stakeholders were asked these questions and other similar ones, in the process of testing the viability of each option, as summarised in the sections below.

Option A: Tailored Report Series

Figure 7 shows what RIIA is essentially doing at present, although without specifically associating the activity or the information it generates with CSR. In other words, RIIA could keep doing what it has always done, and organise some of its events and research specifically around CSR themes. This would meet some demand in the market without inappropriately stretching resources.

It would not, however, be forward-looking. Part of RIIA's purpose is to be advanced, to prepare members for what is in the pipeline. This option is more reactive than pro-active, and as such does not really match RIIA's general remit.

Option B: CSR Leaders Forum

This option (Figure 8) is also very similar to what RIIA does at present, with the difference of a revenue model based on membership dues. The ability to gauge market demand and then meet it more precisely would also be enhanced by this option, in that members of the forum would be able to communicate with each other and with RIIA their precise requirements. For example, if the membership decided to commission focused reports on the post-conflict reconstruction of Afghanistan and Iraq as the issue of most immediate concern, then RIIA could concentrate its resources there with the

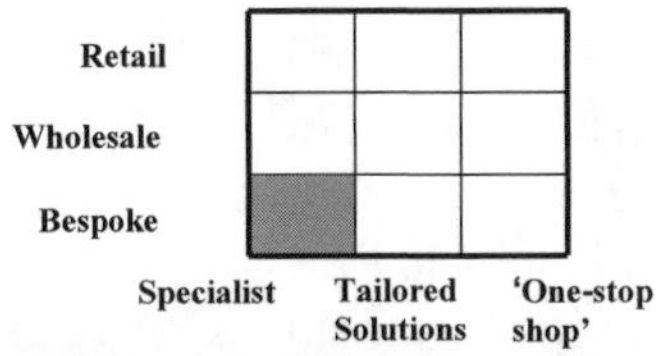

Target Market
- Relationship
- Current core supporters of Sustainable Development programme plus others??

Breadth of Content
- Defined by consultation process between RIIA and core supporters with a defined timeline

Depth of Content
- Distilled research and analysis of issues and developments, including strategic implications

Delivery Mechanism
- Report series published regularly to agreed schedule
- Associated events, as required

Partner
- Not required?

Revenue Model
- Annual fee for reports

Figure 7

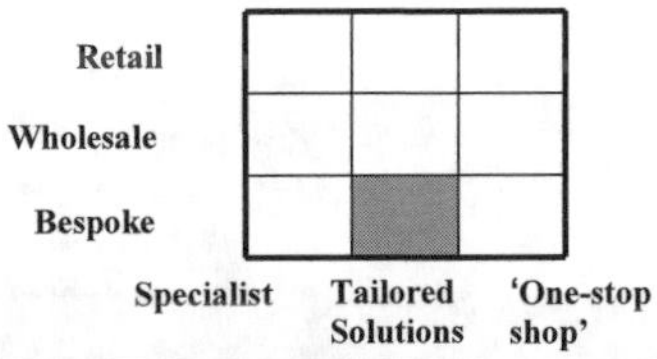

Target Market
- Relationship
- Membership by invitation?
- Limited to 20-30? real peers at Chairman/CEO level (corporate, government, NGO)

Breadth of Content
- Defined by need of forum members (within the capabilities of RIIA)

Depth of Content
- Distilled research and analysis of issues and developments, including strategic implications

Delivery Mechanism
- Regular meeting schedule (say 6 times a year)
- Pre-reading of background paper plus final briefing paper

Partner
- Helpful, but not necessary
- E.g. Conference Board for sourcing of forum members due to managerial credibility
- Initial funding source?

Revenue Model
- Membership dues

Figure 8

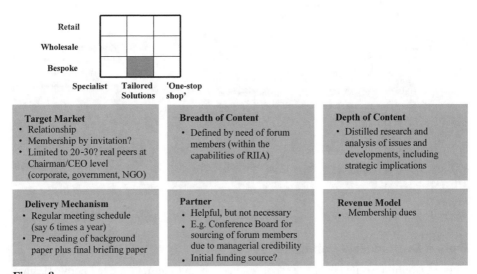

confidence that the market for that material would hold. A chief advantage of this is the increased focus it brings, in an area problematic for its vagueness.

To function properly, this system would require careful selection of members. These would have to be chosen with care, and with a view to achieving greatest leverage in appropriate organisations. From several interviews, there is some suggestion that this will come from a very particular target group: Non-Executive Directors of Multi-National Corporations based in London.

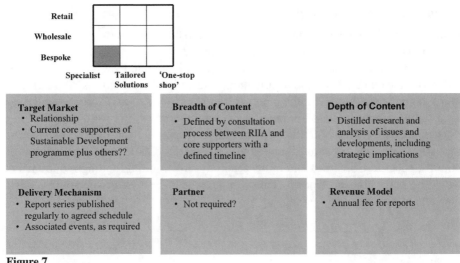

Option C: Global Standards Bulletin

In this option (Figure 9), the notion of a "membership base" is essentially replaced with a larger number of wholesale clients: organisations that pay to distribute RIIA's information through their own networks. Clients might include news agencies, providers of financial analysis and information, and similar organisations. Marketing to this potential client base would be more difficult, as it begins to diverge from RIIA's accustomed constituency. Also, there is substantial competition from consultancies (Sustainability), research entities (Global Ethics Monitor), and even automatic information retrieval software (Autonomy, Moreover Technologies)—this applies at both the specific CSR level and more generally. Also, initial funding requirements would be fairly high, so that financing would have to be raised from sources other than operating revenues.

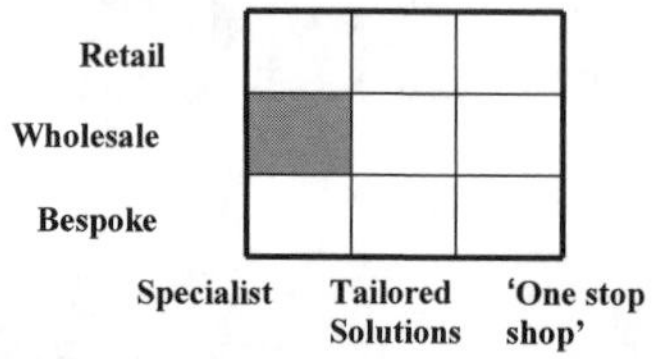

Target Market
- Wholesale
- Top 500 global companies

Breadth of Content
- Geographic (e.g. China, India, Brazil, South Africa)
- Industries and issues? (e.g. green labelling, AIDS, supply chain, etc.)

Depth of Content
- Distilled analysis of news, highlighting good practice and strategic implications

Delivery Mechanism
- Three times a year
- Newsletter bulletin
- Hardcopy and softcopy?

Partner
- Conference Board
- Provide managerial credibility abroad
- Research/admin resources?
- Initial funding source?

Revenue Model
- Subscription access for an annual fee

Figure 9

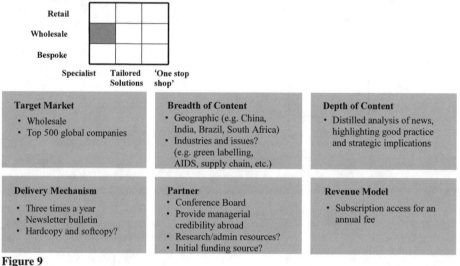

Option D: Broader Retail Roll-Out

This final option would be the most complicated, both to initiate and to operate (Figure 10). It also seems to depart furthest from RIIA's resource base for various reasons:

- the information produced would not be rich
- the delivery system and dissemination would be outside of RIIA's control
- there is considerable competition in this space from established brand-name providers, such as the Economist Intelligence Unit, and even conference organisers such as Ethical Corporation

This option appealed to no one; there was unilateral suspicion of its ability to add any value to RIIA's mission, or indeed of its actual feasibility in terms of RIIA's intellectual resources.

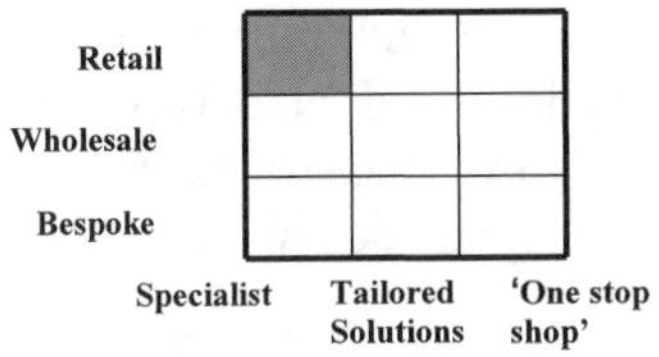

Target Market
- Retail
- Corporates , government and NGOs

Breadth of Content
- Share smaller articles / summaries of tailored work with a broader audience

Depth of Content
- Highlights and key findings of the in -depth analysis

Delivery Mechanism
- Released as online content on an ad -hoc basis when analysis complete

Partner
- Helpful, but not necessary
- Distribution (e.g. Global Ethics Monitor, Reuters)

Revenue Model
- Retail revenues from individual purchases of material

Figure 10

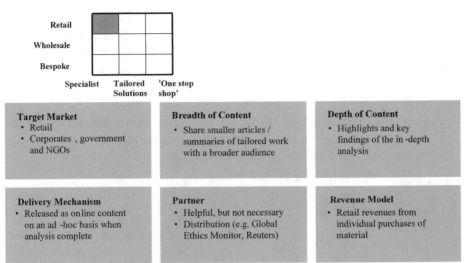

Competitive Landscape

Crucial to any strategic evaluation process is a sense of what other players in the field are doing. A summary of competitive activity grouped according to the four various options is given in the table below. Some function as true competitors (C), in that they would deflect potential revenues away from RIIA were it to operate in the same space; others are more by way of being substitutes (S), or similar products that do not provide exactly the same benefits (Table 4).

Table 4. Competitive Activity

Competitor	*Tailored Report Series*	*CSR Leaders Forum*	*Global Standards Bulletin*	*Broad Retail Rollout*
	Option A	*Option B*	*Option C*	*Option D*
Sustainability	C	S	S	C
Business for Social Responsibility	S	S	C	C
IBLF: Prince of Wales's International Business Leaders Forum	S	C	S	S
World Economic Forum	S	C	C	S
World Business Council for Sustainable Development	C	C	C	S
Global Ethics Monitor	S	C	S	C
Centre for Corporate Citizenship	S	C	S	S
Triple Bottom Line	S	C	S	S

The high threat of substitutes in all options other than B, indicates that this option is the one with a more predictable, controllable competitive landscape. This suggests a strategy based on differentiating the product sufficiently from those of the competitors, while also retaining connection to the evidently high market demand in this space.

Costs and Revenues

While each option would require a different level of investment in time and resources, the decision to implement any one should also be related to market need and level of RIIA commitment. Potential costs and revenues are thus compared in Tables 5 and 6.

Table 5. Costs

Cost items	*Estimate*	*Tailored Report Series*	*CSR Leaders Forum*	*Global Standards Bulletin*	*Broad Retail Rollout*
		Option A	*Option B*	*Option C*	*Option D*
Staff [FTE] (research, management, authors, facilitators)	£60,000	1 – 3 [2]	1 – 4 [2.5]	2 – 4 [3]	1* [0.5]
Events (per year) (catering, mgt.)	£10,000	1 – 2	6 – 8	0	0
Publishing reports (editing, design, layout)	£5,000	6 – 8	6 – 8	3	0
Number of members	n.a.	~20	~20	~500	~5,000
Number of reports printer	£10	~200	~200	~500	0
On-line (formatting and IT administration time)	low	low	low	medium	high
TOTAL (excluding online and travel)		~£250,000	~400,000	~£250,000	£50,000

*assumes partner carries all marketing and distribution costs, and additional staff costs with staff to be accommodated outside RIIA

These figures are complete estimates, and have not been derived from any specific enquiry. Further study is required to clarify exact cost and benefit implications of each option—although as will be seen below, there may be reasons not to engage in the effort of researching some of the options, as they can be eliminated from consideration for reasons prior to financial considerations. It is also clear from the wide range of cost and revenue implications, that implementing any given options will require a very different financial profile and initial funding.

Scalability

In addition to the simple notion of where RIIA ought to situate itself with respect to CSR, there is the question of where—having made the first move—it should aim next. While the issue of growth or scalability in any strategy is important to consider